THE
BOOK
®

FIAT Bravo & Brava
Service and Repair Manual

AK Legg LAE MIMI, Spencer Drayton & RM Jex

Models covered

(3572 - 336 - 11AG1)

FIAT Bravo and Brava models with 4-cylinder petrol engines, including special/limited editions
1.2 litre (1242 cc), 1.4 litre (1370 cc), 1.6 litre (1581 cc) and 1.8 litre (1747 cc)

Covers major mechanical features of 1.6 and 1.8 litre Marea/Weekend models
Does not cover 2.0 litre (HGT) models, or Diesel engine versions

© Haynes Publishing 2004

ABCDE
FGHIJ
KLMN

A book in the **Haynes Service and Repair Manual Series**

ISBN **1 85960 572 9**

British Library Cataloguing in Publication Data
A catalogue record for this book is available from the British Library.

Printed in the USA

Haynes Publishing
Sparkford, Yeovil, Somerset BA22 7JJ, England

Haynes North America, Inc
861 Lawrence Drive, Newbury Park, California 91320, USA

Editions Haynes
4, Rue de l'Abreuvoir
92415 COURBEVOIE CEDEX, France

Haynes Publishing Nordiska AB
Box 1504, 751 45 UPPSALA, Sverige

Contents

LIVING WITH YOUR FIAT BRAVO/BRAVA

Roadside repairs

Weekly checks

Lubricants and fluids

Tyre pressures

MAINTENANCE

Routine maintenance and servicing

Contents

The 3-door FIAT Bravo and 5-door Brava models were introduced at the end of 1995, as part of a new range of FIAT models which began with the successful Punto a year earlier. The elegant all-new design won the coveted Car of the Year award in 1996.

The engines are all fuel-injected, in-line, multi-valve four-cylinder units of 1370 cc, 1581 cc or 1747 cc displacement, and all feature a comprehensive engine management system with extensive emission control equipment. In early 1999, the range received a minor facelift, and the 1370 cc 12-valve engine was replaced by the 1242 cc 16-valve engine from the FIAT Punto.

The 3- and 5-door bodyshells are extensively galvanised and particularly rigid, and offer spacious accommodation. The cars have many crash safety measures, such as a driver's airbag, side impact bars, anti-submarine seats, and front seat belt pre-tensioners.

Transmissions are either 5-speed manual, or 4-speed automatic with computer control. The automatic transmission features mode control selection, allowing the driver to alter the transmission characteristics to suit normal, sport or winter driving requirements.

Braking is by discs at the front, and drums at the rear, with the handbrake acting on the rear drums. Anti-lock braking (ABS) is available as an option. The suspension is conventional, with struts and wishbones at the front, and a torsion beam rear axle. Power-assisted rack and pinion steering is standard on all models.

A high level of standard equipment, and a wide range of optional equipment, is available within the range to suit virtually all tastes. All models have a driver's airbag, tinted glass, high-level brake light and central locking, with several featuring electric windows, electric sunroof and alloy wheels.

Provided that regular servicing is carried out in accordance with the manufacturer's recommendations, the FIAT Bravo and Brava will provide reliable and economical family motoring. The engine compartment is relatively spacious, and most of the items requiring frequent attention are easily accessible.

FIAT Bravo 1.4 SX

FIAT Brava 1.8 ELX

The Fiat Bravo/Brava Team

Haynes manuals are produced by dedicated and enthusiastic people working in close co-operation. The team responsible for the creation of this book included:

Authors	AK Legg LAE MIMI
	Spencer Drayton
	RM Jex
Page Make-up	Steve Churchill
	James Robertson
Workshop manager	Paul Buckland
Photo Scans	John Martin
Cover illustration & Line Art	Roger Healing
Wiring diagrams	Steve Tanswell

We hope the book will help you to get the maximum enjoyment from your car. By carrying out routine maintenance as described you will ensure your car's reliability and preserve its resale value.

Your FIAT Bravo/Brava manual

The aim of this manual is to help you get the best value from your vehicle. It can do so in several ways. It can help you decide what work must be done (even should you choose to get it done by a garage). It will also provide information on routine maintenance and servicing, and give a logical course of action and diagnosis when random faults occur. However, it is hoped that you will use the manual by tackling the work yourself. On simpler jobs it may even be quicker than booking the car into a garage and going there twice, to leave and collect it. Perhaps most important, a lot of money can be saved by avoiding the costs a garage must charge to cover its labour and overheads.

The manual has drawings and descriptions to show the function of the various components so that their layout can be understood. Tasks are described and photographed in a clear step-by-step sequence. The illustrations are numbered by the Section number and paragraph number to which they relate - if there is more than one illustration per paragraph, the sequence is denoted alphabetically.

References to the 'left' or 'right' of the vehicle are in the sense of a person in the driver's seat, facing forwards.

Acknowledgements

Thanks are due to Draper Tools Limited, who provided some of the workshop tools, and to all those people at Sparkford who helped in the production of this manual.

We take great pride in the accuracy of information given in this manual, but vehicle manufacturers make alterations and design changes during the production run of a particular vehicle of which they do not inform us. No liability can be accepted by the authors or publishers for loss, damage or injury caused by any errors in, or omissions from the information given.

Working on your car can be dangerous. This page shows just some of the potential risks and hazards, with the aim of creating a safety-conscious attitude.

General hazards

Scalding

• Don't remove the radiator or expansion tank cap while the engine is hot.
• Engine oil, automatic transmission fluid or power steering fluid may also be dangerously hot if the engine has recently been running.

Burning

• Beware of burns from the exhaust system and from any part of the engine. Brake discs and drums can also be extremely hot immediately after use.

Crushing

• When working under or near a raised vehicle, always supplement the jack with axle stands, or use drive-on ramps. *Never venture under a car which is only supported by a jack.*

• Take care if loosening or tightening high-torque nuts when the vehicle is on stands. Initial loosening and final tightening should be done with the wheels on the ground.

Fire

• Fuel is highly flammable; fuel vapour is explosive.
• Don't let fuel spill onto a hot engine.
• Do not smoke or allow naked lights (including pilot lights) anywhere near a vehicle being worked on. Also beware of creating sparks (electrically or by use of tools).
• Fuel vapour is heavier than air, so don't work on the fuel system with the vehicle over an inspection pit.
• Another cause of fire is an electrical overload or short-circuit. Take care when repairing or modifying the vehicle wiring.
• Keep a fire extinguisher handy, of a type suitable for use on fuel and electrical fires.

Electric shock

• Ignition HT voltage can be dangerous, especially to people with heart problems or a pacemaker. Don't work on or near the ignition system with the engine running or the ignition switched on.

• Mains voltage is also dangerous. Make sure that any mains-operated equipment is correctly earthed. Mains power points should be protected by a residual current device (RCD) circuit breaker.

Fume or gas intoxication

• Exhaust fumes are poisonous; they often contain carbon monoxide, which is rapidly fatal if inhaled. Never run the engine in a confined space such as a garage with the doors shut.

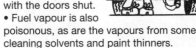

• Fuel vapour is also poisonous, as are the vapours from some cleaning solvents and paint thinners.

Poisonous or irritant substances

• Avoid skin contact with battery acid and with any fuel, fluid or lubricant, especially antifreeze, brake hydraulic fluid and Diesel fuel. Don't syphon them by mouth. If such a substance is swallowed or gets into the eyes, seek medical advice.
• Prolonged contact with used engine oil can cause skin cancer. Wear gloves or use a barrier cream if necessary. Change out of oil-soaked clothes and do not keep oily rags in your pocket.
• Air conditioning refrigerant forms a poisonous gas if exposed to a naked flame (including a cigarette). It can also cause skin burns on contact.

Asbestos

• Asbestos dust can cause cancer if inhaled or swallowed. Asbestos may be found in gaskets and in brake and clutch linings. When dealing with such components it is safest to assume that they contain asbestos.

Special hazards

Hydrofluoric acid

• This extremely corrosive acid is formed when certain types of synthetic rubber, found in some O-rings, oil seals, fuel hoses etc, are exposed to temperatures above 400°C. The rubber changes into a charred or sticky substance containing the acid. *Once formed, the acid remains dangerous for years. If it gets onto the skin, it may be necessary to amputate the limb concerned.*
• When dealing with a vehicle which has suffered a fire, or with components salvaged from such a vehicle, wear protective gloves and discard them after use.

The battery

• Batteries contain sulphuric acid, which attacks clothing, eyes and skin. Take care when topping-up or carrying the battery.
• The hydrogen gas given off by the battery is highly explosive. Never cause a spark or allow a naked light nearby. Be careful when connecting and disconnecting battery chargers or jump leads.

Air bags

• Air bags can cause injury if they go off accidentally. Take care when removing the steering wheel and/or facia. Special storage instructions may apply.

Diesel injection equipment

• Diesel injection pumps supply fuel at very high pressure. Take care when working on the fuel injectors and fuel pipes.

⚠️ *Warning: Never expose the hands, face or any other part of the body to injector spray; the fuel can penetrate the skin with potentially fatal results.*

Remember...

DO

• Do use eye protection when using power tools, and when working under the vehicle.

• Do wear gloves or use barrier cream to protect your hands when necessary.

• Do get someone to check periodically that all is well when working alone on the vehicle.

• Do keep loose clothing and long hair well out of the way of moving mechanical parts.

• Do remove rings, wristwatch etc, before working on the vehicle – especially the electrical system.

• Do ensure that any lifting or jacking equipment has a safe working load rating adequate for the job.

DON'T

• Don't attempt to lift a heavy component which may be beyond your capability – get assistance.

• Don't rush to finish a job, or take unverified short cuts.

• Don't use ill-fitting tools which may slip and cause injury.

• Don't leave tools or parts lying around where someone can trip over them. Mop up oil and fuel spills at once.

• Don't allow children or pets to play in or near a vehicle being worked on.

The following pages are intended to help in dealing with common roadside emergencies and breakdowns. You will find more detailed fault finding information at the back of the manual, and repair information in the main chapters.

If your car won't start and the starter motor doesn't turn

☐ If it's a model with automatic transmission, make sure the selector is in P or N.
☐ Open the bonnet and make sure that the battery terminals are clean and tight.
☐ Switch on the headlights and try to start the engine. If the headlights go very dim when you're trying to start, the battery is probably flat. Get out of trouble by jump starting (see next page) using a friend's car.

If your car won't start even though the starter motor turns as normal

☐ Is there fuel in the tank?
☐ Is there moisture on electrical components under the bonnet? Switch off the ignition, then wipe off any obvious dampness with a dry cloth. Spray a water-repellent aerosol product (WD-40 or equivalent) on ignition and fuel system electrical connectors like those shown in the photos. Pay special attention to the ignition coil wiring connector and HT leads.

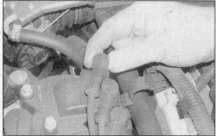

A Check that the HT leads are securely connected to the spark plugs and ignition coil pack, where applicable.
1.8 litre models do not have conventional HT leads.

B Check that the LT wiring plug is securely attached to the ignition coil.
On some models, the HT leads and ignition coil are concealed under a plastic cover, secured by a number of screws.

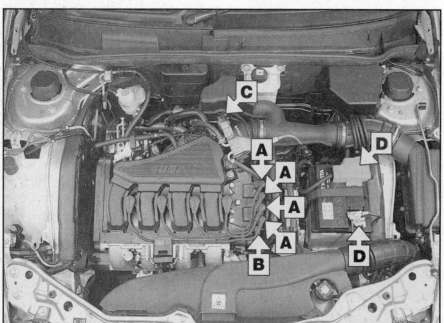

Check that electrical connections are secure (with the ignition switched off) and spray them with a water dispersant spray like WD-40 if you suspect a problem due to damp

C Check the airflow meter and/or inlet air temperature sensor wiring connector for security.

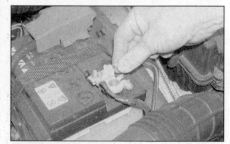

D Check the security and condition of the battery terminals.

Jump starting

HAYNES HiNT *Jump starting will get you out of trouble, but you must correct whatever made the battery go flat in the first place. There are three possibilities:*

1 The battery has been drained by repeated attempts to start, or by leaving the lights on.

2 The charging system is not working properly (alternator drivebelt slack or broken, alternator wiring fault or alternator itself faulty).

3 The battery itself is at fault (electrolyte low, or battery worn out).

When jump-starting a car using a booster battery, observe the following precautions:

✔ Before connecting the booster battery, make sure that the ignition is switched off.

✔ Ensure that all electrical equipment (lights, heater, wipers, etc) is switched off.

✔ Take note of any special precautions printed on the battery case.

✔ Make sure that the booster battery is the same voltage as the discharged one in the vehicle.

✔ If the battery is being jump-started from the battery in another vehicle, the two vehicles MUST NOT TOUCH each other.

✔ Make sure that the transmission is in neutral (or PARK, in the case of automatic transmission).

1 Connect one end of the red jump lead to the positive (+) terminal of the flat battery

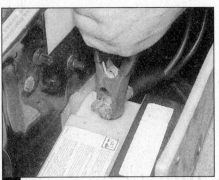

2 Connect the other end of the red lead to the positive (+) terminal of the booster battery.

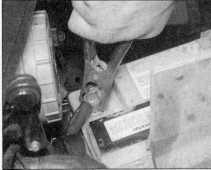

3 Connect one end of the black jump lead to the negative (-) terminal of the booster battery

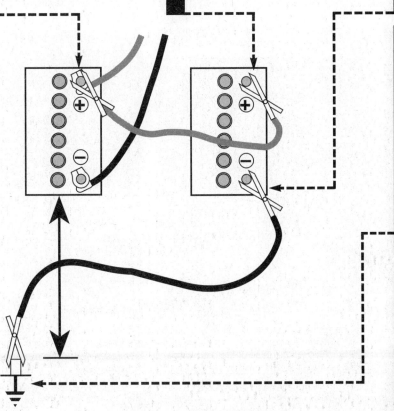

4 Connect the other end of the black jump lead to a bolt or bracket on the engine block, well away from the battery, on the vehicle to be started.

5 Make sure that the jump leads will not come into contact with the fan, drive-belts or other moving parts of the engine.

6 Start the engine using the booster battery and run it at idle speed. Switch on the lights, rear window demister and heater blower motor, then disconnect the jump leads in the reverse order of connection. Turn off the lights etc.

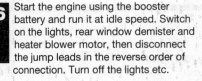

Wheel changing

 Warning: Do not change a wheel in a situation where you risk being hit by another vehicle. On busy roads, try to stop in a lay-by or a gateway. Be wary of passing traffic while changing the wheel - it is easy to become distracted by the job in hand.

Preparation

☐ When a puncture occurs, stop as soon as it is safe to do so.

☐ Park on firm level ground, if possible, and well out of the way of other traffic.

☐ Use hazard warning lights if necessary.

☐ If you have one, use a warning triangle to alert other drivers of your presence.

☐ Apply the handbrake and engage first or reverse gear (or Park on models with automatic transmission).

☐ Chock the wheel diagonally opposite the one being removed – a couple of large stones will do for this.

☐ If the ground is soft, use a flat piece of wood to spread the load under the jack.

Changing the wheel

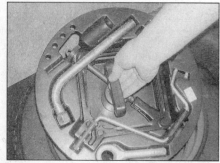

1 The spare wheel and tools are stored in the luggage compartment under the carpet. Unscrew the handle and lift out the tool tray, then take out the jack and spare wheel.

2 Remove the wheel trim (where fitted) by prising up the edges and pulling it straight off. Slacken each wheel bolt by a half turn, using the wheelbrace. If the bolts are too tight, DON'T stand on the wheelbrace to undo them - call for assistance.

3 The jack head engages with the bottom lip on the side sills. If a front wheel is being changed, position the jack head approximately 30 cm back from the front wheel arch. If a rear wheel is being changed, the jack head should be 20 cm forward of the rear wheel arch. Don't jack the vehicle at any other point of the sill.

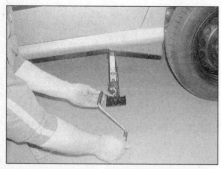

4 Turn the handle clockwise until the wheel is raised clear of the ground. Unscrew the wheel bolts and remove the wheel.

5 Fit the spare wheel, noting that there are two locating pegs on the wheel hub, which must fit through the holes in the spare wheel. Fit and screw in the bolts.

6 Lightly tighten the bolts with the wheelbrace, then lower the vehicle to the ground. Securely tighten the wheel bolts. Note that the wheel trim will not fit the spare wheel. The wheel bolts should be slackened and retightened to the specified torque at the earliest possible opportunity.

Finally...

☐ Remove the wheel chocks.

☐ Stow the punctured wheel and tools in the correct locations in the car.

☐ Check the tyre pressure on the tyre just fitted. If it is low, or if you don't have a pressure gauge with you, drive slowly to the next garage and inflate the tyre to the correct pressure. Particularly in the case of the narrow space-saver spare wheel, this pressure is much higher than for a normal tyre.

☐ Have the punctured wheel repaired as soon as possible, or another puncture will leave you stranded.

Note: *Some models are supplied with a special lightweight 'space-saver' spare wheel, the tyre being narrower than standard. The space-saver spare wheel is intended only for temporary use, and **must** be replaced with a standard wheel as soon as possible. Drive with particular care with this wheel fitted, especially through corners and when braking - FIAT recommend a maximum speed of 50 mph (80 km/h) when the special spare wheel is in use. The temporary spare also has a maximum recommended life of 1800 miles.*

Identifying leaks

Puddles on the garage floor or drive, or obvious wetness under the bonnet or underneath the car, suggest a leak that needs investigating. It can sometimes be difficult to decide where the leak is coming from, especially if the engine bay is very dirty already. Leaking oil or fluid can also be blown rearwards by the passage of air under the car, giving a false impression of where the problem lies.

 Warning: Most automotive oils and fluids are poisonous. Wash them off skin, and change out of contaminated clothing, without delay.

 The smell of a fluid leaking from the car may provide a clue to what's leaking. Some fluids are distinctively coloured. It may help to clean the car carefully and to park it over some clean paper overnight as an aid to locating the source of the leak. Remember that some leaks may only occur while the engine is running.

Sump oil

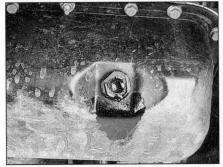

Engine oil may leak from the drain plug...

Oil from filter

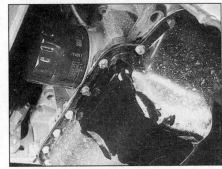

...or from the base of the oil filter.

Gearbox oil

Gearbox oil can leak from the seals at the inboard ends of the driveshafts.

Antifreeze

Leaking antifreeze often leaves a crystalline deposit like this.

Brake fluid

A leak occurring at a wheel is almost certainly brake fluid.

Power steering fluid

Power steering fluid may leak from the pipe connectors on the steering rack.

Towing

When all else fails, you may find yourself having to get a tow home – or of course you may be helping somebody else. Long-distance recovery should only be done by a garage or breakdown service. For shorter distances, DIY towing using another car is easy enough, but observe the following points:

☐ Use a proper tow-rope – they are not expensive. The vehicle being towed must display an ON TOW sign in its rear window.
☐ Always turn the ignition key to the 'on' position when the vehicle is being towed, so that the steering lock is released, and that the direction indicator and brake lights will work.

☐ The screw-in towing eye is provided with the wheel changing tools in the boot. The towing eye is screwed into the threaded hole in the front bumper, below the right-hand headlight, or into the right-hand side of the rear bumper after prising out the trim cover.
☐ Before being towed, release the handbrake and select neutral on the transmission.
☐ Note that greater-than-usual pedal pressure will be required to operate the brakes, since the vacuum servo unit is only operational with the engine running.
☐ On models with power steering, greater-than-usual steering effort will also be required.
☐ The driver of the car being towed must

keep the tow-rope taut at all times to avoid snatching.
☐ Make sure that both drivers know the route before setting off.
☐ Only drive at moderate speeds and keep the distance towed to a minimum. Drive smoothly and allow plenty of time for slowing down at junctions.
☐ On models with automatic transmission, the car must not be towed (with the front wheels on the ground) further than 12 miles (20 km), or faster than 18 mph (30 km/h). If in doubt, do not tow with the driven wheels on the ground, or transmission damage may result.

Introduction

There are some very simple checks which need only take a few minutes to carry out, but which could save you a lot of inconvenience and expense.

These "Weekly checks" require no great skill or special tools, and the small amount of time they take to perform could prove to be very well spent, for example;

☐ Keeping an eye on tyre condition and pressures, will not only help to stop them wearing out prematurely, but could also save your life.

☐ Many breakdowns are caused by electrical problems. Battery-related faults are particularly common, and a quick check on a regular basis will often prevent the majority of these.

☐ If your car develops a brake fluid leak, the first time you might know about it is when your brakes don't work properly. Checking the level regularly will give advance warning of this kind of problem.

☐ If the oil or coolant levels run low, the cost of repairing any engine damage will be far greater than fixing the leak, for example.

Underbonnet check points

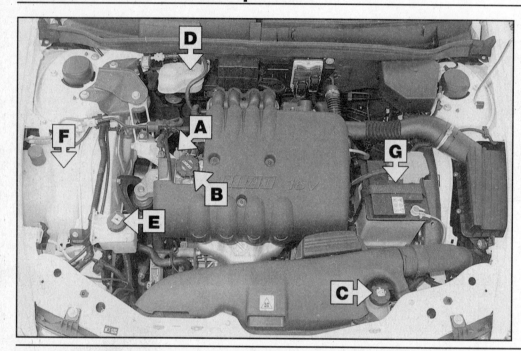

◄ **1.2 litre engine**

A Engine oil level dipstick

B Engine oil filler cap

C Coolant expansion tank

D Brake and clutch fluid reservoir

E Power steering fluid reservoir

F Screen washer fluid reservoir

G Battery

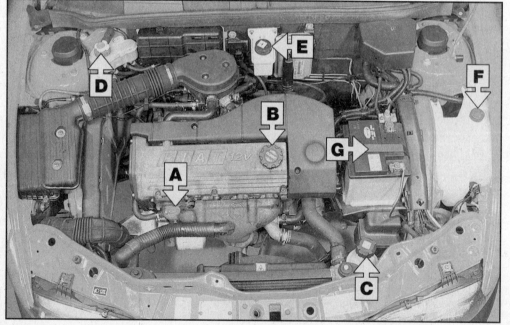

◄ **1.4 litre engine**

A Engine oil level dipstick

B Engine oil filler cap

C Coolant expansion tank

D Brake and clutch fluid reservoir

E Power steering fluid reservoir

F Screen washer fluid reservoir

G Battery

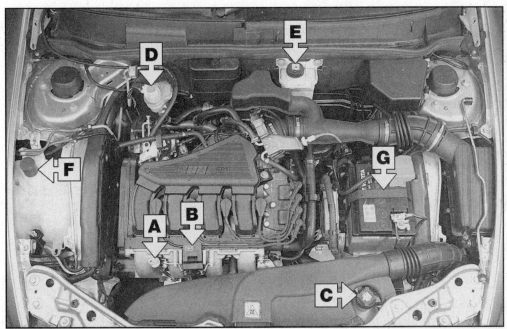

◀ **1.6 litre engine**

A *Engine oil level dipstick*

B *Engine oil filler cap*

C *Coolant expansion tank*

D *Brake and clutch fluid reservoir*

E *Power steering fluid reservoir*

F *Screen washer fluid reservoir*

G *Battery*

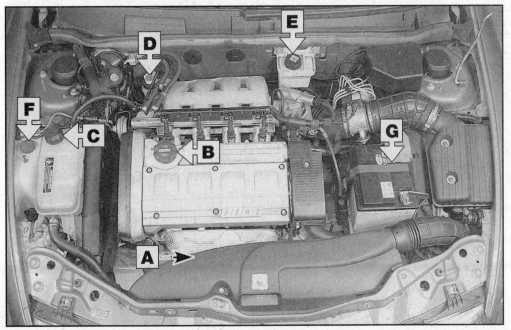

◀ **1.8 litre engine**

A *Engine oil level dipstick*

B *Engine oil filler cap*

C *Coolant expansion tank*

D *Brake and clutch fluid reservoir*

E *Power steering fluid reservoir*

F *Screen washer fluid reservoir*

G *Battery*

Engine oil level

Before you start

✔ Make sure that your car is on level ground.
✔ Check the oil level before the car is driven, or at least 5 minutes after the engine has been switched off.

 HAYNES HiNT *If the oil is checked immediately after driving the vehicle, some of the oil will remain in the upper engine components, resulting in an inaccurate reading on the dipstick!*

The correct oil

Modern engines place great demands on their oil. It is very important that the correct oil for your car is used (See Lubricants and fluids on page 0•17).

Car Care

● If you have to add oil frequently, you should check whether you have any oil leaks. Place some clean paper under the car overnight, and check for stains in the morning. If there are no leaks, the engine may be burning oil.

● Always maintain the level between the upper and lower dipstick marks (see photo 3). If the level is too low severe engine damage may occur. Oil seal failure may result if the engine is overfilled by adding too much oil.

1 The dipstick top is brightly coloured for easy identification, and is situated at the front of the engine compartment (see *Underbonnet check points* on pages 0•10 and 0•11). Withdraw the dipstick

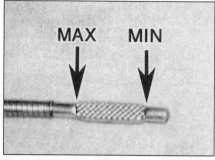

3 Note the oil level on the end of the dipstick, which should be in the hatched area between the upper (MAX) mark and lower (MIN) mark. Approximately 1.0 litre of oil will raise the level from the lower mark to the upper mark.

2 Using a clean rag or paper towel remove all oil from the dipstick. Insert the clean dipstick into the tube as far as it will go, then withdraw it again.

4 Oil is added through the filler cap. Unscrew the cap and top-up the level; a funnel may help to reduce spillage. Add the oil slowly, checking the level on the dipstick often. Don't overfill (see '*Car Care*' left).

Coolant level

⚠ *Warning: DO NOT attempt to remove the expansion tank pressure cap when the engine is hot, as there is a very great risk of scalding. Do not leave open containers of coolant about, as it is poisonous.*

Car Care

● With a sealed-type cooling system, adding coolant should not be necessary on a regular basis. If frequent topping-up is required, it is likely there is a leak. Check the radiator, all hoses and joint faces for signs of staining or wetness, and rectify as necessary.

● It is important that antifreeze is used in the cooling system all year round, not just during the winter months. Don't top-up with water alone, as the antifreeze will become too diluted.

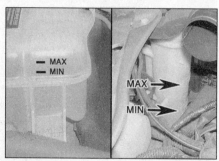

1 The coolant expansion tank is located in one of two places (see *Underbonnet check points* on pages 0•10 and 0•11). The coolant level can vary with engine temperature. When cold, it should be between the MAX and MIN marks. When the engine is hot, the level may rise slightly above the MAX mark.

2 If topping up is necessary, **wait until the engine is cold**. Slowly unscrew the expansion tank cap, to release any pressure present in the cooling system, and remove it.

3 Add a mixture of water and antifreeze to the expansion tank until the coolant level is halfway between the level marks. Refit the cap and tighten it securely.

Brake (and clutch*) fluid level

*On models with a hydraulically-operated clutch, this information is also applicable to the clutch fluid level.

Warning:
● **Brake fluid can harm your eyes and damage painted surfaces, so use extreme caution when handling and pouring it.**

● **Do not use fluid that has been standing open for some time, as it absorbs moisture from the air, which can cause a dangerous loss of braking effectiveness.**

 HAYNES HiNT
● *Make sure that your car is on level ground.*
● *The fluid level in the reservoir will drop slightly as the brake pads wear down, but the fluid level must never be allowed to drop below the MIN mark.*

Safety First!

● If the reservoir requires repeated topping-up this is an indication of a fluid leak somewhere in the system, which should be investigated immediately.

● If a leak is suspected, the car should not be driven until the braking system has been checked. Never take any risks where brakes are concerned.

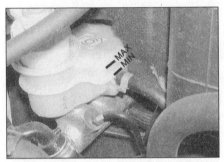

1 The MAX and MIN marks are indicated on the reservoir. The fluid level must be kept between the marks at all times

2 If topping-up is necessary, first wipe clean the area around the filler cap to prevent dirt entering the hydraulic system. Unscrew the reservoir cap and carefully lift it out of position, holding the wiring connector plug and taking care not to damage the level sender float. Inspect the reservoir; if the fluid is dirty, the hydraulic system should be bled through (see Chapter 1).

3 Carefully add fluid, taking care not to spill it onto the surrounding components. Use only the specified fluid; mixing different types can cause damage to the system. After topping-up to the correct level, securely refit the cap and wipe off any spilt fluid. Reconnect the fluid level wiring connector.

Power steering fluid level

Before you start:

✔ Park the vehicle on level ground.
✔ Set the steering wheel straight-ahead.
✔ The engine should be turned off.

 HAYNES HiNT
For the check to be accurate, the steering must not be turned once the engine has been stopped.

Safety First!

● The need for frequent topping-up indicates a leak, which should be investigated immediately.

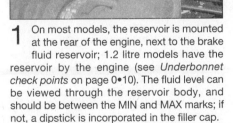

1 On most models, the reservoir is mounted at the rear of the engine, next to the brake fluid reservoir; 1.2 litre models have the reservoir by the engine (see *Underbonnet check points* on page 0•10). The fluid level can be viewed through the reservoir body, and should be between the MIN and MAX marks; if not, a dipstick is incorporated in the filler cap.

2 If topping-up is necessary, use the specified type of fluid - do not overfill the reservoir. When the level is correct, securely refit the cap.

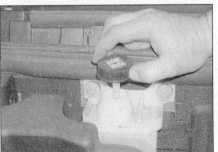

3 Start the engine and wait for the fluid level in the reservoir to stabilise before proceeding. With the engine running, turn the steering wheel fully left and right several times, returning to the straight-ahead position. Wait for the level to stabilise, then check the fluid level once more, and top-up if necessary. Switch off the engine on completion.

Tyre condition and pressure

It is very important that tyres are in good condition, and at the correct pressure - having a tyre failure at any speed is highly dangerous. Tyre wear is influenced by driving style - harsh braking and acceleration, or fast cornering, will all produce more rapid tyre wear. As a general rule, the front tyres wear out faster than the rears. Interchanging the tyres from front to rear ("rotating" the tyres) may result in more even wear. However, if this is completely effective, you may have the expense of replacing all four tyres at once!

Remove any nails or stones embedded in the tread before they penetrate the tyre to cause deflation. If removal of a nail does reveal that the tyre has been punctured, refit the nail so that its point of penetration is marked. Then immediately change the wheel, and have the tyre repaired by a tyre dealer.

Regularly check the tyres for damage in the form of cuts or bulges, especially in the sidewalls. Periodically remove the wheels, and clean any dirt or mud from the inside and outside surfaces. Examine the wheel rims for signs of rusting, corrosion or other damage. Light alloy wheels are easily damaged by "kerbing" whilst parking; steel wheels may also become dented or buckled. A new wheel is very often the only way to overcome severe damage.

New tyres should be balanced when they are fitted, but it may become necessary to re-balance them as they wear, or if the balance weights fitted to the wheel rim should fall off. Unbalanced tyres will wear more quickly, as will the steering and suspension components. Wheel imbalance is normally signified by vibration, particularly at a certain speed (typically around 50 mph). If this vibration is felt only through the steering, then it is likely that just the front wheels need balancing. If, however, the vibration is felt through the whole car, the rear wheels could be out of balance. Wheel balancing should be carried out by a tyre dealer or garage.

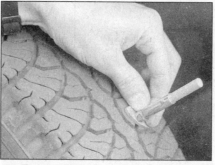

1 Tread Depth - visual check
The original tyres have tread wear safety bands (B), which will appear when the tread depth reaches approximately 1.6 mm. The band positions are indicated by a triangular mark on the tyre sidewall (A).

2 Tread Depth - manual check
Alternatively, tread wear can be monitored with a simple, inexpensive device known as a tread depth indicator gauge.

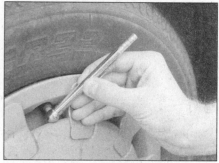

3 Tyre Pressure Check
Check the tyre pressures regularly with the tyres cold. Do not adjust the tyre pressures immediately after the vehicle has been used, or an inaccurate setting will result. Tyre pressures are shown on page 0•17.

Tyre tread wear patterns

Shoulder Wear

Underinflation (wear on both sides)
Under-inflation will cause overheating of the tyre, because the tyre will flex too much, and the tread will not sit correctly on the road surface. This will cause a loss of grip and excessive wear, not to mention the danger of sudden tyre failure due to heat build-up.
Check and adjust pressures
Incorrect wheel camber (wear on one side)
Repair or renew suspension parts
Hard cornering
Reduce speed!

Centre Wear

Overinflation
Over-inflation will cause rapid wear of the centre part of the tyre tread, coupled with reduced grip, harsher ride, and the danger of shock damage occurring in the tyre casing.
Check and adjust pressures

If you sometimes have to inflate your car's tyres to the higher pressures specified for maximum load or sustained high speed, don't forget to reduce the pressures to normal afterwards.

Uneven Wear

Front tyres may wear unevenly as a result of wheel misalignment. Most tyre dealers and garages can check and adjust the wheel alignment (or "tracking") for a modest charge.
Incorrect camber or castor
Repair or renew suspension parts
Malfunctioning suspension
Repair or renew suspension parts
Unbalanced wheel
Balance tyres
Incorrect toe setting
Adjust front wheel alignment
Note: *The feathered edge of the tread which typifies toe wear is best checked by feel.*

Battery

Caution: Before carrying out any work on the vehicle battery, read the precautions given in Safety first! at the start of this manual.

✔ Make sure that the battery tray is in good condition, and that the clamp is tight. Corrosion on the tray, retaining clamp and the battery itself can be removed with a solution of water and baking soda. Thoroughly rinse all cleaned areas with water. Any metal parts damaged by corrosion should be covered with a zinc-based primer, then painted.

✔ Periodically (approximately every three months), check the charge condition of the battery as described in Chapter 5A.

✔ On batteries which are not of the maintenance-free type, periodically check the electrolyte level in the battery - see Chapter 1.

✔ If the battery is flat, and you need to jump start your vehicle, see *Roadside repairs*.

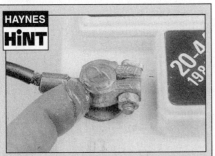

Battery corrosion can be kept to a minimum by applying a layer of petroleum jelly to the clamps and terminals after they are reconnected.

1 The battery is located at the front of the engine compartment on the left-hand side. The exterior of the battery should be inspected periodically for damage such as a cracked case or cover

2 Lift off the terminal covers, and check the tightness of battery clamps to ensure good electrical connections. Also check each cable for cracks and frayed conductors.

3 If corrosion (white, fluffy deposits) is evident, remove the cables from the battery terminals, clean them with a small wire brush, then refit them. Automotive stores sell a tool for cleaning the battery post . . .

4 . . . as well as the battery cable clamps

Bulbs and fuses

✔ Check all external lights and the horn. Refer to the appropriate Sections of Chapter 12 for details if any of the circuits are found to be inoperative.

✔ Visually check all accessible wiring connectors, harnesses and retaining clips for security, and for signs of chafing or damage.

HAYNES HiNT *If you need to check your brake lights and indicators unaided, back up to a wall or garage door and operate the lights. The reflected light should show if they are working properly.*

1 If a single indicator light, stop-light or headlight has failed, it is likely that a bulb has blown and will need to be replaced. Refer to Chapter 12 for details. If both stop-lights have failed, it is possible that the stop-light switch is faulty (see Chapter 9).

2 If more than one indicator light or headlight has failed, it is likely that either a fuse has blown or that there is a fault in the circuit (see Chapter 12). The main fuses are located in the fusebox situated to the right of the steering wheel. Additional fuses are located behind the glovebox, with several engine-related fuses on the engine compartment bulkhead or next to the battery.

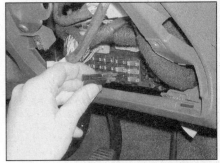

3 To replace a blown fuse, simply pull it out using the plastic tweezers provided. Fit a new fuse of the same rating (see Chapter 12). If the fuse blows again, it is important that you find out why - a complete checking procedure is given in Chapter 12.

Washer fluid level

● The windscreen washer reservoir also supplies the tailgate washer jet. On models so equipped, the same reservoir also serves the headlight washers.

● Screenwash additives not only keep the windscreen clean during foul weather, they also prevent the washer system freezing in cold weather - which is when you are likely to need it most. Don't top up using plain water as the screenwash will become too diluted, and will freeze during cold weather.

On no account use coolant antifreeze in the washer system - this could discolour or damage paintwork.

1 On most models, the washer fluid reservoir filler is located at the rear right-hand side of the engine compartment; 1.4 litre models have the reservoir on the left-hand side. Release the cap and observe the level in the reservoir by looking down the filler neck. Models with headlight washers have a dipstick which can be used to verify the level.

2 To top-up the level, pull the filter inside the filler neck upwards until it clicks - this can now be used as a funnel. When topping-up the reservoir, a screenwash additive should be added in the quantities recommended on the bottle.

Wiper blades

Caution: Take care during the fitting of new blades that the wiper arms do not accidentally strike the windscreen or tailgate glass.

Note: *Fitting details for wiper blades vary according to model, and according to whether genuine FIAT wiper blades have been fitted. Use the procedures and illustrations shown as a guide for your car.*

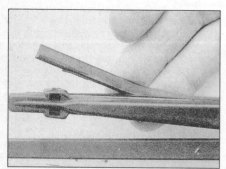

1 Check the condition of the wiper blades; if they are cracked or show any signs of deterioration, or if the glass swept area is smeared, renew them. Wiper blades should be renewed annually.

2 To remove a wiper blade, pull the arm fully away from the glass until it locks. Swivel the blade through 90°, press the locking tab with your fingers and slide the blade out of the arm's hooked end.

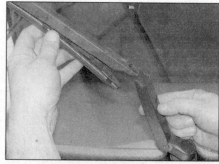

3 Don't forget to check the rear wiper blade as well. To remove the blade, press in the catch at the base of the arm, and slide the blade and upper section of the arm out.

Lubricants and fluids

Engine	Synthetic-based multigrade engine oil, viscosity SAE 10W/40, to ACEA A3, API SJ or better
Cooling system	Ethylene glycol-based antifreeze
Manual transmission	Gear oil, viscosity SAE 75W/80, to API GL5
Automatic transmission	Dexron II type automatic transmission fluid
Braking system	Brake and clutch fluid to DOT 4
Power steering	Dexron type ATF

Choosing your engine oil

Engines need oil, not only to lubricate moving parts and minimise wear, but also to maximise power output and to improve fuel economy.

HOW ENGINE OIL WORKS

• Beating friction

Without oil, the moving surfaces inside your engine will rub together, heat up and melt, quickly causing the engine to seize. Engine oil creates a film which separates these moving parts, preventing wear and heat build-up.

• Cooling hot-spots

Temperatures inside the engine can exceed 1000° C. The engine oil circulates and acts as a coolant, transferring heat from the hot-spots to the sump.

• Cleaning the engine internally

Good quality engine oils clean the inside of your engine, collecting and dispersing combustion deposits and controlling them until they are trapped by the oil filter or flushed out at oil change.

OIL CARE - FOLLOW THE CODE

To handle and dispose of used engine oil safely, always:

OIL CARE
FOLLOW THE CODE

OIL BANK LINE
0800 66 33 66
www.oilbankline.org.uk

• *Avoid skin contact with used engine oil. Repeated or prolonged contact can be harmful.*
• *Dispose of used oil and empty packs in a responsible manner in an authorised disposal site. Call 0800 663366 to find the one nearest to you. Never tip oil down drains or onto the ground.*

Tyre pressures (cold)

Note: *Pressures apply only to original-equipment tyres, and may vary if other makes or type is fitted; check with the tyre manufacturer or supplier for correct pressures if necessary.*

	Front	Rear
Normal load:		
Except 185/55 R15 and 195/50 R15 tyres	2.2 bar (32 psi)	2.2 bar (32 psi)
185/55 R15 and 195/50 R15 tyres	2.2 bar (32 psi)	2.3 bar (33 psi)
Full load	2.3 bar (33 psi)	2.5 bar (36 psi)
Spare wheel:		
Normal (full-width) wheel	2.8 bar (41 psi)	2.8 bar (41 psi)
Space saver (narrow) wheel	4.2 bar (61 psi)	4.2 bar (61 psi)

Advanced driving

Many people see the words 'advanced driving' and believe that it won't interest them or that it is a style of driving beyond their own abilities. Nothing could be further from the truth. Advanced driving is straightforward safe, sensible driving - the sort of driving we should all do every time we get behind the wheel.

An average of 10 people are killed every day on UK roads and 870 more are injured, some seriously. Lives are ruined daily, usually because somebody did something stupid. Something like 95% of all accidents are due to human error, mostly driver failure. Sometimes we make genuine mistakes - everyone does. Sometimes we have lapses of concentration. Sometimes we deliberately take risks.

For many people, the process of 'learning to drive' doesn't go much further than learning how to pass the driving test because of a common belief that good drivers are made by 'experience'.

Learning to drive by 'experience' teaches three driving skills:

☐ Quick reactions. (Whoops, that was close!)
☐ Good handling skills. (Horn, swerve, brake, horn).
☐ Reliance on vehicle technology. (Great stuff this ABS, stop in no distance even in the wet...)

Drivers whose skills are 'experience based' generally have a lot of near misses and the odd accident. The results can be seen every day in our courts and our hospital casualty departments.

Advanced drivers have learnt to control the risks by controlling the position and speed of their vehicle. They avoid accidents and near misses, even if the drivers around them make mistakes.

The key skills of advanced driving are **concentration,** effective all-round **observation, anticipation** and **planning.** When **good vehicle handling** is added to these skills, all driving situations can be approached and negotiated in a safe, methodical way, leaving nothing to chance.

Concentration means applying your mind to safe driving, completely excluding anything that's not relevant. Driving is usually the most dangerous activity that most of us undertake in our daily routines. It deserves our full attention.

Observation means not just looking, but seeing and seeking out the information found in the driving environment.

Anticipation means asking yourself what is happening, what you can reasonably expect to happen and what could happen unexpectedly. (One of the commonest words used in compiling accident reports is 'suddenly'.)

Planning is the link between seeing something and taking the appropriate action. For many drivers, planning is the missing link.

If you want to become a safer and more skilful driver and you want to enjoy your driving more, contact the Institute of Advanced Motorists at www.iam.org.uk, phone 0208 996 9600, or write to IAM House, 510 Chiswick High Road, London W4 5RG for an information pack.

Chapter 1
Routine maintenance & servicing

Contents

Degrees of difficulty

Easy, suitable for novice with little experience	**Fairly easy,** suitable for beginner with some experience	**Fairly difficult,** suitable for competent DIY mechanic	**Difficult,** suitable for experienced DIY mechanic	**Very difficult,** suitable for expert DIY or professional

Lubricants and fluids

Refer to end of *Weekly checks* on page 0•17

Capacities

Engine oil (including filter):
1.2 litre engine	2.8 litres
1.4 litre engine	4.1 litres
1.6 litre engine	3.8 litres
1.8 litre engine	4.3 litres

Cooling system (approximate):
1.2 and 1.4 litre engines	6.0 litres
1.6 and 1.8 litre engines	7.0 litres

Transmission (approximate):
Manual transmission:
1.2 and 1.4 litre engine models	1.65 litres
1.6 and 1.8 litre engine models	2.0 litres
Automatic transmission (fluid change)	4.3 litres

Fuel tank (approximate):
Except 1.8 litre models	50 litres
1.8 litre models	60 litres

Washer reservoir:
Models with headlight washers	6.4 litres
Models without headlight washers	5.0 litres

Cooling system

Antifreeze mixture:
40% antifreeze	Protection down to -25°C
50% antifreeze	Protection down to -35°C

Note: *Refer to antifreeze manufacturer for latest recommendations.*

Ignition system

Ignition timing .... Refer to Chapter 5B

Spark plugs:

	Type	Electrode gap
1.2 litre engine	Bosch YR 7 DE	0.9 mm
1.4 litre engine	Bosch FR 7 LD+	0.9 mm
1.6 litre engine	Bosch FR 8 D+	0.8 mm
1.8 litre engine	Bosch FR 7 LD+	0.9 mm

Clutch

Clutch pedal stroke (see Section 22):
1.2 and 1.4 litre models (where applicable)	155 ± 10 mm
1.6 and 1.8 litre models	170 ± 10 mm

Brakes

Brake pad/shoe friction material minimum thickness .... 1.5 mm

Torque wrench settings

	Nm	lbf ft
Manual transmission drain plug	46	34
Manual transmission filler/level plug	46	34
Roadwheel bolts	86	63
Spark plugs:		
All except 1.6 litre engine	25	18
1.6 litre engine	27	20
Sump drain plug:		
1.2 litre engine	10	7
1.4 litre engine	25	18
1.6 litre engine	50	37
1.8 litre engine	20	15

Maintenance schedule

The maintenance intervals in this manual are provided with the assumption that you, not the dealer, will be carrying out the work. These are the minimum intervals recommended for vehicles driven daily. If you wish to keep your vehicle in peak condition at all times, you may wish to perform some of these procedures more often. We encourage frequent maintenance, since it enhances the efficiency, performance and resale value of your vehicle.

When the vehicle is new, it should be serviced by a dealer service department, in order to preserve the factory warranty.

Every 250 miles (400 km) or weekly

☐ Refer to *Weekly checks*

Every 12 000 miles (20 000 km) or 12 months

In addition to the items listed in the previous services, carry out the following:

☐ Renew the engine oil and filter (Section 3)
☐ Check the front brake pad thickness (Section 4)
☐ Check the automatic transmission fluid level (Section 5)
☐ Check battery electrolyte level - where applicable (Section 6)
☐ Check the tension of the auxiliary drivebelt(s) (Section 7)
☐ Renew the pollen filter element (Section 8)
☐ Check all underbonnet/underbody components and hoses for fluid leaks (Section 9)
☐ Check the transmission and driveshaft gaiters for leaks and damage (Section 10)
☐ Check the brake pipes and hoses for leaks and damage (Section 11)
☐ Check the condition of the exhaust system and its mountings (Section 12)
☐ Check the steering and suspension components for condition and security (Section 13)
☐ Check underbody protection for damage (Section 14)
☐ Check operation of all lights and horn (Section 15)
☐ Lubricate all hinges, locks and door check straps (Section 16)
☐ Carry out a road test (Section 17)

Every 24 000 miles (40 000 km) or 2 years

In addition to the items listed in the previous services, carry out the following:

☐ Renew the spark plugs (Section 18)
☐ Renew the air filter element (Section 19)
☐ Renew the fuel filter, where applicable (Section 20)

Every 24 000 miles (40 000 km) or 2 years (continued)

☐ Check the condition of the auxiliary drivebelt(s), and renew if necessary (Section 21)
☐ Check clutch cable adjustment, where applicable (Section 22)
☐ Check handbrake adjustment (Section 23)
☐ Check exhaust gas emissions (Section 24)
☐ Check engine management system for fault codes (Section 25)

Every 36 000 miles (60 000 km) or 2 years

In addition to the items listed in the previous services, carry out the following:

☐ Renew the brake fluid (Section 26)
☐ Check the manual transmission oil level (Section 27)
☐ Check the rear brake shoe lining thickness (Section 28)

Every 48 000 miles (80 000 km) or 4 years

In addition to the items listed in the previous services, carry out the following:

☐ Check the evaporative emissions control system (Section 29)

Every 72 000 miles (120 000 km)

In addition to all the items listed above, carry out the following:

☐ Renew the timing belt (Section 30)

Note: *It is strongly recommended that the interval is halved to 36 000 miles (60 000 km), particularly on vehicles which are subjected to intensive use, ie. mainly short journeys or a lot of stop-start driving. The actual belt renewal interval is therefore very much up to the individual owner, but bear in mind that severe engine damage will result if the belt breaks.*

Every 2 years (regardless of mileage)

☐ Renew the coolant (Section 31)

Underbonnet view of 1.2 litre model

1   Brake and clutch fluid
    reservoir
2   Fuse and relay box
3   Engine top cover (remove
    for access to coils and
    spark plugs)
4   Engine management
    system ECU
5   Auxiliary fusebox
6   Air inlet duct
7   Air cleaner
8   Battery
9   Cooling system expansion
    tank
10 Engine oil dipstick
11 Oil filler cap
12 Power steering reservoir
13 Washer reservoir

Underbonnet view of 1.4 litre model

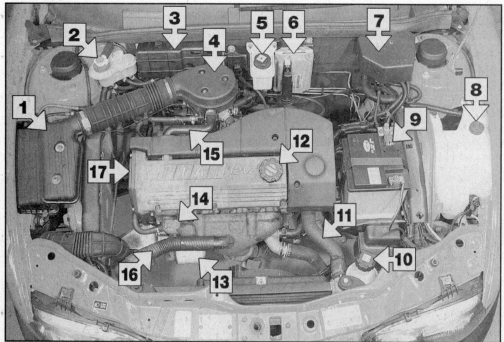

1   Air cleaner
2   Brake and clutch fluid
    reservoir
3   Fuse and relay box
4   Throttle body airbox
5   Power steering reservoir
6   Engine management
    system ECU
7   Auxiliary fusebox
8   Washer reservoir
9   Battery
10 Cooling system expansion
    tank
11 Radiator top hose
12 Oil filler cap
13 Oil filter
14 Engine oil dipstick
15 Crankcase breather hose
16 Warm-air inlet duct
17 Timing belt cover

Underbonnet view of 1.6 litre model

1 Washer reservoir
2 Inlet manifold (upper section)
3 Brake and clutch fluid reservoir
4 Fuse and relay box
5 Inlet air resonator box
6 Power steering reservoir
7 Air inlet duct
8 Auxiliary fusebox
9 Air cleaner
10 Battery
11 Engine management system ECU
12 Accelerator cable
13 Cooling system expansion tank
14 Ignition coil
15 Inlet manifold (lower section)
16 Oil filler cap
17 Engine oil dipstick
18 No 1 spark plug HT lead
19 Timing belt cover

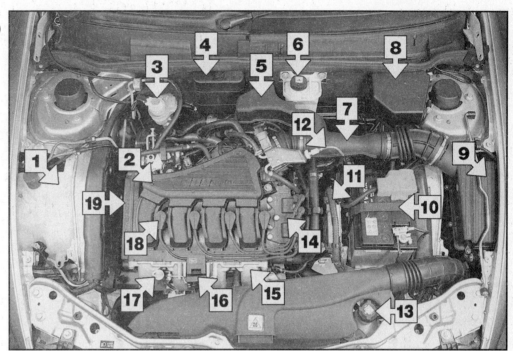

Underbonnet view of 1.8 litre model

1 Washer reservoir
2 Cooling system expansion tank
3 Fuel hoses, fuel rail and injectors
4 Brake and clutch fluid reservoir
5 Inlet manifold
6 Power steering reservoir
7 Idle speed control valve
8 Anti-lock braking system (ABS) modulator
9 Airflow meter
10 Auxiliary fusebox
11 Air inlet duct
12 Air cleaner
13 Battery
14 Engine top cover (remove for access to coils and spark plugs)
15 Oil filler cap
16 Engine oil dipstick
17 Timing belt cover

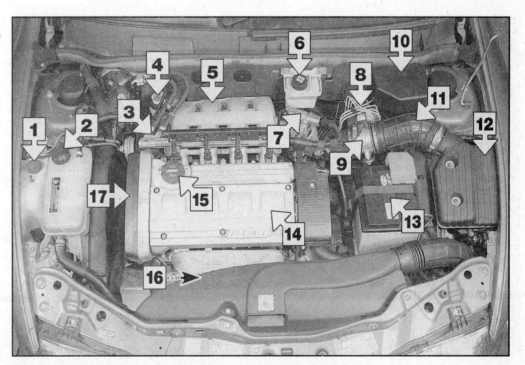

Front underside view of 1.6 litre model

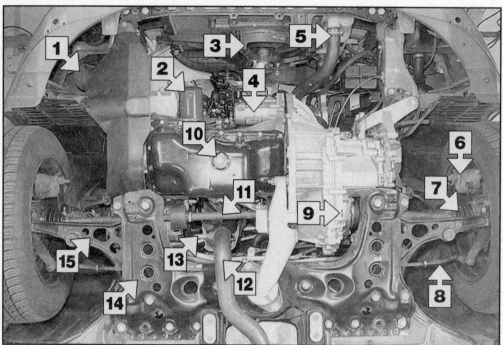

1 Horn unit
2 Oil filter
3 Radiator cooling fan
4 Starter motor
5 Radiator bottom hose
6 Front brake caliper
7 Driveshaft CV joint gaiter
8 Track rod end
9 Manual transmission drain plug
10 Engine oil drain plug
11 Right-hand driveshaft
12 Exhaust downpipe
13 Oxygen sensor
14 Subframe
15 Suspension arm

Rear underside view of 1.6 litre model

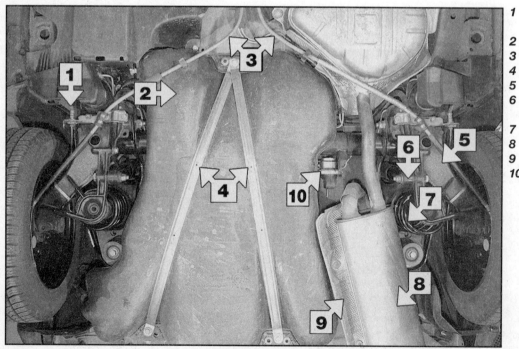

1 Brake pipe/hose connection
2 Fuel tank
3 Handbrake cables
4 Fuel tank retaining straps
5 Rear suspension arm
6 Rear shock absorber mounting
7 Rear coil spring
8 Exhaust rear silencer
9 Exhaust heat shield
10 Brake pressure proportioning valve

1 Introduction

General information

This Chapter is designed to help the home mechanic maintain his/her vehicle for safety, economy, long life and peak performance.

The Chapter contains a master maintenance schedule, followed by Sections dealing specifically with each task in the schedule. Visual checks, adjustments, component renewal and other helpful items are included. Refer to the accompanying illustrations of the engine compartment and the underside of the vehicle for the locations of the various components.

Servicing your vehicle in accordance with the mileage/time maintenance schedule and the following Sections will provide a planned maintenance programme, which should result in a long and reliable service life. This is a comprehensive plan, so maintaining some items but not others at the specified service intervals, will not produce the same results.

As you service your vehicle, you will discover that many of the procedures can - and should - be grouped together, because of the particular procedure being performed, or because of the proximity of two otherwise unrelated components to one another. For example, if the vehicle is raised for any reason, the exhaust can be inspected at the same time as the suspension and steering components.

The first step in this maintenance programme is to prepare yourself before the actual work begins. Read through all the Sections relevant to the work to be carried out, then make a list and gather all the parts and tools required. If a problem is encountered, seek advice from a parts specialist, or a dealer service department.

2 Regular maintenance

1 If, from the time the vehicle is new, the routine maintenance schedule is followed closely, and frequent checks are made of fluid levels and high-wear items, as suggested throughout this manual, the engine will be kept in relatively good running condition, and the need for additional work will be minimised.

2 It is possible that there will be times when the engine is running poorly due to the lack of regular maintenance. This is even more likely if a used vehicle, which has not received regular and frequent maintenance checks, is purchased. In such cases, additional work may need to be carried out, outside of the regular maintenance intervals.

3 If engine wear is suspected, a compression test (refer to the relevant part of Chapter 2) will provide valuable information regarding the overall performance of the main internal components. Such a test can be used as a basis to decide on the extent of the work to be carried out. If, for example, a compression test indicates serious internal engine wear, conventional maintenance as described in this Chapter will not greatly improve the perform-

ance of the engine, and may prove a waste of time and money, unless extensive overhaul work is carried out first.

4 The following series of operations are those most often required to improve the performance of a generally poor-running engine:

Primary operations

a) Clean, inspect and test the battery (See Weekly checks and Section 6, where applicable).
b) Check all the engine-related fluids (See Weekly checks).
c) Check the condition and tension of the auxiliary drivebelt (Sections 7 and 21).
d) Renew the spark plugs (Section 18).
e) Check the condition of the air filter, and renew if necessary (Section 19).
f) Check the fuel filter, where applicable (Section 20).
g) Check the condition of all hoses, and check for fluid leaks (Section 9).
h) Check the exhaust gas emissions (Section 24).

5 If the above operations do not prove fully effective, carry out the following secondary operations:

Secondary operations

All items listed under Primary operations, plus the following:
a) Check the charging system (see Chapter 5A, Section 4).
b) Check the ignition system (see Chapter 5B).
c) Check the fuel system (see relevant Part of Chapter 4).
d) Renew the ignition HT leads, if applicable.

Every 12 000 miles (20 000 km)

3 Engine oil and filter renewal

1 Frequent oil and filter changes are the most important maintenance procedures which can be undertaken by the DIY owner. As engine oil ages, it becomes diluted and contaminated, which leads to premature engine wear.

2 The oil change interval given in this Manual is the same as quoted by the manufacturer, but owners of older vehicles (or those covering a small annual mileage) may feel justified in changing the oil and filter more frequently, perhaps every 6000 miles, or every 6 months. The quality of engine oil used is a significant factor in this - the 12 000-mile interval **only** applies if a high-quality synthetic-based oil is used.

3 Before starting this procedure, gather all the necessary tools and materials. Also make sure that you have plenty of clean rags and newspapers handy, to mop up any spills. Ideally, the engine oil should be warm, as it will drain better, and more built-up sludge will be removed with it. Take care, however, not to

touch the exhaust or any other hot parts of the engine when working under the vehicle. To avoid any possibility of scalding, and to protect yourself from possible skin irritants and other harmful contaminants in used engine oils, it is advisable to wear gloves when carrying out this work.

4 Remove the oil filler cap **(see illustration)**, and take out the dipstick.

5 Access to the underside of the vehicle will be greatly improved if it can be raised on a lift, driven onto ramps, or jacked up and

3.4 Removing the oil filler cap on a 1.6 litre model

supported on axle stands (see *Jacking and vehicle support*). Whichever method is chosen, make sure that the vehicle remains level, or if it is at an angle, that the drain plug is at the lowest point.

6 Where applicable, unscrew the fasteners and remove the engine undertray, for access to the drain plug. On 1.8 litre engines, the drain plug can be reached from the back of the engine, and a panel is provided in the undertray, which can be hinged down to get to the filter **(see illustration)**.

3.6 Removing the oil filter access panel on a 1.8 litre model

3.7 On some models, a special socket is required to loosen the sump drain plug

3.8 Draining the engine oil

3.11 Removing the oil filter on a 1.8 litre model

7 Using a special socket where necessary, slacken the drain plug (on the base of the sump) about half a turn **(see illustration)**. Position the draining container under the drain plug, then remove the plug completely. Recover the sealing ring from the drain plug.

8 Allow some time for the old oil to drain, noting that it may be necessary to reposition the container as the oil flow slows to a trickle **(see illustration)**.

9 After all the oil has drained, wipe off the drain plug with a clean rag, and fit a new sealing washer. Clean the area around the drain plug opening, and refit the plug. Tighten the plug securely.

10 Move the container into position under the oil filter, which is located on the front of the cylinder block.

11 Using an oil filter removal tool if necessary, slacken the filter initially, then unscrew it by hand the rest of the way **(see illustration)**. Empty the oil in the filter into the container.

12 Use a clean rag to remove all oil, dirt and sludge from the filter sealing area on the engine. Check the old filter to make sure that the rubber sealing ring has not stuck to the engine. If it has, carefully remove it.

13 Apply a light coating of clean engine oil to the sealing ring on the new filter, then screw it into position on the engine **(see illustration)**. Tighten the filter firmly by hand only - **do not use any tools**.

14 Remove the old oil from under the car, then refit the undertray or access panel (as applicable). Lower the car to the ground.

15 With the car on level ground, fill the engine, using the correct grade and type of oil (see *Lubricants and fluids*). An oil can spout or funnel may help to reduce spillage **(see illustration)**. Pour in half the specified quantity of oil first, then wait a few minutes for the oil to fall to the sump.

16 Continue adding oil a small quantity at a time until the level is up to the MIN mark on the dipstick. Adding around 1.0 litre of oil will now bring the level up to the MAX on the dipstick - do not worry if a little too much goes in, as some of the apparent excess will be taken up in filling the oil filter. Refit the dipstick and the filler cap.

17 Start the engine and run it for a few minutes; check for leaks around the oil filter seal and the sump drain plug. Note that there may be a few seconds' delay before the oil pressure warning light goes out when the engine is started, as the oil circulates through the engine oil galleries and the new oil filter before the pressure builds up.

18 Switch off the engine, and wait a few minutes for the oil to settle in the sump once more. With the new oil circulated and the filter completely full, recheck the level on the dipstick, and add more oil as necessary.

19 Dispose of the used engine oil safely, with reference to *General repair procedures* in the *Reference* section of this manual.

4 Front brake pad check

1 Firmly apply the handbrake, loosen the front roadwheel bolts, then jack up the front of the car and support it securely on axle stands. Remove the front roadwheels.

2 For a comprehensive check, the brake pads should be removed and cleaned. The operation of the caliper can then also be checked, and the condition of the brake disc itself can be fully examined on both sides. Refer to Chapter 9.

3 If any pads friction material is worn to the specified thickness or less, *all four pads must be renewed as a set*.

4 Check the operation of the pad wear warning light by disconnecting the wiring plug

adjacent to the brake caliper. With the ignition on, touch the wiring plug to earth, and check that the warning light comes on.

5 Automatic transmission fluid level check

1 Ideally, the fluid level must be checked with the engine/transmission at operating temperature. This can be achieved by checking the level after a journey of at least 10 miles. If the level is checked when cold, follow this up with a level check when the fluid is hot.

2 Park the car on level ground, and apply the handbrake very firmly. As an added precaution, chock the front and rear wheels, so that the car cannot move.

3 With the engine idling, move the selector lever gently from position P to position 1, and back to P.

4 The fluid level dipstick is located on the front of the transmission. Before removing the dipstick, thoroughly clean the area around it - no dirt or debris must be allowed to enter the transmission.

5 Extract the dipstick, and wipe it clean using a clean piece of rag or tissue. Re-insert the dipstick completely, then pull it out once more. The fluid level should be between the reference marks on the side of the dipstick marked HOT (if the level is checked when cold, use the markings on the COLD side of the dipstick).

6 If topping-up is required, this is done via the dipstick tube. It is most important that no dirt

3.13 Fit and tighten the new oil filter by hand only - do not use any tools

3.15 Filling the engine with oil

6.3 Topping-up the battery electrolyte

or debris enters the transmission as this is done - use a clean funnel (preferably with a filter) and fresh fluid from a clean container.

7 Pour the fresh fluid a little at a time down the dipstick tube, checking the level frequently.

8 When the level is correct, refit the dipstick and switch off the engine.

6   Battery electrolyte level check

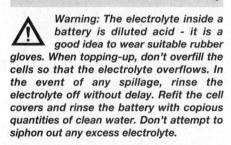

⚠️ *Warning: The electrolyte inside a battery is diluted acid - it is a good idea to wear suitable rubber gloves. When topping-up, don't overfill the cells so that the electrolyte overflows. In the event of any spillage, rinse the electrolyte off without delay. Refit the cell covers and rinse the battery with copious quantities of clean water. Don't attempt to siphon out any excess electrolyte.*

1 Models covered by this Manual are fitted with a 'limited-maintenance' battery as standard equipment (or may have had a 'maintenance-free' one fitted as a replacement). If the battery in your vehicle is marked 'Freedom', 'Maintenance-Free' or similar, no electrolyte level checking is required (the battery is often completely sealed, preventing any topping-up).

2 Batteries which do require their electrolyte level to be checked can be recognised by the presence of level markings and removable covers over the six battery cells - the battery casing is also sometimes translucent, so that the electrolyte level can be more easily checked. Some of the batteries fitted by FIAT have level markings, but no means of topping-up!

3 Remove the cell covers and either look down inside the battery to see the level web, or check the level using any markings provided on the battery casing. The electrolyte should at least cover the battery plates. If necessary, top up a little at a time with distilled (de-ionised) water until the level in all six cells is correct - don't fill the cells up to the brim **(see illustration)**. Wipe up any spillage, then refit the cell covers.

4 On batteries where the level can be checked but not topped-up, if the level is low, consult a dealer or automotive electrical specialist as to the best course of action (likely to be fitting a replacement battery).

7   Auxiliary drivebelt tension check

Note: *On models with 1.4 and 1.8 litre engines, an automatic belt tensioner is used, and regular tension checks are not required. Check the belt condition at the specified intervals, however, as described in Section 21.*

1 The only belt tension specifications quoted by FIAT are for use with their dedicated belt tensioning equipment, and are not of great practical help. The advice given below should be treated as a rough guide, and should be adequate in most cases. If there is serious concern over belt tension, refer to a FIAT dealer for advice.

2 If a drivebelt is set too tight, it will subject the driven unit to excess load, resulting in premature wear of the unit (and of the belt). If the belt is too slack, it will not transmit drive properly, and the belt will suffer wear due to slippage.

1.2 litre engine

3 Two or three separate belts are used on this engine, depending on whether or not air conditioning is fitted.

4 For improved access to the belts, remove the three bolts securing the engine top cover, and lift the cover away.

5 Each of the drivebelts is checked and adjusted in much the same way. To check the power steering pump drivebelt, remove the bolt securing the belt upper cover, and remove the cover. To access the air conditioning compressor drivebelt, refer to paragraphs 16 to 18.

6 Press on the belt at the centre-point between the two pulleys, and the drivebelt should deflect by approximately 5 mm.

Alternator drivebelt

7 If adjustment is required, loosen the nuts and bolts on the two adjuster slots, and the lower mounting through-bolt. Pivot the alternator as necessary using a suitable lever to set the belt tension, then re-tighten all the fasteners **(see illustration)**. Take care when levering the alternator that no damage is caused to the alternator or surrounding components.

8 On models with air conditioning, note that if the air conditioning compressor drivebelt needs adjusting, this will affect the alternator belt tension.

Air conditioning compressor drivebelt

9 If adjustment is required, loosen the nut and bolt on the adjuster slot, and the lower mounting through-bolt. Pivot the compressor as necessary using a suitable lever to set the belt tension, then re-tighten all the fasteners. Take care when levering the compressor that no damage is caused to the compressor or surrounding components.

10 Note that if the air conditioning compressor drivebelt needs adjusting, this will affect the alternator belt tension.

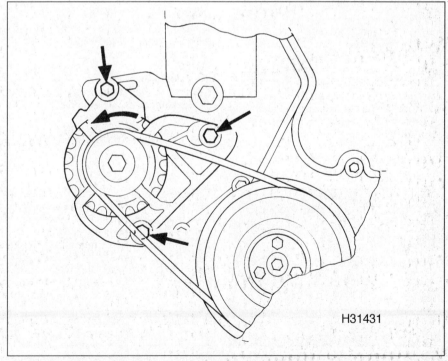

H31431

7.7 Loosen the alternator mountings (arrowed) and pivot the alternator to tension the belt

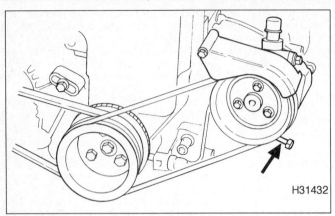

7.11 Power steering pump adjuster bolt (arrowed)

7.13 To improve access to the power steering pump drivebelt, remove the belt guard

Power steering pump drivebelt

11 If adjustment is required, loosen the nuts and bolts on the two adjuster slots, and the upper mounting through-bolt. The belt tension is set by now turning the adjuster bolt at the front of the pump mounting bracket **(see illustration)**. When the belt tension is correct, re-tighten all the fasteners and refit the belt upper cover.

1.6 litre engine

12 Two or three separate belts are used on this engine, depending on whether or not air conditioning is fitted.

Power steering pump drivebelt

13 Check the power steering pump drivebelt

first - to improve access, unbolt and remove the drivebelt guard **(see illustration)**. Press on the belt at the centre-point between the two pulleys, and the drivebelt should deflect by approximately 5 mm.

14 If adjustment is required, loosen the pump mountings, the nut and bolt on the adjuster slot, and the adjuster locknut. Turn the adjuster bolt as required to set the belt tension, then re-tighten the locknut and the nut and bolt on the adjuster slot **(see illustrations)**.

15 With all fixings re-tightened, turn the belt clockwise through one complete revolution, using a spanner on the crankshaft pulley bolt. Re-check the belt tension, and re-adjust if necessary. Refit the drivebelt guard on completion.

Alternator/coolant pump drivebelt

16 With the car parked on a level surface, apply the handbrake and chock the rear wheels. Loosen the right-hand front wheel bolts.

17 Raise the front of the vehicle, rest it securely on axle stands and remove the right-hand front roadwheel.

18 Unscrew and release the fasteners securing the wheelarch inner panel, to gain access to the belt run **(see illustration)**.

19 Press firmly on the belt, midway between the crankshaft and water pump pulleys **(see illustration)**. The belt should deflect by approximately 5 mm.

20 Refer to the advice given in paragraph 2, noting that the lower drivebelt drives the alternator and coolant pump.

21 If adjustment is required, loosen the tensioner upper and lower bolts. Using an Allen key, turn the hex adjuster as required to set the belt tension, then re-tighten the tensioner bolts **(see illustration)**.

22 Turn the belt clockwise through one complete revolution, using a spanner on the crankshaft pulley bolt. Re-check the belt tension, and re-adjust if necessary.

23 On completion, refit the wheelarch access panel and the roadwheel, and lower the car to the ground. Tighten the wheel bolts to the specified torque.

7.14a Loosen the pump mounting bolts . . .

7.14b . . . and the nut and bolt on the adjuster slot . . .

7.14c . . . then turn the adjuster bolt as required before tightening the locknut

7.18 Removing the wheelarch inner panel

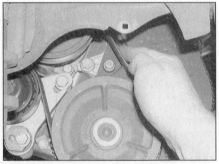

7.19 Checking the drivebelt tension

7.21 Set the belt tension, then tighten the tensioner bolts

8.3 Lift up the weatherstrip which fits over the filter access panel

8.4a Undo the two screws . . .

Air conditioning compressor drivebelt

24 Press on the belt at the centre-point between the two pulleys, on the opposite side to the tensioner wheel. The drivebelt should deflect by approximately 5 mm.

25 If adjustment is required, loosen the bolt on the adjuster slot, and the pivot bolt at the top of the tensioner arm.

26 Loosen the locknut at the front of the arm, and turn the adjuster bolt as required to move the tensioner wheel and set the belt tension.

27 On completion, re-tighten all the fasteners. With all fixings re-tightened, turn the belt clockwise through one complete revolution, using a spanner on the crankshaft pulley bolt. Re-check the belt tension, and re-adjust if necessary.

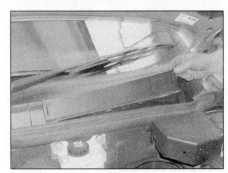

8.4b . . . and lift out the access panel

7 Fit the new filter into position, and secure with the two clips.

8 Refit the access panel, secure with the two bolts, and clip the weatherstrip into position.

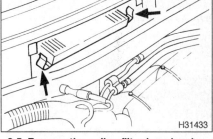

H31433

8.5 Remove the pollen filter by releasing the two clips (arrowed)

8 Pollen filter renewal

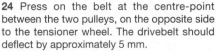

Note: *A pollen filter is not fitted to all models, and one was not actually fitted to our main project vehicle seen in the workshop.*

1 The air entering the vehicle's ventilation system is passed through a very fine pleated-paper air filter element, which removes particles of pollen, dust and other airborne foreign matter. To ensure its continued effectiveness, this filter's element must be renewed at regular intervals. Failure to renew the element will also result in greatly-reduced airflow into the passenger compartment, reducing demisting and ventilation.

2 The pollen filter is located in the air intake at the base of the windscreen. Open the bonnet for access.

3 Lift up the separate section of weatherstrip which fits over the top edge of the pollen filter access panel **(see illustration)**.

4 Unscrew and remove the two retaining bolts, and pull out the pollen filter access panel **(see illustrations)**.

5 Reach in through the access panel, and release the two spring clips which retain the pollen filter. Lower the filter out of its location, noting which way up it fits **(see illustration)**.

6 As far as possible, clean the inside of the filter housing, and the inside of the access panel.

9 Hose and fluid leak check

1 Visually inspect the engine joint faces, gaskets and seals for any signs of water or oil leaks. Pay particular attention to the areas around the cylinder head, oil filter and sump joint faces. Bear in mind that, over a period of time, some very slight seepage from these areas is to be expected - what you are really

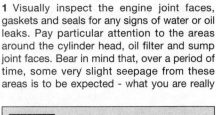

A leak in the cooling system will usually show up as white- or rust-coloured deposits on the areas adjoining the leak.

looking for is any indication of a serious leak **(see Haynes Hint)**. Should a leak be found, renew the offending gasket or oil seal by referring to the appropriate Chapters in this manual.

2 Also check the security and condition of all the engine-related pipes and hoses. Ensure that all cable-ties or securing clips are in place and in good condition. Clips that are broken or missing can lead to chafing of the hoses, pipes or wiring, which could cause more serious problems in the future.

3 Carefully check the radiator hoses and heater hoses along their entire length. Renew any hose that is cracked, swollen or deteriorated. Cracks will show up better if the hose is squeezed. Pay close attention to the hose clips that secure the hoses to the cooling system components. Hose clips can pinch and puncture hoses, resulting in cooling system leaks **(see illustration)**.

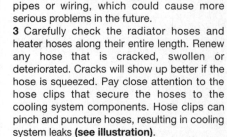

9.3 Check all hoses and their retaining clips

4 Inspect all the cooling system components (hoses, joint faces etc.) for leaks. A leak in the cooling system will usually show up as white- or rust-coloured deposits on the area adjoining the leak. Where any problems of this nature are found on system components, renew the component or gasket with reference to Chapter 3.

5 Where applicable, inspect the automatic transmission fluid cooler hoses for leaks or deterioration.

6 With the vehicle raised, inspect the fuel tank and filler neck for punctures, cracks and other damage. The connection between the filler neck and tank is especially critical. Sometimes a rubber filler neck or connecting hose will leak due to loose retaining clamps or deteriorated rubber.

7 Carefully check all rubber hoses and metal fuel lines leading away from the fuel tank. Check for loose connections, deteriorated hoses, crimped lines, and other damage. Pay particular attention to the vent pipes and hoses, which often loop up around the filler neck and can become blocked or crimped. Follow the lines to the front of the vehicle, carefully inspecting them all the way. Renew damaged sections as necessary.

8 From within the engine compartment, check the security of all fuel hose attachments and pipe unions, and inspect the fuel hoses and vacuum hoses for kinks, chafing and deterioration **(see illustration)**.

9 Check the condition of the power steering fluid hoses and pipes.

10 Transmission and driveshaft gaiter check

1 Raise the front of the vehicle and support on axle stands. Alternatively, drive the car onto ramps.

2 Inspect around the transmission for any sign of leaks or damage. In particular, check the area around the driveshaft oil/fluid seals for leakage. Slight seepage should not be of great concern, but a serious leak should be investigated further, with reference to Chapter 7A or 7B.

3 Check the security and condition of the wiring and wiring plugs on the transmission housing.

4 With the vehicle raised and securely supported on stands, turn the steering onto full lock, then slowly rotate the roadwheel. Inspect the condition of the outer constant velocity (CV) joint rubber gaiters, squeezing the gaiters to open out the folds. Check for signs of cracking, splits or deterioration of the rubber, which may allow the grease to escape, and lead to water and grit entry into the joint. Also check the security and condition of the retaining clips. Repeat these checks on the inner CV joints. If any damage or deterioration is found, the gaiters should be renewed (see Chapter 8).

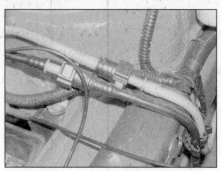

9.8 Check all fuel and vacuum hoses

5 At the same time, check the general condition of the CV joints themselves by first holding the driveshaft and attempting to rotate the wheel. Repeat this check by holding the inner joint and attempting to rotate the driveshaft. Any appreciable movement indicates wear in the joints, wear in the driveshaft splines, or a loose driveshaft retaining nut.

11 Braking system pipes and hoses check

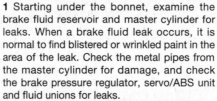

1 Starting under the bonnet, examine the brake fluid reservoir and master cylinder for leaks. When a brake fluid leak occurs, it is normal to find blistered or wrinkled paint in the area of the leak. Check the metal pipes from the master cylinder for damage, and check the brake pressure regulator, servo/ABS unit and fluid unions for leaks.

2 With the vehicle raised and securely supported on stands, first inspect each front brake caliper. In particular, check the flexible hose leading to the caliper for signs of damage or leaks, especially where the hose enters the metal end fitting. Make sure that the hose is not twisted or kinked, and that it cannot come into contact with any other components when the steering is on full lock.

3 From the caliper, trace the metal brake pipes back along the car. Again, look for leaks from the fluid unions or signs of damage, but additionally check the pipes for signs of corrosion **(see illustration)**. Make sure the

11.3 Check all brake pipes and fittings for corrosion

pipes are securely located by the clips provided on the vehicle underside.

4 At the rear of the vehicle, inspect each rear brake and its flexible hose, where applicable. Examine the handbrake cable, tracing it back from each rear brake and checking for frayed cables or other damage. Lubricate the handbrake cable guides, pivots and other moving parts with general-purpose grease.

5 If any damage is found, refer to Chapter 9 for further information.

12 Exhaust system check

1 With the engine cold (at least an hour after the vehicle has been driven), check the complete exhaust system from the engine to the end of the tailpipe. The exhaust system is most easily checked with the vehicle raised on a hoist, or suitably supported on axle stands, so that the exhaust components are readily visible and accessible.

2 Check the exhaust pipes and connections for evidence of leaks, severe corrosion and damage **(see illustration)**. Make sure that all brackets and mountings are in good condition, and that all relevant nuts and bolts are tight. Leakage at any of the joints or in other parts of the system will usually show up as a black sooty stain in the vicinity of the leak.

3 Rattles and other noises can often be traced to the exhaust system, especially the brackets and mountings **(see illustration)**.

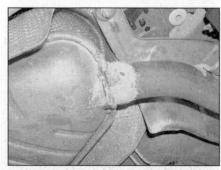

12.2 Check all exhaust joints for signs of corrosion damage

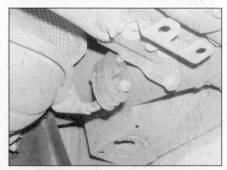

12.3 Check the condition of all exhaust mounting brackets and rubbers

Try to move the pipes and silencers. If the components are able to come into contact with the body or suspension parts, secure the system with new mountings. Otherwise separate the joints (if possible) and twist the pipes as necessary to provide additional clearance.

13 Steering and suspension check

Front suspension and steering check

1 Raise the front of the vehicle, and securely support it on axle stands. Where necessary for improved access, release the fasteners and remove the engine undertray (where applicable).
2 Visually inspect the balljoint dust covers and the steering rack-and-pinion gaiters for splits, chafing or deterioration. Any wear of these components will cause loss of lubricant, together with dirt and water entry, resulting in rapid deterioration of the balljoints or steering gear **(see illustration)**.
3 Check the power steering fluid hoses for chafing or deterioration, and the pipe and hose unions for fluid leaks. Also check for signs of fluid leakage under pressure from the steering gear rubber gaiters, which would indicate failed fluid seals within the steering gear.
4 Grasp the roadwheel at the 12 o'clock and 6 o'clock positions, and try to rock it. Very slight free play may be felt, but if the movement is appreciable, further investigation is necessary to determine the source. Continue rocking the wheel while an assistant depresses the footbrake. If the movement is now eliminated or significantly reduced, it is likely that the hub bearings are at fault. If the free play is still evident with the footbrake depressed, then there is wear in the suspension joints or mountings. Before condemning any components, however, check that the roadwheel bolts are tightened to the specified torque.
5 Now grasp the wheel at the 9 o'clock and 3 o'clock positions, and try to rock it as before. Any movement felt now may again be caused by wear in the hub bearings or the steering track-rod balljoints. If the inner or outer balljoint is worn, the visual movement will be obvious.
6 Using a large screwdriver or flat bar, check for wear in the suspension mounting bushes by levering between the relevant suspension component and its attachment point. Some movement is to be expected as the mountings are made of rubber, but excessive wear should be obvious. Also check the condition of any visible rubber bushes, looking for splits, cracks or contamination of the rubber.
7 With the car standing on its wheels, have an assistant turn the steering wheel back and forth about an eighth of a turn each way. There should be very little, if any, lost movement between the steering wheel and

roadwheels. If this is not the case, closely observe the joints and mountings previously described, but in addition, check the steering column universal joints for wear, and the rack-and-pinion steering gear itself.

Suspension strut/shock absorber check

8 Check for any signs of fluid leakage around the suspension strut/shock absorber body, or from the rubber gaiter around the piston rod. Should any fluid be noticed, the suspension strut/shock absorber is defective internally, and should be renewed. **Note:** *Suspension struts/shock absorbers should always be renewed in pairs on the same axle.*
9 The efficiency of the suspension strut/shock absorber may be checked by bouncing the vehicle at each corner. Generally speaking, the body will return to its normal position and stop after being depressed. If it rises and returns on a rebound, the suspension strut/shock absorber is probably suspect. Examine also the suspension strut/shock absorber upper and lower mountings for any signs of wear.

14 Underbody protection check

Raise and support the vehicle on axle stands. Using an electric torch or lead light, inspect the entire underside of the vehicle, paying particular attention to the wheelarches. Look for any damage to the flexible underbody coating, which may crack or flake off with age, leading to corrosion. Also check that the wheelarch liners are securely attached with any clips provided - if they come loose, dirt may get in behind the liners and defeat their purpose. If there is any damage to the underseal, or any corrosion, it should be repaired before the damage gets too serious.

15 Lights and horn operation check

1 With the ignition switched on where necessary, check the operation of all exterior lights.
2 Check the brake lights with the help of an assistant, or by reversing up close to a reflective door. Make sure that all the rear lights are capable of operating independently, without affecting any of the other lights - for example, switch on as many rear lights as possible, then try the brake lights. If any unusual results are found, this is usually due to an earth fault or other poor connection at that rear light unit.
3 Again with the help of an assistant or using a reflective surface, check as far as possible that the headlights work on both main and dipped beam.
4 Replace any defective bulbs with reference to Chapter 12.

13.2 Check the condition of the balljoint rubber covers

HAYNES HiNT *Particularly on older vehicles, bulbs can stop working as a result of corrosion build-up on the bulb or its holder - fitting a new bulb may not cure the problem in this instance. When replacing any bulb, if you find any green or white-coloured powdery deposits, these should be cleaned off using emery cloth.*

5 Check the operation of all interior lights, including the glovebox and luggage area illumination lights. Switch on the ignition, and check that all relevant warning lights come on as expected - the vehicle handbook should give details of these. Now start the engine, and check that the appropriate lights go out. When you are next driving at night, check that all the instrument panel and facia lighting works correctly. If any problems are found, refer to Chapter 12, Section 5.
6 Finally, choose an appropriate time of day to test the operation of the horn.

16 Hinge and lock lubrication

Lubricate the hinges of the bonnet, doors and tailgate with light general-purpose oil. Similarly, lubricate all latches, locks and lock strikers, and the door check straps with general-purpose oil or grease **(see illustration)**. At the same time, check the

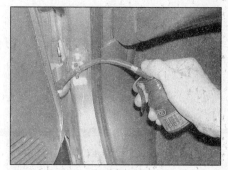

16.1 Lubricate the door hinges and check straps

security and operation of all the locks, adjusting them if necessary (see Chapter 11).

Lightly lubricate the bonnet release mechanism and cable with suitable grease.

Do not attempt to lubricate the steering lock.

17 Road test

Instruments and electrical equipment

1 Check the operation of all instruments and electrical equipment.
2 Make sure that all instruments read correctly, and switch on all electrical equipment in turn, to check that it functions properly.

Steering and suspension

3 Check for any abnormalities in the steering, suspension, handling or road 'feel'.
4 Drive the vehicle, and check that there are no unusual vibrations or noises.
5 Check that the steering feels positive, with no excessive 'sloppiness', or roughness, and check for any suspension noises when cornering and driving over bumps.

Drivetrain

6 Check the performance of the engine, clutch (where applicable), transmission and driveshafts.
7 Listen for any unusual noises from the engine, clutch and transmission.
8 Make sure the engine runs smoothly at idle, and there is no hesitation on accelerating.
9 Check that, where applicable, the clutch action is smooth and progressive, that the drive is taken up smoothly, and that the pedal travel is not excessive. Also listen for any noises when the clutch pedal is depressed.
10 On manual transmission models, check that all gears can be engaged smoothly without noise, and that the gear lever action is not abnormally vague or 'notchy'.
11 On automatic transmission models, make sure that all gearchanges occur smoothly, without snatching, and without an increase in engine speed between changes. Check that all the gear positions can be selected with the vehicle at rest. If any problems are found, they should be referred to a FIAT dealer.
12 Listen for a metallic clicking sound from the front of the vehicle, as the vehicle is driven slowly in a circle with the steering on full-lock. Carry out this check in both directions. If a clicking noise is heard, this indicates wear in a driveshaft joint, in which case renew the joint if necessary.

Braking system

13 Make sure that the vehicle does not pull to one side when braking, and that the wheels do not lock prematurely when braking hard.
14 Check that there is no vibration through the steering when braking.
15 Check that the handbrake operates correctly without excessive movement of the lever, and that it holds the vehicle stationary on a slope.
16 Test the operation of the brake servo unit as follows. With the engine off, depress the footbrake four or five times to exhaust the vacuum. Hold the brake pedal depressed, then start the engine. As the engine starts, there should be a noticeable 'give' in the brake pedal as vacuum builds up. Allow the engine to run for at least two minutes, and then switch it off. If the brake pedal is depressed now, it should be possible to detect a hiss from the servo as the pedal is depressed. After about four or five applications, no further hissing should be heard, and the pedal should feel considerably harder.

Every 24 000 miles (40 000 km)

18 Spark plug renewal

1 The correct functioning of the spark plugs is vital for the correct running and efficiency of the engine. It is essential that the plugs fitted are appropriate for the engine (a suitable type is specified at the beginning of this Chapter). If this type is used and the engine is in good condition, the spark plugs should not need attention between scheduled replacement intervals. Spark plug cleaning is rarely necessary, and should not be attempted unless specialised equipment is available, as damage can easily be caused to the firing ends.
2 Before removing the spark plugs, allow the engine time to cool.

1.2 and 1.4 litre engines

3 Remove the three bolts securing the engine top cover, loosen the fourth bolt at the rear of the timing cover (where applicable), and lift away the cover for access to the spark plugs and leads **(see illustrations)**.

1.2, 1.4 and 1.6 litre engines

4 Release the HT leads from the retaining clips on the top of the cylinder head as necessary.
5 If the marks on the original-equipment spark plug (HT) leads cannot be seen, mark the leads 1 to 4, to correspond to the cylinder the lead serves (No 1 cylinder is at the timing belt end of the engine).

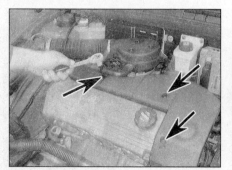

18.3a Remove the three screws (arrowed) . . .

18.3b . . . loosen the screw behind the timing cover . . .

18.3c . . . and remove the engine top cover - 1.4 litre engine

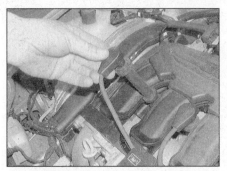

18.6 Pull the HT leads off the spark plugs

18.7a Removing one of the Allen screws under the oil filler cap

18.7b Lifting off the engine top cover

6 Carefully pull the lead end fittings upwards from the plugs, and (where applicable) out of the recesses in the cylinder head. Grip the end fitting, not the lead, otherwise the lead connection may be fractured **(see illustration)**.

1.8 litre engine

7 Unscrew the oil filler cap, and remove the two Allen screws concealed underneath. Remove the six main cover bolts, and lift off the engine top cover, for access to the ignition coil assemblies **(see illustrations)**.
8 Disconnect the wiring plugs from the ignition coil which fits over each spark plug **(see illustration)**.
9 To avoid transposing the ignition coils, it is advisable to work on one assembly at a time. Alternatively, mark the coil assemblies for position, noting that No 1 coil is nearest the timing belt end of the engine.

10 Starting with No 1 coil, unscrew the two bolts securing the coil to the cylinder head **(see illustration)**.
11 Carefully pull the coil and plug connector upwards off the plug, and withdraw it from the cylinder head recess **(see illustration)**.

All engines

12 It is advisable to remove the debris from the spark plug recesses using a clean brush, vacuum cleaner or compressed air before removing the plugs. If this is not done, this debris will drop into the cylinders or lodge in the spark plug threads.
13 Unscrew the plugs using a spark plug spanner, suitable box spanner or a deep socket and extension bar **(see illustrations)**. Keep the socket aligned with the spark plug - if it is forcibly moved to one side, the ceramic insulator may be broken off. As each plug is removed, examine it as follows.

14 Examination of the spark plugs will give a good indication of the condition of the engine. If the insulator nose of the spark plug is clean and white, with no deposits, this is indicative of a weak mixture or too hot a plug (a hot plug transfers heat away from the electrode slowly, a cold plug transfers heat away quickly).
15 If the tip and insulator nose are covered with hard black-looking deposits, then this is indicative that the mixture is too rich. Should the plug be black and oily, then it is likely that the engine is fairly worn, as well as the mixture being too rich.
16 If the insulator nose is covered with light-coloured deposits, then the mixture is correct and it is likely that the engine is in good condition.
17 The spark plug electrode gap is of considerable importance as, if it is too large or too small, the size of the spark and its efficiency will be seriously impaired. Where the

18.8 Disconnect the wiring plug from each coil

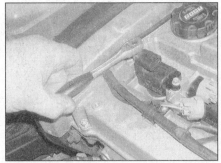

18.10 Unscrew the two coil retaining bolts

18.11 Pull the coil upwards off its spark plug

18.13a Unscrew the plugs using a socket and extension bar - 1.6 litre engine . . .

18.13b . . . and on the 1.4 litre engine

18.13c . . . and remove them from the engine - note the twin-earth electrode plug

HAYNES HiNT

It is very often difficult to insert spark plugs into their holes without cross-threading them. To avoid this possibility, fit a short length of 5/16 inch internal diameter rubber hose over the end of the spark plug. The flexible hose acts as a universal joint to help align the plug with the plug hole. Should the plug begin to cross-thread, the hose will slip on the spark plug, preventing thread damage to the aluminium cylinder head

gap can be adjusted, it should be set to the value specified at the start of this Chapter.
Note: *Spark plugs with multiple earth electrodes are becoming an increasingly common fitment, especially to vehicles equipped with catalytic converters. Unless there is clear information to the contrary, no attempt should be made to adjust the plug gap on a spark plug with more than one earth electrode.*

18 To set the gap, measure it with a feeler blade and then bend open, or closed, the outer plug electrode until the correct gap is achieved. The centre electrode should never be bent, as this may crack the insulator and cause plug failure, if nothing worse. If using feeler blades, the gap is correct when the appropriate-size blade is a firm sliding fit.
19 Special spark plug electrode gap adjusting tools are available from most motor accessory shops, or from some spark plug manufacturers.
20 Before fitting the spark plugs, check that the threaded connector sleeves are tight, and that the plug exterior surfaces and threads are clean. It's often difficult to screw in new spark plugs without cross-threading them - this can be avoided using a piece of rubber hose **(see Haynes Hint)**.
21 Remove the rubber hose (if used), and tighten the plug to the specified torque using the spark plug socket and a torque wrench. If a torque wrench is not available, tighten the plug by hand until it just seats, then tighten it by no more than a quarter of a turn further with the plug socket and handle. Refit the remaining spark plugs in the same manner.
22 Refit the HT leads (or ignition coils) securely in their correct order.
23 Where applicable, refit the engine top cover, using a reversal of the removal procedure.

19.1 Loosen the securing clip, and pull off the air inlet duct . . .

19.2b . . . and remove the air cleaner lid

19 Air filter renewal

1 Release the metal retaining band securing the air inlet duct to the air cleaner lid, and separate the duct from the lid **(see illustration)**.
2 Remove the screws securing the air cleaner lid, and lift the lid away **(see illustrations)**.
3 Lift out the filter element, noting which way round it fits **(see illustration)**.
4 Remove any debris that may have collected inside the air cleaner.
5 Fit a new air filter element in position, noting any direction-of-fitting markings and ensuring that the edges are securely seated.
6 Refit the air cleaner lid and secure with the screws. Refit the air inlet duct, and secure with the retaining band.

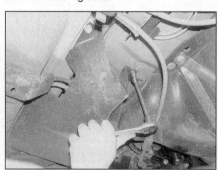

20.3 Unscrew the bolts securing the filter cover panel

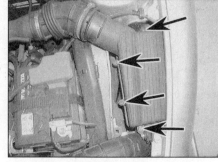

19.2a Loosen the securing screws (arrowed) . . .

19.3 Lift out the air filter element, noting which way round it fits

20 Fuel filter renewal

Warning: Refer to the notes in Safety first!, and follow them implicitly. Petrol is a highly-dangerous and volatile liquid, and the precautions necessary when handling it cannot be overstressed.

Note: *On later 1.6 litre models, and all 1.2 litre models, an in-line fuel filter is not fitted (even though the plastic cover panel still appears under the car). On these models, the only filters are fitted to the base of the fuel pump/sender unit, inside the fuel tank - these are not routinely replaced.*

1 The fuel filter is situated underneath the rear of the vehicle, next to the fuel tank. To gain access to the filter, chock the front wheels, then jack up the rear of the vehicle and support it securely on axle stands.
2 Depressurise the fuel system with reference to the relevant Part of Chapter 4.
3 To gain access to the filter, unbolt and remove the plastic cover panel fitted underneath it **(see illustration)**.
4 If you have them, fit hose clamps to the filter inlet and outlet hoses. These are not essential, but even with the system depressurised, there will still be an amount of petrol in the pipes (and the old filter), and this will siphon out when the pipes are disconnected. Even with hose clamps fitted, the old filter will contain some fuel, so have some rags ready to soak up any spillage.

5 Before removing the filter, note any direction-of-flow markings on the filter body, and check against the new filter - the arrow should point in the direction of fuel flow (following the hose leading to the front of the car) **(see illustration)**.

6 The inlet and outlet hoses are equipped with quick-release connectors. To release the connectors, squeeze them together at the sides, then pull apart **(see illustration)**.

7 Loosen the retaining clamp bolt and remove the old filter **(see illustration)**.

8 If the fuel hoses show any sign of damage, or if the quick-release connectors are not making a secure fit, seek the advice of a FIAT dealer on renewing the hoses.

9 Fit the new filter into position, with the flow marking arrow correctly orientated, and tighten the retaining clamp bolt **(see illustration)**.

10 Reconnect the fuel hoses, ensuring that no dirt is allowed to enter the hoses or filter connections, and that the quick-release connectors click together fully.

11 Start the engine (there may be a delay as the system re-pressurises and the new filter fills with fuel). Let the engine run for several minutes while you check the filter hose connections for leaks.

12 Refit the cover panel below the filter, secure with the bolts, then lower the vehicle to the ground.

 Warning: Dispose safely of the old filter; it will be highly flammable, and may explode if thrown on a fire.

21 Auxiliary drivebelt check and renewal

1.2 litre engine

1 Remove the three bolts securing the engine upper cover, and remove the cover for access to the belts.

2 With the car parked on a level surface, apply the handbrake and chock the rear wheels. Loosen the right-hand front wheel bolts.

3 Raise the front of the vehicle, rest it securely on axle stands and remove the right-hand front roadwheel.

4 Unscrew and release the fasteners securing the wheelarch inner panel, to gain access to the belt run.

Power steering pump drivebelt

5 The power steering pump is located at the front of the engine. Check the condition of the pump drivebelt as follows.

6 Look for cracks, splitting and fraying on the surface of the belt; check also for signs of glazing (shiny patches) and separation of the belt plies. If damage or wear is visible, the belt should be renewed. If there is any evidence of contamination by oil, grease or coolant, the reason should be investigated without delay.

20.5 Note the flow direction arrow before removing the old filter

7 Note that it is not unusual for a ribbed belt to exhibit small cracks in the edges of the belt ribs, and unless these are extensive or very deep, belt renewal is not essential.

8 Using a socket and wrench on the crankshaft pulley bolt, rotate the crankshaft so that the full length of the drivebelt can be examined.

9 If the belt is to be removed, loosen the fasteners described in Section 7 and slip the drivebelt from the pulleys.

10 Refitting the belt is a reversal of removal, making sure that the belt ribs engage properly with the pulley grooves. Tension the belt using the information in Section 7.

Air conditioning compressor drivebelt

11 Where fitted, the drivebelt is the 'middle' drivebelt of three. The compressor is mounted at the rear of the engine, below the alternator.

12 Check the belt using the information in paragraphs 6 to 8.

13 If the belt is to be removed, first remove the power steering pump drivebelt as described previously. Loosen the fasteners on the compressor as described in Section 7, and slip the drivebelt from the pulleys.

14 Refitting the belt is a reversal of removal, making sure that the belt ribs engage properly with the pulley grooves. Tension the compressor and pump drivebelts using the information in Section 7.

Alternator drivebelt

15 The alternator is fitted at the rear of the engine.

16 Check the belt using the information in paragraphs 6 to 8.

20.6 Disconnecting one of the quick-release hoses

17 If the belt is to be removed, first remove the air conditioning compressor drivebelt (where applicable) as described previously. Loosen the fasteners on the alternator as described in Section 7, and slip the drivebelt from the pulleys.

18 Refitting the belt is a reversal of removal, making sure that the belt ribs engage properly with the pulley grooves. On models with air conditioning, loosely fit the alternator drivebelt first, then fit and tension the compressor drivebelt before tensioning the alternator belt. Tension the drivebelts using the information in Section 7.

1.6 litre engine

19 To improve access, remove the wheelarch inner panel as described in paragraphs 2 to 4.

Air conditioning compressor drivebelt

20 The air conditioning compressor is mounted at the front of the engine.

21 Check the belt using the information in paragraphs 6 to 8.

22 Loosen the fasteners on the tensioner pulley as described in Section 7, and slip the drivebelt from the pulleys.

23 Refitting the belt is a reversal of removal, noting the following points:

a) Fit the belt around the pulleys as noted on removal, with the flat side of the belt over the tensioner wheel. Make sure that the belt ribs engage properly with the pulley grooves. Make sure that any slack in the belt is adjacent to the tensioner.

b) Tension the belt using the information in Section 7.

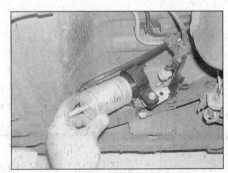

20.7 Removing the fuel filter

20.9 Tighten the filter clamp bolt securely

21.25a Loosen the tensioner bolts . . .

21.25b . . . and remove the auxiliary drivebelt from the pulleys

c) *Refit the wheelarch access panel and the roadwheel, and lower the car to the ground. Tighten the wheel bolts to the specified torque.*

Alternator/coolant pump drivebelt

24 Check the belt using the information in paragraphs 6 to 8.

25 If the belt is to be removed, either for servicing work or renewal, remove the air conditioning compressor belt (where applicable) as described previously. Loosen the tensioner bolts, and release the belt tension. Noting how the belt is fitted around the pulleys, slip the belt off and remove it **(see illustrations)**.

26 Refitting the belt is a reversal of removal, noting the following points:

a) *Fit the belt around all the pulleys as noted on removal, apart from the tensioner pulley, making sure that the belt ribs engage properly with the pulley grooves.*

Make sure that any slack in the belt is adjacent to the tensioner.

b) *Turn the tensioner pulley fully anti-clockwise, then slip the flat side of the belt over the tensioner pulley.*

c) *Tension the belt using the information in Section 7.*

d) *Where applicable, refit the air conditioning compressor drivebelt as described previously.*

e) *Refit the wheelarch access panel and the roadwheel, and lower the car to the ground. Tighten the wheel bolts to the specified torque.*

Power steering pump drivebelt

27 Check the belt using the information in paragraphs 6 to 8.

28 If the belt is to be removed, either for servicing work or renewal, the lower belt (which drives the alternator and coolant pump) must

be removed first, as described previously. Loosen the pump mountings, the nut and bolt on the adjuster slot, and the adjuster locknut. Turn the adjuster bolt to slacken the belt tension, then slip the belt from the power steering pump pulley **(see illustrations)**.

29 Refitting the belt is a reversal of removal, making sure that the belt ribs engage properly with the pulley grooves. Tension the belt using the information in Section 7.

1.4 and 1.8 litre engines

30 To improve access, remove the wheelarch inner panel as described in paragraphs 2 to 4. Also remove the upper guard from the drivebelt, which is secured by two bolts - release the hose which is also clipped to the belt guard **(see illustration)**.

31 Check the belt using the information in paragraphs 6 to 8.

32 If the belt is to be removed, either for servicing work or renewal, first note how the belt is fitted around the pulleys. Using a spanner on the drivebelt tensioner bolt, rotate the tensioner anti-clockwise to release the belt tension, then slip the belt from the pulleys **(see illustration)**.

33 Refitting the belt is a reversal of removal, noting the following points:

a) *Fit the belt around all the pulleys as noted on removal, apart from the tensioner pulley, making sure that the belt ribs engage properly with the pulley grooves. Make sure that any slack in the belt is adjacent to the tensioner.*

b) *Turn the tensioner pulley fully anti-clockwise, then slip the flat side of the belt over the tensioner pulley.*

c) *Release the tensioner, and allow it to tension the belt.*

d) *Using a spanner on the crankshaft pulley bolt, turn the belt clockwise through one complete revolution, checking that the belt runs true, and that the belt ribs stay located in the pulley grooves.*

e) *Refit the wheelarch access panel and the roadwheel, and lower the car to the ground. Tighten the wheel bolts to the specified torque.*

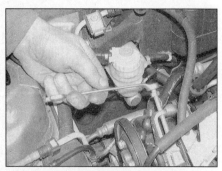

21.28a Turn the adjuster to release the belt tension . . .

21.28b . . . and remove the drivebelt from the steering pump pulley

22 Clutch cable adjustment

Note: *This check does not apply to models with a hydraulically-operated clutch - the clutch on these models is self-adjusting.*
Refer to Chapter 6, Section 2.

23 Handbrake adjustment

1 The handbrake should be fully applied by the fifth click from the handbrake lever ratchet mechanism.

21.30 Removing the drivebelt upper guard

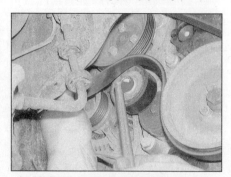

21.32 Release the belt tension, then slip the belt from the pulleys

2 To fully check the operation of the handbrake, chock the front wheels, then jack up the rear of the car and support it on axle stands.

3 Release the handbrake completely, and check that both rear wheels are free to turn. If this is not the case, either the handbrake has been over-adjusted, the cable is binding, or there is a problem with the rear drums (investigate using the information in Chapter 9).

4 Apply the handbrake by three clicks of the ratchet. By this point, both rear wheels should become difficult to turn by hand. By the time the lever has been set to the fifth notch (if not before) the wheels should be completely locked.

5 In practice, it may be found that the lever will not travel five notches - provided the handbrake releases completely, and can be fully applied, it is perhaps unnecessary to adjust the cable in this instance. If the lever travels more than five notches, adjustment is required, as follows.

6 Remove the gaiter from the handbrake lever, for access to the adjuster nut. The gaiter clips into a collar/groove at the base of the handbrake grip, and has a lip around its base which clips into the hole in the centre console. Release the gaiter, and lift it over the handbrake lever.

7 Adjust the nut at the base of the lever as required, until the operation of the handbrake is satisfactory. On completion, lower the rear of the car to the ground.

24 Exhaust emissions check

This check is part of the manufacturer's maintenance schedule, and involves testing the exhaust emissions using an exhaust gas analyser. Unless a fault is suspected, this test is not essential, although it should be noted that it is recommended by the manufacturers. In the majority of cases, adjusting the idle speed and mixture is either not possible, or requires access to dedicated FIAT test equipment. Exhaust emissions testing is included as part of the MoT test.

25 Engine management system fault code check

1 This check is part of the manufacturer's maintenance schedule, and involves 'interrogating' the engine management control unit (and those for the automatic transmission and/or ABS, as applicable) using special dedicated test equipment. Such testing will allow the test equipment to read any fault codes stored in the electronic control unit memory **(see illustration)**.

25.1 Connector plug for use with diagnostic equipment - 1.6 litre model shown

2 Unless a fault is suspected, this test is not essential, although it should be noted that it is recommended by the manufacturers.

3 It is possible for quite serious faults to occur in the engine management system without the owner being aware of it. Certain engine management system faults will cause the system to enter an emergency back-up mode, which is often so sophisticated that engine performance is not apparently much affected. If a problem has caused the system to enter its back-up mode, this will usually be most apparent when starting and running from cold.

Every 36 000 miles (60 000 km)

26 Brake fluid renewal

⚠ **Warning: Brake hydraulic fluid can harm your eyes and damage painted surfaces, so use extreme caution when handling and pouring it. Do not use fluid that has been standing open for some time, as it absorbs moisture from the air. Excess moisture can cause a dangerous loss of braking effectiveness.**

1 The procedure is similar to that for the bleeding of the hydraulic system as described in Chapter 9. The brake fluid reservoir should be emptied by siphoning, using a clean poultry baster or similar before starting, and allowance should be made for the old fluid to be expelled when bleeding a section of the circuit.

2 Working as described in Chapter 9, open the first bleed screw in the sequence, and pump the brake pedal gently until nearly all the old fluid has been emptied from the master cylinder reservoir.

HAYNES HiNT *Old hydraulic fluid is often much darker in colour than the new, making it easy to distinguish the two.*

3 Top-up to the MAX level with new fluid, and continue pumping until only the new fluid remains in the reservoir, and new fluid can be seen emerging from the bleed screw. Tighten the screw, and top the reservoir level up to the MAX level line.

4 Work through all the remaining bleed screws in the sequence until new fluid can be seen at all of them. Be careful to keep the master cylinder reservoir topped-up to above the MIN level at all times, or air may enter the system and greatly increase the length of the task.

5 When the operation is complete, check that all bleed screws are securely tightened, and that their dust caps are refitted. Wash off all traces of spilt fluid, and recheck the fluid level.

27.3 Unscrewing the transmission oil filler/level plug

6 Check the operation of the brakes before taking the car on the road.

27 Manual transmission oil level check

1 Park the car on a level surface. The oil level must be checked before the car is driven, or at least 5 minutes after the engine has been switched off. If the oil is checked immediately after driving the car, some of the oil will remain distributed around the transmission components, resulting in an inaccurate level reading.

2 The filler/level plug is on the front of the transmission housing, typically next to the reversing light switch. Access is possible from above, but is better from below, once the engine undertray has been removed (where applicable).

3 Wipe clean the area around the filler/level plug. A large Allen key or socket will be required to remove the plug, which will probably be quite tight **(see illustration)**.

4 Remove the plug, and check the oil level. This can be done with your finger; alternatively, a piece of bent wire can be inserted through the plug hole to assess the oil level inside the transmission - if this is

27.4a Remove the filler/level plug . . .

27.4b . . . and check the oil level using a suitable probe

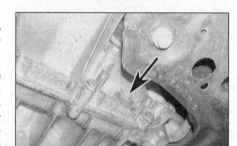

27.5 If necessary, top-up the oil level, until oil just starts to trickle out

done, make sure that whatever is used cannot break off or fall inside **(see illustrations)**.
5 The oil level should reach the lower edge of the filler/level hole. A certain amount of oil will have gathered behind the filler/level plug, and will trickle out when it is removed; this does **not** necessarily indicate that the level is correct. To ensure that a true level is established, wait until the initial trickle has stopped, then add oil through the hole as necessary until a trickle of new oil can be seen emerging **(see illustration)**. The level will be correct when the flow ceases; use only good-quality oil of the specified type.
6 Filling the transmission with oil is an extremely awkward operation; above all, allow plenty of time for the oil level to settle properly before checking it. If a large amount is added to the transmission, and a large amount flows out on checking the level, refit the filler/level plug; take the vehicle on a short journey so that the new oil is distributed fully around the transmission components, then recheck the level when it has settled again.
7 If the transmission has been overfilled so that oil flows out when the filler/level plug is removed, check that the car is completely level (front-to-rear and side-to-side), and allow the surplus to drain off into a suitable container.

8 When the level is correct, refit the plug, tightening it to the specified torque, and wipe off any spilt oil. Refit the engine undertray (where removed).
9 FIAT do not state that the transmission oil need ever be drained and refilled as part of the routine maintenance schedule. However, a car which has covered a large mileage would clearly benefit from this being done. For those owners who wish to change the transmission oil, a drain plug is provided on the base of the transmission housing **(see illustration)**. Once the oil has been drained, tighten the plug to the specified torque, and refill until the level is correct.

28 Rear brake shoe check

1 On some models, the thickness of friction material remaining on one of the brake shoes can be observed through an inspection window in the brake backplate.
2 Loosen the rear wheel bolts and chock the front wheels. Jack up the rear of the car and support on axle stands. Remove the rear wheels.

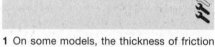

27.9 Transmission oil drain plug (arrowed)

3 The Inspection window in the brake backplate may be plugged with a sealing grommet, which can be prised out. A torch or inspection light will probably be required, as well as a small mirror if access is difficult. If the friction material on any shoe is worn down to the specified minimum thickness or less, all four shoes must be renewed as a set.
4 For a comprehensive check (or on cars where no inspection window is provided), the brake drum should be removed and cleaned. This will also allow the wheel cylinders to be checked, and the condition of the brake drum itself to be fully examined (see Chapter 9).

Every 48 000 miles (80 000 km)

29 Evaporative emission control system check

Check all the engine vacuum and fuel vapour hoses associated with the system (typically blue in colour) for signs of cracking, leaks, and general deterioration. For more information, see Chapter 4C. This check is

particularly relevant if any fuel smells have been noted, in which case all fuel pipes and connections should be closely inspected.

Every 72 000 miles (120 000 km)

30 Timing belt renewal

Refer to the relevant Part of Chapter 2.

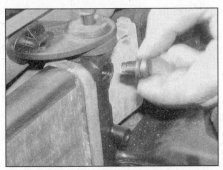

31.3a Opening the radiator bleed screw on a 1.4 litre engine . . .

31.3b . . . and on a 1.6 litre engine

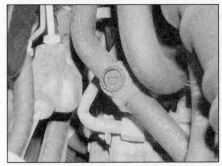

31.3c Typical heater hose bleed screw - 1.4 litre engine shown

Every 2 years (regardless of mileage)

31 Coolant renewal

Cooling system draining

⚠️ **Warning: Wait until the engine is cold before starting this procedure. Do not allow antifreeze to come in contact with your skin, or with the painted surfaces of the vehicle. Rinse off spills immediately with plenty of water. Never leave antifreeze lying around in an open container, or in a puddle in the driveway or on the garage floor. Children and pets are attracted by its sweet smell, but antifreeze can be fatal if ingested.**

1 With the engine completely cold, cover the expansion tank cap with a wad of rag, and slowly turn the cap anti-clockwise to relieve the pressure in the cooling system (a hissing sound will normally be heard). Wait until any pressure remaining in the system is released, then continue to turn the cap until it can be removed.

2 Where necessary, release the fasteners and remove the engine undertray. On all models except those with the 1.4 litre engine, access to the radiator and cooling system bleed screws may be improved by removing the two screws securing the air inlet shroud over the radiator.

3 Open all the cooling system bleed screws.

Depending on model, there will be one or two on or around the radiator, and one in each of the hoses leading to the heater (towards the engine compartment bulkhead) **(see illustrations)**.

4 Position a suitable container beneath the radiator bottom hose connection, then release the retaining clip and ease the hose from the radiator stub **(see illustrations)**. Some models have hose clips which cannot be re-used, as they have to be cut off. Take care not to damage the hose as this is done, and obtain new clips for refitting.

5 If the hose joint has not been disturbed for some time, it will be necessary to gently manipulate the hose to break the joint. Do not use excessive force, or the radiator stub could be damaged. Allow the coolant to drain into the container. Some models also have a drain tap at the base of the radiator.

6 On 1.6 litre models, a cylinder block drain plug is provided on the front of the engine, next to the starter motor **(see illustration)**. Removing this plug will allow more complete draining to be carried out.

7 On 1.6 and 1.8 litre models, loosen the clip securing the small-diameter hose to the thermostat housing - this hose leads back to the expansion tank. FIAT state that this hose must be blown through (with compressed air) to ensure that all coolant has drained from it. If compressed air is not available, disconnect the hose and allow it to drain - antifreeze may be harmful if ingested.

8 If the coolant has been drained for a reason other than renewal, then provided it is clean and less than two years old, it can be re-used, though this is not recommended (see *Antifreeze type and mixture* later in this Section).

9 Once all the coolant has drained, reconnect the hose to the radiator and secure it in position with the retaining clip. Where applicable, apply a little sealant to the block drain plug threads, then fit and tighten it securely.

Cooling system flushing

10 If coolant renewal has been neglected, or if the antifreeze mixture has become diluted, then in time, the cooling system may gradually lose efficiency, as the coolant passages become restricted due to rust, scale deposits, and other sediment. Flushing the system clean can restore the cooling system efficiency.

11 The radiator should be flushed independently of the engine, to avoid unnecessary contamination.

Radiator flushing

12 To flush the radiator, disconnect the top and bottom hoses and any other relevant hoses from the radiator, with reference to Chapter 3.

13 Insert a garden hose into the radiator top inlet. Direct a flow of clean water through the radiator, and continue flushing until clean water emerges from the radiator bottom outlet.

31.4a Loosen the radiator bottom hose clip . . .

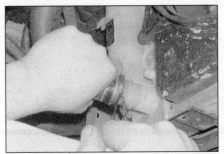

31.4b . . . then release the bottom hose from the radiator, and drain the coolant into a container

31.6 Cylinder block drain plug (arrowed) on 1.6 litre engine

31.24a Remove the expansion tank cap . . .

31.24b . . . and fill the system slowly

14 If after a reasonable period, the water still does not run clear, the radiator can be flushed with a good proprietary cooling system cleaning agent. It is important that their manufacturer's instructions are followed carefully. If the contamination is particularly bad, insert the hose in the radiator bottom outlet, and reverse-flush the radiator.

Engine flushing

15 To flush the engine, remove the thermostat as described in Chapter 3, then temporarily refit the thermostat cover.

16 With the top and bottom hoses disconnected from the radiator, insert a garden hose into the radiator top hose. Direct a clean flow of water through the engine, and continue flushing until clean water emerges from the radiator bottom hose.

17 On completion of flushing, refit the thermostat and reconnect the hoses with reference to Chapter 3.

Antifreeze type and mixture

18 The antifreeze should always be renewed at the specified intervals. This is necessary not only to maintain the antifreeze properties, but also to prevent corrosion which would otherwise occur as the corrosion inhibitors become progressively less effective.

19 Always use ethylene-glycol-based antifreeze suitable for use in mixed-metal cooling systems. The total system capacity is quoted in the Specifications, as well as the percentage of neat antifreeze required to give adequate protection against freezing (and corrosion).

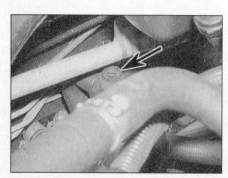

31.27 Bleed screw (arrowed) on heater hose

20 Before adding antifreeze, the cooling system should be completely drained, preferably flushed, and all hoses checked for condition and security.

21 After filling with antifreeze, a label should be attached to the expansion tank, stating the type and concentration of antifreeze used, and the date installed. Any subsequent topping-up should be made with the same type and concentration of antifreeze.

22 Do not use engine antifreeze in the washer system, as it will cause damage to the vehicle paintwork.

Cooling system filling

23 Before attempting to fill the cooling system, make sure that all hoses and clips are in good condition, and that the clips are tight. Note that an antifreeze mixture must be used all year round, to prevent corrosion of the engine components (see following sub-Section).

24 Remove the expansion tank filler cap, and fill the system by slowly pouring the coolant into the expansion tank to prevent airlocks from forming **(see illustrations)**.

25 If the coolant is being renewed, begin by pouring in a litre of water, followed by the correct quantity of antifreeze to make up the required mixture, then top-up with more water. The best option, if suitable clean containers are available, is to make up the mixture before pouring it in. Bear in mind that the system capacities quoted are only approximate - it is unlikely that all the old coolant will have drained, so allowance must be made when refilling.

26 During the initial stages of filling, squeeze the radiator top and bottom hoses to help expel any trapped air in the system. Fill the system until coolant (free of air bubbles) emerges from the radiator bleed screw(s), then tighten them securely.

27 Continue filling the system until coolant emerges from the bleed screws on the heater hoses, then tighten the screws **(see illustration)**.

28 Now top-up the coolant level to the MAX mark and refit the expansion tank cap loosely. Particularly on models with air conditioning, it is important not to overfill the expansion tank at this stage.

29 Start the engine and run it at idle.

30 Particularly on models with air conditioning, have an assistant raise the engine speed to approximately 3000 rpm every 30 seconds while the engine is warming-up. When this is done, carefully open the bleed screw on the heater hose - bear in mind the dangers of hot coolant - and bleed out any trapped air.

31 Initially, add more coolant as necessary to keep the level up to the MAX mark, but only for the first few minutes after the engine is started.

32 Once the coolant level has stabilised, refit the expansion tank cap securely. Let the engine continue to warm up until normal operating temperature is reached, indicated by the temperature gauge, or by the radiator fan cutting in. Keep the engine running for a few more minutes, then switch it off and allow it to cool for several hours (preferably, overnight).

33 Check for leaks, particularly around disturbed components.

34 Check the coolant level in the expansion tank, and top-up if necessary. Note that the system must be cold before an accurate level is indicated in the expansion tank.

Airlocks

35 If, after draining and refilling the system, symptoms of overheating are found which did not occur previously, then the fault is almost certainly due to trapped air at some point in the system, causing an airlock and restricting the flow of coolant; usually, the air is trapped because the system was refilled too quickly.

36 If an airlock is suspected, first try gently squeezing all visible coolant hoses. A coolant hose which is full of air feels quite different to one full of coolant, when squeezed. After refilling the system, most airlocks will clear once the system has cooled, and been topped up.

37 While the engine is running at operating temperature, switch on the heater and heater fan, and check for heat output. Provided there is sufficient coolant in the system, lack of heat output could be due to an airlock in the system.

38 Airlocks can have more serious effects than simply reducing heater output - a severe airlock could reduce coolant flow around the engine. Check that the radiator top hose is hot when the engine is at operating temperature - a top hose which stays cold could be the result of an airlock (or a non-opening thermostat).

39 If the problem persists, stop the engine and allow it to cool down **completely**, before unscrewing the expansion tank filler cap or opening the bleed screws and squeezing the hoses to bleed out the trapped air. In the worst case, the system will have to be at least partially drained (this time, the coolant can be saved for re-use) and flushed to clear the problem.

Chapter 2 Part A:
1.2 litre engine in-car repair procedures

Contents

Degrees of difficulty

Easy, suitable for novice with little experience		Fairly easy, suitable for beginner with some experience		Fairly difficult, suitable for competent DIY mechanic		Difficult, suitable for experienced DIY mechanic		Very difficult, suitable for expert DIY or professional	

Specifications

General

Engine code*	182.B2.000
Bore	70.8 mm
Stroke	78.86 mm
Capacity	1242 cc
Compression ratio	10.2:1
Firing order	1-3-4-2
No 1 cylinder location	Timing belt end of engine

*Note: See 'Vehicle Identification numbers' for the location of code marking on the engine.

Lubrication system

Oil pump type	Bi-rotor driven from front of crankshaft
Outer rotor-to-housing clearance	0.100 to 0.210 mm
Axial clearance	0.025 to 0.070 mm

Camshafts

Drive	Toothed belt to exhaust camshaft, gear drive to inlet camshaft
No of bearings	3
Camshaft bearing journal diameters:	
No 1 bearing	35.000 to 35.015 mm
No 2 bearing	48.000 to 48.015 mm
No 3 bearing	49.000 to 49.015 mm
Camshaft bearing journal running clearance	0.030 to 0.070 mm
Camshaft endfloat	0.15 to 0.34 mm

Cylinder head extensions

Camshaft bearing diameters:	
No 1 bearing	35.045 to 35.070 mm
No 2 bearing	48.045 to 48.070 mm
No 3 bearing	49.045 to 49.070 mm
Hydraulic tappet diameter	28.353 to 28.370 mm
Hydraulic tappet bore diameter	28.400 to 28.421 mm
Hydraulic tappet running clearance	0.046 to 0.051 mm

Torque wrench settings

	Nm	lbf ft
Air conditioning compressor mounting bracket-to-block	50	37
Auxiliary drivebelt pulley bolts	22	16
Big-end (connecting rod) bearing cap bolts	41	30
Camshaft bearing caps	15	11
Camshaft gears	120	89
Camshaft sprocket	120	89
Crankshaft sprocket centre bolt (left-hand thread):		
Stage 1	20	15
Stage 2	Angle-tighten a further 90°	
Cylinder head:		
Stage 1	20	15
Stage 2	30	22
Stage 3	Angle-tighten a further 90°	
Stage 4	Angle-tighten a further 90°	
Cylinder head extension to cylinder head	15	11
Dipstick tube nut and bolt	9	7
Engine/transmission mountings:		
Mounting brackets to transmission:		
M10 bolts	50	37
M12 bolts	85	63
Mounting through-bolts	80	59
Mountings to bodyshell	32	24
Right-hand mounting bracket to block	50	37
Right-hand mounting reaction rod	28	21
Exhaust manifold nuts	27	20
Flywheel*	44	32
Inlet manifold nuts	15	11
Main bearing cap bolts:		
Stage 1	40	30
Stage 2	Angle-tighten a further 90°	
Oil pressure switch	32	24
Oil pump bolts	9	7
Sump bolts	10	7
Timing belt tensioner nut	25	18

*Although not specifically recommended by FIAT, use locking fluid.

1 General information

Using this Chapter

Chapter 2 is divided into five Parts: A to E. Repair operations that can be carried out with the engine in the vehicle are described in Parts A to D. Part E covers the removal of the engine/transmission as a unit, and describes the engine dismantling and overhaul procedures.

In Parts A to D, the assumption is made that the engine is installed in the vehicle, with all ancillaries connected. If the engine has been removed for overhaul, the preliminary dismantling information which precedes each operation may be ignored.

Engine description

The 1.2 litre engine is a water-cooled, double overhead camshaft, in-line four-cylinder unit, with cast-iron cylinder block and aluminium-alloy cylinder head. The unit is mounted transversely at the front of the vehicle, with the transmission bolted to the left-hand side of the engine.

The cylinder head houses the eight inlet and eight exhaust valves, which are closed by single coil springs, and which run in guides pressed into the cylinder head. The two camshafts are housed in a cylinder head extension which is bolted to the top of the cylinder head. The exhaust camshaft is driven by a toothed timing belt and in turn drives the inlet camshaft via a pair of gears located at the left-hand end of the cylinder head extension. The camshafts each have three bearings, and actuate the valves directly via self-adjusting hydraulic tappets mounted in the cylinder head extension.

The crankshaft is supported by five main bearings, and endfloat is controlled by the thrust flanges fitted to the upper half of the centre main bearing shell.

Engine coolant is circulated by a pump, driven by the timing belt. For details of the cooling system, refer to Chapter 3.

Lubricant is circulated under pressure by a pump, driven from the front of the crankshaft. Oil is drawn from the sump through a strainer, and then forced through an externally-mounted, replaceable screw-on filter. From there, it is distributed to the cylinder head and cylinder head extension, where it lubricates the camshaft journals and tappets, and also to the crankcase, where it lubricates the main bearings, connecting rod big and small-ends, gudgeon pins and cylinder bores. Oil jets are fitted to the base of each cylinder bore - these spray oil onto the underside of the pistons, to improve cooling.

Repair operations possible with the engine in the car

The following work can be carried out with the engine in the car:
a) Auxiliary drivebelt - removal and refitting (refer to Chapter 1).
b) Oil pump and pick-up tube assembly - removal, inspection and refitting.
c) Timing belt and covers - removal and refitting.
d) Timing belt tensioner and sprockets - removal and refitting.
e) Cylinder head - removal and refitting*.
f) Cylinder head extension - removal and refitting.
g) Camshaft and tappets - removal and refitting.
h) Camshaft oil seal - renewal.
i) Crankshaft oil seals - renewal.
j) Flywheel - removal, inspection and refitting.
k) Engine mountings - inspection and renewal.
l) Sump - removal and refitting.

*Cylinder head dismantling procedures are detailed in Chapter 2E.

Note 1: *It is possible to remove the pistons and connecting rods (after removing the cylinder head and sump) without removing the engine. However, this is not recommended. Work of this nature is more easily and thoroughly completed with the engine on the bench, as described in Chapter 2E.*

Note 2: *Many of the procedures in this Chapter entail the use of numerous special tools. Where possible, suitable alternatives are described with details of their fabrication. Before starting any operations on the engine, read through the entire procedure first to familiarise yourself with the work involved, tools to be obtained and new parts that may be necessary.*

2 Engine assembly/ valve timing holes - general information and usage

Note: *Do not attempt to rotate the engine whilst the camshafts are locked in position. If the engine is to be left in this state for a long period of time, it is a good idea to place suitable warning notices inside the vehicle, and in the engine compartment. This will reduce the possibility of the engine being accidentally cranked on the starter motor, which is likely to cause damage with the locking tools in place.*

1 To accurately set the valve timing for all operations requiring removal and refitting of the timing belt, timing holes are drilled in the camshafts and cylinder head extension. The holes are used in conjunction with camshaft locking tools and crankshaft positioning rods to lock the camshafts when all the pistons are positioned at the mid-point of their stroke. This arrangement prevents the possibility of the valves contacting the pistons when refitting the cylinder head or timing belt, and also ensures that the correct valve timing can be obtained. The design of the engine is such that there are no conventional timing marks on the crankshaft or camshaft sprockets to indicate the normal TDC position. Therefore, for any work on the timing belt, camshafts or cylinder head, the locking and positioning tools must be used.

2 The special FIAT tools for setting the camshafts and pistons consist of two rods which slide in sleeves that are screwed into No 1 and No 2 cylinder spark plug holes. The rods are pushed down to contact the pistons, and the crankshaft is then turned until both rods protrude from their sleeves by the same amount. With the crankshaft correctly set, two camshaft locking pins are used, one for the inlet camshaft and one for the exhaust camshaft. The pins are screwed into holes on each side of the cylinder head extension so that they engage with slots machined in the camshafts. The arrangement of the FIAT special tools are shown **(see illustrations)**. The tool numbers are as follows:

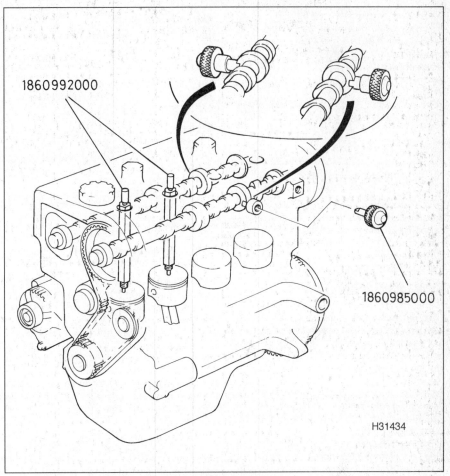

2.2a Arrangement of FIAT special tools for setting the piston position and locking the camshafts

Camshaft locking tools - 1860985000
Piston positioning tool - 1860992000

3 Although the special FIAT tools are relatively inexpensive and should be readily available from FIAT dealers, it is possible to fabricate suitable alternatives, with the help of a local machine shop, as described below. Once the tools have been made up, their usage is described in the relevant Sections of this Chapter where the tools are required.

Camshaft locking tool fabrication

4 Remove the air cleaner, inlet air duct and resonator as described in Chapter 4B.

5 Unscrew the sealing plug from the front face of the cylinder head extension.

6 Using the sealing plug as a pattern, obtain a length of threaded dowel rod or two suitable bolts to screw into the sealing plug hole. With

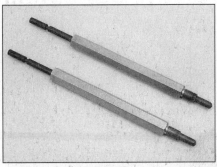

2.2b FIAT special tool for setting piston position . . .

2.2c . . . and locking the camshafts

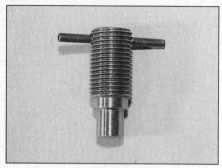

2.6a To make an alternative camshaft locking tool . . .

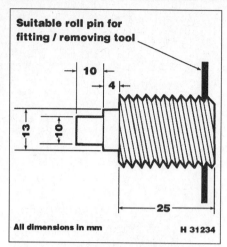

Suitable roll pin for fitting / removing tool

10

4

13

10

25

All dimensions in mm   **H 31234**

2.6b . . . have suitable dowel rods or bolts machined to the dimensions shown

the help of a machine shop or engineering works, make up the camshaft locking tools by having the dowel rod or bolts machined to the dimensions shown **(see illustrations)**. Note that two will be needed, one for each camshaft.

Crankshaft setting tool fabrication

7 To make the crankshaft setting tools, four old spark plugs will be required, together with four lengths of dowel rod. The length of each dowel rod is not critical, but it must be long enough to protrude about 100 mm above the top of the cylinder head extension when resting on top of a piston located half way down its bore. What is critical, however, is that all four dowel rods must be **exactly** the same length.

8 Break off the ceramic upper section of each plug, and remove the centre electrode and earth tip. The easiest way to do this is to mount each spark plug in a vice (after removing the ceramic upper plug section) and drill a hole down through the centre of the plug. The diameter of the drill bit should be the same as the diameter of the dowel rod to be used. When finished, you should have four spark plug bodies and four equal-length dowel rods which will slide through the centre of the spark plugs.

3 Cylinder compression test

1 When engine performance is down, or if misfiring occurs which cannot be attributed to the ignition or fuel systems, a compression test can provide diagnostic clues as to the engine's condition. If the test is performed regularly, it can give warning of trouble before any other symptoms become apparent.
2 The engine must be fully warmed-up to normal operating temperature, the battery must be fully charged, and all the spark plugs must be removed (Chapter 1). The aid of an assistant will also be required.
3 Disable the ignition system by disconnecting the LT wiring plug to the ignition coil unit.

4 Fit a compression tester to the No 1 cylinder spark plug hole - the type of tester which screws into the plug thread is to be preferred.
5 Have the assistant hold the throttle wide open, and crank the engine on the starter motor; after one or two revolutions, the compression pressure should build up to a maximum figure, and then stabilise. Record the highest reading obtained.
6 Repeat the test on the remaining cylinders, recording the pressure in each.
7 All cylinders should produce very similar pressures; any excessive difference indicates the existence of a fault. Note that the compression should build up quickly in a healthy engine; low compression on the first stroke, followed by gradually increasing pressure on successive strokes, indicates worn piston rings. A low compression reading on the first stroke, which does not build up during successive strokes, indicates leaking valves or a blown head gasket (a cracked head could also be the cause).
8 If the pressure in any cylinder is very low, carry out the following test to isolate the cause. Introduce a teaspoonful of clean oil into that cylinder through its spark plug hole and repeat the test.
9 If the addition of oil temporarily improves the compression pressure, this indicates that

4.8 Undo the three bolts and remove the crankshaft pulley from the sprocket

bore or piston wear is responsible for the pressure loss. No improvement suggests that leaking or burnt valves, or a blown head gasket, may be to blame.
10 A low reading from two adjacent cylinders is almost certainly due to the head gasket having blown between them; the presence of coolant in the engine oil will confirm this.
11 If one cylinder is about 20 percent lower than the others and the engine has a slightly rough idle, a worn camshaft lobe could be the cause.
12 On completion of the test, refit the spark plugs and reconnect the ignition LT wiring plug.

4 Timing belt and covers - removal and refitting

General information

1 The function of the timing belt is to drive the camshafts and coolant pump. Should the belt slip or break in service, the valve timing will be disturbed and piston-to-valve contact will occur, resulting in serious engine damage.
2 The timing belt should be renewed at the specified intervals (see Chapter 1), or earlier if it is contaminated with oil, or if it is at all noisy in operation (a scraping noise due to uneven wear).
3 If the timing belt is being removed, it is a wise precaution to check the condition of the coolant pump at the same time (check for signs of coolant leakage). This may avoid the need to remove the timing belt again at a later stage, should the coolant pump fail.
4 Before carrying out this procedure, it will be necessary to obtain or fabricate suitable camshaft locking tools and piston positioning tools as described in Section 2. The procedures contained in this Section depict the use of the home-made alternative tools described in Section 2, which were fabricated in the Haynes workshop. If the manufacturers tools are being used instead, the procedures are virtually identical. Do not attempt to remove the timing belt unless the special tools or their alternatives are available.

Removal

5 Disconnect the battery negative terminal (refer to *Disconnecting the battery*).
6 Remove the auxiliary drivebelts as described in Chapter 1.
7 Remove the air cleaner, inlet air duct and resonator as described in Chapter 4B.
8 Undo the three bolts and remove the crankshaft pulley from the sprocket **(see illustration)**.
9 Undo the retaining bolt in the centre of the lower timing cover **(see illustration)**.
10 Undo the upper timing cover upper retaining bolt, and the rear retaining bolt located above the alternator **(see illustration)**.

4.9 Undo the retaining bolt in the centre of the lower timing cover

4.10 Undo the upper timing cover upper retaining bolt, and the rear retaining bolt

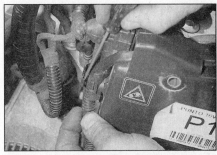

4.11a Release the crankshaft TDC sensor wiring from the clip on the upper timing cover . . .

4.11b . . . then slide the wiring plug and socket from the timing cover slot

4.12a Remove the upper . . .

4.12b . . . and lower timing covers

11 Release the crankshaft TDC sensor wiring from the clip on the upper timing cover, then withdraw the cover slightly and slide the wiring plug and socket from the timing cover slot **(see illustrations)**.

12 Release the TDC sensor wiring from the periphery of the upper and lower timing covers, and remove both covers **(see illustrations)**.

13 Free the accelerator inner cable from the throttle cam, remove the outer cable spring clip, then pull the outer cable out from its mounting bracket rubber grommet.

14 From the side of the throttle body, disconnect the wiring connectors from the throttle potentiometer and the idle control stepper motor. Disconnect the coolant temperature sensor wiring connector located in the inlet manifold below the throttle body,

and disconnect the brake servo vacuum hose.

15 Disconnect the wiring connectors for the fuel injector harness and the intake air temperature/pressure sensor, then disconnect the fuel pressure regulator vacuum hose and the EVAP purge valve hose.

16 Undo the two bolts securing the plastic inlet manifold upper section to the lower section. Release the spark plug HT lead from the location groove in the manifold upper section, then lift the upper section, complete with throttle body, off the engine. Recover the O-rings from the manifold ports.

17 Unscrew the two bolts securing the fuel rail assembly to the inlet manifold lower section, then carefully pull the injectors from the manifold. Lift the fuel rail and injector assembly, with fuel hoses still connected, and position it to one side.

18 Undo the bolts securing the engine management ECU mounting brackets to the body, and move the ECU to one side without disconnecting the wiring connector.

19 Remove the spark plugs as described in Chapter 1.

20 Unscrew the two sealing plugs from the front and rear of the cylinder head extension to enable the camshaft locking tools to be inserted.

21 Screw the spark plug bodies of the home-made piston positioning tools into each spark plug hole, and insert the dowel rods into each body. To keep the dowel rods vertical, locate a suitable washer or similar over the rod and into the recess at the top of the spark plug hole. In the photos shown here, an old valve stem oil seal housing was used, but anything similar will suffice **(see illustrations)**.

4.21a Screw the spark plug bodies of the home-made piston positioning tools into each spark plug hole . . .

4.21b . . . place a suitable washer or similar into the recess to keep the dowel rod vertical . . .

4.21c . . . then insert the dowel rods

4.22 Place a straight edge along the top of the rods and turn the crankshaft until the straight edge contacts all four rods

4.24a Screw in the camshaft locking tools into the timing holes in the cylinder head extension

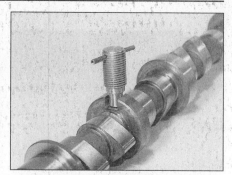

4.24b The tools engage in the camshaft slots when fitted (shown removed for clarity)

22 Using a socket on the crankshaft sprocket centre bolt, turn the crankshaft in the normal direction of rotation until all four dowel rods are protruding from the top of the cylinder head extension by the same amount. As the engine is turned, two of the rods will move up, and two will move down until the position is reached where they are all at the same height. The best way to check this is to place a straight-edge along the top of the rods and turn the crankshaft very slowly until the straight-edge contacts all four rods (see illustration).

23 When all four rods are at the same height, all the pistons will be at the mid-point of their stroke. Using a screwdriver or similar inserted into the front timing hole in the cylinder head extension, check that the timing slot in the exhaust camshaft is approximately aligned with the timing hole. If the camshaft slot cannot be felt, turn the crankshaft through one complete revolution and realign the dowel rods using the straight-edge. Check again for the camshaft slot. Note that, although the pistons can be at the mid-point of their stroke twice for each cycle of the engine, the camshaft slots will only be positioned correctly once per cycle.

24 With the pistons correctly set, it should now be possible to screw in the camshaft locking tools into the timing holes in the cylinder head extension. To provide the necessary degree of timing accuracy, the machined ends of the locking tools are a very close fit in the slots machined in the

camshafts. To allow the tools to be screwed fully into engagement, it may be necessary to move the crankshaft in one direction or another *very slightly* until the tools are felt to engage fully (see illustrations).

25 Release the nut on the timing belt tensioner to release the tension on the belt (see illustration).

26 If the timing belt is to be re-used, use white paint or chalk to mark the direction of rotation on the belt (if markings do not already exist), then slip the belt off the sprockets (see illustration). Note that the crankshaft must not be rotated whilst the belt is removed.

27 Check the timing belt carefully for any signs of uneven wear, splitting, or oil contamination. Pay particular attention to the roots of the teeth. Renew it if there is the slightest doubt about its condition. If the engine is undergoing an overhaul, renew the belt as a matter of course, regardless of its apparent condition. The cost of a new belt is nothing compared with the cost of repairs, should the belt break in service. If signs of oil contamination are found, trace the source of the oil leak and rectify it. Wash down the engine timing belt area and all related components, to remove all traces of oil.

Refitting

28 Before refitting, thoroughly clean the timing belt sprockets. Check that the tensioner pulley rotates freely, without any sign of roughness. If necessary, renew the tensioner pulley as described in Section 5.

29 The camshaft sprocket retaining bolt must now be slackened to allow the sprocket to move as the timing belt is refitted and tensioned. To hold the sprocket stationary while the retaining bolt is loosened, make up a tool as follows and engage it with the holes in the sprocket (see Tool Tip). With the sprocket held, slacken the retaining bolt.

30 Check that the pistons are still correctly positioned at the mid-point of their stroke and that the camshafts are locked with the locking tools.

31 Ensuring that the direction markings on the timing belt point in the normal direction of engine rotation, engage the timing belt with the crankshaft sprocket first, then place it around the coolant pump sprocket and the camshaft sprocket (see illustration). Finally slip the belt around the tensioner pulley.

TOOL TiP

To make a camshaft sprocket holding tool, obtain two lengths of steel strip about 6 mm thick by 30 mm wide or similar, one 600 mm long, the other 200 mm long (all dimensions approximate). Bolt the two strips together to form a forked end, leaving the bolt slack so that the shorter strip can pivot freely. At the end of each 'prong' of the fork, secure a bolt with a nut and a locknut, to act as the fulcrums; these will engage with the cut-outs in the sprocket, and should protrude by about 30 mm

4.25 Release the nut on the timing belt tensioner (arrowed)

4.26 Slip the timing belt off the sprockets

4.31 Fit the new belt around the sprockets observing the direction markings

4.32 Using right-angled circlip pliers, turn the tensioner pulley to fully tension the belt

4.33 Holding the camshaft sprocket with the tool described previously while tightening the sprocket bolt

32 Insert the jaws of a pair of right-angled circlip pliers (or similar) into the two holes on the front face of the tensioner pulley **(see illustration)**. Rotate the pulley to tension the belt until the belt is quite taut. Maintain the effort applied to the tensioner pulley, then tighten the pulley retaining nut.

33 Tighten the camshaft sprocket retaining bolt to the specified torque while holding the camshaft stationary using the method described previously **(see illustration)**.

34 Remove the piston positioning tools and camshaft locking tools, and turn the crankshaft through two complete turns in the normal direction of rotation.

35 Slacken the tensioner pulley retaining nut and reposition the tensioner to align the mobile indicator with the fixed reference mark on the pulley face **(see illustration)**. Hold the pulley in this position, and tighten the retaining nut to the specified torque.

36 Turn the crankshaft through a further two complete turns in the normal direction of rotation. Check that the timing is correct by refitting the piston positioning tools and camshaft locking tools as described previously.

37 When all is correct, remove the setting and locking tools and refit the sealing plugs to the cylinder head extension, using new O-rings if necessary. Tighten the plugs securely.

38 Refit the spark plugs as described in Chapter 1.

39 Refit the ECU and secure with the mounting bolts.

40 Renew the injector O-ring seals, smear them with a little Vaseline, then locate the injectors and fuel rail onto the inlet manifold lower section. Secure the fuel rail with the two retaining bolts.

41 Refit the inlet manifold upper section using new sealing O-rings if necessary, and secure with the two bolts.

42 Reconnect the wiring connectors for the fuel injector harness and the intake air temperature/pressure sensor, then connect the fuel pressure regulator vacuum hose and the EVAP purge valve hose.

43 Reconnect the wiring connectors for the throttle potentiometer, idle control stepper motor and coolant temperature sensor. Reconnect the brake servo vacuum hose.

44 Refit and adjust the accelerator cable as described in Chapter 4B.

45 Refit the upper and lower timing belt covers together with the TDC sensor wiring.

46 Refit the crankshaft pulley and tighten the three retaining bolts securely.

47 Refit the air cleaner, inlet air duct and resonator as described in Chapter 4B.

48 Refit the auxiliary drivebelts as described in Chapter 1, then reconnect the battery negative terminal.

---

5 Timing belt tensioner and sprockets - removal and refitting

Timing belt tensioner

Removal

1 Remove the timing belt as described in Section 4.

2 Completely unscrew the tensioner nut and slide the tensioner off the mounting stud.

Inspection

3 Wipe the tensioner clean, but do not use solvents that may contaminate the bearings.

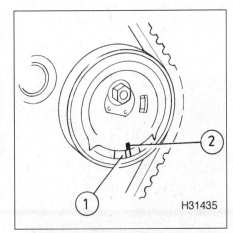

4.35 Position the tensioner so that the mobile indicator (1) is aligned with the fixed reference mark (2)

Spin the tensioner pulley on its hub by hand. Stiff movement or excessive freeplay is an indication of severe wear; the tensioner is not a serviceable component, and should be renewed.

Refitting

4 Slide the tensioner pulley over the mounting stud and fit the securing nut.

5 Refit the timing belt as described in Section 4.

Exhaust camshaft sprocket

Removal

6 Remove the timing belt as described in Section 4.

7 Unscrew the bolt and slide the sprocket from the end of the camshaft.

Inspection

8 With the sprocket removed, examine the camshaft oil seal for signs of leaking. If necessary, refer to Section 6 and renew it.

9 Check the sprocket teeth for damage.

10 Wipe clean the sprocket and camshaft mating surfaces.

Refitting

11 Locate the sprocket on the end of the camshaft, then refit the retaining bolt finger-tight only at this stage.

12 Refit the timing belt as described in Section 4.

Crankshaft sprocket

Removal

13 Remove the timing belt as described in Section 4.

14 Working beneath the engine, unbolt and remove the flywheel lower cover, then hold the flywheel stationary preferably using a tool which engages the flywheel starter ring gear. Alternatively, have an assistant engage a wide-bladed screwdriver with the starter ring gear.

15 Unscrew the crankshaft sprocket retaining bolt, and slide the sprocket off the end of the crankshaft. The sprocket may have an integral location key on its inner face, or a separate key which locates in a groove in the crankshaft nose may be fitted.

Inspection

16 With the sprocket removed, examine the crankshaft oil seal for signs of leaking. If necessary, refer to Section 7 and renew it.
17 Check the sprocket teeth for damage.
18 Wipe clean the sprocket and crankshaft mating surfaces.

Refitting

19 Slide the sprocket onto the crankshaft, making sure it engages the integral key or separate key. Refit the bolt and washer, and tighten the bolt to the specified torque while holding the crankshaft stationary using the method described in paragraph 14.
20 Refit the timing belt as described in Section 4.

---

6 Camshaft oil seal - renewal

1 Remove the timing belt and camshaft sprocket as described in Sections 4 and 5.
2 Punch or drill a small hole in the oil seal. Screw a self-tapping screw into the hole, and pull on the screws with pliers to extract the seal.
3 Clean the seal housing, and polish off any burrs or raised edges, which may have caused the seal to fail in the first place.
4 Lubricate the lips of the new seal with clean engine oil, and drive it into position until it seats on its locating shoulder. Use a suitable tubular drift, such as a socket, which bears only on the hard outer edge of the seal. Take care not to damage the seal lips during fitting. Note that the seal lips should face inwards.
5 Refit the camshaft sprocket and timing belt as described in Sections 5 and 4.

---

7 Crankshaft oil seals - renewal

Front (right-hand side) oil seal

1 The front oil seal is located in the oil pump on the front of the crankshaft. Remove the timing belt as described in Section 4 and the crankshaft sprocket as described in Section 5.
2 Using a hooked instrument, remove the oil seal from the oil pump casing, taking care not to damage the surface of the crankshaft.
3 Clean the seating in the housing and the surface of the crankshaft. To prevent damage to the new oil seal as it is being fitted, wrap some adhesive tape around the end of the crankshaft and lightly oil it.
4 Dip the new oil seal in oil, then offer it up to the oil pump casing, making sure that the sealing lips are facing inwards.
5 Using a suitable tubular drift, drive the oil seal squarely into the casing. Remove the adhesive tape.
6 Refit the crankshaft sprocket and timing belt with reference to Sections 5 and 4.

Rear (left-hand side) oil seal

Note: *The following paragraphs describe renewal of the rear oil seal leaving the housing in position. Refer to Chapter 2E for details of removing the housing.*

7 Remove the flywheel as described in Section 11.
8 Using a suitable hooked instrument, remove the oil seal from the rear oil seal housing taking care not to damage the surface of the crankshaft.
9 Clean the seating in the housing and the surface of the crankshaft. Check the crankshaft for burrs which may damage the sealing lip of the new seal, and if necessary use a fine file to remove them.

10 Dip the new seal in clean engine oil and carefully locate it over the crankshaft rear flange, making sure that it is the correct way round (lips facing inwards).
11 Progressively tap the oil seal into the housing, keeping it square to prevent distortion. A block of wood is useful for this purpose.
12 Refit the flywheel (see Section 11).

---

8 Cylinder head extension - removal and refitting

Removal

1 Remove the timing belt as described in Section 4.
2 Identify the HT leads for position, then disconnect them from the coil HT terminals.
3 Disconnect the LT wiring plug from the ignition coil unit, then unscrew the mounting bolts and remove the ignition coil assembly from the end of the cylinder head extension.
4 Undo the bolt and remove the resonator support bracket from the top of the cylinder head extension.
5 Unscrew the protective caps covering the cylinder head extension retaining bolts **(see illustration)**.
6 To retain the tappets in place as the cylinder head extension is removed, FIAT special tool No 1860988000 will be required. This tool is two strips of suitably slotted thin metal angle bracket which slip between the cylinder head extension and cylinder head mating faces as the extension is lifted off. The tool holds the tappets in place in the extension, allowing the assembly to be withdrawn without fouling the inlet and exhaust valves. The tools are relatively inexpensive and readily available from FIAT dealers. Suitable alternatives can be fabricated, if desired, using thin metal angle strip cut to the dimensions shown **(see Tool Tip)**.

8.5 Unscrew the protective caps covering the cylinder head extension retaining bolts

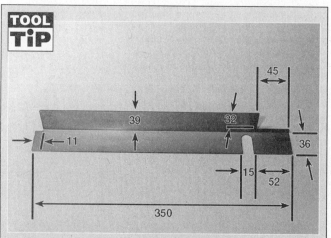

To make a cam follower retaining tool, obtain two lengths of thin metal angle and cut both to the dimensions (in mm) shown

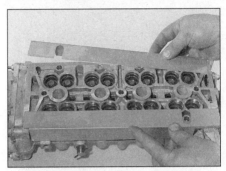

8.8a Lift the cylinder head extension slightly and insert the tools (shown with cylinder head removed for clarity) . . .

8.8b . . . then remove the cylinder head extension

8.10 Locate a new gasket on the cylinder head

7 Progressively slacken and remove the bolts securing the cylinder head extension to the cylinder head.

8 Lift the cylinder head extension up very slightly, keeping it square to the cylinder head. Slip the tools in place to hold the tappets, then lift the extension off the cylinder head **(see illustrations)**. Recover the gasket between the two assemblies.

9 Dismantling and inspection procedures for the cylinder head extension and camshafts are given in Section 9.

Refitting

10 Ensure that the mating faces of the cylinder head and extension are thoroughly cleaned, with all traces of old gasket removed, then locate a new gasket on the cylinder head **(see illustration)**.

11 Locate the tappet retaining tools in position, then lower the extension assembly onto the cylinder head. When all the tappets have engaged their respective valves, remove the tools.

12 Refit the retaining bolts and tighten them progressively to pull the extension down onto the cylinder head. Do this slowly and carefully - the valve springs will be compressed during this operation, and it is essential to keep the extension square and level as the bolts are tightened. Once all the bolts are initially tightened, progressively tighten them further to the specified torque **(see illustration)**.

13 If necessary, renew the O-ring seals on the protective caps covering the cylinder head extension retaining bolts **(see illustration)**.

8.12 Refit the cylinder head extension retaining bolts and tighten them to the specified torque

Refit the caps and tighten them securely.

14 Refit the resonator support bracket to the top of the cylinder head extension.

15 Refit the ignition coil assembly and reconnect the wiring.

16 Refit the timing belt as described in Section 4.

9 Camshafts and tappets - removal, inspection and refitting

Removal

1 Remove the cylinder head extension as described in Section 8.

2 Place the assembly upside-down on a bench, and lift off the tappet retaining tools.

3 Remove the tappets from their locations in

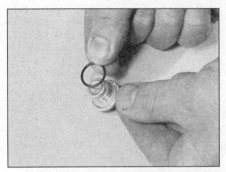

8.13 Renew the O-ring seals on the protective caps covering the cylinder head extension retaining bolts

the cylinder head extension, and place them in an oil-tight compartmented box labelled 1 to 8 (inlet) and 1 to 8 (exhaust) **(see illustration)**. Alternatively, place them into individual storage jars or containers, suitably marked. Fill the box or the jars with clean engine oil until each tappet is just submerged.

4 Undo the camshaft sprocket retaining bolt while holding the sprocket with a suitable tool as described in Section 4.

5 Remove the camshaft sprocket, then undo the bolt and nut and remove the cover plate over the inlet camshaft **(see illustrations)**.

6 At the other end of the cylinder head extension, undo the nuts and remove the end cover **(see illustration)**. Recover the gasket.

7 Undo the two bolts securing the camshaft drive gears to the inlet and exhaust camshafts **(see illustration)**. The camshaft locking tools used in the timing belt removal procedure

9.3 Remove the cam followers from their locations in the cylinder head extension

9.5a Remove the camshaft sprocket . . .

9.5b . . . then undo the bolt and nut and remove the cover plate over the inlet camshaft

9.6 Undo the nuts and remove the end cover

9.7 Undo the two bolts securing the camshaft drive gears to the inlet and exhaust camshafts

9.9 Carefully remove the inlet camshaft from the cylinder head extension

(which should still be in place) are sufficient to prevent the camshafts rotating while the gear retaining bolts are undone. Remove the bolts and withdraw the camshaft gears.

8 Remove the camshaft locking tools.

9 Carefully remove the inlet camshaft from the cylinder head extension **(see illustration)**. Suitably mark the camshaft IN to avoid confusion when refitting.

10 Punch or drill a small hole in the exhaust camshaft oil seal. Screw a self-tapping screw into the hole, and pull on the screw with pliers to extract the seal **(see illustration)**.

11 Carefully remove the exhaust camshaft from the cylinder head extension **(see illustration)**. Suitably mark the camshaft EX to avoid confusion when refitting.

Inspection

12 Examine the camshaft bearing surfaces

and cam lobes for signs of wear ridges and scoring. Renew the camshaft if any of these conditions are apparent. Examine the condition of the bearing surfaces, both on the camshaft journals and in the cylinder head extension. If the head extension bearing surfaces are worn excessively, the extension will need to be renewed. If suitable measuring equipment is available, camshaft bearing journal wear can be checked by direct measurement.

13 Examine the tappet bearing surfaces which contact the camshaft lobes for wear ridges and scoring. Renew any tappet on which these conditions are apparent. If a tappet bearing surface is badly scored, also examine the corresponding lobe on the camshaft for wear, as it is likely that both will be worn. Renew worn components as necessary.

Refitting

14 Liberally lubricate the camshaft journals and cylinder head extension bearings, then locate both camshafts in position. Note that the exhaust camshaft is nearest to the front facing side of the engine.

15 With the camshafts in position, rotate them as necessary until the camshaft locking tools can be re-inserted **(see illustration)**.

16 Lubricate the lips of a new exhaust camshaft oil seal with clean engine oil, and drive it into position until it seats on its locating shoulder **(see illustration)**. Use a suitable tubular drift, such as a socket, which bears only on the hard outer edge of the seal. Take care not to damage the seal lips during fitting. Note that the seal lips should face inwards.

17 Refit the inlet camshaft drive gear and retaining bolt, then tighten the bolt to the specified torque **(see illustration)**.

18 Refit the exhaust camshaft drive gear to the exhaust camshaft. As the gear is being fitted, it will be necessary to align the anti-backlash inner gear teeth using a screwdriver to enable the teeth of both the gears to mesh **(see illustration)**.

19 At this stage, it is advisable to check the camshaft endfloat using a dial gauge mounted on the cylinder head extension, with its probe in contact with the camshaft being checked. Move the camshaft one way, zero the gauge, then move the camshaft as far as it will go the other way. Record the reading on the dial gauge, and compare the figure with that given

9.10 Extract the exhaust camshaft oil seal . . .

9.11 . . . then remove the exhaust camshaft from the cylinder head extension

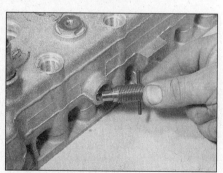

9.15 Refit the camshaft locking tools

9.16 Fit a new exhaust camshaft oil seal

9.17 Tighten the inlet camshaft drive gear retaining bolt to the specified torque

9.18 Refit the exhaust camshaft drive gear while aligning the anti-backlash inner gear teeth

9.20a Locate a new gasket on the cylinder head extension end cover . . .

9.20b . . . then wrap round the protruding tangs to retain the gasket

in the Specifications. Repeat on the other camshaft. If either of the readings exceeds the tolerance given, a new cylinder head extension will probably be required.

20 Locate a new gasket on the cylinder head extension end cover, then wrap round the protruding tangs on the gasket to retain it in position **(see illustrations)**.

21 Locate the end cover on the cylinder head extension, and secure with the retaining nuts securely tightened.

22 Locate a new O-ring on the inlet camshaft cover plate, then apply RTV gasket sealant to the cover plate contact face **(see illustrations)**. Fit the cover plate and secure with the nut and bolt.

23 Refit the camshaft sprocket, and secure with the retaining bolt tightened finger-tight only at this stage.

24 Liberally lubricate the tappets and place them in position in their respective cylinder head extension bores **(see illustration)**.

25 Locate the tappet retaining tools in position and refit the cylinder head extension as described in Section 8.

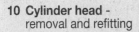

10 Cylinder head - removal and refitting

Removal

Note: *The cylinder head bolts are of special splined design and a FIAT tool should be obtained to unscrew them. A Torx key will not fit however in practise it was found that a*

close-fitting Allen key could be used as an alternative.

1 Drain the cooling system as described in Chapter 1.

2 Remove the cylinder head extension as described in Section 8.

3 Disconnect the radiator hose from the thermostat housing on the left-hand end of the cylinder head.

4 Disconnect the heater hose from the outlet at the rear of the cylinder head.

5 Disconnect the coolant temperature sensor and temperature gauge sensor wiring plugs from the left-hand end of the cylinder head.

6 Undo the engine oil dipstick tube bracket retaining bolt, and the two bolts securing the wiring harness support clips to the inlet manifold lower section.

7 Undo the retaining nuts, and separate the exhaust system front pipe from the exhaust manifold flange.

8 Check that nothing remains attached to the cylinder head likely to impede removal. It is assumed that the head will be removed complete with exhaust manifold and inlet manifold lower section.

9 Unscrew the cylinder head bolts half a turn at a time in the reverse order to that shown in illustration 10.25a. When the bolts are free, remove them from their locations..

10 Lift the cylinder head from the block. If it is stuck tight, rock the head to break the joint by means of the manifolds. On no account drive levers into the gasket joint, nor attempt to tap the head sideways, as it is located on positioning dowels.

11 Remove and discard the cylinder head gasket.

12 If necessary, refer to Chapter 2E for cylinder head dismantling and inspection procedures.

Preparation for refitting

13 The mating faces of the cylinder head and cylinder block must be perfectly clean before refitting the head. Use a hard plastic or wooden scraper to remove all traces of gasket and carbon; also clean the piston crowns.

14 Take particular care when cleaning the piston crowns, as the soft aluminium alloy is easily damaged.

15 Make sure that the carbon is not allowed to enter the oil and water passages - this is particularly important for the lubrication system, as carbon could block the oil supply to the engine's components. Using adhesive tape and paper, seal the water, oil and bolt holes in the cylinder block.

16 To prevent carbon entering the gap between the pistons and bores, smear a little grease in the gap. After cleaning each piston, use a small brush to remove all traces of grease and carbon from the gap, then wipe away the remainder with a clean rag. Clean all the pistons in the same way.

17 Check the mating surfaces of the cylinder block and the cylinder head for nicks, deep scratches and other damage. If slight, they may be removed carefully with a file, but if excessive, machining may be the only alternative to renewal.

9.22a Locate a new O-ring on the inlet camshaft cover plate . . .

9.22b . . . then apply RTV gasket sealant to the cover plate contact face

9.24 Lubricate the cam followers and place them in position in their respective bores

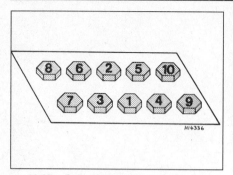

10.25a Cylinder head bolt tightening sequence

10.25b Tighten the cylinder head bolts to the Stage 1 torque setting . . .

10.25c . . . then through the Stage 2 and Stage 3 angle

18 If warpage of the cylinder head gasket surface is suspected, use a straight-edge to check it for distortion. Refer to Part E of this Chapter if necessary.

19 Check the condition of the cylinder head bolts, and particularly their threads, whenever they are removed. Wash the bolts in a suitable solvent, and wipe them dry. Check each bolt for any sign of visible wear or damage, renewing them if necessary.

Refitting

20 Before refitting the assembled cylinder head, make sure that the head and block mating surfaces are perfectly clean, and that the bolt holes in the cylinder block have been mopped out to clear any oil or coolant. If the

To lock the flywheel, make up a pointed tool to engage the ring gear teeth, and bolt it to the engine using one of the bellhousing bolts

bolt holes have any significant amount of liquid in them, the block could be cracked by hydraulic pressure when the head bolts are tightened.

21 The new gasket should not be removed from its plastic bag until required for use. Fit the gasket dry - no grease or sealant should be used.

22 Place the gasket on the cylinder block so that the word ALTO (TOP) can be read from above.

23 Lower the cylinder head onto the block so that it locates on the positioning dowels.

24 Ensure that the cylinder head bolts are cleaned of all debris, and check the threads for signs of damage. Especially if it is known that the bolts have been removed previously, it is advisable to renew all ten bolts as a set, rather than risk the bolts shearing when tightened.

25 Lightly oil the bolt threads. Screw the bolts in finger-tight, and tighten them in the sequence shown to the Stage 1 torque (**see illustrations**).

26 When all ten bolts have been tightened to the Stage 1 torque, go round again in sequence and tighten to the Stage 2 torque.

27 Again working in sequence, tighten the bolts through the specified Stage 3 angle. Note that 90° is equivalent to a quarter-turn or right-angle, making it easy to judge by noting the initial position of the socket handle. If available, use an angle gauge fitted to the socket handle for maximum accuracy.

28 With all ten bolts tightened to Stage 3, go round once more and tighten all bolts in sequence to the Stage 4 angle.

29 Further refitting is a reversal of removal. Ensure that all wiring and hoses are correctly routed and securely reconnected. Refer to Section 4 when refitting the timing belt, and to Chapter 1 when refitting the spark plugs and auxiliary drivebelt, and when refilling the cooling system.

11 Flywheel - removal, inspection and refitting

Removal

1 Remove the transmission as described in Chapter 7A, and the clutch as described in Chapter 6.

2 Mark the position of the flywheel with respect to the crankshaft using a dab of paint. Note that on some models although there is only one location dowel on the flywheel, there are two holes in the end of the crankshaft and it is therefore possible to locate the flywheel 180° out.

3 The flywheel must now be held stationary while the bolts are loosened. A home-made locking tool may be fabricated from a piece of scrap metal and used to lock the ring gear. Bolt the tool to one of the transmission bellhousing mounting holes (**see Tool Tip**).

4 Support the flywheel as the bolts are loosened - the flywheel is very heavy. Unscrew and remove the mounting bolts, take off the spacer plate, then lift off the flywheel (**see illustrations**).

Inspection

5 If the flywheel's clutch mating surface is deeply scored, cracked or otherwise damaged, the flywheel must be renewed. However, it may be possible to have it surface-ground; seek the advice of a FIAT dealer or engine reconditioning specialist.

6 If the ring gear is badly worn or has missing teeth, the flywheel must be renewed.

Refitting

7 Clean the mating surfaces of the flywheel and crankshaft. Remove any remaining locking compound from the threads of the crankshaft holes, using the correct-size tap, if available.

11.4a Unscrew the flywheel bolts . . .

11.4b . . . and remove the spacer plate

HAYNES HiNT *If a suitable tap is not available, cut two slots down the threads of one of the old bolts with a hacksaw, and use the bolt to remove the locking compound from the threads.*

8 Clean the flywheel bolt threads, then apply a suitable thread-locking compound to the threads of each bolt.

9 Offer up the flywheel onto the crankshaft, using the alignment marks made during removal; engage the dowel and fit the retaining bolts (together with the spacer plate) **(see illustrations)**.

10 Lock the flywheel using the method employed on dismantling, and tighten the retaining bolts to the specified torque.

11 Refit the clutch as described in Chapter 6, and the transmission as described in Chapter 7A.

12 Engine mountings - inspection and renewal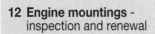

Inspection

1 Jack up the front of the vehicle and support on axle stands (see *Jacking and vehicle support*).

2 Check the mounting rubbers to see if they are cracked, hardened or separated from the metal at any point; renew the mounting if any such damage or deterioration is evident.

3 Check that all the mounting's fasteners are securely tightened; use a torque wrench to check if possible.

4 Using a large screwdriver or a crowbar, check for wear in the mounting by carefully levering against it to check for free play. Where this is not possible enlist the aid of an assistant to move the engine/transmission back and forth, or from side to side, while you watch the mounting. While some free play is to be expected even from new components, excessive wear should be obvious. If excessive free play is found, check first that the fasteners are correctly secured, then renew any worn components as described below.

Renewal

Right-hand mounting

5 Raise the front of the vehicle and support on axle stands (see *Jacking and vehicle support*).

6 Place a trolley jack beneath the right-hand side of the engine, with a block of wood on the jack head. Raise the jack until it is supporting the weight of the engine.

7 Unscrew the through-bolt and nut securing the reaction rod to the engine mounting bracket.

8 Lower the engine sufficiently to disengage the reaction rod from the mounting, then remove the bolts securing the mounting to the body, and remove it.

11.9a Location dowel on the flywheel

9 Locate the new mounting on the body, then insert the mounting-to-body bolts and tighten by hand.

10 Raise the engine and locate the reaction rod on the mounting. Refit the through-bolt and nut, tighten to the specified torque, then tighten the mounting-to-body bolts.

11 Remove the trolley jack and lower the vehicle to the ground.

Left-hand/rear mounting

12 Raise the front of the vehicle and support on axle stands (see *Jacking and vehicle support*).

13 Place a trolley jack beneath the transmission, with a block of wood on the jack head. Raise the jack until it is supporting the weight of the engine/transmission.

14 Unscrew the through-bolt securing the transmission bracket to the mounting, and recover the washers.

15 Unscrew the two bolts securing the left-hand mounting to the body.

16 Lower the transmission sufficiently to remove the mounting from the transmission bracket.

17 Locate the new mounting in position, and loosely refit the mounting-to-body bolts.

18 Raise the engine/transmission and refit the through-bolt securing the bracket to the mounting. Tighten the bolt to the specified torque, then tighten the mounting-to-body bolts.

19 Remove the trolley jack and lower the vehicle to the ground.

Front mounting

20 Raise the front of the vehicle and support on axle stands (see *Jacking and vehicle support*).

21 Place a trolley jack beneath the engine/transmission flange, with a block of wood on the jack head. Raise the jack until it is supporting the weight of the engine and transmission.

22 Working from below, unscrew the nut securing the bracket to the mounting.

23 Lower the engine sufficiently to disengage the bracket from the mounting, then remove the bolts securing the mounting to the body, and remove it.

24 Locate the new mounting on the body, then insert the mounting-to-body bolts and tighten by hand.

25 Raise the engine and locate the bracket on the mounting. Refit the nut and tighten to

11.9b Inserting the flywheel bolts

the specified torque, then tighten the mounting-to-body bolts.

26 Remove the trolley jack and lower the vehicle to the ground.

13 Sump - removal and refitting

Removal

1 Jack up the front of the vehicle and support on axle stands. Drain the engine oil.

2 Unscrew the sump securing nuts and bolts, and pull the sump downwards to remove it. The joint sealant will require cutting with a sharp knife to release the pan.

3 The sump is located on four studs, which may unscrew from the crankcase when the nuts are loosened - this poses no great problem, and the studs can be refitted if they are in good condition. To screw a stud back into position, lock two nuts against each other on the stud threads, then use one of the nuts to tighten the stud firmly.

Refitting

4 Clean away all old gasket material, from the sump pan and from the base of the block.

5 Apply a bead of RTV silicone instant gasket 3 mm in diameter to the sump flange. The bead of sealant should pass around the inside of the sump bolt holes.

6 Fit the sump, screw in the fixing bolts and nuts, and tighten securely in a diagonal sequence.

7 Wait one hour for the gasket compound to harden before filling with oil.

8 Lower the vehicle to the ground and fill the engine with oil (see Chapter 1). Check the oil level after running the engine for a few minutes, as described in *Weekly checks*.

14 Oil pump and pick-up tube - removal and refitting

Removal

1 Drain the engine oil and remove the sump as described in Section 13.

2 Unbolt and remove the oil pick-up/filter screen assembly. Note the sealing O-ring.

14.8 Using an impact screwdriver to remove the oil pump rear cover plate screws

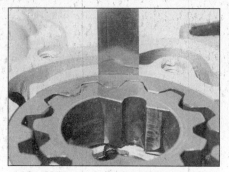

14.9a Measuring oil pump outer gear-to-pump housing clearance

14.9b Measuring oil pump gear endfloat

3 Unscrew and remove the oil filter cartridge (see Chapter 1).

4 Remove the timing belt as described in Section 4.

5 Remove the crankshaft sprocket as described in Section 5.

6 Extract the oil pump fixing bolts, noting their locations (there is one long bolt, and four short ones with washers). Withdraw the pump and remove the gasket.

Inspection

7 The oil pump incorporates a pressure relief valve, which can be removed for examination by unscrewing the plug and pulling out the spring and valve.

8 If pump wear is suspected, check the gears in the following way. Extract the five fixing screws and remove the rear cover plate. The

screws are very tight, and will probably require the use of an impact screwdriver (see illustration).

9 Check the clearance between the outer gear and the pump housing using feeler blades. Check the gear endfloat by placing a straight-edge across the pump body, and checking the gap between the straight-edge and gear face (see illustrations). If the clearances are outside the specified tolerance, renew the oil pump complete.

10 If the pump is unworn, refit the rear cover plate and tighten the screws fully.

11 Apply air pressure from a tyre pump to the oil pump oil ducts, to clear any sludge or other material. If any solvents are used, the pump must be allowed to dry thoroughly before refitting.

12 Prime the pump by pouring clean engine

oil into its inlet duct, at the same time turning the oil pump inner gear with your fingers.

13 Lever out the oil seal, and drive a new one squarely into the oil pump casing. Lubricate the oil seal lips (see illustrations).

Refitting

14 Clean all traces of old gasket from the pump and the mating surfaces on the cylinder block.

15 Bolt the pump into position, using a new joint gasket (see illustrations). Insert the longer bolt into the position noted on removal, and tighten all to the specified torques.

16 Bolt on the oil pick-up assembly using a new sealing washer.

17 Refit the crankshaft sprocket as described in Section 5.

18 Fit and tension the timing belt as described in Section 4.

19 Fit the sump as described in Section 13.

20 Screw on a new oil filter cartridge, and fill the engine with oil (see Chapter 1).

21 Run the engine for a few minutes, then check and top-up the oil level as described in *Weekly checks*.

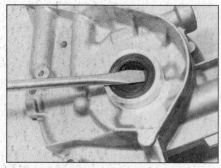

14.13a Removing the oil pump oil seal (crankshaft front oil seal)

14.13b Using a socket to fit a new oil seal to the oil pump

14.15a Using a new gasket . . .

14.15b . . . refit the oil pump

15 Oil pressure switch - removal and refitting

Removal

1 The oil pressure switch is located on the oil pump housing at the front of the engine block, behind the oil filter.

2 Disconnect the switch wiring connector.

3 Unscrew the switch from the oil pump, and remove it.

4 Clean the switch location as far as possible. If the switch is to be refitted, clean its threads.

5 Examine the switch for signs of cracking or splits. If the top part of the switch is loose, this is an early indication of impending failure.

Refitting

6 Apply a smear of sealant to the threads of the switch, then screw it into place and tighten to the specified torque.

7 Reconnect the switch wiring on completion.

Chapter 2 Part B:
1.4 litre engine in-car repair procedures

Contents

Degrees of difficulty

Easy, suitable for novice with little experience		Fairly easy, suitable for beginner with some experience		Fairly difficult, suitable for competent DIY mechanic		Difficult, suitable for experienced DIY mechanic		Very difficult, suitable for expert DIY or professional	

Specifications

General

Engine code*	182 A3.000
Bore	82.0 mm
Stroke	64.9 mm
Compression ratio	9.85:1
Firing order	1-3-4-2
No 1 cylinder location	Timing (right-hand) end of engine

*Note: See 'Vehicle identification numbers' for the location of code marking on the engine.

Lubrication system

Oil pump type	Bi-rotor driven from front of crankshaft
Outer rotor-to-housing clearance	0.080 to 0.186 mm
Axial clearance	0.025 to 0.061 mm
Oil pressure (at operating temperature)	15 psi at idle, to 58 psi at 4000 rpm

Torque wrench settings

	Nm	lbf ft
Air conditioning compressor mounting bracket-to-block	50	37
Alternator mounting bracket to block:		
M8 bolts	25	18
M10 bolts	70	52
Big-end (connecting rod) bearing cap bolts:		
Stage 1	20	15
Stage 2	Angle-tighten a further 40°	
Camshaft caps	15	11
Camshaft cover	9	7
Camshaft sprocket	120	89
Coolant pipe to block:		
M6 bolts	9	7
M8 bolts	25	18
Crankshaft pulley-to-sprocket bolts	25	18
Crankshaft sensor	9	7
Crankshaft sprocket bolt (left-hand thread)	360	266
Cylinder head:		
Stage 1	20	15
Stage 2	40	30
Stage 3	Angle-tighten a further 90°	
Stage 4	Angle-tighten a further 90°	

Torque wrench settings (continued)

	Nm	lbf ft
Engine oil dipstick tube	9	7
Engine/transmission mountings:		
Front mounting through-bolt	38	28
Left-hand mounting bracket to transmission:		
M10 bolts	45	33
M12 bolts	85	63
Mounting nuts	80	59
Mountings to bodyshell	32	24
Right-hand mounting bracket to block	70	52
Exhaust manifold nuts	25	18
Flywheel*	160	118
Inlet manifold nuts	25	18
Knock sensor	25	18
Main bearing cap bolts:		
Stage 1	20	15
Stage 2	Angle-tighten a further 100°	
Oil pressure switch	32	24
Oil pump bolts:		
M6 bolt	9	7
M8 bolt	25	18
Sump bolts:		
M6 bolt	9	7
M8 bolt	25	18
Timing belt covers	9	7
Thermostat housing bolts	25	18

*Although not specifically recommended by FIAT, use new bolts and locking fluid.

1 General information

Using this Chapter

Chapter 2 is divided into five Parts; A to E. Repair operations that can be carried out with the engine in the vehicle are described in Parts A to D. Part E covers the removal of the engine/transmission as a unit, and describes the engine dismantling and overhaul procedures.

In Parts A to D, the assumption is made that the engine is installed in the vehicle, with all ancillaries connected. If the engine has been removed for overhaul, the preliminary dismantling information which precedes each operation may be ignored.

Engine description

The 1.4 litre engine is a water-cooled, single overhead camshaft, in-line four-cylinder unit, with cast-iron cylinder block and aluminium-alloy cylinder head. The engine is a 12-valve unit, with two inlet valves per cylinder. The engine is mounted transversely at the front of the vehicle, with the transmission bolted to the left-hand side of the engine.

The cylinder head carries the camshaft, which is driven by a toothed timing belt and runs in five bearings. It also houses the inlet and exhaust valves, which are closed by single coil springs, and which run in guides pressed into the cylinder head. The camshaft actuates the valves directly via cam followers; the valve clearances are maintained by hydraulic tappets mounted in the cylinder head. The cylinder head contains integral oilways which supply and lubricate the tappets.

The crankshaft is supported by five main bearings, and endfloat is controlled by thrust washers fitted either side of the centre main bearing.

Engine coolant is circulated by a pump, driven by the timing belt. For details of the cooling system, refer to Chapter 3.

Lubricant is circulated under pressure by a pump, driven from the front of the crankshaft. Oil is drawn from the sump through a strainer, and then forced through an externally-mounted, replaceable screw-on filter. From there, it is distributed to the cylinder head, where it lubricates the camshaft journals and tappets, and also to the crankcase, where it lubricates the main bearings, connecting rod big and small-ends, gudgeon pins and cylinder bores.

Repair operations possible with the engine in the car

The following work can be carried out with the engine in the car:
a) Auxiliary drivebelt - removal and refitting (see Chapter 1).
b) Camshaft - removal and refitting*.
c) Camshaft oil seals - renewal.
d) Camshaft sprocket - removal and refitting.
e) Coolant pump - removal and refitting (refer to Chapter 3).
f) Crankshaft oil seals - renewal.
g) Crankshaft sprocket - removal and refitting.
h) Cylinder head - removal and refitting.
i) Engine mountings - inspection and renewal.
j) Oil pump and pickup assembly - removal and refitting.

k) Sump.
l) Timing belt, sprockets and cover - removal, inspection and refitting.

*Cylinder head dismantling procedures are detailed in Chapter 2E, Section 4, with details of camshaft and tappet removal.

Note: It is possible to remove the pistons and connecting rods (after removing the cylinder head and sump) without removing the engine. However, this is not recommended. Work of this nature is more easily and thoroughly completed with the engine on the bench, as described in Chapter 2E.

2 Location of TDC on No 1 cylinder

1 With the car parked on a level surface, apply the handbrake and chock the rear wheels. Loosen the right-hand front wheel bolts.
2 Raise the front of the vehicle, rest it securely on axle stands and remove the right-hand front roadwheel.
3 Unscrew and release the fasteners, and remove the wheelarch inner panel, to gain access to the crankshaft pulley.
4 To make the engine easier to turn, remove all four spark plugs, as described in Chapter 1. If preferred, however, it is sufficient to remove just No 1 spark plug (nearest the timing belt end of the engine).
5 Have an assistant turn the engine using a spanner or socket on the crankshaft pulley centre bolt. As this is done, place a finger over No 1 spark plug hole, and feel for pressure build-up.

6 Once pressure is felt, continue turning the engine until the crankshaft pulley timing mark is aligned with the mark on the oil pump cover or timing belt lower cover **(see illustration)**.

7 For further confirmation that the engine is at TDC with No 1 cylinder on compression, remove the camshaft cover as described in Section 6. The camshaft lobes for No 1 cylinder will be just above horizontal (valves closed, cylinder on compression), while those for No 4 cylinder will be pointing downwards, opening the exhaust valve **(see illustration)**.

8 The engine is now set at TDC on No 1 cylinder.

3 Cylinder compression test

1 When engine performance is down, or if misfiring occurs which cannot be attributed to the ignition or fuel systems, a compression test can provide diagnostic clues as to the engine's condition. If the test is performed regularly, it can give warning of trouble before any other symptoms become apparent.

2 The engine must be fully warmed-up to normal operating temperature, the battery must be fully charged, and all the spark plugs must be removed (Chapter 1). The aid of an assistant will also be required.

3 Disable the ignition system by disconnecting the LT wiring plug to the ignition coil.

4 To prevent possible damage to the catalytic converter, depressurise and disable the fuel injection system by removing the fuel pump fuse or relay (see Chapter 4A, Section 8).

5 Fit a compression tester to the No 1 cylinder spark plug hole - the type of tester which screws into the plug thread is to be preferred.

6 Have the assistant hold the throttle wide open, and crank the engine on the starter motor; after one or two revolutions, the compression pressure should build up to a maximum figure, and then stabilise. Record the highest reading obtained.

7 Repeat the test on the remaining cylinders, recording the pressure in each.

8 All cylinders should produce very similar pressures; any excessive difference indicates the existence of a fault. Note that the compression should build up quickly in a healthy engine; low compression on the first stroke, followed by gradually increasing pressure on successive strokes, indicates worn piston rings. A low compression reading on the first stroke, which does not build up during successive strokes, indicates leaking valves or a blown head gasket (a cracked head could also be the cause).

9 If the pressure in any cylinder is very low, carry out the following test to isolate the cause. Introduce a teaspoonful of clean oil into that cylinder through its spark plug hole and repeat the test.

10 If the addition of oil temporarily improves

2.6 Notch in crankshaft pulley aligned with rib mark on timing belt lower cover

the compression pressure, this indicates that bore or piston wear is responsible for the pressure loss. No improvement suggests that leaking or burnt valves, or a blown head gasket, may be to blame.

11 A low reading from two adjacent cylinders is almost certainly due to the head gasket having blown between them; the presence of coolant in the engine oil will confirm this.

12 If one cylinder is about 20 percent lower than the others and the engine has a slightly rough idle, a worn camshaft lobe could be the cause.

13 On completion of the test, refit the spark plugs and restore the ignition and fuel systems.

4 Timing belt and covers - removal and refitting

Note: *If the timing belt is being removed, it is a wise precaution to check the condition of the coolant pump at the same time (check for signs of coolant leakage). This may avoid the need to remove the timing belt again at a later stage, should the coolant pump fail.*

General information

1 The function of the timing belt is to drive the camshaft and coolant pump. Should the belt slip or break in service, the valve timing will be disturbed and piston-to-valve contact will occur, resulting in serious engine damage.

2 For this reason, it is important that a new timing belt is fitted at or before the specified mileage (see Chapter 1). If the car has been

2.7 Camshaft lobes for No 1 cylinder (arrowed) pointing upwards

purchased second-hand, and its history is unknown, renewing the timing belt should be treated as a priority.

3 FIAT garages use a pair of special tools to keep the camshaft and crankshaft sprockets at the TDC position, since it is possible that the sprockets may turn as the old belt is removed and the new one fitted. If they turn independently, the valve timing will be lost, and the engine will not run properly when restarted - worse, piston-to-valve contact may occur.

4 In the absence of the special tools, great care must be taken when removing and refitting the belt that the sprockets do not move. Marks may be found on the sprockets, which align with markings on the cylinder head or oil pump housing. If none are present, take care to make your own, using typists correction fluid or similar, **before** removing the belt.

5 If the special tools are not used, the procedure given below will suffice to change the belt successfully, but if care is not taken and the camshaft timing is slightly out, the engine may not run very well on completion. It is advisable to have a FIAT dealer confirm the camshaft timing after a new belt is fitted, if the special tools are not used.

Removal

6 To improve access, remove the air cleaner cover and air ducting as described in Chapter 4A.

7 Remove the spark plugs (refer to Chapter 1).

8 Remove the two bolts securing the coolant hose mounting brackets to the timing belt cover, then unclip the hose and move it out of the way **(see illustrations)**.

4.8a Unscrew the two mounting bracket bolts . . .

4.8b . . . then unclip the hose and remove the mounting bracket

4.9 Removing the timing belt upper cover

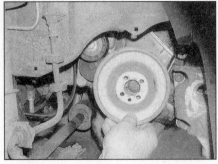

4.13 Removing the crankshaft pulley

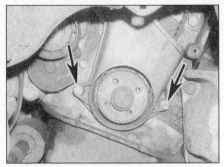

4.14a Remove the two bolts (arrowed) . . .

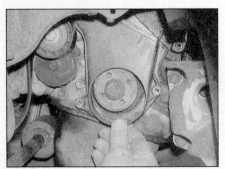

4.14b . . . and take off the timing belt lower cover

4.15a Alignment mark made between the camshaft and the end bearing cap . . .

4.15b . . . and between the camshaft and sprocket - useful if the sprocket is to be removed

9 Unbolt and remove the timing belt upper cover, which is secured by six bolts **(see illustration)**.

10 Remove the camshaft cover as described in Section 6. With the cover removed, the camshaft can be marked for position (or the special FIAT locking tool can be fitted). In addition, removing the cover enables confirmation that the engine is at TDC on No 1 cylinder, as the camshaft lobes for No 1 cylinder will be just above horizontal (valves closed, cylinder on compression).

11 Set the engine to TDC as described in Section 2, then engage top gear; if the handbrake is firmly applied, this should prevent the crankshaft from moving.

12 Remove the auxiliary drivebelt from the crankshaft pulley as described in Chapter 1.

13 Remove the four small bolts and take off the crankshaft pulley **(see illustration)**.

14 Remove the two bolts securing the timing

belt lower cover, and remove the cover **(see illustrations)**.

15 If the special holding tools are not available, make your own sprocket alignment marks as necessary before removing the belt (see paragraph 4). If the camshaft cover is removed, an accurate mark can be made across the left-hand end of the camshaft and the left-hand bearing cap (left as seen from the driver's seat) **(see illustrations)**.

16 The FIAT tool (1860899000) for holding the camshaft stationary is a modified No 2 camshaft bearing cap which locates over one of the camshaft lobes, preventing rotation and maintaining the camshaft timing **(see illustration)**. It is fitted after removing the camshaft cover, and loosening the other bearing cap bolts securing the camshaft oil feed pipe assembly. When the tool has been fitted, tighten all the bearing cap bolts to 10 Nm (7 lbf ft).

4.15c Use a ruler to mark the inside of the sprocket relative to the top of the cylinder head

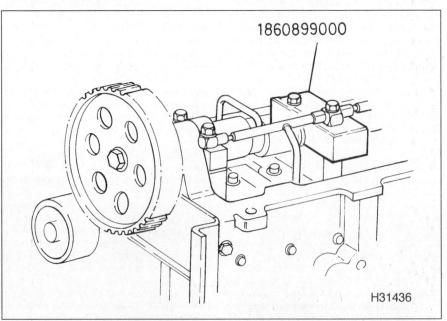

1860899000

H31436

4.16 FIAT special tool used to lock the camshaft

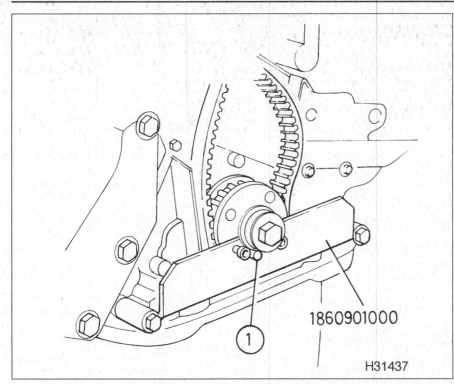

4.18 Release the timing belt tensioner nut

4.17 FIAT special tool used to lock the crankshaft sprocket and locating peg (1)

4.19 Removing the timing belt

17 The tool used to lock and time the crankshaft sprocket (1869901000) is a metal plate which bolts across the lower half of the sprocket, secured using the oil pump lower bolt holes **(see illustration)**. The plate has two holes through which two of the crankshaft pulley bolts can be screwed into the crankshaft sprocket, and a smaller hole between the bolt holes, through which a locating peg can be inserted into a corresponding recess in the sprocket face, for timing.

18 Release the nut on the timing belt tensioner, move the pulley away from the belt and retighten the nut to hold the pulley in the retracted position **(see illustration)**.

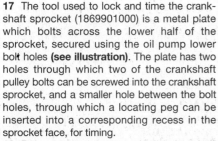

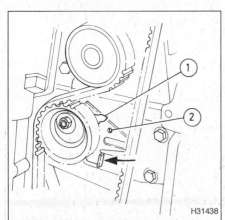

4.23a Timing belt tensioner details - vertical rib (arrowed), tensioner pointer (1) and alignment hole (2)

19 Slide the timing belt from the sprockets, taking great care not to turn them if locking tools have not been used **(see illustration)**.

Refitting

20 When refitting the new belt, first make sure that the sprocket timing marks are still in alignment.

21 If the special locking tools are being used, the camshaft sprocket bolt should be loosened to allow the sprocket to move slightly as the timing belt is refitted and tensioned. To hold the sprocket stationary while the retaining bolt is loosened, make up a tool as described in Section 5.

22 If the special locking tools are not being used, it is not advisable to loosen the camshaft sprocket bolt unless absolutely necessary. If the timing belt teeth will not engage the camshaft sprocket satisfactorily, it is permissible to loosen the bolt and turn the sprocket *very slightly*.

23 Fit the belt so that the arrows on the belt (where applicable) point in the direction of engine rotation. Also where applicable, the lines painted on the belt should coincide with marks on the sprockets.

22 Engage the timing belt with the crankshaft sprocket first, then place it around the camshaft sprocket and the coolant pump pulley. Finally, slip the belt around the tensioner sprocket. Ensure that any slack in the belt is on the tensioner side of the belt run.

23 Release the tensioner nut and push the pulley anti-clockwise against the belt, using

the small vertical rib on the tensioner backplate **(see illustrations)**.

24 Initially, the belt should be set to the maximum tension possible using reasonable force, indicated by the tensioner pointer moving past the alignment hole in the tensioner backplate. Tighten the tensioner nut securely.

25 If the camshaft sprocket bolt was loosened, tighten it to the specified torque, holding the sprocket in the same way as when it was loosened.

26 Remove any locking tools used, and/or select neutral. Using a spanner or socket on the crankshaft pulley bolt, turn the engine through two complete turns in the normal direction of rotation. Check (as far as possible) that the sprocket timing marks come back into alignment.

27 Loosen the tensioner nut, and align the

4.23b Using a screwdriver to set the belt tensioner

4.27 Belt tensioner correctly set - pointer aligned with hole

tensioner pointer with the small hole on the tensioner backplate. Hold the tensioner in this position, and tighten the tensioner nut securely **(see illustration)**.

28 Refit the timing belt lower cover, and secure with the two bolts.

29 Refit the crankshaft pulley, locating the pulley over the peg on the crankshaft sprocket and tightening the four bolts to the specified torque.

30 If the crankshaft has not turned, check that the mark on the crankshaft pulley aligns with the mark on the belt lower cover.

31 Further refitting is a reversal of removal. Refit and tension the auxiliary drivebelt as described in Chapter 1.

---

5 Timing belt sprockets and tensioner - removal and refitting

Timing belt tensioner

Removal

1 Remove the air cleaner and air ducting as described in Chapter 4A.

2 Remove the auxiliary drivebelt as described in Chapter 1.

3 Remove the two bolts securing the coolant hose mounting bracket to the timing belt cover, and move the hose out of the way.

4 Unbolt and remove the timing belt upper cover, which is secured by six bolts.

Caution: Provided the timing belt is kept fully engaged with the camshaft, crankshaft and coolant pump sprockets during the

following procedure, it is not necessary to align the timing TDC marks. However if any doubt exists, read through the full procedure given in Section 4, noting the advice on setting to TDC, and ensuring that the timing is not lost. The timing belt does not have to be removed for this procedure, but if the belt slips from the sprockets, the timing could be lost.

5 Loosen the nut on the timing belt tensioner and move the pulley away from the belt. If necessary, keep the belt engaged with the sprockets using cable-ties, elastic bands or string.

6 Completely unscrew the nut, and slide the tensioner off the mounting stud.

Inspection

7 Wipe the tensioner clean, but do not use excessive amounts of solvent, as these may contaminate the bearings. Spin the tensioner pulley on its hub by hand. Stiff movement or excessive freeplay is an indication of severe wear; the tensioner is not a serviceable component, and should be renewed if its condition is suspect, or as a precaution at the time of a major engine overhaul.

Refitting

8 Hold the timing belt aside, then slide the tensioner over the mounting stud and secure loosely with the nut. Ensuring that all slack is taken out of the belt, engage the timing belt with tensioner sprocket.

9 Set the belt tension with reference to Section 4, paragraphs 20 to 23.

10 Refit the timing belt cover and tighten the bolts. Refit the bolts securing the coolant hose to the timing belt cover.

11 Refit and tension the auxiliary drivebelt as described in Chapter 1.

12 Refit the air cleaner and air ducting as described in Chapter 4A.

Camshaft sprocket

Removal

13 Remove the timing belt as described in Section 4. It is essential that an alignment mark is made between the sprocket and the cylinder head, to preserve the camshaft timing - make your own if none are present, particularly if the camshaft holding tool described in Section 4 is not available.

14 The camshaft sprocket must now be held stationary while the retaining bolt is loosened; if the sprocket turns very far, there is a risk that the valves will hit the pistons. Make up a tool as follows and engage it with the holes in the sprocket **(see illustration)**.

> **TOOL TiP** *To make a camshaft sprocket holding tool, obtain two lengths of steel strip about 6 mm thick by 30 mm wide or similar, one 600 mm long, the other 200 mm long (all dimensions approximate). Bolt the two strips together to form a forked end, leaving the bolt slack so that the shorter strip can pivot freely. At the end of each 'prong' of the fork, secure a bolt with a nut and a locknut, to act as the fulcrums; these will engage with the cut-outs in the sprocket, and should protrude by about 30 mm.*

15 Alternatively, pass a rod through one of the holes in the camshaft sprocket to prevent it rotating. Position a pad of rag or a piece of wood under the rod to avoid damaging the cylinder head.

16 Unscrew the bolt, and slide the sprocket from the end of the camshaft. Note the integral location key on the inner face of the sprocket **(see illustrations)**.

Inspection

17 With the sprocket removed, examine the camshaft oil seal for signs of leaking. If necessary, refer to Section 7 and renew it.

18 Check the sprocket teeth for damage.

19 Wipe clean the sprocket and camshaft mating surfaces.

Refitting

20 Locate the sprocket on the end of the camshaft. Refit the bolt and tighten to the specified torque while holding the camshaft stationary using the method described previously.

21 Align the marks made between the camshaft sprocket and cylinder head, then refit the timing belt as described in Section 4.

Crankshaft sprocket

Removal

22 Remove the timing belt as described in

5.14 Hold the camshaft sprocket as the bolt is loosened

5.16a Remove the camshaft sprocket bolt . . .

5.16b . . . and remove the sprocket - note keyway (arrowed)

Section 4. It is essential that an alignment mark is made between the sprocket and the oil pump housing, to preserve the timing - make your own if none are present, particularly if the sprocket holding tool described in Section 4 is not available.

23 Working beneath the engine, unbolt and remove the flywheel lower cover, then hold the flywheel stationary, preferably using a tool which engages the flywheel starter ring gear (see Section 10). Alternatively, have an assistant engage a wide-bladed screwdriver with the starter ring gear.

24 Unscrew the crankshaft sprocket retaining bolt - this is tightened to a particularly high torque, so ensure that the car is adequately supported. Use only good-quality, close-fitting tools, and take precautions against personal injury, especially when the bolt eventually loosens (wear gloves to protect your hands). The bolt has a **left-hand thread** - ie it unscrews **clockwise**.

25 Slide the sprocket off the end of the crankshaft. If it is tight, remove it using a puller or a pair of suitable screwdrivers. The sprocket may have an integral location key on its inner face, or a separate key which locates in a groove in the crankshaft nose.

Inspection

26 With the sprocket removed, examine the crankshaft oil seal for signs of leaking. If necessary, refer to Section 8 and renew it.

27 Wipe clean the sprocket and crankshaft mating surfaces. Check the sprocket teeth for damage.

Refitting

28 Slide the sprocket onto the crankshaft, making sure it engages the integral key or separate key. Fit the washer to a new bolt - do not lubricate the threads. It is not advisable to re-use the old bolt, given the extremely high torque to which it is tightened.

29 Fit the new bolt and washer, tightening the bolt to the specified torque while holding the crankshaft stationary using the method described in paragraph 23. Also bear in mind the advice in paragraph 24.

30 Refit the timing belt as described in Section 4.

6.1 Disconnecting the breather hose from the camshaft cover

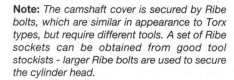

6 Camshaft cover - removal and refitting

Note: *The camshaft cover is secured by Ribe bolts, which are similar in appearance to Torx types, but require different tools. A set of Ribe sockets can be obtained from good tool stockists - larger Ribe bolts are used to secure the cylinder head.*

Removal

1 Remove the air cleaner top cover and inlet duct as described in Chapter 4A **(see illustration)**.

2 Remove the three bolts securing the engine top cover, and loosen the fourth bolt at the rear of the engine, behind the timing belt cover. Remove the top cover from the engine compartment.

3 Loosen and remove the two bolts securing the wiring harness brackets to the rear of the cylinder head, and move the harness back out of the way **(see illustration)**.

> **HAYNES HINT**
> *If the spark plugs have been removed as part of another procedure, place rags over the spark plug holes, to prevent the bolts falling into the engine.*

6.3 Remove the two wiring harness brackets from the rear of the head

4 Remove the two top Allen bolts securing the timing belt upper cover to the camshaft cover - there is no need to remove the timing belt upper cover completely.

5 Progressively unscrew the six Ribe bolts from the top of the camshaft cover and lift off the cover - note the location of any supports on the bolts **(see illustrations)**. If it sticks, do not attempt to lever it off - instead free it by working around the cover and tapping it lightly with a soft-faced mallet.

6 Recover the camshaft cover gasket. Inspect the gasket carefully, and renew it if damage or deterioration is evident.

7 Clean the mating surfaces of the cylinder head and camshaft cover thoroughly, removing all traces of oil and old gasket - take care to avoid damaging the surfaces as you do this.

Refitting

8 Before refitting the cover, pull out the breather filter from the breather hose connection stub **(see illustration)**. Clean the filter using suitable solvent, then refit it.

9 Locate a new gasket on the cylinder head and make sure it is correctly seated.

10 Lower the cover onto the gasket, making sure the gasket is not displaced.

11 Insert the mounting bolts and tighten them progressively to the specified torque.

12 Refit the components removed for access using a reversal of the relevant removal procedure.

6.5a Unscrew the camshaft cover bolts . . .

6.5b . . . and lift off the cover

6.8 Removing the breather filter from the camshaft cover

7.4 Lubricate the new seal, then fit over the camshaft

7.5 Tap the camshaft seal home using a large socket

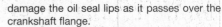

damage the oil seal lips as it passes over the crankshaft flange.

11 Progressively tap the oil seal into the housing, keeping it square to prevent distortion. A block of wood is useful for this purpose.

12 Refit the flywheel with reference to Section 10.

9 Cylinder head - removal and refitting

Note: *The cylinder head is secured by Ribe bolts, which are similar in appearance to Torx types, but require different tools. A set of Ribe sockets can be obtained from good tool stockists - Ribe bolts are also used on other parts of the engine.*

Removal

1 Depressurise the fuel system, and remove the air cleaner cover, air inlet duct and airbox as described in Chapter 4A.

2 Disconnect the battery negative terminal (refer to *Disconnecting the battery*).

3 Drain the cooling system as described in Chapter 1.

4 Remove the auxiliary drivebelt as described in Chapter 1.

5 Remove the spark plugs as described in Chapter 1.

6 Remove the timing belt from the camshaft sprocket, using the information in Section 4. Unless the belt has been changed recently, remove it completely and fit a new one on reassembly.

7 Disconnect the accelerator cable from the throttle body as described in Chapter 4A.

8 Taking precautions against fuel spillage, disconnect the fuel supply and return hoses from the throttle body (the fuel supply hose is at the front, and has an arrow indicating direction of fuel flow) **(see illustrations)**.

9 Disconnect the charcoal canister hose, either at the throttle body, or at the connection above the inner wing **(see illustration)**.

10 Disconnect the warm-air supply duct from the heat shield over the exhaust manifold. If the manifold is to be removed from the head (see

7 Camshaft oil seal - renewal

1 Remove the timing belt and camshaft sprocket as described in Sections 4 and 5.

2 Using a suitable hooked instrument, remove the oil seal from the cylinder head, taking care not to damage the surface of the camshaft.

3 Clean the seating in the cylinder head and the end of the camshaft. To prevent damage to the new oil seal as it is being fitted, wrap some adhesive tape around the end of the camshaft and lightly oil it.

4 Dip the new oil seal in oil then locate it over the camshaft, making sure that the sealing lips are facing inwards **(see illustration)**.

5 Using a suitable tubular drift, drive the oil seal squarely into the cylinder head **(see illustration)**. Remove the adhesive tape from the camshaft.

6 Refit the camshaft sprocket and timing belt with reference to Sections 5 and 4.

8 Crankshaft oil seals - renewal

Front (right-hand side) oil seal

1 The front oil seal is located in the oil pump on the front of the crankshaft. Remove the timing belt as described in Section 4 and the crankshaft sprocket as described in Section 5.

2 Using a hooked instrument, remove the oil seal from the oil pump housing, taking care not to damage the surface of the crankshaft.

3 Clean the seating in the housing and the surface of the crankshaft. To prevent damage to the new oil seal as it is being fitted, wrap some adhesive tape around the end of the crankshaft and lightly oil it.

4 Dip the new oil seal in oil then offer it up to the oil pump casing making sure that the sealing lips are facing inwards.

5 Using a suitable tubular drift, drive the oil seal squarely into the casing. Remove the adhesive tape.

6 Refit the crankshaft sprocket and timing belt with reference to Sections 5 and 4.

Rear (left-hand side) oil seal

Note: *The following paragraphs describe renewal of the rear oil seal leaving the housing in position. Refer to Chapter 2E for details of removing the housing.*

7 Remove the flywheel as described in Section 10.

8 Using a suitable hooked instrument, remove the oil seal from the rear oil seal housing, taking care not to damage the surface of the crankshaft.

9 Clean the seating in the housing and the surface of the crankshaft. Check the crankshaft for burrs which may damage the oil seal lip of the new seal, and if necessary use a fine file to remove them.

10 Dip the new seal in clean engine oil and carefully locate it over the crankshaft rear flange, making sure that it is the correct way round (lips facing inwards). Take care not to

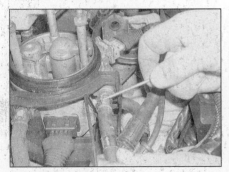

9.8a Release the hose clips . . .

9.8b . . . and disconnect the fuel supply . . .

9.8c . . . and return hoses from the throttle body

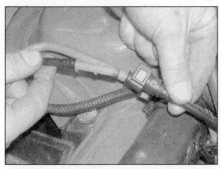

9.9 Disconnecting the charcoal canister hose at the inner wing

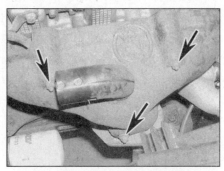

9.10 Exhaust manifold heat shield securing nuts (arrowed)

9.11a Disconnect the hoses at the front . . .

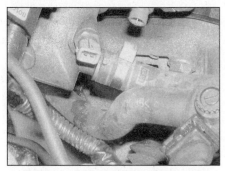

9.11b . . . and rear of the thermostat housing

9.12a Unscrew the hose clip . . .

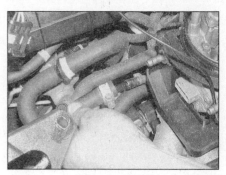

9.12b . . . and disconnect the brake servo hose

paragraph 17), then remove the heat shield itself, which is secured by three nuts **(see illustration)**.
11 Disconnect the coolant hoses from the

front and rear of the thermostat housing **(see illustrations)**.
12 Unscrew the hose clip and disconnect the brake servo vacuum pipe **(see illustrations)**.

13 Disconnect the following wiring:
a) *Ignition coil (small wiring plug). Also disconnect the large fuel injection system wiring plug just behind the ignition coil **(see illustrations)**.*
b) *Reversing light switch - on the front of the transmission **(see illustration)**.*
c) *Detach the HT leads from the clip behind the ignition coil **(see illustration)**.*
d) *Three wiring plugs on the throttle housing **(see illustration)**.*
e) *Coolant temperature senders - on the left-hand end of the cylinder head (left as seen from the driver's seat) **(see illustrations)**.*
f) *Oxygen sensor wiring plug - clipped to a bracket at the front of the engine, below the thermostat housing **(see illustration)**.*

9.13a Disconnect the ignition coil LT wiring plug . . .

9.13b . . . and the fuel injection wiring connector

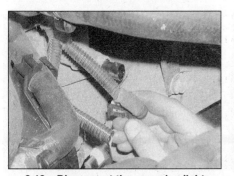

9.13c Disconnect the reversing light switch . . .

9.13d . . . unclip the HT leads . . .

9.13e . . . and unplug the wiring connectors at the throttle body

9.13f Unplug the fuel system coolant temperature sender . . .

9.13g . . . and the temperature gauge sender

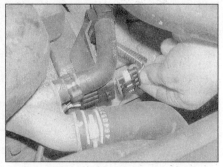

9.13h Disconnecting the oxygen sensor wiring plug

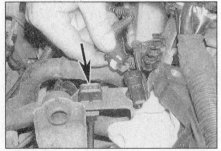

9.13i Disconnect the two wiring plugs behind the ignition coil - one seen disconnected (arrowed)

9.14a Unscrew the top bolt (which also secures the injection wiring connector) . . .

9.14b . . . and the lower bolt securing the ignition coil wiring bracket

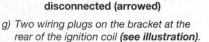

g) Two wiring plugs on the bracket at the rear of the ignition coil (see illustration).

14 Remove the two bolts securing the wiring bracket at the rear of the ignition coil **(see illustrations)**. Move the bracket clear of the

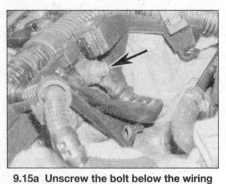

9.15a Unscrew the bolt below the wiring harness mounting bracket (arrowed) . . .

9.15b . . . and disconnect the earth lead

cylinder head, unclipping the connector plug halves from it as necessary.

15 If not already done, working along the wiring harness at the rear of the cylinder head, unscrew the harness clip mounting bolts and

release the harness from the head. A further bolt secures the engine earth lead, which must also be disconnected. When the harness is free, lift it from the rear of the head, and move it to the right of the engine compartment **(see illustrations)**.

16 Free the wiring harness which runs along the base of the inlet manifold by prising open the plastic guide channel (some models may have a cable-tie holding the channel together) **(see illustrations)**. Work along the harness towards the timing belt end of the engine. The fluid pipe(s) from the power steering pump hamper removal of the harness, but we found that disconnecting the pipes was unnecessary.

17 There are various potential options concerning the exhaust manifold. It is possible to remove the head with the exhaust manifold attached; alternatively, unbolt the manifold from the head and leave the manifold attached

9.15c Check that the harness is free, and move it clear of the head

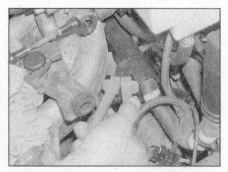

9.16a Cut the cable-tie (where fitted) . . .

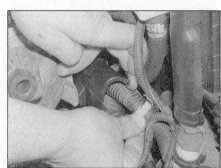

9.16b . . . and separate the plastic guide channel to release the wiring harness

to the downpipe. The safest option (although involving more work) is to remove the exhaust manifold completely, as described.

18 Working under the car, unscrew the four exhaust manifold-to-downpipe nuts, and separate the joint **(see illustration)**. Recover the gasket.

19 Unscrew the manifold-to-cylinder head nuts, and withdraw the manifold from the cylinder head, recovering the gasket.

20 In some cases, the manifold studs will come out with the nuts - this poses no great problem, and the studs can be refitted if they are in good condition. For preference, however, a complete set of manifold and downpipe studs and nuts should be obtained as required, as the old ones are likely to be in less-than-perfect condition.

21 If the downpipe is lowered to the floor, check that the wiring to the oxygen sensor (at the top of the downpipe) is not placed under strain. The wiring plug has already been disconnected, so feed the wiring through.

22 Remove the bolt securing the upper end of the engine oil dipstick tube to the cylinder head, then pull the tube upwards to remove it **(see illustration)**. Removing the tube may displace the seal at the base of the tube - if so, refit it now or store it with the tube for refitting.

23 Check around the head that there are no further wires, hoses or other obstructions which will prevent the head from being lifted off.

24 Unscrew the cylinder head Ribe bolts half a turn at a time, in the reverse order to that shown in illustration 9.42. When the bolts are free, remove them with their washers.

25 Lift the cylinder head from the block, together with the inlet manifold. If it is stuck tight, insert pieces of wood into the exhaust ports (if possible), and use them as levers to rock the head off the block. On no account drive levers into the gasket joint, nor attempt to tap the head sideways, as it is located on positioning dowels.

26 Remove and discard the cylinder head gasket and the manifold gaskets.

27 The cylinder head can be dismantled after removing the camshaft and cam followers as described in Chapter 2E. Further dismantling and decarbonising are also described in Chapter 2E.

Preparation for refitting

28 The mating faces of the cylinder head and cylinder block must be perfectly clean before refitting the head. Use a hard plastic or wooden scraper to remove all traces of gasket and carbon; also clean the piston crowns.

29 Take particular care when cleaning the piston crowns, as the soft aluminium alloy is easily damaged.

30 Make sure that the carbon is not allowed to enter the oil and water passages - this is particularly important for the lubrication system, as carbon could block the oil supply

9.18 Exhaust manifold-to-downpipe joint

to the engine's components. Using adhesive tape and paper, seal the water, oil and bolt holes in the cylinder block.

31 To prevent carbon entering the gap between the pistons and bores, smear a little grease in the gap. After cleaning each piston, use a small brush to remove all traces of grease and carbon from the gap, then wipe away the remainder with a clean rag. Clean all the pistons in the same way.

32 Check the mating surfaces of the cylinder block and the cylinder head for nicks, deep scratches and other damage. If slight, they may be removed carefully with a file, but if excessive, machining may be the only alternative to renewal.

33 If warpage of the cylinder head gasket surface is suspected, use a straight-edge to check it for distortion. Refer to Part E of this Chapter if necessary.

34 Check the condition of the cylinder head bolts, and particularly their threads, whenever they are removed. Wash the bolts in a suitable solvent, and wipe them dry. Check each bolt for any sign of visible wear or damage, renewing them if necessary.

Refitting

35 Before refitting the assembled cylinder head, make sure that the head and block mating surfaces are perfectly clean.

36 The bolt holes in the cylinder block must be mopped out to clear any oil or coolant. If the bolt holes have any significant amount of

9.22 Dipstick tube mounting bolt

liquid in them, the block could be cracked by hydraulic pressure when the head bolts are tightened.

37 Check that the camshaft marks made during dismantling (see Section 4) are aligned.

38 The new gasket should not be removed from its plastic bag until required for use. Fit the gasket dry - no grease or sealant should be used.

39 Place the gasket on the cylinder block so that the word ALTO can be read from above.

40 Lower the cylinder head onto the block so that it locates on the positioning dowels.

41 Ensure that the cylinder head bolts are cleaned of all debris, and check the threads for signs of damage. Especially if it is known that the bolts have been removed previously, it is advisable to renew all ten bolts as a set, rather than risk the bolts shearing when tightened.

42 Lightly oil the bolt threads. Screw the bolts in finger-tight, and tighten them in the sequence shown to the Stage 1 torque **(see illustration)**.

43 When all ten bolts have been tightened to the Stage 1 torque, go round again in sequence and tighten to the Stage 2 torque.

44 Again working in sequence, tighten the bolts through the specified Stage 3 angle. Note that 90° is equivalent to a quarter-turn or right-angle, making it easy to judge by noting the initial position of the socket handle. If available, use an angle gauge fitted to the socket handle for maximum accuracy.

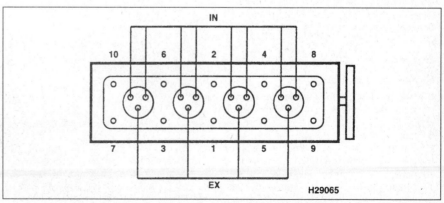

9.42 Cylinder head bolt tightening sequence

45 With all ten bolts tightened to Stage 3, go round once more and tighten all bolts in sequence to the Stage 4 angle.

46 When all the bolts are fully tightened, refit the camshaft cover as described in Section 6.

47 Refit the exhaust manifold, using new gaskets, studs and nuts, as appropriate according to how the manifold was separated. Tighten all nuts securely.

48 Further refitting is a reversal of removal. Ensure that all wiring and hoses are correctly routed and securely reconnected. Refer to Section 4 when refitting the timing belt, and to Chapter 1 when refitting the spark plugs and auxiliary drivebelt, and when refilling the cooling system.

10 Flywheel - removal, inspection and refitting

Refer to Part A, Section 11.

11 Engine mountings - inspection and renewal

Inspection

1 Jack up the front of the vehicle and support on axle stands (see *Jacking and vehicle support*).

2 Check the mounting rubbers to see if they are cracked, hardened or separated from the metal at any point; renew the mounting if any such damage or deterioration is evident.

3 Check that all the mounting's fasteners are securely tightened; use a torque wrench to check if possible.

4 Using a large screwdriver or a crowbar, check for wear in the mounting by carefully levering against it to check for free play. Where this is not possible enlist the aid of an assistant to move the engine/transmission back and forth, or from side to side, while you watch the mounting. While some free play is to be expected even from new components, excessive wear should be obvious. If excessive free play is found, check first that the fasteners are correctly secured, then renew any worn components as described below.

Renewal

Right-hand mounting

5 Raise the front of the vehicle and support on axle stands (see *Jacking and vehicle support*).

6 Place a trolley jack beneath the right-hand side of the engine, with a block of wood on the jack head. Raise the jack until it is supporting the weight of the engine.

7 Working from below, unscrew the nut securing the engine bracket to the mounting.

8 Lower the engine sufficiently to disengage the engine bracket from the mounting, then

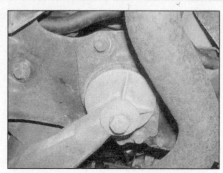

11.15 View of the rear engine mounting, showing the through-bolt (centre) and two mounting-to-body bolts

remove the three bolts securing the mounting to the body, and remove it.

9 Locate the new mounting on the body, then insert the mounting-to-body bolts and tighten by hand.

10 Raise the engine and locate the bracket on the mounting. Refit the nut and tighten to the specified torque, then tighten the mounting-to-body bolts.

11 Remove the trolley jack and lower the vehicle to the ground.

Left-hand/rear mounting

12 Raise the front of the vehicle and support on axle stands (see *Jacking and vehicle support*).

13 Place a trolley jack beneath the transmission, with a block of wood on the jack head. Raise the jack until it is supporting the weight of the engine/transmission.

14 Unscrew the through-bolt securing the transmission bracket to the mounting, and recover the washers.

15 Unscrew the two bolts securing the left-hand mounting to the body **(see illustration)**.

16 Lower the transmission sufficiently to remove the mounting from the transmission bracket.

17 Locate the new mounting in position, and loosely refit the mounting-to-body bolts.

18 Raise the engine/transmission and refit the through-bolt securing the bracket to the mounting. Tighten the bolt to the specified torque, then tighten the mounting-to-body bolts.

19 Remove the trolley jack and lower the vehicle to the ground.

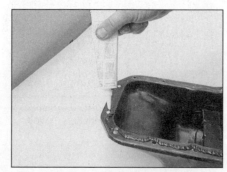

12.4 Applying sealant to the sump flange

Front mounting

20 Raise the front of the vehicle and support on axle stands (see *Jacking and vehicle support*).

21 Place a trolley jack beneath the engine/transmission flange, with a block of wood on the jack head. Raise the jack until it is supporting the weight of the engine and transmission.

22 Working from below, unscrew the nut securing the bracket to the mounting.

23 Lower the engine sufficiently to disengage the bracket from the mounting, then remove the three bolts securing the mounting to the body, and remove it.

24 Locate the new mounting on the body, then insert the mounting-to-body bolts and tighten by hand.

25 Raise the engine and locate the bracket on the mounting. Refit the nut and tighten to the specified torque, then tighten the mounting-to-body bolts.

26 Remove the trolley jack and lower the vehicle to the ground.

12 Sump - removal and refitting

Removal

1 Jack up the front of the vehicle and support on axle stands. Drain the engine oil.

2 Unscrew the sump securing bolts and pull the sump downwards past the exhaust pipe to remove it. The joint sealant will require cutting with a sharp knife to release the pan.

Refitting

3 Clean away all old gasket material, from the sump pan and from the base of the block.

4 Apply a bead of RTV silicone instant gasket 3 mm in diameter to the sump flange. The bead of sealant should pass around the inside of the sump bolt holes **(see illustration)**.

5 Fit the sump, screw in the fixing bolts and tighten in a diagonal sequence to the specified torque.

6 Wait one hour for the gasket compound to harden before filling with oil.

7 Lower the vehicle to the ground and fill the engine with oil (see Chapter 1). Check the oil level after running the engine for a few minutes, as described in *Weekly checks*.

13 Oil pump and pick-up tube - removal and refitting

Removal

1 Drain the engine oil and remove the sump as described in Section 12.

2 Unbolt and remove the oil pick-up/filter screen assembly. Note the sealing washer.

3 Unscrew and remove the oil filter cartridge (see Chapter 1).

13.8 Using an impact screwdriver to remove the oil pump rear cover plate screws

13.9a Measuring oil pump outer gear-to-pump housing clearance

13.9b Measuring oil pump gear endfloat

4 Remove the timing belt as described in Section 4.

5 Remove the crankshaft sprocket as described in Section 5.

6 Extract the oil pump fixing bolts, noting their locations (there are four long bolts, and four short ones). Withdraw the pump and remove the gasket.

Inspection

7 The oil pump incorporates a pressure relief valve, which can be removed for examination by unscrewing the plug and pulling out the spring and valve.

8 If pump wear is suspected, check the gears in the following way. Extract the five fixing screws and remove the rear cover plate. The screws are very tight, and will probably require the use of an impact screwdriver **(see illustration)**.

9 Check the clearance between the outer gear and the pump housing using feeler blades. Check the gear endfloat by placing a straight-edge across the pump body, and checking the gap between the straight-edge and gear face **(see illustrations)**. If the clearances are outside the specified tolerance, renew the oil pump complete.

10 If the pump is unworn, refit the rear cover plate and tighten the screws fully.

11 Apply air pressure from a tyre pump to the oil pump oil ducts, to clear any sludge or other material. If any solvents are used, the pump must be allowed to dry thoroughly before refitting.

12 Prime the pump by pouring clean engine oil into its inlet duct, at the same time turning the oil pump inner gear with your fingers.

13 Lever out the oil seal, and drive a new one squarely into the oil pump casing **(see illustration)**. Lubricate the oil seal lips.

Refitting

14 Clean all traces of old gasket from the pump and the mating surfaces on the cylinder block.

15 Bolt the pump into position using a new joint gasket. Insert the four longer bolts into the positions noted on removal, and tighten all to the specified torques.

16 Bolt on the oil pick-up assembly using a new sealing washer.

17 Refit the crankshaft sprocket as described in Section 5.

18 Fit and tension the timing belt as described in Section 4.

19 Fit the sump as described in Section 12.

20 Screw on a new oil filter cartridge, and fill the engine with oil (see Chapter 1).

21 Run the engine for a few minutes, then check and top-up the oil level as described in *Weekly checks*.

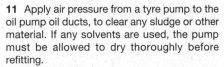

14 Oil pressure switch -
removal and refitting

Removal

1 The oil pressure switch is located at the rear of the engine block, next to the knock sensor **(see illustration)**. Access to the switch is hampered by the inlet manifold.

2 Disconnect the switch wiring connector **(see illustration)**.

3 Unscrew the switch from the block, and remove it.

4 Clean the switch location in the block as far as possible. If the switch is to be refitted, clean its threads.

5 Examine the switch for signs of cracking or splits. If the top part of the switch is loose, this is an early indication of impending failure.

Refitting

6 Apply a smear of sealant to the threads of the switch, then screw it into place and tighten to the specified torque.

7 Reconnect the switch wiring on completion.

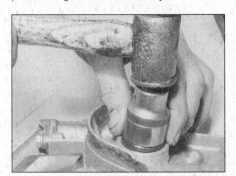

13.13 Using a socket to fit a new oil seal to the oil pump

14.1 Oil pressure switch (arrowed) - seen with inlet manifold removed

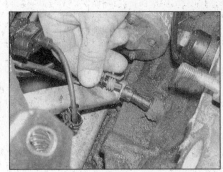

14.2 Disconnect the switch wiring connector

Notes

Chapter 2 Part C:
1.6 litre engine in-car repair procedures

Contents

Degrees of difficulty

Easy, suitable for novice with little experience	**Fairly easy,** suitable for beginner with some experience 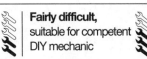	**Fairly difficult,** suitable for competent DIY mechanic	**Difficult,** suitable for experienced DIY mechanic 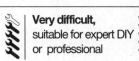	**Very difficult,** suitable for expert DIY or professional

Specifications

General

Engine code*	182 A4.000
Bore	86.4 mm
Stroke	67.4 mm
Compression ratio	10.15:1
Firing order	1-3-4-2
No 1 cylinder location	Timing (right-hand) end of engine

*Note: See 'Vehicle identification numbers' for the location of code marking on the engine.

Lubrication system

Oil pump type	Gear type, driven from auxiliary shaft
Gear teeth-to-cover clearance	0.110 to 0.180 mm
Gear side-to-cover clearance	0.040 to 0.106 mm
Gear side-to-side play	0.015 to 0.048 mm
Drive gear to driven gear clearance	0.30 mm
Oil pressure (at operating temperature)	15 psi at idle, to 54 psi at 4000 rpm

Camshafts

Drive	Toothed belt
No of bearings	5
Camshaft bearing journal diameters:	
No 1 bearing	29.944 to 29.960 mm
No 2 bearing	52.400 to 52.415 mm
No 3 bearing	52.800 to 52.815 mm
No 4 bearing	53.200 to 53.215 mm
No 5 bearing	53.600 to 53.615 mm
Camshaft bearing journal running clearance	0.030 to 0.070 mm
Camshaft endfloat (typical)	0.15 to 0.34 mm

Camshaft housings

Camshaft bearing diameters:	
No 1 bearing	29.989 to 30.014 mm
No 2 bearing	52.445 to 52.470 mm
No 3 bearing	52.845 to 52.870 mm
No 4 bearing	53.245 to 53.270 mm
No 5 bearing	53.645 to 53.670 mm
Hydraulic tappet diameter	32.959 to 32.975 mm
Hydraulic tappet bore diameter	33.000 to 33.025 mm
Hydraulic tappet running clearance	0.025 to 0.066 mm

Torque wrench settings

	Nm	lbf ft
Alternator mounting bracket to block	50	37
Auxiliary drivebelt tensioner	48	35
Auxiliary shaft sprocket bolt	80	59
Big-end (connecting rod) bearing cap nuts	51	38
Camshaft housing bolts	15	11
Camshaft sprocket	115	85
Coolant pipe to block	25	18
Crankcase breather pipe:		
M8 bolts	23	17
M10 bolts	48	35
Crankshaft sprocket nut*	220	162
Cylinder head:		
Stage 1	20	15
Stage 2	40	30
Stage 3	Angle-tighten a further 90°	
Stage 4	Angle-tighten a further 90°	
Engine/transmission mountings:		
Mounting brackets to transmission:		
M10 bolts	50	37
M12 bolts	85	63
Mounting through-bolts:		
M10 bolts	50	37
M12 bolts	80	59
Mountings to bodyshell/subframe	32	24
Right-hand mounting bracket to block:		
M8 bolts	25	18
M10 bolts	48	35
M12 bolts	80	59
Exhaust manifold nuts	30	22
Flywheel/driveplate**	83	61
Inlet manifold:		
M7 bolts	15	11
M8 bolts	30	22
Main bearing cap bolts	80	59
Oil pressure switch	32	24
Oil pump mounting bolts	25	18
Sump bolts	9	7
Thermostat housing bolts	25	18
Timing belt covers:		
M6 bolts	9	7
M8 bolts	25	18
M10 bolts	50	37
Timing belt guide pulley bolt	87	64
Timing belt tensioner mounting plate:		
M8 bolts	23	17
M10 bolts	48	35
Timing belt tensioner nut	23	17

*Although not specifically recommended by FIAT, use a new nut and locking fluid.
** Use locking fluid.

1 General information

Using this Chapter

Chapter 2 is divided into five Parts; A to E. Repair operations that can be carried out with the engine in the vehicle are described in Parts A to D. Part E covers the removal of the engine/transmission as a unit, and describes the engine dismantling and overhaul procedures.

In Parts A to D, the assumption is made that the engine is installed in the vehicle, with all ancillaries connected. If the engine has been removed for overhaul, the preliminary dismantling information which precedes each operation may be ignored.

Engine description

The 1.6 litre engine is a water-cooled, double overhead camshaft, in-line four-cylinder unit, with cast-iron cylinder block and aluminium-alloy cylinder head. The engine is a 16-valve unit, with two inlet and two exhaust valves per cylinder. The engine is mounted transversely at the front of the vehicle, with the transmission bolted to the left-hand side of the engine.

The cylinder head contains the valve assemblies, while the camshafts run in two separate housings bolted on top of the engine. The camshafts are driven by a toothed timing belt, and each one runs in five bearings. The inlet and exhaust valves are closed by single coil springs, and run in guides pressed into the cylinder head. The camshafts actuate the valves directly via hydraulic tappets mounted in the camshaft housings.

The crankshaft is supported by five main bearings, and endfloat is controlled by thrust washers fitted around No 5 main bearing.

Engine coolant is circulated by a pump, driven by an auxiliary drivebelt. For details of the cooling system, refer to Chapter 3.

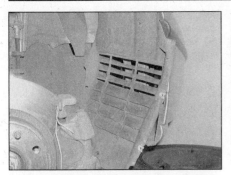

2.3a Remove the front section of the wheelarch liner . . .

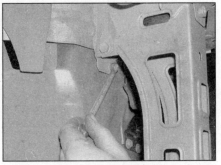

2.3b . . . for access to the inner panel's front securing screw

2.3c Removing the wheelarch inner panel

Lubricant is circulated under pressure by a gear-type pump, driven via an auxiliary shaft which itself is driven by the timing belt. Oil is drawn from the sump through a strainer, and then forced through an externally-mounted, replaceable screw-on filter. From there, it is distributed to the cylinder head, where it lubricates the camshaft journals and tappets, and also to the crankcase, where it lubricates the main bearings, connecting rod big and small-ends, gudgeon pins and cylinder bores.

Models from 1999 onwards may be fitted with the revised 'Step A' engine, which features a number of minor modifications. The engine seen in our 1.6 litre project vehicle was a Step A engine.

Repair operations possible with the engine in the car

The following work can be carried out with the engine in the car:

2.4 Remove the screw securing the timing belt upper access cover

2.6 Using a dial gauge and probe to establish TDC on No 1 piston

a) *Auxiliary drivebelts - removal and refitting (see Chapter 1).*
b) *Camshafts - removal and refitting.*
c) *Camshaft oil seals - renewal.*
d) *Auxiliary shaft oil seal - renewal.*
e) *Camshaft sprockets - removal and refitting.*
f) *Coolant pump - removal and refitting (refer to Chapter 3).*
g) *Crankshaft oil seals - renewal.*
h) *Crankshaft sprocket - removal and refitting.*
i) *Cylinder head - removal and refitting.*
j) *Engine mountings - inspection and renewal.*
k) *Oil pump and pickup assembly - removal and refitting.*
l) *Sump.*
m) *Timing belt, sprockets and cover - removal, inspection and refitting.*

Note: *It is possible to remove the pistons and connecting rods (after removing the cylinder head and sump) without removing the engine. However, this is not recommended. Work of this nature is more easily and thoroughly completed with the engine on the bench, as described in Chapter 2E.*

2 Location of TDC on No 1 cylinder

1 With the car parked on a level surface, apply the handbrake and chock the rear wheels. Loosen the right-hand front wheel bolts.

2 Raise the front of the vehicle, rest it securely on axle stands and remove the right-hand front roadwheel.

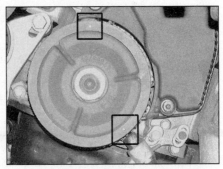

2.8a Crankshaft pulley timing marks aligned at TDC

3 Remove the screws securing the inner panel under the right-hand wheelarch, to gain access to the crankshaft pulley. Removing this cover entails removing the screws securing the wheelarch front liner to the end of the bumper, and removing the front liner, for access to the inner panel's front securing screw **(see illustrations)**.

4 Remove the single screw securing the small access cover in the timing belt cover **(see illustration)**, and remove the access cover to view the camshaft sprockets.

5 To make the engine easier to turn, remove all four spark plugs, as described in Chapter 1. If preferred, however, it is sufficient to remove just No 1 spark plug (nearest the timing belt end of the engine).

6 Insert a suitable large screwdriver (or, if available, a dial gauge and probe) down No 1 spark plug hole, taking care to keep it vertical, so that it does not bind as the piston rises **(see illustration)**. Do not use any tool which might break off or fall down inside the engine.

7 Have an assistant turn the engine slowly, using a spanner or socket on the crankshaft pulley nut.

8 Once the screwdriver (or dial gauge reading) starts to rise, continue turning the engine until the crankshaft pulley timing mark is aligned with the mark on the timing belt lower cover. Note that there are actually two marks - the other mark aligns with the centre of the crankshaft timing sensor **(see illustrations)**.

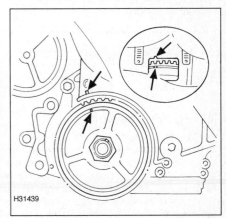

2.8b Crankshaft pulley and flywheel marks (arrowed) aligned at TDC

2.9 Camshaft sprocket painted marks aligned with lines on access hole

9 The engine will be at TDC on compression only when the painted marks on the camshaft sprockets are visible in the timing belt cover access hole **(see illustration)**. The painted marks on the sprockets should align with the steeply-angled lines at either side of the access hole - judging the alignment is not easy, however.

10 A further TDC mark is provided on the flywheel, and this can be viewed through the aperture in the transmission bellhousing (remove the aperture cover first). When the flywheel mark aligns with the 0 notch on the bellhousing, the engine is set to TDC. In practice, however, viewing the marks is impossible without first removing the ignition coil assembly and thermostat housing **(see illustration)**.

11 As a further confirmation, the screwdriver will stop rising (or the reading on the dial gauge will stop increasing) when TDC is reached.

12 The engine is now set at TDC on No 1 cylinder.

3 Cylinder compression test

1 When engine performance is down, or if misfiring occurs which cannot be attributed to the ignition or fuel systems, a compression test can provide diagnostic clues as to the engine's condition. If the test is performed regularly, it can give warning of trouble before any other symptoms become apparent.

2 The engine must be fully warmed-up to normal operating temperature, the battery must be fully charged, and all the spark plugs must be removed (Chapter 1). The aid of an assistant will also be required.

3 Disable the ignition system by disconnecting the LT wiring plug to the ignition coil assembly **(see illustration)**.

4 To prevent possible damage to the catalytic converter, depressurise and disable the fuel injection system by removing the fuel pump fuse or relay (see Chapter 4B, Section 7).

5 Fit a compression tester to the No 1 cylinder spark plug hole - the type of tester which screws into the plug thread is to be preferred.

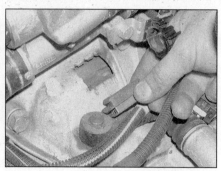

2.10 Remove the cover from the bellhousing to view the timing marks

6 Have the assistant hold the throttle wide open, and crank the engine on the starter motor; after one or two revolutions, the compression pressure should build up to a maximum figure, and then stabilise. Record the highest reading obtained.

7 Repeat the test on the remaining cylinders, recording the pressure in each.

8 All cylinders should produce very similar pressures; any excessive difference indicates the existence of a fault. Note that the compression should build up quickly in a healthy engine; low compression on the first stroke, followed by gradually increasing pressure on successive strokes, indicates worn piston rings. A low compression reading on the first stroke, which does not build up during successive strokes, indicates leaking valves or a blown head gasket (a cracked head could also be the cause).

9 If the pressure in any cylinder is very low, carry out the following test to isolate the cause. Introduce a teaspoonful of clean oil into that cylinder through its spark plug hole and repeat the test.

10 If the addition of oil temporarily improves the compression pressure, this indicates that bore or piston wear is responsible for the pressure loss. No improvement suggests that leaking or burnt valves, or a blown head gasket, may be to blame.

11 A low reading from two adjacent cylinders is almost certainly due to the head gasket having blown between them; the presence of coolant in the engine oil will confirm this.

12 If one cylinder is about 20 percent lower than the others and the engine has a slightly

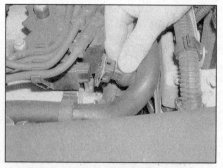

3.3 Disconnecting the ignition coil LT wiring plug

rough idle, a worn camshaft lobe could be the cause.

13 On completion of the test, refit the spark plugs and restore the ignition and fuel systems.

4 Timing belt and covers - removal and refitting

General information

1 The function of the timing belt is to drive the camshafts and auxiliary shaft (which drives the oil pump). Should the belt slip or break in service, the valve timing will be disturbed and piston-to-valve contact will occur, resulting in serious engine damage.

2 For this reason, it is important that a new timing belt is fitted at or before the specified mileage (see Chapter 1). If the car has been purchased second-hand, and its history is unknown, renewing the timing belt should be treated as a priority.

3 FIAT garages use various special tools to set and keep the camshaft and crankshaft sprockets at the TDC position, since it is possible that the sprockets may turn as the old belt is removed and the new one fitted. If they turn independently, the valve timing will be lost, and the engine will not run properly when restarted - worse, piston-to-valve contact may occur.

4 A special tool is also needed to set the timing belt tensioner pulley - it is not possible to set the tension using ordinary workshop tools. A simple alternative tool can be made easily, however, from a strip of metal plate.

5 In the absence of the special locking tools, great care must be taken when removing and refitting the belt that the sprockets do not move. Marks may be found on the sprockets, which align with markings on the cylinder head or block. If none are present, take care to make your own, using typists correction fluid or similar, **before** removing the belt.

6 If the special locking tools are not used, the procedure given below will suffice to change the belt successfully, but if care is not taken and the camshaft timing is slightly out, the engine may not run very well on completion. It is advisable to have a FIAT dealer confirm the camshaft timing after a new belt is fitted, if the special tools are not used.

Removal

7 Remove the auxiliary drivebelt(s) from the crankshaft pulley, then remove the spark plugs (refer to Chapter 1).

8 Working beneath the engine, unbolt and remove the flywheel lower cover **(see illustration)**, then hold the flywheel stationary, preferably using a tool which engages the flywheel starter ring gear (see Section 12). Alternatively, have an assistant engage a wide-bladed screwdriver with the starter ring gear.

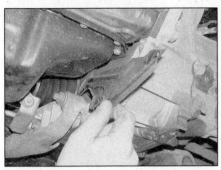

4.8 Removing the flywheel lower cover

4.12a Unscrew the crankshaft pulley nut . . .

4.12b . . . and remove the pulley

9 Loosen the crankshaft pulley retaining nut - this is tightened to a particularly high torque, so ensure that the car is adequately supported. Use only good-quality, close-fitting tools, and take precautions against personal injury, especially when the nut eventually loosens (wear gloves to protect your hands). Loosen the nut only at this stage - do not remove it.

10 Use the marks on the crankshaft pulley and timing belt cover to reset the engine to TDC, as described in Section 2. Engage top gear; if the handbrake is firmly applied, this should prevent the crankshaft from moving.

11 To further aid refitting, paint an alignment mark between the timing sensor (below and in front of the pulley) and one of the teeth on the sensor pickup wheel.

12 Unscrew the crankshaft pulley nut, and remove the pulley **(see illustrations)**.

13 Unbolt and remove the timing belt cover,

4.13 Removing the timing belt cover

which is secured by a total of eight bolts (one additional bolt is used to secure the camshaft sprocket access panel - see Section 2) **(see illustration)**. Note the location of each bolt (and any washers) as it is removed, as they are of different sizes. Where applicable, also recover the rubber gasket fitted between the outer and inner covers.

14 If the special holding tools are not available, make your own sprocket alignment marks as necessary before removing the belt (see paragraph 5).

15 In particular, mark the relative positions of the camshaft sprockets. The best way to do this is to place a straight edge across the centres of the two sprockets, and to draw a line (or several short lines) across the sprockets using an indelible marker **(see illustration)**.

16 The crankshaft sprocket should also be marked for position, if no timing marks are evident. The sprocket is keyed to the crankshaft, so can only be fitted in one position, but a timing mark would be useful as confirmation.

17 The FIAT tools (1860874000) for holding the camshafts stationary are modified camshaft housing end covers, with a keyway set into the inner face, which when fitted engage with slots in the end of the camshafts, preventing rotation and maintaining the camshaft timing. To gain access to the camshaft housing end covers, disconnect the coil LT wiring, remove the bolts securing the ignition coil, and lift the coil away from the engine complete with HT leads.

18 Release the nut on the timing belt tensioner, move the pulley away from the belt, and retighten the nut to hold the pulley in the retracted position **(see illustration)**. If the locking tools are not fitted, the tension of the valve springs will move the camshafts very slightly as the belt tension is released - watch how the sprockets move, and compensate for this when fitting the new belt.

19 Slide the drivebelt from the sprockets, taking great care not to turn them if locking tools have not been used **(see illustration)**. Note that the crankshaft sprocket is a sliding fit only over the end of the crankshaft - try not to remove the sprocket with the belt.

Refitting

20 When refitting the new belt, first make sure that the sprocket timing marks are still in alignment (the camshaft sprocket marks should be as close as possible).

21 If the special locking tools are being used, the camshaft sprocket bolts should be loosened to allow the sprockets to move slightly as the timing belt is refitted and tensioned. To hold each sprocket stationary while the retaining bolt is loosened, make up a tool as described in Section 5.

22 If the special locking tools are not being used, it is not advisable to loosen the camshaft sprocket bolts unless absolutely necessary. If the timing belt teeth will not engage the camshaft sprockets satisfactorily, it is permissible to loosen the bolts and turn the sprockets *very slightly,* both in the same direction.

4.15 Mark the camshaft sprockets in relation to each other

4.18 Loosening the timing belt tensioner nut

4.19 Removing the timing belt

4.25a If the locking tools are not used, the belt will not engage the exhaust camshaft sprocket . . .

4.25b . . . until the sprocket is turned to align the marks made on the sprockets

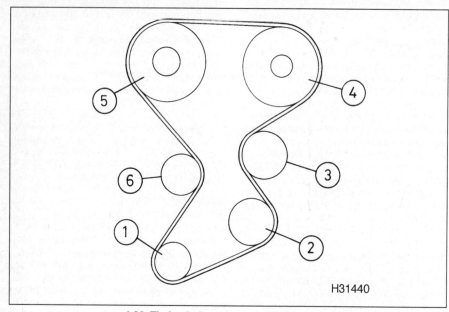

4.26 Timing belt run/sprocket fitting order

1 Crankshaft sprocket	*4 Inlet camshaft sprocket*
2 Auxiliary shaft sprocket (oil pump drive)	*5 Exhaust camshaft sprocket*
3 Fixed guide pulley	*6 Timing belt tensioner pulley*

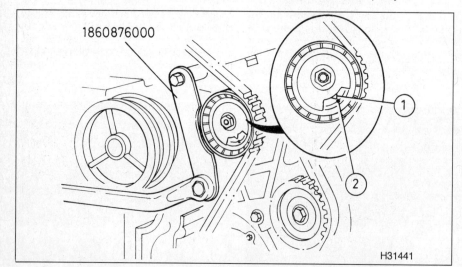

4.27 Tensioner pointer (1) should align with punched mark (2) - note use of spanner and FIAT tool

23 Fit the belt so that the arrows on the belt (where applicable) point in the direction of engine rotation. Also where applicable, the lines painted on the belt should coincide with marks on the sprockets.

24 Engage the timing belt with the crankshaft sprocket first, then place it around the auxiliary shaft sprocket, fixed guide pulley, and inlet (front) camshaft sprocket.

25 If the special locking tools are not used, turn the exhaust camshaft sprocket slightly (against the valve spring tension) to bring the timing marks made into alignment, and slip the belt onto the sprocket teeth **(see illustrations)**.

26 Finally, slip the belt around the tensioner pulley. Ensure that any slack in the belt is on the tensioner side of the belt run **(see illustration)**.

Tensioning

With the special tool

27 To tension the timing belt, a special FIAT tool (no 1860876000) is used to turn the tensioner, and to set the tensioner spring tension, in one movement. The tool is bolted into position as shown **(see illustration)**.

28 Release the tensioner nut and use the tool to push the pulley anti-clockwise against the belt.

29 Initially, the belt should be set to the maximum tension possible using reasonable force, indicated by the mark on the tensioner moving past the pointer. Tighten the tensioner nut securely.

30 If the camshaft sprocket bolts were loosened, tighten them to the specified torque, holding each sprocket in the same way as when they were loosened.

31 Remove any locking tools used, and/or select neutral. Temporarily fit the crankshaft pulley nut, and turn the engine through two complete turns in the normal direction of rotation. Check (as far as possible) that the sprocket timing marks come back into alignment.

32 Loosen the tensioner nut, and align the tensioner pointer with the punched marking. Hold the tensioner in this position, and tighten the tensioner nut to the specified torque.

Without the special tool

33 Make up a thin strip of thick metal (to be levered against), with two holes drilled 125 mm apart. Remove two of the tensioner backplate bolts, and bolt the metal strip into position **(see illustrations)**.

34 Loosen the tensioner nut, but leave it fitted.

35 Locate the end of a suitable screwdriver or large pin punch in the slot in the tensioner backplate, then lever against the metal strip **(see illustration)**. Do not lever against the plastic surface of the tensioner pulley, or it will be damaged.

36 Initially, take up the slack in the belt, but then pull on the belt while levering against the strip so that the mark on the tensioner moves

4.33a Make up a metal strip with two drilled holes . . .

4.33b . . . and bolt it into position as shown

4.35 Locate the end of a suitable tool in the notch in the backplate, below the slot, and lever against the metal strip

beyond the pointer, to the full extent of its travel **(see illustration)**. Tighten the tensioner nut to hold the tensioner spring in position.

37 If the camshaft sprocket bolts were loosened, tighten them to the specified torque, holding each sprocket in the same way as when they were loosened.

38 Remove any locking tools used, and/or select neutral. Temporarily fit the crankshaft pulley nut, and turn the engine through two complete turns in the normal direction of rotation. Check (as far as possible) that the sprocket timing marks come back into alignment **(see illustration)**.

39 Using a screwdriver (or pin punch) again as described in paragraph 35, lever against the metal strip to take up the spring pressure in the tensioner.

40 Carefully loosen the tensioner nut, and let the tensioner spring relax gradually until the mark on the tensioner is aligned with the

pointer **(see illustration)**. Tighten the tensioner nut to the specified torque.

Final refitting

41 Refit the timing belt cover and rubber gasket, and secure with the eight bolts, correctly refitted to their original locations.

42 Refit the crankshaft pulley, locating the pulley over the crankshaft sprocket and ensuring that the marks made between the timing sensor and pickup wheel are aligned. Holding the flywheel stationary as described in paragraph 8, fit and tighten the (new) nut securely **(see illustrations)**.

43 If the crankshaft has not turned, check that the mark on the crankshaft pulley aligns with the mark on the belt cover.

44 Further refitting is a reversal of removal. Refit and tension the auxiliary drivebelt as described in Chapter 1.

5 Timing belt sprockets and tensioner -
removal and refitting

Timing belt tensioner

Removal

1 Remove the auxiliary drivebelt(s) from the crankshaft pulley, then remove the spark plugs (refer to Chapter 1).

2 Unbolt and remove the timing belt cover, which is secured by a total of eight bolts. Note the location of each bolt (and any washers) as it is removed, as they are of different sizes. Also recover the rubber gasket fitted between the outer and inner covers.

Caution: Provided the timing belt is kept fully engaged with all the sprockets during the following procedure, it is not necessary to align the timing TDC marks. However if any doubt exists, read through the full procedure given in Section 4, noting the advice on the various TDC alignment markings to ensure that the timing is not lost. The timing belt does not have to be removed for this procedure, but if the belt slips from the sprockets, the timing could be lost.

3 Loosen the nut on the timing belt tensioner and move the pulley away from the belt. If necessary, keep the belt engaged with the sprockets using cable-ties, elastic bands or string.

4.36 Pull on the belt with one hand, while levering the tensioner, so that the tensioner marking moves

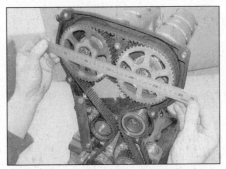

4.38 Checking that the camshaft sprocket marks made are in alignment

4.40 Release the tensioner gradually, so that the mark aligns with the pointer

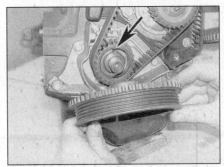

4.42a Fit the crankshaft pulley onto the key (arrowed) on the crankshaft sprocket . . .

4.42b . . . and secure using a new nut

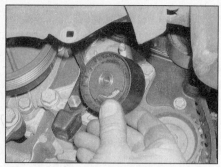

5.4 Removing the timing belt tensioner pulley

4 Completely unscrew the nut, and slide the tensioner off the mounting stud **(see illustration)**. If required, the tensioner mounting plate can be unbolted from the engine, noting the location of each bolt, as they are of different sizes.

Inspection

5 Wipe the tensioner clean, but do not use excessive amounts of solvent, as these may contaminate the bearings. Spin the tensioner

To make a camshaft sprocket holding tool, obtain two lengths of steel strip about 6 mm thick by 30 mm wide or similar, one 600 mm long, the other 200 mm long (all dimensions approximate). Bolt the two strips together to form a forked end, leaving the bolt slack so that the shorter strip can pivot freely. At the end of each 'prong' of the fork, secure a bolt with a nut and a locknut, to act as the fulcrums; these will engage with the cut-outs in the sprocket, and should protrude by about 30 mm.

pulley on its hub by hand. Stiff movement or excessive freeplay is an indication of severe wear; the tensioner is not a serviceable component, and should be renewed if its condition is suspect, or as a precaution at the time of a major engine overhaul.

Refitting

6 Hold the timing belt aside, then slide the tensioner over the mounting stud and secure loosely with the nut. Ensuring that all slack is taken out of the belt, engage the timing belt with tensioner sprocket.

7 Set the belt tension with reference to Section 4, paragraphs 21 to 24.

8 Refit the timing belt cover and rubber gasket, and secure with the eight bolts, correctly refitted to their original locations.

9 Refit and tension the auxiliary drivebelt as described in Chapter 1.

Camshaft sprockets

Removal

10 Remove the timing belt as described in Section 4. In addition to the alignment marks suggested in Section 4, it is useful to have a mark between each sprocket and the cylinder head - make your own if none are present, particularly if the camshaft holding tools described in Section 4 are not available.

11 The camshaft sprocket must now be held stationary while the retaining bolt is loosened; if the sprocket turns very far, there is a risk that the valves will hit the pistons. Make up a tool as follows and engage it with the holes in the sprocket **(see Tool Tip)**.

12 Alternatively, pass a rod through one of the holes in the camshaft sprocket to prevent it rotating. Position a pad of rag or a piece of wood under the rod to avoid damaging the cylinder head.

13 Unscrew the bolt (recover the washer), and slide the sprocket from the end of the camshaft. Note the integral location key on the inner face of the sprocket, and the notch on the end of the camshaft into which it fits **(see illustrations)**.

Inspection

14 With the sprockets removed, examine the camshaft oil seals for signs of leaking. If necessary, refer to Section 7 and renew them.

15 Check the sprocket teeth for damage.

16 Wipe clean the sprocket and camshaft mating surfaces.

Refitting

17 Locate the sprocket on the end of the camshaft, noting that it is (loosely) keyed. Refit the bolt and washer, and tighten to the specified torque while holding the camshaft stationary using the method described previously.

18 Align the marks made between the camshaft sprockets and cylinder head, then refit the timing belt as described in Section 4.

Crankshaft sprocket

Removal

19 Remove the timing belt as described in Section 4.

20 Slide the sprocket off the end of the crankshaft **(see illustration)**. If it is tight, remove it using a puller or a pair of suitable screwdrivers. The sprocket has a separate key which locates in a groove in the crankshaft nose - recover the key if it is loose.

Inspection

21 With the sprocket removed, examine the crankshaft oil seal for signs of leaking. If necessary, refer to Section 10 and renew it.

22 Wipe clean the sprocket and crankshaft mating surfaces. Check the sprocket teeth for damage.

Refitting

23 Slide the sprocket fully onto the crankshaft, making sure it engages the key.

24 Refit the timing belt as described in Section 4.

Auxiliary shaft sprocket

Removal

25 Remove the timing belt as described in Section 4. There is no need to make any alignment marks to show the auxiliary shaft sprocket fitted position.

26 The sprocket must now be held stationary while the bolt is loosened. Locking up the flywheel will not help in this case, as the sprocket turns the oil pump driveshaft. One solution would be to hold the sprocket using a strap wrench, as used for oil filter removal;

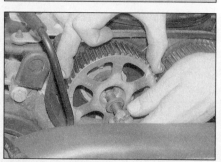

5.13a Unscrew and remove the bolt and washer, and remove the camshaft sprocket . . .

5.13b . . . noting how the sprocket locates on the end of the camshaft

5.20 Slide the crankshaft sprocket off, noting the location of the locating key

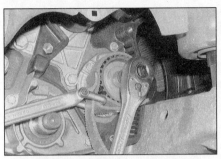

5.26 Using a strap wrench to hold the auxiliary shaft sprocket as the bolt is loosened

5.27 Removing the auxiliary shaft sprocket

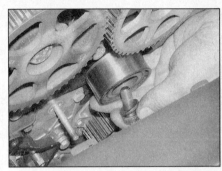

5.33 Removing the fixed guide pulley

alternatively, a means must be devised for jamming the sprocket teeth. If a chain wrench must be used, wrap a cloth around the sprocket first, to prevent damage to the sprocket teeth **(see illustration)**.

27 Once the bolt has been loosened, remove it and its washer, and take off the sprocket **(see illustration)**. Recover the locating dowel fitted between the sprocket and shaft.

Inspection

28 With the sprocket removed, examine the auxiliary shaft oil seal for signs of leaking. If necessary, refer to Section 9 and renew it.
29 Wipe clean the sprocket and shaft mating surfaces. Check the sprocket teeth for damage.

Refitting

30 Fit the locating dowel, then slide the sprocket fully onto the shaft, making sure the dowel engages correctly.

31 Refit the timing belt as described in Section 4.

Fixed guide pulley

Removal

32 Remove the timing belt as described in Section 4.
33 Loosen and remove the pulley bolt and its washer, and take off the pulley **(see illustration)**.

Inspection

34 Check the pulley for any sign of damage, and check that it spins freely, with no sign of roughness. Wipe the pulley clean before fitting.

Refitting

35 Offer the pulley up to the engine, and secure with the retaining bolt and washer. Tighten the bolt to the specified torque.

36 Refit the timing belt as described in Section 4.

6 Camshaft housings and camshafts - removal and refitting

Note: *The camshaft housings are secured by Ribe bolts, which are similar in appearance to Torx types, but require different tools. A set of Ribe sockets can be obtained from good tool stockists - larger Ribe bolts are used to secure the cylinder head.*

Removal

1 Making sure that they are labelled for position, disconnect the HT leads from the spark plugs.
2 Referring to Chapter 5B, remove the ignition coil assembly, and place it to one side without disconnecting the HT leads from it.
3 To improve working room, remove the two bolts securing the air intake at the front of the engine compartment, and lift the intake out of position, detaching it from the intake duct **(see illustrations)**.
4 Remove both sections of the inlet manifold as described in Chapter 4B.
5 Set the engine to TDC, as described in Section 2.
6 Remove the four nuts securing the ignition coil mounting bracket; note that these nuts also serve to secure the camshaft housing end covers themselves. Lift away the coil mounting bracket, and remove it from the engine **(see illustrations)**.

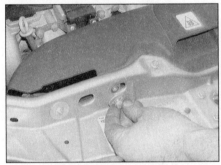

6.3a Remove the right-hand . . .

6.3b . . . and left-hand securing bolts . . .

6.3c . . . and lift out the air intake

6.6a Unscrew the four mounting nuts (arrowed) . . .

6.6b . . . and remove the ignition coil mounting bracket

6.7a With the coil bracket removed, the end covers are each secured by one nut (arrowed) . . .

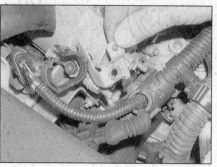

6.7b . . . which also secures a hose/wiring harness bracket

6.8 Carefully prise off the camshaft housing end covers

7 Noting their respective fitted positions, remove the hose and wiring harness brackets from the housing end covers (one nut remaining per cover) - note the earth lead

6.12a Remove the four bolts (arrowed) . . .

which may be fitted to the rear cover **(see illustrations)**.

8 Prise off and remove the end covers from the camshaft housings **(see illustration)**.

9 If the camshaft locking tools described in Section 4 are available, fit them now. If not, make accurate alignment marks between the ends of the camshafts and their housings, for use when refitting.

10 Remove the camshaft sprockets and the fixed guide pulley as described in Section 5.

11 On early models, remove the two bolts securing the inlet camshaft timing sensor. Withdraw the sensor from the engine, and disconnect the wiring plug.

12 Unbolt and remove the upper half of the inner timing belt cover, unclip the fuel line plastic guide channel, and remove the inner cover and channel from the top of the engine **(see illustrations)**.

13 Loosen the ten Ribe bolts securing each camshaft housing by a quarter-turn at a time, in a diagonal sequence **(see illustration)**. As the bolts are loosened, some of the valve springs will be released.

14 When all the bolts are loose, carefully tilt the housings towards the front of the car, noting that the housings are each located on two small dowels. Some of the hydraulic tappets may try and fall out; it is important that the tappets are not interchanged, so turn the housings upside-down as soon as they are removed. Recover the gaskets from the top of the cylinder head **(see illustrations)**.

15 Lift the hydraulic tappets from their bores and store them with the valve contact surface facing downwards, to prevent the oil from draining out. Alternatively, place the tappets in a tray full of oil, sufficiently deep to prevent the tappets draining **(see illustration)**.

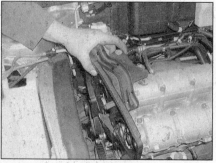

6.12b . . . unclip the fuel line guide channel . . .

6.12c . . . and remove the timing belt inner cover

6.13 Top view of the camshaft housings, showing the ten bolts securing each one

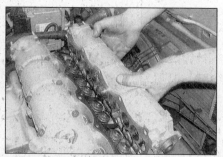

6.14a When removing the housings, tip them over, to prevent the tappets falling out . . .

6.14b . . . and recover the gasket from the cylinder head, noting the two dowels

6.15 Immerse the hydraulic tappets in oil, in a numbered container

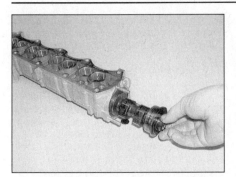

6.17 Withdrawing one of the camshafts

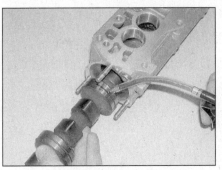

6.21 Oil the camshaft lobes as the camshaft is inserted

6.24 Place a new housing gasket over the locating dowels

6.25 Oil and refit the hydraulic tappets

16 Make a note of the position of each tappet, as they must be fitted to the same valves on reassembly - accelerated wear leading to early failure may result if they are interchanged.

17 Carefully withdraw the camshafts from their respective housings, turning them as necessary so that the camshaft lobes do not hang up on the bearings inside the housing **(see illustration)**. Keep the camshaft horizontal as it is withdrawn; force should not be used, or required, otherwise the camshaft and bearings could be damaged.

18 Suitably mark the camshafts (and housings) to avoid confusion when refitting. The camshafts may be found to be marked A and S, which stands for Aspirazione (Inlet) and Scario (Exhaust). Note that the inlet camshaft is nearest to the front facing side of the engine. On the car seen in the workshop, the inlet camshaft had a blue paint mark, while the exhaust camshaft was marked with green paint.

Inspection

19 Examine the camshaft bearing surfaces and cam lobes for signs of wear ridges and scoring. Renew the camshafts if any of these conditions are apparent. As far as possible, check the condition of the bearing surfaces in the camshaft housings. If suitable measuring equipment is available, camshaft bearing journal wear can be checked by direct measurement.

20 Examine the tappet bearing surfaces which contact the camshaft lobes for wear ridges and scoring. Renew any tappet on which these conditions are apparent. If a tappet bearing surface is badly scored, also examine the

corresponding lobe on the camshaft for wear, as it is likely that both will be worn. Renew worn components as necessary.

Refitting

21 Liberally lubricate the camshaft lobes, and as far as possible, the bearing surfaces in each camshaft housing **(see illustration)**.

22 Carefully insert the camshafts back into their respective housings, taking the same precautions described in paragraph 17.

23 At this stage, it is advisable to check the camshaft endfloat using a dial gauge mounted on the camshaft housing, with its probe in contact with the camshaft being checked. Move the camshaft one way, zero the gauge, then move the camshaft as far as it will go the other way. Record the reading on the dial gauge, and repeat on the other camshaft and housing. FIAT do not quote a figure for camshaft endfloat, but the figure given in the Specifications can be used as a guide. If either of the readings exceeds the tolerance given, a pair of new camshaft housings will probably be required.

24 Clean all traces of gasket from the mating faces on the housings and cylinder head, then place new gaskets in position over the locating dowels **(see illustration)**.

25 Fit the hydraulic tappets back in their original positions **(see illustration)**.

26 If the FIAT special tools for holding the camshafts were not available, turn the camshafts (if necessary) so that the marks made on removal are aligned, and try not to let the camshafts turn as the housings are refitted.

27 Check that the engine is still set to TDC as described in Sections 2 and 4.

28 Offer the housings into position over the two dowels, ensuring that the tappets engage correctly with the valves. Take care that none of the tappets fall out as the housings are refitted - offer the housing into place on its side initially, and use a ruler to hold the tappets in place **(see illustrations)**.

29 Insert the housing bolts. Note that as the housings are tightened down, some of the valve springs will be compressed - it is important that tightening is done progressively.

30 Working in a diagonal sequence and keeping the housing as level as possible, tighten each housing bolt by a quarter-turn at a time until the housing just seats on the head.

31 Again working in a diagonal sequence, tighten all bolts to the specified torque **(see illustration)**.

32 Refit all components removed for access, using a reversal of the removal procedure.

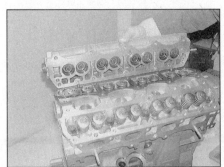

6.28a Offer the housing into position on its side . . .

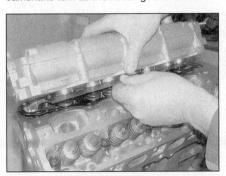

6.28b . . . using a ruler to keep the tappets from falling out

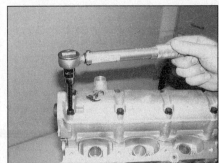

6.31 Tighten the housing bolts to the specified torque

7.5 Levering out the old seal

7.7 Oil the new seal before fitting

12 Referring to the information in Chapter 5B, remove the ignition coil assembly, and move it clear without disconnecting the HT leads from it.

13 Refer to Section 6, paragraphs 6 to 8, and remove the camshaft end covers.

14 Using a suitable hooked instrument if necessary, remove the large O-ring seal from each end cover. Even if only one seal is known to be leaking, it is advisable to renew both.

15 Clean the seating in the end cover, and inside the end of the camshaft housing.

16 Dip the new oil seal in oil, then fit it into the groove in the camshaft end cover **(see illustration)**.

17 Refit the end covers, and all components removed for access, using a reversal of the relevant removal procedure.

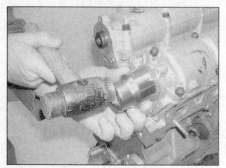

7.8 Tap the new seal into place using a socket or similar

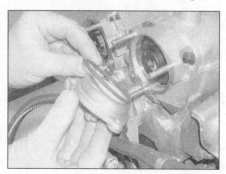

7.16 Fit the O-ring into the groove in the end cover

8 Auxiliary shaft - removal and refitting

There appears to be insufficient clearance to withdraw the auxiliary shaft while the engine is in the car. For this reason, the procedure is covered in Chapter 2E.

7 Camshaft oil seals - renewal

Front oil seals

1 Remove the camshaft sprockets and the fixed guide pulley as described in Section 5.

2 Unbolt and remove the upper half of the inner timing belt cover (four bolts), unclip the fuel line plastic guide channel, and remove the inner cover and channel from the top of the engine.

3 If necessary, to improve access, remove the upper section of the inlet manifold as described in Chapter 4B.

4 Even if only one seal is found to be leaking, it is advisable to renew both.

5 Carefully drill a hole in the old seal, taking care not to drill too deep. Use a suitable pointed tool and a block of wood to lever

against, lever the seal out of its housing **(see illustration)**.

6 Clean the seating in the housing and the end of the camshaft. To prevent damage to the new oil seal as it is being fitted, wrap some adhesive tape around the end of the camshaft and lightly oil it.

7 Lubricate the new oil seal **(see illustration)**, then locate it over the camshaft, making sure that the sealing lips are facing inwards.

8 Using a tubular drift, drive the oil seal squarely into the housing **(see illustration)**. Remove the adhesive tape from the camshaft.

9 Renew the seal in the other camshaft housing (as required) using the same procedure.

10 Refit all components removed for access, using a reversal of the removal procedure.

Rear oil seals

11 Ensuring that they are labelled for position, disconnect the HT leads from the spark plugs.

9 Auxiliary shaft oil seal - renewal

1 Remove the auxiliary shaft sprocket as described in Section 5.

2 Unscrew the three bolts, and withdraw the auxiliary shaft flange from the engine **(see illustration)**. Recover the gasket.

3 Mount the flange in a vice with protected jaws. Taking care not to mark the flange sealing surfaces, drive the seal out from inside using a suitable punch **(see illustration)**.

4 Wipe clean the oil seal location in the flange, and use a file or emery paper to clean up any sharp edges which might cause the new seal to fail.

5 Dip the new oil seal in oil, then carefully tap it into the flange, lips facing inwards. Once the seal has started, use a large socket to drive the seal squarely into position **(see illustrations)**.

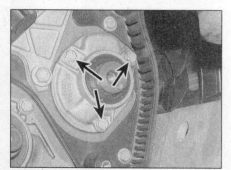

9.2 Auxiliary shaft flange bolts (arrowed)

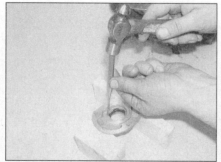

9.3 Tap out the old seal using a punch

9.5a Fit the new seal with lips facing inwards . . .

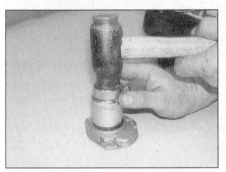

9.5b . . . and tap in with a suitable socket

9.6a Fit a new auxiliary flange gasket . . .

9.6b . . . then fit the flange over the auxiliary shaft

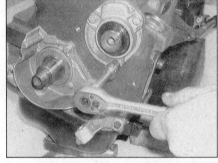

9.7 Tightening the auxiliary flange bolts

6 Fit a new auxiliary flange gasket. Lightly oil the end of the auxiliary shaft, then carefully feed the seal and flange over it **(see illustrations)**.

7 Refit the flange bolts, and tighten securely **(see illustration)**.

8 Refit the shaft sprocket, and all other components removed for access, using a reversal of the relevant removal procedure.

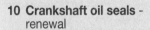

10 Crankshaft oil seals -
renewal

Front (right-hand side) oil seal

1 The front oil seal is located in a flange on the front of the crankshaft. Remove the timing belt as described in Section 4 and the crankshaft sprocket as described in Section 5.

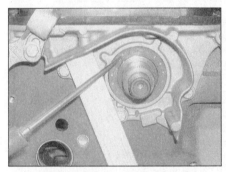

10.4 Levering out the old seal

2 There are two possible methods for renewing the oil seal. If the engine is in the car, try the first method first, as this involves much less dismantling.

Method 1

3 Taking care not to damage the crankshaft timing sensor, use a sharp-pointed tool (such as a bradawl) to pierce the seal and thus provide a leverage point. Take care that the tool does not score the crankshaft, and do not penetrate too far, as the seal seat may be damaged.

4 Using the hole made, lever the seal out of position, taking care not to damage the crankshaft **(see illustration)**.

5 As far as possible, clean the oil seal location, and remove any sharp edges which might damage the new seal.

6 Dip the new seal in oil, and carefully feed it over the end of the crankshaft **(see illustration)**.

7 Tap the new seal into its seat, then drive it squarely home using a large socket **(see illustration)**. This is the most difficult part, as there is limited room to use a hammer or mallet. If care is taken, it may be possible to press the seal into place, working progressively around the seal so that is does not distort.

Method 2

8 Remove the sump as described in Section 14.

9 Trace the wiring back from the crankshaft timing sensor, and disconnect it at the wiring plug. Remove the screw securing the sensor to its mounting bracket, and remove it.

10 Unscrew and remove the bolts securing the crankshaft front flange to the block. Take care not to unscrew the two mounting bolts for the crankshaft timing sensor bracket (one is a shear-head bolt) - if these must be removed for any reason, mark around them very carefully with paint or a sharp tool, so that the sensor position is not lost.

11 Withdraw the flange from the front of the crankshaft, and mount it in a vice with protected jaws. Recover the flange gasket from the engine.

12 Taking care not to mark the flange sealing surfaces, drive the seal out from inside using a suitable punch **(see illustration)**.

13 Wipe clean the oil seal location in the flange, and use a file or emery paper to clean up any sharp edges which might cause the new seal to fail.

14 Dip the new oil seal in oil, then carefully tap it into the flange, lips facing inwards. Once

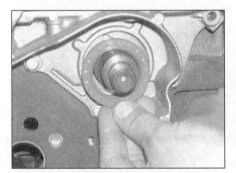

10.6 Lubricate the new seal, and fit it over the crankshaft

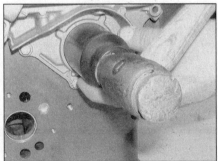

10.7 Tap the new seal into place using a large socket

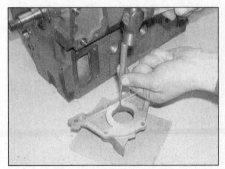

10.12 Tap out the old seal using a pin punch

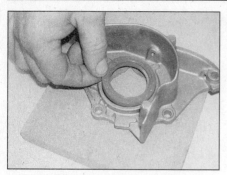

10.14a Oil the new seal, and fit it to the flange . . .

10.14b . . . then drive it in with a large socket

10.15 Use a little grease to stick the new flange gasket in place

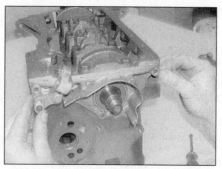

10.16 Fit the flange into place, then fit and tighten the bolts

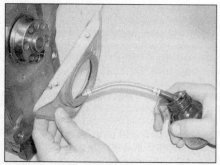

10.27a Oil the new seal . . .

10.27b . . . fit the flange and seal over the end of the crankshaft . . .

10.27c . . . then fit and tighten the flange bolts

10.28 Check that the flange is square to the base of the engine

the seal has started, use a large socket to drive the seal squarely into position **(see illustrations)**.

15 Fit a new flange gasket, sticking it in place with a little grease **(see illustration)**.

16 Lightly oil the end of the crankshaft, then carefully feed the seal and flange over it **(see illustration)**. Use a straight edge to ensure that the flange is aligned with the bottom of the engine.

17 Refit the flange bolts, and tighten evenly and securely, ensuring that the flange does not twist out of alignment.

All methods

18 Refit the crankshaft sprocket, and all other components removed for access, using a reversal of the relevant removal procedure.

Rear (left-hand side) oil seal

Note: *On early models (up to approximately 1999, before the introduction of the 'Step A' engine) the rear oil seal is available separately from the housing. On later models, the seal is integral with its housing.*

19 Remove the flywheel/driveplate as described in Section 12.

Early models

20 Using a suitable hooked instrument, remove the oil seal from the rear oil seal housing, taking care not to damage the surface of the crankshaft. Alternatively, carefully drill the seal and screw in two self-tapping screws on either side of the seal; using pliers on the screws, pull the seal from its seat.

21 Clean the seating in the housing and the surface of the crankshaft. Check the crankshaft for burrs which may damage the oil seal lip of the new seal, and if necessary use a fine file to remove them.

22 Dip the new seal in clean engine oil and carefully locate it over the crankshaft rear flange, making sure that it is the correct way round (lips facing inwards). Take care not to damage the oil seal lips as it passes over the crankshaft flange.

23 Progressively tap the oil seal into the housing, keeping it square to prevent distortion. A block of wood is useful for this purpose.

Later models

24 Remove the sump as described in Section 14.

25 Unbolt the oil seal flange from the engine, and remove it from the end of the crankshaft.

26 Clean the flange mating surface on the engine, and the surface of the crankshaft. Check the crankshaft for burrs which may damage the oil seal lip of the new seal, and if necessary use a fine file to remove them.

27 Oil the new seal, and fit the flange with the gasket side to the engine **(see illustrations)**.

28 Use a straight edge to align the base of the flange with the bottom of the engine **(see illustration)**.

29 Fit the flange securing bolts, and tighten evenly and securely, ensuring that the flange does not twist out of alignment.

30 Refit the sump as described in Section 14.

All models

31 Refit the flywheel/driveplate with reference to Section 12.

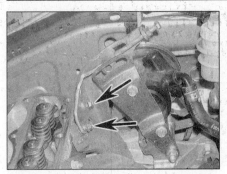

11.9a Remove the two nuts securing the power steering pump mounting bracket . . .

11.9b . . . and remove the bracket from the manifold

11.11a Unscrew the retainer and remove the relay box cover . . .

11 Cylinder head -
removal and refitting

Note: *The cylinder head is secured by Ribe bolts, which are similar in appearance to Torx types, but require different tools. A set of Ribe sockets can be obtained from good tool stockists - smaller Ribe bolts are used to secure the camshaft housings.*

Removal

1 Depressurise the fuel system as described in Chapter 4B, Section 7.
2 Disconnect the battery negative terminal (refer to *Disconnecting the battery*).
3 Drain the cooling system as described in Chapter 1.
4 Remove the auxiliary drivebelts as described in Chapter 1.

11.12a Unscrew the manifold-to-cylinder head nuts . . .

5 Remove the spark plugs as described in Chapter 1.
6 To improve working room, remove the two bolts securing the air intake at the front of the engine compartment, and lift the intake out of position, detaching it from the intake duct.
7 Loosen the hose clips and disconnect the air duct which runs from the air cleaner to the inlet manifold, also disconnecting the breather pipe which runs to the oil filler tube.
8 Remove the camshaft housings as described in Section 6.
9 Loosen/remove the power steering pump mounting bolts, and tip the pump to the rear, clear of the mounting bracket attached to the exhaust manifold. Remove the nuts securing the power steering pump mounting bracket to the manifold, and remove the bracket **(see illustrations)**.
10 Unbolt the exhaust manifold heat shield (three bolts), and remove the shield.
11 To avoid the possibility of straining the oxygen sensor wiring when the exhaust manifold is detached, trace the wiring back to the connector plug inside the relay box on the bulkhead, and disconnect it **(see illustrations)**.
12 Unscrew the exhaust manifold-to-cylinder head nuts, and the bolt from the manifold support bracket at the downpipe joint **(see illustrations)**.
13 Withdraw the manifold from the cylinder head, recovering the gasket. Tie the manifold back clear of the head **(see illustration)**.
14 In some cases, the manifold studs will come out with the nuts - this poses no great

11.11b . . . then locate and disconnect the wiring plug for the oxygen sensor

problem, and the studs can be refitted if they are in good condition. For preference, however, a complete set of manifold studs and nuts should be obtained as required, as the old ones are likely to be in less-than-perfect condition.
15 Disconnect the coolant hoses from the thermostat housing, noting their fitted positions **(see illustration)**.
16 Check around the head that there are no further wires, hoses or other obstructions which will prevent the head from being lifted off.
17 Unscrew the cylinder head Ribe bolts half a turn at a time, in the reverse order to that shown in illustration 11.33. When the bolts are free, remove them **(see illustrations)**.
18 Lift the cylinder head from the block. If it is stuck tight, insert pieces of wood into the exhaust or inlet ports, and use them as levers to rock the head off the block. On no account

11.12b . . . and the bolt (arrowed) from the manifold support bracket

11.13 Move the manifold clear of the cylinder head studs, and recover the gasket

11.15 Disconnect the hoses from the thermostat housing

11.17a Unscrew the cylinder head bolts . . .

11.17b . . . and remove them

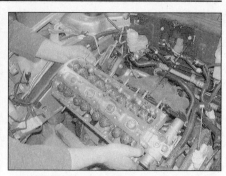

11.18a Lifting the cylinder head from the block

drive levers into the gasket joint, nor attempt to tap the head sideways, as it is located on positioning dowels **(see illustrations)**.

19 Remove and discard the cylinder head gasket.

20 The cylinder head can be dismantled as described in Chapter 2E.

Preparation for refitting

21 The mating faces of the cylinder head and cylinder block must be perfectly clean before refitting the head. Use a hard plastic or wooden scraper to remove all traces of gasket and carbon; also clean the piston crowns.

22 Take particular care when cleaning the piston crowns, as the soft aluminium alloy is easily damaged.

23 Make sure that the carbon is not allowed to enter the oil and water passages - this is particularly important for the lubrication system, as carbon could block the oil supply

to the engine's components. Using adhesive tape and paper, seal the water, oil and bolt holes in the cylinder block.

24 To prevent carbon entering the gap between the pistons and bores, smear a little grease in the gap. After cleaning each piston, use a small brush to remove all traces of grease and carbon from the gap, then wipe away the remainder with a clean rag. Clean all the pistons in the same way.

25 Check the mating surfaces of the cylinder block and the cylinder head for nicks, deep scratches and other damage. If slight, they may be removed carefully with a file, but if excessive, machining may be the only alternative to renewal.

26 If warpage of the cylinder head gasket surface is suspected, use a straight-edge to check it for distortion. Refer to Part E of this Chapter if necessary.

27 Check the condition of the cylinder head

bolts, and particularly their threads, whenever they are removed. Wash the bolts in a suitable solvent, and wipe them dry. Check each bolt for any sign of visible wear or damage, renewing them if necessary.

Refitting

28 Before refitting the assembled cylinder head, make sure that the head and block mating surfaces are perfectly clean, and that the bolt holes in the cylinder block have been mopped out to clear any oil or coolant. If the bolt holes have any significant amount of liquid in them, the block could be cracked by hydraulic pressure when the head bolts are tightened.

29 Fit the two dowels to their locations on the cylinder block **(see illustration)**.

30 The new gasket should not be removed from its plastic bag until required for use. Fit the gasket dry - no grease or sealant should be used. Place the gasket on the cylinder block so that the word ALTO can be read from above **(see illustrations)**.

31 Lower the cylinder head onto the block so that it locates on the positioning dowels **(see illustration)**.

32 Ensure that the cylinder head bolts are cleaned of all debris, and check the threads for signs of damage. Especially if it is known that the bolts have been removed previously, it is advisable to renew all ten bolts as a set, rather than risk the bolts shearing when tightened.

11.18b The head is located on two dowels - one shown

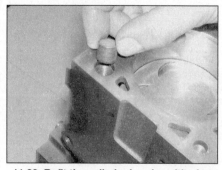

11.29 Refit the cylinder head positioning dowels

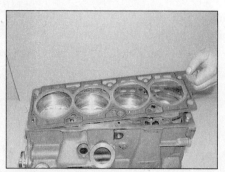

11.30a Fit the gasket over the dowels . . .

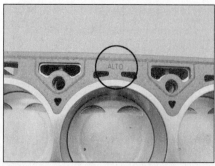

11.30b . . . so that the word ALTO is visible

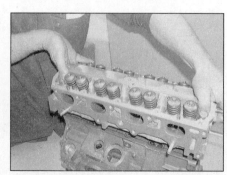

11.31 Lower the cylinder head into position

33 Lightly oil the bolt threads. Screw the bolts in finger-tight, and tighten them in the sequence shown to the Stage 1 torque **(see illustration)**.
34 When all ten bolts have been tightened to the Stage 1 torque, go round again in sequence and tighten to the Stage 2 torque **(see illustration)**.
35 Again working in sequence, tighten the bolts through the specified Stage 3 angle. Note that 90° is equivalent to a quarter-turn or right-angle, making it easy to judge by noting the initial position of the socket handle. If available, use an angle gauge fitted to the socket handle for maximum accuracy **(see illustration)**.
36 With all ten bolts tightened to Stage 3, go round once more and tighten all bolts in sequence to the Stage 4 angle.
37 Refit the exhaust manifold, using new gaskets, studs and nuts, as appropriate. Tighten all nuts securely.
38 Further refitting is a reversal of removal. Ensure that all wiring and hoses are correctly routed and securely reconnected. Refer to Section 4 when refitting the timing belt, and to Chapter 1 when refitting the spark plugs and auxiliary drivebelt, and when refilling the cooling system.

---

12 Flywheel/driveplate -
removal, inspection and refitting

Removal

1 Remove the transmission as described in Chapter 7A or 7B. On manual transmission models, also remove the clutch as described in Chapter 6.
2 Mark the position of the flywheel/driveplate with respect to the crankshaft using a dab of paint. Note that on some models although there is only one location dowel on the flywheel/driveplate, there are two holes in the end of the crankshaft and it is therefore possible to locate the flywheel 180° out.
3 The flywheel/driveplate must now be held stationary while the bolts are loosened. A home-made locking tool may be fabricated from a piece of scrap metal and used to lock the ring gear. Bolt the tool to one of the transmission bellhousing mounting holes **(see Tool Tip)**.
4 Support the flywheel as the bolts are loosened - the flywheel is very heavy. Unscrew and remove the mounting bolts, take off the mounting plate, then lift off the flywheel/driveplate. Where applicable, recover the spacer fitted between the flywheel and crankshaft.

Inspection

Manual transmission models

5 If the flywheel's clutch mating surface is deeply scored, cracked or otherwise damaged, the flywheel must be renewed.

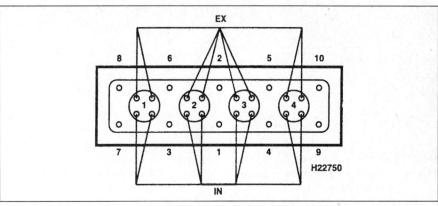

11.33 Cylinder head bolt tightening sequence

11.34 Tightening the cylinder head bolts

11.35 Use an angle gauge if possible for the latter stages of tightening

---

However, it may be possible to have it surface-ground; seek the advice of a FIAT dealer or engine reconditioning specialist.
6 If the ring gear is badly worn or has missing teeth, the flywheel must be renewed.

Automatic transmission models

7 Check the driveplate for signs of damage and renew it if necessary. If the ring gear is badly worn or has missing teeth, the driveplate must be renewed.

Refitting

8 Clean the mating surfaces of the flywheel/driveplate and crankshaft. Remove any remaining locking compound from the threads

To lock the flywheel, make up a pointed tool to engage the ring gear teeth, and bolt it to the engine using one of the bellhousing bolts

---

of the crankshaft holes, using the correct-size tap, if available.

> **HAYNES HINT** *If a suitable tap is not available, cut two slots down the threads of one of the old bolts with a hacksaw, and use the bolt to remove the locking compound from the threads.*

9 Clean the flywheel bolt threads, then apply a suitable thread-locking compound to the threads of each bolt.
10 Offer up the flywheel/driveplate to the crankshaft (with the spacer behind, where applicable). Use the alignment marks made during removal to ensure correct refitting **(see illustrations)**.

12.10a Fit the flywheel into position . . .

12.10b . . . making sure the marks made on removal are aligned

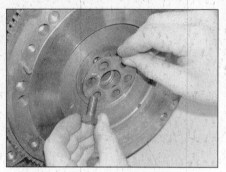

12.11a Refit the mounting plate and flywheel bolts . . .

12.11b . . . and tighten the bolts to the specified torque

11 Fit the mounting plate and secure the flywheel/driveplate loosely with the bolts. Lock the flywheel/driveplate using the method employed on dismantling, and tighten the retaining bolts to the specified torque **(see illustrations)**.
12 Refit the clutch on manual transmission models as described in Chapter 6.
13 Refit the transmission as described in Chapter 7A or 7B.

13 Engine mountings - inspection and renewal

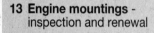

Inspection

1 Jack up the front of the vehicle and support on axle stands (see *Jacking and vehicle support*).
2 Check the mounting rubbers to see if they are cracked, hardened or separated from the metal at any point; renew the mounting if any such damage or deterioration is evident.
3 Check that all the mounting's fasteners are securely tightened; use a torque wrench to check if possible.
4 Using a large screwdriver or a crowbar, check for wear in the mounting by carefully levering against it to check for free play. Where this is not possible enlist the aid of an assistant to move the engine/transmission back and forth, or from side to side, while you watch the mounting. While some free play is to be expected even from new components, excessive wear should be obvious. If

excessive free play is found, check first that the fasteners are correctly secured, then renew any worn components as described below.

Renewal

Note: *Left and right are as seen from the driver's seat.*

Right-hand mounting

5 Raise the front of the vehicle and support on axle stands (see *Jacking and vehicle support*).
6 Place a trolley jack beneath the right-hand side of the engine, with a block of wood on the jack head. Raise the jack until it is supporting the weight of the engine.
7 Working from below, unscrew the through-bolt (and washers) securing the engine bracket to the mounting **(see illustration)**.
8 Lower the engine sufficiently to disengage the engine bracket from the mounting, then remove the bolts securing the mounting to the body, and remove it.
9 Locate the new mounting on the body, then insert the mounting-to-body bolts and tighten by hand.
10 Raise the engine and locate the bracket on the mounting. Refit the through-bolt (and washers) and tighten to the specified torque, then tighten the mounting-to-body bolts.
11 Remove the trolley jack and lower the vehicle to the ground.

Rear mounting

12 Raise the front of the vehicle and support on axle stands (see *Jacking and vehicle support*).

13 Place a trolley jack beneath the transmission, with a block of wood on the jack head. Raise the jack until it is supporting the weight of the engine/transmission.
14 Unscrew the through-bolt securing the transmission bracket to the mounting, and recover the washer **(see illustration)**.
15 Unscrew the two bolts securing the mounting to the subframe.
16 Lower the transmission sufficiently to remove the mounting from the transmission bracket.
17 Locate the new mounting in position, and loosely refit the mounting-to-body bolts.
18 Raise the engine/transmission and refit the through-bolt (and washer) securing the bracket to the mounting. Tighten the bolt to the specified torque, then tighten the mounting-to-subframe bolts.
19 Remove the trolley jack and lower the vehicle to the ground.

Left-hand mounting

20 Raise the front of the vehicle and support on axle stands (see *Jacking and vehicle support*).
21 Place a trolley jack beneath the engine/transmission flange, with a block of wood on the jack head. Raise the jack until it is supporting the weight of the engine and transmission.
22 Working from below, unscrew the through-bolt securing the bracket to the mounting **(see illustration)**.
23 Lower the engine sufficiently to disengage the bracket from the mounting, then remove the bolts securing the mounting to the body, and remove it.

13.7 Engine right-hand mounting (seen from below) - through-bolt arrowed

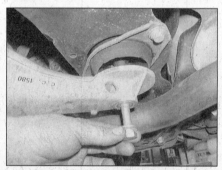

13.14 Removing the engine rear mounting through-bolt

13.22 Engine left-hand mounting (seen from below)

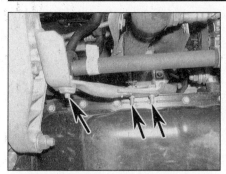

14.2a Unscrew the bolts (arrowed) . . .

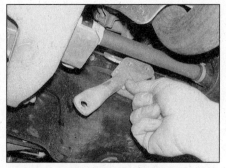

14.2b . . . and remove the support bracket from the rear mounting

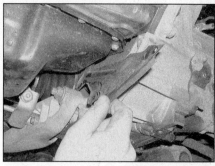

14.2c Removing the flywheel lower cover

24 Locate the new mounting on the body, then insert the mounting-to-body bolts and tighten by hand.

25 Raise the engine and locate the bracket on the mounting. Refit the through-bolt (and washers) and tighten to the specified torque, then tighten the mounting-to-body bolts.

26 Remove the trolley jack and lower the vehicle to the ground.

14 Sump -
removal and refitting

Removal

1 Jack up the front of the vehicle and support on axle stands. Drain the engine oil.

2 To improve access to some of the sump bolts, unbolt and remove the support bracket fitted to the engine rear mounting. It is also helpful to remove the flywheel lower cover **(see illustrations)**.

3 Unscrew the sump securing bolts, and recover the elongated washers fitted under the head of each. We found that a flexible extension piece was required to reach the bolts at the transmission end of the sump **(see illustrations)**.

4 A conventional sump gasket is not used - the sump is sealed using liquid gasket. Use a sharp knife to cut around the bead of sealant, then pull the sump downwards to remove it **(see illustration)**.

Refitting

5 Clean away all the old sealant, from the sump pan and from the base of the block.

Also clean any sealant from the sump bolts.

6 Where removed, refit the oil spill tube to the base of the engine, tightening its retaining bolt securely **(see illustration)**.

7 Apply a bead of RTV silicone instant gasket 3 mm in diameter to the sump flange. The bead of sealant should pass around the inside of the sump bolt holes. Also apply a little sealant to the joints between the front and rear oil seal flanges and the engine block **(see illustrations)**.

8 Fit the sump, then screw in the fixing bolts (and washers) and tighten in a diagonal sequence to the specified torque.

9 Wait one hour for the gasket compound to cure before filling with oil.

10 Lower the vehicle to the ground and fill the engine with oil (see Chapter 1). Check the oil level after running the engine for a few minutes, as described in *Weekly checks*.

14.3a Removing the sump bolts

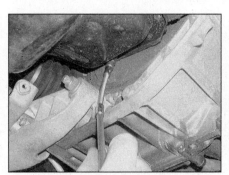

14.3b Using a flexible extension to reach the sump bolts at the transmission end

14.4 Removing the sump - note oil spill tube (arrowed)

14.6 Tightening the oil spill tube bolt

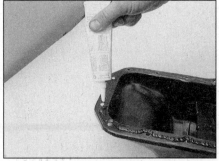

14.7a Run a bead of sealant around the sump flange . . .

14.7b . . . and across the oil seal flange joints

15.2 Oil pick-up/pump assembly retaining bolts (arrowed)

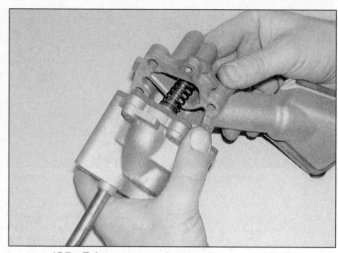

15.7a Take care removing the oil pump cover . . .

15 Oil pump and pick-up tube - removal and refitting

Removal

1 Drain the engine oil and remove the sump as described in Section 14.

2 Unbolt and remove the oil pick-up/pump assembly, which is secured by the three larger bolts visible (the smaller bolts retain the oil pump cover) **(see illustration)**. Remove the assembly, withdrawing the driveshaft from the idler gear. Recover the gasket.

3 Removing the oil pump idler gear requires the auxiliary shaft to be removed first. There is insufficient room to withdraw the auxiliary shaft with the engine fitted; removal of the auxiliary shaft is covered in Chapter 2E.

4 Once the shaft has been removed, the plug fitted over the idler gear must be removed from the cylinder block. The plug is driven into position, and is fitted using sealant, so removal will not be easy.

5 With the plug removed, the idler gear and its guide can be tapped out from below, using a long drift of diameter slightly larger than the oil pump driveshaft.

Inspection

6 If pump wear is suspected, dismantle the pump as follows.

7 Extract the three fixing bolts and remove the cover plate. Take care as the cover is removed, and recover the oil pressure relief valve, spring and spring seat **(see illustrations)**.

8 Lift off the adaptor plate fitted between the cover and pump body **(see illustration)**.

9 Check the clearance between the outer gear and the pump housing using feeler blades. Check the gear endfloat by placing a straight-edge across the pump body, and checking the gap between the straight-edge and gear face **(see illustrations)**. If the

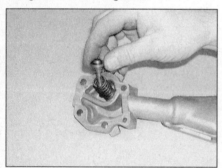

15.7b . . . retrieve the oil pressure relief valve . . .

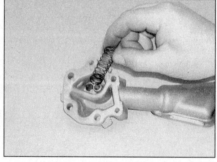

15.7c . . . valve spring . . .

15.7d . . . and spring seat

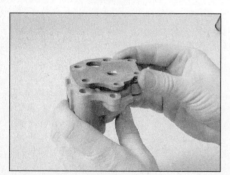

15.8 Remove the adaptor plate from the oil pump body

15.9a Checking the pump gear-to-body clearance . . .

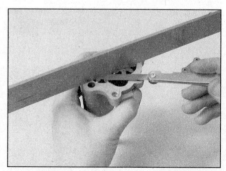

15.9b . . . and the gear endfloat

15.14a Fit a new oil pump gasket . . .

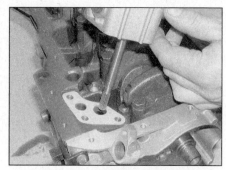

15.14b . . . then fit the pump into position . . .

15.14c . . . and tighten the mounting bolts to the specified torque

clearances are outside the specified tolerance, renew the oil pump complete.

10 If the pump is unworn, refit all removed components in reverse order to removal, and tighten the cover bolts fully.

11 Apply air pressure from a tyre pump to the oil pump oil ducts, to clear any sludge or other material. If any solvents are used, the pump must be allowed to dry thoroughly before refitting.

12 Where the idler gear has been removed, check the condition of the gear teeth, and of those on the auxiliary shaft. Renewal of both components will be necessary if either is worn. Use a new plug when refitting the idler gear.

Refitting

13 Clean all traces of old gasket from the pump and the mating surfaces on the crankcase.

14 Fit a new joint gasket, then offer the pump into position. Tighten the mounting bolts to the specified torque **(see illustrations)**.

15 Fit the sump as described in Section 14.

16 Fill the engine with oil (see Chapter 1).

17 Run the engine for a few minutes, then check and top-up the oil level as described in *Weekly checks*.

16.1 Oil pressure switch (arrowed)

16 Oil pressure switch - removal and refitting

Removal

1 The oil pressure switch is located at the front of the engine block, next to the oil filler tube **(see illustration)**.

2 Disconnect the switch wiring connector.

3 Unscrew the switch from the block, and remove it **(see illustration)**.

16.3 Removing the oil pressure switch

4 Clean the switch location in the block as far as possible. If the switch is to be refitted, clean its threads.

5 Examine the switch for signs of cracking or splits. If the top part of the switch is loose, this is an early indication of impending failure.

Refitting

6 Apply a smear of sealant to the threads of the switch, then screw it into place and tighten to the specified torque.

7 Reconnect the switch wiring on completion.

Notes

Chapter 2 Part D:
1.8 litre engine in-car repair procedures

Contents

Degrees of difficulty

| Easy, suitable for novice with little experience | | Fairly easy, suitable for beginner with some experience | | Fairly difficult, suitable for competent DIY mechanic | | Difficult, suitable for experienced DIY mechanic | | Very difficult, suitable for expert DIY or professional | |

Specifications

General

Engine code*	182 A2.000
Bore	82.0 mm
Stroke	82.7 mm
Compression ratio	10.3:1
Firing order	1-3-4-2
No 1 cylinder location	Timing (right-hand) end of engine

*Note: See 'Vehicle identification numbers' for the location of code marking on the engine.

Lubrication system

Oil pump type	Bi-rotor driven from front of crankshaft
Outer rotor-to-housing clearance	0.080 to 0.186 mm
Axial clearance	0.025 to 0.070 mm
Oil pressure (at operating temperature)	15 psi at idle, 50 to 72 psi at 4000 rpm

Torque wrench settings

	Nm	lbf ft
Air conditioning compressor mounting bracket-to-block	50	37
Alternator mounting bracket-to-block:		
M8 bolts	25	18
M10 bolts	70	52
Big-end (connecting rod) bearing cap bolts:		
Stage 1	25	18
Stage 2	Angle-tighten a further 60°	
Camshaft bearing caps	15	11
Camshaft cover	9	7
Camshaft sprocket bolt	120	89
Coolant pipe to block	9	7
Crankshaft pulley-to-sprocket bolts	32	24
Crankshaft sensor	9	7
Crankshaft sprocket bolt (left-hand thread)	360	266
Cylinder head:		
Stage 1	20	15
Stage 2	40	30
Stage 3	Angle-tighten a further 90°	
Stage 4	Angle-tighten a further 90°	
Stage 5	Angle-tighten a further 90°	

Torque wrench settings (continued)

	Nm	lbf ft
Engine/transmission mountings:		
Mounting brackets-to-transmission:		
M10 bolts	50	37
M12 bolts	80	59
Mounting through-bolts:		
Front mounting	38	28
Left- and right-hand mountings	80	59
Reaction rod through-bolt	25	18
Mountings to bodyshell	32	24
Right-hand mounting brackets-to-block	70	52
Right-hand mounting reaction rod to strut bracket	50	37
Exhaust manifold nuts	25	18
Flywheel*	160	118
Inlet manifold nuts	25	18
Knock sensor	25	18
Main bearing cap bolts:		
Stage 1	25	18
Stage 2	Angle-tighten a further 100°	
Oil pressure switch	32	24
Oil pump bolts:		
M6 bolt	9	7
M8 bolt	25	18
Sump bolts:		
M6 bolt	9	7
M8 bolt	25	18
Thermostat housing bolts	25	18
Timing belt covers	9	7
Timing belt fixed guide pulley bolt	25	18
Timing belt tensioner nut	25	18

Although not specifically recommended by FIAT, use new bolts and locking fluid.

1 General information

Using this Chapter

Chapter 2 is divided into five Parts; A to E. Repair operations that can be carried out with the engine in the car are described in Parts A to D. Part E covers the removal of the engine/transmission as a unit, and describes the engine dismantling and overhaul procedures.

In Parts A to D, the assumption is made that the engine is installed in the car, with all ancillaries connected. If the engine has been removed for overhaul, the preliminary dismantling information which precedes each operation may be ignored.

Engine description

The 1.8 litre engine is a water-cooled, double overhead camshaft, in-line four-cylinder unit, with cast-iron cylinder block and aluminium-alloy cylinder head. The engine is a 16-valve unit, with two inlet valves and two exhaust valves per cylinder. The engine is mounted transversely at the front of the car, with the transmission bolted to the left-hand side of the engine.

The cylinder head carries the camshafts, which are driven by a toothed timing belt. Each camshaft runs in six bearings. The cylinder head also houses the inlet and exhaust valves, which are closed by single coil springs, and which run in guides pressed into the cylinder head. The camshafts actuate the valves directly via hydraulic tappets mounted in the cylinder head. The cylinder head contains integral oilways which supply and lubricate the tappets.

The crankshaft is supported by five main bearings, and endfloat is controlled by thrust washers fitted either side of the centre main bearing.

Engine coolant is circulated by a pump, driven by the timing belt. For details of the cooling system, refer to Chapter 3.

Lubricant is circulated under pressure by a pump, driven from the front of the crankshaft. Oil is drawn from the sump through a strainer, and then forced through an externally-mounted, replaceable screw-on filter. From there, it is distributed to the cylinder head, where it lubricates the camshaft journals and tappets, and also to the crankcase, where it lubricates the main bearings, connecting rod big and small-ends, gudgeon pins and cylinder bores. Four jets mounted on the base of the crankcase spray oil onto the undersides of the pistons, to aid cooling.

Note: *Several components are secured by Ribe bolts, which are similar in appearance to Torx types, but require different tools. A set of Ribe sockets can be obtained from good tool stockists. Among the components affected are the camshaft cover, sump and cylinder head.*

Repair operations possible with the engine in the car

The following work can be carried out with the engine in the car:

a) Auxiliary drivebelt - removal and refitting (see Chapter 1).
b) Camshafts - removal and refitting*.
c) Camshaft oil seals - renewal.
d) Camshaft sprockets - removal and refitting.
e) Coolant pump - removal and refitting (refer to Chapter 3).
f) Crankshaft oil seals - renewal.
g) Crankshaft sprocket - removal and refitting.
h) Cylinder head - removal and refitting.
i) Engine mountings - inspection and renewal.
j) Oil pump and pickup assembly - removal and refitting.
k) Sump.
l) Timing belt, sprockets and cover - removal, inspection and refitting.

Cylinder head dismantling procedures are detailed in Chapter 2E, with details of camshaft and tappet removal.

Note: *It is possible to remove the pistons and connecting rods (after removing the cylinder head and sump) without removing the engine. However, this is not recommended. Work of this nature is more easily and thoroughly completed with the engine on the bench, as described in Chapter 2E.*

2 Location of TDC on No 1 cylinder

1 Remove the camshaft cover as described in Section 6.

2 With the car parked on a level surface, apply the handbrake and chock the rear wheels. Loosen the right-hand front wheel bolts.

3 Raise the front of the car, rest it securely on axle stands and remove the right-hand front roadwheel.

4 Unscrew and release the fasteners, and remove the wheelarch inner panel, to gain access to the crankshaft pulley.

5 Have an assistant turn the engine using a spanner or socket on the crankshaft pulley bolt. As this is done, place your hand over No 1 spark plug hole, and feel for pressure build-up.

6 Once pressure is felt, insert the shaft of a large screwdriver (or, if available, a dial gauge and probe) down No 1 spark plug hole. When TDC is reached, the screwdriver will stop rising (or the reading on the dial gauge will stop increasing).

7 Once the screwdriver (or dial gauge reading) starts to rise, continue turning the engine until the crankshaft pulley timing mark is aligned with the mark on the timing belt lower cover **(see illustration)**.

8 A further TDC mark is provided on the flywheel, and this can be viewed through the aperture in the transmission bellhousing (remove the aperture cover, where fitted) **(see illustrations)**. When the flywheel mark aligns with the notch on the bellhousing, the engine is set to TDC. This mark is quite difficult to see, however, without further dismantling.

9 The engine is now set at TDC on No 1 cylinder.

3 Cylinder compression test

1 When engine performance is down, or if misfiring occurs which cannot be attributed to the ignition or fuel systems, a compression test can provide diagnostic clues as to the engine's condition. If the test is performed regularly, it can give warning of trouble before any other symptoms become apparent.

2 The engine must be fully warmed-up to normal operating temperature, the battery must be fully charged, and all the spark plugs must be removed (Chapter 1). The aid of an assistant will also be required.

3 Disable the ignition system by disconnecting the LT wiring plug to the ignition coil.

4 To prevent possible damage to the catalytic converter, depressurise and disable the fuel injection system by removing the fuel pump fuse or relay (see Chapter 4B, Section 7).

5 Fit a compression tester to the No 1 cylinder spark plug hole - the type of tester which

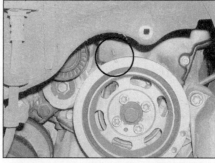

2.7 Camshaft pulley timing mark aligned with mark on timing belt lower cover

screws into the plug thread is to be preferred.

6 Have the assistant hold the throttle wide open, and crank the engine on the starter motor; after one or two revolutions, the compression pressure should build up to a maximum figure, and then stabilise. Record the highest reading obtained.

7 Repeat the test on the remaining cylinders, recording the pressure in each.

8 All cylinders should produce very similar pressures; any excessive difference indicates the existence of a fault. Note that the compression should build up quickly in a healthy engine; low compression on the first stroke, followed by gradually increasing pressure on successive strokes, indicates worn piston rings. A low compression reading on the first stroke, which does not build up during successive strokes, indicates leaking valves or a blown head gasket (a cracked head could also be the cause).

2.8a Removing the flywheel aperture cover - seen with the airflow meter removed

9 If the pressure in any cylinder is very low, carry out the following test to isolate the cause. Introduce a teaspoonful of clean oil into that cylinder through its spark plug hole and repeat the test.

10 If the addition of oil temporarily improves the compression pressure, this indicates that bore or piston wear is responsible for the pressure loss. No improvement suggests that leaking or burnt valves, or a blown head gasket, may be to blame.

11 A low reading from two adjacent cylinders is almost certainly due to the head gasket having blown between them; the presence of coolant in the engine oil will confirm this.

12 If one cylinder is about 20 percent lower than the others and the engine has a slightly rough idle, a worn camshaft lobe could be the cause.

13 On completion of the test, refit the spark plugs and restore the ignition and fuel systems.

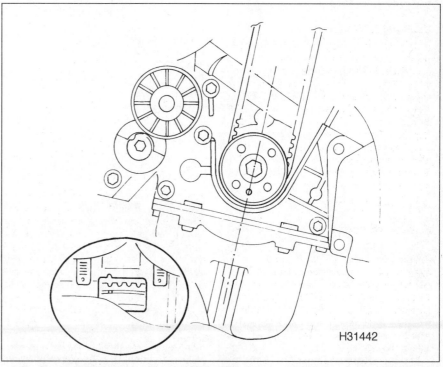

H31442

2.8b Showing flywheel alignment at TDC - also shows crankshaft sprocket alignment with sump

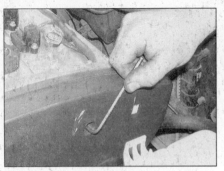

4.7a Removing one of the timing belt cover bolts

4.7b Removing the timing belt cover

4.9 Remove the four small bolts and take off the crankshaft pulley

4 Timing belt and covers - removal and refitting

Note: *If the timing belt is being removed, it is a wise precaution to check the condition of the coolant pump at the same time (check for signs of coolant leakage). This may avoid the need to remove the timing belt again at a later stage, should the coolant pump fail.*

General information

1 The function of the timing belt is to drive the camshafts and coolant pump. Should the belt slip or break in service, the valve timing will be disturbed and piston-to-valve contact will occur, resulting in serious engine damage.

2 For this reason, it is important that a new timing belt is fitted at or before the specified mileage (see Chapter 1). If the car has been

4.11 Mark the camshaft sprockets for TDC position

purchased second-hand, and its history is unknown, renewing the timing belt should be treated as a priority.

3 FIAT garages use a number of special tools to keep the camshaft sprockets and crankshaft sprocket (flywheel) at the TDC position, since it is possible that the sprockets may turn as the old belt is removed and the new one fitted. If they turn independently, the valve timing will be lost, and the engine will not run properly when restarted - worse, piston-to-valve contact may occur.

4 In the absence of the special tools, great care must be taken when removing and refitting the belt that the sprockets do not move. Marks may be found on the sprockets, which align with markings on the cylinder head or oil pump housing. If none are present, take care to make your own, using typists correction fluid or similar, **before** removing the belt.

5 If the special tools are not used, the procedure given below will suffice to change the belt successfully, but if care is not taken and the camshaft timing is slightly out, the engine may not run very well on completion. It is advisable to have a FIAT dealer confirm the camshaft timing after a new belt is fitted, if the special tools are not used.

Removal

6 Remove the auxiliary drivebelt, then remove the spark plugs (refer to Chapter 1).

7 Unbolt and remove the timing belt cover, which is secured by a total of eight bolts **(see illustrations)**. Two of the bolts are longer than

the rest - note their locations as they are removed. Recover the rubber gasket fitted between the outer and inner covers, if it is loose.

8 Set the engine to TDC as described in Section 2, then engage top gear; if the handbrake is firmly applied, this should prevent the crankshaft from moving.

9 Remove the four small Ribe bolts and take off the crankshaft pulley **(see illustration)**. Note that the pulley fits over a locating peg on the crankshaft sprocket.

10 If the special holding tools are not available, make your own sprocket alignment marks as necessary before removing the belt (see paragraph 4).

11 In particular, mark the relative positions of the camshaft sprockets. When the engine is at TDC, it should be found that the teeth on each sprocket line up with each other at the point where the sprockets are closest - if one tooth on each sprocket is marked for horizontal alignment, this can be used to confirm the TDC position. Alternatively, refit the camshaft cover, and mark each sprocket at the top, in relation to the edge of the cover **(see illustration)**.

12 The crankshaft sprocket should also be marked for position, if no timing marks are evident. The sprocket is keyed to the crankshaft, so can only be fitted in one position, but a timing mark would be useful as confirmation. When the engine is at TDC, the locating peg for the crankshaft pulley should be perpendicular to the sump mating flange **(see illustrations)**.

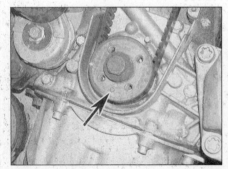

4.12a Locating peg in crankshaft sprocket (arrowed) . . .

4.12b . . . should be aligned vertically with indent in sump (perpendicular to sump flange)

4.12c We made alignment marks between the sprocket and oil pump flange

4.13a Removing No 3 exhaust camshaft bearing cap

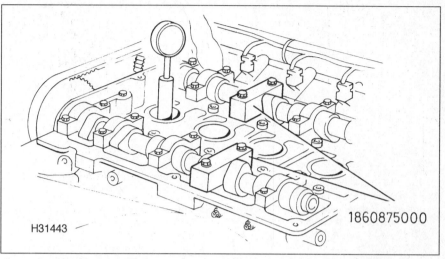

4.13b Showing FIAT special tools for locking and timing the camshafts

13 The FIAT tools (1860875000) for holding the camshafts stationary are modified No 2 inlet (rear) and No 3 exhaust camshaft bearing caps which locate over their respective camshaft lobes, preventing rotation and maintaining the camshaft timing. If available, the tools are fitted after removing the camshaft cover, as described in Section 6 **(see illustrations)**.

14 The tool used to lock the flywheel (1860898000) is a metal plate which is fitted after removing the lower access plate from the base of the flywheel. The tool engages the flywheel ring gear teeth, and prevents the flywheel (and therefore, the crankshaft sprocket) from turning. The same effect could be achieved by jamming a suitable screwdriver blade in the flywheel ring gear. However, if the procedure in paragraph 8 is followed, even this should not be necessary.

15 Release the nut on the timing belt tensioner, move the sprocket away from the belt and retighten the nut to hold the sprocket in the retracted position.

16 Slide the timing belt from the sprockets, taking great care not to turn them if locking tools have not been used.

Refitting

17 When refitting the new belt, first make sure that the sprocket timing marks are still in alignment.

18 If the special locking tools are being used, the camshaft sprocket bolts should be loosened to allow the sprockets to move slightly as the timing belt is refitted and tensioned. To hold each sprocket stationary

while the retaining bolt is loosened, make up a tool as described in Section 5.

19 If the special locking tools are not being used, it is not advisable to loosen the camshaft sprocket bolts unless absolutely necessary. If the timing belt teeth will not engage the camshaft sprockets satisfactorily, it is permissible to loosen the bolts and turn the sprockets *very slightly*, both in the same direction.

20 Fit the belt so that the arrows on the belt (where applicable) point in the direction of engine rotation. Also where applicable, the lines painted on the belt should coincide with marks on the sprockets.

21 Engage the timing belt with the crankshaft sprocket first, then place it around the fixed guide pulley, exhaust (front) camshaft sprocket, inlet camshaft sprocket and the tensioner sprocket. Finally, slip the belt around the coolant pump sprocket. Ensure that any slack in the belt is on the tensioner side of the belt run **(see illustration)**.

22 Release the tensioner nut and push the sprocket against the belt, using the raised rib on the tensioner backplate. Inserting an 8 mm bolt into the hole next to the tensioner will provide a levering point. This hole could also be used to locate the tool we made from an 8 mm bolt, two nuts and an oversize washer **(see illustrations below and Tool Tip overleaf)**.

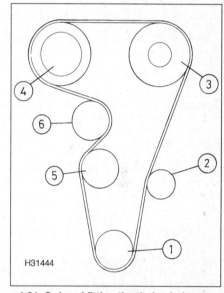

4.21 Order of fitting the timing belt over the sprockets

1 Crankshaft sprocket	4 Inlet camshaft sprocket
2 Fixed guide pulley	5 Tensioner
3 Exhaust camshaft sprocket	6 Coolant pump sprocket

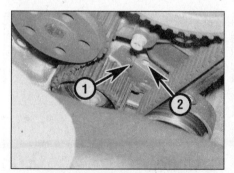

4.22a Rib (1) on tensioner backplate and hole (2) for inserting bolt or tool

4.22b Levering against an 8 mm bolt

4.22c Workshop tool inserted in hole

TOOL TiP

The timing belt tensioning tool consists of an 8 mm bolt, two 8 mm nuts, and an oversize washer. Clamp the washer so that it is off-centre, using the two nuts VERY firmly tightened (use two smaller washers either side of the main washer, if wished). The short end of the bolt locates in the hole already shown. The off-centre washer acts like an eccentric against the tensioner rib - as the bolt is turned, the washer bears on the rib and pushes the tensioner, thus tensioning the timing belt

23 Initially, the belt should be set to the maximum tension possible using reasonable force. Tighten the tensioner nut securely.

24 If the camshaft sprocket bolts were loosened, tighten them to the specified torque, holding each sprocket in the same way as when they were loosened.

25 Remove any locking tools used, and/or select neutral. Using a spanner or socket on the crankshaft pulley bolt, turn the engine through two complete turns in the normal direction of rotation. Check (as far as possible) that the sprocket timing marks come back into alignment.

26 Loosen the tensioner nut, and align the pointer with the small hole on the tensioner backplate **(see illustration)**. Hold the tensioner in this position, and tighten the tensioner nut to the specified torque.

27 Refitting the components removed for access is a reversal of removal.

---

5 Timing belt sprockets and tensioner -
removal and refitting

Timing belt tensioner

Removal

1 Remove the auxiliary drivebelt as described in Chapter 1.

2 Unbolt and remove the timing belt cover, which is secured by a total of eight bolts. Two of the bolts are longer than the rest - note their locations as they are removed. Recover the rubber gasket fitted between the outer and inner covers, if it is loose.

Caution: Provided the timing belt is kept

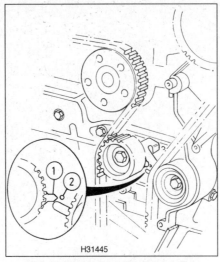

4.26 Timing belt tensioner details - pointer (1) must align with hole (2)

fully engaged with the camshaft, crankshaft and coolant pump sprockets during the following procedure, it is not necessary to align the timing TDC marks. However if any doubt exists, read through the full procedure given in Section 4, noting the advice on setting to TDC, and ensuring that the timing is not lost. The timing belt does not have to be removed for this procedure, but if the belt slips from the sprockets, the timing could be lost.

3 Loosen the nut on the timing belt tensioner and move the pulley away from the belt **(see illustration)**. If necessary, keep the belt engaged with the sprockets using cable-ties, elastic bands or string.

4 Completely unscrew the nut, recover the washer, and slide the tensioner off the mounting stud.

Inspection

5 Wipe the tensioner clean, but do not use excessive amounts of solvent, as these may contaminate the bearings. Spin the tensioner pulley on its hub by hand. Stiff movement or excessive freeplay is an indication of severe wear; the tensioner is not a serviceable component, and should be renewed if its condition is suspect, or as a precaution at the time of a major engine overhaul.

5.3 Timing belt tensioner - securing nut arrowed

Refitting

6 Hold the timing belt aside, then slide the tensioner over the mounting stud and secure loosely with the nut. Ensuring that all slack is taken out of the belt, engage the timing belt with tensioner sprocket.

7 Set the belt tension with reference to Section 4, paragraphs 22 to 26.

8 Refit the timing belt cover (and gasket) and tighten the bolts.

9 Refit the auxiliary drivebelt as described in Chapter 1.

Camshaft sprockets

Removal

10 Remove the timing belt as described in Section 4. In addition to the alignment marks suggested in Section 4, it is useful to have a mark between each sprocket and the cylinder head - make your own if none are present, particularly if the camshaft holding tools described in Section 4 are not available.

11 The camshaft sprocket must now be held stationary while the retaining bolt is loosened; if the sprocket turns very far, there is a risk that the valves will hit the pistons. Make up a tool and engage it with the holes in the sprocket **(see Tool Tip below)**.

12 Alternatively, pass a rod through one of the holes in the camshaft sprocket to prevent it rotating. Position a pad of rag or a piece of wood under the rod to avoid damaging the cylinder head.

13 Unscrew the bolt, and slide the sprocket from the end of the camshaft. Note the integral location key on the inner face of the sprocket.

Inspection

14 With the sprockets removed, examine the

TOOL TiP

To make a camshaft sprocket holding tool, obtain two lengths of steel strip about 6 mm thick by 30 mm wide or similar, one 600 mm long, the other 200 mm long (all dimensions approximate). Bolt the two strips together to form a forked end, leaving the bolt slack so that the shorter strip can pivot freely. At the end of each 'prong' of the fork, secure a bolt with a nut and a locknut, to act as the fulcrums; these will engage with the cut-outs in the sprocket, and should protrude by about 30 mm.

camshaft oil seals for signs of leaking. If necessary, refer to Section 7 and renew them.

15 Check the sprocket teeth for damage.

16 Wipe clean the sprocket and camshaft mating surfaces.

Refitting

17 Locate the sprocket on the end of the camshaft, then refit the bolt and washer and tighten to the specified torque while holding the camshaft stationary using the method described previously.

18 Align the marks made between the camshaft sprockets and cylinder head, then refit the timing belt as described in Section 4.

Crankshaft sprocket

Removal

19 Remove the timing belt as described in Section 4. It is essential that an alignment mark is made between the sprocket and the engine, to preserve the timing - make your own if none are present.

20 Working beneath the engine, unbolt and remove the flywheel lower cover, then hold the flywheel stationary, preferably using a tool which engages the flywheel starter ring gear (see Section 10). Alternatively, have an assistant engage a wide-bladed screwdriver with the starter ring gear.

21 Unscrew the crankshaft sprocket retaining bolt - this is tightened to a particularly high torque, so ensure that the car is adequately supported. Use only good-quality, close-fitting tools, and take precautions against personal injury, especially when the bolt eventually loosens (wear gloves

5.29 Timing belt fixed guide pulley

to protect your hands). The bolt has a **left-hand thread** - ie it unscrews **clockwise**.

22 Slide the sprocket off the end of the crankshaft. If it is tight, remove it using a puller or a pair of suitable screwdrivers. The sprocket may have an integral location key on its inner face, or a separate key which locates in a groove in the crankshaft nose. Recover the spacer fitted behind the sprocket.

Inspection

23 With the sprocket removed, examine the crankshaft oil seal for signs of leaking. If necessary, refer to Section 8 and renew it.

24 Wipe clean the sprocket and crankshaft mating surfaces. Check the sprocket teeth for damage.

Refitting

25 Slide the sprocket and spacer onto the crankshaft, making sure the sprocket engages the integral key or separate key. Fit a new bolt

\- do not lubricate the threads. It is not advisable to re-use the old bolt, given the extremely high torque to which it is tightened.

26 Fit the new bolt and washer, tightening the bolt to the specified torque while holding the crankshaft stationary using the method described in paragraph 20. Also bear in mind the advice in paragraph 21.

27 Refit the timing belt as described in Section 4.

Fixed guide pulley

Removal

28 Remove the timing belt as described in Section 4.

29 Loosen and remove the pulley bolt and its washer, and take off the pulley **(see illustration)**.

Inspection

30 Check the pulley for any sign of damage, and check that it spins freely, with no sign of roughness. Wipe the pulley clean before fitting.

Refitting

31 Offer the pulley up to the engine, and secure with the retaining bolt and washer. Tighten the bolt to the specified torque.

32 Refit the timing belt as described in Section 4.

6 Camshaft cover - removal and refitting

Removal

1 Unscrew the two bolts securing the plastic cover at the left-hand end of the cylinder head, and remove the cover **(see illustrations)**.

2 Disconnect the breather hose from the left-hand end of the camshaft cover, then unscrew the retaining bolt and remove the breather pipe stub from the end of the cover **(see illustrations)**.

3 Unclip the wiring plugs from the bracket at the left-hand end of the cover, and lay them to one side (note that, unless further work is being carried out, there should be no need to separate the wiring plugs) **(see illustration)**.

6.1a Unscrew the two bolts (arrowed) . . .

6.1b . . . and take off the plastic end cover

6.3 Unclip the wiring plugs from the end of the cover

6.2a Unscrew the retaining bolt . . .

6.2b . . . and remove the breather pipe stub

6.4 Removing one of the Allen screws under the oil filler cap

6.5 Removing the engine top cover

6.6 Disconnecting No 1 coil wiring plug

4 Unscrew and remove the oil filler cap, and remove the two Allen screws concealed underneath **(see illustration)**.

5 Remove the six main bolts securing the

engine top cover, then lift the cover away **(see illustration)**.

6 Label the ignition coil connector plugs for position (No 1 is at the timing belt end of the engine), then disconnect them **(see illustration)**.

7 Ensuring that they are marked for position, remove each of the ignition coils by unscrewing the two mounting bolts and pulling them upwards off the spark plugs **(see illustrations)**.

8 Disconnect the earth lead between coil Nos 2 and 3, unscrew the two bolts securing the harness brackets, then move the harness aside **(see illustrations)**.

9 On models with air conditioning, trace the wiring back from the compressor, and disconnect it at the wiring plug.

10 The camshaft cover is secured by a total of nine Ribe bolts - eight around the sides,

and one in the centre **(see illustration)**. Progressively unscrew the bolts in a diagonal sequence. When all the bolts are loose, remove them, noting their locations, as one is longer than the rest.

11 Lift off the cover, and recover the main seal **(see illustration)**. If the cover sticks, do not attempt to lever it off - instead free it by working around the cover and tapping it lightly with a soft-faced mallet.

12 Peel off the main rubber seal from around the inside of the cover, and check its condition. It is permissible to re-use it, provided it is not perished, crushed or otherwise damaged. Clean the mating surfaces of the cylinder head and camshaft cover thoroughly.

13 Check the condition of the four round seals fitted to the inside of the cover, which fit over the ignition coils.

6.7a Unscrew the two mounting bolts . . .

6.7b . . . and pull the each coil upwards off its spark plug

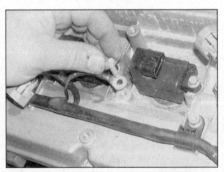

6.8a Disconnect the central earth lead . . .

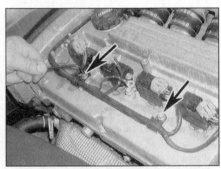

6.8b . . . unscrew the harness bracket bolts (arrowed) . . .

6.8c . . . and move the harness clear of the cover

6.10 Removing the camshaft cover bolts

6.11 Lifting off the camshaft cover

14 If necessary, remove and clean the baffle plate fitted inside the cover. If this is particularly in need of cleaning, also check the breather pipe stub which was removed in paragraph 2. When refitting the stub, check the condition of the O-rings which seal the stub to the cover, and renew if necessary.

Refitting

15 Locate the main seal in the cover, making sure it is correctly seated in its groove **(see illustration)**.

16 Apply a little sealant to the joints between the camshaft front bearing cap (nearest the sprockets) and the cylinder head **(see illustration)**.

17 Lower the cover into position on the cylinder head, making sure the seals are not displaced.

18 Insert the bolts and tighten them progressively in a diagonal sequence to the specified torque.

19 Refit all components removed for access, using a reversal of the removal procedure.

---

7 Camshaft oil seals - renewal

1 Remove the camshaft sprockets as described in Section 5.

2 Using a suitable hooked instrument, remove each oil seal as required, taking care not to damage the surface of the camshaft or the front bearing cap. Even if only one seal is found to be leaking, it is advisable to renew both.

3 Clean the seating in the cylinder head and front bearing cap, and the end of the camshaft. To prevent damage to the new oil seal as it is being fitted, wrap some adhesive tape around the end of the camshaft and lightly oil it.

4 Dip the new oil seal in oil then locate it over the camshaft, making sure that the sealing lips are facing inwards.

5 Using a suitable tubular drift, drive the oil seal squarely into the housing. Remove the adhesive tape from the camshaft.

6 Renew the other seal (as required) using the same procedure.

7 Refit all components removed for access, using a reversal of the relevant removal procedure.

---

8 Crankshaft oil seals - renewal

Front (right-hand side) oil seal

1 The front oil seal is located in the oil pump on the front of the crankshaft. Remove the timing belt as described in Section 4 and the crankshaft sprocket as described in Section 5.

2 Using a hooked instrument, remove the oil seal from the oil pump housing, taking care not to damage the surface of the crankshaft.

6.15 Check the condition of the cover main seal, and of the four round seals

3 Clean the seating in the housing and the surface of the crankshaft. To prevent damage to the new oil seal as it is being fitted, wrap some adhesive tape around the end of the crankshaft and lightly oil it.

4 Dip the new oil seal in oil then offer it up to the oil pump casing making sure that the sealing lips are facing inwards.

5 Using a suitable tubular drift, drive the oil seal squarely into the casing. Remove the adhesive tape.

6 Refit the crankshaft sprocket and timing belt with reference to Sections 5 and 4.

Rear (left-hand side) oil seal

Note: *The following paragraphs describe renewal of the rear oil seal leaving the housing in position. Refer to Chapter 2E for details of removing the housing.*

7 Remove the flywheel as described in Section 10.

8 Using a suitable hooked instrument, remove the oil seal from the rear oil seal housing, taking care not to damage the surface of the crankshaft.

9 Clean the seating in the housing and the surface of the crankshaft. Check the crankshaft for burrs which may damage the oil seal lip of the new seal, and if necessary use a fine file to remove them.

10 Dip the new seal in clean engine oil and carefully locate it over the crankshaft rear flange, making sure that it is the correct way round (lips facing inwards). Take care not to damage the oil seal lips as it passes over the crankshaft flange.

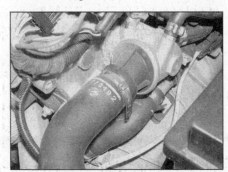

9.9a Disconnect the hoses from the thermostat housing . . .

6.16 Applying sealant to the joint at the camshaft front bearing cap

11 Progressively tap the oil seal into the housing, keeping it square to prevent distortion. A block of wood is useful for this purpose.

12 Refit the flywheel with reference to Section 10.

---

9 Cylinder head - removal and refitting

Removal

1 Depressurise the fuel system as described in Chapter 4B, Section 7.

2 Disconnect the battery negative terminal (refer to *Disconnecting the battery*). Remove the battery as described in Chapter 5A.

3 Drain the cooling system as described in Chapter 1. Disconnect the top and bottom hoses, and the expansion tank hoses, from the engine.

4 Remove the auxiliary drivebelt as described in Chapter 1.

5 Remove the spark plugs as described in Chapter 1.

6 Remove the timing belt from the camshaft sprockets, using the information in Section 4. Unless the belt has been changed recently, remove it completely and fit a new one on reassembly.

7 To improve working room, remove the two bolts securing the air intake shroud at the front of the engine compartment, and lift the shroud out of position, detaching it from the intake duct.

8 Remove the inlet manifold as described in Chapter 4B. Alternatively, disconnect all hoses and connections from the inlet manifold, including the manifold support brackets at the rear of the engine, using the manifold removal procedure in Chapter 4B.

9 Disconnect the hoses from the thermostat housing, and the coolant temperature sensor wiring plug on top of the housing. Also disconnect the (smaller) temperature gauge sender wiring plug from the end of the head **(see illustrations)**.

10 Unbolt the cable clip in front of the thermostat housing - this retains the oxygen sensor wiring. Trace the wiring back to the

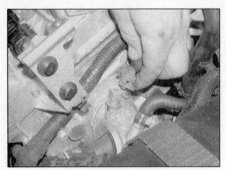

9.9b . . . the coolant temperature sensor on top of the housing . . .

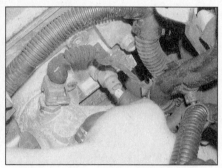

9.9c . . . and the temperature gauge sender on the head

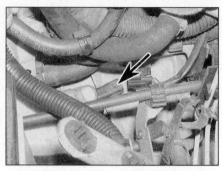

9.10 Disconnecting the oxygen sensor wiring plug

connector plug below the thermostat housing, and disconnect it **(see illustration)**.

11 Remove the camshaft cover as described in Section 6.

12 Working just behind the inlet camshaft sprocket, remove the bolt securing the ignition coil wiring bracket to the cylinder head, and remove the bracket.

13 Remove the nut securing the engine oil dipstick to the exhaust manifold. Remove the dipstick, and move the tube clear of the head.

14 Working under the car, unscrew the exhaust manifold-to-downpipe nuts, and separate the downpipe from the manifold, recovering the gasket **(see illustration)**.

15 Unscrew the manifold-to-cylinder head nuts, and withdraw the manifold from the engine compartment, recovering the gasket.

16 In some cases, the manifold studs will come out with the nuts - this poses no great problem, and the studs can be refitted if they are in good condition. For preference, however, a complete set of manifold and downpipe studs and nuts should be obtained as required, as the old ones are likely to be in less-than-perfect condition.

17 Check around the head that there are no further wires, hoses or other obstructions which will prevent the head from being lifted off.

18 Unscrew the cylinder head bolts half a turn at a time, in the reverse order to that shown in illustration 9.35a - a suitable Ribe socket will be required **(see illustration)**. When the bolts are free, remove them with their washers.

19 Lift the cylinder head from the block. If it is

stuck tight, insert pieces of wood into the exhaust or inlet ports, and use them as levers to rock the head off the block. On no account drive levers into the gasket joint, nor attempt to tap the head sideways, as it is located on positioning dowels.

20 Remove and discard the cylinder head gasket and the manifold gaskets.

21 The cylinder head can be dismantled after removing the camshafts and tappets as described in Chapter 2E. Further dismantling and decarbonising are also described in Chapter 2E.

Preparation for refitting

22 The mating faces of the cylinder head and cylinder block must be perfectly clean before refitting the head. Use a hard plastic or wooden scraper to remove all traces of gasket and carbon; also clean the piston crowns.

23 Take particular care when cleaning the piston crowns, as the soft aluminium alloy is easily damaged.

24 Make sure that the carbon is not allowed to enter the oil and water passages - this is particularly important for the lubrication system, as carbon could block the oil supply to the engine's components. Using adhesive tape and paper, seal the water, oil and bolt holes in the cylinder block.

25 To prevent carbon entering the gap between the pistons and bores, smear a little grease in the gap. After cleaning each piston, use a small brush to remove all traces of grease and carbon from the gap, then wipe away the remainder with a clean rag. Clean all the pistons in the same way.

26 Check the mating surfaces of the cylinder block and the cylinder head for nicks, deep scratches and other damage. If slight, they may be removed carefully with a file, but if excessive, machining may be the only alternative to renewal.

27 If warpage of the cylinder head gasket surface is suspected, use a straight-edge to check it for distortion. Refer to Part E of this Chapter if necessary.

28 Check the condition of the cylinder head bolts, and particularly their threads, whenever they are removed. Wash the bolts in a suitable solvent, and wipe them dry. Check each bolt for any sign of visible wear or damage, renewing them if necessary.

Refitting

29 Before refitting the assembled cylinder head, make sure that the head and block mating surfaces are perfectly clean, and that the bolt holes in the cylinder block have been mopped out to clear any oil or coolant. If the bolt holes have any significant amount of liquid in them, the block could be cracked by hydraulic pressure when the head bolts are tightened.

30 The camshaft sprocket timing marks should be aligned with the mark on the cylinder head.

31 The new gasket should not be removed from its plastic bag until required for use. Fit the gasket dry - no grease or sealant should be used.

32 Place the gasket on the cylinder block so that the word ALTO can be read from above.

33 Lower the cylinder head onto the block so that it locates on the positioning dowels.

34 Ensure that the cylinder head bolts are cleaned of all debris, and check the threads for signs of damage. Especially if it is known that the bolts have been removed previously, it is advisable to renew all ten bolts as a set, rather than risk the bolts shearing when tightened.

35 Lightly oil the bolt threads. Screw the bolts in finger-tight, and tighten them in the sequence shown to the Stage 1 torque **(see illustrations)**.

36 When all ten bolts have been tightened to the Stage 1 torque, go round again in sequence and tighten to the Stage 2 torque.

9.14 Exhaust manifold-to-downpipe nuts

9.18 A Ribe socket is needed to unscrew the cylinder head bolts

37 Again working in sequence, tighten the bolts through the specified Stage 3 angle. Note that 90° is equivalent to a quarter-turn or right-angle, making it easy to judge by noting the initial position of the socket handle. If available, use an angle gauge fitted to the socket handle for maximum accuracy **(see illustration)**.

38 With all ten bolts tightened to Stage 3, go round once more and tighten all bolts in sequence to the Stage 4 angle.

39 When all ten bolts have been tightened to Stage 4, finally tighten all bolts in sequence to the Stage 5 angle.

40 When all the bolts are fully tightened, refit the camshaft cover as described in Section 6.

41 Refit the exhaust manifold, using new gaskets, studs and nuts, as necessary. Tighten all nuts securely.

42 Further refitting is a reversal of removal. Ensure that all wiring and hoses are correctly routed and securely reconnected. Refer to Section 4 when refitting the timing belt, and to Chapter 1 when refitting the spark plugs and auxiliary drivebelt, and when refilling the cooling system.

10 Flywheel -
removal, inspection and refitting

Refer to Part A, Section 11.

11 Engine mountings -
inspection and renewal

Inspection

1 Jack up the front of the car and support on axle stands (see *Jacking and vehicle support*).

2 Check the mounting rubbers to see if they are cracked, hardened or separated from the metal at any point; renew the mounting if any such damage or deterioration is evident.

3 Check that all the mounting's fasteners are securely tightened; use a torque wrench to check if possible.

4 Using a large screwdriver or a crowbar, check for wear in the mounting by carefully levering against it to check for free play. Where this is not possible enlist the aid of an assistant to move the engine/transmission back and forth, or from side to side, while you watch the mounting. While some free play is to be expected even from new components, excessive wear should be obvious. If excessive free play is found, check first that the fasteners are correctly secured, then renew any worn components as described below.

Renewal

Note: *Left and right are as seen from the driver's seat.*

Right-hand mounting

5 Raise the front of the car and support on

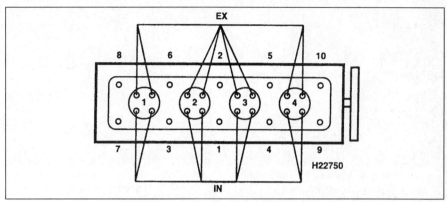

9.35a **Cylinder head bolt tightening sequence**

9.35b **Tightening the cylinder head bolts using a torque wrench**

9.37 **Angle-tightening the cylinder head bolts**

axle stands (see *Jacking and vehicle support*).

6 Place a trolley jack beneath the right-hand side of the engine, with a block of wood on the jack head. Raise the jack until it is supporting the weight of the engine.

7 Working from below, unscrew the through-bolt (and washers) securing the engine bracket to the mounting **(see illustration)**.

8 Lower the engine sufficiently to disengage the engine bracket from the mounting, then remove the bolts securing the mounting to the body, and remove it.

9 Locate the new mounting on the body, then insert the mounting-to-body bolts and tighten by hand.

10 Raise the engine and locate the bracket on the mounting. Refit the through-bolt (and washers) and tighten to the specified torque, then tighten the mounting-to-body bolts.

11 Remove the trolley jack and lower the car to the ground.

Right-hand reaction rod

12 Raise the front of the car and support on axle stands (see *Jacking and vehicle support*).

13 Place a trolley jack beneath the right-hand side of the engine, with a block of wood on the jack head. Raise the jack until it is supporting the weight of the engine.

14 Unscrew the through-bolt and nut from the engine mounting, and remove the bolt securing the rod to the suspension strut mounting plate **(see illustrations)**. Separate the rod from the mounting on the engine and suspension strut mounting, and remove it.

15 If required, the engine mounting and/or strut mounting plate can be unbolted and removed. Note that the strut mounting plate is

11.7 **Engine right-hand mounting (seen from below) - through-bolt arrowed**

11.14a **View of reaction rod**

11.14b Reaction rod through-bolt (arrowed)

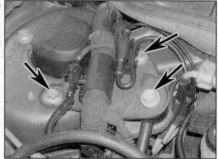

11.15 Reaction rod strut mounting plate bolts (arrowed)

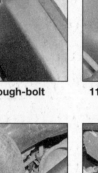

11.19 Engine rear mounting

11.26 Engine left-hand mounting (seen from below)

secured by two of the three suspension strut mounting bolts **(see illustration)**.

16 Refitting is a reversal of removal. Tighten all bolts to the specified torque, then remove the trolley jack and lower the car to the ground.

Rear mounting

17 Raise the front of the car and support on axle stands (see *Jacking and vehicle support*).
18 Place a trolley jack beneath the engine/transmission flange, with a block of wood on the jack head. Raise the jack until it is supporting the weight of the engine and transmission.
19 Working from below, unscrew the through-bolt securing the bracket to the mounting **(see illustration)**.
20 Lower the engine sufficiently to disengage the bracket from the mounting, then remove the two bolts securing the mounting to the body, and remove it.

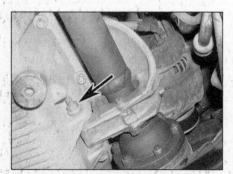

12.5a Right-hand driveshaft support/shield-to-sump nut and bolt (arrowed)

21 Locate the new mounting on the body, then insert the mounting-to-body bolts and tighten by hand.
22 Raise the engine and locate the bracket on the mounting. Refit the through-bolt and tighten to the specified torque, then tighten the mounting-to-body bolts.
23 Remove the trolley jack and lower the car to the ground.

Left-hand mounting

24 Raise the front of the car and support on axle stands (see *Jacking and vehicle support*).
25 Place a trolley jack beneath the transmission, with a block of wood on the jack head. Raise the jack until it is supporting the weight of the engine/transmission.
26 Unscrew the through-bolt securing the transmission bracket to the mounting, and recover the washers **(see illustration)**.

12.5b Access to one of the sump bolts (arrowed) is hampered by the driveshaft

27 Unscrew the two bolts securing the left-hand mounting to the subframe.
28 Lower the transmission sufficiently to remove the mounting from the transmission bracket.
29 Locate the new mounting in position, and loosely refit the mounting-to-body bolts.
30 Raise the engine/transmission and refit the through-bolt securing the bracket to the mounting. Tighten the bolt to the specified torque, then tighten the mounting-to-body bolts.
31 Remove the trolley jack and lower the car to the ground.

12 Sump - removal and refitting

Removal

1 Jack up the front of the car and support on axle stands. Drain the engine oil as described in Chapter 1.
2 Unscrew and remove the various fasteners, and completely remove the engine undertray.
3 Remove the exhaust downpipe as described in Chapter 4C, Section 5.
4 Support the weight of the engine/transmission using a trolley jack with a block of wood under the engine-to-transmission flange. Unbolt and remove the engine rear mounting from the rear of the sump.
5 Removing the sump will be made easier by removing the right-hand driveshaft and support/shield, using the information in Chapter 8. However, although access to one of the sump bolts is hampered by the right-hand driveshaft, it is sufficient to unbolt the driveshaft support/shield from the rear of the sump **(see illustrations)**.
6 Unscrew the Ribe bolts, and pull the sump downwards to remove it. The joint sealant will require cutting with a sharp knife to release the pan.

Refitting

7 Clean away all old gasket material, from the sump pan and from the base of the block.
8 Apply a bead of RTV silicone instant gasket 3 mm in diameter to the sump flange. The bead of sealant should pass around the inside of the sump bolt holes. Also apply a little sealant to the joints between the front and rear oil seal flanges and the engine block.
9 Fit the sump, screw in the fixing bolts, and tighten securely in a diagonal sequence.
10 Wait one hour for the gasket compound to harden before filling with oil.
11 Lower the car to the ground and fill the engine with oil (see Chapter 1). Check the oil level after running the engine for a few minutes, as described in *Weekly checks*.

13.8 Using an impact screwdriver to remove the oil pump rear cover plate screws

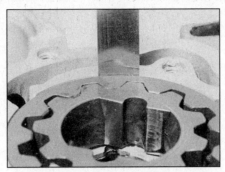

13.9a Measuring oil pump outer gear-to-pump housing clearance

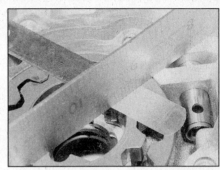

13.9b Measuring oil pump gear endfloat

13 Oil pump and pick-up tube - removal and refitting

Removal

1 Drain the engine oil and remove the sump as described in Section 12.
2 Unbolt and remove the oil pick-up/filter screen assembly. Note the sealing washer.
3 Unscrew and remove the oil filter cartridge (see Chapter 1).
4 Remove the timing belt as described in Section 4.
5 Remove the crankshaft sprocket as described in Section 5.
6 Extract the oil pump fixing bolts, noting their locations (there are nine bolts in all, of three different lengths). Withdraw the pump and remove the gasket.

Inspection

7 The oil pump incorporates a pressure relief valve, which can be removed for examination by depressing the spring plunger and pulling out the keeper plate.
8 If pump wear is suspected, check the gears in the following way. Extract the five fixing screws and remove the rear cover plate. The screws are very tight, and will probably require the use of an impact screwdriver **(see illustration)**.
9 Check the clearance between the outer gear and the pump housing using feeler blades. Check the gear endfloat by placing a straight-edge across the pump body, and checking the gap between the straight-edge

and gear face **(see illustrations)**. If the clearances are outside the specified tolerance, renew the oil pump complete.
10 If the pump is unworn, refit the rear cover plate and tighten the screws fully.
11 Apply air pressure from a tyre pump to the oil pump oil ducts, to clear any sludge or other material. If any solvents are used, the pump must be allowed to dry thoroughly before refitting.
12 Prime the pump by pouring clean engine oil into its inlet duct, at the same time turning the oil pump inner gear with your fingers.
13 Lever out the oil seal, and drive a new one squarely into the oil pump casing **(see illustration)**. Lubricate the oil seal lips.

Refitting

14 Clean all traces of old gasket from the pump and the mating surfaces on the cylinder block.
15 Bolt the pump into position using a new joint gasket. Insert the bolts into the positions noted on removal, and tighten all to the specified torques.
16 Bolt on the oil pick-up assembly using a new sealing washer.
17 Refit the crankshaft sprocket as described in Section 5.
18 Fit and tension the timing belt as described in Section 4.
19 Fit the sump as described in Section 12.
20 Screw on a new oil filter cartridge, and fill the engine with oil (see Chapter 1).
21 Run the engine for a few minutes, then check and top-up the oil level as described in *Weekly checks*.

13.13 Using a socket to fit a new oil seal to the oil pump

14 Oil pressure switch - removal and refitting

Removal

1 The oil pressure switch is located at the rear of the cylinder head.
2 Disconnect the switch wiring connector.
3 Unscrew the switch from the block, and remove it.
4 Clean the switch location in the block as far as possible. If the switch is to be refitted, clean its threads.
5 Examine the switch for signs of cracking or splits. If the top part of the switch is loose, this is an early indication of impending failure.

Refitting

6 Apply a smear of sealant to the threads of the switch, then screw it into place and tighten to the specified torque.
7 Reconnect the switch wiring on completion.

Notes

Chapter 2 Part E:
Engine removal and overhaul procedures

Contents

Degrees of difficulty

| **Easy,** suitable for novice with little experience | | **Fairly easy,** suitable for beginner with some experience | | **Fairly difficult,** suitable for competent DIY mechanic | | **Difficult,** suitable for experienced DIY mechanic | | **Very difficult,** suitable for expert DIY or professional | |

Specifications

Engine codes
Refer to Specifications in relevant Part of Chapter 2.

Cylinder head
Camshaft bearing diameters:
  1.2 and 1.6 litre engines . . . . See Chapter 2A or 2C
  1.4 and 1.8 litre engines . . . . 26.045 to 26.070 mm
Valve seat angle:
  Except 1.2 litre engine . . . . 45° ± 5'
  1.2 litre engine . . . . 45° ± 20'
Tappet running clearance in head:
  1.4 litre engine . . . . 0.016 to 0.055 mm
  1.8 litre engine . . . . 0.025 to 0.066 mm

Valves
Valve stem diameter:
  Inlet:
    1.2 litre engine . . . . 5.974 to 5.992 mm
    1.4 and 1.6 litre engines . . . . 6.982 to 7.000 mm
    1.8 litre engine . . . . 6.975 to 6.990 mm
  Exhaust:
    1.2 litre engine . . . . 5.974 to 5.992 mm
    1.4 litre engine . . . . 6.982 to 7.000 mm
    1.6 litre engine . . . . 6.974 to 6.992 mm
    1.8 litre engine . . . . 6.960 to 6.975 mm
Valve face angle:
  Except 1.2 litre engine . . . . 45° 30' ± 5'
  1.2 litre engine . . . . 45° 30' ± 20'
Valve stem-to-guide clearance:
  1.2 litre engine . . . . 0.030 to 0.066 mm
  1.4 and 1.6 litre engines . . . . 0.022 to 0.058 mm
  1.8 litre engine . . . . 0.032 to 0.065 mm

Camshaft
Camshaft bearing running clearance (1.4 and 1.8 litre engines) . . . . . . 0.030 to 0.070 mm
Camshaft endfloat (1.4 and 1.8 litre engines) . . . . 0.100 to 0.230 mm

Auxiliary shaft (1.6 litre engine)
Shaft bearing running clearance . . . . 0.040 to 0.091 mm
Shaft bearing diameters:
  Innermost bearing . . . . 35.593 to 35.618 mm
  Outermost bearing . . . . 31.940 to 31.960 mm

Cylinder block

Bore diameter:
1.2 litre engine	70.800 to 70.830 mm
1.6 litre engine	86.400 to 86.430 mm
1.4 and 1.8 litre engines	70.800 to 70.830 mm
Undersizes	Increments of 0.010 mm

Pistons and piston rings

Piston diameter:

Grade A:
1.2 litre engine	70.760 to 70.770 mm
1.6 litre engine	86.352 to 86.362 mm
1.4 and 1.8 litre engines	81.952 to 81.962 mm

Grade B:
1.2 litre engine	70.770 to 70.780 mm
1.6 litre engine	86.359 to 86.371 mm
1.4 and 1.8 litre engines	81.959 to 81.971 mm

Grade C:
1.2 litre engine	70.780 to 70.790 mm
1.6 litre engine	86.368 to 86.378 mm
1.4 and 1.8 litre engines	81.968 to 81.978 mm

Piston-to-bore clearance:
Except 1.2 litre engine	0.038 to 0.062 mm
1.2 litre engine	0.030 to 0.050 mm
Maximum difference in weight between pistons	± 5g

Gudgeon pin diameter:
1.2 litre engine	17.970 to 17.974 mm
1.6 litre engine	21.990 to 21.995 mm
1.4 and 1.8 litre engines	19.996 to 20.000 mm

Gudgeon pin to piston clearance:
Except 1.2 litre engine	0.002 to 0.011 mm
1.2 litre engine	0.008 to 0.016 mm

Piston ring-to-ring wall clearance:

Top compression ring:
1.2 litre engine	0.000 to 0.060 mm
1.4 litre engine	0.050 to 0.090 mm
1.6 litre engine	0.035 to 0.075 mm
1.8 litre engine	0.050 to 0.085 mm

2nd compression ring:
1.2 litre engine	0.000 to 0.055 mm
1.4 litre engine	0.040 to 0.075 mm
1.6 litre engine	0.020 to 0.060 mm
1.8 litre engine	0.040 to 0.075 mm

Oil scraper ring:
1.2 litre engine	0.000 to 0.055 mm
1.4 litre engine	0.075 to 0.105 mm
1.6 litre engine	0.065 to 0.095 mm
1.8 litre engine	0.030 to 0.065 mm

Piston ring end gap:

Top compression ring:
1.2 litre engine	0.200 to 0.400 mm
1.4 litre engine	0.250 to 0.500 mm
1.6 litre engine	0.200 to 0.450 mm
1.8 litre engine	0.300 to 0.500 mm

2nd compression ring:
1.2 litre engine	0.250 to 0.450 mm
1.4 litre engine	0.300 to 0.500 mm
1.6 litre engine	0.250 to 0.500 mm
1.8 litre engine	0.300 to 0.500 mm

Oil scraper ring:
1.2 litre engine	0.200 to 0.450 mm
1.4 litre engine	0.400 to 1.400 mm
1.6 litre engine	0.400 to 1.400 mm
1.8 litre engine	0.250 to 0.450 mm

Connecting rods

Gudgeon pin-to-small end clearance:
1.4 litre engine	0.006 to 0.016 mm
1.6 litre engine	0.009 to 0.020 mm
1.8 litre engine	0.006 to 0.020 mm

Crankshaft

Main bearing journal diameters:
- 1.2 litre engine:
  - Grade 1 . . . .   47.982 to 47.988 mm
  - Grade 2 . . . .   47.988 to 47.994 mm
  - Grade 3 . . . .   47.994 to 48.000 mm
- 1.6 litre engine:
  - Grade 1 . . . .   50.790 to 50.800 mm
  - Grade 2 . . . .   50.780 to 50.790 mm
- 1.4 and 1.8 litre engines:
  - Grade 1 . . . .   52.994 to 53.000 mm
  - Grade 2 . . . .   52.988 to 52.994 mm
  - Grade 3 . . . .   52.982 to 52.988 mm

Crankpin journal diameters:
- 1.2 litre engine:
  - Grade A . . . .   41.990 to 42.008 mm
- 1.4 litre engine:
  - Grade A . . . .   40.884 to 40.890 mm
  - Grade B . . . .   40.878 to 40.884 mm
  - Grade C . . . .   40.872 to 40.878 mm
- 1.6 litre engine:
  - Grade A . . . .   45.513 to 45.523 mm
  - Grade B . . . .   45.503 to 45.513 mm
- 1.8 litre engine:
  - Grade A . . . .   50.799 to 50.805 mm
  - Grade B . . . .   50.793 to 50.799 mm
  - Grade C . . . .   50.787 to 50.793 mm

Main bearing running clearance:
- 1.2 litre engine . . . .   0.025 to 0.040 mm
- 1.6 litre engine . . . .   0.019 to 0.050 mm
- 1.4 and 1.8 litre engines . . . .   0.025 to 0.052 mm

Big-end bearing running clearance:
- 1.2 litre engine . . . .   0.024 to 0.060 mm
- 1.6 litre engine . . . .   0.025 to 0.063 mm
- 1.4 and 1.8 litre engines . . . .   0.030 to 0.056 mm

Crankshaft endfloat:
- 1.2 and 1.6 litre engines . . . .   0.055 to 0.265 mm
- 1.4 and 1.8 litre engines . . . .   0.059 to 0.161 mm

Torque wrench settings

Refer to Specifications in relevant Part of Chapter 2.

---

1 Engine and transmission removal - preparation and precautions

If you have decided the engine must be removed for overhaul or major repair work, several preliminary steps should be taken.

Locating a suitable place to work is extremely important. Adequate work space, along with storage space for the vehicle, will be needed. If a workshop or garage isn't available, at the very least a flat, level, clean work surface is required.

If possible, clear some shelving close to the work area, and use it to store the engine components and ancillaries as they are removed and dismantled. In this manner, the components stand a better chance of staying clean and undamaged during the overhaul. Laying out components in groups together with their retaining nuts and bolts, etc will save time and avoid confusion when the engine is refitted.

Clean the engine compartment and engine/transmission before beginning the removal procedure; this will help visibility and help to keep tools clean.

The help of an assistant should be available; there are certain instances when one person cannot safely perform all of the operations required to remove the engine from the vehicle. Safety is of primary importance, considering the potential hazards involved in this kind of operation. A second person should always be in attendance to offer help in an emergency. If this is the first time you have removed an engine, advice and aid from someone more experienced would also be beneficial.

Plan the operation ahead of time. Before starting work, obtain (or arrange for the hire of) all of the tools and equipment you will need. Access to the following items will allow the task of removing and refitting the engine/transmission to be completed safely and with relative ease; a heavy-duty trolley jack - rated in excess of the combined weight of the engine and transmission, complete sets of spanners and sockets (see Tools and working facilities), wooden blocks, and plenty of rags and cleaning solvent for mopping up spilled oil, coolant and fuel. A selection of different-sized plastic storage boxes will also prove useful for keeping dismantled components grouped together. If any of the equipment must be hired, make sure that you arrange for it in advance, and perform all of the operations possible without it beforehand; this may save you time and money.

Plan on the vehicle being out of use for quite a while, especially if you intend to carry out an engine overhaul. Read through the whole of this section and work out a strategy based on your own experience and the tools, time and workspace available to you. Some of the overhaul processes may have to be carried out by a FIAT dealer or an engineering works - these establishments often have busy schedules, so it would be prudent to consult them before removing or dismantling the engine, to get an idea of the amount of time required to carry out the work.

When removing the engine from the vehicle, be methodical about the disconnection of

2.7a Removing the battery drip tray

2.7b Lift off the fuse/relay carrier lid . . .

2.7c . . . for access to the mounting nuts

external components. Labelling cables and hoses as they are removed will greatly assist the refitting process.

Always be extremely careful when lifting the engine/transmission assembly from the engine bay. Serious injury can result from careless actions. If help is required, it is better to wait until it is available rather than risk personal injury and/or damage to components by continuing alone. By planning ahead and taking your time, a job of this nature, although major, can be accomplished successfully and without incident.

On all models described in this manual, the engine and transmission are removed as a complete assembly downwards from the engine compartment.

2 Engine and transmission - removal, separation, connection and refitting

Note 1: *The engine is lowered from the engine compartment as a complete unit with the transmission; the two are then separated for overhaul.*

Note 2: *On 1.2 and 1.8 litre models with air conditioning, the air conditioning system must be discharged before the engine is removed. This work MUST be carried out by a FIAT dealer or air conditioning specialist, and it is advisable to have this done before starting to remove the engine.*

Removal

1 Select a solid, level surface to park the

vehicle upon. Give yourself enough space to move around it easily. Apply the handbrake, and securely chock the rear wheels as an added precaution - the front of the car has to be raised significantly to withdraw the engine, so the car will be at quite an angle.

2 On models not fitted with alloy wheels, remove the front wheel trims and loosen the driveshaft nuts. The nuts are tightened to a very high torque, so only use good-quality, close-fitting tools to loosen them. This task is most safely performed while the front wheels are still on the ground. Leave the nuts in place, hand-tight.

3 Depressurise the fuel system as described in the relevant part of Chapter 4.

4 Remove the battery as described in Chapter 5A.

5 Where applicable, unscrew the nuts and disconnect any additional wiring attached to the battery positive terminal, noting its location for refitting.

6 On 1.6 litre models, remove the engine management ECU as described in Chapter 4B, Section 4.

7 Remove the plastic drip tray from the main battery tray, disconnecting the drain tube from it. Remove the fuse/relay carrier from the battery tray, labelling and disconnecting the wiring plugs as necessary **(see illustrations)**.

8 Unscrew the bolts securing the battery tray to the body, and remove the tray from the engine compartment **(see illustration)**.

9 Drain the cooling system as described in Chapter 1.

10 Disconnect the hoses from the radiator, expansion tank and thermostat housing. At

the rear of the engine compartment, disconnect the hoses leading through the bulkhead to the heater. Label any hose whose fitted location is not obvious.

11 To improve working room, remove the two bolts securing the air intake at the front of the engine compartment, and lift the intake out of position, detaching it from the intake duct.

12 To avoid any possibility of damage to the radiator as the engine is removed, refer to Chapter 3 and remove the radiator.

13 Loosen the hose clips and disconnect the air duct which runs from the air cleaner to the inlet manifold; also disconnect any associated breather pipes.

14 Taking precautions against fuel spillage, disconnect the fuel supply and return connections with reference to the relevant part of Chapter 4.

15 Again referring to Chapter 4, disconnect the fuel injection wiring from the throttle body or fuel rail.

16 Disconnect the LT wiring plug from the ignition coil assembly **(see illustration)**. On 1.8 litre models, refer to Chapter 5B and unbolt the coil wiring harness from the cylinder head; disconnect the harness at the large wiring connector at the left-hand end of the cylinder head.

17 Disconnect the accelerator cable as described in the relevant part of Chapter 4.

18 Trace the (blue) pipes from the charcoal canister (mounted in the right-hand rear corner of the engine compartment, or under the right-hand wheel arch), and disconnect the pipes at the connections on the inner wing **(see illustration)**.

2.8 Removing the battery tray

2.16 Disconnecting the LT wiring plug

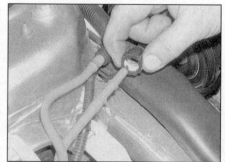

2.18 Disconnecting the charcoal canister pipes

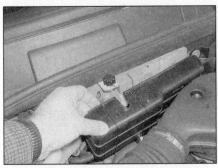

2.20a Removing the cover from the bulkhead fuse/relay bracket

2.20b On 1.4 litre models, disconnect the ECU multi-plug

2.21a On 1.4 litre models, disconnect the flexible hot-air duct . . .

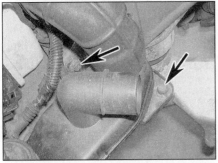

2.21b . . . then remove the mounting bolts (arrowed) and remove the air inlet elbow from the inner wing

2.22a Disconnecting the reversing light switch . . .

2.22b . . . and the earth lead at the front of the transmission

19 Disconnect the vacuum pipe from the brake servo.

20 At the engine compartment bulkhead, loosen the screw and remove the plastic cover

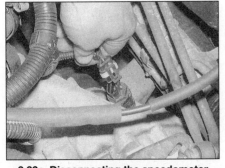

2.22c Disconnecting the speedometer wiring plug

from the relay carrier bracket. Labelling the wiring if necessary, disconnect the wiring plugs from the relays and other components. On 1.4 litre models, also disconnect the ECU wiring plug from the bulkhead **(see illustrations)**.

21 On 1.4 litre models, disconnect the hot-air flexible duct from the shroud over the exhaust manifold. To make room for the engine to be removed, unbolt the air inlet elbow from the right-hand inner wing **(see illustrations)**.

22 On manual transmission models, carry out the following:

a) *Disconnect the reversing light switch, earth lead and reverse gear inhibitor cable (as applicable) from the transmission housing, noting their locations* **(see illustrations)**.

b) *Disconnect the speedometer wiring plug from the rear of the transmission* **(see illustration)**.

c) *On models with a cable clutch, disconnect the clutch cable from the transmission (refer to Chapter 6).*

d) *On models with a hydraulic clutch, unbolt the clutch slave cylinder from the top of the transmission, then fit a cable-tie around it to prevent the piston coming out. Position the cylinder to one side* **(see illustrations)**.

e) *Disconnect the gearchange control cables and rods, referring to Chapter 7A as necessary. Details vary according to model, but dismantling procedures are self-evident. Disconnecting the cable end fittings either involves prising off the ball-and-socket joint, or unscrewing the through-bolt and nut* **(see illustrations)**. *Mark the components if necessary, to aid refitting.*

f) *Drain the transmission oil using the information in Chapter 7A* **(see illustration)**.

2.22d Unbolt the clutch slave cylinder . . .

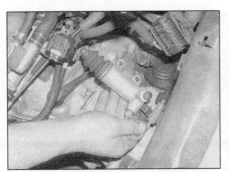

2.22e . . . and move it to one side

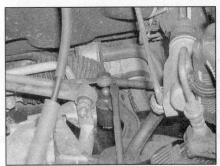

2.22f Prising off the ball-and-socket joint, using a screwdriver

2.22g Unscrew the through-bolt and nut . . .

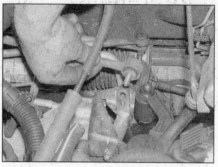

2.22h . . . and separate the gearchange rods

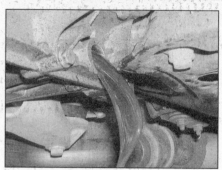

2.22i Draining the transmission oil

23 On automatic transmission models, carry out the following:
a) *Remove the three bolts securing the selector cable mounting bracket to the top of the transmission, prise off the cable end fitting, and move the bracket aside (see illustration).*
b) *Disconnect the earth lead from below the transmission selector lever (see illustration).*
c) *Disconnect the three wiring plugs in the immediate vicinity of the transmission.*
d) *Disconnect the speedometer wiring plug from the rear of the transmission.*
e) *Unbolt the pipe and wiring harness support bracket fitted just behind the transmission selector lever.*
f) *Drain the transmission fluid as described in Chapter 7B, Section 2.*

24 Where applicable, prise up the cover over the starter motor. Disconnect the starter motor wiring, noting the location of each wire, and the fitted sequence of the nuts and washers **(see illustration)**.
25 Drain or syphon the fluid from the power steering reservoir, then refer to Chapter 10, Section 22, and disconnect the fluid pipes (and wiring, where applicable) from the power steering pump, taking precautions against further fluid spillage. Cover the pump connections, to prevent the ingress of dirt. On some models (such as those with the 1.6 litre engine), it is possible to unbolt the steering pump from the engine, and leave it in the engine compartment.
26 On 1.8 litre models, carry out the following:
a) *Unbolt the power steering fluid reservoir*

from the bulkhead, and tie it to the engine for removal.
b) *Disconnect the oxygen sensor wiring from the clip at the front of the thermostat housing. Trace the wiring back to the wiring plug, and disconnect it.*
c) *Unbolt the engine oil dipstick from the exhaust manifold.*
d) *Where applicable, have the air conditioning system discharged by a FIAT dealer or suitable specialist.*
e) *Pull up the weatherstrip from the rear of the engine compartment, then remove the four screws securing the section of plastic scuttle panel on the passenger side. To remove the panel, it will also be necessary to remove the passenger wiper blade.*
f) *Remove the glovebox as described in Chapter 11. Working in the glovebox aperture, disconnect the wiring plugs from the engine management ECU, and from the various relays, etc, marking each as necessary for position. Approximately eight plugs must be disconnected, according to model. Feed the wiring harness through the aperture created by removing the plastic scuttle panel, into the engine compartment, and tie it to the engine.*

27 If not already done, loosen the front wheel bolts, then jack up the front of the car and support it on axle stands. Remove the front wheels. Note that the car must (eventually, if not now) be raised to a sufficient height that the engine/transmission can be removed from below.
28 Locate the oxygen sensor at the top of the exhaust downpipe, immediately below the exhaust manifold. Trace the wiring from the sensor back to its wiring plug, and disconnect it.
29 Referring to Chapter 4C as required, loosen the bolts securing the exhaust downpipe to the catalytic converter.
30 Remove the manifold-to-downpipe nuts, and separate the downpipe from the manifold **(see illustration)**. In some cases, the manifold studs will come out with the nuts - this poses no great problem, and the studs can be refitted if they are in good condition. For preference, however, a complete set of studs and nuts should be obtained as required, as the old ones are likely to be in less-than-perfect condition.

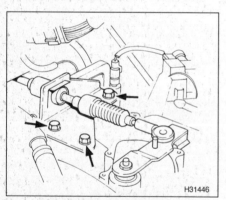

2.23a Remove the selector cable mounting bracket bolts (arrowed)

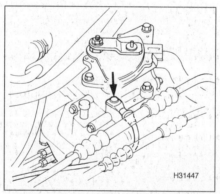

2.23b Disconnect the transmission earth lead

2.24 Disconnecting the starter motor wiring

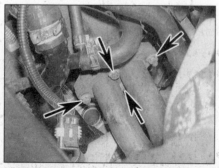

2.30 Exhaust manifold-to-downpipe nuts (arrowed)

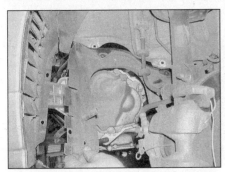

2.33 Removing the left-hand wheelarch inner access panel

2.34 Separating a track rod end balljoint

2.35 Pull the brake hose from the clip on the suspension strut

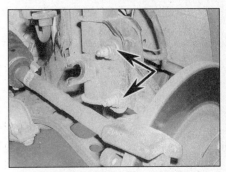

2.36 Suspension strut-to-swivel hub securing nuts (arrowed)

31 Remove the exhaust downpipe-to-catalytic converter bolts, and remove the downpipe from under the car. Take care while the downpipe is removed that the oxygen sensor is not knocked - it is fragile. Also, if necessary, tie the catalytic converter up at the front, to support it while the downpipe is removed.

32 If not already done, loosen the driveshaft nuts. The nuts are tightened to a very high torque, so only use good-quality, close-fitting tools to loosen them. If the job is being done with the car raised, make sure that it is securely supported, as considerable force may be needed to loosen the nuts.

33 To improve access to the suspension components and the driveshafts, remove the access panels fitted in the inner wheel arch liners. It will be necessary on most models to remove the front section of the liner, as well as the inner section. The access panels are secured by a combination of bolts and plastic studs (see illustration). It may be necessary to disconnect the brake pad wear sensor wiring to remove the panels.

34 Unscrew the nuts retaining the track rod ends on the swivel hubs, and use a balljoint separator tool to disconnect them (see illustration).

35 Release the flexible brake fluid hoses and ABS/pad wear sensor wiring from the front suspension struts (see illustration).

36 Unscrew the two nuts/bolts securing the right-hand swivel hub assembly to the front suspension strut, then move the hub assembly outwards, taking care not to strain

the flexible brake hose (see illustration). Release the outer end of the driveshaft from the hub assembly.

37 Move the driveshaft to one side, then temporarily refit the hub assembly to the strut. Note that it is not recommended to allow the driveshaft to hang down under its own weight, or to turn the inner or outer joints through too acute an angle, or the joints may separate and be damaged.

38 Disconnect the left-hand driveshaft using the procedure described in paragraphs 36 and 37.

39 On 1.6 litre models, remove the three bolts securing the inner end of the left-hand driveshaft (see illustration). At the inner end of the right-hand driveshaft, release the inner CV boot from the transmission.

40 On 1.8 litre models, loosen and remove the socket-headed flange bolts securing the inner ends of the driveshafts (see illustration).

41 Using a suitable flat-bladed tool between the driveshaft inner joint and the transmission housing as necessary, prise out and separate the inner ends of the driveshafts from the transmission (see illustration). Be prepared for oil or fluid spillage if the transmission was not drained. Remove the driveshafts from under the car.

42 On automatic transmission models, loosen the union nuts and disconnect the fluid pipes at the side of the transmission. Again, be prepared for fluid spillage. Move the pipes out of the way, so that they are not damaged as the engine is lowered.

43 At this stage, the front of the car must be raised sufficiently to allow the engine/transmission assembly to be lowered and removed from under the front of the car. This will entail raising the car much higher than would normally be the case for most servicing work. Do not, however, be tempted to use makeshift means of support - before proceeding further, make sure the car is stable.

44 Connect a hoist and raise it so that the weight of the engine and transmission are just supported. Arrange the hoist and sling so that the engine and transmission are kept level when they are being withdrawn from the vehicle.

45 Unscrew and remove the engine and transmission mountings, referring to the relevant Part of Chapter 2 as necessary. Where possible, leave the bonded rubber mountings attached to the support points; this

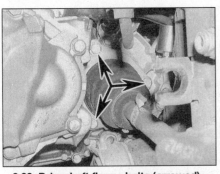

2.39 Driveshaft flange bolts (arrowed) - 1.6 litre model

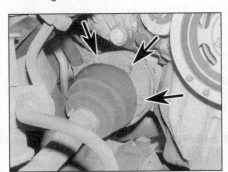

2.40 Driveshaft flange bolts on a 1.8 litre model

2.41 Using a large flat-bladed screwdriver to separate the driveshaft inner ends from the transmission

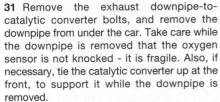

2.48a As the engine is lowered, guide it past the subframe

2.48b Lowering the engine out of the car

2.61 Apply grease to the transmission input shaft splines

will avoid the need for realignment during refitting. On models fitted with a reaction rod on the right-hand mounting, the rod should be removed completely, to make engine removal easier.

46 Check around the engine and transmission assembly from above and below, to ensure that all associated attachments are disconnected and positioned out of the way. Engage the services of an assistant to help in guiding the assembly clear of surrounding components.

47 Consider how the engine will be removed from under the car, before lowering it. If a wheeled trolley is available, this makes the task of moving the engine much easier. If the engine is dropped onto its sump, the sump may be damaged; a piece of old foam or carpet will offer some protection. If the engine is lowered onto a piece of carpet or a sheet of wood, this can be used to drag the engine out from under the car, without damage.

48 Carefully lower the engine/transmission assembly clear of the mountings, guiding the assembly past any obstructions, and taking care that surrounding components are not damaged. Remove the assembly from the front of the car **(see illustrations)**.

49 Once the engine/transmission assembly is clear of the vehicle, move it to an area where it can be cleaned and worked on.

Separation

50 Rest the engine and transmission assembly on a firm, flat surface, and use

wooden blocks as wedges to keep the unit steady.

51 Note the routing and location of any wiring on the engine/transmission assembly, then methodically disconnect it.

52 Remove the starter motor (Chapter 5A).

53 Unscrew the remaining bolts and remove the transmission lower cover.

Manual transmission models

54 Support the transmission with blocks of wood. The transmission is secured to the engine by a combination of bolts, and studs and nuts. A locating dowel is fitted to the top bolt location. Unscrew the transmission-to-engine nuts and bolts, noting their locations.

55 Lift the transmission directly from the engine, taking care to keep it level so that the transmission input shaft does not hang on the clutch. Recover the backplate, which will fall out as the engine and transmission are separated.

56 Refer to Chapter 6, and remove the clutch release mechanism, pressure plate and friction plate.

Automatic transmission models

57 Mark the position of the torque converter with respect to the driveplate, using chalk or a marker pen. Remove the six socket-head bolts that secure the driveplate to the torque converter; turn the engine over using a socket and wrench on the crankshaft sprocket to rotate the driveplate and expose each nut in turn.

58 The transmission is secured to the engine by ten bolts of three different lengths - note

their positions as they are removed.

59 Starting at the bottom, remove all the bolts, then carefully draw the transmission away from the engine, resting it securely on wooden blocks. Recover the backplate, which will fall out as the engine and transmission are separated.

Caution: Take care to prevent the torque converter from sliding off the transmission input shaft - hold it in place as the transmission is withdrawn.

60 Place a length of batten across the open face of the bellhousing, fastening it with cable-ties, to keep the torque converter in place in its housing.

Reconnection

Manual transmission models

61 Smear a little high-melting-point grease on the splines of the transmission input shaft **(see illustration)**. Do not use an excessive amount, as there is the risk of contaminating the clutch friction plate.

62 Refit the backplate, then carefully offer up the transmission to the cylinder block, guiding it onto the dowel **(see illustrations)**.

63 Refit the bellhousing bolts and nuts, hand-tightening them to secure the transmission in position **(see illustration)**. **Note:** *Do not tighten them to force the engine and transmission together.* Ensure that the bellhousing and cylinder block mating faces will butt together evenly without obstruction, before tightening the bolts and nuts fully.

2.62a Refitting the backplate

2.62b To ease fitting, apply a little grease to the locating dowel

2.62c Fitting the transmission back on the engine

Automatic transmission models

64 Remove the torque converter restraint from the face of the bellhousing. Check that the torque converter is still fully engaged with the transmission fluid pump.

65 Refit the backplate, then carefully offer up the transmission to the cylinder block. Observe the markings made during the removal, to ensure correct alignment between the torque converter and the driveplate.

66 Refit the bellhousing bolts to the positions noted on removal, hand-tightening them to secure the transmission in position. **Note:** *Do not tighten them to force the engine and transmission together.* Ensure that the bellhousing and cylinder block mating faces will butt together evenly without obstruction, before tightening the bolts and nuts fully.

All models

67 Refit the transmission lower cover, tightening the bolts securely.

68 Refit the starter motor, referring to Chapter 5A if necessary.

69 Reconnect any wiring on the engine/transmission assembly, routing it as noted on removal.

Refitting

70 Manoeuvre the engine and transmission into place under the front of the car.

71 Attach the hoist or engine support bar to the engine.

72 With the help of an assistant, carefully lift the assembly up into the engine compartment and onto the engine mountings, taking care not to damage the surrounding components.

73 Reconnect the engine/transmission mountings, and tighten the nuts and bolts.

74 When the engine is securely reconnected, disconnect the hoist from the engine.

75 The remainder of the refitting procedure is the direct reverse of the removal procedure, noting the following points:

a) *Ensure that all sections of the wiring harness follow their original routing; use new cable-ties to secure the harness in position, keeping it away from sources of heat and abrasion.*

b) *On vehicles with manual transmission, check and if necessary adjust the gearchange linkage with reference to Chapter 7A.*

c) *On vehicles with automatic transmission, check and if necessary adjust the kick-down and selector cables with reference to Chapter 7B.*

d) *Ensure that all hoses are correctly routed and are secured with the correct hose clips, where applicable. If the hose clips cannot be used again; proprietary worm-drive clips should be fitted in their place.*

e) *Refill the cooling system as described in Chapter 1.*

f) *Refill the engine with appropriate grade and quantity of oil (Chapter 1).*

g) *Refill or top-up the transmission oil or fluid (see Chapter 1 or Chapter 7).*

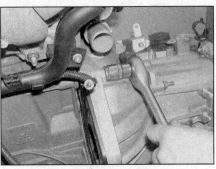

2.63 Fit and tighten the engine-to-bellhousing bolts

h) *Check and if necessary adjust the auxiliary drivebelt(s) with reference to Chapter 1.*

i) *Check and if necessary adjust the accelerator cable with reference to Chapter 4.*

j) *When the engine is started for the first time, check for air, coolant, lubricant and fuel leaks from manifolds, hoses etc. If the engine has been overhauled, read the notes in Section 12 before attempting to start it.*

3 Engine overhaul - preliminary information

It is much easier to dismantle and work on the engine if it is mounted on a portable engine stand. These stands can often be hired from a tool hire shop. Before the engine is mounted on a stand, the flywheel should be removed, so that the stand bolts can be tightened into the end of the cylinder block/crankcase.

If a stand is not available, it is possible to dismantle the engine with it blocked up on a sturdy workbench, or on the floor. Be very careful not to tip or drop the engine when working without a stand.

If you intend to obtain a reconditioned engine, all ancillaries must be removed first, to be transferred to the replacement engine (just as they will if you are doing a complete engine overhaul yourself). These components include the following:

a) *Power steering pump if removed with the engine (Chapter 10).*

b) *Air conditioning compressor (Chapter 3) - where applicable.*

c) *Alternator (including mounting brackets) and starter motor (Chapter 5A).*

d) *The ignition system and HT components including all sensors, HT leads (where applicable) and spark plugs (Chapters 1 and 5).*

e) *The fuel injection system components (Chapter 4A and 4B).*

f) *All electrical switches, actuators and sensors, and the engine wiring harness (Chapter 4A and 4B, and Chapter 5B).*

g) *Inlet and exhaust manifolds (Chapter 4).*

h) *Engine oil dipstick and tube (relevant Part of Chapter 2).*

i) *Engine mountings (relevant Part of Chapter 2).*

j) *Flywheel/driveplate (relevant Part of Chapter 2).*

k) *Clutch components (Chapter 6) - manual transmission.*

l) *Coolant pump (Chapter 3).*

Note: *When removing the external components from the engine, pay close attention to details that may be helpful or important during refitting. Note the fitted position of gaskets, seals, spacers, pins, washers, bolts, and other small components.*

If you are obtaining a 'short' engine (the engine cylinder block/crankcase, crankshaft, pistons and connecting rods), all fully assembled), then the cylinder head, sump, oil pump, timing belt (together with its tensioner, guide pulleys and covers), auxiliary belt(s), coolant pump, thermostat housing, and coolant outlet elbows (as applicable) will also have to be removed.

If you are planning a full overhaul, the engine can be dismantled in the order given below:

a) *Flywheel/driveplate.*

b) *Timing belt, sprockets, and tensioner.*

c) *Inlet and exhaust manifolds.*

d) *Cylinder head.*

e) *Sump.*

f) *Oil pump.*

g) *Pistons and crankshaft.*

4 Cylinder head - dismantling, cleaning, inspection and reassembly

Note 1: *New and reconditioned cylinder heads are available from the manufacturer or engine overhaul specialists. Be aware that some specialist tools are required for the dismantling and inspection procedures, and new components may not be readily available. It may therefore be more practical and economical for the home mechanic to purchase a reconditioned head, rather than dismantle, inspect and recondition the original head.*

Note 2: *On 1.2 and 1.6 litre engines, camshaft and tappet removal is described in Chapter 2A or 2C respectively.*

Dismantling

1 On 1.4 and 1.8 litre engines, remove the camshaft sprocket with reference to Chapter 2B or 2D.

2 Remove the cylinder head as described in the relevant Part of this Chapter.

3 If not already done, remove the inlet and exhaust manifolds with reference to the relevant Part of Chapter 4.

4 Unbolt and remove the ignition coil mounting.

4.7 Mark the camshaft bearing caps for position and orientation - 1.4 litre engine shown

4.8a Unbolt the oil feed pipe . . .

4.8b . . . then prise out the oil feed stub (location arrowed) and remove it

5 On 1.2 litre engines, unscrew the coolant temperature sensor from the thermostat housing on the left-hand end of the cylinder head. Unbolt and remove the thermostat housing, and recover the gasket.

1.4 and 1.8 litre engines

6 Unbolt and remove the coolant pump from the right-hand end of the cylinder head, and recover the gasket.
7 Mark the positions of the camshaft bearing caps, numbering them from the timing end, and marking them so they are refitted the right way round (on 1.4 litre engines, the curved surface on the caps faces the rear) **(see illustration)**.
8 On 1.4 litre engines, unbolt and remove the lubrication pipe (prise the oil feed stub out with a screwdriver). Recover the oil feed pipe seals which fit into the cylinder head - new

4.8c Recover the oil feed pipe oil seals

seals must be fitted on completion **(see illustrations)**.
9 Unscrew the remaining bolts and take off the bearing caps **(see illustration)**.
10 Lift the camshaft(s) carefully from the cylinder head, checking that the hydraulic tappets (and followers on 1.4 litre engines) are not withdrawn by the 'adhesion' of the oil **(see illustration)**. On 1.4 litre engines, note that the pair of inlet valves per cylinder are operated by the wider camshaft lobes.
11 Remove the hydraulic tappets (and followers on 1.4 litre engines), but keep them in their originally fitted order. Stand the hydraulic tappets in an oil bath, so that the oil does not drain from them.

All engines

12 Stand the cylinder head on its end. Using a valve spring compressor, compress each valve spring in turn, extracting the split collets when the upper valve spring seat has been pushed far enough down the valve stem to free them. If the spring seat sticks, lightly tap the upper jaw of the spring compressor with a hammer to free it.
13 Release the valve spring compressor and remove the upper spring seat, valve spring(s), and lower spring seat. The 1.2 and 1.4 litre engines have one spring per valve - the other engines have two; note how they are fitted. Also identify the upper and lower spring seats, to avoid confusion on refitting.
14 Withdraw the valve from the head gasket side of the cylinder head, then use a pair of pliers to extract the valve stem oil seal from

the top of the guide. If the valve sticks in the guide, carefully deburr the end face with fine abrasive paper. Repeat this process for the remaining valves.
15 It is essential that each valve is stored together with its collets, spring(s), and spring seats. The valves should also be kept in their correct sequence, unless they are so badly worn that they are to be renewed. If they are going to be kept and used again, place each valve assembly in a labelled polythene bag or similar small container, labelled as follows **(see illustration)**:

a) No 1 valve is at the timing end of the engine.
b) On 1.4 litre engines, there are two inlet valves per cylinder - the inlet valves are smaller than the exhaust valve, and are operated by the wider camshaft lobes. Number the inlet valves 1 to 8, the exhaust valves 1 to 4.
c) On 1.2 and 1.8 litre engines, exhaust valves are at the front, inlet valves at the rear. Number the inlet and exhaust valves 1 to 8.
d) On 1.6 litre engines, inlet valves are at the front, exhaust valves at the rear. Number the inlet and exhaust valves 1 to 8.

Cleaning

16 Using a suitable degreasing agent, remove all traces of oil deposits from the cylinder head, paying particular attention to the journal bearings, valve follower bores, valve guides and oilways. Scrape off any traces of old gasket from the mating surfaces,

4.9 Removing one of the camshaft bearing caps

4.10 Lifting out the camshaft on a 1.4 litre engine

4.15 Keep the valve components together in a labelled bag or box

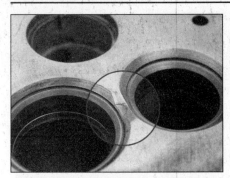

4.20 Look for cracking between the valve seats

4.21 Measuring the distortion of the cylinder head gasketed surface

4.23a Measure the deflection of the valve in its guide, using a dial gauge

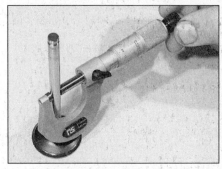

4.23b Measuring the diameter of a valve stem

taking care not to score or gouge them. If using emery paper, do not use a grade of less than 100. Turn the head over and using a blunt blade, scrape any carbon deposits from the combustion chambers and ports.

Caution: Do not erode the sealing surface of the valve seat.

17 Finally, wash the entire head casting with a suitable solvent to remove the remaining debris.

18 Clean the valve heads and stems using a fine wire brush. If the valve is heavily coked, scrape off the majority of the deposits with a blunt blade first, then use the wire brush.

Caution: Do not erode the sealing surface of the valve face.

19 Thoroughly clean the remainder of the components using solvent, and allow them to dry completely. Discard the oil seals, as new items must be fitted when the cylinder head is reassembled.

Inspection

Cylinder head

20 Inspect the head very carefully for cracks, evidence of coolant leakage, and other damage **(see illustration)**. If cracks are found, a new cylinder head should be obtained.

21 Use a straight-edge and feeler blade to check that the cylinder head gasket surface is not distorted **(see illustration)**. If it is, it may be possible to have it machined (skimmed), provided not too much material is removed. Minimum head heights are not quoted by FIAT, so seek the advice of an engine overhaul specialist.

22 Examine the valve seats in each of the combustion chambers. If they are severely pitted, cracked, or burned, they will need to be renewed or re-cut by an engine overhaul specialist. If they are only slightly pitted, this can be removed by grinding-in the valve heads and seats with fine valve-grinding compound, as described below.

23 Check the valve guides for wear by inserting the relevant valve, and checking for side-to-side motion of the valve. A very small amount of movement is acceptable. If the movement seems excessive, remove the valve. Measure the valve stem diameter at several points, and renew the valve if it is worn **(see illustrations)**. If the valve stem is not worn, the wear must be in the valve guide, and the guide must be renewed. The renewal of valve guides is best carried out by an engine overhaul specialist, who will have the necessary tools available.

24 If renewing the valve guides, the valve seats should be re-cut or re-ground only *after* the guides have been fitted.

Camshaft(s), tappets and followers - 1.4 and 1.8 litre engines

25 Inspect the camshaft(s) for wear on the surfaces of the lobes and journals. Normally their surfaces should be smooth and have a dull shine; look for scoring and pitting. Accelerated wear will occur once the hardened exterior of the camshaft has been damaged **(see illustration)**.

26 Examine the bearing cap and journal surfaces for signs of wear **(see illustration)**.

27 If excessive cam lobe wear is noted, examine the relevant tappet and/or follower(s) for similar signs of wear. It is advisable to renew the camshaft, tappets (and followers, on the 1.4 litre engine) as a set, even if only one lobe is worn; this is particularly true if the car has completed a large mileage.

28 To measure the camshaft endfloat, temporarily refit the camshaft, then push the camshaft to one end of the cylinder head as far as it will travel. Attach a dial test indicator to the cylinder head and zero it, then push the camshaft as far as it will go to the other end of the cylinder head and record the gauge reading **(see illustration)**. Verify the reading by pushing the camshaft back to its original position and checking that the gauge indicates zero again.

29 The camshaft bearing running clearance may be checked using Plastigauge as described later in this Chapter.

4.25 An example of a badly-worn camshaft lobe

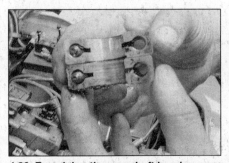

4.26 Examining the camshaft bearing caps - the top one is fine, the bottom one is badly worn

4.28 Checking the camshaft endfloat using a dial gauge

4.37 Grinding-in a valve

4.41 Checking the squareness of a valve spring

4.43a Fit the lower spring seat . . .

30 Where the camshaft and bearings are worn excessively, consider renewing the complete cylinder head together with camshaft(s), tappets (and followers, on the 1.4 litre engine). A reconditioned head may be available from engine repairers. Tappet (and/or follower) wear serious enough to warrant new components will be obvious on inspection.

31 On 1.4 litre engines, clean out the camshaft oil feed pipe assembly before refitting. This can be achieved using an aerosol can of engine degreasant, or carburettor cleaner. Make sure the solvent is drained off before the pipe is refitted.

Valves and associated components

32 Examine the head of each valve for pitting, burning, cracks, and general wear. Check the valve stem for scoring and wear ridges. Rotate the valve, and check for any obvious indication that it is bent. Look for pits or excessive wear on the tip of each valve stem. Renew any valve that shows any such signs of wear or damage.

33 If the valve appears satisfactory at this stage, measure the valve stem diameter at several points using a micrometer. Any significant difference in the readings obtained indicates wear of the valve stem. Should any of these conditions be apparent, the valve(s) must be renewed.

34 If the valves are in satisfactory condition, they should be ground (lapped) into their respective seats, to ensure a smooth, gastight seal. To complete this process, you will need a quantity of fine/coarse grinding paste

and a grinding tool - this can either be of the dowel and rubber sucker type, or the automatic type which are driven by a rotary power tool.

35 If the seat is only lightly pitted, or if it has been re-cut, fine grinding compound *only* should be used to produce the required finish. Coarse valve-grinding compound should *not* be used, unless a seat is badly burned or deeply pitted. If this is the case, the cylinder head and valves should be inspected by an expert, to decide whether seat re-cutting, or even the renewal of the valve or seat insert (where possible) is required.

36 Valve grinding is carried out as follows. Place the cylinder head upside-down on a bench.

37 Smear a trace of (the appropriate grade of) valve-grinding compound on the seat face, and attach the grinding tool onto the valve head. With a semi-rotary action, grind the valve head to its seat, lifting the valve occasionally to redistribute the grinding compound **(see illustration)**. A light spring placed under the valve head will greatly ease this operation.

38 If coarse grinding compound is being used, work only until a dull, matt even surface is produced on both the valve seat and the valve, then wipe off the used compound, and repeat the process with fine compound. When a smooth unbroken ring of light grey matt finish is produced on both the valve and seat, the grinding operation is complete. *Do not* grind-in the valves any further than absolutely necessary, or the seat will be prematurely

sunk into the cylinder head.

39 When all the valves have been ground-in, carefully wash off *all* traces of grinding compound using paraffin or a suitable solvent, before reassembling the cylinder head.

40 Examine the valve springs for signs of damage and discoloration. If possible, compare the length of the springs with new ones, and renew them if necessary.

41 Stand each spring on a flat surface, and check it for squareness **(see illustration)**. If any of the springs are damaged, distorted or have lost their tension, obtain a complete new set of springs. It is normal to renew the valve springs as a matter of course if a major overhaul is being carried out.

42 Renew the valve stem oil seals regardless of their apparent condition.

Reassembly

43 Refit the lower spring seat then, working on the first valve, dip the new valve stem seal in fresh engine oil. Carefully locate it onto the guide. Take care not to damage the seal as it is passed over the valve stem. Use a suitable socket or metal tube to press the seal firmly onto the guide **(see illustrations)**.

44 Lubricate the stems of the valves, and insert the valves into their original locations **(see illustration)**. If new valves are being fitted, insert them into the locations to which they have been ground.

45 Locate the valve spring (or the inner and outer springs, on 1.6 and 1.8 litre engines) on top of the lower seat, then refit the upper spring seat **(see illustrations)**.

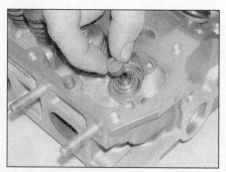

4.43b . . . then the valve stem oil seal . . .

4.43c . . . pressing the seal home using a deep socket

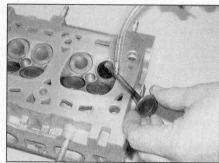

4.44 Oil the valve stems before fitting

4.45a Locate the inner . . .

4.45b . . . and outer valve springs
(1.6 litre engine shown) . . .

4.45c . . . then fit the upper spring seat

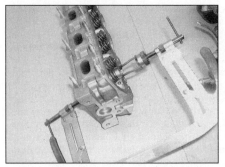

4.46a Fit the valve spring compressor . . .

4.46b . . . then insert the split collets, using
a small screwdriver to guide them in

4.47 Using a hide mallet to settle the valve
components

46 Compress the valve spring(s), and locate the split collets in the recess in the valve stem **(see illustrations)**. Release the compressor, then repeat the procedure on the remaining valves.

HAYNES HiNT *Use a dab of grease to hold the collets in position on the valve stem while the spring compressor is released.*

47 With all the valves installed, place the cylinder head flat on the bench and, using a hammer and interposed block of wood (or a hide mallet), tap the end of each valve stem to settle the components **(see illustration)**.

1.4 and 1.8 litre engines

48 Fit the hydraulic tappets (to their original positions, if they were not renewed). On 1.4 litre engines, similarly refit the followers **(see illustrations)**. Lubricate all components with fresh oil as they are fitted.
49 Oil the journals, then locate the camshaft(s) in the cylinder head. The cam lobes of No 1 cylinder should be facing upwards (ie No 1 cylinder at TDC).
50 Refit the bearing caps in their correct positions, together with new camshaft oil seal(s). On 1.4 litre engines, locate the lubrication pipe and new end seals on the head, and press in the oil feed stub before refitting the bolts. Tighten the bearing cap bolts by a quarter-turn at a time, to the specified torque.
51 On the 1.4 litre engine, FIAT state that the camshaft should be turned so that each of the

hydraulic tappets is held fully compressed for 15 minutes - this will bleed any air from the tappets, which would otherwise impair their correct operation when the engine is eventually started.
52 Refit the coolant pump, using a new gasket. Refer to Chapter 3 as necessary.

All engines

53 Further refitting is a reversal of the relevant removal procedure.

---

5 Pistons and connecting rods
- removal, inspection, and big-end running clearance check

Removal

1 Remove the sump and oil pump pick-up with reference to the relevant Part of Chapter 2.

4.48a On 1.4 litre engines, refit the
hydraulic tappets . . .

On 1.6 litre engines, remove the oil pump completely, as described in Chapter 2C.
2 The big-end bearing shells can be renewed without having to remove the cylinder head, if the caps are unbolted and the piston/connecting rod pushed gently about one inch up the bore (the crankpin being at its lowest point). If these shells are worn, however, the main bearing shells will almost certainly be worn as well. In this case, the crankshaft should be removed for inspection.
3 To remove the pistons and connecting rods, remove the cylinder head first, as described in the relevant Part of Chapter 2.
4 On the 1.2 litre engine, to improve access, remove the ten bolts securing the vibration damping plate to the main bearing caps, and remove the plate, noting which way round it fits.
5 The big-end caps and the connecting rods should be numbered 1, 2, 3 and 4 from the

4.48b . . . and followers

5.5 No 3 connecting rod and bearing cap markings

5.11a Using a feeler blade to remove the second compression ring

5.11b Removing the oil scraper expander ring

timing belt cover end of the engine. Note which side the marks appear, relative to the front- or rear-facing side of the engine, for use when refitting. If no marks are present, make your own marks using a centre-punch **(see illustration)**.

6 Turn the crankshaft as necessary to bring the first crankpin to its lowest point, then unscrew the bolts (or nuts, on the 1.6 litre engine) and remove the big-end cap and shell bearing.

7 On the 1.6 litre engine, wrap a piece of tape around the big-end cap bolts (which remain in the connecting rod). The tape is intended to prevent the bolt threads from scratching the crankshaft journals as the connecting rods are removed.

8 Push the piston/rod assembly up the bore and out of the cylinder block. There is one reservation; if a wear ridge has developed at the top of the bores, remove this by careful scraping before trying to remove the piston/rod assemblies. The ridge will otherwise prevent removal, or will break the piston rings during the attempt.

9 Remove the remaining pistons/rods in a similar way. If the bearing shells are to be used again, tape them to their respective caps or rods.

Inspection

10 Before the inspection process can begin, the piston/connecting rod assemblies must be cleaned, and the original piston rings removed from the pistons.

11 Carefully expand the old rings over the top of the pistons. The use of two or three old

5.15 Piston size class marking (arrowed) on underside of piston

feeler blades will be helpful in preventing the rings dropping into empty grooves. Be careful not to scratch the piston with the ends of the ring. The rings are brittle, and will snap if they are spread too far. They are also very sharp - protect your hands and fingers. Always remove the rings from the top of the piston. Keep each set of rings with its piston if the old rings are to be re-used. Note the fitted order of all components, which ring is fitted to which groove, and which way up each is fitted **(see illustrations)**.

12 Scrape away all traces of carbon from the top of the piston. A hand-held wire brush (or a piece of fine emery cloth) can be used, once the majority of the deposits have been scraped away.

13 Remove the carbon from the ring grooves in the piston, using an old ring. Break the ring in half to do this (be careful not to cut your fingers - piston rings are sharp). Be careful to remove only the carbon deposits - do not remove any metal, and do not nick or scratch the sides of the ring grooves.

14 Once the deposits have been removed, clean the piston/connecting rod assembly with paraffin or a suitable solvent, and dry thoroughly. Make sure that the oil return holes in the ring grooves are clear. Fit the rings to their respective grooves, making sure they are positioned the correct way round where applicable.

15 If the pistons and cylinder bores are not damaged or worn excessively, and if the cylinder block does not need to be rebored, the original pistons can be refitted **(see illustration)**. Normal piston wear shows up as even vertical wear on the piston thrust surfaces, and slight looseness of the top ring in its groove. New piston rings should always be used when the engine is reassembled.

16 Carefully inspect each piston for cracks around the skirt, around the gudgeon pin holes, and at the piston ring 'lands' (between the ring grooves).

17 Look for scoring and scuffing on the piston skirt, holes in the piston crown, and burned areas at the edge of the crown. If the skirt is scored or scuffed, the engine may have been suffering from overheating, and/or abnormal combustion which caused excessively high operating temperatures. The

cooling and lubrication systems should be checked thoroughly.

18 Scorch marks on the sides of the pistons show that piston ring blow-by has occurred. A hole in the piston crown, or burned areas at the edge of the piston crown, indicates that abnormal combustion has been occurring. If any of the above problems exist, the causes must be investigated and corrected, or the damage will occur again. The causes may include incorrect ignition timing, or a fuel system fault which has led to the engine running on too weak a fuel/air mixture.

19 Corrosion of the piston, in the form of pitting, indicates that coolant has been leaking into the combustion chamber and/or the crankcase. Again, the cause must be corrected, or the problem may persist in the rebuilt engine.

20 Examine each connecting rod carefully for signs of damage, such as cracks around the big-end and small-end bearings. Check that the rod is not bent or distorted. Damage is highly unlikely, unless the engine has been seized or badly overheated. Detailed checking of the connecting rod assembly can only be carried out by an engine repair specialist with the necessary equipment.

21 Although not essential, it is highly recommended that the big-end cap bolts (and nuts, on 1.6 litre engines) are renewed as a complete set prior to refitting. On 1.6 litre engines, the bolts can be tapped out of the connecting rods for renewal.

22 On 1.2 litre engines, piston and/or connecting rod renewal should be entrusted to an engine repair specialist, who will have the necessary facilities to remove and install the gudgeon pins. The gudgeon pins can only be removed or refitted after heating the pistons and connecting rods to 240°C.

23 On engines except the 1.2 litre, the gudgeon pins are of the floating type, secured in position by two circlips. On these engines, the pistons and connecting rods can be separated as follows.

24 Using a small flat-bladed screwdriver, prise out the circlips, and remove the gudgeon pin **(see illustrations)**. Identify the piston and rod to ensure correct reassembly. Discard the circlips - new ones *must* be used on refitting.

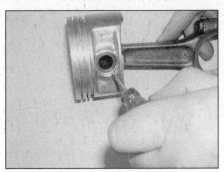

5.24a Using a small screwdriver . . .

5.24b . . . prise out the gudgeon pin circlip . . .

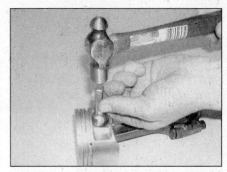

5.24c . . . and using a suitable socket if necessary . . .

25 Examine the gudgeon pin and connecting rod small-end bearing for signs of wear or damage. Bush renewal should be entrusted to an engine overhaul specialist.

26 The connecting rods themselves should not be in need of renewal, unless seizure or some other major mechanical failure has occurred. Check the alignment of the connecting rods visually, and if the rods are not straight, take them to an engine overhaul specialist for a more detailed check.

27 Examine all components, and obtain any new parts as necessary. If new pistons are purchased, they will be supplied complete with gudgeon pins and circlips.

28 On reassembly, position the piston on the connecting rod. Apply a smear of clean engine oil to the gudgeon pin. Slide it (or tap it) into the piston and through the connecting rod small-end. Check that the piston pivots freely on the rod, then secure the gudgeon pin in position with two new circlips. Ensure that each circlip is correctly located in its groove in the piston.

Refitting and big-end bearing running clearance check

29 Prior to refitting the piston/connecting rod assemblies, it is recommended that the big-end bearing running clearance is checked as follows.

Big-end bearing running clearance check

30 Clean the backs of the bearing shells, and the bearing locations in both the connecting rod and bearing cap.

31 Press the bearing shells into their locations, ensuring that the tab on each shell engages in the notch in the connecting rod and cap **(see illustrations)**. Take care not to touch any shell's bearing surface with your fingers. If the original bearing shells are being used for the check, ensure that they are refitted in their original locations. The clearance can be checked in either of two ways.

32 One method is to refit the big-end bearing cap to the connecting rod, ensuring that they are fitted the correct way around, with the bearing shells in place. With the cap retaining nuts/bolts correctly tightened, use an internal micrometer or vernier caliper to measure the internal diameter of each assembled pair of bearing shells. If the diameter of each corresponding crankshaft journal is measured and then subtracted from the bearing internal diameter, the result will be the big-end bearing running clearance.

33 The second, and more accurate method is to use a product called Plastigauge. Ensure that the bearing shells are correctly fitted, then place a strand of Plastigauge on each (cleaned) crankpin journal.

34 Refit the (clean) piston/connecting rod assemblies to the crankshaft, and refit the big-end bearing caps, using the marks made or noted on removal to ensure that they are fitted the correct way around.

35 Tighten the bearing cap nuts/bolts, taking care not to disturb the Plastigauge or rotate the connecting rod during the tightening sequence.

36 Dismantle the assemblies without rotating the connecting rods. Use the scale printed on the Plastigauge envelope to measure the crushed Plastigauge strand, and thus obtain the big-end bearing running clearance.

37 If the clearance is significantly different from that expected, the bearing shells may be the wrong size (or excessively worn, if the original shells are being re-used). Make sure that no dirt or oil was trapped between the bearing shells and the caps or block when the clearance was measured. If the Plastigauge was wider at one end than at the other, the crankshaft journal may be tapered.

38 On completion, carefully scrape away all traces of the Plastigauge material from the crankshaft and bearing shells. Use your fingernail, or some other object which is unlikely to score the bearing surfaces.

Final piston/connecting rod refitting

39 Ensure that the bearing shells are correctly fitted. If new shells are being fitted, ensure that all traces of the protective grease are cleaned off using paraffin. Wipe dry the shells and connecting rods with a lint-free cloth.

40 Lubricate the cylinder bores, the pistons, and piston rings, then lay out each

5.24d . . . tap or push out the gudgeon pin

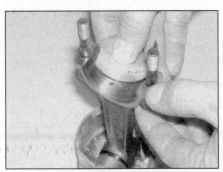

5.31a Fit the bearing shells to the connecting rods . . .

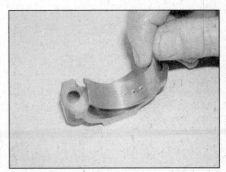

5.31b . . . and big-end bearing caps

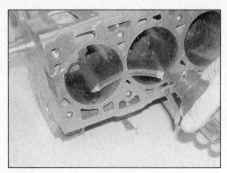

5.40a Lubricate the cylinder bores . . .

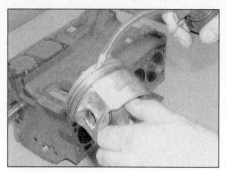

5.40b . . . pistons, and piston rings

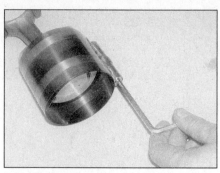

5.41 Clamp the piston rings using a piston ring compressor

piston/connecting rod assembly in its respective position (see illustrations).
41 Start with assembly No 1. Position the piston ring gaps 120° apart, then clamp them

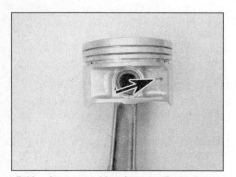

5.42a Arrow marking (arrowed) on piston indicates direction of rotation

5.42b Punch mark (arrowed) on piston crown

in position with a piston ring compressor (see illustration).
42 Insert the piston/connecting rod assembly into the top of cylinder, making sure it is the correct way round, as follows:
a) On 1.2 litre engines, the arrows on the piston crowns point to the timing belt end of the engine.
b) On 1.4 and 1.6 litre engines, the arrow markings on the base of the pistons indicate the direction of engine rotation, and should point to the front of the engine (as seen installed in the car). Some models may have a punched mark off-centre in the piston crown, which should be nearest the timing belt end and front of the engine (see illustrations).
c) On 1.8 litre engines, the larger recesses in the piston crowns are for the inlet valves, so these must be positioned on the inlet

side of the engine (the rear of the engine, as seen installed in the car).
43 Using a block of wood or hammer handle against the piston crown, tap the assembly into the cylinder until the piston crown is flush with the top of the cylinder (see illustration).
44 Ensure that the bearing shell is still correctly installed. Liberally lubricate the crank-pin and both bearing shells (see illustration). Taking care not to mark the cylinder bores, pull the piston/connecting rod assembly down the bore and onto the crankpin.
45 On 1.6 litre engines, remove the tape from the connecting rod bolt threads (where used).
46 Refit the big-end bearing cap, tightening its retaining bolts or nuts finger-tight at first (see illustrations). Note that the faces with the identification marks must match (which means that the bearing shell locating tabs abut each other).

5.42c Inserting the piston/connecting rod assembly

5.43 Tapping the assembly into the cylinder

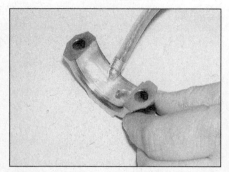

5.44 Lubricating a big-end bearing shell

5.46a Refit the big-end bearing caps . . .

5.46b . . . and secure with the nuts (as on 1.6 litre engine shown) or bolts

5.47 Tightening the big-end bearing caps

6.4 Checking crankshaft endfloat with a dial gauge

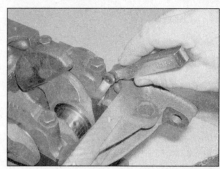

6.5 Using feeler blades to assess crankshaft endfloat - 1.6 litre engine shown

47 Tighten the bearing cap retaining nuts or bolts evenly and progressively to the specified torque setting **(see illustration)**. On 1.4 and 1.8 litre engines, tighten the bolts to the Stage 1 torque, then angle-tighten them to the specified angle using an angle-measuring gauge.

48 Once the bearing caps have been correctly tightened, rotate the crankshaft. Check that it turns freely; some stiffness is to be expected if new components have been fitted, but there should be no signs of binding or tight spots.

49 Refit the remaining three piston/connecting rod assemblies in the same way.

50 On 1.2 litre models, refit the vibration damping plate to the main bearing caps, tightening the bolts securely.

51 Refit the cylinder head, oil pump (or pick-up) and sump with reference to the relevant Part of Chapter 2.

6 Crankshaft - removal and inspection

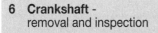

Removal

1 Remove the sump, oil pump and pick-up tube, and the flywheel/driveplate as described in the relevant Part of Chapter 2. Where applicable, unbolt and remove the oil spill tube from the base of the engine.

2 Remove the pistons and connecting rods, as described in Section 5. However, if no work is to be done on the pistons and connecting rods, there is no need to remove the cylinder head, or to push the pistons out of the cylinder bores. The pistons should just be pushed far enough up the bores that they are positioned clear of the crankshaft journals.

3 Unbolt the crankshaft rear oil seal housing from the cylinder block, and recover the gasket (where fitted).

4 Before removing the crankshaft, check the endfloat using a dial gauge **(see illustration)**. Push the crankshaft fully one way, and then zero the gauge. Push the crankshaft fully the other way, and check the endfloat. The result can be compared with the specified amount, and will give an indication as to whether new thrustwashers are required.

5 If a dial gauge is not available, feeler blades can be used. First push the crankshaft fully towards the flywheel end of the engine, then use feeler blades to measure the gap - on all engines except the 1.6 litre, measure between the centre main bearing thrustwasher and the crankshaft web; on 1.6 litre engines, measure between the rear main bearing and the crankshaft web **(see illustration)**.

6 Note the markings on the main bearing caps. There should be one line on the cap nearest the timing end, two on the second cap, C on the centre cap, then three and four lines on the remaining caps. Alternatively, on some engines there are no notches on the cap nearest the timing end (No 1 cylinder), one notch on No 2 cap, two notches on No 3 cap, and three notches on No 4 cap. If you are in any doubt about the markings on your engine, make your own using paint or a centre-punch **(see illustrations)**.

7 Loosen and remove the main bearing cap retaining bolts, and lift off each bearing cap. Recover the lower bearing shells, and tape them to their respective caps for safe-keeping.

8 Lift the crankshaft from the crankcase, and remove the upper bearing shells from the crankcase. If the shells are to be used again, keep them identified for position. Where applicable, also remove the thrustwashers from their position either side of the centre main bearing (1.4 and 1.8 litre engines) or rear main bearing (1.6 litre engines). On 1.2 litre engines, the upper half of the centre main bearing shell has thrust flanges.

Inspection

9 Wash the crankshaft in a suitable solvent and allow it to dry. Flush the oil holes thoroughly, to ensure that are not blocked - use a pipe cleaner or a needle brush if necessary. Remove any sharp edges from the edge of the holes which may damage the new bearings when they are installed.

10 Inspect the main bearing and crankpin journals carefully; if uneven wear, cracking, scoring or pitting are evident, the crankshaft should be reground by an engineering workshop, and refitted to the engine with undersize bearings.

11 Use a micrometer to measure the diameter of each main bearing journal **(see illustration)**. Taking a number of measurements on the surface of each journal will reveal if it is worn unevenly. Differences in diameter measured at 90° intervals indicate that the journal is out-of-round. Differences in

6.6a Showing the notches identifying the main bearing cap locations

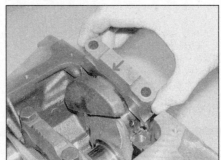

6.6b On this engine, we marked the rear cap to show its fitted direction

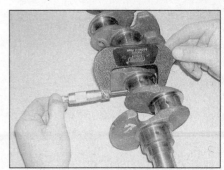

6.11 Checking the crankshaft journals using a micrometer

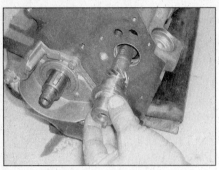

7.3 Withdrawing the auxiliary shaft

diameter measured along the length of the journal, indicate that the journal is tapered. Again, if wear is detected, the crankshaft can be reground by an engineering workshop and refitted with undersize bearings.

12 Check the oil seal journals at either end of the crankshaft. If they appear excessively scored or damaged, they may cause the new seals to leak when the engine is reassembled. It may be possible to repair the journal; seek the advice of an engineering workshop.

13 Measure the crankshaft runout by setting up a DTI gauge on the centre main bearing journal and rotating the shaft in V - blocks. The maximum deflection of the gauge will indicate the runout. Take precautions to protect the bearing journals and oil seal mating surfaces from damage during this procedure. A maximum runout figure is not quoted by the manufacturer, but use the figure of 0.05 mm as a rough guide. If the runout exceeds this figure, crankshaft renewal should be considered - consult your FIAT dealer or an engine rebuilding specialist for advice.

14 Refer to Section 9 for details of main and big-end bearing inspection.

**7 Auxiliary shaft
(1.6 litre engines) -
removal, inspection and refitting**

Removal

1 Remove the auxiliary shaft sprocket as described in Chapter 2C, Section 5.

7.5 Auxiliary shaft oil pump driven gear

2 Unscrew the three bolts, and withdraw the auxiliary shaft flange from the engine. Recover the gasket.

3 The auxiliary shaft can now be withdrawn from the engine **(see illustration)**. Note that, if the oil pump has not been removed, the oil pump driveshaft will turn as the shaft is removed.

4 Turn the auxiliary shaft as necessary so that it does not hang up on the bearings inside the engine. Keep the shaft horizontal as it is withdrawn; force should not be used, or required, otherwise the shaft and bearings could be damaged.

Inspection

5 Check the condition of the oil pump drivegear. If the teeth are excessively worn, it is likely that a new shaft will be needed, but consult an engine rebuilding specialist first. Also check the condition of the driven gear mounted in the crankcase **(see illustration)**.

6 Examine the shaft's two bearings for signs of scoring or excessive wear. If a micrometer is available, the bearing diameters can be checked against the specified values.

7 If the shaft bearings are worn, it is likely that the shaft bushes in the cylinder block will also be worn. Renewal is possible, but a press will be required, making this a job for an engine specialist.

Refitting

8 Refitting is a reversal of removal, using a new flange gasket. It is advisable to fit a new auxiliary shaft oil seal, as described in Chapter 2C, Section 9. If the oil pump has not been removed, check (by turning the auxiliary shaft) that the oil pump drive is working properly.

**8 Cylinder block/crankcase -
cleaning and inspection**

Cleaning

1 Remove all external components and brackets from the block, including (as applicable) the rear engine plate, oil pressure switch, breather pipe, coolant pump and alternator/power steering pump/air conditioning compressor mounting brackets.

2 For complete cleaning, the core plugs should ideally be removed. Drill a small hole in the plugs, then insert a self-tapping screw into the hole. Pull out the plugs by pulling on the screw with a pair of grips, or by using a slide hammer.

3 Where applicable, undo the retaining bolts and remove the piston oil jet spray tubes from inside the cylinder block.

4 Scrape all traces of gasket from the cylinder block/crankcase, taking care not to damage the gasket/sealing surfaces.

5 Remove all oil gallery plugs (where fitted). The plugs are usually very tight - they may have to be drilled out, and the holes re-

tapped. Use new plugs when the engine is reassembled.

6 If the block is very dirty have it steam-cleaned, otherwise use paraffin to clean it.

7 Clean all oil holes and oil galleries again and dry thoroughly, then apply a light film of oil to all mating surfaces, to prevent rusting. Smear the cylinder bores with a light coating of oil.

8 All threaded holes must be clean, to ensure accurate torque readings during reassembly. To clean the threads, run the correct-size tap into each of the holes to remove rust, corrosion, thread sealant or sludge, and to restore damaged threads **(see illustration)**. If possible, use compressed air to clear the holes of debris produced by this operation.

9 Apply suitable sealant to the new oil gallery plugs, and insert them into the holes in the block. Tighten them securely.

10 Where applicable, refit the piston oil jet spray tubes to the cylinder block, and securely tighten the retaining bolts. Bend over the tabs to lock the bolts.

11 Fit the new core plugs with sealant applied to their perimeters before using a suitable metal tube to drive them squarely into position.

Inspection

12 Visually check the cylinder block for cracks and corrosion. Look for stripped threads in the threaded holes. If there has been any history of internal water leakage, it may be worthwhile having an engine overhaul specialist check it with special equipment.

13 Check each cylinder bore for scuffing and scoring. Check for signs of a wear ridge at the top of the cylinder, indicating that the bore is excessively worn.

14 If the necessary measuring equipment is available, measure the bore diameters at the top (just under the wear ridge), centre, and bottom, parallel to the crankshaft axis **(see illustration)**.

15 Next, measure the bore diameters at the same three locations, at right-angles to the crankshaft axis. If there is any doubt about the condition of the cylinder bores, seek the advice of a FIAT dealer or suitable engine reconditioning specialist.

16 If the engine is not going to be reassembled right away, cover it with a large plastic

8.8 To clean the cylinder block bolt threads, run a correct-size tap into the holes

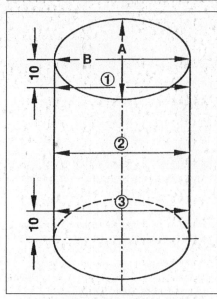

8.14 Three bore measurement points - dimensions in mm

A Measure at right-angles to the crankshaft axis
B Measure in line with the crankshaft axis

bag to keep it clean and prevent rusting. If the engine is ready for reassembly, refit all the components and brackets removed.

9 Main and big-end bearings - inspection and selection

Inspection

1 Even though the main and big-end bearings should be renewed during the engine overhaul, the old bearings should be retained for close examination, as they may reveal valuable information about the condition of the engine **(see illustration)**. The bearing shells are available in different thicknesses to match the diameter of the journal.
2 Bearing failure can occur due to lack of lubrication, the presence of dirt or other foreign particles, overloading the engine, or corrosion. Regardless of the cause of bearing failure, the cause must be corrected (where applicable) before the engine is reassembled, to prevent it from happening again.
3 When examining the bearing shells, remove them from the cylinder block/crankcase, the main bearing caps, the connecting rods and the connecting rod big-end bearing caps. Lay them out on a clean surface in the same general position as their location in the engine. This will enable you to match any bearing problems with the corresponding crankshaft journal. Do not touch any shell's bearing surface with your fingers while checking it.
4 Dirt and other foreign matter gets into the engine in a variety of ways. It may be left in the engine during assembly, or it may pass through filters or the crankcase ventilation

system. It may get into the oil, and from there into the bearings. Metal chips from machining operations and normal engine wear are often present. Abrasives are sometimes left in engine components after reconditioning, especially when parts are not thoroughly cleaned using the proper cleaning methods.
5 Whatever the source, these foreign objects often end up embedded in the soft bearing material, and are easily recognised. Large particles will not embed in the bearing, and will score or gouge the bearing and journal. The best prevention for this cause of bearing failure is to clean all parts thoroughly, and keep everything spotlessly-clean during engine assembly. Regular engine oil and filter changes are also recommended.
6 Lack of lubrication (or lubrication break-down) has a number of interrelated causes. Excessive heat (which thins the oil), overloading (which squeezes the oil from the bearing face) and oil leakage (from excessive bearing clearances, worn oil pump or high engine speeds) all contribute to lubrication breakdown. Blocked oil passages, which can be the result of misaligned oil holes in a bearing shell, will also oil-starve a bearing, and destroy it.
7 When lack of lubrication is the cause of bearing failure, the bearing material is wiped or extruded from the steel backing of the bearing. Temperatures may increase to the point where the steel backing turns blue from overheating.
8 Driving habits can have a definite effect on bearing life. Full-throttle, low-speed operation (labouring the engine) puts very high loads on bearings, tending to squeeze out the oil film. These loads cause the bearings to flex, which produces fine cracks in the bearing face (fatigue failure). Eventually, the bearing material will loosen in pieces, and tear away from the steel backing.

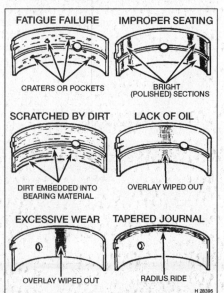

9.1 Typical bearing failures

9 Short-distance driving leads to corrosion of bearings, because insufficient engine heat is produced to drive off the condensed water and corrosive gases. These products collect in the engine oil, forming acid and sludge. As the oil is carried to the engine bearings, the acid attacks and corrodes the bearing material.
10 Incorrect bearing installation during engine assembly will lead to bearing failure as well. Tight-fitting bearings leave insufficient bearing running clearance, and will result in oil starvation. Dirt or foreign particles trapped behind a bearing shell result in high spots on the bearing, which lead to failure.
11 Do not touch any shell's bearing surface with your fingers during reassembly; there is a risk of scratching the delicate surface, or of depositing particles of dirt on it.
12 As mentioned at the beginning of this Section, the bearing shells should be renewed as a matter of course during engine overhaul; not to do so is false economy.

Selection

13 Main and big-end bearings are available in standard sizes and a range of undersizes to suit reground crankshafts - refer to Specifications for details. The engine reconditioner will select the correct bearing shells for machined crankshaft.
14 The running clearances can be checked when the crankshaft is refitted with its new bearings.

10 Engine overhaul - reassembly sequence

1 Before reassembly begins, ensure that all new parts have been obtained, and that all necessary tools are available. Read through the entire procedure to familiarise yourself with the work involved, and to ensure that all items necessary for reassembly of the engine are at hand. In addition to all normal tools and materials, thread-locking compound will be needed. A tube of sealant will also be required for the joint faces that are fitted without gaskets.
2 In order to save time and avoid problems, engine reassembly can be carried out in the following order:
  a) Crankshaft (Section 11).
  b) Piston/connecting rod assemblies (Section 5).
  c) Oil pump (relevant Part of Chapter 2).
  d) Sump (relevant Part of Chapter 2).
  e) Flywheel (relevant Part of Chapter 2).
  f) Cylinder head (relevant Part of Chapter 2).
  g) Coolant pump (see Chapter 3)
  h) Timing belt tensioner and sprockets, and timing belt (relevant Part of Chapter 2).
  i) Engine external components.
3 At this stage, all engine components should be absolutely clean and dry, with all faults repaired. The components should be laid out on a completely clean work surface.

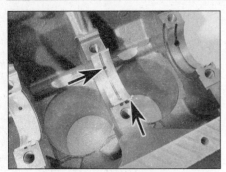

11.3 Bearing shell partially fitted, showing lug and oil hole (arrowed)

11.5 Fitting the plain centre bearing on a 1.6 litre engine

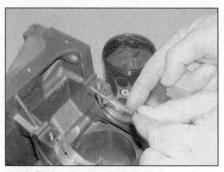

11.6 Fitting the crankshaft thrustwashers on a 1.6 litre engine

11 Crankshaft - refitting and main bearing running clearance check

Crankshaft - initial refitting

1 Crankshaft refitting is the first stage of engine reassembly following overhaul. At this point, it is assumed that the crankshaft, cylinder block/crankcase and bearings have been cleaned, inspected and reconditioned or renewed.

2 Place the cylinder block on a clean, level work surface, with the crankcase facing upwards. Where necessary, unbolt the bearing caps and lay them out in order to ensure correct reassembly. If they are still in place, remove the bearing shells from the caps and the crankcase, and wipe out the inner surfaces with a clean rag - they must be kept spotlessly clean. Clean the bearing cap bolts, and check their threads for signs of damage.

3 Clean the rear surface of the new bearing shells with a rag, and fit them on the bearing saddles. Ensure that the orientation lugs on the shells engage with the recesses in the saddles, and that the oil holes are correctly aligned **(see illustration)**. Do not hammer or otherwise force the bearing shells into place. It is critically important that the surfaces of the bearings are kept free from damage and contamination.

4 On 1.2 litre engines, locate the bearing shell with the thrust flanges into the centre main bearing position.

5 On 1.6 litre engines, the centre main bearings are plain - ie they do not have lubrication grooves **(see illustration)**.

6 On engines except the 1.2 litre, fit the crankshaft thrustwashers to their relevant locations (where necessary, stick them in position with a little grease). On 1.6 litre engines, the washers are fitted to No 5 main bearing; on the 1.4 and 1.8 litre engines, the washers fit around the centre main bearing **(see illustration)**.

7 Give the newly-fitted bearing shells and the crankshaft journals a final clean with a rag. Check that the oil holes in the crankshaft are free from dirt, as any left here will become embedded in the new bearings when the engine is first started.

8 Carefully lay the crankshaft in the crankcase, taking care not to dislodge the bearing shells.

Main bearing running clearance check

9 When the crankshaft and bearings are refitted, a clearance must exist between them to allow lubricant to circulate. This clearance is impossible to check using feeler blades, but a product called Plastigauge can be used. This consists of a thin strip of soft plastic that is crushed between the bearing shells and journals when the bearing caps are tightened up. The width of the crushed strip then indicates the size of the clearance gap.

10 Cut off five pieces of Plastigauge, just shorter than the length of the crankshaft journal. Lay a piece on each journal, in line with its axis **(see illustration)**.

11 Wipe off the rear surfaces of the new lower half main bearing shells and fit them to the main bearing caps, again ensuring that the locating lugs engage correctly.

12 Fit the caps in their correct locations on the bearing saddles, using the manufacturers markings as a guide. Ensure that they are correctly orientated - the caps should be fitted such that the recesses for the bearing shell locating lugs are on the same side as those in the bearing saddle.

13 On engines except the 1.2 litre, fit the remaining crankshaft thrustwashers, using the information in paragraph 6.

14 Insert and tighten the main bearing bolts until they are all correctly torqued. Do not allow the crankshaft to rotate at all whilst the Plastigauge is in place. Progressively unbolt the bearing caps and remove them, taking care not to dislodge the Plastigauge.

15 The width of the crushed Plastigauge can now be measured, using the scale provided **(see illustration)**. Use the correct scale, as both imperial and metric are printed. This measurement indicates the running clearance - compare it with that listed in *Specifications*.

16 If the clearance is outside the tolerance, it may be due to dirt or debris trapped under the bearing surface; try cleaning them again and repeat the clearance check. If the results are still unacceptable, re-check the journal diameters and the bearing sizes. Note that if the Plastigauge is thicker at one end, the journals may be tapered and as such, will require regrinding.

17 When you are satisfied that the clearances are correct, carefully remove the remains of the Plastigauge from the journals and bearing faces. Use a soft, plastic or wooden scraper, as anything metallic is likely to damage the surfaces.

Crankshaft - final refitting

18 Lift the crankshaft out of the crankcase. Wipe off the surfaces of the bearings in the crankcase and the bearing caps. Where applicable (see paragraph 6), fit the thrust washers, using grease to hold them in position. Ensure they are seated correctly in the machined recesses, with the oil grooves facing outwards

11.10 Lay a piece of Plastigauge on each journal, in line with the crankshaft axis

11.15 Measure the width of the crushed Plastigauge, using the scale provided

11.19 Lubricate the crankcase main bearing shells

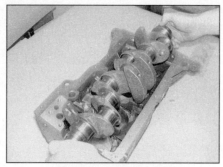

11.20 Fitting the crankshaft

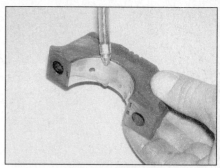

11.21 Lubricate the main bearing cap shells - plain No 3 shell on a 1.6 litre engine shown

19 Liberally coat the bearing shells in the crankcase with clean engine oil **(see illustration)**.

20 Lower the crankshaft into position in the crankcase **(see illustration)**.

21 Lubricate the lower bearing shells in the main bearing caps with clean engine oil. Make sure that the locating lugs on the shells are still engaged with the corresponding recesses in the caps **(see illustration)**.

22 Fit the main bearing caps in the correct order and orientation. Lightly oil the bearing cap bolt threads, then insert the bolts, and hand-tighten them only **(see illustrations)**.

23 Working from the centre bearing cap outwards, tighten the main bearing bolts to their specified torque **(see illustration)**. On all engines except the 1.6 litre, the bolts are tightened in two stages - tighten all the bolts to the Stage 1 setting before tightening further through the specified angle (use an angle-measuring gauge if possible, to ensure accuracy).

24 Fit a new oil seal to the crankshaft rear oil seal housing (or fit a new oil seal housing, as applicable). Apply grease to the seal lips. Where applicable, tighten the housing bolts securely, ensuring that the edge of the housing is kept square to the edge of crankcase. On 1.6 litre engines, similarly refit

the front oil seal flange, using a new seal - refer to Chapter 2C.

25 Check that the crankshaft rotates freely by turning it by manually. If resistance is felt, re-check the running clearances, as described above.

26 Carry out a check of the crankshaft endfloat as described in Section 6. If the thrust surfaces of the crankshaft have been checked and new thrust bearings (or main bearings, on the 1.2 litre engine) have been fitted, then the endfloat should be within specification.

27 Refit the pistons and connecting rods as described in Section 5.

28 Refit the flywheel/driveplate, oil pump and pick-up tube, and sump with reference to the relevant Parts of Chapter 2. Where applicable, refit the oil spill tube to the base of the engine before fitting the sump.

12 Engine - initial start-up after overhaul and reassembly

1 With the engine refitted in the vehicle, double-check the engine oil and coolant levels. Make a final check that everything has been reconnected, and that there are no tools

or rags left in the engine compartment.

2 Remove the spark plugs, then remove the fuel pump fuse or relay (refer to Chapter 12 if necessary).

3 Turn the engine on the starter until the oil pressure warning light goes out. Refit the spark plugs, and reconnect the ECU.

4 Start the engine, noting that this may take a little longer than usual, due to the fuel system components having been disturbed.

5 While the engine is idling, check for fuel, water and oil leaks. Don't be alarmed if there are some odd smells and smoke from parts getting hot and burning off oil deposits.

6 Assuming all is well, keep the engine idling until hot water is felt circulating through the top hose, then switch off the engine.

7 Recheck the oil and coolant levels as described in Chapter 1, and top-up as necessary.

8 There is no need to re-tighten the cylinder head bolts once the engine has first run after reassembly.

9 If new pistons, rings or crankshaft bearings have been fitted, the engine must be treated as new, and run-in for the first 500 miles (800 km). *Do not* operate the engine at full-throttle, or allow it to labour at low engine speeds in any gear. It is recommended that the oil and filter be changed at the end of this period.

11.22a Fit the main bearing caps . . .

11.22b . . . and loosely fit the retaining bolts

11.23 Tighten the main bearing cap bolts to the specified torque

Chapter 3
Cooling, heating and ventilation systems

Contents

Degrees of difficulty

Easy, suitable for novice with little experience	**Fairly easy,** suitable for beginner with some experience	**Fairly difficult,** suitable for competent DIY mechanic 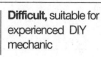	**Difficult,** suitable for experienced DIY mechanic	**Very difficult,** suitable for expert DIY or professional

Specifications

General

Expansion tank relief valve opening pressure	0.98 bar
Coolant pump impeller-to-casing clearance (1.6 litre engine only)	0.3 to 1.1 mm

Thermostat

Opening temperature:

1.2 litre engine:	
Starts to open	81 to 85°C
Fully open	103°C
1.4 litre engine:	
Starts to open	81 to 85°C
Fully open	101 to 105°C
1.6 litre engine:	
Starts to open	81 to 85°C
Fully open	99 to 103°C
1.8 litre engine:	
Starts to open	81 to 85°C
Fully open	98 to 102°C
Maximum thermostat lift (approximate):	
1.2 litre engine	9.5 mm
1.4 litre engine	9.5 mm
1.6 litre engine	9.5 mm
1.8 litre engine	$\geq$ 7.5 mm

Electric cooling fan thermoswitch

Note: *1.6 litre models manufactured from April 1998-on are not fitted with a thermoswitch because the electric cooling fan is switched on by the control unit.*

Models without air conditioning:	
Cut-in temperature	90 to 94°C
Cut-out temperature	85 to 89°C
Models with air conditioning:	
Cut-in temperature:	
1st stage	90 to 94°C
2nd stage	95 to 99°C
Cut-out temperature:	
1st stage	85 to 89°C
2nd stage	90 to 94°C

Coolant temperature sensor

Temperature:	Resistance (approx)
0°	6000 ohms
20°	2300 ohms
40°	1000 ohms
60°	550 ohms
80°	300 ohms
100°	180 ohms
120°	100 ohms

Torque wrench settings

	Nm	lbf ft
Air conditioning compressor bracket to cylinder block	50	37
Coolant pump:		
M8 bolt	25	18
M8 nut with flange	20	15
Coolant temperature sensor:		
M12	25	18
M14	30	22
M16	34	25
Inlet pipe to cylinder head:		
M6 bolt on 1.4 and 1.8 litre models	9	7
M8 bolt on 1.4 and 1.6 litre models	25	18
Thermostat to cylinder head:		
M8 bolt	25	18
M8 nut	20	15
Timing belt guard brackets (1.8 litre engine)	9	7

1 General information and precautions

General information

The engine cooling/interior heating system is of pressurised type, comprising a coolant pump, a crossflow radiator, a coolant expansion tank, an electric cooling fan, a thermostat, heater matrix, and all associated hoses and switches. On 1.2 litre models, the coolant pump is driven by the toothed timing belt. On 1.4 litre models, the coolant pump is driven off the back of the timing belt. On 1.6 litre models the coolant pump is driven by the auxiliary drivebelt from the crankshaft pulley. On 1.8 litre models, the coolant pump is driven off the back of the timing belt.

The system functions as follows. The coolant pump circulates cold water around the cylinder block and head passages, through the heater matrix, returning it to the pump. On certain engines it also circulates it through the inlet manifold and throttle body.

When the engine is cold, the thermostat remains closed and prevents coolant from circulating through the radiator. When the coolant reaches a predetermined temperature, the thermostat opens, and the coolant passes through the top hose to the radiator. As the coolant circulates through the radiator, it is cooled by the in-rush of air when the car is in forward motion. The airflow is supplemented by the action of the electric cooling fan, when necessary. From the bottom of the radiator the coolant is returned to the coolant pump, and the cycle is repeated.

When the engine reaches normal operating temperature, the coolant expands, and some of it is displaced into the expansion tank. Coolant collects in the tank, and is returned to the radiator when the system cools. On 1.2 litre models without air conditioning, all 1.4 litre models, and 1.6 litre models with manual transmission, the expansion tank is integrated into the side of the radiator. On 1.2 litre models with air conditioning, 1.6 litre models with automatic transmission, and 1.8 litre models, a separate expansion tank is located on the right-hand side of the engine compartment.

The electric cooling fan mounted on the rear of the radiator is controlled by a thermostatic switch except on 1.6 litre models manufactured from April 1998-on. At a predetermined coolant temperature, the switch/sensor actuates the fan to provide additional airflow through the radiator. The switch cuts the electrical supply to the fan when the coolant temperature has dropped below a preset threshold (see Specifications). On 1.6 litre models manufactured from April 1998-on, the electric cooling fan is switched on by the control unit.

Precautions

Warning: Do not attempt to remove the expansion tank pressure cap, or to disturb any part of the cooling system, while the engine is hot, as there is a high risk of scalding. If the expansion tank pressure cap must be removed before the engine and radiator have fully cooled (even though this is not recommended), the pressure in the cooling system must first be relieved. Cover the cap with a thick layer of cloth, to avoid scalding, and slowly unscrew the pressure cap until a hissing sound is heard. When the hissing stops, indicating that the pressure has reduced, slowly unscrew the pressure cap until it can be removed; if more hissing sounds are heard, wait until they have stopped before unscrewing the cap completely. At all times, keep your face well away from the pressure cap opening, and protect your hands.

Warning: Do not allow antifreeze to come into contact with your skin, or with the painted surfaces of the vehicle. Rinse off spills immediately, with plenty of water. Never leave antifreeze lying around in an open container, or in a puddle in the driveway or on the garage floor. Children and pets are attracted by its sweet smell, but antifreeze can be fatal if ingested.

Warning: If the engine is hot, the electric cooling fan may start rotating even if the engine and ignition are switched off. Be careful to keep your hands, hair, and any loose clothing well clear when working in the engine compartment.

Warning: Refer to Section 10 for precautions to be observed when working on models equipped with air conditioning.

2 Cooling system hoses - disconnection and renewal

Note: *Refer to the warnings given in Section 1 of this Chapter before proceeding. Hoses should only be disconnected once the engine has cooled sufficiently to avoid scalding.*

1 If the checks described in Chapter, Section 9,

reveal a faulty hose, it must be renewed as described in the following paragraphs.

2 First drain the cooling system (see Chapter 1). If the coolant is not due for renewal, it may be re-used, providing it is collected in a clean container.

3 To disconnect a hose, use a screwdriver to slacken the clips, then move them along the hose, clear of the relevant inlet/outlet. Carefully work the hose free. The hoses can be removed with relative ease when new - on an older car, they may have stuck.

4 If a hose proves to be difficult to remove, try to release it by twisting its ends before attempting to free it. Gently prise the end of the hose with a blunt instrument (such as a flat-bladed screwdriver), but do not apply too much force, and take care not to damage the pipe stubs or hoses. Note in particular that the radiator inlet stub is fragile; do not use excessive force when attempting to remove the hose. If all else fails, cut the hose with a sharp knife, then slit it so that it can be peeled off in two pieces. Although this may prove expensive if the hose is otherwise undamaged, it is preferable to buying a new radiator. Check first, however, that a new hose is readily available.

5 When fitting a hose, first slide the clips onto the hose, then ease the hose into position.

TOOL TiP *If the hose is stiff, use a little soapy water as a lubricant, or soften the hose by soaking it in hot water. Do not use oil or grease, which may attack the rubber.*

6 Ensure the hose is correctly routed, then slide each clip back along the hose until it passes over the end of the relevant inlet/outlet, before tightening the clip securely.

7 Refill the cooling system with reference to Chapter 1.

8 Check thoroughly for leaks as soon as possible after disturbing any part of the cooling system.

3 Radiator -
removal, inspection and refitting

Removal

Note: *If leakage is the reason for removing the radiator, bear in mind that minor leaks can often be cured using proprietary radiator sealing compound, with the radiator in situ.*

1 Disconnect the battery negative (earth) lead (see *Disconnecting the battery*).

2 Drain the cooling system as described in Chapter 1.

1.2 litre models

3 Loosen the clips and disconnect the top and bottom coolant hoses from the radiator.

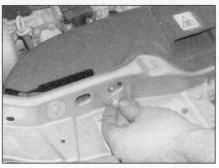
3.11a Unscrew the mounting bolts . . .

4 On the rear of the radiator, disconnect the wiring plugs leading to the electric cooling fan. The plugs are located on the cowl.

5 Unbolt the air inlet duct from the engine compartment front crossmember, and also disconnect it from the air cleaner.

6 On models with air conditioning, release the clip and disconnect the expansion tank purge hose from the top right-hand side of the radiator.

7 Remove the electric cooling fan assembly from the rear of the radiator with reference to Section 5.

8 On models with air conditioning, unscrew and remove the bolts securing the radiator to the air conditioning condenser and front valance.

1.4 litre models

9 Loosen the clips and disconnect the top and bottom coolant hoses from the radiator.

10 On the rear of the radiator, disconnect the wiring plug leading to the electric cooling fan. The plug is located on the cowl.

1.6 litre models

11 Unscrew the mounting bolts on the engine compartment front crossmember, and remove the air inlet shroud from over the radiator **(see illustrations)**.

12 Loosen the clips and disconnect the top and bottom coolant hoses from the radiator **(see illustrations)**.

13 On models with automatic transmission and/or air conditioning, release the clip and disconnect the expansion tank purge hose from the top of the radiator.

3.12a Disconnecting the top . . .

3.11b . . . and remove the air inlet shroud from over the radiator

14 If necessary for additional working room, remove the electric cooling fan assembly from the rear of the radiator with reference to Section 5.

15 On models with air conditioning, unscrew and remove the bolts securing the radiator to the air conditioning condenser and front valance.

1.8 litre models

16 Loosen the clips and disconnect the top and bottom coolant hoses from the radiator.

17 Unscrew the mounting bolts on the engine compartment front crossmember, and remove the air inlet shroud from over the radiator.

18 Remove the electric cooling fan assembly from the rear of the radiator with reference to Section 5.

19 Release the clip and disconnect the expansion tank purge hose from the top of the radiator.

20 Unscrew and remove the upper bolts securing the air conditioning condenser to the front of the radiator. Loosen only the condenser lower mounting bolts.

All models

21 Unscrew and remove the two radiator upper mounting nuts located on the engine compartment front crossmember. Remove the upper mounting brackets and rubbers from the top of the radiator **(see illustrations)**.

22 Carefully lift the radiator (together with the electric fan unit where applicable) from the lower mounting rubbers in the engine compartment, taking care not to damage the radiator fins as they are easily dented **(see illustrations)**.

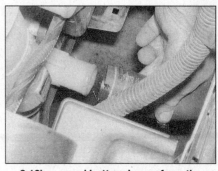
3.12b . . . and bottom hoses from the radiator

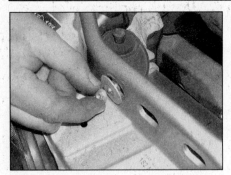

3.21a Unscrew the mounting nuts . . .

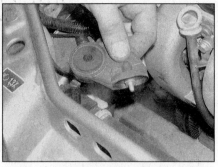

3.21b . . . and remove the upper mounting brackets and rubbers

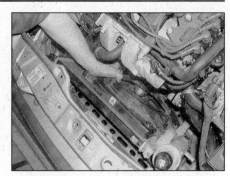

3.22a Removing the radiator from the engine compartment

23 With the radiator on the bench, disconnect the wiring from the thermoswitch where fitted. As applicable, unscrew the bolts and remove the electric fan unit from the radiator, and unbolt the lower front air duct from the radiator. Remove the lower mounting rubbers **(see illustration)**.

Inspection

24 If the radiator has been removed due to suspected blockage, it may be flushed out as described in Chapter 1, Section 31. Clean dirt and debris from the radiator fins, using an air line (in which case, wear eye protection) or a soft brush. Be careful, as the fins are sharp, and can also be easily damaged.
25 If necessary, a radiator specialist can perform a 'flow test' on the radiator, to establish whether an internal blockage exists.
26 A leaking radiator must be referred to a specialist for permanent repair. **Note:** *In an emergency, minor leaks from the radiator can often be cured by using a suitable radiator sealing compound, in accordance with its manufacturer's instructions, with the radiator in situ.*
27 If the radiator is to be sent for repair or is to be renewed, remove all hoses and, where applicable, the cooling fan thermoswitch.
28 Inspect the radiator mounting rubbers, and renew them if necessary.

Refitting

29 Refitting is a reversal of removal, but securely tighten the radiator mounting bolts and hose clips. On completion, refill the cooling system as described in Chapter 1.

4.4 Thermostat housing and top hose - distributor removed for clarity (1.2 litre models)

3.22b Radiator and electric fan unit removed from the car

---

4 Thermostat -
removal, testing and refitting

General

1 The thermostat housing is bolted to the left hand end of the cylinder head. The thermostat itself cannot be separated from the housing and can only be renewed as a complete assembly.

Removal

2 Drain the cooling system as described in Chapter 1.
3 For improved access, remove the battery as described in Chapter 5A.

1.2 litre models

4 Loosen the clip and disconnect the radiator top hose from the thermostat housing on the

4.5 Removing the thermostat housing (1.2 litre models)

3.23 One of the radiator bottom mounting rubbers

left-hand end of the cylinder head **(see illustration)**.
5 Unscrew the mounting bolts and remove the thermostat housing from the cylinder head **(see illustration)**. Recover the gasket.

1.4, 1.6 and 1.8 litre models

6 Loosen the clip and disconnect the radiator top hose from the thermostat housing on the left-hand end of the cylinder head, below the ignition coil.
7 Loosen the clip and disconnect the throttle body coolant hose from the rear of the thermostat housing. Also disconnect the by-pass hose from the bottom of the housing.
8 Disconnect the wiring from the temperature sender(s) on the thermostat housing.
9 Unscrew the mounting bolts and remove the thermostat housing from the cylinder head. Recover the gasket/O-ring.

Testing

10 A rough test of the thermostat may be made by suspending it with a piece of string in a container full of water. Heat the water to bring it to the boil - the thermostat must open by the time the water boils. If not, renew the complete thermostat/housing assembly.
11 If a thermometer is available, the precise opening temperature of the thermostat may be determined; compare with the figures given in the *Specifications*. The opening temperature should also be marked on the thermostat housing.
13 Note that a thermostat which fails to close completely as the water cools must also be renewed.

Refitting

14 Ensure that the cylinder head and thermostat housing mating surfaces are completely clean and free from all traces of the old gasket material.

15 Locate a new gasket in position on the cylinder head, then fit the thermostat housing and insert retaining bolts, tightening them securely.

16 The remaining procedure is a reversal of removal, but refill the cooling system as described in Chapter 1.

5 Electric cooling fan - testing, removal and refitting

Testing

1 Detailed fault diagnosis should be carried out by a FIAT dealer using dedicated test equipment, but basic diagnosis can be carried out as follows. Note that on models equipped with air conditioning, two fans are fitted together with a two-speed control unit.

2 If the fan does not appear to work, run the engine until normal operating temperature is reached, then allow it to idle. The fan should cut in just before the temperature gauge needle enters the red section. If not, switch off the ignition and disconnect the cooling fan motor wiring connector.

3 The motor can be tested by disconnecting it from the wiring loom, and connecting a 12-volt supply and an earth wire directly to it. The motor should operate - if not, the motor, or the motor wiring, is faulty.

4 If the motor operates when tested as described, the fault must lie in the engine wiring harness or the temperature sensor. The temperature sensor/switch can be tested as described in Section 6. Any further fault diagnosis should be referred to a suitably-equipped FIAT dealer - **do not** attempt to test the electronic control unit.

Removal

5 Make sure that the ignition switch is turned off, and that the engine is cold.

⚠️ **Warning: The electric fan could start to operate if the engine is hot, even if the ignition is switched off.**

6 On 1.6 and 1.8 litre models, unscrew the bolts and remove the inlet air duct from over the radiator.

7 Disconnect the electric cooling fan wiring from the loom and where necessary from the thermoswitch **(see illustration)**.

8 On 1.8 litre models, improved access to the lower mounting bolts may be gained by raising the front of the vehicle. Apply the handbrake, then jack up the front of the vehicle and support it on axle stands (see *Jacking and vehicle support*). Remove the splash shield from under the engine compartment.

5.7 Disconnecting the wiring from the electric cooling fan unit on the radiator

9 Support the electric cooling fan assembly, then unscrew the bolts securing it to the rear of the radiator. Carefully lift the assembly from the engine compartment, taking care not to damage the radiator cooling fins.

Refitting

10 Refitting is a reversal of removal.

6 Cooling fan thermoswitch - testing, removal and refitting

Note: *1.6 litre models manufactured from April 1998-on are not fitted with a thermoswitch because the electric cooling fan is switched on by the control unit.*

Testing

1 Where fitted, the switch is threaded into the lower left hand corner of the radiator.

2 The switch can be tested by removing it, and checking that the switching action occurs at the correct temperature (heat the sensor in a container of water, and monitor the temperature with a thermometer).

3 There should be no continuity between the switch terminals until the specified cooling fan cut-in temperature is reached, when continuity (and zero resistance) should exist between the terminals.

Removal

4 Make sure that the ignition switch is turned off, and that the engine is cold.

⚠️ **Warning: The electric fan could start to operate if the engine is hot, even if the ignition is switched off.**

5 Drain the cooling system as described in Chapter 1.

6 Disconnect the wiring from the thermoswitch.

7 Carefully unscrew the sensor and, where applicable, recover the sealing ring.

Refitting

8 If the thermoswitch was originally fitted using sealing compound, clean the sensor threads thoroughly, and coat them with fresh sealing compound. If the thermoswitch was originally fitted using a sealing ring, locate a new sealing ring on the sensor. Screw the thermoswitch into the radiator and tighten securely.

9 Reconnect the wiring.

10 Reconnect the battery negative (earth) lead (see *Disconnecting the battery*).

11 Refill the cooling system as described in Chapter 1.

7 Coolant temperature sensor - testing, removal and refitting

Testing

1 The coolant temperature sensor is located on the thermostat housing on the left-hand side of the cylinder head.

2 The sensor is a thermistor - an electronic component whose electrical resistance decreases at a predetermined rate as its temperature rises. The fuel injection/engine management ECU supplies the sensor with a set voltage, and by measuring the current flowing in the sensor circuit, it determines the engine temperature.

3 If the sensor circuit should fail to provide adequate information, the ECU back-up facility will override the sensor signal. In this event, the ECU assumes a predetermined setting which will allow the fuel injection/engine management system to run, albeit at reduced efficiency. When this occurs, the engine warning light on the instrument panel will come on, and the advice of a FIAT dealer should be sought.

4 The sensor can be tested by removing it, and checking that its resistance is correct at different temperatures (see Specifications). Heat the sensor in a container of water, and monitor the temperature and resistance using a thermometer and ohmmeter.

Caution: Do not attempt to test the ECU circuit. This must be entrusted to a FIAT dealer using special diagnostic equipment.

Removal

5 Drain the cooling system as described in Chapter 1. Alternatively, if a new sensor has already been obtained, it is possible to fit the new unit immediately after removing the old one. If this method is used, make sure that the engine is cold, then release any remaining pressure in the cooling system by removing the expansion tank filler cap and refitting it.

6 If necessary for improved access, remove the battery as described in Chapter 5A.

7 Disconnect the wiring from the sensor. Where necessary, remove the rubber boot from the top of the sensor and disconnect the fly lead/terminal.

8 Unscrew the sensor and, where applicable, recover the sealing ring.

Refitting

9 Screw the sensor into the thermostat housing (together with a new sealing ring

8.5a Unscrew the securing bolts . . .

8.5b . . . and withdraw the coolant pump (1.2 litre models)

where applicable) and tighten to the specified torque. The manufacturers recommend applying anaerobic sealant to the tapered threads of the sensor before refitting it.

10 Reconnect the wiring, and where removed, refit the battery as described in Chapter 5A.

11 Refill the cooling system as described in Chapter 1.

8 Coolant pump - removal, inspection and refitting

Removal

1.2 litre models

1 Disconnect the battery negative (earth) lead (see *Disconnecting the battery*).

2 Drain the cooling system as described in Chapter 1.

3 Remove the auxiliary drivebelt(s) as described in Chapter 1.

4 Remove the timing belt as described in Chapter 2A.

5 Unscrew the mounting bolts/nuts, and withdraw the coolant pump from the cylinder block casting **(see illustrations)**. If the pump is stuck, tap it gently using a soft-faced mallet to release the sealing compound.

1.4 litre models

6 Disconnect the battery negative (earth) lead (see *Disconnecting the battery*).

7 Drain the cooling system as described in Chapter 1.

8.25 Coolant pump location (1.6 litre models)

8 Remove the auxiliary drivebelt as described in Chapter 1.

9 Remove the timing belt as described in Chapter 2B.

10 Remove the camshaft sprocket as described in Chapter 2B, Section 5.

11 Unscrew the mounting bolts, and withdraw the coolant pump from the cylinder head. Recover the O-ring seal.

1.6 litre models

Note: *The coolant pump is mounted on a housing, which is bolted to the engine. A new pump may be supplied with a new housing, but removing the pump AND housing is quite difficult, and involves more dismantling then simply unbolting the pump from the housing. Both methods are described below.*

12 Disconnect the battery negative (earth) lead (see *Disconnecting the battery*).

13 Drain the cooling system as described in Chapter 1.

14 Apply the handbrake, then jack up the front of the vehicle and support it on axle stands (see *Jacking and vehicle support*). Remove the front right-hand side roadwheel.

15 Undo the fastenings and remove the wheel arch liner from under the front wing.

16 Remove the auxiliary drivebelt as described in Chapter 1, then unbolt and completely remove the drivebelt tensioner assembly. Loosen the alternator lower mounting bolt.

17 Where fitted, remove the alternator cooling hose from the right-hand side of the engine compartment.

18 On early models, unbolt the fuel supply

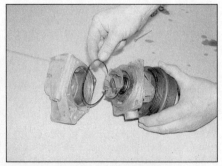

8.26 Separating the coolant pump from its housing (1.6 litre models)

and return hose bracket from the inlet manifold, then loosen the union nuts and disconnect the fuel lines for access to the power steering pump.

19 Unbolt the power steering pump drivebelt guard from the pump.

20 Loosen the power steering pump pivot and adjustment nuts, then back off the adjustment bolt and release the drivebelt. Completely remove the mounting nuts and position the power steering pump to one side. **Do not** disconnect the hydraulic lines from the pump.

Method 1 - pump and housing removal

21 Unbolt the heat shrouds from the exhaust manifold and downpipe.

22 Unbolt and remove the alternator upper mounting bracket, noting that one of the bolts secures the coolant pump housing.

23 Loosen the alternator lower mounting bolt and swivel the alternator backwards to provide access to the coolant pump.

24 Unscrew the bolts securing the coolant pipe to the rear of the coolant pump, and free the pipe. Access to the bolt nearest the back of the engine is particularly difficult - in the workshop, we had to use a socket and very long extension bar. Recover the O-ring seal from the end of the coolant pipe.

25 Unscrew the remaining three bolts securing the coolant pump housing to the cylinder block, and withdraw the assembly. Recover the gasket **(see illustration)**.

26 Note that a new coolant pump may be supplied together with the housing - however, it is possible to obtain the pump-to-housing O-ring seal separately. Unscrew the four bolts and separate the pump from its housing **(see illustration)**.

Method 2 - pump removal from housing

27 Remove the alternator upper mounting bolt, then loosen the alternator lower mounting bolt and swivel the alternator backwards to provide access to the coolant pump.

28 Remove the four bolts securing the coolant pump to the housing, and withdraw the pump. Recover the large O-ring seal, and discard it - a new seal must be used when refitting.

1.8 litre models

29 Disconnect the battery negative (earth) lead (see *Disconnecting the battery*).

30 Drain the cooling system as described in Chapter 1.

31 Remove the auxiliary drivebelt as described in Chapter 1.

32 Apply the handbrake, then jack up the front of the vehicle and support it on axle stands (see *Jacking and vehicle support*). Remove the right-hand front roadwheel.

33 Undo the fastenings and remove the wheel arch liner from under the front wing.

34 Remove the timing belt as described in Chapter 2D.

35 Remove the inlet (rear) camshaft sprocket as described in Chapter 2D, Section 5.

36 Unbolt and remove the timing belt guard brackets from over the coolant pump. One is located on the rear of the engine and the other is located below the exhaust camshaft sprocket.

37 Unscrew the mounting bolts and withdraw the coolant pump from the cylinder head. Recover the O-ring seal.

Inspection

38 Check the pump body and impeller for signs of excessive corrosion. Turn the impeller, and check for stiffness due to corrosion, or roughness due to excessive end play.

39 On 1.6 litre engines, check the clearance between the pump impeller and the casing. Either use vernier calipers to calculate the clearance, or use a feeler blade inserted through the aperture at the rear of the pump housing. If the clearance is different to that given in the *Specifications*, the pump must be renewed.

Refitting

40 Commence refitting by thoroughly cleaning the mating faces of the pump and cylinder block/head/housing.

1.2 litre models

41 Apply a continuous bead of sealant (liquid gasket) to the cylinder block mating face of the pump **(see illustration)**.

42 Locate the pump in the cylinder block casting and insert the mounting bolts/nuts. Progressively tighten them to the specified torque.

43 Refit the timing belt as described in Chapter 2A.

44 Refit the auxiliary drivebelt(s) as described in Chapter 1.

45 Refill the cooling system as described in Chapter 1.

46 Reconnect the battery negative (earth) lead (see *Disconnecting the battery*).

1.4 litre models

47 Locate a new O-ring seal on the coolant pump, then locate it on the cylinder head and insert the mounting bolts. Progressively tighten the bolts to the specified torque.

48 Refit the camshaft sprocket as described in Chapter 2B, Section 5.

49 Refit the timing belt as described in Chapter 2B.

50 Refit the auxiliary drivebelt as described in Chapter 1.

51 Refill the cooling system as described in Chapter 1.

52 Reconnect the battery negative (earth) lead (see *Disconnecting the battery*).

1.6 litre models

Method 1

53 Locate the coolant pump in its housing together with a new O-ring. Insert the bolts and tighten them securely.

54 Locate the pump housing on the cylinder block together with a new gasket, then refit the three shorter bolts and tighten them to the specified torque.

55 Locate the coolant pipe on the rear of the coolant pump together with a new O-ring seal, insert the bolts and tighten them securely.

56 Refit the alternator upper mounting bracket and tighten the bolts securely.

57 Refit the heat shrouds to the exhaust manifold and downpipe, and tighten the bolts.

Method 2

58 Locate the coolant pump in its housing together with a new O-ring. Insert the bolts and tighten them securely.

59 Refit the alternator upper mounting bolt, tightening it securely.

All methods

60 Refit the power steering pump and tension the drivebelt with reference to Chapters 10 and 1. Refit the drivebelt guard and tighten the bolts.

61 On early models, reconnect the fuel lines and tighten the union nuts. Refit the hose bracket to the inlet manifold and tighten the bolts.

62 Where applicable, refit the alternator cooling hose to the right-hand side of the engine compartment.

63 Refit the drivebelt tensioner, and tension the alternator drivebelt with reference to Chapter 1.

64 Refit the wheel arch liner under the right-hand front wing, then refit the roadwheel and lower the vehicle to the ground.

65 Refill the cooling system as described in Chapter 1.

66 Reconnect the battery negative (earth) lead (see *Disconnecting the battery*).

1.8 litre models

67 Locate the coolant pump on the cylinder head together with a new O-ring seal. Insert the bolts and tighten them to the specified torque.

68 Refit the timing belt guard brackets and tighten the bolts to the specified torque.

69 Refit the inlet camshaft sprocket as described in Chapter 2D, Section 5.

70 Refit the timing belt as described in Chapter 2D.

71 Refit the wheel arch liner under the front wing and tighten the fastenings.

72 Refit the right-hand front roadwheel.

73 Refit the auxiliary drivebelt as described in Chapter 1.

74 Refill the cooling system as described in Chapter 1.

8.41 Apply a continuous bead of sealant (liquid gasket) to the pump mating face (1.2 litre models)

75 Reconnect the battery negative (earth) lead (see *Disconnecting the battery*).

9 Heater/ventilation components - removal and refitting

Complete heater assembly (models without air conditioning)

⚠️ *Warning: On models fitted with air conditioning, do not attempt to remove the evaporator, which is located between the heater blower motor and the heater matrix. Removal of the evaporator entails disconnection of refrigerant lines, and this work should be entrusted to a FIAT dealer or refrigeration engineer.*

Removal

1 Disconnect the battery negative (earth) lead (see *Disconnecting the battery*).

2 Drain the cooling system as described in Chapter 1.

3 Remove the facia and centre console as described in Chapter 11.

4 At the rear of the engine compartment, loosen the clips and disconnect the heater hoses from the heater matrix supply and return stubs **(see illustration)**.

5 Inside the vehicle, release the airbag wiring from the retainers on the bulkhead **(see illustration)**. Note the position of the wiring to ensure correct refitting.

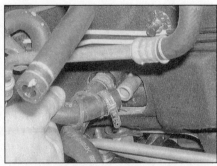

9.4 Disconnecting the heater hoses from the heater matrix supply and return stubs

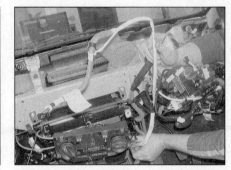

9.5 Releasing the airbag wiring from the retainers

9.7 Disconnect the wiring near the heater motor

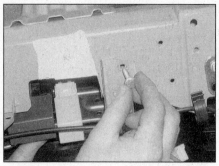

9.9a Undo the support bracket screws . . .

9.9b . . . and move the relays to one side

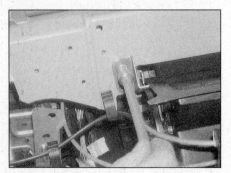

9.9c Heater upper mounting bolt

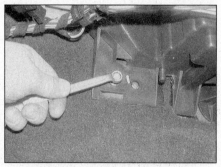

9.9d Heater lower mounting bolt

9.9e Removing the heater assembly from inside the car

6 Disconnect the wiring at the plug located next to the clutch pedal.

7 Disconnect the wiring at the plug located next to the heater blower motor on the left-hand side of the heater assembly (see illustration).

9.10 Bulkhead rubber grommet for the heater matrix pipes

8 Place some cloth rags on the passenger floor to absorb any spilt coolant.

9 Unscrew the mounting bolts and withdraw the complete heater assembly, including the heater controls and the blower motor. There are five bolts accessible from the top of the assembly, and two accessible under the left-hand side. For access to the left-hand bolts, move the relays to one side. Remove the assembly from the vehicle (see illustrations).

Refitting

10 Refitting is a reversal of removal, with reference to Chapter 11 and 1 for the refitting of the facia and refilling of the cooling system. Check that the bulkhead rubber grommet (see illustration) is in good condition before refitting the heater. Make sure that all wiring and cables are routed as noted during dismantling.

Heater blower motor

Removal

11 The heater blower motor is located below the left-hand side of the facia. First make sure that the ignition and heater controls are switched off. For improved access, remove the glovebox as described in Chapter 11.

12 Disconnect the wiring from the blower motor (see illustration).

13 Undo the mounting screw and lower the blower motor from the housing (see illustrations).

Refitting

14 Refitting is a reversal of removal.

Heater matrix

Removal

15 Remove the complete heater assembly as described earlier in this Section.

9.12 Disconnect the wiring . . .

9.13a . . . then undo the mounting screw . . .

9.13b . . . and remove the heater blower motor (heater removed for clarity)

9.16a Remove the sealing packing . . .

9.16b . . . then remove the pipe support . . .

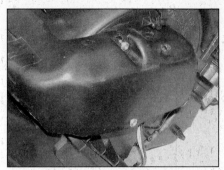

9.16c . . . and matrix end cover

16 Unscrew the bolt and remove the pipe support from the heater body. Also remove the sealing packing and the matrix end cover **(see illustrations)**.

17 Identify the two pipes for position, then undo the screw and remove the holding plate. Ease the pipes from the matrix and recover the O-ring seals **(see illustrations)**.

18 Undo the securing screw and withdraw the matrix from the heater body taking care not to damage the delicate fins **(see illustration)**.

Refitting

19 Refitting is a reversal of removal.

Heater blower motor resistor

Removal

20 The resistor is located at the bottom of the heater casing, behind the blower motor.

21 For improved access, remove the blower motor as described in the previous sub-Section.

22 Disconnect the wiring plug from the resistor **(see illustration)**.

23 Remove the securing screws, and withdraw the resistor **(see illustrations)**.

Refitting

24 Refitting is a reversal of removal.

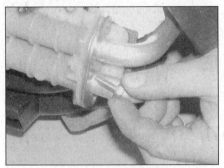

9.17a Undo the screw . . .

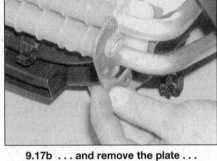

9.17b . . . and remove the plate . . .

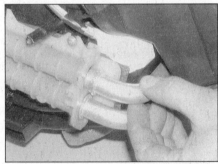

9.17c . . . then remove the pipes

9.18a Undo the screw . . .

9.18b . . . and withdraw the matrix from the heater body

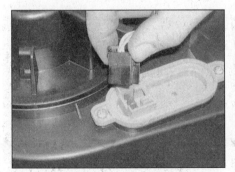

9.22 Disconnect the wiring . . .

9.23a . . . then remove the securing screws . . .

9.23b . . . and withdraw the blower motor resistor (heater removed for clarity)

9.29 Removing the fresh air control knob

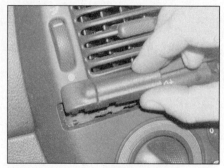

9.30 Prise out the small covers from each end of the facia switches

9.36a Control cable on the side of the heater

Heater control panel

Removal

25 Disconnect the battery negative (earth) lead (see *Disconnecting the battery*).
26 Remove the radio/cassette player as described in Chapter 12.
27 Remove the glovebox as described in Chapter 11.
28 Open the ashtray, then unscrew the heater control panel surround mounting screws. There are two in the ashtray aperture and two more above the radio position.
29 Carefully pull off the heater ventilation centre control knob, using a pair of pliers and a piece of card to protect the knob. Unscrew the panel mounting screw located beneath it. Also pull off the fresh air control knob **(see illustration)**.
30 Using a small screwdriver, carefully prise out the small covers from each end of the facia switches located above the heater control knobs **(see illustration)**. Also, prise out the cover at the centre of the switches noting that on some models the alarm system warning light is located in this position.
31 Undo the screws and withdraw the switch panel from the front of the facia. Disconnect the wiring and remove the switches from the facia.
32 Withdraw the heater control panel surround from the facia and disconnect the wiring from the hazard warning switch.
33 With the ashtray closed, undo the lower mounting screws, then open the ashtray lid and unscrew the upper mounting screws. Withdraw the ashtray from the facia and disconnect the wiring from the cigar lighter.
34 Undo the screws securing the heater controls to the facia. There are four screws.
35 Working in the front footwells, remove the inner trim panels for access to the heater body.
36 Identify the heater control cables for position, then disconnect them and withdraw the heater control panel from the facia **(see illustrations)**.

Refitting

37 Refitting is a reversal of removal.

10 Air conditioning system - general information and precautions

General information

Air conditioning is available as an option on certain models. It enables the temperature of incoming air to be lowered, and also dehumidifies the air, which allows rapid demisting and increased comfort.

The cooling side of the system works in the same way as a domestic refrigerator. Refrigerant gas is drawn into a belt-driven compressor where the increase in pressure causes the refrigerant gas to turn to liquid. It then passes through a condenser mounted on the front of the radiator, where it is cooled. The liquid then passes through an expansion valve to an evaporator, where it changes from liquid under high pressure to gas under low pressure. This change is accompanied by a drop in temperature, which cools the evaporator and hence the air passing over it. The refrigerant returns to the compressor, and the cycle begins again.

The air blown through the evaporator passes to the air distribution unit where it is mixed, if required, with hot air blown through the heater matrix to achieve the desired temperature in the passenger compartment.

The heating side of the system works in the same way as on models without air conditioning (see Section 9).

The system is electronically-controlled. Any problems with the system should be referred to a FIAT dealer.

Precautions

With an air conditioning system, it is necessary to observe special precautions whenever dealing with any part of the system, or its associated components. If for any

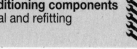

9.36b Heater control panel

reason the system must be disconnected, it is essential that you entrust this task to your FIAT dealer or a refrigeration engineer.

⚠ *Warning: The refrigeration circuit contains a liquid refrigerant, and it is dangerous to disconnect any part of the system without specialised knowledge and equipment.*

11 Air conditioning components - removal and refitting

⚠ *Warning: Do not attempt to open the refrigerant circuit. Refer to the precautions given in Section 10.*

The only operation which can be carried out easily without discharging the refrigerant is renewal of the compressor drivebelt - this procedure is described in Chapter 1, Section 21. All other operations must be referred to a FIAT dealer or an air conditioning specialist.

If necessary for access to other components, the compressor can easily be unbolted and moved aside, *without disconnecting its flexible hoses*, after removing the drivebelt. Access is gained by jacking up the front of the vehicle and support it on axle stands (see *Jacking and vehicle support*), then removing the wheel arch liner.

Chapter 4 Part A:
Fuel system - single-point injection

Contents

Degrees of difficulty

Easy, suitable for novice with little experience	**Fairly easy,** suitable for beginner with some experience	**Fairly difficult,** suitable for competent DIY mechanic	**Difficult,** suitable for experienced DIY mechanic 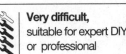	**Very difficult,** suitable for expert DIY or professional

Specifications

System type
1.4 litre models . . . . Bosch Mono-Motronic

Fuel injection system data
Fuel pump type . . . . Electric, immersed in fuel tank
Fuel pump delivery rate . . . . 120 litres/hour minimum
Regulated fuel pressure . . . . 1.0 ± 0.2 bar
Inlet air temperature sensor resistance (approx.):
    At 20°C . . . . 2300 ohms
    At -10°C . . . . 9000 ohms
Coolant temperature sensor resistance (approx.):
    At -10°C . . . . 9000 ohms
    At 20°C . . . . 2300 ohms
    At 100°C . . . . 180 ohms
Injector duration (at idle) . . . . 1.5 ms
Engine idle speed (not adjustable) . . . . 850 ± 50 rpm
Exhaust emissions limits:
    CO . . . . 0.35 % maximum
    HC . . . . 90 ppm maximum
    CO_2 . . . . 13 % maximum
Accelerator cable throttle disc cam-to-stop clearance . . . . 0.2 to 0.5 mm

Recommended fuel
Minimum octane rating . . . . 95 RON unleaded (Premium unleaded)

Torque wrench settings

	Nm	lbf ft
Coolant temperature sensor	25	18
Fuel filter collar nut	5	4
Fuel tank	28	21
Idle control stepper motor	4	3
Inlet manifold	25	18
Inlet union to filter	31	23
Outlet union to filter	15	11
Throttle body-to-manifold bolts:		
M6 bolts	9	7
M8 bolts	25	18
Throttle potentiometer	25	18

2.2a Unscrew the air box securing nuts . . .

2.2b . . . and pull off the breather hose from the camshaft cover

1 General information and precautions

General information

The Bosch Mono-Motronic single point injection (SPI) system fitted only to 1.4 litre engine models is a self-contained engine management system, which controls both the fuel injection and ignition. This Chapter deals with the fuel supply and fuel injection system components only - refer to Chapter 5B for details of the ignition system components.

The fuel supply system comprises a fuel tank, an electric fuel pump, a fuel filter, fuel supply and return lines. The fuel injection system components include the throttle body with an integral electromagnetic fuel injector, and an Electronic Control Unit (ECU) together with its associated sensors, actuators and wiring.

The fuel pump is mounted inside the fuel tank, submerged in the fuel. It delivers a constant supply of fuel through a cartridge filter, mounted underneath the floorpan, to the throttle body. The fuel pressure regulator (integral with the throttle body) maintains a constant fuel pressure at the fuel injector and returns excess fuel to the tank via the return line. This constant flow system also helps to reduce fuel temperature and prevents vaporisation.

The fuel injector is opened and closed by an Electronic Control Unit (ECU), which

calculates the injection timing and duration according to engine speed, throttle position and rate of opening, inlet air temperature, coolant temperature and exhaust gas oxygen content information, received from sensors mounted on the engine.

Inlet air is drawn into the engine through the air cleaner, which contains a renewable paper filter element. The inlet air temperature is regulated by a vacuum operated valve mounted in the air ducting, which blends air at ambient temperature with hot air, drawn from over the exhaust manifold.

Idle speed is controlled principally by a stepper motor located on the side of the throttle body. In addition, fine control of the idle speed is achieved by the ECU advancing or retarding the ignition timing in small increments, to adjust the torque produced by the engine. The ECU provides cold starting enrichment by monitoring the coolant and inlet air temperature parameters and increasing the injector opening duration accordingly.

The exhaust gas oxygen content is constantly monitored by the ECU via the oxygen (or lambda) sensor, which is mounted in the exhaust downpipe. The ECU then uses this information to modify the injection timing and duration to maintain the optimum air/fuel ratio. An exhaust catalyst is fitted to all SPI models. The ECU also controls the operation of the activated charcoal filter evaporative loss system - refer to Chapter 4C for further details.

It should be noted that fault diagnosis of the

Bosch Mono-Motronic system is only possible with dedicated electronic test equipment. Problems with the system should therefore be referred to a FIAT dealer for assessment. Once the fault has been identified, the appropriate removal/refitting procedures detailed in the following Sections can then be followed.

Precautions

Many procedures in this Chapter require the disconnection and/or removal of fuel lines, which may result in fuel spillage. Before carrying out any work on the fuel system, refer to the precautions given in *Safety first!* at the beginning of this manual, and follow them implicitly. Petrol is a highly dangerous and volatile liquid, and the precautions necessary when handling it cannot be overstressed.

Note that residual pressure will remain in the fuel lines long after the vehicle was last used. When disconnecting any fuel line, first depressurise the fuel system as described in Section 8.

2 Air cleaner and inlet system - removal and refitting

Removal

1 Remove the air cleaner element as described in Chapter 1.
2 Slacken and withdraw the three nuts and release the air box from the top of the throttle body. Release the clips and disconnect the breather hoses from the side of the air box or from the camshaft cover (see illustrations).
3 Disconnect the air duct from the air cleaner, then lift the air box and duct from the engine compartment (see illustrations). Recover the sealing ring from the throttle body aperture.
4 Disconnect the vacuum hoses from the throttle body and the air temperature control valve (see illustration).
5 Detach the warm-air inlet hose from the exhaust manifold cowl. Undo the securing screws and detach the air inlet elbow from the inner wing; pull off the (front) air inlet duct which fits between the elbow and the air cleaner lid (see illustrations).

2.3a Release the clip securing the air inlet duct . . .

2.3b . . . and lift the duct and air box from the throttle body

2.4 Disconnect the vacuum hoses from the temperature control valve

6 Slacken and withdraw the securing screws and remove the air cleaner from the engine compartment **(see illustrations)**.

Refitting

7 Refitting is a reversal of removal.

3 Inlet air temperature regulator -
removal and refitting

Flap valve

Checking

1 The flap valve is located in the section of intake ducting that runs between the intake scoop, at the front of the engine compartment, and the front of the air cleaner.
2 To check the operation of the valve, disconnect the hot-air inlet hose with the engine cold, and use a mirror to check that the flap is positioned horizontally, to admit only air from the hot-air inlet hose exhaust manifold.
3 Next, warm up the engine and check that the flap moves to admit a mixture of cold air and hot air from the inlet ducts. If no movement is observed, apply vacuum directly to the flap valve vacuum hose and check for movement. If the valve now operates, the thermostatic vacuum valve may be faulty.

Removal

4 Remove the front intake duct from the air cleaner lid as described in Section 2.
5 Unscrew the retaining screw and remove the flap valve unit from the air duct.

Refitting

6 Refitting is a reversal of removal.

Temperature control valve

Removal

7 Remove the lid from the air cleaner, as described in the air filter renewal procedure in Chapter 1 **(see illustration)**.
8 Disconnect the vacuum hoses from the valve ports **(see illustration)**. Make a careful note of their order of fitment - on the project car, the brown end fitting was the lower connection.
9 Carefully prise off the metal retaining clip and release the valve from the air cleaner lid **(see illustration)**. Recover the gasket and renew it.

Refitting

10 Refitting is a reversal of removal.

4 Accelerator cable -
removal, refitting and adjustment

Removal

1 Disconnect the battery negative cable and position it away from the terminal.

2.5a Pull off the warm-air inlet duct . . .

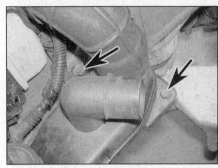

2.5b . . . and unscrew the air inlet elbow from the inner wing

2.6a Air cleaner mounting bolt at the front . . .

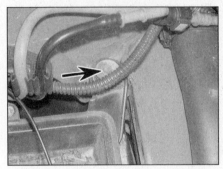

2.6b . . . and the rear of the inner wing (arrowed)

2 Remove the air box from the top of the throttle body as described in Section 2.
3 Relieve the strain from the accelerator cable by grasping the remote throttle disc cam and turning it by hand. Unhook the nipple at the end of the cable inner from the throttle disc cam **(see illustration)**.
4 Remove the outer cable locking clip, then

3.7 View of the temperature control valve with the air cleaner lid removed

3.8 Disconnecting the temperature control valve vacuum hoses from the air cleaner

3.9 Carefully prise off the valve retaining clip

4.3 Unhook the throttle cable from the cam

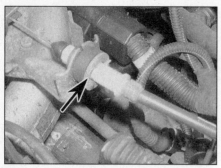

4.4a Remove the outer cable locking clip (arrowed) . . .

4.4b . . . and release the cable from the mounting bracket

4.5 Removing the fuse panel cover

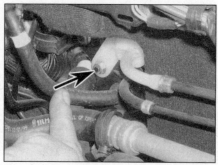

4.7 Accelerator cable guide securing nut (arrowed)

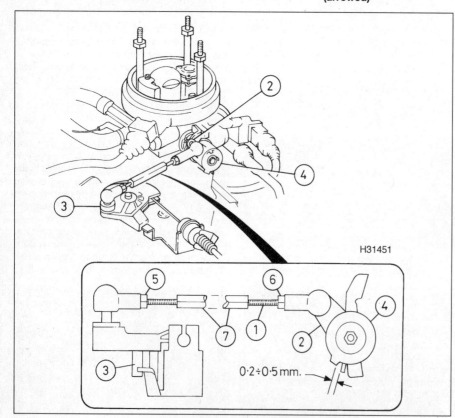

4.18 Accelerator cable and linkrod adjustment details

1	Linkrod	3	Remote throttle disc cam	5	Locknut
2	Throttle body throttle lever	4	Throttle body throttle disc cam	6	Locknut
				7	Hexagonal section

disengage the inner cable from the remote throttle disc cam, and release the outer cable from its mounting bracket **(see illustrations)**. Mark the slot in which the locking clip was fitted, to ensure correct refitting.

5 Undo the securing screw and remove the protective cover from the fuse panel at the rear of the engine compartment **(see illustration)**. Slacken and withdraw the bolts then detach the fuse panel from the bulkhead and position it one side. There is no need to unplug the harness connectors, but take care to avoid straining the wiring.

6 Prise out the stud and detach the right-hand end of the padding panel from the bulkhead, at the rear of the engine compartment.

7 Undo the nut and detach the accelerator cable guide from the bulkhead **(see illustration)**. Prise the rubber grommet from the bulkhead aperture.

8 Release the accelerator cable from the clip located underneath the engine management system ECU, at the rear of the engine compartment.

9 Working in the driver's footwell, undo the three securing screws and remove the footrest.

10 Remove the trim panels from the underside of the facia, as necessary to gain access to the foot pedal mountings. Release the nipple at the end of the accelerator cable from the spigot at the top of the accelerator pedal linkage.

11 Withdraw the accelerator cable through the bulkhead aperture from the inside of the vehicle into the engine compartment.

Refitting

12 Refitting is a reverse of the removal process

Adjustment

13 Disconnect the linkrod from the throttle disc cam by pressing off one of the ball joints.

14 Remove the locking clip from the accelerator cable outer.

15 Adjust the position of the cable in its mounting bracket such that all slack is removed from the cable inner, then refit the clip by sliding it into the slot closest to the surface of the cable mounting bracket.

16 Check that throttle disc is positioned against its end stop - if it is not, there is too much tension in the accelerator cable; reposition the locking clip to slacken the cable slightly. When correctly adjusted, the accelerator cable should eliminate any free movement at the accelerator pedal; check this by moving the pedal by hand.

17 Reconnect the linkrod to the throttle disc cam by pressing the balljoint back onto its spigot. Start the engine and allow it to reach operating temperature, then switch the engine off.

18 At the throttle body, with the accelerator pedal in the rest position, check that the clearance between the throttle disc cam and its stop is as listed in the Specifications. If

5.1 Disconnect the breather hose from the throttle body

5.2a Release the hose clips . . .

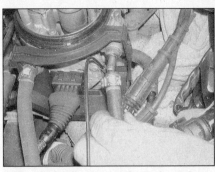

5.2b . . . and disconnect the fuel supply . . .

necessary, adjust the length of the linkrod by slackening the locknuts and rotating the hexagonal section of the rod, to obtain the correct clearance. On completion, tighten the locknuts securely **(see illustration)**.

19 With the engine switched off, have an assistant depress the accelerator pedal fully, then check that the throttle disc is wide open by looking down into the throttle body. Repeat the adjustment process if this is not the case.

---

5 Engine management system components - removal and refitting

Note: *Refer to the precautions in Section 1 before proceeding. Also, check parts availability before dismantling - new parts may have to be sourced from a Bosch agent, rather than from a FIAT dealer.*

5.2c . . . and return hoses from the throttle body

Throttle body assembly

Removal

1 Remove the air box and the associated air ducting from the top of the throttle body as described in Section 2. Disconnect the crankcase breather hose from the front of the throttle body **(see illustration)**.

2 Depressurise the fuel system with reference to Section 8, then release the retaining clips and disconnect the fuel feed and return hoses from the throttle body assembly (the fuel supply hose is at the front, and has an arrow indicating direction of fuel flow). If the original FIAT retaining clips are still fitted, cut the clips and discard them; replace them with standard fuel hose clips on refitting **(see illustrations)**.

3 Unplug the wiring connectors for the idle control stepper motor, fuel injector, and throttle potentiometer **(see illustrations)**. Label each connector to avoid confusion on refitting.

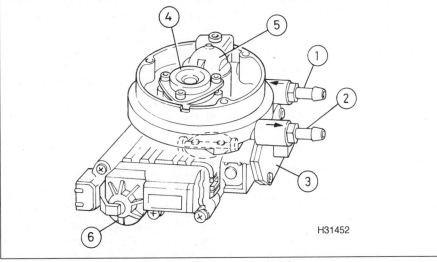

5.3a Throttle body components

1 *Fuel inlet fitting*
2 *Fuel return fitting*
3 *Throttle potentiometer*

4 *Fuel pressure regulator*
5 *Fuel injector*
6 *Idle control stepper motor*

5.3b Disconnect the idle control stepper motor . . .

5.3c . . . fuel injector . . .

5.3d . . . and throttle potentiometer wiring plugs

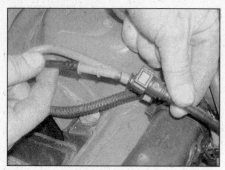

5.5 Disconnecting the charcoal canister hose at the inner wing

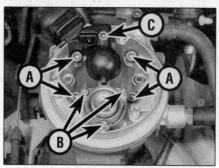

5.6 Throttle body through-bolts (A), fuel pressure regulator screws (B) and injector securing screw (C)

4 Disconnect the accelerator cable inner from the remote throttle disc cam as described in Section 4, then disconnect the link rod from the spigot on the throttle disc cam.

5 Disconnect the vacuum hoses that serve the EVAP purge valve and intake air flap valve from the throttle body. Alternatively, the EVAP hose can be disconnected at the connector above the inner wing **(see illustration)**.

6 Slacken and remove the four through-bolts securing the throttle body assembly to the inlet manifold, then remove the assembly along with its insulating spacer **(see illustration)**. Unless specifically required, it is not recommended that the upper and lower halves of the throttle body are separated - these are held together by two inner through-bolts. If the two halves are split, a new gasket must be used on reassembly.

Refitting

7 Refitting is a reversal of the removal procedure, bearing in mind the following points:
  a) Examine the insulating spacer for signs of damage, and renew if necessary.
  b) Ensure that the throttle body, inlet manifold and insulating spacer mating surfaces are clean and dry, then fit the throttle body and spacer, and securely tighten the retaining bolts.
  c) Ensure that all hoses are correctly reconnected and, where necessary, that their retaining clips are securely tightened.
  d) Adjust the accelerator cable as described in Section 4.

Fuel injector

Note: *If a faulty injector is suspected, before condemning the injector, it is worth trying the effect of one of the proprietary injector cleaning treatments.*

Removal

8 Remove the air box and the associated air ducting from the top of the throttle body as described in Section 2.

9 Refer to Section 8 and depressurise the fuel system, then disconnect the battery negative lead and position it away from the terminal.

10 Unplug the wiring harness from the injector.

11 Remove the screw and lift off the injector retaining cap/inlet air temperature sensor housing. Recover the gasket.

12 Release the securing washer, then lift the injector out of the throttle body, recovering the O-ring seals **(see illustration)**.

Refitting

13 Refit the injector by following the removal procedure in reverse, renewing all O-ring seals and gaskets. Apply a suitable sealant to the screw threads, then insert and tighten the retaining screw.

Fuel pressure regulator

Removal

14 Remove the air box and the associated air ducting from the top of the throttle body as described in Section 2.

15 Using a marker pen, make alignment marks between the regulator cover and the throttle body, then undo the three Torx retaining screws. As the screws are loosened, place a rag over the cover to catch any fuel spray which may be released.

16 Lift off the cover, then remove the spring and withdraw the diaphragm, noting its correct fitted orientation. Remove all traces of dirt, and examine the diaphragm for signs of splitting. If damage is found, it may be necessary to renew the complete throttle body assembly - consult a FIAT dealer or Bosch agent.

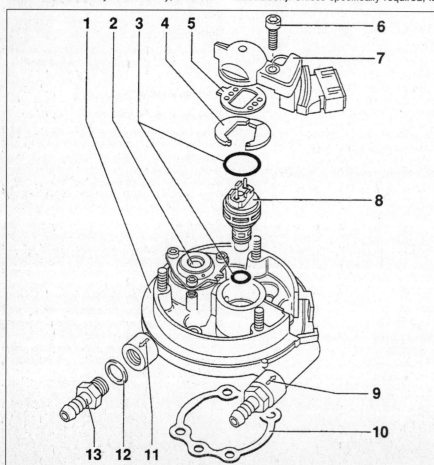

5.12 Upper half of throttle body, showing injector fitting details

1 Throttle body upper section	6 Injector/air inlet temperature sensor securing screw	9 Fuel supply connection
2 Fuel pressure regulator	7 Air inlet temperature sensor	10 Upper-to lower section gasket
3 O-ring	8 Fuel injector	11 Fuel return connection
4 Securing washer		12 Seal
5 Gasket		13 Fuel hose connection stub

Refitting

17 Refitting is a reversal of removal, ensuring that the diaphragm and cover are fitted the correct way round, and that the retaining screws are securely tightened.

Idle control stepper motor

Removal

18 Remove the air box and the associated air ducting from the top of the throttle body as described in Section 2.

19 Using a crosshead screwdriver, unscrew the three mounting screws and remove the stepper motor from the throttle body. Recover the gasket.

20 Clean the unit and check for damage and wear.

Refitting

21 When refitting the unit, use a new gasket and make sure that the plunger is inserted correctly using the following procedure:

a) *Insert the unit and refit the mounting screws loosely.*

b) *Reconnect the wiring, then switch on the ignition several times so that the unit centralises itself.*

c) *Securely tighten the mounting screws.*

d) *Disconnect the battery negative cable, and leave it disconnected for about 20 minutes - the injection/ignition ECU will then position the idle control stepper motor correctly when the battery is reconnected and the engine is started for the first time.*

Throttle potentiometer

22 The position of the throttle potentiometer with respect to the throttle disc is pre-set at the factory. Consequently, if the potentiometer is found to be faulty, the entire throttle body must be renewed.

Inlet air temperature sensor

23 The inlet air temperature sensor is an integral part of the fuel injector assembly, and cannot apparently be renewed separately - check with a FIAT dealer or Bosch agent.

Coolant temperature sensor

Removal

24 The coolant temperature sensor is located

5.26 Disconnect the wiring from the coolant temperature sensor

on the left-hand side of the cylinder head, threaded into the coolant outlet elbow.

25 Drain the cooling system with reference to Chapter 1.

26 Unplug the wiring from the sensor at the connector **(see illustration)**.

27 Unscrew the sensor and remove it from the cylinder head. Recover the sealing washer where fitted. If using a socket, take care not to damage the wiring connector on the sensor.

Refitting

28 Refitting is a reversal of removal. Where applicable, fit a new sealing washer. Tighten the sensor to the specified torque. Do not exceed the specified torque otherwise the unit's threads may be damaged.

Crankshaft TDC sensor

29 Refer to Chapter 5B, Section 6.

Electronic control unit (ECU)

Note: *The ECU communicates with the anti-theft/immobiliser system when the vehicle is started; once the ignition key electronic code has been stored by the ECU, it cannot be used on any other vehicle. For this reason, do not attempt to diagnose problems with the engine management system by connecting the ECU to another vehicle, or by substituting an ECU from another vehicle.*

Removal

30 The ECU (electronic control unit) is mounted on the bulkhead at the rear of the engine compartment.

31 Prior to removal, disconnect the battery negative cable from its terminal. Discon-

5.32 Engine management ECU

necting the ECU multi-plug while there is any power connected to it may well result in damage to the ECU.

32 Release the locking clip at the lower end of the multiway connector, then unhook the upper end by pivoting the connector away from the ECU. Undo the retaining screws and remove the ECU from its bracket **(see illustration)**.

Refitting

33 Refitting is a reversal of removal, making sure that the wiring connector is securely reconnected.

Inertia switch

Removal - early models

34 The inertia safety switch is located underneath the driver's seat. Slide the seat back as far as possible then pull back the carpet for access.

35 Unscrew the two securing bolts, then disconnect the wiring and remove the switch from the vehicle.

Refitting

36 Refitting is a reversal of removal. If the switch was tripped during removal, reset it after refitting by depressing the centre of the rubber cap.

Removal - later models

37 On later models, the inertia switch is located behind a plastic panel to the left of the passenger's footwell.

38 Remove the sill trim panel by removing the two screws and releasing the securing clips **(see illustrations)**.

5.38a Remove the screw at the front . . .

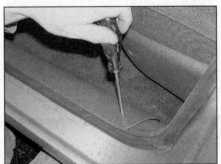

5.38b . . . and at the rear . . .

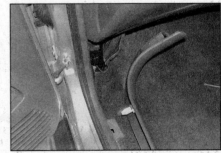

5.38c . . . then release the clips and remove the sill trim panel

5.39 View of the inertia switch, showing the wiring plug and one of the securing bolts

5.40 The inertia switch can be reset without removing the sill trim panel, if required

5.41a Remove the screw and lift off the engine compartment fusebox outer cover . . .

5.41b . . . then lift off the inner cover for access to the fuses

5.42a Unscrew the knob and remove the cover . . .

39 Unscrew the two securing bolts, then disconnect the wiring and remove the switch from the vehicle **(see illustration).**

Refitting

40 Refitting is a reversal of removal. If the switch was tripped during removal, reset it after refitting by depressing the centre of the rubber cap **(see illustration).**

Fuel injection system fuses and relays

Removal

41 The main system 30A fuse is located underneath a plastic cover at the left-hand

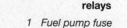

5.42b . . . for access to the fuses and relays

1 *Fuel pump fuse*
2 *Injection/ignition system fuse*
3 *Injection/ignition system relay*
4 *Fuel pump relay*

rear corner of the engine compartment **(see illustrations).**
42 Individual fuses for the fuel pump and the injection/ignition system are mounted in the relay box, located to the rear of the engine compartment, directly behind the throttle body intake air box. To gain access, unscrew the knob and lift off the cover **(see illustrations).**
43 To renew a fuse, ensure that the battery negative cable is disconnected, then pull the existing fuse from its socket and press a new one into place.
44 To remove a relay, ensure that the battery negative cable is disconnected, then unclip the relay from its mountings and unplug the wiring connector.

Refitting

45 Refitting is a reversal of removal.

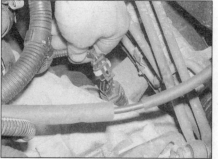

5.47 Unplug the connector for the speedometer sensor

Vehicle speed (speedometer) sensor

Removal

46 The vehicle speed sensor is mounted on the top of the transmission casing.
47 Unplug the wiring connector, then unscrew the sensor from the transmission casing **(see illustration).**

Refitting

48 Refitting is a reversal of removal.

---

6 Fuel pump/ fuel gauge sender unit - removal and refitting

Removal

Note: *Refer to the precautions in Section 1 before proceeding.*
1 Disconnect the negative cable from the battery terminal.
2 Remove the press-stud fixings and detach the carpet from the load space floor.
3 Undo the screws and remove the dust cover from the access aperture in the floorpan **(see illustrations).**
4 Bearing in mind the warning given in Section 1, disconnect the fuel supply and return lines from the fuel pump/gauge sender unit by pressing the tabs **(see illustration).** Plug the ends of the lines or cover them with adhesive tape, to prevent the ingress of

6.3a Remove the screws . . .

6.3b . . . and take off the dust cover for access to the sender unit

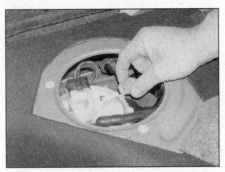

6.4 Disconnecting the fuel supply pipe from the sender unit

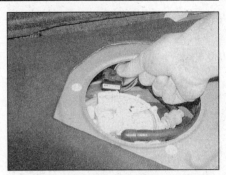

6.5 Unplug the wiring connector from the sender unit

debris. Label the fuel lines to ensure correct refitting.

5 Unplug the wiring connector from the top of the fuel pump/gauge sender unit **(see illustration)**.

6 Where applicable, remove the nut securing the breather pipe to the tank, then prise the pipe end fitting out of the tank **(see illustration)**.

7 Using a suitable tool, unscrew the large ring nut that secures the pump/sender unit to the top of the fuel tank **(see Tool Tip)**.

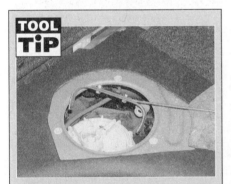

TOOL TiP

With the limited access available to the sender unit ring nut, and the fact that the nut is very tight, we had to make up a tool to unscrew it. The tool is made from two metal strips - one bent to fit across the ring nut to provide two 'legs' which engage in the ribs on the ring nut, and one bolted to the first, to act as a handle.

8 Carefully withdraw the unit from the fuel tank. Some careful manipulation will be required, to allow the sender unit float arm to exit the tank without snagging. Suspend the unit above the tank aperture for a few minutes, to allow the excess fuel to drain away **(see illustration)**.

9 Recover the sealing ring from the fuel tank aperture.

HAYNES HiNT *If the pump/sender unit is not being refitted immediately, screw the retaining nut back onto the tank temporarily, as the fittings may swell over a period of time, making refitting difficult.*

10 The sender unit fuel filter can be inspected by unclipping the round cover at the base of the unit. The float assembly can

6.8 Removing the pump/sender unit

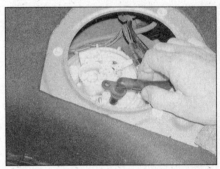

6.6 Disconnecting the fuel tank breather pipe

also be unclipped from the side of the unit, and the wiring disconnected **(see illustrations)**. The pump unit hoses must be disconnected before it too is unclipped from the base of the unit - it appears, however, that separating the hose connections may destroy them, so have replacement hoses available for refitting.

11 From the FIAT information available at the time of writing, it appears that no pump/sender unit components are available separately.

Refitting

12 Refitting is a reversal of the removal procedure, noting the following points:

a) It is advisable to use a new sealing ring.

b) Refit the ring nut loosely to the top of the sender unit before offering it into position **(see illustration)**.

c) Take care as the unit is fitted that the

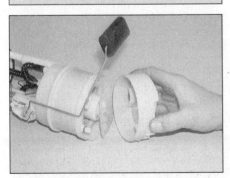

6.10a Once the base of the unit has been unclipped . . .

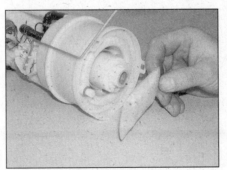

6.10b . . . the pump filter can also be unclipped and removed

6.10c Removing the float assembly

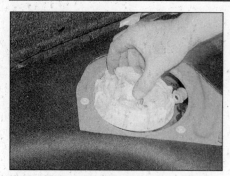

6.12a Make sure the ring nut is in position before fitting the unit

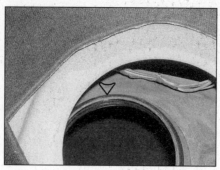

6.12b Arrowhead marking on top of the fuel tank

sealing ring does not get pushed into the tank.

d) Align the arrowhead marking on top of the tank with the similar mark on the sender unit **(see illustration)**.

e) Prior to refitting the access cover, reconnect the battery, then start the engine and check the unions for signs of leakage.

7 Fuel tank - removal and refitting

Note: *Refer to the precautions in Section 1 before proceeding.*

Removal

1 Before removing the fuel tank, all fuel must be drained from the tank. Since a fuel tank drain plug is not provided, it is therefore preferable to carry out the removal operation when the tank is nearly empty. Before proceeding, disconnect the battery negative lead and syphon or hand-pump the remaining fuel from the tank.

2 Remove the fuel pump/fuel gauge sender unit as described in Section 6.

3 Chock the front wheels, then jack up the rear of the vehicle and support on axle stands (see *Jacking and vehicle support*).

4 Open the fuel filler flap and carefully release the filler neck flexible gaiter from the bodywork.

5 To improve access, remove the fasteners securing the rear wheel arch liner(s). Working

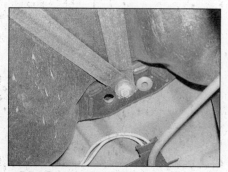

7.7a Fuel tank retaining strap front . . .

via the wheel arch, undo the screw and release the filler neck from the bodywork.

6 Position a trolley jack or similar centrally underneath the fuel tank and raise it until it is just supporting the weight of the tank. Prevent damage to the underside of the tank by placing a block of wood between the jack head and the tank.

7 Undo the front and rear fuel tank strap securing bolts, recover the spacer washers, then carefully lower the fuel tank away from the floorpan **(see illustrations)**. Loosen the clips and disconnect the EVAP purge hose and breather hose from the fuel tank as they become accessible.

8 Check that all hoses and wiring are disconnected, then lower the tank to the ground and remove it from underneath the vehicle.

Refitting

9 Refitting is a reversal of the removal procedure, ensuring all hoses are correctly routed and securely reconnected.

8 Fuel injection system - depressurisation

Note: *Refer to the precautions in Section 1 before proceeding.*

1 The fuel supply system referred to in this Section is defined as the tank-mounted fuel pump, the fuel filter, the throttle body and pressure regulator components, and the metal pipes and flexible hoses of the fuel lines

7.7b . . . and rear bolts

between these components. All these contain fuel which will be under pressure while the engine is running and/or while the ignition is switched on. The pressure will remain for some time after the ignition has been switched off, and must be relieved before any of these components are disturbed for servicing work.

2 Make sure that the ignition is switched off (take out the key). Unscrew the knob and remove the cover from the fuse/relay holder directly behind the throttle body air box.

3 Referring to Section 5, pull out the fuse for the fuel pump. If the injection/ignition fuse or the main system fuse are removed, the injector will not open, so defeating the purpose of this exercise.

4 Try to start the engine, keeping the engine cranking for several seconds. It may fire and run for a little while - if so, let it run until it stops.

5 Once the injector has opened and closed several times, this will reduce the fuel pressure to a safer level. However, fuel will still be present in the system, and care should still be taken.

6 Disconnect the negative cable from the battery terminal, then refit the fuel pump fuse and the fuse/relay box cover.

7 Place a container beneath the relevant connection/union to be disconnected, and have a large rag ready to soak up any escaping fuel not being caught by the container.

8 Slowly loosen the connection or union nut (as applicable) to avoid a sudden release of fuel, and wrap the rag around the connection to catch any fuel which may be expelled. Once the fuel has been soaked up, disconnect the fuel line, and insert plugs to minimise fuel loss and prevent the entry of dirt into the fuel system.

9 Inlet manifold - removal and refitting

Note: *Refer to the precautions in Section 1 before proceeding.*

Removal

1 Remove the throttle body assembly as described in Section 5. Alternatively, using the information in Section 5, disconnect the wiring plugs and hoses from the throttle body, and remove with the manifold as an assembly.

2 Drain the cooling system as described in Chapter 1.

3 Disconnect the wiring connector from the coolant temperature sensor (situated on the left-hand side of the manifold).

4 Undo the bolt securing the accelerator cable mounting bracket to the manifold, and position it clear of the manifold.

5 Slacken the retaining clip and disconnect the coolant hose from the rear of the manifold. Alternatively, this hose can be disconnected

9.5 Disconnect the inlet manifold coolant supply hose

9.6 Unscrew the clip and disconnect the brake servo vacuum hose

9.7a Unscrew the manifold retaining nuts (seven of eight arrowed) . . .

9.7b . . . withdraw the manifold from the cylinder head studs . . .

9.7c . . . and remove it from the engine

9.7d Removing the inlet manifold gasket

at the coolant elbow in front of the timing belt cover **(see illustration)**.

6 Disconnect the brake vacuum hose **(see illustration)**.

7 Undo the eight manifold retaining nuts, recover the split washers, and remove the manifold from the engine. Remove the gasket and discard it; a new one should be used on refitting **(see illustrations)**. Note the plastic locating pins used to secure the gasket to the inlet manifold - transfer them to the new gasket.

Refitting

8 Refitting is a reverse of the removal procedure, noting the following points:

 a) *Check the condition of the core plugs fitted to the base of the manifold. If signs of leakage are evident, the plugs should be removed, and new ones tapped in.*

 b) *Ensure that the manifold and cylinder head mating surfaces are clean and dry, and fit a new manifold gasket. Use the plastic locating pins to secure the gasket to the manifold - tap them in with a pin punch until they are flush with the gasket surface* **(see illustrations)**.

 c) *Refit the manifold and washers over the cylinder head studs, and securely tighten the retaining nuts.*

 d) *Ensure that all relevant hoses are reconnected to their original positions and are securely held (where necessary) by the retaining clips.*

 e) *Refit (or reconnect) the throttle body with reference to Section 5.*

 f) *On completion, refill the cooling system as described in Chapter 1.*

10 Fuel injection system - checking and adjustment

Checking

Note: *Also see Chapter 5B, Section 3.*

1 Before disconnecting any of the injection system wiring, ensure that the ignition is switched off (take out the key).

2 If a fault appears in the fuel injection system, first ensure that all the system wiring connectors are securely connected and free of corrosion. Also check the wiring harness for signs of damage, such as may result if the wiring is routed too close to a hot component, for example.

3 Remove the cover from the fuse/relay box behind the throttle body, and check the connections to the fuses and relays. With the

ignition switched off, remove the fuses and relays in turn, and check that the fuse and relay contacts, and their sockets in the box, are clean. Refit the fuses and relays securely. Similarly check the 30A fuse in the box at the left rear corner of the engine compartment (refer to Section 5).

4 The system's main earth point is located at the right-hand rear of the cylinder head, just in front of No 1 spark plug. Remove the bolt securing the earth terminal, and clean all contact surfaces thoroughly **(see illustrations)**. Refit the terminal and bolt, and tighten it securely.

5 Then ensure that the fault is not due to poor maintenance; ie, check that the air cleaner filter element is clean, the spark plugs are in good condition and correctly gapped, the HT leads are securely connected and in good condition, and that the engine breather hoses are clear and undamaged.

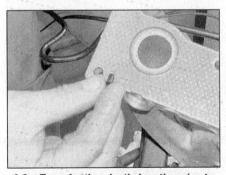

9.8a Transfer the plastic locating pins to the new gasket . . .

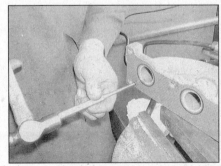

9.8b . . . and tap them in flush with a pin punch

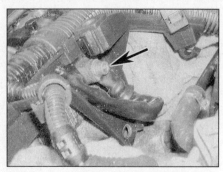

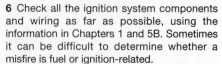

10.4a Unscrew the bolt (arrowed) below the wiring harness bracket . . .

10.4b . . . and take off the earth lead

10.8 Diagnostic connector (arrowed) located behind the throttle body

6 Check all the ignition system components and wiring as far as possible, using the information in Chapters 1 and 5B. Sometimes it can be difficult to determine whether a misfire is fuel or ignition-related.

7 If the engine is difficult to start, or runs poorly, when cold, the problem may be that the engine management system has gone into emergency back-up mode. This, and the nature of the fault that caused it to happen, can only be determined using diagnostic equipment such as a fault code reader.

8 A diagnostic connector is located behind the throttle body, into which a fault code reader can be plugged **(see illustration)**. The test equipment is capable of 'interrogating' the engine management system electronically and accessing its internal fault log.

9 Fault codes can only be extracted from the ECU using a dedicated fault code reader. A FIAT dealer will obviously have such a reader, but they are also available from other suppliers, including Haynes. It is unlikely to be cost-effective for the private owner to purchase a fault code reader, but a well-equipped local garage or auto electrical specialist will have one.

10 Using this equipment, faults can be pinpointed quickly and simply, even if their occurrence is intermittent. Testing all the system components individually in an attempt to locate the fault by elimination is a time-consuming operation that is unlikely to be fruitful (particularly if the fault occurs dynamically), and carries high risk of damage to the ECU's internal components.

Adjustment

11 Experienced home mechanics equipped with an accurate tachometer and a carefully-calibrated exhaust gas analyser may be able to check the exhaust gas CO content and the engine idle speed; if these are found to be out of specification, then the vehicle must be taken to a suitably-equipped FIAT dealer for assessment.

12 Neither the air/fuel mixture (exhaust gas CO content) nor the engine idle speed are manually adjustable; incorrect test results indicate the need for maintenance (possibly, injector cleaning) or a fault within the fuel injection system.

11 Unleaded petrol - general information and usage

Note: *The information given in this Chapter is correct at the time of writing. If updated information is thought to be required, check with a FIAT dealer. If travelling abroad, consult one of the motoring organisations (or a similar authority) for advice on the fuel available.*

1 The fuel recommended by FIAT is given in the Specifications at the start of this Chapter, followed by the equivalent petrol currently on sale in the UK.

2 All models are fitted with a catalytic converter and must be run on unleaded fuel **only**, with a minimum octane rating of 95 RON. Under no circumstances should leaded fuel (eg UK 4-star) or lead replacement petrol (LRP) be used, as this may damage the converter.

3 Super unleaded petrol (98 octane) can also be used in all models if desired.

Chapter 4 Part B:
Fuel system - multi-point injection

Contents

Degrees of difficulty

Easy, suitable for novice with little experience	**Fairly easy,** suitable for beginner with some experience	**Fairly difficult,** suitable for competent DIY mechanic 	**Difficult,** suitable for experienced DIY mechanic	**Very difficult,** suitable for expert DIY or professional

Specifications

System type

1.2 litre models	Bosch Motronic 1.5.5 engine management system
1.6 litre models	Weber IAW engine management system
1.8 litre models	Hitachi engine management system

Fuel system data

Fuel pump type	Electric, immersed in fuel tank
Fuel pump delivery rate	120 litres/hour
Regulated fuel pressure	3.0 bar
Coolant temperature sensor:	
At -10°C	9000 to 10 000 ohms
At 0°C	5700 to 6300 ohms
At 30°C	1600 to 1700 ohms
At 100°C	137 to 133 ohms
Inlet air temperature sensor:	
At 0°C	5300 to 6500 ohms
At 10°C	3400 to 4200 ohms
At 20°C	2300 to 2700 ohms
Injector electrical resistance:	
1.2 litre models	16.2 ohms
1.6 litre models	13.7 to 15.2 ohms
1.8 litre models	10.8 to 13.2 ohms
Engine idle speed (non-adjustable):	
1.2 litre models	800 ± 30 rpm
1.6 litre models	800 ± 30 rpm
1.8 litre models	850 ± 50 rpm
Exhaust emissions limit:	
CO	0.35 % maximum

Recommended fuel

Minimum octane rating	95 RON unleaded (Premium unleaded)

Torque wrench settings

	Nm	lbf ft
Coolant temperature sensor	25	18
Inlet manifold:		
1.2 litre	15	11
1.6 litre	30	22
1.8 litre	25	18

1 General information and precautions

General information

Three different types of engine management system are fitted to the multi-point fuel injection models covered in this Chapter. Each of the systems covered here is a self-contained engine management system, controlling both the fuel injection and ignition functions. This Chapter deals with the fuel injection system components only - refer to Chapter 5B for details of the ignition system components. Chapter 4A covers the fuel injection system components fitted to 1.4 litre models with single-point fuel injection.

The engine management systems are very similar in their design and operation; similarities and differences are outlined in the following text.

The fuel injection system comprises a fuel tank with an electric fuel pump, a fuel filter, fuel supply and return lines, a throttle body, a fuel rail with four electromagnetic fuel injectors, and an Electronic Control Unit (ECU) together with its associated sensors, actuators and wiring.

The fuel pump has an integrated fuel gauge level sender and is mounted inside the fuel tank, immersed in the fuel. It delivers a constant supply of fuel through a cartridge filter to the throttle body and fuel pressure regulator (which is mounted on the fuel rail). The pressure regulator maintains a near-constant fuel pressure at the fuel injectors, and returns excess fuel to the tank via the return line. This constant-flow system also helps to prevent localised fuel heating in the engine compartment, reducing the fuel vaporisation that can cause difficult hot starting. Note that all 1.2 litre, and later 1.6 litre, models do not have a fuel return line or fuel rail-mounted pressure regulator; the pressure regulator is housed inside the fuel pump itself, in the fuel tank.

The electromagnetic, pintle-type fuel injectors are opened and closed by an Electronic Control Unit (ECU), which calculates the injection timing and duration according to engine speed, throttle position and rate of opening, engine load, coolant temperature and exhaust gas oxygen content information, received from sensors mounted on and around the engine. The injectors are operated sequentially, so that the required quantity of fuel for each cylinder is injected once per cycle, on the induction stroke only. During starting, engine timing cannot be established until the crankshaft has started and rotated at least twice. During this time, banked injection is employed, ie fuel is injected into all cylinders simultaneously until the correct timing can be established.

1.2 and 1.6 litre models measure engine load by calculating the mass of air entering

2.1 Removing the air intake

the engine. This is achieved by monitoring signals from the inlet air temperature and inlet manifold vacuum sensors; air volume and density measurements can be derived from these sensors, allowing air mass to be calculated.

1.8 litre models use a different approach - the mass of air entering the engine is measured directly by a hot-wire type mass airflow meter. Air passing through the meter cools an electrically-heated wire filament, the amount of cooling is proportional to the air mass flow rate. The cooling has the effect of altering the electrical resistance of the filament and this in turn alters the signal voltage produced by the meter and sent to the ECU. As the mass air mass flow rate is measured directly, there is no requirement for an inlet air temperature sensor or a manifold absolute pressure sensor.

Inlet air is drawn into the engine through the air cleaner, which contains a renewable paper filter element.

Idle speed is controlled principally by an idle speed actuator, mounted on the side of the throttle body. On 1.6 litre and 1.8 litre models, the actuator controls a valve which alters the amount of air that bypasses the main throttle valve. On 1.2 litre models, the idle actuator acts directly on the throttle valve, rather than controlling a separate bypass valve. In addition, fine control of the idle speed is achieved by the ECU advancing or retarding the ignition timing in small increments, to adjust the torque produced by the engine. Loads that can have a sudden significant effect on engine idle speed (such

2.2 Removing the first section of air inlet duct

as the air conditioning, power steering and automatic transmission systems) are monitored via additional sensors. When such loads are detected, the ECU increases the engine idle speed to prevent stalling.

Information on the degree of throttle opening, and the rate of its change, is provided by the throttle potentiometer (or position sensor). This device is effectively a variable resistor attached to the throttle valve. Its most important function is to signal the ECU when the throttle is in the idle (closed) or full-throttle (wide open) positions.

The ECU provides cold starting fuel mixture enrichment by monitoring the coolant and inlet air temperature parameters and increasing the injector opening duration accordingly.

The exhaust gas oxygen content is constantly monitored by the ECU via the oxygen (lambda) sensor, which is mounted in the exhaust downpipe. The ECU then uses this information to modify the injection timing and duration to maintain the optimum air/fuel ratio. An exhaust catalyst is fitted to all models. The ECU also controls the operation of the activated charcoal filter evaporative loss system - refer to Chapter 4D for further details.

Precautions

Many procedures in this Chapter require the removal of fuel lines and connections, which may result in fuel spillage. Before carrying out any operation on the fuel system, refer to the precautions given in *Safety first!* at the beginning of this manual, and follow them implicitly. Petrol is a highly dangerous and volatile liquid, and the precautions necessary when handling it cannot be overstressed.

Note that residual pressure will remain in the fuel lines long after the vehicle was last used. When disconnecting any fuel line, first depressurise the fuel system (see Section 7).

2 Air cleaner and inlet system - removal and refitting

Removal

1 Unscrew and remove the two bolts from the front crossmember, and lift out the air intake, disconnecting it from the air inlet duct leading to the air cleaner (slacken the securing clip, where applicable) **(see illustration)**.

2 The first section of the air inlet duct can be removed from the air cleaner either by slackening the securing clip, or by pulling and twisting the duct to release it **(see illustration)**.

3 On 1.8 litre models, a resonator box is fitted under the front crossmember. This can be removed if required by slackening the clip securing the air hose to the air cleaner elbow, and then removing the bolt securing the resonator to the front crossmember.

2.5 Disconnecting the breather hose from the air inlet duct

2.6 Disconnecting the air inlet duct from the air cleaner lid

2.7a Unscrew and remove the airflow meter mounting bolts . . .

2.7b . . . then disconnect the airflow meter wiring plug

2.8 Removing the air inlet duct

2.9a To remove the air cleaner, undo the bolt at the front . . .

4 Remove the air cleaner element as described in Chapter 1.

5 Where applicable, slacken the clips and disconnect the crankcase ventilation hoses from the main air inlet duct that connects the throttle body to the air cleaner **(see illustration)**.

6 If not already done, release the clip and detach the main air inlet duct from the air cleaner lid **(see illustration)**.

7 On 1.8 litre models, unscrew the two bolts securing the airflow meter to its mounting bracket, then disconnect the wiring plug **(see illustrations)**. Unless the airflow meter is being worked on, it is best to remove the meter with the inlet duct - otherwise the two clips at either end of the meter must be disturbed.

8 Release the hose clips securing the main intake duct to the throttle body, then pull the duct away from the throttle body **(see illustration)**. Recover the sealing ring (where fitted). Check the ring for condition and renew it if necessary.

9 Slacken and withdraw the securing bolts **(see illustrations)** and lift the air cleaner from the engine compartment, noting the following points:

a) On 1.2 litre models, it will be necessary to disconnect the secondary resonator pipe before removing the intake duct.

b) On the models seen in our workshop, it was found that the air cleaner would not come out upwards, and in fact the left-hand wheelarch liner had to be removed to lower the air cleaner from its location.

Refitting

10 Refitting is a reversal of removal.

3 Accelerator cable - removal, refitting and adjustment

Removal

1 Disconnect the battery negative cable and position it away from the terminal as described in Chapter 5A.

2 Working in the driver's footwell, undo the three securing screws and remove the footrest. Remove the trim panels from the underside of the facia, as necessary to gain access to the foot pedal mountings.

3 Release the plastic eyelet at the end of the accelerator cable from the spigot at the top of the accelerator pedal linkage.

4 Relieve the tension from the accelerator cable by grasping the throttle quadrant and turning it by hand. Unhook the nipple at the end of the cable inner from the throttle quadrant **(see illustration)**.

5 Working at the accelerator cable mounting bracket, unscrew the adjuster sleeve (or remove the adjustment clip), then withdraw the accelerator cable outer from the bracket grommet. Prise the grommet from the bracket (where necessary) and move the cable away from the throttle body **(see illustration)**. Note that on earlier 1.6 litre models, the cable outer is secured to the bracket by means of a metal spring clip. Slide the clip free to release the cable from the bracket, but note the slot to which clip was fitted, to aid refitting.

6 Release the accelerator cable from the clip located underneath the power steering fluid reservoir, at the rear of the engine compartment.

2.9b . . . and at the rear, securing the air cleaner to the inner wing

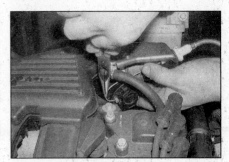

3.4 Open the throttle by hand, and unhook the cable end fitting from the throttle quadrant

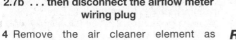

7 Unscrew and remove the nut securing the plastic cable mounting to the bulkhead, and release the mounting from the grommet in the bulkhead **(see illustration)**.

8 Withdraw the accelerator cable through the bulkhead aperture from the inside of the vehicle into the engine compartment.

Refitting

9 Refitting is a reverse of the removal process. On completion, adjust the cable as described in the next sub-Section.

Adjustment - early 1.6 litre models

10 Working at the cable mounting bracket adjacent to the throttle body in the engine compartment, remove the spring clip from the slotted section of the accelerator cable outer.

11 Pull the cable lightly through the mounting bracket to tension it, so that all slack in the cable inner is taken up, however do apply so much tension that the throttle disc starts to turn.

12 Press the spring clip into the nearest accessible slot in cable outer, so that the clip bears against the surface of the mounting bracket.

13 Check that throttle disc is positioned against its end stop - if it is not, there is too

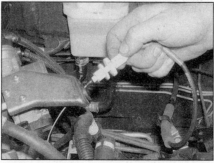

3.5 Unscrew the adjuster and release the cable end fitting from its mounting bracket

much tension in the accelerator cable - correct this by repositioning the spring clip in the adjacent slot **(see illustration)**. When correctly adjusted, the accelerator cable should eliminate any free movement at the accelerator pedal; check this by moving the pedal by hand.

Adjustment - 1.2 litre, later 1.6 litre and 1.8 litre models

14 Working at the cable mounting bracket adjacent to the throttle body in the engine compartment, loosen the locknut (where fitted) and turn the adjustment sleeve until all

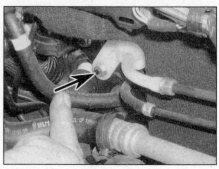

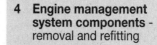

3.7 Accelerator cable guide securing nut (arrowed)

slack is removed from the cable inner **(see illustration)**.

15 Check that throttle disc is positioned against its end stop - if it is not, there is too much tension in the accelerator cable - slacken the adjustment sleeve slightly. When correctly adjusted, the accelerator cable should eliminate any free movement at the accelerator pedal; check this by moving the pedal by hand.

16 With the engine switched off, have an assistant depress the accelerator pedal fully, then check that the throttle disc is wide open by looking down into the throttle body. Repeat the adjustment process if this is not the case. Where applicable, tighten the locknut on completion.

4 Engine management system components - removal and refitting

Note: Refer to the precautions in Section 1 before proceeding.

Throttle body assembly

Removal

1 Disconnect the negative cable from the battery terminal.

2 With reference to Section 2, remove the section of air inlet duct that connects the throttle body to the air cleaner.

3 Unplug the wiring connectors from the idle air control valve and the throttle potentiometer **(see illustrations)**.

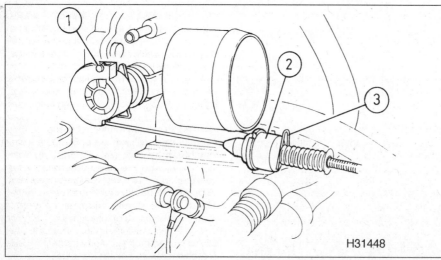

H31448

3.13 Cable end fitting (1), grooved cable outer (2) and spring clip (3)

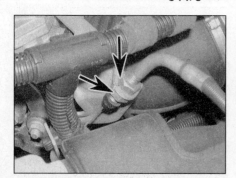

3.14 Accelerator cable locknut and adjuster nut (arrowed) - 1.8 litre model

4.3a Disconnect the idle air control valve . . .

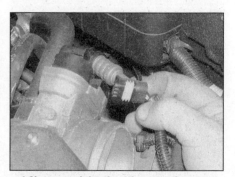

4.3b . . . and the throttle potentiometer (1.6 litre model)

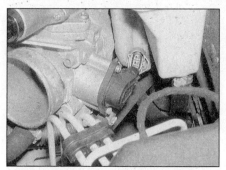

4.3c Disconnecting the throttle potentiometer on a 1.8 litre model

4.6a Release the hose clips . . .

4.6b . . . then disconnect the coolant hoses from the throttle body

4 With reference to Section 3, release the accelerator cable inner from the throttle quadrant, then free the cable outer from its retaining bracket. Position the cable clear of the throttle body.

5 Where applicable, release the clips and disconnect the EVAP purge valve and crankcase ventilation hoses from the throttle body.

6 On 1.6 litre and 1.8 litre models, apply clamps to the coolant hoses leading to and from the throttle body, then release the clips and disconnect the hoses from the throttle body ports **(see illustrations)**.

7 Release the wiring harness as necessary from the clips in the vicinity of the throttle body, noting how it is routed.

8 Slacken and remove the bolts securing the throttle body assembly to the inlet manifold, then remove the assembly along with its insulating spacer (where fitted). On later 1.6 litre

models, note the wiring harness bracket which is retained by one of the throttle body bolts - move it to one side **(see illustrations)**.

Refitting

9 Refitting is a reversal of the removal procedure, bearing in mind the following points:

a) *Examine the insulating spacer for signs of damage, and renew if necessary.*

b) *Ensure the throttle body, inlet manifold and insulating spacer mating surfaces are clean and dry, then fit the throttle body and spacer, and securely tighten the retaining bolts.*

c) *Where applicable, ensure all hoses are correctly reconnected and that their retaining clips are securely tightened.*

d) *Adjust the accelerator cable as described in Section 3.*

Fuel rail and injectors

Removal

⚠️ *Warning: Ensure that the engine has cooled completely before starting work.*

10 Depressurise the fuel system as described in Section 7.

11 On 1.2 and 1.6 litre models, remove the throttle body assembly as described earlier in this Section.

12 On 1.2 and 1.6 litre models, remove the upper section of the inlet manifold as described in Section 8. On 1.6 litre models, the lower section of the inlet manifold must also be removed - see Section 8.

13 Loosen the clips and disconnect the fuel inlet and outlet hoses from the fuel rail, or at the rear of the engine compartment - be prepared for some fuel spillage. Note the fitted positions of the hoses to aid refitting later. Later models are equipped with quick-release fuel hose couplings, which are released by squeezing the sides of the coupling, and pulling apart **(see illustrations)**.

14 Unplug the main injector wiring harness connector, where applicable **(see illustration)**.

15 Disconnect the vacuum hose from the fuel pressure regulator (early 1.6 litre models, and all 1.8 litre models) **(see illustration)**.

16 Unscrew the bolts securing the fuel rail assembly to the inlet manifold, then carefully pull the fuel rail, together with the fuel injectors, from the inlet manifold **(see illustrations)**.

4.8a Throttle body securing bolts (arrowed) - 1.6 litre model

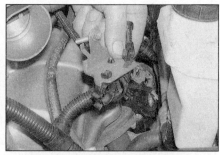

4.8b On 1.6 litre models, one of the throttle body bolts secures this wiring harness bracket

4.8c Removing the throttle body

4.13a Fuel hose connections and arrow markings - 1.8 litre model

4.13b Disconnecting a quick-release fuel line - 1.6 litre model

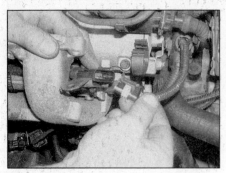

4.14 Disconnecting the injector wiring -
1.6 litre model

4.15 Disconnecting the fuel pressure
regulator vacuum hose - 1.8 litre model

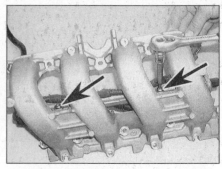

4.16a Unscrew the fuel rail mounting bolts
(arrowed) . . .

17 Remove the assembly from the engine
and remove the injector lower O-ring seals
(see illustrations).
18 The injectors can be removed individually
from the fuel rail by unplugging the relevant

wiring connector, sliding out the metal clip
(where fitted) and easing the injector from the
rail. Remove the injector upper O-ring seals
(see illustrations).
19 On models so equipped, remove the

retaining clip, or undo the securing screws
(as applicable) and withdraw the fuel
pressure regulator from the fuel rail **(see
illustration)**. Recover the seal, and renew if
necessary.

4.16b . . . and remove the fuel rail assembly
from the inlet manifold - 1.6 litre model

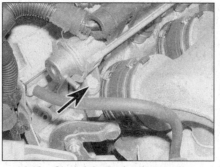

4.16c One of the fuel rail mounting
bolts . . .

4.16d . . . and removing the fuel rail on a
1.8 litre model

4.17a Removing the injector lower O-ring
seals on a 1.6 litre model . . .

4.17b . . . and prising them out on a
1.8 litre model

4.18a Disconnect the injector wiring
plug . . .

4.18b . . . slide out the locking clip (where
fitted) . . .

4.18c . . . and remove the injector from the
fuel rail (O-ring seal arrowed)

4.19 Prise off the pressure regulator
retaining clip to remove it

Refitting

20 Refit the injectors and fuel rail by following the removal procedure, in reverse, noting the following points:
  a) *Renew the O-ring seals before refitting the injectors. Take care when fitting the injectors to the fuel rail, and do not press them in further than required to fit the retaining clip, otherwise the O-ring seal may be damaged.*
  b) *Ensure that the injector retaining clips are securely seated.*
  c) *Make sure the fuel supply hose (and where applicable, the fuel return hose) are correctly fitted as noted on removal.*
  d) *Check that all vacuum and electrical connections are remade correctly and securely.*
  e) *On completion check the fuel rail and injectors for fuel leaks.*

Fuel pressure regulator

Note: *Later models with the 'returnless' fuel system (see Section 1) have their pressure regulator mounted inside the fuel pump/ sender unit in the fuel tank. Refer to Section 5 for details of pump/sender unit removal.*

Removal

Early 1.6 litre models
21 Remove the throttle body assembly as described earlier in this Section.
22 Depressurise the fuel system as described in Section 7.
23 Unplug the wiring connectors from the inlet air temperature and manifold pressure sensors.
24 Release the clip and disconnect the EVAP hose from the inlet manifold port.
25 Remove the upper section of the inlet manifold with reference to Section 8.
26 Disconnect the vacuum hose from the port on the side of the regulator.
27 Extract the retaining clip and pull the pressure regulator out of the fuel rail; recover the O-ring seal.

1.8 litre models
28 Remove the fuel rail and injectors as described earlier in this Section.
29 Disconnect the vacuum hose from the port on the side of the regulator.
30 Extract the retaining clip and pull the pressure regulator out of the fuel rail; recover the O-ring seal.

Refitting

31 Refit the fuel pressure regulator by following the removal procedure in reverse. Renew the O-ring seal and refit the vacuum hose securely.

Idle air control valve (1.6 and 1.8 litre models)

Removal

32 Disconnect the battery negative cable, then unplug the wiring connector from the actuator valve **(see illustration)**.
33 On early models, undo the securing screws

4.32 Disconnect the idle air control valve wiring plug

and withdraw the valve from the throttle body **(see illustration)**; on later models, unscrew the unit itself.

Refitting

34 Refit the actuator by following the removal procedure in reverse. Noting the following points:
  a) *Clean the threads of the screws or valve body, and apply a coat of locking compound to the threads before refitting.*
  b) *Take great care to ensure that the plunger is correctly aligned with its bore, before tightening the actuator securing screws.*
  c) *Delay reconnecting the battery negative cable for about 20 minutes. After this, the ECU will correctly reposition the idle actuator valve when the engine is started for the first time.*

Idle actuator (1.2 litre models)

Note: *On 1.2 litre models, the throttle potentiometer is integral with the idle actuator.*
35 Disconnect the battery negative cable, then unplug the wiring connector from the actuator valve.
36 Undo the securing screws and withdraw the valve from the throttle body.

Refitting

37 Refit the actuator by following the removal procedure in reverse.

Throttle potentiometer

Note: *On 1.2 litre models, the throttle potentiometer is integral with the idle actuator.*
38 Disconnect the battery negative cable, then unplug the wiring connector from the potentiometer.
39 On early models, undo the securing screws and withdraw the valve from the throttle body **(see illustration)**; on later models, the potentiometer appears to be integral with the throttle body.

Refitting

40 Refit the potentiometer by following the removal procedure in reverse, noting the following points:
  a) *Note that the mounting holes are not slotted; no adjustment of the potentiometer's position is possible or necessary, as the ECU adapts to the potentiometer and 'learns' the idle and full throttle positions.*

4.33 Idle air control valve retaining screws (arrowed)

  b) *On 1.8 litre models, ensure that drive dog on the sensor rotor is above the corresponding pin on the throttle disc shaft, when the sensor is refitted.*
  c) *Clean the threads of the screws or valve body, and apply a coat of locking compound to the threads before refitting.*

Intake air temperature sensor

Removal

41 On 1.2 litre and later 1.6 litre models, the intake air temperature sensor is integral with the manifold absolute pressure (MAP) sensor. On 1.8 litre models, an intake air temperature sensor is not fitted (see Section 1). On early 1.6 litre models, the sensor is mounted at the rear of the upper section of the inlet manifold.
42 Ensure that the ignition is switched off, then unplug the wiring from the sensor at the connector.
43 Unscrew the sensor from the manifold, taking care to avoid damaging the plastic connector.

Refitting

44 Refit the sensor by following the removal procedure in reverse.

Manifold absolute pressure (MAP) sensor

Removal

45 On early 1.6 litre models, the MAP sensor is mounted on a bracket at the rear of the engine compartment. Ensure that the ignition is switched off, then unplug the vacuum hose and wiring connector from the sensor, undo

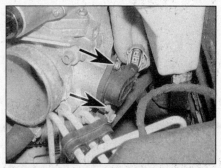

4.39 Disconnect the throttle potentiometer wiring plug - securing screws arrowed

4.46a Unplug the wiring connector . . .

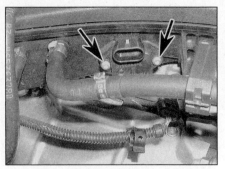

4.46b . . . then unscrew the retaining screws (arrowed) . . .

4.46c . . . and remove the MAP sensor from the inlet manifold

the three securing screws and remove the sensor from its bracket. Refitting is a reversal of removal.

46 On 1.2 litre models and later 1.6 litre models, the combined MAP/inlet air temperature sensor is fitted to the right-hand end of the inlet manifold. Ensure that the ignition is switched off, then unplug the wiring connector from the sensor, undo the securing screws and remove the sensor **(see illustrations)**.

47 A MAP sensor is not fitted to 1.8 litre models (see Section 1).

Refitting

49 Refitting is a reversal of removal.

Coolant temperature sensor

50 On 1.2 litre models, the coolant temperature sensor is located at the rear of the cylinder head on the left-hand side. On 1.6 litre

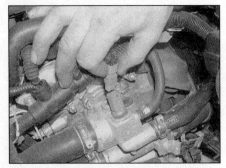

4.51a Disconnecting the coolant temperature sensor on a 1.6 litre model . . .

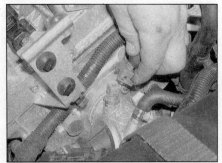

4.51b . . . and on a 1.8 litre model

and 1.8 litre models, the sensor is located at the left-hand end of the engine, on the thermostat housing.

51 Drain the cooling system with reference to Chapter 1, or be prepared for coolant spillage. Ensure that the ignition is switched off, then unplug the wiring from the sensor at the connector **(see illustrations)**.

52 Unscrew the sensor and remove it from the cylinder head. Recover the sealing washer where fitted. If using a socket, take care not to damage the wiring connector on the sensor.

Refitting

53 Refitting is a reversal of removal. Where applicable, fit a new sealing washer. Tighten the sensor to the specified torque. Do not exceed the specified torque, otherwise the unit's threads may be damaged.

Electronic control unit (ECU)

Note: *The ECU communicates with the anti-theft/immobiliser system when the vehicle is started. Once the ignition key electronic code has been stored by the ECU, the unit cannot be used on any other vehicle. For this reason, do not attempt to diagnose problems with the engine management system by connecting the ECU to another vehicle, or by substituting an ECU from another vehicle.*

54 Disconnect the negative cable from the battery terminal as described in Chapter 5A, before starting work.

1.2 litre models

55 On 1.2 litre models, the ECU is mounted at the rear left-hand corner of the engine compartment. The multiway harness

connectors are secured in position by locking bars. To release the connectors, pivot the locking bars upwards and then pull the connectors squarely away from the ECU. The ECU can then be removed by slackening and withdrawing its securing bolts.

56 Refitting is a reversal of removal - ensure that the connector locking bars are pressed firmly home.

1.6 litre models

57 On early 1.6 litre models, the ECU is mounted at the side of the battery, in the front left-hand corner of the engine compartment. To remove it, unplug the wiring connector then slacken and withdraw the four securing bolts. Access to the lower two bolts is limited, and may be improved by raising and supporting the front of the vehicle.

58 On later 1.6 litre models, the ECU is mounted in the same place, but there are two ECU wiring connectors, both secured by locking bars which must be slid to one side to allow disconnection. The upper section of the ECU mounting bracket must be unbolted moved to one side to allow the removal of the ECU itself **(see illustrations)**.

59 Refitting is a reversal of removal - where applicable, ensure that the connector locking bars are pressed firmly home.

1.8 litre models

60 The ECU is mounted inside the right-hand footwell, at the base of the A-pillar behind a plastic trim panel. Remove the trim panel; note that on left-hand drive models, it will be necessary to remove the glovebox assembly from the facia, with reference to Chapter 11.

4.58a Release the locking clip and disconnect the large multi-plug . . .

4.58b . . . then release the harness clips . . .

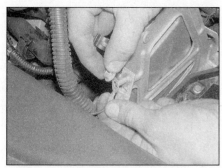

4.58c . . . and disconnect the earth lead

4.58d Unscrew the mounting nuts . . .

4.58e . . . remove the upper mounting plate . . .

4.58f . . . disconnect the lower multi-plug . . .

4.58g . . . and remove the ECU

4.64a Remove the fusebox lid at the rear of the engine compartment . . .

Unplug the wiring connectors and unscrew the earth cable from the bodywork. Undo the mounting bracket securing screws and remove the ECU from the vehicle.

61 Refitting is a reversal of removal.

Inertia switch

62 Refer to the information given in Chapter 4A, Section 5.

Fuel injection system fuses and relays

63 The injection system relays are located in similar positions to those described in Chapter 4A, Section 5.

64 The main system fuse is located underneath a plastic cover at the left-hand rear corner of the engine compartment **(see illustrations)**.

65 The individual fuses for the fuel pump and injection/ignition are located in one of the fuse locations inside the car - refer to Chapter 12 and/or the wiring diagrams for details **(see illustration)**.

Airflow meter (1.8 litre models)

Removal

66 Disconnect the battery negative lead as described in Chapter 5A.

67 Unplug the wiring connector from the airflow meter.

68 Release the hose clips and remove the meter from the inlet air ducting.

Refitting

69 Refitting is a reversal of removal.

Camshaft position sensor

1.6 litre models

70 The camshaft position sensor is only fitted to pre-1999 models, prior to the introduction of the Step A engine.

71 Remove the timing belt and inlet camshaft sprocket as described in Chapter 2C, Sections 4 and 5.

72 Remove the two bolts securing the sensor **(see illustration)**. Withdraw the sensor from the engine, and disconnect the wiring plug.

73 Refitting is a reversal of removal.

4.64b . . . and pull out the main system fuse

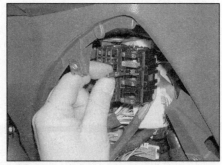

4.65 Removing the fuel pump fuse on a 1.6 litre model

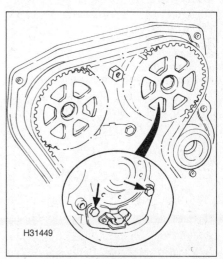

H31449

4.72 Camshaft position sensor location and securing bolts - 1.6 litre model

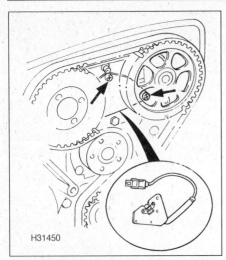

H31450

4.75 Camshaft position sensor location and securing bolts - 1.8 litre model

1.8 litre models

74 Remove the timing belt and exhaust camshaft sprocket as described in Chapter 2D, Sections 4 and 5.

75 Remove the two bolts securing the sensor **(see illustration)**. Withdraw the sensor from the engine, and disconnect the wiring plug at the rear of the timing belt cover.

76 Refitting is a reversal of removal.

Vehicle speed (speedometer) sensor

77 Refer to the information given in Chapter 4A, Section 5.

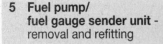

5   Fuel pump/ fuel gauge sender unit - removal and refitting

Removal

Note: *Refer to the precautions in Section 1 before proceeding.*

1 Disconnect the negative cable from the battery terminal.

2 Remove the press stud fixings and detach the carpet from the load space floor.

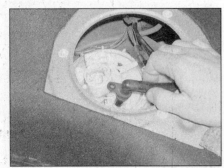

5.6 Disconnecting the fuel tank breather pipe

5.3a Remove the screws . . .

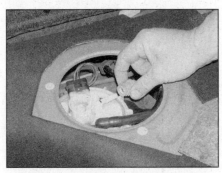

5.4 Disconnecting the fuel supply pipe from the sender unit

3 Undo the screws and remove the dust cover from the access aperture in the floorpan **(see illustrations)**.

4 Bearing in mind the warning given in Section 1, disconnect the fuel supply line by pressing the tabs and separating the quick-release connection **(see illustration)**. Plug the end of the line or cover with adhesive tape, to prevent the ingress of debris.

5 Unplug the wiring connectors from the top of the fuel pump/gauge sender unit **(see illustration)**.

With the limited access available to the sender unit ring nut, and the fact that the nut is very tight, we had to make up a tool to unscrew it. The tool is made from two metal strips - one bent to fit across the ring nut to provide two 'legs' which engage in the ribs on the ring nut, and one bolted to the first, to act as a handle.

5.3b . . . and take off the dust cover for access to the sender unit

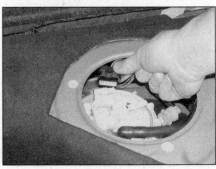

5.5 Unplug the wiring connector from the sender unit

6 As applicable, disconnect the breather pipe and/or return line from the sender unit. The breather pipe on later models is secured by a nut, and is then pulled out of the tank **(see illustration)**.

7 Using a suitable tool, unscrew the large ring nut that secures the pump/sender unit to the top of the fuel tank. We made up a simple claw tool in the workshop, which engages in the ribs around the edge of the ring nut **(see Tool Tip)**.

8 Carefully withdraw the unit from the fuel tank. Some careful manipulation will be required, to allow the sender unit float arm to exit the tank without snagging. Suspend the unit above the tank aperture for a few minutes, to allow the excess fuel to drain away **(see illustration)**.

9 Recover the sealing ring from the fuel tank aperture, if it wasn't removed with the sender unit.

5.8 Removing the pump/sender unit

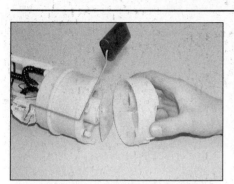

5.10a Once the base of the unit has been unclipped . . .

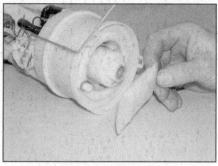

5.10b . . . the pump filter can also be unclipped and removed

5.10c Removing the float assembly

 If the pump/sender unit is not being refitted immediately, screw the retaining nut back onto the tank temporarily, as the fittings may swell over a period of time, making refitting difficult.

10 The sender unit fuel filter can be inspected by unclipping the round cover at the base of the unit. The float assembly can also be unclipped from the side of the unit, and the wiring disconnected **(see illustrations)**. The pump unit hoses must be disconnected before it too is unclipped from the base of the unit - it appears, however, that separating the hose connections may destroy them, so have replacement hoses available for refitting.

11 From the FIAT information available at the time of writing, it appears that no pump/ sender unit components are available separately. On later models with a 'returnless' fuel system, the pressure regulator fitted to top of the sender unit is not available, nor was it even clear how it might be removed **(see illustration)**.

Refitting

12 Refitting is a reversal of the removal procedure, noting the following points:

  a) It is advisable to use a new sealing ring.
  b) Refit the ring nut loosely to the top of the sender unit before offering it into position **(see illustration)**.
  c) Take care as the unit is fitted that the sealing ring does not get pushed into the tank.

  d) Align the arrowhead marking on top of the tank with the similar mark on the sender unit **(see illustration)**.
  e) Prior to refitting the dust cover, reconnect the battery, then start the engine and check the unions for signs of leakage.

6 Fuel tank - removal and refitting

Refer to Section 7 in Chapter 4A.

7 Fuel injection system - depressurisation

Note 1: Refer to the precautions in Section 1 before proceeding.

Note 2: On later models with a 'returnless' fuel supply system, the fuel pressure can be relieved via the quick-release coupling at the end of the fuel rail. This should carried out using a FIAT fuel pressure discharge kit; it may be possible to hire or borrow a kit from you local dealer, if required.

1 The fuel supply system referred to in this Section is defined as the tank-mounted fuel pump, the fuel filter, the throttle body and pressure regulator components, and the metal pipes and flexible hoses of the fuel lines between these components. All these contain fuel which will be under pressure while the engine is running and/or while the ignition is switched on. The pressure will remain for some

time after the ignition has been switched off, and must be relieved before any of these components are disturbed for servicing work.

2 Make sure that the ignition is switched off (take out the key).

3 Referring to Section 4, pull out the fuse for the fuel pump (or remove the fuel pump relay). If the injection/ignition fuse or the main system fuse are removed, the injectors will not open, so defeating the purpose of this exercise.

4 Try to start the engine, keeping the engine cranking for several seconds. It may fire and run for a little while - if so, let it run until it stops.

5 Once the injectors have opened and closed several times, this will reduce the fuel pressure to a safer level. However, fuel will still be present in the system, and care should still be taken.

6 Disconnect the negative cable from the battery terminal, then refit the fuel pump fuse (or relay).

7 On later models, a Schrader-type valve (like a tyre valve) is fitted to the end of the fuel rail, and this may be used to depressurise the system. Unscrew the plastic valve cap, then place rags around the valve, to soak up spilt fuel **(see illustration)**. Use a suitable tool to depress the centre of the valve, and release the fuel under pressure. Once the pressure has dissipated, refit the plastic valve cap.

8 Even when the pressure has been released, care should still be taken when opening a fuel line connection. Place a container beneath the relevant connection/union to be disconnected, and have a large rag ready to soak up any escaping fuel not being caught by the container.

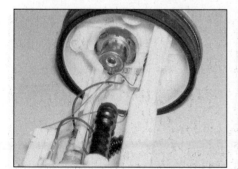

5.11 View of the pressure regulator and its wiring connections

5.12a Make sure the ring nut is in position before fitting the unit

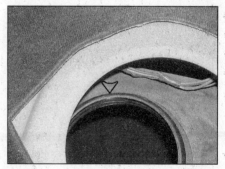

5.12b Arrowhead marking on top of the fuel tank

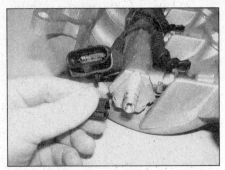

7.7 Plastic cap removed from fuel rail pressure relief valve - seen on a 1.6 litre model, with the inlet manifold removed

9 Slowly open the connection or union nut (as applicable) to avoid a sudden release of fuel, and wrap the rag around the connection to catch any fuel which may be expelled. Once the

fuel has been soaked up, disconnect the fuel line, and insert plugs to minimise fuel loss and prevent the entry of dirt into the fuel system.

8 Inlet manifold - removal and refitting

Note: *Refer to the warning given in Section 1 before proceeding.*

Removal - 1.2 and 1.6 litre models

Upper section

1 Remove the throttle body assembly as described in Section 4.
2 Unplug the wiring connector from the inlet air temperature and manifold pressure (MAP) sensor **(see illustration)**.

8.2 Disconnecting the MAP sensor wiring plug

8.3 Disconnecting the EVAP (charcoal canister) hose at the inner wing connection

3 Release the clip and disconnect the EVAP hose from the inlet manifold port. Alternatively on later models, trace the EVAP hose back, and separate the quick-release connection at the right-hand side of the engine compartment (this saves destroying another hose clip) **(see illustration)**.

1.6 litre models

4 As applicable, disconnect the crankcase breather pipe and brake servo vacuum pipe from the rear of the manifold, identifying them for location if necessary **(see illustrations)**. On early models, disconnect the vacuum pipe for the fuel pressure regulator.
5 To gain access to some of the manifold bolts, it is necessary to unbolt the oil filler tube from the front of the engine; one of the bolts also secures the oil dipstick tube **(see illustration)**.
6 On later models, also unbolt the bracket for the knock sensor **(see illustration)**.
7 Move the oil filler tube forwards, clear of the engine - it can be removed completely if preferred **(see illustration)**.

All models

8 Progressively slacken and withdraw the securing bolts or nuts, and detach the upper section of the inlet manifold from the lower section. Note the location of any wiring harness or hose brackets fitted to the bolts, and recover the gasket(s) **(see illustrations)**.

Lower section

1.2 litre models

9 Unplug the wiring connector from the coolant temperature sensor (situated on the left-hand side of the manifold).

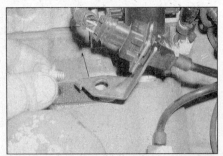

8.4a Disconnect the breather hoses . . .

8.4b . . . and the brake servo vacuum hose

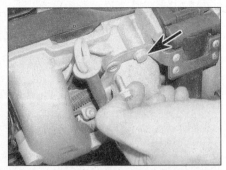

8.5 Remove the bolts securing the oil filler tube

8.6 Remove the knock sensor mounting bracket bolt, and move the bracket to one side

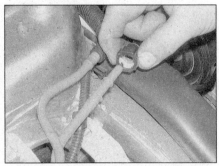

8.7 Move the oil filler tube clear of the inlet manifold

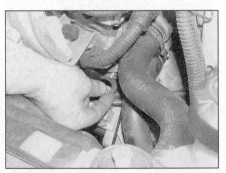

8.8a On 1.6 litre models, unscrew this nut . . .

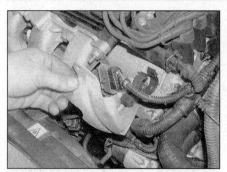

8.8b . . . and remove this wiring harness bracket . . .

8.8c . . . for access to one of the manifold bolts

8.8d Remove the remaining bolts (arrowed) . . .

8.8e . . . and remove the upper section of the inlet manifold

10 Undo the bolt securing the accelerator cable mounting bracket to the manifold, and position it clear of the manifold.
11 Slacken the retaining clip and disconnect the coolant hose from the rear of the manifold.

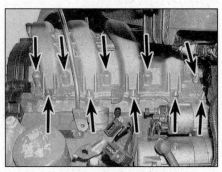

8.15 Lower inlet manifold fasteners (arrowed)

12 Disconnect the brake vacuum hose.

1.6 litre models
13 Remove the upper section of the manifold as described above.
14 Disconnect the wiring plug and fuel

hose(s) from the fuel rail and injectors, using the information in Section 4.
15 The lower section of the manifold is secured by eight bolts and two studs/nuts **(see illustration)**. Note that the manifold is slotted where it fits over the studs, to make removal and refitting easier.

All models
16 Undo the retaining nuts and bolts, and remove the lower section of the manifold from the cylinder head. Remove the gasket and discard it; a new one should be used on refitting **(see illustrations)**.

Removal - 1.8 litre models

17 The upper and lower sections of the manifold are removed together, and can be separated after removal if required.
18 Remove the throttle body, and the fuel rail and injectors, as described in Section 4. Unbolt the fuel hose guide bracket from the top of the manifold **(see illustration)**.
19 Disconnect the coolant hose at the rear of the expansion tank, and unclip it from the support brackets at the right-hand end of the manifold (right as seen from the driver's seat) **(see illustrations)**.
20 Disconnect the EVAP hose (coloured blue) from the manifold by depressing the hose collar with a small screwdriver, and pulling out the hose **(see illustration)**.
21 Noting their locations, disconnect the two wiring plugs from the ignition power module at the right-hand end of the manifold **(see illustration)**.
22 Jack up the front of the car, and support on axle stands (see *Jacking and vehicle support*).

8.16a Remove the inlet manifold lower section . . .

8.16b . . . and recover the gasket

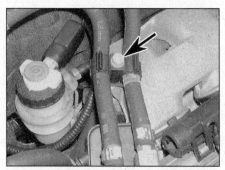

8.18 Fuel hose guide bracket bolt (arrowed)

8.19a Disconnect the coolant hose at the rear of the expansion tank . . .

8.19b . . . and unclip the hose from the support brackets (arrowed) on the manifold

8.20 Disconnecting the EVAP hose from the inlet manifold

23 Unbolt the two manifold support brackets from the rear of the engine. The two bolts securing each one are not easy to get to - the first pair is just above the bearing/shield for the right-hand driveshaft, with the second pair (on an alloy bracket) directly above the first.

24 Returning to the engine compartment, progressively loosen and remove the nuts securing the inlet manifold assembly to the cylinder head. Carefully withdraw the manifold from the studs, and out from the engine compartment. Recover the gasket.

Refitting - all models

25 Refitting is a reverse of the removal procedure, noting the following points:
 a) Ensure that the manifold and cylinder head mating surfaces are clean and dry, and fit a new manifold gasket. Refit the manifold and securely tighten its retaining nuts.
 b) Ensure all relevant hoses are reconnected to their original positions and are securely held (where necessary) by the retaining clips.
 c) Refit the fuel rail and injectors, and the throttle body assembly (Section 4).
 d) On completion, refill the cooling system as described in Chapter 1.

9 Fuel injection system - checking and adjustment

Checking

Note: Also see Chapter 5B, Section 3.

1 Before disconnecting any of the injection system wiring, ensure that the ignition is switched off (take out the key).

9.9a Diagnostic connector on 1.6 litre model

8.21 Ignition power module wiring plugs (arrowed)

2 If a fault appears in the fuel injection system, first ensure that all the system wiring connectors are securely connected and free of corrosion. Also check the wiring harness for signs of damage, such as may result if the wiring is routed too close to a hot component, for example.

3 Remove the cover(s) from the fuse/relay box(es) on the engine compartment bulkhead, and check the connections to the fuses and relays. With the ignition switched off, remove the fuses and relays in turn, and check that the fuse and relay contacts, and their sockets in the box, are clean. Refit the fuses and relays securely.

4 The system's main earth point varies according to model, as follows:
 1.2 litre engine - adjacent to the knock sensor, at the rear of the engine, between cylinders 2 and 3.
 1.6 litre engine - on the rear bolt securing the exhaust camshaft housing end cover.
 1.8 litre engine - at the rear of the cylinder block, just behind the timing belt cover.

5 Remove the nut or bolt securing the earth terminal, and clean all contact surfaces thoroughly. Refit the terminal, and tighten the nut or bolt securely.

6 Then ensure that the fault is not due to poor maintenance; ie, check that the air cleaner filter element is clean, the spark plugs are in good condition and correctly gapped, the HT leads are securely connected and in good condition, and that the engine breather hoses are clear and undamaged.

7 Check all the ignition system components and wiring as far as possible, using the information in Chapters 1 and 5B. Sometimes

9.9b Diagnostic connector on 1.8 litre model

it can be difficult to determine whether a misfire is fuel or ignition-related.

8 If the engine is difficult to start, or runs poorly, when cold, the problem may be that the engine management system has gone into emergency back-up mode. This, and the nature of the fault that caused it to happen, can only be determined using diagnostic equipment such as a fault code reader.

9 A diagnostic connector is provided, into which a fault code reader can be plugged. The test equipment is capable of 'interrogating' the engine management system electronically and accessing its internal fault log. The location of the diagnostic connector varies according to model, as follows:
 1.2 litre engine - on the fuse/relay box at the left-hand rear of the engine compartment.
 1.6 litre engine - adjacent to the injection/ignition ECU, or on the fuse/relay box at the left-hand rear of the engine compartment (see illustration).
 1.8 litre engine - at the rear right-hand side of the engine compartment, just in front of the suspension strut top mounting, or between the battery and air cleaner (see illustration).

10 Fault codes can only be extracted from the ECU using a dedicated fault code reader. A FIAT dealer will obviously have such a reader, but they are also available from other suppliers, including Haynes. It is unlikely to be cost-effective for the private owner to purchase a fault code reader, but a well-equipped local garage or automotive electrical specialist will have one.

11 Using this equipment, faults can be pinpointed quickly and simply, even if their occurrence is intermittent. Testing all the system components individually in an attempt to locate the fault by elimination is a time-consuming operation that is unlikely to be fruitful (particularly if the fault occurs dynamically), and carries high risk of damage to the ECU's internal components.

Adjustment

12 Experienced home mechanics equipped with an accurate tachometer and a carefully-calibrated exhaust gas analyser may be able to check the exhaust gas CO content and the engine idle speed; if these are found to be out of specification, then the vehicle must be taken to a suitably-equipped FIAT dealer for assessment.

13 Neither the air/fuel mixture (exhaust gas CO content) nor the engine idle speed are manually adjustable; incorrect test results indicate the need for maintenance (possibly, injector cleaning) or a fault within the fuel injection system.

10 Unleaded petrol - general information and usage

Refer to Section 11 in Chapter 4A.

Chapter 4 Part C:
Exhaust and emission control systems

Contents

Degrees of difficulty

Easy, suitable for novice with little experience	Fairly easy, suitable for beginner with some experience	Fairly difficult, suitable for competent DIY mechanic	Difficult, suitable for experienced DIY mechanic	Very difficult, suitable for expert DIY or professional

Specifications

Torque wrench settings	Nm	lbf ft
Exhaust manifold nuts:		
1.2 litre	27	20
1.4 and 1.8 litre	25	18
1.6 litre	30	22
Exhaust manifold-to-downpipe nuts	30	22
Exhaust system clamp nuts/bolts	25	18
Oxygen sensor:		
1.2 litre	36	27
1.4 litre	55	41
1.6 and 1.8 litre	40	30

1 General information

1 All models use unleaded petrol, and have various features built into the fuel system to help minimise harmful emissions. All models are equipped with a crankcase emission-control system, a catalytic converter, and an evaporative emission control system to minimise fuel vapour emissions.

Crankcase emission control

2 To reduce the emission of unburned hydrocarbons from the crankcase into the atmosphere, the engine is sealed and the blow-by gases and oil vapour are drawn from inside the crankcase, through an oil separator, into the inlet tract to be burned by the engine during normal combustion.

3 Under conditions of high manifold depression (idling, deceleration) the gases will be sucked positively out of the crankcase. Under conditions of low manifold depression (acceleration, full-throttle running) the gases are forced out of the crankcase by the (relatively) higher crankcase pressure; if the engine is worn, the raised crankcase pressure (due to increased blow-by) will cause some of the flow to return under all manifold conditions.

Exhaust emission control

4 To minimise the amount of pollutants which escape into the atmosphere, all models are fitted with a catalytic converter in the exhaust system. The system is of the closed-loop type, in which an oxygen sensor in the exhaust system provides the fuel-injection/ignition system ECU with constant feedback, enabling the ECU to adjust the mixture to provide the best possible conditions for the converter to operate.

5 The oxygen sensor's tip is sensitive to oxygen, and sends the ECU a varying voltage depending on the amount of oxygen in the exhaust gases; if the intake air/fuel mixture is too rich, the exhaust gases are low in oxygen so the sensor sends a low-voltage signal, the voltage rising as the mixture weakens and the amount of oxygen rises in the exhaust gases.

6 Peak conversion efficiency of all major pollutants occurs if the intake air/fuel mixture is maintained at the chemically-correct ratio for the complete combustion of petrol of 14.7 parts (by weight) of air to 1 part of fuel (the 'Stoichiometric ratio'). The sensor output voltage alters in a large step at this point (known as the Lambda point), the ECU using the signal change as a reference point and correcting the intake air/fuel mixture accordingly by altering the fuel injector pulse width.

Evaporative emission control

7 To minimise the escape into the atmosphere of unburned hydrocarbons, an evaporative emissions control system is also fitted to all models. The fuel tank filler cap is sealed and a charcoal canister is mounted behind the right-hand front wing. The canister collects the petrol vapours released from the fuel in the tank when the car is parked and stores them until they can be cleared from the canister (under the control of the engine management system ECU) via the purge valve into the inlet tract to be burned by the engine during normal combustion.

8 To ensure that the engine runs correctly when it is cold and/or idling and to protect the catalytic converter from the effects of an over-rich mixture, the purge control valve is not opened by the ECU until the engine has warmed up, and the engine is under load; the valve solenoid is then modulated on and off to allow the stored vapour to pass into the inlet tract.

2.4a Remove the retaining screws and other fasteners . . .

2.4b . . . and unclip the wheelarch liner

2.6 Charcoal canister seen from front wheelarch - retaining bolt arrowed

2 Emission control systems - testing and component renewal

Crankcase emission control

1 The components of this system require no attention other than to check that the hose(s) are clear and undamaged at regular intervals. Note that the hoses contain 'flame trap' inserts, to prevent the flame front from vapour, ignited in the inlet manifold, from travelling back to the crankcase.

Evaporative emission control system

Testing

2 If the system is thought to be faulty, disconnect the hoses from the charcoal canister and purge control valve and check that they are clear by blowing through them. Full testing of the system can only be carried out using specialist electronic equipment which is connected to the engine management system diagnostic wiring connector (see Chapter 4A or 4B). If the purge control valve or charcoal canister are thought to be faulty, they must be renewed.

Charcoal canister

3 The charcoal canister is located behind the right-hand front wing. To gain access to the canister, loosen the right-hand front wheel bolts, firmly apply the handbrake, then jack up the front of the vehicle and support it on axle stands. Remove the right-hand front wheel.
4 Remove the retaining screws and fasteners and remove the wheelarch liner to gain access to the canister (see illustrations).
5 Mark the vapour hoses for identification purposes, then disconnect them from the canister ports.
6 Unscrew the retaining bolt, recover the washers, then remove the canister from the vehicle (see illustration).
7 Refitting is a reverse of the removal procedure, ensuring the hoses are correctly and securely reconnected.

Purge valve

8 On 1.2 litre models, the valve is mounted on

a bracket, at the rear right-hand corner of the engine compartment. On all other models, it is mounted on a bracket next to the charcoal canister, inside the right-hand front wheelarch cavity. To remove the valve, unplug the wiring connector, then prise the valve from its mounting bracket.

Fuel tank safety valve

9 A safety valve mounted on the upper surface of the fuel tank controls the flow of fuel vapour to the charcoal canister. It contains a one-way valve that prevents liquid fuel from flowing out, if the fuel level in the tank is very high, or if the vehicle overturns in an accident. It also permits ventilation of the fuel tank, preventing the build up of vacuum that can occur as the fuel level in the tank drops.
10 Access to the valve can only be gained by first removing the fuel tank; removal is then self-evident.

Exhaust emission control

Testing

11 The performance of the catalytic converter can be checked only by measuring the exhaust gases using a good-quality, carefully-calibrated exhaust gas analyser, in accordance with the manufacturers instructions.
12 If the CO level at the tailpipe is too high, the vehicle should be taken to a FIAT dealer so that the complete fuel injection and ignition systems, including the oxygen sensor, can be thoroughly checked using the special diagnostic equipment.

Catalytic converter

13 Refer to Section 5.

Oxygen sensor

14 Refer to Section 6.

3 Catalytic converter - general information and precautions

1 The catalytic converter is a reliable and simple device which needs no maintenance in itself, but there are some facts of which an owner should be aware if the converter is to

function properly for its full service life:
a) *DO NOT use leaded petrol (or lead-replacement petrol) in a car equipped with a catalytic converter - the lead (or other additives) will coat the precious metals, reducing their converting efficiency and will eventually destroy the converter.*
b) *Always keep the ignition and fuel systems well-maintained in accordance with the manufacturer's schedule (see Chapter 1).*
c) *If the engine develops a misfire, do not drive the car at all (or at least as little as possible) until the fault is cured.*
d) *DO NOT push- or tow-start the car - this will soak the catalytic converter in unburned fuel, causing it to overheat when the engine does start.*
e) *DO NOT switch off the ignition at high engine speeds - ie do not 'blip' the throttle immediately before switching off the engine.*
f) *DO NOT use fuel or engine oil additives - these may contain substances harmful to the catalytic converter.*
g) *DO NOT continue to use the car if the engine burns oil to the extent of leaving a visible trail of blue smoke.*
h) *Remember that the catalytic converter operates at very high temperatures. DO NOT, therefore, park the car in dry undergrowth, over long grass or piles of dead leaves after a long run.*
i) *Remember that the catalytic converter is FRAGILE - do not strike it with tools during servicing work, and take care handling it when removing it from the car for any reason.*
j) *In some cases, a sulphurous smell (like that of rotten eggs) may be noticed from the exhaust. This is common to many catalytic converter-equipped cars, and has more to do with the sulphur content of the brand of fuel being used than the converter itself.*
k) *The catalytic converter, used on a well-maintained and well-driven car, should last for between 50 000 and 100 000 miles - if the converter is no longer effective it must be renewed.*

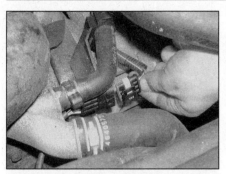

4.3 Disconnect the oxygen sensor wiring plug - 1.4 litre model shown

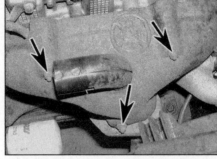

4.5a Exhaust manifold hot-air shroud nuts (arrowed) on a 1.4 litre model . . .

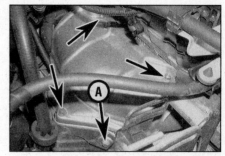

4.5b . . . and on a 1.6 litre model - also remove bolt (A) which secures the downpipe shroud

4.5c Removing the exhaust manifold shroud - 1.6 litre model

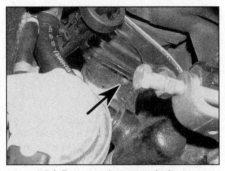

4.5d Remove the upper bolt . . .

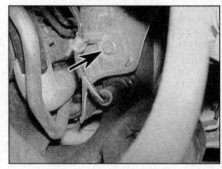

4.5e . . . and lower bolt . . .

4 Exhaust manifold - removal and refitting

Removal

1 Jack up the front of the vehicle and support on axle stands. The exhaust manifold is located at the front of the engine on all models except those with the 1.6 litre engine.

2 On 1.6 litre models, access to the exhaust manifold is improved by removing the upper section of the inlet manifold as described in Chapter 4B.

3 Locate the oxygen sensor, which is at the top of the exhaust downpipe, just below the manifold. Trace the wiring from the sensor back to the connector plug and disconnect it **(see illustration)**. Alternatively, remove the sensor completely (see Section 6).

4 Where applicable, disconnect the hot-air duct from the shroud above the exhaust manifold.

5 Unscrew the studs and nuts securing the manifold shrouds, and remove the shrouds from the manifold and/or downpipe **(see illustrations)**. If any of the fasteners proves difficult to unscrew, don't use excessive force, or the stud may shear - try a little penetrating oil, and if necessary, try tightening the fastener slightly before loosening it once more.

6 Where applicable, unscrew the nuts/bolts and separate the halves of the downpipe support bracket **(see illustration)**.

7 Unscrew the nuts and disconnect the exhaust downpipe from the exhaust manifold flange **(see illustration)**. Recover the gasket.

8 Progressively slacken and remove the manifold mounting nuts **(see illustration)**. Use plenty of penetrating oil if the studs are rusty. If a nut appears to be sticking, do not try to force it; turn the nut back half a turn, apply some more penetrating oil to the stud threads, wait several seconds for it to soak in, then gradually unscrew the nut by one turn. Repeat this process until the nut is free.

4.5f . . . and remove the downpipe shroud - 1.6 litre model

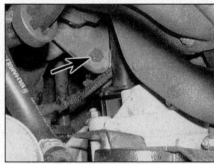

4.6 Exhaust downpipe support bracket bolt (arrowed)

4.7 Exhaust manifold-to-downpipe joint nuts

4.8 Unscrewing the manifold nuts - 1.6 litre engine shown

5.7 Disconnecting the oxygen sensor on a 1.8 litre model - seen with the airflow meter removed

5.9 Four nuts secure this plate fitted below the exhaust downpipe

9 Remove the washers, then withdraw the manifold from the cylinder head and recover the gaskets from the studs.

10 In some cases, the manifold studs will come out with the nuts - this poses no great problem, and the studs can be refitted if they are in good condition. For preference, however, a complete set of manifold and downpipe studs and nuts should be obtained as required, as the old ones are likely to be in less-than-perfect condition.

Refitting

11 Refitting is a reversal of the removal procedure, noting the following points:

a) *Always fit new manifold gaskets.*

b) *If any studs were broken when removing, drill out the remains of the stud, and fit new studs and nuts.*

c) *It is recommended that new studs and nuts are used as a matter of course - even if the old ones came off without difficulty, they may not stand being re-tightened. New components will be much easier to remove in future, should this be necessary.*

d) *If the old studs are re-used, clean the threads thoroughly to remove all traces of rust.*

e) *Apply a little copper grease to the nut and stud threads - this may make subsequent removal easier.*

f) *Tighten the manifold securing nuts to the specified torque.*

5.13 Catalytic converter on a 1.8 litre model

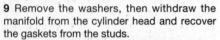

5 Exhaust system - general information and component renewal

General information

1 A three-section exhaust system is fitted, consisting of a downpipe, a catalytic converter, and a tailpipe section containing one centre silencer (two on 1.8 litre models), and a tailpipe with an integral silencer. The downpipe-to-manifold and downpipe-to-catalytic converter joints are both of flange and gasket type, whereas the remaining joints are sleeve type joints, secured with a clamp ring.

2 The system is suspended along its entire length by rubber mountings.

Removal

3 Each exhaust section can be removed individually or, alternatively, the complete system can be removed as a unit. Where separation of the rear sleeve joint is necessary, it may be more practical to remove the entire system rather than try and separate the joint in position.

4 To remove the system or part of the system, first jack up the front of the vehicle and support on axle stands (see *Jacking and vehicle support*). Alternatively, position the vehicle over an inspection pit or on car ramps.

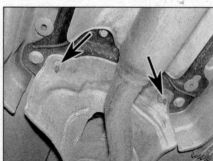

5.21 Typical exhaust heatshield - securing nuts arrowed

Downpipe

5 Where applicable, remove the nuts/bolts securing the downpipe heat shield, and remove the shield to improve access.

6 Support the catalytic converter using an axle stand or blocks of wood.

7 Locate the oxygen sensor, which is at the top of the exhaust downpipe, just below the manifold. Trace the wiring from the sensor back to the connector plug and disconnect it **(see illustration)**. Alternatively, remove the sensor completely (see Section 6).

8 Where applicable, unscrew the nuts/bolts and separate the halves of the downpipe support bracket.

9 On 1.8 litre models, remove the four nuts securing the plate which fits across the downpipe, where it passes under the sump **(see illustration)**.

10 Unscrew and remove the bolts securing the downpipe to the catalytic converter, then separate the joint and recover the gasket.

11 Bend back the locktabs (where fitted) then unscrew the nuts securing the downpipe to the exhaust manifold, and lower the downpipe. Recover the gasket.

Catalytic converter

12 Support the centre silencers and tailpipe section using axle stands or blocks of wood.

13 Unscrew and remove the bolts securing the downpipe to the catalytic converter, then separate the joint and recover the gasket **(see illustration)**.

14 Unscrew the clamp bolt and separate the converter from the tailpipe section.

15 Release the mounting rubber and remove the converter from under the vehicle.

Centre silencer(s) and tailpipe

16 Support the catalytic converter using an axle stand or blocks of wood.

17 Unscrew the clamp bolts and separate the catalytic converter from the tailpipe section.

18 Release the mounting rubbers and remove the tailpipe section from under the vehicle.

Complete system

19 Disconnect the downpipe from the exhaust manifold as described previously.

20 With the aid of an assistant, free the system from all its mounting rubbers and manoeuvre it out from underneath the vehicle.

Heatshields

21 The heatshields are secured to the underbody by a combination of screws and nuts **(see illustration)**. They are easily removed once the exhaust system has been lowered away from the underside of the floorpan, although in most cases, they can be removed with the system still in place.

6.2a On 1.6 litre models, unscrew the retainer and remove the relay box cover . . .

6.2b . . . then locate and disconnect the wiring plug for the oxygen sensor

6.3 Oxygen sensor on a 1.8 litre model

Refitting

22 Each section is refitted by a reverse of the removal sequence, noting the following points:

a) *Ensure that all traces of corrosion have been removed from the flanges and renew all necessary gaskets.*

b) *Inspect the rubber mountings for signs of damage or deterioration and renew as necessary.*

c) *Before refitting the tailpipe joint, smear some exhaust system jointing paste to the joint mating surfaces to ensure an air-tight seal. Tighten the clamp bolt.*

d) *Prior to fully tightening the rear joint clamp, ensure that all rubber mountings are correctly located and that there is adequate clearance between the exhaust system and vehicle underbody.*

6 Oxygen (lambda) sensor - removal and refitting

Note: *The oxygen sensor is delicate component, and may be damaged if it is dropped or knocked, or if any cleaning materials are used on it.*

Removal

1 The sensor is threaded into the exhaust downpipe. Access if best gained from underneath the vehicle. Apply the handbrake, then jack up the front of the vehicle and support on axle stands (see *Jacking and vehicle support*).

2 Ensure that the ignition is switched off, then trace the wiring from the sensor back to the connector in the engine compartment and unplug it **(see illustrations)**.

3 Working beneath the vehicle, unscrew the sensor, taking care to avoid damaging the sensor probe as it is removed **(see illustration)**. **Note:** *As a flying lead remains connected to the sensor after it has been disconnected, if the correct spanner is not available, a slotted socket will be required to remove the sensor.*

Refitting

4 Apply a little anti-seize grease to the sensor threads - avoid contaminating the probe tip.

5 Refit the sensor to the downpipe, tightening it to the specified torque.

6 Reconnect the wiring and lower the vehicle to the ground.

Chapter 5 Part A:
Starting and charging systems

Contents

Degrees of difficulty

| **Easy,** suitable for novice with little experience | | **Fairly easy,** suitable for beginner with some experience | | **Fairly difficult,** suitable for competent DIY mechanic | | **Difficult,** suitable for experienced DIY mechanic | | **Very difficult,** suitable for expert DIY or professional | |

Specifications

General
System type . . . . 12-volt, negative-earth

Starter motor
Type . . . . Magneti-Marelli pre-engaged
Rating . . . . 12 volts, 0.9 to 1.4 kW, depending on model

Battery
Capacity . . . . 40 to 50 amp-hours

Alternator
Type . . . . Bosch or Magneti-Marelli
Output . . . . 65 to 80 amps, depending on model
Regulated voltage . . . . 14.3 to 14.6 volts

Torque wrench settings	Nm	lbf ft
Alternator:		
M8 nuts/bolts	25	18
M10 nuts/bolts	50	37
M12 nuts/bolts	70	52
Battery support tray	29	21

1 General information and precautions

General information

The engine electrical system consists mainly of the charging and starting systems. Because of their engine-related functions, these components are covered separately from the body electrical devices such as the lights, instruments, etc (which are covered in Chapter 12). Refer to Part B for information on the ignition system.

The electrical system is of 12-volt negative-earth type.

The battery fitted as original equipment is of 'limited-maintenance' type and is charged by the alternator, which is belt-driven from the crankshaft pulley. The original-equipment battery does not require regular topping-up, and some of the types fitted cannot be topped-up (see Chapter 1).

The starter motor is of the pre-engaged type, incorporating an integral solenoid. On starting, the solenoid moves the drive pinion into engagement with the flywheel ring gear before the starter motor is energised. Once the engine has started, a one-way clutch prevents the motor armature being driven by the engine until the pinion disengages from the flywheel.

Further details of the various systems are given in the relevant Sections of this Chapter. While some repair procedures are given, the usual course of action is to renew the component concerned. The owner whose interest extends beyond mere component renewal should obtain a copy of the *Automobile Electrical & Electronic Systems Manual*, available from the publishers of this manual.

Precautions

 Warning: It is necessary to take extra care when working on the electrical system to avoid damage to semi-conductor devices (diodes and transistors), and to avoid the risk of personal injury. In addition to the precautions given in Safety first!, observe the following when working on the system:

Always remove rings, watches, etc before working on the electrical system. Even with the battery disconnected, capacitive discharge could occur if a component's live terminal is earthed through a metal object. This could cause a shock or nasty burn.

Do not reverse the battery connections. Components such as the alternator, electronic control units, or any other components having semi-conductor circuitry could be irreparably damaged.

Never disconnect the battery terminals, the alternator, any electrical wiring or any test instruments when the engine is running.

Do not allow the engine to turn the alternator when the alternator is not connected.

Never 'test' for alternator output by 'flashing' the output lead to earth.

Always ensure that the battery negative lead is disconnected when working on the electrical system.

If the engine is being started using jump leads and a slave battery, connect the batteries *positive-to-positive* and *negative-to-negative* (see *Jump starting*). This also applies when connecting a battery charger.

Never use an ohmmeter of the type incorporating a hand-cranked generator for circuit or continuity testing.

Before using electric-arc welding equipment on the car, *disconnect the battery, alternator and components such as the electronic control units* (where applicable) to protect them from the risk of damage.

The radio/cassette unit fitted as standard equipment by FIAT is equipped with a built-in security code, to deter thieves. If the power source to the unit is cut, the anti-theft system will activate - see *Disconnecting the battery* in the Reference section for more information.

2 Battery - testing and charging

Standard or limited-maintenance battery - testing

Note: *Some models are fitted with a limited-maintenance battery which is sealed, meaning that the electrolyte specific gravity cannot be checked. The condition of the battery can therefore only be tested using a voltmeter - refer to paragraphs 6 to 8.*

1 If the vehicle covers a small annual mileage, it is worthwhile checking the specific gravity of the electrolyte every three months to determine the state of charge of the battery. Use a hydrometer to make the check, and compare the results with the following table. Note that the specific gravity readings assume an electrolyte temperature of 15°C (60°F); for every 10°C (18°F) below 15°C (60°F) subtract 0.007. For every 10°C (18°F) above 15°C (60°F) add 0.007.

	Above 25°C	Below 25°C
Fully charged	1.210 to 1.230	1.270 to 1.290
70% charged	1.170 to 1.190	1.230 to 1.250
Discharged	1.050 to 1.070	1.110 to 1.130

2 If the battery condition is suspect, first check the specific gravity of electrolyte in each cell. A variation of 0.040 or more between any cells indicates loss of electrolyte or deterioration of the internal plates.

3 If the specific gravity variation is 0.040 or more, the battery should be renewed. If the cell variation is satisfactory but the battery is discharged, it should be charged as described later in this Section.

Maintenance-free battery - testing

4 In cases where a 'sealed for life' maintenance-free battery is fitted, topping-up and testing of the electrolyte in each cell is not possible. The condition of the battery can therefore only be assessed using the battery condition indicator or a voltmeter.

5 Certain models may have been fitted with a maintenance-free battery with a built-in charge condition indicator. The indicator is located in the top of the battery casing, and indicates the condition of the battery from its colour. If the indicator shows green, then the battery is in a good state of charge. If the indicator turns darker, eventually to black, then the battery requires charging, as described later in this Section. If the indicator shows clear/yellow, then the electrolyte level in the battery is too low to allow further use, and the battery should be renewed. **Do not** attempt to charge, load or jump start a battery when the indicator shows clear or yellow.

6 If testing the battery using a voltmeter, connect the voltmeter across the battery terminals. The test is only accurate if the battery has not been subjected to any kind of charge for the previous six hours. If this is not the case, switch on the headlights for 30 seconds, then wait four to five minutes before testing the battery after switching off the headlights. All other electrical circuits must be switched off, so check that the doors and tailgate are fully shut when making the test.

7 If the voltage reading is less than 12 volts, then the battery is discharged, whilst a reading of 12.0 to 12.4 volts indicates a partially-discharged condition.

8 If the battery is to be charged, remove it from the vehicle (Section 3) and charge it as described later in this Section.

Standard or limited-maintenance battery - charging

Note: *The following is intended as a guide only. Always refer to the manufacturer's recommendations (often printed on a label attached to the battery) before charging a battery.*

9 Charge the battery at a rate of 3.5 to 4 amps and continue to charge the battery at this rate until no further rise in specific gravity is noted over a 4-hour period.

10 Alternatively, a trickle charger charging at the rate of 1.5 amps can safely be used overnight.

11 Specially rapid 'boost' charges which are claimed to restore the power of the battery in 1 to 2 hours are not recommended, as they can cause serious damage to the battery plates through overheating.

12 While charging the battery, note that the temperature of the electrolyte should never exceed 37.8°C (100°F).

3.1 Disconnecting the battery negative terminal

3.2a Lift off the cover for access to the positive terminal . . .

3.2b . . . then unscrew the clamp and disconnect it

3.3a Unscrew the clamp plate bolt . . .

3.3b . . . then lift away the holding strap

3.4 Removing the battery

Maintenance-free battery - charging

Note: *The following is intended as a guide only. Always refer to the manufacturer's recommendations (often printed on a label attached to the battery) before charging a battery.*

13 This battery type takes considerably longer to fully recharge than the standard type, the time taken being dependent on the extent of discharge, but it can take anything up to three days.

14 A constant voltage type charger is required, to be set, when connected, to 13.9 to 14.9 volts with a charger current below 25 amps. Using this method, the battery should be usable within three hours, giving a voltage reading of 12.5 volts, but this is for a partially discharged battery and, as mentioned, full charging can take considerably longer.

15 If the battery is to be charged from a fully discharged state (condition reading less than 12 volts), have it recharged by your FIAT dealer or local automotive electrician, as the charge rate is higher and constant supervision during charging is necessary.

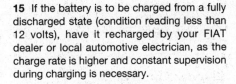

3 Battery - removal and refitting

Note: *If the vehicle has a security-coded radio, check that you have a copy of the code number before disconnecting the battery cable; refer to Disconnecting the battery in the Reference section for details.*

Removal

1 Loosen the clamp bolt and disconnect the battery negative cable from the terminal **(see illustration)**.
2 Lift up the plastic cover, and disconnect the positive cable in the same manner **(see illustrations)**.
3 At the base of the battery, unscrew the bolt from the battery holding clamp plate, and lift away the clamp plate and battery holding strap **(see illustrations)**.
4 Remove the battery from the engine compartment **(see illustration)**.
5 If necessary, the plastic tray beneath the battery can be lifted out. The main battery tray may be removed by unscrewing the bolts - note, however, that on 1.6 litre models, this also entails removing the ECU - see Chapter 4B, Section 4. Before removing the tray completely, unbolt the relay holder(s) (where applicable) and place to one side **(see illustrations)**.

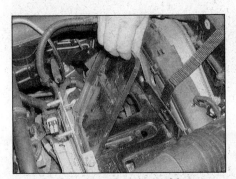

3.5a Removing the battery drip tray

3.5b Lift off the fuse/relay carrier lid . . .

3.5c . . . for access to the mounting nuts

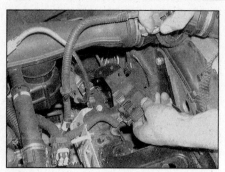

3.5d Removing the rear fuse/relay carrier

Not shown caption

5.9 Remove the plastic cover from the alternator connections

Refitting

6 Refitting is a reversal of removal, but make sure that the positive terminal is connected first, followed by the negative terminal.

---

4 Alternator/charging system - testing in vehicle

Note: _Refer to the warnings given in Safety first! and in Section 1 of this Chapter before starting work._

1 If the ignition warning light fails to illuminate when the ignition is switched on, first check the alternator wiring connections for security. If satisfactory, check that the warning light bulb has not blown, and that the bulbholder is secure in its location in the instrument panel. If the light still fails to illuminate, check the continuity of the warning light feed wire from the alternator to the bulbholder. If all is satisfactory, the alternator is at fault and should be renewed or taken to an auto-electrician for testing and repair.

2 If the ignition warning light illuminates when the engine is running, stop the engine and check that the drivebelt is correctly tensioned (see Chapter 1) and that the alternator connections are secure. If all is so far satisfactory, have the alternator checked by an auto-electrician.

3 If the alternator output is suspect even though the warning light functions correctly, the regulated voltage may be checked as follows.

4 Connect a voltmeter across the battery terminals and start the engine.

5 Increase the engine speed until the voltmeter reading remains steady; the reading should be approximately 12 to 13 volts, and no more than 14 volts.

6 Switch on as many electrical accessories (eg, the headlights, heated rear window and heater blower) as possible, and check that the alternator maintains the regulated voltage at around 13 to 14 volts.

7 If the regulated voltage is not as stated, the fault may be due to worn brushes, weak brush springs, a faulty voltage regulator, a faulty diode, a severed phase winding or worn or damaged slip rings. The alternator should be renewed or taken to an automotive electrician for testing and repair.

---

5 Alternator - removal and refitting

1.2 and 1.4 litre models

Removal

1 Disconnect the battery negative cable and position it away from the terminal.

2 Refer to Chapter 1 and remove the auxiliary drivebelt which drives the alternator.

3 Unplug the wiring from the rear of the alternator at the connectors.

4 Unscrew and remove the bolts securing the upper mounting bracket to the alternator and the engine, then remove the bracket from the engine compartment.

5 Slacken and withdraw the lower mounting

bolt then remove the alternator from the engine compartment.

Refitting

6 Refitting is a reversal of removal. Refer to Chapter 1 for details of refitting and tensioning the auxiliary drivebelt. On completion, tighten all mounting bolts securely.

1.6 and 1.8 litre models without air conditioning

Removal

7 Disconnect the battery negative cable and position it away from the terminal.

8 Refer to Chapter 1 and remove the auxiliary drivebelt which drives the alternator.

9 Remove the plastic cover which fits over the alternator wiring connections **(see illustration)**. Noting the locations of the wiring, and of any washers used, unscrew the terminal nuts and disconnect the wiring from the rear of the alternator.

10 Slacken and remove the alternator upper mounting nut and bolt **(see illustrations)**.

11 Slacken the nut on the alternator's captive lower mounting bolt, noting that this was found to be extremely tight on the project car, and with the limited access, loosening it was not easy. Success was finally achieved using a socket and very long extension bar, working to the left of the exhaust downpipe.

1.6 litre models

12 Remove the lower mounting bolt nut and two washers. Supporting the alternator (which is quite heavy), withdraw the lower mounting bolt, and move the alternator to the rear, resting it on the subframe **(see illustration)**.

5.12 Withdraw the lower mounting bolt, and move the alternator to the rear

Bottom left caption: **5.10a Remove the upper mounting nut . . .**

Bottom middle caption: **5.10b . . . and withdraw the bolt**

5.13a Unscrew the bolts securing the alternator lower mounting bracket . . .

5.13b . . . and remove the bracket

5.14 Withdraw the alternator through the inner wheelarch

13 Remove the four bolts securing the alternator mounting bracket to the engine block, and remove the mounting **(see illustrations)**. Access to the bolts is hampered by the driveshaft, but they are less tight than the alternator lower mounting bolt.

14 With the mounting bracket removed, the alternator can be removed through the inner wheelarch, and out from under the car **(see illustration)**.

1.8 litre models

15 In order for the alternator to be withdrawn, the right-hand driveshaft and its support bracket/shield must be removed, with reference to Chapter 8 **(see illustration)**.

16 With the driveshaft removed, support the alternator, then remove the lower mounting bolt and lower the alternator out of position.

Refitting

17 Refitting is a reversal of removal. Refer to Chapter 1 for details of refitting and tensioning the auxiliary drivebelt. On completion, tighten all mounting bolts securely.

1.8 litre models with air conditioning

Removal

18 Disconnect the battery negative cable and position it away from the terminal.

19 Refer to Chapter 1 and remove the auxiliary drivebelt.

20 Unbolt and remove the exhaust system downpipe from the exhaust manifold and catalytic converter, as described in Chapter 4C.

21 Prise open the protective plastic cover and unplug the wiring from the rear of the alternator at the connectors.

22 Support the engine and transmission on a trolley jack, then unbolt the rear engine mounting from the engine, with reference to Chapter 2D. Lower the rear of the engine slightly using the trolley jack, to allow the alternator to be withdrawn without obstruction.

23 Undo the upper and lower alternator mounting bolts and remove the alternator from the engine compartment.

Refitting

24 Refitting is a reversal of removal. Refer to Chapter 1 for details of refitting and tensioning the auxiliary drivebelt. On completion, tighten the mounting bolts securely.

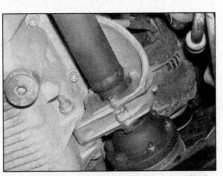

5.15 Right-hand driveshaft support/shield, with alternator visible above (seen from below)

6 Alternator - brush holder/regulator module renewal

1 Remove the alternator as described in Section 5.

2 Where applicable, remove the screw and nut securing the alternator rear cover, and take off the cover **(see illustrations)**.

3 Extract the two small screws (marked with green paint, on our project vehicles) and withdraw the brush holder **(see illustrations)**.

4 Using a steel rule check the length of the brushes. If less than 5.0 mm, the complete brush holder assembly should be renewed. **Note:** *On Bosch alternators, it may be possible to obtain the brushes separately, in which case the brush leads should be*

6.2a Remove the cover screw . . .

6.2b . . . and the nut . . .

6.2c . . . and remove the alternator rear cover

6.3a Unscrew the brush holder screws (arrowed) . . .

6.3b . . . and withdraw the brush holder from the alternator

8.4a Unscrew the nut . . .

8.4b . . . and disconnect the smaller wire from the solenoid

unsoldered from the terminals and the new brush leads soldered onto the terminals. Refer to an automotive electrical specialist for advice.

5 Check the slip rings for excessive wear and clean them with a cloth; do not use coarse abrasives that may damage the contact surface.

6 Fit the new holder using a reversal of the removal procedure, but make sure that each brush moves freely.

7 Starting system - testing

Note: *Refer to the precautions given in Safety first! and in Section 1 of this Chapter before starting work.*

1 If the starter motor fails to operate when the ignition key is turned to the appropriate position, the following possible causes may be to blame.
  a) *The battery is faulty.*
  b) *The electrical connections between the switch, solenoid, battery and starter motor are somewhere failing to pass the necessary current from the battery through the starter to earth.*
  c) *The solenoid is faulty.*
  d) *The starter motor is mechanically or electrically defective.*
  e) *On models fitted with an ignition immobiliser or anti-theft alarm, either the immobiliser has not been deactivated, or is faulty.*

2 To check the battery, switch on the headlights. If they dim after a few seconds, this indicates that the battery is discharged - recharge (see Section 2) or renew the battery. If the headlights glow brightly, operate the ignition switch and observe the lights. If they dim, then this indicates that current is reaching the starter motor, therefore the fault must lie in the starter motor. If the lights continue to glow brightly (and no clicking sound can be heard from the starter motor solenoid), this indicates that there is a fault in the circuit or solenoid - see following paragraphs.

3 If the starter motor turns slowly when

operated, but the battery is in good condition, then this indicates that either the starter motor is faulty, or there is considerable resistance somewhere in the circuit.

4 If a fault in the circuit is suspected, disconnect the battery leads (including the earth connection to the body), the starter/solenoid wiring and the engine/transmission earth strap. Thoroughly clean the connections, and reconnect the leads and wiring, then use a voltmeter or test light to check that full battery voltage is available at the battery positive lead connection to the solenoid, and that the earth is sound. Smear petroleum jelly around the battery terminals to prevent corrosion - corroded connections are amongst the most frequent causes of electrical system faults.

5 If the battery and all connections are in good condition, check the circuit by disconnecting the wire from the solenoid blade terminal. Connect a voltmeter or test light between the wire end and a good earth (such as the battery negative terminal), and check that the wire is live when the ignition switch is turned to the 'start' position. If it is, then the circuit is sound - if not, the circuit wiring can be checked as described in Chapter 12.

6 The solenoid contacts can be checked by connecting a voltmeter or test light across the solenoid. When the ignition switch is turned to the 'start' position, there should be a reading or lighted bulb, as applicable. If there is no reading or lighted bulb, the solenoid is faulty and should be renewed.

7 If the circuit and solenoid are proved sound, the fault must lie in the starter motor.

In this event, it may be possible to have the starter motor overhauled by a specialist, but check on the cost of spares before proceeding, as it may prove more economical to obtain a new or exchange motor.

8 Starter motor - removal and refitting

Removal

1 Disconnect the battery negative cable and position it away from the terminal.

2 On 1.8 litre models, carry out the following:
  a) *Remove the battery and its support tray as described in Section 3.*
  b) *Remove the airflow meter and its associated air ducting as described in Chapter 4B, Section 4.*
  c) *Unbolt the throttle body housing from the inlet manifold, as described in Chapter 4B, Section 4, and move it to one side leaving all coolant hoses and wiring attached.*

3 Apply the handbrake, then jack up the front of the vehicle and support on axle stands (see *Jacking and vehicle support*).

4 Working beneath the vehicle, unscrew the nut and disconnect the smaller wire from the solenoid lower terminal **(see illustrations)**.

5 Raise the plastic cover, then disconnect the wiring from the larger solenoid terminal. Note the fitted order of all components, for use when refitting. Separate the wiring connector incorporated into the main battery lead **(see illustrations)**.

8.5a Lift up the outer cover . . .

8.5b . . . unscrew the nut . . .

6 Unscrew and remove the starter motor upper mounting bolts, located at the top of the transmission bellhousing **(see illustration)**. Note that on 1.8 litre models, access is extremely limited - a cranked ring spanner will be required to reach the bolt heads.

7 Unscrew the starter motor lower mounting bolt(s), then withdraw the starter motor from the engine **(see illustration)**. Note that on 1.6 litre models, the three starter mounting bolts are all accessible from the transmission side of the bellhousing.

Refitting

8 Refit the starter motor by following the removal procedure in reverse. Tighten the mounting bolts securely.

9	Starter motor - testing and overhaul

If the starter motor is thought to be suspect, it should be removed from the vehicle and taken to an auto-electrician for testing. Most automotive electricians will be able to supply and fit brushes at a reasonable cost. However, check on the cost of repairs before proceeding, as it may prove more economical to obtain a new or exchange motor.

8.5c . . . and disconnect the wiring from the larger solenoid terminal

8.5d Separate the wiring plug in the battery supply lead

8.6 Removing the starter motor upper mounting bolt

8.7 Withdrawing the starter motor from the engine

Chapter 5 Part B:
Ignition system

Contents

Degrees of difficulty

| Easy, suitable for novice with little experience | | Fairly easy, suitable for beginner with some experience | | Fairly difficult, suitable for competent DIY mechanic | | Difficult, suitable for experienced DIY mechanic | | Very difficult, suitable for expert DIY or professional | |

Specifications

General

System type:
1.2 litre models	Bosch Motronic 1.5.5 engine management system
1.4 litre models	Bosch Mono-Motronic engine management system
1.6 litre models	Weber IAW engine management system
1.8 litre models	Hitachi engine management system
Firing order	1-3-4-2 (No 1 at timing belt end)
Ignition timing at idle	Under ECU control, constantly changing according to engine load, to maintain idle speed

Ignition coil winding resistance (at 20°C):
Primary:
1.2 and 1.4 litre models	0.45 to 0.55 ohms
1.6 litre models	0.55 to 0.61 ohms
1.8 litre models	0.6 ohms

Secondary:
1.2 and 1.4 litre models	12 000 to 14 600 ohms
1.6 litre models	8645 to 9555 ohms
1.8 litre models	N/A

Crankshaft TDC sensor:
Electrical resistance:
1.2 litre models	9600 ohms
1.4 litre models	774 to 946 ohms
1.6 litre models	575 to 750 ohms
1.8 litre models	440 to 570 ohms

Air gap:
1.4 litre models	0.8 to 1.5 mm
1.8 litre models	0.8 ± 0.4 mm
All other models	0.5 to 1.5 mm

Torque wrench settings

	Nm	lbf ft
Knock sensor	25	18
Spark plugs:		
All except 1.6 litre engine	25	18
1.6 litre engine	27	20

1 General information

The ignition system is integrated with the fuel injection system to form a combined engine management system under the control of one ECU (refer to Chapter 4, Part A or B for information on the fuel injection side of the system).

On all models, the ignition side of the system is of the static (distributorless) type. The ECU uses its inputs from the various sensors to calculate the required ignition advance setting and coil charging time. Some of the sensors described in Parts A or B of Chapter 4 are also used to determine the appropriate ignition firing point for different operating conditions.

The basic timing information is derived from an inductive sensor, positioned above a reluctor wheel mounted on the engine crankshaft. The reluctor wheel has a number of equally-spaced teeth around it, resembling a small flywheel. As the crankshaft turns, the sensor detects the teeth passing it, and sends a pulse signal to the engine management ECU. At the crankshaft TDC position, one of the reluctor teeth is missing, and this creates a variation in the signal produced by the sensor. The ECU uses this information to determine the crankshaft position and speed of rotation, to calculate the optimum firing point for the engine.

All models have a knock sensor, which is used as a safeguard against possible engine damage from pre-ignition (detonation, or 'pinking'). The sensor is bolted to the engine block, adjacent to the top of the combustion chambers. The sensor is sensitive to a particular frequency of vibration, corresponding to that produced during pre-ignition (a condition which can occur when the wrong grade of fuel is used, or when a fuel system problem has resulted in a weak mixture, for example). When the knock sensor detects pre-ignition, it sends a signal to the ECU, which then retards the ignition timing until pre-ignition stops; the timing is then progressively advanced until pre-ignition recurs. This process is repeated many times, until the ECU determines the most efficient running condition for the engine.

In the event of a fault in the system due to loss of a signal from one of the sensors, the ECU reverts to an emergency ('limp-home') program. This will allow the car to be driven, although engine operation and performance will be limited. A warning light on the instrument panel will illuminate if the fault is likely to cause an increase in harmful exhaust emissions.

To facilitate fault diagnosis, the ignition system is provided with an on-board diagnostic facility, which can be interrogated in the same way as for other engine management system faults, as described in Chapter 4A or B.

1.2, 1.4 and 1.6 litre models

On all except 1.8 litre models, the system components consist only of a pair of twin-output ignition coils located on the left-hand side of the cylinder head, and four HT spark plug leads. Note that the ignition coils are housed in a single sealed unit. Each ignition coil supplies two cylinders (one coil supplies cylinders 1 and 4, and the other cylinders 2 and 3).

Under the control of the ECU, the ignition coils operate on the 'wasted spark' principle, ie. each coil produces an HT voltage at both outputs every time its primary coil voltage is interrupted. The result of this is that each spark plug fires twice for every cycle of the engine, once on the compression/ignition stroke and once on the exhaust stroke. The spark voltage is greatest in the cylinder which is on its compression stroke, due to the composition and high density of the air/fuel mixture. The 'wasted' spark occurs in the cylinder that is on its exhaust stroke; the composition and low density of the exhaust charge means that the spark produced is very weak and so has little effect.

1.8 litre models

On 1.8 litre models, each spark plug has its own dedicated 'plug-top' HT coil, which fits directly onto the top of the spark plug (conventional HT leads are therefore not fitted). A power module, driven by the engine management system ECU, controls the supply to the primary circuit in each one of the four coils; unlike the 'wasted spark' system, a spark is generated at each spark plug only once per engine cycle.

2 Ignition system - testing

General

1 The components of the ignition system are normally very reliable; most faults are far more likely to be due to loose or dirty connections, or to 'tracking' of HT voltage due to dirt, dampness or damaged insulation, than to the failure of any of the system's components. **Always** check all wiring thoroughly before condemning an electrical component, and work methodically to eliminate all other possibilities before deciding that a particular component is faulty.

2 The old practice of checking for a spark by holding the live end of an HT lead a short distance away from the engine is **not** recommended; not only is there a high risk of a powerful electric shock, but the ECU, HT coil, or power stage may be damaged. Similarly, **never** try to 'diagnose' misfires by pulling off one HT lead at a time.

3 The following tests should be carried out when an obvious fault such as non-starting or a clearly detectable misfire exists. Some faults, however, are more obscure and are often disguised by the fact that the ECU will adopt an emergency program ('limp-home') mode to maintain as much driveability as possible. Faults of this nature usually appear in the form of excessive fuel consumption, poor idling characteristics, lack of performance, knocking or 'pinking' noises from the engine under certain conditions, or a combination of these conditions. Where problems such as this are experienced, the best course is to refer the car to a suitably-equipped garage for diagnostic testing using dedicated test equipment.

Engine will not start

Note: *Remember that a fault with the anti-theft alarm or immobiliser will give rise to apparent starting problems. Make sure that the alarm or immobiliser has been deactivated, referring to the vehicle handbook for details. If the CODE warning light on the instrument panel is flashing, this indicates that the ignition key being used has not been programmed into the immobiliser control unit - use the master key, and refer to Disconnecting the battery in the Reference section.*

4 If the engine either will not turn over at all, or only turns very slowly, check the battery and starter motor. Connect a voltmeter across the battery terminals (meter positive probe to battery positive terminal) then note the voltage reading obtained while turning the engine over on the starter for (no more than) ten seconds. If the reading obtained is less than approximately 9.5 volts, first check the battery, starter motor and charging system as described in Part A of this Chapter.

5 If the engine turns over at normal speed but will not start, check the HT circuit.

6 Connect a timing light (following its manufacturer's instructions) and turning the engine over on the starter motor; if the light flashes, voltage is reaching the spark plugs, so these should be checked first. If the light does not flash, check the HT leads themselves (where applicable). If there is a spark, continue with the checks described in Section 3 of this Chapter.

7 If there is still no spark, check the condition of the coil(s), if possible by substitution with a known good unit, or by checking the primary and secondary resistances. If the fault persists, the problem lies elsewhere; if the fault is now cleared, a new coil is the obvious cure. However, check carefully the condition of the LT connections themselves before obtaining a new coil, to ensure that the fault is not due to dirty or poorly-fastened connectors.

8 If the coil is in good condition, the fault is probably within the power stage (built into the ECU, on all except 1.8 litre models), one of the system sensors, or related components (as applicable). In this case, a fault code should be logged in the diagnostic unit, which could

2.8 Diagnostic connector plug location on a 1.4 litre model

be read using a fault code reader **(see illustration)**.

9 Fault codes can only be extracted from the ECU using a dedicated fault code reader. A FIAT dealer will obviously have such a reader, but they are also available from other suppliers, including Haynes. It is unlikely to be cost-effective for the private owner to purchase a fault code reader, but a well-equipped local garage or automotive electrical specialist will have one.

Engine misfires

10 An irregular misfire is probably due to a loose connection to one of the ignition coils or system sensors.

11 With the ignition switched off, check carefully through the system, ensuring that all connections are clean and securely fastened.

12 Where applicable (not 1.8 litre models), check the condition of the spark plug HT leads. Ensure that the leads are routed and clipped so that they come into contact with fewest possible metal surfaces, as this may encourage the HT voltage to 'leak', via poor or damaged insulation. If there is any sign of damage to the insulation, renew the leads as a set.

13 Unless the HT leads are known to have been recently replaced, it is considered good practice to eliminate the HT leads from fault diagnosis in cases of misfiring, by fitting a new set as a matter of course.

14 When fitting new leads, remove one lead at a time, so that confusion over their fitted positions does not arise. If the old leads were

damaged, take steps to ensure that the new leads do not become similarly damaged.

15 If the HT leads are sound, regular misfiring indicates a problem with the ignition coil(s) or spark plugs. Fit new plugs as described in Chapter 1, or test the coil(s) as described in Section 4. A dirty or faulty crankshaft sensor could also be to blame - see Section 6.

16 Any further checking of the system components should be carried out after first checking the ECU for fault codes - see paragraph 9.

3 Fault finding - general information and preliminary checks

Note: *Both the ignition and fuel systems must ideally be treated as one inter-related engine management system. Although the contents of this section are mainly concerned with the ignition side of the system, many of the components perform dual functions, and some of the following procedures of necessity relate to the fuel system.*

General information

1 The fuel and ignition systems on all engines covered by this manual incorporate an on-board diagnostic system to facilitate fault finding and system testing. Should a fault occur, the ECU stores a series of signals (or fault codes) for subsequent read-out via the diagnostic connector (see the Section on testing the fuel injection system, in Chapter 4A or 4B).

2 If driveability problems have been experienced and engine performance is suspect, the on-board diagnostic system can be used to pinpoint any problem areas, but this requires special test equipment. Once this has been done, further tests may often be necessary to determine the exact nature of the fault; ie, whether a component itself has failed, or whether it is a wiring or other inter-related problem.

3 Apart from visually checking the wiring and connections, any testing will require the use of a fault code reader at least. A FIAT dealer will obviously have such a reader, but they are also available from other suppliers, including

Haynes. It is unlikely to be cost-effective for the private owner to purchase a fault code reader, but a well-equipped local garage or automotive electrical specialist will have one.

Preliminary checks

Note: *When carrying out these checks to trace a fault, remember that if the fault has appeared only a short time after any part of the vehicle has been serviced or overhauled, the first place to check is where that work was carried out, however unrelated it may appear, to ensure that no carelessly-refitted components are causing the problem.*

If you are tracing the cause of a 'partial' engine fault, such as lack of performance, in addition to the checks outlined below, check the compression pressures. Check also that the fuel filter and air cleaner element have been renewed at the recommended intervals. Refer to Chapter 1 and the appropriate Part of Chapter 2 for details of these procedures.

Remember that any fault codes which have been logged will have to be cleared from the ECU memory using a dedicated fault code reader (see paragraph 3) before you can be certain the cause of the fault has been fixed.

4 Open the bonnet and check the condition of the battery connections - remake the connections or renew the leads if a fault is found. Use the same techniques to ensure that all earth points in the engine compartment provide good electrical contact through clean, metal-to-metal joints, and that all are securely fastened **(see illustrations)**.

5 Next work methodically around the engine compartment, checking all visible wiring, and the connections between sections of the wiring loom. What you are looking for at this stage is wiring that is obviously damaged by chafing against sharp edges, or against moving suspension/transmission components and/or the auxiliary drivebelt, by being trapped or crushed between carelessly-refitted components, or melted by being forced into contact with hot engine castings, coolant pipes, etc. In almost all cases, damage of this sort is caused in the first instance by incorrect routing on reassembly after previous work has been carried out (see the note at the beginning of this sub-Section).

6 Obviously, wires can break or short together

3.4a Engine earth point behind the camshaft cover - 1.4 litre model . . .

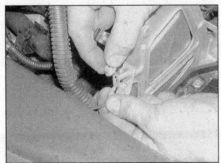

3.4b . . . on the ECU mounting bracket - 1.6 litre model . . .

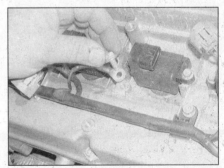

3.4c . . . and between the ignition coils - 1.8 litre model

inside the insulation so that no visible evidence betrays the fault, but this usually only occurs where the wiring loom has been incorrectly routed so that it is stretched taut or kinked sharply; either of these conditions should be obvious on even a casual inspection. If this is thought to have happened and the fault proves elusive, the suspect section of wiring should be checked very carefully during the more detailed checks which follow.

7 Depending on the extent of the problem, damaged wiring may be repaired by rejoining the break or splicing-in a new length of wire, using solder to ensure a good connection, and remaking the insulation with adhesive insulating tape or heat-shrink tubing, as desired. If the damage is extensive, given the implications for the vehicle's future reliability, the best long-term answer may well be to renew that entire section of the loom, however expensive this may appear.

8 When the actual damage has been repaired, ensure that the wiring loom is re-routed correctly, so that it is clear of other components, is not stretched or kinked, and is secured out of harm's way using the plastic clips, guides and ties provided.

9 Check all electrical connectors, ensuring that they are clean, securely fastened, and that each is locked by its plastic tabs or wire clip, as appropriate. If any connector shows external signs of corrosion (accumulations of white or green deposits, or streaks of 'rust'), or if any is thought to be dirty, it must be unplugged and cleaned using electrical contact cleaner. If the connector pins are severely corroded, the connector must be renewed; note that this may mean the renewal of that entire section of the loom.

10 If the cleaner completely removes the corrosion to leave the connector in a satisfactory condition, it would be wise to pack the connector with a suitable material which will exclude dirt and moisture, and prevent the corrosion from occurring again; a FIAT dealer may be able to recommend a suitable product.

11 All models have an inductive sensor which determines crankshaft speed and TDC position. On an older engine, it is possible that the tip of the sensor may become contaminated with oil and/or dirt, interfering with its operation and giving rise to a misfire. Similarly, if the sensor air gap is incorrect, this may result in a misfire (at best). Refer to Section 6 for sensor removal and refitting information.

12 Working methodically around the engine compartment, check carefully that all vacuum hoses and pipes are securely fastened and correctly routed, with no signs of cracks, splits or deterioration to cause air leaks, or of hoses that are trapped, kinked, or bent sharply enough to restrict air flow. Check with particular care at all connections and sharp bends, and renew any damaged or deformed lengths of hose.

13 Check the crankcase breather hoses for splits, poor connections or blockages. Details of the breather system vary according to which engine is fitted, but all models have at least one hose running from the top of the engine connected to the air inlet duct or inlet manifold (see illustrations). The breather hoses run from the engine block (or from the oil filler tube) and carry oil fumes into the engine, to be burned with the fuel/air mixture. A variety of poor-running problems (especially unstable idling) can result from blocked or damaged breather hoses.

14 Working from the fuel tank, via the filter, to the fuel rail (and including the feed and return), check the fuel lines, and renew any that are found to be leaking, trapped or kinked. Check particularly the ends of the hoses - these can crack and perish sufficiently to allow leakage.

15 Check that the accelerator cable is correctly secured and adjusted, and that it is routed with as few sharp turns as possible. Renew the cable if there is any doubt about its condition, or if it appears to be stiff or jerky in operation. Refer to Chapter 4A or 4B for further information, if required.

16 Remove the air cleaner cover as described in Chapter 1, and check that the air filter is not clogged or soaked. A clogged air filter will obstruct the inlet air flow, causing a noticeable effect on engine performance. Renew the filter if necessary; refer to the relevant Sections of Chapter 1 for further information, if required.

17 Start the engine and allow it to idle.

Caution: Working in the engine compartment while the engine is running requires great care if the risk of personal injury is to be avoided; among the dangers are burns from contact with hot components, or contact with moving components such as the radiator cooling fan or the auxiliary drivebelt. Refer to Safety first! at the front of this manual before starting, and ensure that your hands, and any long hair or loose clothing, are kept well clear of hot or moving components at all times.

18 Working from the air inlet, via the air cleaner assembly and the airflow sensor (or air mass meter) to the throttle housing and inlet manifold (and including the various vacuum hoses and pipes connected to these), check for air leaks. Usually, these will be revealed by sucking or hissing noises, but minor leaks may be traced by spraying a solution of soapy water on to the suspect joint; if a leak exists, it will be shown by the change in engine note and the accompanying air bubbles (or sucking-in of the liquid, depending on the pressure difference at that point). If a leak is found at any point, tighten the fastening clamp and/or renew the faulty components, as applicable.

19 Similarly, work from the cylinder head, via the manifold to the tailpipe, to check that the exhaust system is free from leaks. The simplest way of doing this, if the vehicle can be raised and supported safely and with complete security while the check is made, is to temporarily block the tailpipe while listening for the sound of escaping exhaust gases; any leak should be evident. If a leak is found at any point, tighten the fastening clamp bolts and/or nuts, renew the gasket, and/or renew the faulty section of the system, as necessary, to seal the leak.

20 It is possible to make a further check of the electrical connections by wiggling each electrical connector of the system in turn as the engine is idling; a faulty connector will be immediately evident from the engine's response as contact is broken and remade. A faulty connector should be renewed to ensure that the future reliability of the system; note that this may mean the renewal of that entire section of the loom.

21 If the preliminary checks have failed to reveal the fault, the car must be taken to a FIAT dealer or suitably-equipped garage for diagnostic testing using electronic test equipment.

4 Ignition HT coil(s) -
removal, testing and refitting

1.2, 1.4 and 1.6 litre models

Removal

1 On 1.2 and 1.4 litre models, remove the three bolts securing the engine top cover, and lift away the cover for access to the spark plug HT leads.

3.13a Disconnecting a breather hose from the camshaft cover - 1.4 litre model

3.13b On 1.4 litre models, the breather hose stub contains a filter which can be removed for cleaning

4.4 Pull the HT leads off the spark plugs

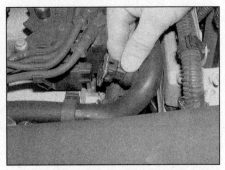

4.5 Disconnect the LT wiring plug from the ignition coil

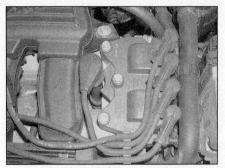

4.6a On 1.6 litre models, the coil is secured by three bolts

4.6b Removing the ignition coil

2 Before removing the ignition coil unit, attach labels to the spark plug HT leads to indicate which plug they serve. Number the leads 1 to 4, starting from the timing belt end of the engine.

3 As an added precaution, check to see whether there are any cylinder numbers marked next to the HT lead terminals on the coil assembly itself - if not, make your own marks, to correspond with the HT lead numbering.

4 Disconnect the HT leads from the spark plugs, and unclip the leads from their locations on the top of the engine **(see illustration)**. Place the leads to one side.

5 Disconnect the LT wiring plug from the ignition coil assembly **(see illustration)**.

6 The ignition coil assembly is secured by four bolts from the side on 1.2 and 1.4 litre models, and by three bolts from the top on 1.6 litre models. Remove the bolts, and recover the washers **(see illustrations)**.

7 Lift the ignition coil assembly away from the engine, complete with HT leads. Recover the support plate fitted to 1.4 litre models.

Testing

8 The only testing which can be carried out without special test equipment is to measure the coil primary and secondary resistance values.

9 The primary resistances are checked on the pins for the LT wiring plug. Connect an ohmmeter between the centre (+) pin of the three, and each of the outer pins in turn **(see illustrations)**. Both tests should give virtually

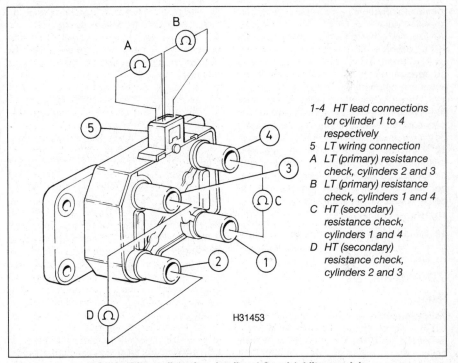

1-4 HT lead connections for cylinder 1 to 4 respectively
5 LT wiring connection
A LT (primary) resistance check, cylinders 2 and 3
B LT (primary) resistance check, cylinders 1 and 4
C HT (secondary) resistance check, cylinders 1 and 4
D HT (secondary) resistance check, cylinders 2 and 3

H31453

4.9a Ignition coil testing details - 1.2 and 1.4 litre models

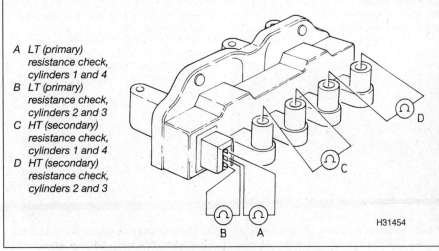

A LT (primary) resistance check, cylinders 1 and 4
B LT (primary) resistance check, cylinders 2 and 3
C HT (secondary) resistance check, cylinders 1 and 4
D HT (secondary) resistance check, cylinders 2 and 3

H31454

4.9b Ignition coil testing details - 1.6 litre models

4.14 Removing the engine top cover

4.15 Disconnect the coil wiring plug

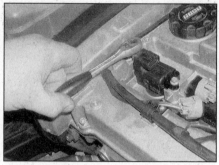

4.17 Unscrew the coil retaining bolts

identical readings - compare with the specified value.

10 To check the secondary resistances, the HT leads must be disconnected from the coil HT terminals. Ensure that the cylinder number markings are visible, so that the leads can be correctly refitted.

11 Check the secondary resistance between the HT terminals for cylinders 1 and 4, then between those for cylinders 2 and 3. Again, both tests should give near-identical readings.

12 If the test results are not as expected, bear in mind that a fault is normally only indicated by a zero or infinity reading. Do not condemn the coil without consulting a FIAT dealer or automotive electrician first.

Refitting

13 Refitting is a reversal of removal, making sure that the LT and HT wiring is correctly and securely reconnected.

1.8 litre models

Removal

14 Unscrew the oil filler cap, and remove the two bolts concealed underneath. Remove the six main cover bolts, and lift off the engine top cover, for access to the ignition coil assemblies **(see illustration)**.

15 Disconnect the wiring plugs from the ignition coil which fits over each spark plug **(see illustration)**.

16 If all four coils are to be removed, mark the coil assemblies for position, noting that No 1 coil is nearest the timing belt end of the engine.

17 Unscrew the two bolts securing the coil to the cylinder head **(see illustration)**.

18 Carefully pull the coil and plug connector upwards off the plug, and withdraw it from the cylinder head recess **(see illustration)**.

Testing

19 The primary resistances are checked on the pins for the LT wiring plug. Connect an ohmmeter between the two outer pins - compare the result with the specified value.

20 If the test results are not as expected, bear in mind that a fault is normally only indicated by a zero or infinity reading. Do not condemn the coil without consulting a FIAT dealer or automotive electrician first.

21 At the time of writing, details for checking the coil secondary resistance were not available - seek the advice of a FIAT dealer.

Refitting

22 Refitting is a reversal of removal, making sure that the coils are refitted to the correct spark plugs, and that the wiring plug is securely reconnected.

---

5 Ignition timing - checking and adjustment

Note 1: *No ignition timing specifications are available from FIAT, so the results will be of academic interest only.*

Note 2: *Checking the timing on 1.8 litre models may not be possible with a*

conventional stroboscopic timing light, as there are no HT leads.

1 When the engine is running, the ignition timing is constantly being monitored and adjusted by the engine management system. When the engine is idling, small changes are made to the ignition timing, to help maintain a constant idle speed.

2 Although it is possible to observe the base ignition timing using a standard timing light, it is not possible to adjust it. The reading obtained will only be approximate, due to the constantly changing ignition timing.

3 On most models, timing marks are provided on the flywheel, accessed after removing a rubber bung from the transmission bellhousing **(see illustration)**. However, it is generally not possible to view the marks without significant further dismantling - the marks are only intended for setting up the camshaft timing, and are not ideal for this check. On the 1.6 litre engine, for example, the thermostat housing and battery tray must be removed for proper access to the flywheel marks.

4 For those wishing to observe the ignition timing, a stroboscopic timing light will be required. The light will need to be the type which incorporates a variable delay, so that the advance angle can be determined from a single TDC marking on the flywheel. It is recommended that the timing mark is highlighted as follows.

5 Remove the rubber bung from the top of the transmission casing, then turn the engine slowly (using a spanner on the crankshaft pulley bolt) until the timing mark scribed on the edge of the flywheel appears in the aperture. Highlight the line with quick-drying white paint; typist's correction fluid is ideal. If marks are not present, set the engine to TDC as described in the relevant Part of Chapter 2, and make your own TDC markings on the flywheel and transmission casing.

6 Start the engine and run it to normal operating temperature, then stop it.

7 Connect the timing light to No 1 cylinder spark plug lead (No 1 cylinder is at the transmission end of the engine) as described in the timing light manufacturer's instructions.

8 Start the engine, allow it to idle, and point the timing light at the transmission housing

4.18 Pull the coil upwards off its spark plug

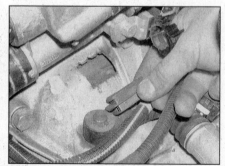

5.3 Remove the rubber bung for access to the flywheel timing marks

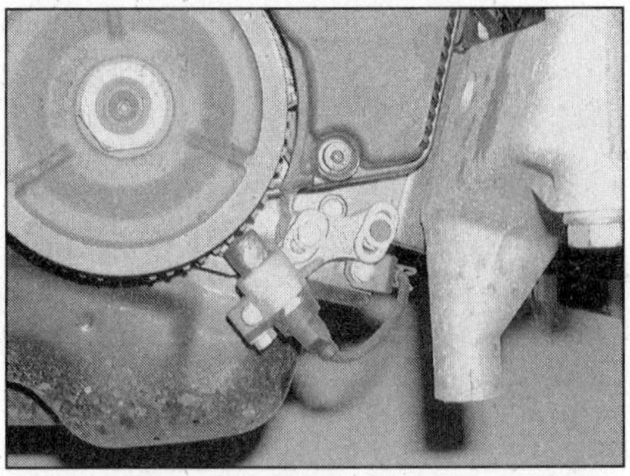

6.1 Crankshaft sensor on 1.6 litre model (1.2 litre similar)

aperture/crankshaft pulley. Adjust the timing light firing point using the variable delay function, until the TDC marks are aligned with each other, and read off the corresponding ignition advance figure.

9 No ignition timing figures are available from FIAT. If there are symptoms which suggest the ignition timing is incorrect, it may be that the engine management system has detected a fault, and entered its emergency running mode. When this happens, the timing is usually set to a fixed value, which may not be ideal for all conditions. In this case, take the car for testing using special diagnostic equipment.

10 After making the check stop the engine, disconnect the timing light, and refit the rubber bung to the top of the transmission casing, and the wheel arch liner and roadwheel, if removed.

6 Ignition system sensors - removal and refitting

Note: *Certain other engine management system sensors are used in calculating the optimum ignition setting, but the two listed here have the most direct influence on the ignition system, and so appear in this Chapter, rather than in Chapter 4A or 4B.*

Crankshaft TDC/engine RPM sensor

1 On 1.2 and 1.6 litre models, the sensor is located at the right-hand end of the engine, mounted on a bracket, adjacent to the crankshaft pulley **(see illustration)**.

2 On 1.4 and 1.8 litre models, the sensor is mounted at the flywheel end of the engine, to the rear **(see illustration)**. Access to the sensor may be found easier from below, in which case, jack up the front of the car and support on axle stands (see *Jacking and vehicle support*).

Removal

3 Ensure that the ignition is switched off, then trace the wiring from the sensor back to the connector and unplug it from the main harness.

4 Unscrew the securing bolt and remove the sensor from the engine **(see illustration)**. On 1.4 and 1.8 litre models, recover any shims fitted between the sensor and the engine.

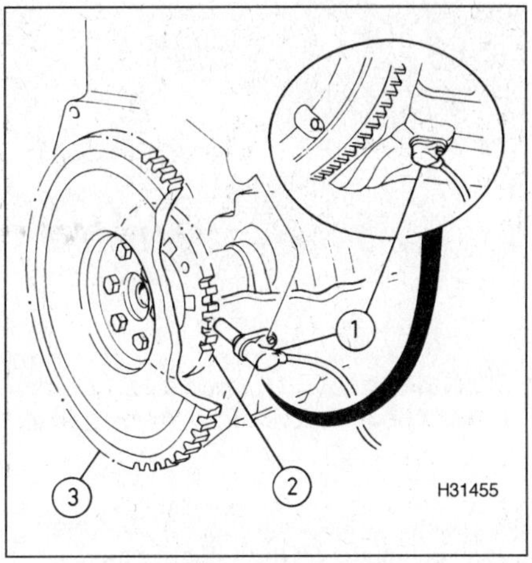

6.2 Crankshaft sensor on 1.4 litre model (1.8 litre similar)

1 Sensor 2 Pickup wheel 3 Flywheel

5 On 1.6 litre models, note that the sensor bracket must not be removed, otherwise the sensor setting will be lost. One of the bolts securing the sensor bracket is of shear-head type, to discourage removal. A special FIAT tool is required to reset the sensor position, if the bracket is disturbed.

Refitting

6 Refitting is a reversal of removal, noting the following points:

a) *The sensor must be clean - any oil or dirt on the sensor tip may interfere with the sensor's operation.*
b) *Ensure that the sensor mounting bolt is securely tightened, and the sensor wiring is correctly routed and securely reconnected.*
c) *Check the sensor air gap as described below.*

Air gap checking

1.2 and 1.6 litre models

7 On 1.2 and 1.6 litre models, using a feeler gauge, check the air gap between the end of the sensor and the tips of the teeth on the reluctor wheel, mounted behind the crankshaft pulley **(see illustration)**.

8 If the gap is not within the tolerance given in the Specifications, this can only mean that the sensor mounting bracket has been disturbed, or that the sensor is damaged.

9 If the mounting bracket has been moved, FIAT special tools will be required to accurately re-position it.

10 If the engine runs satisfactorily, it is not wise to move the bracket to correct a small discrepancy in the air gap.

1.4 and 1.8 litre models

11 Checking the air gap on these models is less easy, as there is no access to the sensor tip and reluctor teeth once the sensor has been fitted.

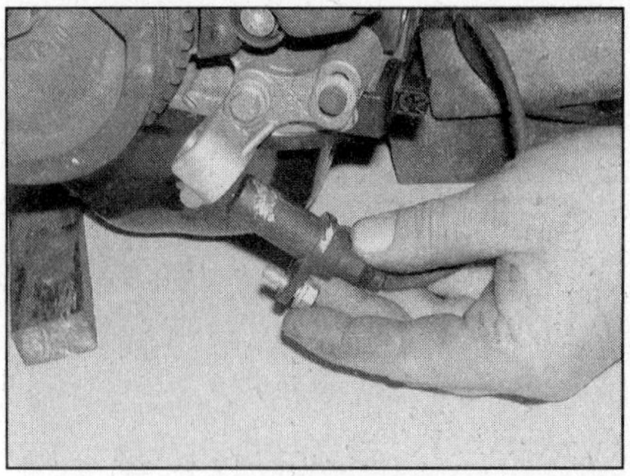

6.4 Removing the crankshaft sensor - 1.6 litre model

12 One way to check the air gap is to remove the flywheel, as described in the relevant Part of Chapter 2. This should provide sufficient access to check the air gap using a feeler blade, as for 1.2 and 1.6 litre models.

13 The only way to avoid removing the flywheel for this check would be to use an accurate depth gauge inserted through the sensor hole, to measure the depth to the reluctor wheel teeth from the outer surface of the engine. By then measuring the fitted depth of the sensor itself (allowing for any shims used), the air gap could be established.

14 As mentioned in paragraph 10, air gap measurement is only essential if the engine is not running well, and fault diagnosis is being carried out.

15 If the air gap proves to be incorrect, it would be possible to alter it using suitable shims below the sensor. Refer to a FIAT dealer for advice.

Knock sensor

Removal

16 On all models except the 1.6 litre, the knock sensor is fitted on the rear of the engine, between Nos 2 and 3 cylinders; access is poor from above, but better from

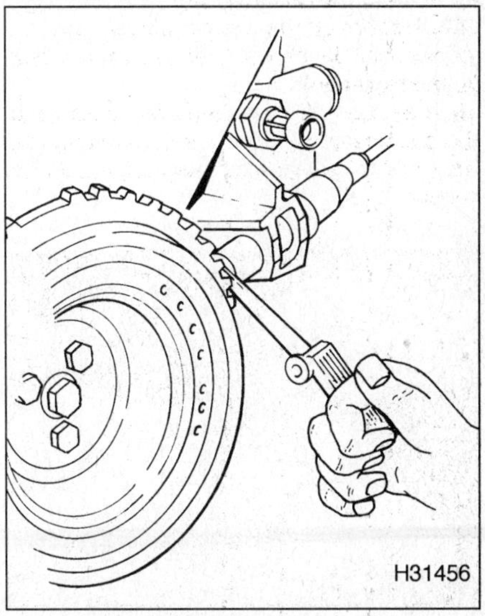

6.7 Checking the sensor air gap on a 1.2 litre model

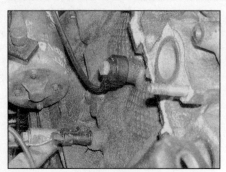

6.16a Knock sensor on a 1.4 litre model - seen with inlet manifold removed

6.16b Knock sensor on a 1.6 litre model

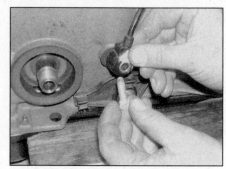

6.18 Removing the knock sensor

below - jack up the front of the car if necessary, and support it on axle stands (see *Jacking and vehicle support*). On 1.6 litre models, the knock sensor is on the front of the engine, next to the oil filter **(see illustrations)**.

17 Trace the wiring for the knock sensor back from its location on the engine, and disconnect its wiring connector. Where applicable, release the wiring connector from its mounting bracket.

18 Unscrew the bolt securing the sensor to the engine, and remove the sensor from the engine compartment **(see illustration)**.

Refitting

19 Ensure that the sensor and its location on the engine are clean, then refit the securing bolt and tighten to the specified torque. The bolt must be tightened correctly for the sensor to function.

20 Refit the sensor wiring to the mounting bracket (where applicable) and reconnect it.

7 Ignition power module (1.8 litre models) - removal and refitting

Removal

1 The ignition power module is fitted to the right-hand end of the inlet manifold (right as seen from the driver's seat).

2 Ensure that the ignition is switched off (take out the key).

3 Release the clip securing the expansion tank hose to the right-hand end of the inlet manifold, and move the hose out of the way **(see illustration)**.

4 Noting their respective positions, disconnect the wiring plugs at either end of the module **(see illustration)**.

5 Unscrew the two socket-head screws securing the module, and remove the module from the engine.

Refitting

5 Refitting is a reversal of removal, ensuring that the wiring connections are correctly and securely remade.

7.3 Unclip the expansion tank hose

7.4 Ignition power module wiring plugs (arrowed)

Chapter 6
Clutch

Contents

Degrees of difficulty

Easy, suitable for novice with little experience	Fairly easy, suitable for beginner with some experience	Fairly difficult, suitable for competent DIY mechanic	Difficult, suitable for experienced DIY mechanic	Very difficult, suitable for expert DIY or professional

Specifications

General

Type .... Single friction disc with diaphragm spring pressure plate, cable- or hydraulically-operated according to model

Clutch pedal travel (cable-operated type)

1.2 litre models .... 155.0 ± 10 mm
1.4 litre models .... 155.0 ± 10 mm
1.6 litre models .... 170.0 ± 10 mm
1.8 litre models .... 170.0 ± 10 mm

Friction disc diameter

1.2 and 1.4 litre models .... 190.0 mm
1.6 litre models .... 200.0 mm
1.8 litre models .... 215.0 mm

Torque wrench setting	Nm	lbf ft
Pressure plate retaining bolts	25	18

1 General information

Vehicles with manual transmission are fitted with a single friction disc with diaphragm spring pressure plate clutch system. When the clutch pedal is depressed, effort is transmitted to the clutch release mechanism either mechanically by means of a cable, or hydraulically by means of a master cylinder and slave cylinder. The release fork forces the release bearing against the centre of the diaphragm spring, which withdraws the pressure plate from the flywheel and releases the friction disc.

Where applicable, the hydraulic fluid employed in the clutch system is the same as that used in the braking system, hence fluid is supplied to the master cylinder from a tapping on the brake fluid reservoir. The clutch hydraulic system must be sealed before work is carried out on any of its components and then on completion, topped up and bled to purge any accumulated air.

2 Clutch - adjustment

Note: *This procedure applies to models fitted with a cable-operated clutch release mechanism. No adjustment is possible on models with the hydraulically-operated system.*

1 The clutch adjustment is checked by measuring the clutch pedal travel. If a new cable has been fitted, settle it in position by depressing the clutch pedal at least five times.
2 Ensure that there are no obstructions beneath the clutch pedal, then measure the distance from the upper edge of the clutch pedal pad to the floor by resting a ruler on the floor. Position the ruler directly in line with the movement of the clutch pedal.
3 Have an assistant fully depress the pedal, then measure the distance from the same point on the pedal to the floor.

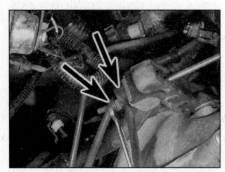

2.6 Clutch cable adjustment

4 Subtract the second measurement from the first to obtain the clutch pedal travel. If this is not within the range given in the Specifications at the start of this Chapter, adjust the clutch as follows.
5 The clutch cable is adjusted by means of the adjuster nut on the transmission end of the cable. Access to the nut is best achieved from under the vehicle. Apply the handbrake, then jack up the front of the vehicle and support it on axle stands (see *Jacking and vehicle support*).
6 Working under the left-hand side of the engine compartment, loosen the locknut on the end of the clutch cable. Adjust the position of the adjuster nut, then depress the clutch pedal several times and re-measure the clutch pedal travel. Repeat this procedure until the clutch pedal travel is as specified **(see illustration)**.
7 Once the adjuster nut is correctly positioned, and the pedal travel is correctly set, securely tighten the cable locknut then lower the vehicle to the ground.

3 Clutch cable - removal and refitting

Note: *This procedure applies to models fitted with a cable-operated clutch release mechanism.*

Removal

1 Remove the battery and battery tray as described in Chapter 5A, and unbolt the battery mounting bracket. Move the relay holder box to one side after removing the cover and unscrewing the mounting bolts.
2 On 1.2 and 1.4 litre models, unscrew the adjustment locknut and adjuster nut from the end of the cable fitting, then release the inner and outer cables from the transmission housing. Note the position of the damper block.
3 On 1.6 and 1.8 litre models, release the outer cable from the transmission and unhook the inner cable from the release lever.
4 Working inside the vehicle, fold back the carpet then unhook the inner cable from the top of the clutch pedal.
5 Returning to the engine compartment, release the cable from the supports then pull it from the bulkhead at the same time releasing the rubber buffer. Withdraw the cable assembly from the engine compartment.

Refitting

6 Apply a smear of multi-purpose grease to the inner cable and end fittings, then pass the cable through the bulkhead. Make sure that the rubber buffer is pressed firmly into the bulkhead before locating the end of the outer cable in it.

7 Inside the vehicle, hook the inner cable onto the top of the clutch pedal.
8 On 1.2 and 1.4 litre models, locate the outer cable on the transmission housing, then refit the adjustment and lock nuts.
9 On 1.6 and 1.8 litre models, hook the inner cable onto the release lever and locate the outer cable on the transmission.
10 Adjust the cable as described in Section 2.
11 Refit the relay holder box, battery and mounting bracket, referring to Chapter 5A as necessary. Also refit the carpet inside the vehicle.

4 Clutch hydraulic system - bleeding

Note: *This procedure applies to models fitted with the hydraulically-operated clutch release mechanism.*

⚠ **Warning: Hydraulic fluid is poisonous; thoroughly wash off spills from bare skin without delay. Seek immediate medical advice if any fluid is swallowed or gets into the eyes. Certain types of hydraulic fluid are inflammable and may ignite when brought into contact with hot components; when servicing any hydraulic system, it is safest to assume that the fluid IS inflammable, and to take precautions against the risk of fire as though it were petrol that was being handled. Hydraulic fluid is an effective paint stripper and will also attack many plastics. If spillage occurs onto painted bodywork or fittings, it should be washed off immediately, using copious quantities of fresh water. It is also hygroscopic - it can absorb moisture from the air, which then renders it useless. Old fluid may have suffered contamination, and should never be re-used. When topping-up or renewing the fluid, always use the recommended grade, and ensure that it comes from a new sealed container.**

General information

1 Whenever the clutch hydraulic lines are disconnected for service or repair, a certain amount of air will enter the system. The presence of air in any hydraulic system will introduce a degree of elasticity, and in the clutch system this will translate into poor pedal feel and reduced travel, leading to inefficient gear changes and even clutch system failure. For this reason, the hydraulic lines must be sealed using hose clamps before any work is carried out and then on completion, topped up and bled to remove any air bubbles.
2 The most effective way of bleeding the clutch hydraulic system is to use a pressure brake bleeding kit. These are readily available in motor accessories shops and are extremely

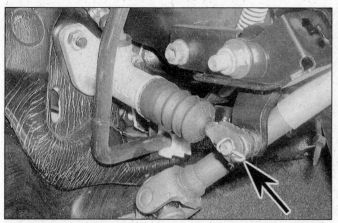

5.7 Clip securing the clutch pedal to the master cylinder pushrod

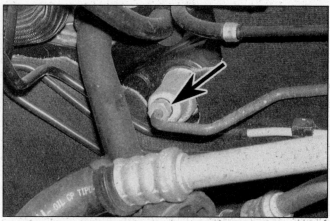

5.8 Union nut on the clutch master cylinder

effective, and the following sub-section describes bleeding the clutch system using such a kit. The alternative method is to bleed the system by depressing the clutch pedal as for bleeding the brake hydraulic system - refer to Chapter 9 for details of this method.

Bleeding

3 Remove the battery and battery tray as described in Chapter 5A, and unbolt the battery mounting bracket for access to the bleed screw on the clutch slave cylinder. Move the relay holder box to one side after removing the cover and unscrewing the mounting bolts. Removal of the air cleaner ducting may also provide additional working room.

4 Remove the protective cap from the bleed screw.

5 Fit a ring spanner over the bleed screw head, but do not slacken it at this point. Connect a length of clear plastic hose over the nipple and insert the other end into a clean container. Pour hydraulic fluid into the container, such that the end of the hose is covered.

6 Following the manufacturer's instructions, pour hydraulic fluid into the bleeding kit container.

7 Unscrew the brake fluid reservoir cap, then connect the bleeding kit fluid supply hose to the reservoir.

8 Connect the pressure hose to a supply of compressed air - a spare tyre is a convenient source.

Caution: Check that the pressure in the tyre does not exceed the maximum supply pressure quoted by the kit manufacturer, let some air escape to reduce the pressure, if necessary. Gently open the air valve and allow the air and fluid pressures to equalise. Check that there are no leaks before proceeding.

9 Using the spanner, loosen the bleed screw until fluid and air bubbles can be seen to flow through the tube, into the container. Maintain a steady flow until the emerging fluid is free of air bubbles, then tighten the bleed screw. Keep a watchful eye on the level of fluid in the bleeding kit container and the brake fluid

reservoir - if it is allowed to drop too low, air may be forced into the system, defeating the object of the exercise. To refill the container, turn off the compressed air supply, remove the lid and pour in an appropriate quantity of clean fluid from a new container - do not re-use the fluid collected in the receiving container. Repeat as necessary until the ejected fluid is bubble-free.

10 On completion, pump the clutch pedal several times to assess its feel and travel. If firm, constant pedal resistance is not felt throughout the pedal stroke, it is probable that air is still present in the system - repeat the bleeding procedure until the pedal feel is restored.

11 Depressurise the bleeding kit and remove it. At this point the fluid reservoir may be 'over-full', and the excess should be removed using a *clean* pipette to reduce the level to the MAX mark.

12 Remove the plastic hose from the bleed screw and refit the protective cap.

13 Refit the battery and mounting bracket, and also the air cleaner ducting if removed.

5 Clutch master cylinder - removal and refitting

Warning: Refer to the warning at the beginning of Section 4.

Note: *This procedure applies to models fitted with the hydraulically-operated clutch release mechanism.*

Removal

1 Where applicable, remove the air cleaner air inlet duct from the engine compartment front crossmember by unscrewing the two bolts.

2 Remove the battery and battery tray as described in Chapter 5A, and unbolt the battery mounting bracket. Release the wiring from the supports on the bracket. Move the relay holder box to one side after removing the cover and unscrewing the mounting bolts.

3 Remove the air cleaner ducting as described in Chapter 4A or 4B. Also remove the air duct

resonator (as applicable) for access to the bulkhead at the rear of the engine compartment.

4 Release the hydraulic hose from its supports over the transmission.

5 At the brake fluid reservoir, fit a hose clamp to the clutch master cylinder supply hose. Alternatively syphon all the fluid from the reservoir.

6 Working inside the vehicle, loosen the clip and disconnect the supply hose from the top of the clutch master cylinder. Anticipate some loss of fluid by placing cloth rags on the floor below the master cylinder.

7 Extract the clip, remove the washer, and disconnect the master cylinder pushrod from the clutch pedal **(see illustration)**.

8 Unscrew the clutch master cylinder mounting nuts and withdraw the master cylinder until the high pressure pipe union nut can be unscrewed from the outlet on the rear of the unit. Alternatively, unscrew the union nut from inside the engine compartment, although access is not easy **(see illustration)**. Withdraw the master cylinder from inside the vehicle and recover the gasket.

9 It is not possible to obtain an overhaul kit from FIAT however some motor factors may be able to supply one. Follow the instructions with the repair kit if obtained.

Refitting

10 Refitting is a reversal of removal, but apply a little grease to the clutch pedal pivot. Tighten the mounting bolts and union nut securely. On completion bleed the clutch hydraulic system as described in Section 4.

6 Clutch slave cylinder - removal and refitting

Warning: Refer to the warning at the beginning of Section 4.

Note: *This procedure applies to models fitted with the hydraulically-operated clutch release mechanism.*

6.4 Clutch slave cylinder location on the transmission

6.6 Removing the clutch slave cylinder from the transmission

7.1 View of the clutch with the transmission removed

Removal

1 Remove the battery and battery tray as described in Chapter 5A, and unbolt the battery mounting bracket. Release the wiring from the supports on the bracket. Move the relay holder box to one side after removing the cover and unscrewing the mounting bolts.

2 Remove the air cleaner ducting as described in Chapter 4A or 4B. Also remove the resonator (as applicable).

3 To seal off the hydraulic supply to the clutch slave cylinder, fit a brake hose clamp to the flexible section of the hose located over the transmission.

4 Unscrew the union nut and disconnect the hydraulic pipe from the slave cylinder **(see illustration)**. Be prepared for some fluid loss by placing rags beneath the cylinder.

5 Unscrew the mounting bolts and release the slave cylinder pushrod from the release arm on the transmission, then remove the slave cylinder from the engine compartment **(see illustration)**.

6 It is not possible to obtain an overhaul kit from FIAT however some motor factors may be able to supply one. Follow the instructions with the repair kit if obtained.

Refitting

7 Refitting is a reversal of removal, but apply a little grease to the tip of the slave cylinder pushrod. Tighten the mounting bolts and union nut securely. On completion bleed the clutch hydraulic system as described in Section 4.

7 Clutch assembly - removal, inspection and refitting

⚠️ *Warning: Dust created by clutch wear and deposited on the clutch components may contain asbestos, which is a health hazard. DO NOT blow it out with compressed air, or inhale any of it. DO NOT use petrol or petroleum-based solvents to clean off the dust. Brake system cleaner or methylated spirit should be used to flush the dust into a suitable receptacle. After the clutch components are wiped clean*

with rags, dispose of the contaminated rags and cleaner in a sealed, marked container.

Note: *Although some friction materials may no longer contain asbestos, it is safest to assume that they DO, and to take precautions accordingly.*

Removal

1 Unless the complete engine/transmission is to be removed from the car and separated for major overhaul (see Chapter 2E), the clutch can be reached by removing the transmission as described in Chapter 7A **(see illustration)**.

2 Before disturbing the clutch, use chalk or a marker pen to mark the relationship of the pressure plate assembly to the flywheel.

3 Working in a diagonal sequence, unscrew the pressure plate bolts by half a turn at a time, until spring pressure is released and the bolts can be removed by hand **(see illustration)**. Note that on some models, the bolts are of Ribe-type, requiring a special key to remove them.

4 Prise the pressure plate assembly off its locating dowels, and collect the friction disc, noting which way round the friction disc is fitted **(see illustration)**.

Inspection

Note: *Due to the amount of work necessary to remove and refit clutch components, it is usually considered good practice to renew the clutch friction disc, pressure plate assembly and release bearing as a matched set, even if only one of these is actually worn enough to*

require renewal. It is also worth considering the renewal of the clutch components on a preventative basis if the engine and/or transmission have been removed for some other reason.

5 Separate the pressure plate and friction disc and place them on the bench.

6 When cleaning clutch components, read first the warning at the beginning of this Section. Remove dust working in a well-ventilated atmosphere.

7 Check the friction disc facings for signs of wear, damage or oil contamination. If the friction material is cracked, burnt, scored or damaged, or if it is contaminated with oil or grease (shown by shiny black patches), the friction disc must be renewed.

8 If the friction material is still serviceable, check that the centre boss splines are unworn, that the torsion springs are in good condition and securely fastened, and that all the rivets are tight. If any wear or damage is found, the friction disc must be renewed.

9 If the friction material is fouled with oil, this must be due to an oil leak from the crankshaft rear (left-hand) oil seal, from the sump-to-cylinder block joint, or from the transmission input shaft. Renew the seal or repair the joint, as appropriate, as described in the relevant part of Chapter 2, before installing the new friction disc.

10 Check the pressure plate assembly for obvious signs of wear or damage. Shake it to check for loose rivets or worn or damaged fulcrum rings, and check that the drive straps securing the pressure plate to the cover do

7.3 Removing the clutch pressure plate bolts

7.4 Removing the clutch pressure plate and friction plate

7.17 Using a clutch friction plate centralising tool

8.2 Removing the release bearing from the fork and guide tube

8.5 Clutch release shaft (1) and upper shaft bush (2)

not show signs (such as a deep yellow or blue discoloration) of overheating. If the diaphragm spring fingers are worn or damaged, or if the spring pressure is in any way suspect, the pressure plate assembly should be renewed.

11 Check that the machined bearing surfaces of the pressure plate and flywheel are clean, completely flat, and free from scratches or scoring. If either is discoloured from excessive heat, or shows signs of cracks, it should be renewed - although minor damage of this nature can sometimes be polished away using emery paper.

12 Check that the release bearing contact surface rotates smoothly and easily, with no sign of noise or roughness. Also check that the surface itself is smooth and unworn, with no sign of cracks, pitting or scoring. If there is any doubt about its condition, the bearing must be renewed as described in Section 8.

Refitting

13 On reassembly, ensure that the bearing surfaces of the flywheel and pressure plate are completely clean. Use solvent to remove any protective grease from new components.

14 Fit the friction disc so that its spring hub assembly faces away from the flywheel. Note that there may also be a marking showing which way round the disc is to be refitted.

15 Refit the pressure plate assembly, aligning the marks made on dismantling (if the original pressure plate is re-used), and locating the pressure plate on its three locating dowels. Fit the pressure plate bolts, but tighten them only finger-tight, so that the friction disc can still be moved.

16 The friction disc must now be centralised, so that when the transmission is refitted, its input shaft will pass through the splines at the centre of the friction disc.

17 Centralisation can be achieved by passing a screwdriver or other long bar through the friction disc and into the hole in the

crankshaft, so that the friction disc can then be moved around until the disc is centred on the crankshaft hole. Alternatively, a clutch-aligning tool can be used to eliminate the guesswork; these can be obtained from most accessory shops **(see illustration)**. A home-made aligning tool can be fabricated from a length of metal rod or wooden dowel which fits closely inside the crankshaft hole, and has insulating tape wound around it to match the diameter of the friction disc splined hole.

18 When the friction disc is centralised, tighten the pressure plate bolts evenly and in a diagonal sequence to the specified torque setting.

19 Apply a smear of high melting point grease to the splines of the friction disc and to the contact points of the diaphragm spring fingers. Also apply a little grease to the release bearing guide tube.

20 Refit the transmission with reference to Chapter 7A.

---

8 Clutch release mechanism - removal, inspection and refitting

Removal

1 Unless the complete engine/transmission is to be removed from the car and separated for major overhaul (see Chapter 2E), the clutch release mechanism can be reached by removing the transmission as described in Chapter 7A.

2 Unhook the release bearing from the fork and slide it off the guide tube **(see illustration)**.

3 Using circlip pliers extract the circlip from the top of the release fork shaft.

4 Note the position of the arm then slide it off the splines.

5 Prise out the release shaft upper bush from the transmission casing **(see illustration)**. If it

is tight, use a thin drift from inside the bellhousing.

6 Lift the release shaft from the lower bush then remove it from inside the transmission bellhousing.

7 Extract the lower bush from the casing.

Inspection

8 Check the release components, renewing any worn or damaged parts. Carefully check all bearing surfaces and points of contact.

9 When checking the release bearing itself, note that it is often considered worthwhile to renew it as a matter of course. Check that the contact surface rotates smoothly and easily, with no sign of roughness, and that the surface itself is smooth and unworn, with no signs of cracks, pitting or scoring. If there is any doubt about its condition, the bearing must be renewed.

Refitting

10 Apply a smear of high melting point grease to the shaft pivot bushes and the contact surfaces of the release fork.

11 Tap the lower bush into the casing and refit the release shaft.

12 Slide the upper bush down the shaft and tap it into the casing making sure that the ridge engages with the cut-out, then slide the arm on the splines the correct way round.

13 Refit the circlip in the shaft groove.

14 Slide the release bearing onto the guide tube and engage it with the fork.

15 Refit the transmission with reference to Chapter 7A.

---

9 Clutch pedal - removal and refitting

The procedure is described as part of the brake pedal removal. Refer to Chapter 9, Section 11.

Chapter 7 Part A:
Manual transmission

Contents

Degrees of difficulty

Easy, suitable for novice with little experience		Fairly easy, suitable for beginner with some experience		Fairly difficult, suitable for competent DIY mechanic		Difficult, suitable for experienced DIY mechanic		Very difficult, suitable for expert DIY or professional	

Specifications

General

Type	Transverse mounted, front wheel drive layout with integral transaxle differential/final drive. 5 forward speeds, 1 reverse speed

Designation:
1242 cc engine	C.514.5.13
1370 cc engine	C.514.5.13, C.513.5.13
1581 cc engine	C.513.5.13
1747 cc engine	C.510.5.17

Lubricant capacity:
1.2 and 1.4 litre models	1.7 litres
1.6 and 1.8 litre models	2.0 litres

Torque wrench settings

	Nm	lbf ft
Flywheel cover	25	18
Gear lever support	15	11
Oil drain and filler plugs	46	34
Reversing light switch	30	22
Speedometer pinion retaining bolt	12	9

1 General information

The manual transmission is bolted to the left-hand end of the engine, and incorporates the main gears and final drive differential. Drive is transmitted from the crankshaft via the clutch to the input shaft, which is splined to accept the clutch friction disc. From the input shaft, drive is transmitted to the output shaft, final drive and differential, then through the driveshafts to the front roadwheels. The differential unit allows the inner roadwheel to rotate at a slower speed than the outer roadwheel when the car is cornering.

The transmission input and output shafts are arranged side by side, so that their gear pinion teeth are in constant mesh. Sliding synchromesh units allow the gears to be locked to their shafts when a gear is selected. In neutral, none of the gears are engaged so the input shaft rotates independently of the output shaft.

Gear selection is via a floor-mounted lever. On 1.2 litre models the gear change consists of two cables. On 1.4 litre models the gear change consists of a gear selector rod, a gear

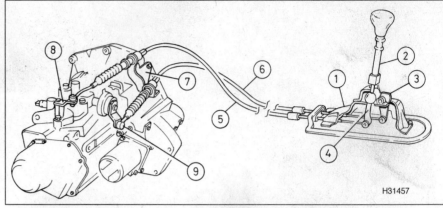

1.3a Gearchange cables and lever (1.2 litre models)

1	Gear lever support	5	Gear engagement cable	8	Selector lever on transmission
2	Gear lever	6	Gear selector cable	9	Engagement lever on transmission
3	Selector linkage	7	Cable mounting bracket		
4	Engagement linkage				

engagement cable, and a reverse inhibitor cable. The rod selects the gear, and the main cable engages the gear. The second cable prevents accidental engagement of reverse gear. On 1.6 and 1.8 litre models the gear change linkage consists of three rods operated by a single control rod. One of the rods acts as a reaction member to ensure the remaining two rods operate at a constant distance from the linkage relay. One of the remaining rods is a gear selector rod, and the other is a gear engagement rod **(see illustrations)**.

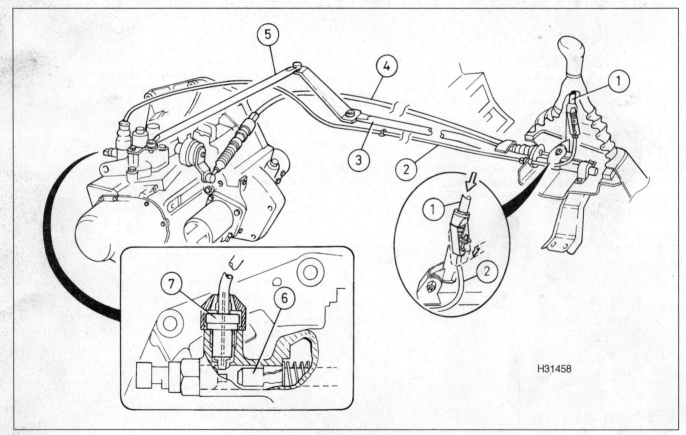

1.3b Gearchange linkage and lever (1.4 litre models)

1	Sliding part of gear lever	4	Gear engagement cable	6	Gear selector and engagement rod
2	Reverse gear inhibitor cable	5	Gear selector link	7	Reverse gear inhibitor device
3	Gear selector rod				

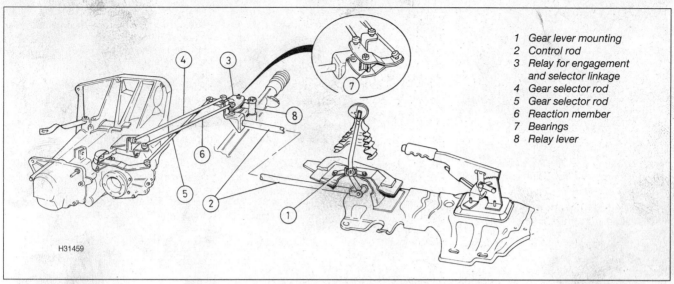

1.3c Gearchange linkage and lever (1.6 and 1.8 litre models)

1 Gear lever mounting
2 Control rod
3 Relay for engagement and selector linkage
4 Gear selector rod
5 Gear selector rod
6 Reaction member
7 Bearings
8 Relay lever

2 Gearchange lever and linkage - removal, overhaul and refitting

1.2 litre models

Removal

1 Apply the handbrake, then jack up the front of the vehicle and support it on axle stands (see *Jacking and vehicle support*).
2 Remove the battery and mounting tray as described in Chapter 5A.
3 Release the wiring from the rear of the battery mounting bracket, then undo the bolt and remove the relay box cover. Unscrew the nuts and remove the relay box from the mounting bracket - position the box to one side.
4 Unbolt and remove the battery mounting bracket.
5 Inside the car, release the gear lever gaiter

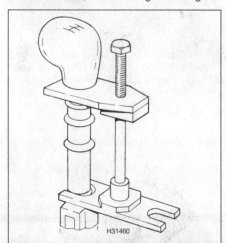

2.17 Tool for removing the knob from the gear lever

from the floor, then release the upper strap and pull the gaiter over the knob.
6 Release the handbrake lever gaiter from the floor, then disconnect the wiring from the handbrake warning light switch.
7 Carefully prise the gear engagement cable end from the lever on the transmission, then unbolt the mounting bracket.
8 Carefully prise the gear selector cable end from the lever on the transmission.
9 Working under the car, disconnect the handbrake cables from the equaliser bar then release them from the rear bracket and tie them to one side.
10 Remove the complete exhaust system from under the car with reference to Chapter 4C.
11 Unscrew the bolts and remove the heat shield assembly from the underbody.
12 Unscrew the mounting bolts from the handbrake and gear lever control assembly. There are 13 bolts in total.
13 Carefully lower the assembly and unscrew the nuts securing the remote control assembly to the gear lever mounting.
14 Withdraw the linkage and cables from the engine compartment, then lower and remove from under the car.

Overhaul

15 With the assembly on the bench, unbolt and remove the gear lever bracket and remove the rubber cover.
16 Extract the clips securing the two outer cables to the mounting, then disconnect the cable ends. The engagement cable end is a press fit on the ball, and the selector cable end is secured with a circlip.
17 Unbolt the gear lever from the bracket. FIAT technicians use a special tool to press the knob from the top of the lever **(see illustration)** however, a tool may be made from two metal plates and a long bolt, using nuts to hold the plates in position.

18 To dismantle the gear lever mechanism, extract the circlip and slide out the shaft and lever. Unscrew the nut to remove the lever from the shaft.
19 Check the components for wear and damage, and renew them as necessary.
20 Reassemble the components using a reversal of the dismantling procedure.

Refitting

21 Refitting is a reversal of removal, but tighten all nuts and bolts securely. Check the operation of the handbrake and if necessary adjust it with reference to Chapter 9.

1.4 litre models

Removal

22 Apply the handbrake, then jack up the front of the vehicle and support it on axle stands (see *Jacking and vehicle support*).
23 Inside the car, release the gear lever gaiter from the floor, then pull the knob together with the gaiter from the top of the gear lever.
24 Release the handbrake lever gaiter from the floor, then disconnect the wiring from the handbrake warning light switch.
25 Remove the clip securing the gear engagement cable to the transmission casing, then carefully lever the cable end fitting from the ball on the engagement lever.
26 Unscrew the bolt and disconnect the reverse gear inhibitor and cable from the top of the transmission. The inhibitor is located beneath the battery position.
27 Unbolt the reaction and gear selector link from the transmission.
28 Working under the car, disconnect the handbrake cables from the equaliser bar then release them from the rear bracket and tie them to one side.
29 Remove the complete exhaust system from under the car with reference to Chapter 4C.
30 Unscrew the bolts and remove the heat shield assembly from the underbody.

2.51 Gearchange relay and rods on the steering gear

31 Unscrew the mounting bolts from the handbrake and gear lever control assembly. There are 13 bolts in total.

32 Carefully lower the assembly and unscrew the nuts securing the remote control assembly to the gear lever mounting.

33 Withdraw the linkage and cables from the engine compartment, then lower and remove from under the car.

Overhaul

34 With the assembly on the bench, extract the circlip and release the reverse inhibitor cable from the gear lever, at the same time unhooking the inner cable end fitting. Release the cable from the base.

35 Extract the circlip and disconnect the gearchange cable from the pin at the bottom of the gear lever. Pull out the retaining clip and release the cable from the base.

36 Unscrew the pivot bolt and remove the gear lever from the gear selector link rod.

37 Unscrew the nuts and remove the gear selector rod rear clamp from the base. Remove the support pad.

38 Withdraw the gear selector rod from the base.

39 Check the components for wear and damage and renew them as necessary.

40 Reassemble the linkage using a reversal of the dismantling procedure, but apply a little multi-purpose grease to the bearing surfaces.

Refitting

41 Refitting is a reversal of removal, but tighten all nuts and bolts securely. Check the operation of the handbrake and if necessary adjust it with reference to Chapter 9.

1.6 and 1.8 litre models

Removal

42 Apply the handbrake, then jack up the front of the vehicle and support it on axle stands (see *Jacking and vehicle support*).

43 Inside the car, release the gear lever gaiter from the floor, then pull the knob together with the gaiter from the top of the gear lever.

44 Unscrew the front mounting bolt for the handbrake and gear lever control assembly. The bolt is located just in front of the lever.

45 Release the handbrake lever gaiter from the floor, then disconnect the wiring from the handbrake warning light switch.

46 Remove the complete exhaust system from under the car with reference to Chapter 4C.

47 Disconnect the handbrake cables from the equaliser bar then release them from the rear bracket and tie them to one side.

48 Unscrew the bolts and remove the heat shield assembly from the underbody.

49 Working in the engine compartment identify the location of the three gearchange rods to ensure correct refitting.

50 Unscrew the nut and disconnect the control rod from the relay lever.

51 Detach the relay lever from the pivot on the top of the steering gear by removing the cap, spring clip and washers, and sliding the lever from the pivot **(see illustration)**.

52 Disconnect the reaction, selector and engagement rods from the transmission, then withdraw the rods as an assembly from the engine compartment.

53 Unscrew the mounting bolts from the handbrake and gear lever control assembly. There are 13 bolts in total.

54 Carefully lower the assembly together with the handbrake lever from the underbody, at the same time withdrawing the control rod from the engine compartment.

Overhaul

55 With the assembly on the bench, unscrew the two bolts securing the gear lever to the mounting, and also unscrew the bolt securing the control rod to the bottom of the lever. Remove the lever from its mounting bracket and also remove the control rod.

56 The relay components may be dismantled by unscrewing the nut. Note the order of removal as the components are removed from the pivot.

57 Check the components for wear and damage and renew them as necessary.

58 Reassemble the components using a reversal of the dismantling procedure, but apply a little multi-purpose grease to the bearing surfaces.

Refitting

59 Refitting is a reversal of removal, but tighten all nuts and bolts securely. Check the operation of the handbrake and if necessary adjust it with reference to Chapter 9.

3 Manual transmission - removal and refitting

1.2 and 1.4 litre models

Removal

1 Select a solid, level surface to park the vehicle on. Give yourself enough space to move around it easily. Apply the handbrake then jack up the front of the vehicle and support it on axle stands (see *Jacking and vehicle support*). Remove both front wheels.

2 Remove the battery and mounting tray as described in Chapter 5A.

3 Release the wiring from the rear of the battery mounting bracket, then undo the bolt and remove the relay box cover. Unscrew the nuts and remove the relay box from the mounting bracket - position the box to one side.

4 Unbolt and remove the battery mounting bracket.

5 On 1.2 litre models, carefully prise the gear engagement cable end from the lever, then unbolt the cable mounting bracket from the transmission.

6 On 1.4 litre models, disconnect the selector rod from the lever on top of the transmission.

7 Disconnect the wiring from the reversing light switch on top of the transmission. Also disconnect the wiring from the speedometer sender.

8 On 1.4 litre models, unscrew the bolt and remove the reverse inhibitor cable from the transmission.

9 Unscrew the nut and disconnect the earth cable.

10 Disconnect the clutch cable from the transmission with reference to Chapter 6.

11 On 1.2 litre models, carefully prise the gear selector cable end from the lever, then position both gearchange cables to one side.

12 On 1.4 litre models, pull out the clip and disconnect the gear engagement outer cable from the transmission, then prise the inner cable end fitting from the ball on the lever. Position the cable to one side.

13 Unscrew the upper bolts securing the starter motor to the transmission.

14 Working on each side at a time, unscrew the nut and use a balljoint separator tool to disconnect the steering track rod ends from the steering arms on the hub carriers. Refer to Chapter 10 if necessary.

15 Remove the inner panel splash guards from under each side of the front wings, then remove the dust guards after disconnecting the wires from the front brake pads.

16 Position a suitable container beneath the transmission, then unscrew and remove the drain plug and allow the oil to drain. On completion, refit and tighten the drain plug.

17 Remove the exhaust front downpipe as described in Chapter 4C.

18 Remove the right- and left-hand driveshafts as described in Chapter 8. Use a suitable lever to prise the driveshafts from the transmission, using a thin piece of wood to prevent damage to the transmission casing.

19 Disconnect the wiring from the starter motor, then unscrew the lower mounting bolt and withdraw the starter motor from the transmission.

20 Unbolt and remove the flywheel cover.

21 Unbolt the exhaust front downpipe securing bracket from the front of the cylinder block for access to the transmission-to-engine mounting bolt. Unscrew and remove the bolt.

22 The engine must now be supported while the transmission is being removed. To do this, remove the engine top cover and attach a hoist to the left-hand end of the inlet manifold, then take the weight of the engine. Make sure that the engine is well supported since only one other engine mounting will still be connected when the transmission is removed. **Do not** support the engine with a trolley jack positioned under the sump because the position of the right-hand front engine mounting dictates that the centre of gravity of the engine mass is high, and it is quite likely that the engine will fall to one side damaging either the radiator or the rear bulkhead. As an additional precaution, position axle stands and a block of wood beneath the engine.

23 Unscrew and remove the upper and lower bolts securing the transmission to the engine, but leave the side nut and bolt at this stage.

24 Support the transmission on a trolley jack.

25 Working under the car, unbolt the rear engine mounting and bracket from the transmission and underbody.

26 Unbolt the front engine mounting and bracket from the front valance and transmission.

27 Lower the transmission and engine slightly until the transmission is clear of the left-hand inner body panels. Unscrew and remove the remaining rear mounting nut and front mounting bolt securing the transmission to the engine, then, with the help of an assistant, withdraw the transmission directly from the left-hand end of the engine. Do not allow the weight of the transmission to rest on the clutch friction disc hub.

28 Lower the transmission to the ground and withdraw from under the car.

Refitting

29 Before refitting the transmission, check the clutch release bearing with reference to Chapter 6 and renew it if necessary.

30 Refitting is a reversal of removal, but first apply a little high-melting-point grease to the clutch friction disc hub splines, taking care not to allow any onto the friction linings. Refer as necessary to the Chapters used for the removal procedures. Tighten the nuts and bolts to the specified torque where given. Fill the transmission with the correct grade and quantity of oil with reference to Chapter 1. Finally, adjust the clutch as described in Chapter 6.

1.6 litre models

Removal

31 Select a solid, level surface to park the vehicle on. Give yourself enough space to move around it easily. Apply the handbrake then jack up the front of the vehicle and support it on axle stands (see *Jacking and vehicle support*). Remove both front wheels.

32 Unbolt the air inlet duct from the engine compartment front crossmember, then disconnect it from the air cleaner and remove.

33 Remove the air inlet duct from between the air cleaner and throttle body by loosening the clips. Also disconnect the crankcase ventilation hose from the front of the cylinder block.

34 Remove the battery and battery tray with reference to Chapter 5A.

35 Release the wiring from the rear of the battery mounting bracket, then undo the bolt and remove the relay box cover. Unscrew the

nuts and remove the relay box from the mounting bracket - position the box to one side.

36 Disconnect the wiring from the engine management ECU by unclipping the connector. Unscrew the nuts and remove the ECU mounting bracket from the battery mounting bracket. The nuts also secure the starter motor and fuel injection wiring.

37 Unbolt and remove the battery mounting bracket and unclip the remaining wiring supports.

38 As applicable, either disconnect the clutch cable or unbolt the slave cylinder from the transmission with reference to Chapter 6 **(see illustration)**.

39 Unscrew the nut and disconnect the earth wire from the transmission **(see illustration)**.

40 Disconnect the gear linkage and reaction rods from the transmission by unscrewing the nuts or separating the rod socket from the ball **(see illustration)**.

41 Disconnect the wiring from the speedometer sender **(see illustration)**.

42 Disconnect the wiring from the reversing light switch **(see illustration)**.

43 Remove the electric cooling fan assembly from the rear of the radiator with reference to Chapter 3.

44 Disconnect the wiring from the starter motor, then unscrew the mounting bolts and remove the starter motor from the transmission. Refer to Chapter 5A if necessary.

45 Position a suitable container beneath the transmission, then unscrew and remove the drain plug and allow the oil to drain **(see illustration)**. On completion, refit and tighten the drain plug.

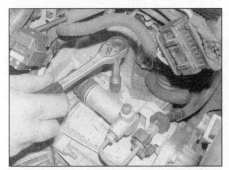

3.38 Unbolting the clutch slave cylinder from the transmission

3.39 Earth wire on the transmission

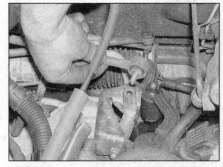

3.40 Disconnecting the gear linkage and reaction rods from the transmission

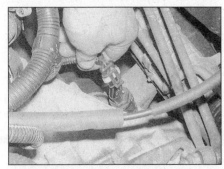

3.41 Disconnecting the wiring from the speedometer sender

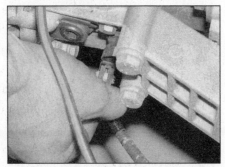

3.42 Disconnecting the wiring from the reversing light switch

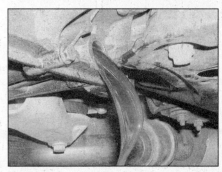

3.45 Draining the oil from the transmission

3.50 Removing the flywheel cover

3.52 Rear engine mounting and bracket

46 Remove the right- and left-hand driveshafts as described in Chapter 8. The clips securing the inner joint gaiters to the transmission side flanges must be removed, and the driveshaft inner tripod joints withdrawn from the differential sun gears.

47 Unscrew and remove the upper and lower bolts securing the transmission to the engine, but leave the side nut and bolt at this stage.

48 The engine must now be supported while the transmission is being removed. FIAT recommend fitting an eyelet to the thermostat housing after unbolting the wiring support bracket from it, however an alternative method is to fit the lifting chain to the left-hand end of the exhaust manifold. If the latter method is used, first remove the engine top cover then attach a hoist to the manifold and take the weight of the engine. **Do not** support the engine with a trolley jack positioned under the sump because the position of the right-hand front engine mounting dictates that the centre of gravity of the engine mass is high, and it is quite likely that the engine will fall to one side damaging either the radiator or the rear bulkhead. As an additional precaution, position axle stands and a block of wood beneath the engine.

49 Support the transmission on a trolley jack.

50 Unbolt and remove the flywheel cover **(see illustration)**.

51 Unbolt the exhaust front downpipe from the exhaust manifold and support on an axle stand. Recover the gasket.

52 Working under the car, unbolt the rear engine mounting and bracket from the transmission and underbody **(see illustration)**.

53 Unbolt the front engine mounting and bracket from the front valance and transmission.

54 Lower the transmission and engine slightly until the transmission is clear of the left-hand inner body panels. Unscrew and remove the remaining rear mounting nut and front mounting bolt securing the transmission to the engine, then, with the help of an assistant, withdraw the transmission directly from the left-hand end of the engine. Do not allow the weight of the transmission to rest on the clutch friction disc hub. The engine may need to be moved forward a little, but make sure that the heater hoses on the bulkhead

are not strained - if necessary, drain the cooling system and disconnect the hoses.

55 Lower the transmission to the ground and withdraw from under the car.

1.8 litre models

56 Select a solid, level surface to park the vehicle on. Give yourself enough space to move around it easily. Apply the handbrake then jack up the front of the vehicle and support it on axle stands (see *Jacking and vehicle support*). Remove both front wheels.

57 Unbolt the air inlet duct from the engine compartment front crossmember, then disconnect it from the air cleaner and remove.

58 Remove the battery and battery tray with reference to Chapter 5A.

59 Remove the inlet duct from the rear of the engine compartment by disconnecting the wiring and crankcase ventilation hose, then loosening the clips and disconnecting the duct from the throttle body and air cleaner.

60 Release the wiring from the rear of the battery mounting bracket, then undo the bolt and remove the relay box cover. Unscrew the nuts and remove the relay box from the mounting bracket - position the box to one side.

61 Unscrew the bolts and disconnect the wiring from the battery positive terminal.

62 Unbolt the remove the battery mounting bracket and unclip the remaining wiring.

63 Disconnect the clutch cable from the transmission with reference to Chapter 6.

64 Unscrew the nut and disconnect the earth wire from the transmission. Also disconnect the wiring from the speedometer sender.

65 Unscrew the nuts and disconnect the gearchange reaction link from the transmission.

66 Remove the electric cooling fan assembly from the rear of the radiator with reference to Chapter 3.

67 Unscrew and remove the two upper bolts securing the transmission to the rear of the engine.

68 At the right-hand side of the engine, unbolt the short engine steady bar between the cylinder head and inner body panel.

69 Remove the right- and left-hand driveshafts as described in Chapter 8. If preferred, the driveshafts can remain attached to the front hub bearings, and tied to one side.

70 Position a suitable container beneath the transmission, then unscrew and remove the drain plug and allow the oil to drain. On completion, refit and tighten the drain plug.

71 Remove the intermediate shaft from the right-hand side of the transmission as described in Chapter 8.

72 Prise the gear engagement and selector rods from the levers on the transmission.

73 Remove the exhaust front downpipe as described in Chapter 4C.

74 Disconnect the wiring from the starter motor, then unscrew the mounting bolts and remove the starter motor from the transmission. Refer to Chapter 5A if necessary.

75 Unbolt the exhaust front downpipe securing bracket from the front of the cylinder block for access to the transmission-to-engine mounting bolt. Unscrew and remove the bolt.

76 The engine must now be supported while the transmission is being removed. FIAT recommend fitting an eyelet to the left-hand side of the cylinder block, however an alternative method is to fit the lifting chain to the left-hand end of the inlet manifold. Attach a suitable hoist and take the weight of the engine. **Do not** support the engine with a trolley jack positioned under the sump because the position of the right-hand front engine mounting dictates that the centre of gravity of the engine mass is high, and it is quite likely that the engine will fall to one side damaging either the radiator or the rear bulkhead. As an additional precaution, position axle stands and a block of wood beneath the engine.

77 Support the transmission on a trolley jack.

78 Working under the car, unbolt the rear engine mounting and bracket from the transmission and underbody.

79 Unbolt the engine left-hand side mounting from the transmission and underbody.

80 Lower the transmission and engine slightly until the transmission is clear of the left-hand inner body panels. Unscrew and remove the remaining bolts and nut securing the transmission to the engine, then, with the help of an assistant, withdraw the transmission directly from the left-hand end of the engine. Do not allow the weight of the transmission to rest on the clutch friction disc hub. The engine may need to be moved forward a little, but make sure that the heater hoses on the bulkhead are not strained - if necessary, drain the cooling system and disconnect the hoses.

81 Lower the transmission to the ground and withdraw from under the car.

Refitting

82 Refitting is a reversal of the removal procedure with reference to the Chapters used for removal, but note the following points.

a) *Check the clutch release bearing with reference to Chapter 6 before refitting the transmission.*

b) *Apply a smear of high-melting-point grease to the clutch friction disc splines; take care to avoid contaminating the friction surfaces.*

c) *Tighten all bolts to the specified torque, where given.*

d) *Observe any special procedures for setting the engine mountings as given in Chapters 2A, 2B, 2C and 2D. In particular, on 1.6 and 1.8 litre engines assemble the left-hand mounting loosely, then tighten the bolts securing the mounting to the left-hand end of the transmission to 5 Nm, followed by the bolts securing the mounting to the front of the transmission tightened to the same torque. Finally, fully tighten the bolts.*

e) *Refill the transmission with the correct quantity and grade of oil with reference to Chapter 1.*

f) *Adjust the clutch as described in Chapter 6.*

4 Manual transmission overhaul - general information

Overhauling a manual transmission is a difficult and involved job for the DIY home mechanic. In addition to dismantling and reassembling many small parts, clearances must be precisely measured and, if necessary, changed by selecting shims and spacers. Internal transmission components are also often difficult to obtain, and in many instances, extremely expensive. Because of this, if the transmission develops a fault or becomes noisy, the best course of action is to have the unit overhauled by a specialist repairer, or to obtain an exchange reconditioned unit.

Nevertheless, it is not impossible for the more experienced mechanic to overhaul the transmission, provided the special tools are available, and the job is done in a deliberate step-by-step manner, so that nothing is overlooked.

The tools necessary for an overhaul include internal and external circlip pliers, bearing pullers, a slide hammer, a set of pin punches, a dial test indicator, and possibly a hydraulic press. In addition, a large, sturdy workbench and a vice will be required.

During dismantling of the transmission, make careful notes of how each component is fitted, to make reassembly easier and more accurate.

Before dismantling the transmission, it will help if you have some idea what area is malfunctioning. Certain problems can be closely related to specific areas in the transmission, which can make component examination and replacement easier. Refer to the *Fault finding section* at the end of this manual for more information.

5 Reversing light switch - testing, removal and refitting

Testing

1 The reversing light circuit is controlled by a plunger-type switch screwed into the front of the transmission casing. If a fault develops, first ensure that the circuit fuse has not blown.

2 To test the switch, disconnect the wiring connector, and use a multimeter (set to the resistance function) or a battery-and-bulb test circuit to check that there is continuity between the switch terminals only when reverse gear is selected. If this is not the case, and there are no obvious breaks or other damage to the wires, the switch is faulty, and must be renewed.

Removal

3 Access to the reversing light switch is best achieved from under the vehicle. Apply the handbrake, then jack up the front of the vehicle and support it on axle stands (see *Jacking and vehicle support*).

4 Position a container beneath the transmission to catch any spilt oil.

5 Disconnect the wiring connector, then unscrew the switch from the transmission casing.

Refitting

6 Refit the switch and tighten securely.

7 Check and if necessary top up the transmission oil level with reference to Chapter 1.

8 Reconnect the wiring then lower the vehicle to the ground.

6 Differential oil seals (except 1.6 litre models) - renewal

1 Apply the handbrake, then jack up the front of the vehicle and support it on axle stands (see *Jacking and vehicle support*).

2 On 1.2 and 1.4 litre models, remove the relevant driveshaft as described in Chapter 8.

3 To renew the left-hand oil seal on 1.8 litre models, remove the driveshaft as described in Chapter 8. Position a container beneath the transmission to catch spilt oil/fluid. Lever out the drive flange, using a suitable lever and piece of thin wood to protect the transmission casing.

4 To renew the right-hand oil seal on 1.8 litre models, remove the driveshaft and intermediate shaft as described in Chapter 8.

5 Wipe clean the old oil seal and note the fitted depth below the casing edge. This is necessary to determine the correct fitted position of the new oil seal.

6 Using a large screwdriver or lever, carefully prise the oil seal out of the transmission casing, taking care not to damage the casing. If the oil seal is reluctant to move, it is sometimes helpful to carefully drive it *into* the transmission a little way, applying the force at one point only. This will have the effect of swivelling the seal out of the casing, and it can then be pulled out. If the oil seal is particularly difficult to remove, an oil seal removal tool may be obtained from a garage or accessory shop.

7 Wipe clean the oil seal seating in the transmission casing, then press the new seal a little way into the casing by hand, making sure that it is square with its seating and its closed end is facing outwards.

8 Using a suitable tube or large socket, carefully drive the oil seal fully into the casing up to its previously-noted fitted depth. Check that the oil seal spring has not been displaced from its location around the inner lip.

9 On 1.8 litre models, either press in the left-hand drive flange until the internal circlip engages the groove, or refit the intermediate shaft with reference to Chapter 8.

10 Refit the driveshaft with reference to Chapter 8, then lower the car to the ground.

Chapter 7 Part B:
Automatic transmission

Contents

Degrees of difficulty

Easy, suitable for novice with little experience		**Fairly easy,** suitable for beginner with some experience		**Fairly difficult,** suitable for competent DIY mechanic		**Difficult,** suitable for experienced DIY mechanic		**Very difficult,** suitable for expert DIY or professional	

Specifications

General

Type	AISIN AW 596/Y024
Ratios:	
1st	2.807 : 1
2nd	1.479 : 1
3rd	1.000 : 1
4th	0.735 : 1
Reverse	2.769 : 1

Vehicle speed sensor

Resistance	648 to 792 ohms

Main shaft speed sensor

Resistance	387 to 473 ohms

Lubrication

Lubricant type	See *Lubricants and fluids*
Lubricant capacity:	
From dry	2.8 litres
Drain and refill	1.9 litres

Torque wrench setting	**Nm**	**lbf ft**
Drain plug	24 to 55	18 to 41

1 General information

General description

The automatic transmission is a four speed unit, incorporating a hydrodynamic torque converter with a planetary gearbox.

Gear selection is achieved by means of a floor-mounted, seven position selector lever. The positions are P (Park), R (Reverse), N (Neutral), D (Drive), 3 (4th gear excluded), 2 (only 1st and 2nd gear selected automatically), 1 (1st gear lock). A SPORT button enables the driver to select an operating mode which provides additional acceleration by shifting up or down at higher engine speeds. 4th gear is not selected in this mode, and top speed is achieved in 3rd gear. Note that increased fuel consumption will occur in this mode. An ICE button may be selected when driving in ice or snow in position D; 2nd gear is used when moving away from rest in this mode.

The transmission incorporates a kick-down feature which provides greater acceleration when the accelerator pedal is depressed to the floor.

The overall operation of the transmission is managed by the engine management electronic control unit (ECU) and as a result there are no manual adjustments **(see illustration)**. Comprehensive fault diagnosis can therefore only be carried out using dedicated electronic test equipment.

Due to the complexity of the transmission and its control system, major repairs and overhaul operations should be left to a FIAT dealer, who will be equipped to carry out fault diagnosis and repair. The information in this Chapter is therefore limited to a description of the removal and refitting of the transmission as a complete unit. The removal, refitting and adjustment of the selector cable is also described.

Precautions

Observe the following precautions to avoid damage to the automatic transmission:
a) Do not attempt to start the engine by pushing or towing the car.
b) If the car has to be towed for recovery, the distance must not exceed 12 miles (20 km), and the speed must not exceed 19 mph (30 kph). If these conditions cannot be met, or if transmission damage is suspected, only tow the car with the front wheels clear of the ground.
c) Only engage P or R when the vehicle is stationary.

2 Automatic transmission - removal and refitting

Removal

1 Select a solid, level surface to park the vehicle on. Give yourself enough space to move around it easily. Apply the handbrake then jack up the front of the vehicle and support it on axle stands (see *Jacking and vehicle support*). Remove both front wheels.
2 Unbolt the air inlet duct from the engine compartment front crossmember, then disconnect it from the air cleaner and remove.
3 Remove the air inlet duct and resonator from between the air cleaner and throttle body by loosening the clips. Also disconnect the crankcase ventilation hose from the front of the cylinder block.
4 Remove the battery and battery tray with reference to Chapter 5A.
5 Release the wiring from the rear of the battery mounting bracket, then undo the bolt and remove the relay box cover. Unscrew the nuts and remove the relay box from the mounting bracket - position the box to one side.
6 Disconnect the wiring from the engine management ECU by unclipping the connector. Unscrew the nuts and remove the ECU mounting bracket from the battery mounting bracket. The nuts also secure the starter motor and fuel injection wiring.
7 Unscrew the nut and disconnect the earth wire from the bracket, then unbolt and remove the battery mounting bracket and unclip the remaining wiring supports.
8 Remove the spring clip and washer, and disconnect the selector cable end from the lever on the transmission. Unbolt the cable mounting bracket and position the cables to one side.
9 Unbolt the earth cable from the transmission.
10 Disconnect the two wiring connectors located on top of the transmission. One is for the selector lever position sensor and the other is for the gear change, lock-up, and pressure control solenoids.
11 Disconnect the oil temperature sensor wiring at the front of the transmission.
12 Disconnect the wiring from the speedometer sender.
13 Unscrew the bolt securing the wiring support to the thermostat housing, and move the wiring to one side.
14 Remove the starter motor as described in Chapter 5A.
15 The engine must now be supported while the transmission is being removed. FIAT technicians fit an engine lifting eye to the bolt hole on the thermostat housing, however an alternative method is to attach a hoist to the left-hand end of the inlet manifold. With the

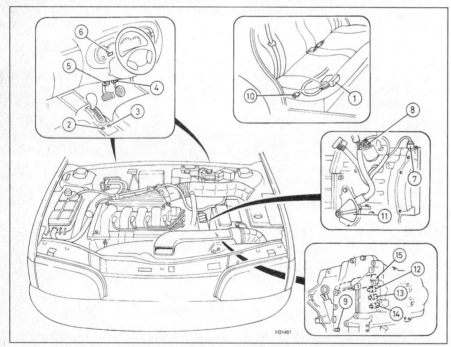

1.4 AISIN AW 596/Y024 automatic transmission component locations

1 Electronic control module
2 NORMAL/SPORT mode switch
3 ICE mode switch
4 Kick-down switch
5 Stop light switch
6 Instrument panel
7 Main shaft RPM sensor (black)
8 Vehicle speed sensor (grey)
9 Transmission fluid temperature sensor
10 Diagnostic socket
11 Selector lever position sensor
12 Solenoid S1, gear engagement
13 Solenoid S2, gear engagement
14 Solenoid SL, lock-up clutch
15 Solenoid STH, pressure control

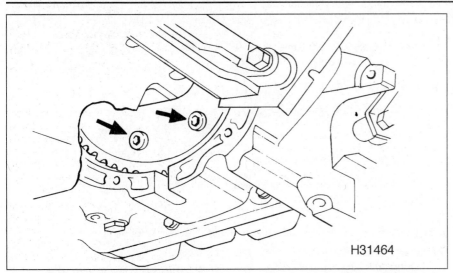

2.19a Two of the six bolts securing the driveplate to the torque converter

hoist in position, take the weight of the engine. Make sure that the engine is well supported since only one other engine mounting will still be connected when the transmission is removed. **Do not** support the engine with a trolley jack positioned under the sump because the position of the right-hand front engine mounting dictates that the centre of gravity of the engine mass is high, and it is quite likely that the engine will fall to one side damaging either the radiator or the rear bulkhead. As an additional precaution, position axle stands and a block of wood beneath the engine.

16 Position a container beneath the transmission, then unscrew the drain plug and allow the fluid to drain from the transmission. On completion, clean the plug and refit it, tightening it to the specified torque.

17 Identify the position of the two hydraulic fluid hoses on the transmission, then unscrew the union nuts and disconnect the hoses. Tie the hoses to one side. To prevent the ingress of dust and dirt, plug the ends of the hoses and apertures in the transmission.

18 Unbolt the driveplate cover from the bottom of the transmission bellhousing for access to the driveplate-to-torque converter bolts.

19 Using an Allen key, unscrew the driveplate-to-converter bolts. The access hole will accommodate two of the bolts, then it will be necessary to turn the crankshaft (using a spanner on the crankshaft pulley bolt) until the next pair bolt appear in the hole. There are 6 bolts in total, and it is important that only these bolts are used on refitting as they are of specific length, measuring 12.5 mm from under the head to the end of the bolt **(see illustrations)**. Bolts which are too long will damage the torque converter, and bolts which are too short may not withstand the rotational torques.

20 Support the transmission on a trolley jack.

21 Working under the car, unbolt the rear engine mounting and bracket from the transmission and underbody.

22 Unbolt the left-hand engine mounting and bracket from the underbody and transmission.

23 Unscrew and remove the bolts securing the transmission to the engine.

24 With the help of an assistant, lower the trolley jack, then withdraw the transmission slightly from the engine. Using a lever, push the torque converter back into the transmission bellhousing so that it remains engaged with the transmission oil pump. It is suggested that a suitable piece of metal is bolted to the bellhousing to ensure the torque converter remains in position **(see illustration)**.

⚠️ *Warning: Make sure that the transmission remains steady on the jack head.*

25 Withdraw the transmission from the engine and lower it to the ground.

Refitting

26 Refitting is a reversal of removal, but note the following points:

a) *Make sure that the torque converter is fully engaged with the transmission pump before lifting the transmission into position.*

b) *Tighten all nuts and bolts to the specified torque where given.*

c) *If there is any sign of oil leaking from the driveshaft oil seals on the sides of the transmission, renew them with reference to Section 11.*

---

3 Automatic transmission - overhaul

In the event of a fault occurring, it will be necessary to establish whether the fault is electrical, mechanical or hydraulic in nature, before repair work can be contemplated. Diagnosis requires detailed knowledge of the transmissions operation and construction, as well as access to specialised test equipment, and so is deemed to be beyond the scope of this manual. It is therefore essential that problems with the automatic transmission are referred to a FIAT dealer for assessment.

Note that a faulty transmission should not be removed before the vehicle has been assessed by a dealer, as fault diagnosis is carried out with the transmission *in situ*.

---

4 Selector cable - removal, refitting and adjustment

Removal

1 Move the selector lever to position P. Chock the front roadwheels, then jack up the rear of the vehicle and support on axle stands (see *Jacking and vehicle support*). For additional working room, raise the front of the car as well.

2 Unbolt the air inlet duct from the engine compartment front crossmember, then disconnect it from the air cleaner and remove.

3 Remove the battery and battery tray with reference to Chapter 5A.

4 Release the wiring from the rear of the battery

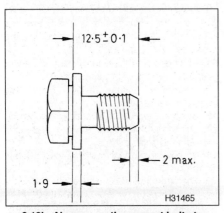

2.19b Always use the correct bolts to secure the torque converter to the driveplate - the dimensions are given in mm

12·5 ± 0·1
2 max.
1·9

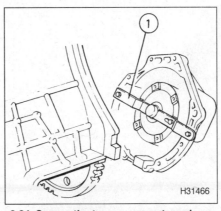

2.24 Secure the torque converter using a piece of metal bolted to the transmission bellhousing

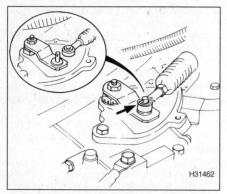

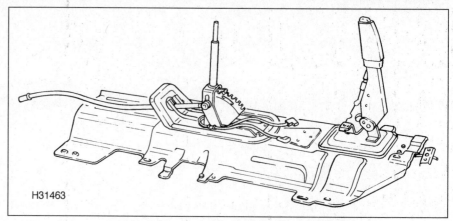

4.7 Disconnecting the selector cable end from the transmission

4.14 Gear selector and handbrake lever mounting

mounting bracket, then undo the bolt and remove the relay box cover. Unscrew the nuts and remove the relay box from the mounting bracket - position the box to one side.

5 Disconnect the wiring from the engine management ECU by unclipping the connector. Unscrew the nuts and remove the ECU mounting bracket from the battery mounting bracket. The nuts also secure the starter motor and fuel injection wiring.

6 Unbolt and remove the battery mounting bracket and unclip the remaining wiring supports.

7 Remove the spring clip and washer, and disconnect the selector cable end from the lever on the transmission **(see illustration)**.

8 Pull out the spring clip and disconnect the outer cable from the cable mounting bracket.

9 Unscrew the bolt from the front of the gear lever knob, then withdraw the knob upwards. Carefully prise the indicator panel from the floor and remove over the gear lever.

10 Carefully prise the driving mode panel from the floor and disconnect the switch wiring.

11 Release the handbrake lever gaiter from the floor, then back off the handbrake lever adjustment nut. Also disconnect the wiring from the handbrake-on warning switch.

12 Working under the car, unscrew the nuts and remove the heat shield for access to the handbrake cables. Unhook the front of the handbrake cables from the equaliser bar, then release the outer cables from the underbody bracket.

13 Remove the exhaust downpipe as described in Chapter 4C.

14 Unscrew the nuts/bolts securing the gear selector and handbrake lever mounting to the underbody, and withdraw it from under the car **(see illustration)**.

15 Extract the clip and disconnect the cable end from the selector lever, then pull out the clip and disconnect the outer cable from the mounting.

16 Unscrew the nuts and remove the selector lever assembly from the mounting.

17 Unscrew the bolt securing the wiring to the side of the assembly.

18 If necessary, unscrew the nuts and remove the PARK position switch and also unbolt the shift-lock device **(see illustration)**.

Refitting and adjustment

19 Refitting is a reversal of removal, but before

attaching the cable end to the selector lever on the transmission, check the adjustment as follows. With the selector lever in position P and the cable attached to the lever inside the car, check that the lever on the transmission is also in position P. Offer the cable end onto the transmission lever and check that the hole in the end correctly aligns with the pin on the lever. If not, loosen the locknut on the cable and turn the end fitting in or out as required until it aligns correctly with the pin, then tighten the locknut. Locate the cable on the pin and secure with the clip. On completion, check that it is only possible to start the engine with the selector lever in positions P or N. Also check that the selector lever position shown on the floor mounted panel matches the positions indicated on the instrument panel.

5 Kick-down switch - removal and refitting

Removal

1 The kick-down switch is mounted on the accelerator pedal bracket. **Note:** *It is quite likely that the switch mounting lugs will be broken as the switch is being removed.*

2 Disconnect the wiring from the switch.

3 Release the mounting lugs and withdraw the switch from the accelerator pedal.

Refitting

4 Refitting is a reversal of removal.

6 Selector lever position sensor - removal and refitting

Removal

1 Move the selector lever to position P.

2 Unbolt the air inlet duct from the engine compartment front crossmember, then disconnect it from the air cleaner and remove.

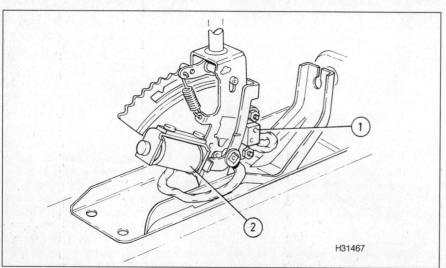

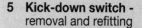

4.18 PARK position switch (1) and shift-lock device (2)

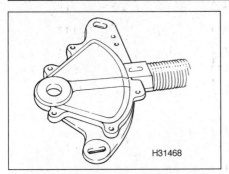

6.11 Selector lever position sensor

3 Remove the battery and battery tray with reference to Chapter 5A.

4 Release the wiring from the rear of the battery mounting bracket, then undo the bolt and remove the relay box cover. Unscrew the nuts and remove the relay box from the mounting bracket - position the box to one side.

5 Disconnect the wiring from the engine management ECU by unclipping the connector. Unscrew the nuts and remove the ECU mounting bracket from the battery mounting bracket. The nuts also secure the starter motor and fuel injection wiring.

6 Unbolt and remove the battery mounting bracket and unclip the remaining wiring supports.

7 Remove the spring clip and washer, and disconnect the selector cable end from the lever on the transmission.

8 Disconnect the selector lever position sensor wiring at the connector.

9 Unscrew the nut and remove the lever from the sensor.

10 Release the special washer from the central nut, then unscrew and remove the nut.

11 Unscrew the mounting bolts and remove the selector lever position sensor from the transmission **(see illustration)**.

Refitting

12 Locate the sensor on the spindle followed by the special washer, then tighten the nut securely and bend up the washer tabs to lock.

13 Insert and tighten the mounting bolts securely.

14 With the sensor adjustment bolts loose, turn the spindle fully clockwise to position P, then turn it two notches anticlockwise to position N.

15 Turn the sensor until the projection on its upper surface is aligned with the machined edges on the spindle **(see illustration)**. Tighten the sensor adjustment bolts without moving the sensor.

16 An alternative method of setting the sensor is to use an ohmmeter. Connect the ohmmeter between terminals 6 and 10 of the wiring connector then turn the sensor to determine the limits of the arc where the meter indicates continuity. Position the sensor in the centre of this arc, then tighten the adjustment bolts. The N and P internal

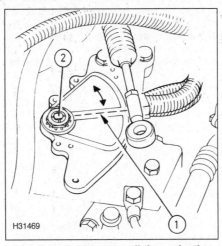

6.15 Turn the sensor until the projection on its upper surface (1) is aligned with the machined edges on the spindle (2)

contacts are both closed with the sensor in its centre position.

17 Refit the lever to the spindle and tighten the nut.

18 Reconnect the wiring.

19 Refer to Section 4 when refitting the selector cable.

20 The remaining procedure is a reversal of removal.

7 Electronic control unit - removal and refitting

Caution: Handle the electronic control unit carefully, and do not touch the connector terminals. Do not attempt to remove the cover from the unit.

Removal

1 The automatic transmission electronic control unit is located beneath the rear passenger seat, on the right-hand side. First,

disconnect the battery negative (earth) lead (see *Disconnecting the battery*).

2 Remove the rear seat cushion as described in Chapter 11, Section 19.

3 Remove the trim for access to the control unit, then unscrew the bolts and nut securing the unit mounting bracket to the floor.

4 Carefully disconnect the wiring from the control unit.

5 Unscrew the nuts and remove the control unit from the mounting bracket **(see illustration)**.

Refitting

6 Refitting is a reversal of removal. Make sure that the wiring connector is firmly pressed on.

8 Safety control unit - removal and refitting

Removal

1 The safety control unit is located under the passenger seat. First, disconnect the battery negative (earth) lead (see *Disconnecting the battery*).

2 Adjust the front passenger seat fully rearwards.

3 Unscrew the mounting bolts, then disconnect the wiring and remove the safety control unit from inside the car.

Refitting

4 Refitting is a reversal of removal.

9 Vehicle and transmission main shaft speed sensors - removal, testing and refitting

Removal

1 Apply the handbrake, then jack up the front of the vehicle and support it on axle stands (see *Jacking and vehicle support*). Remove the front left-hand roadwheel.

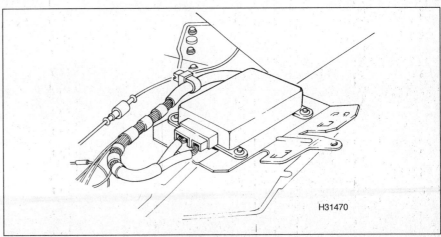

7.5 Electronic control unit

2 Remove the trim (not the wheel arch liner) for access to the rear of the transmission.

3 To remove either the vehicle speed sensor (grey) or main shaft speed sensor (black), disconnect the wiring then unscrew the mounting bolt and withdraw the sensor from the casing.

4 Remove the O-ring seal.

Testing

5 Connect an ohmmeter between the terminals of the sensor, and check that the resistance value is as given in the Specifications.

Refitting

6 Refitting is a reversal of removal, but fit a new O-ring seal and lightly smear it with grease before refitting the sensor.

10 Transmission fluid cooling radiator and fan - removal and refitting

Removal

1 Apply the handbrake, then jack up the front of the vehicle and support it on axle stands (see *Jacking and vehicle support*). Remove the front left-hand roadwheel.

2 Position a container beneath the transmission, then unscrew the drain plug and allow the fluid to drain. On completion, refit and tighten the drain plug, and wipe clean the area around the plug.

3 Unbolt the air inlet duct from the engine compartment front crossmember, then disconnect it from the air cleaner and remove.

4 Behind the battery location, disconnect the wiring for the electric fan.

5 Working under the left-hand wheel arch, unscrew the mounting bolts and remove the electric cooling fan from the rear of the fluid cooling radiator **(see illustration)**. Withdraw the fan from under the car.

6 Position the container beneath the fluid cooling radiator, then unscrew the union nuts and disconnect the fluid feed and return hoses. Plug the ends of the hoses to prevent the ingress of dust and dirt.

7 Unscrew the upper mounting nuts and withdraw the radiator from under the car.

Refitting

8 Refitting is a reversal of removal, but tighten all nuts and bolts securely. Finally, top-up the transmission fluid level with reference to Chapter 1.

11 Differential oil seals - renewal

1 Apply the handbrake, then jack up the front of the vehicle and support it on axle stands (see *Jacking and vehicle support*).

2 Remove the relevant driveshaft as described in Chapter 8.

3 Wipe clean the old oil seal and note the fitted depth below the casing edge. This is necessary to determine the correct fitted position of the new oil seal.

4 Using a large screwdriver or lever, carefully prise the oil seal out of the transmission casing, taking care not to damage the casing. If the oil seal is reluctant to move, it is

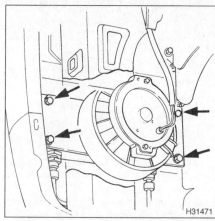

10.5 Electric cooling fan mounting bolts on the rear of the fluid cooling radiator

sometimes helpful to carefully drive it *into* the transmission a little way, applying the force at one point only. This will have the effect of swivelling the seal out of the casing, and it can then be pulled out. If the oil seal is particularly difficult to remove, an oil seal removal tool may be obtained from a garage or accessory shop.

5 Wipe clean the oil seal seating in the transmission casing, then press the new seal a little way into the casing by hand, making sure that it is square with its seating and its closed end is facing outwards.

6 Using a suitable tube or large socket, carefully drive the oil seal fully into the casing up to its previously-noted fitted depth. Check that the oil seal spring has not been displaced from its location around the inner lip.

7 Refit the driveshaft with reference to Chapter 8, then lower the car to the ground.

Chapter 8
Driveshafts

Contents

Degrees of difficulty

Easy, suitable for novice with little experience		Fairly easy, suitable for beginner with some experience		Fairly difficult, suitable for competent DIY mechanic		Difficult, suitable for experienced DIY mechanic		Very difficult, suitable for expert DIY or professional	

Specifications

General

Type . . . . Unequal-length, solid steel shafts, splined to inner and outer constant velocity joints. Intermediate shaft with support bearing on 1.8 litre models with equal length driveshafts.

Damping weight position:
  1.2 and 1.4 litre models . . . . 201 mm from inner end of driveshaft
  1.6 litre models:
    Early models . . . . Either 290 to 295 mm, or 292 to 297 mm from inner end of driveshaft
    Later models . . . . Recess on driveshaft
  1.8 litre models . . . . Recess on driveshaft
Inner gaiter bearing position (1.6 litre models):
  Left-hand driveshaft . . . . Either 133 or 135 mm from inner end of driveshaft
  Right-hand driveshaft . . . . Either 108 or 110 mm from inner end of driveshaft

Lubrication

Lubricant type . . . . FIAT specification grease, supplied with gaiter repair kit

Torque wrench settings

	Nm	lbf ft
Hub (driveshaft) nut (M22)	240	177
Intermediate shaft damping weight	7	5
Intermediate shaft mounting bracket	49	36
Suspension strut-to-hub carrier bolts	70	52
Track-rod balljoint to hub carrier	40	30
Wheel bolts	86	63

1 General information

Power is transmitted from the differential to the roadwheels by the driveshafts, via inboard and outboard constant velocity (CV) joints.

An intermediate shaft, with its own support bearing is fitted between the transmission output and right-hand driveshaft on 1.8 litre models. This has the effect of equalising driveshaft angles at all suspension positions and reduces driveshaft flexing, which improves directional stability, particularly under acceleration.

The outer Rzeppa type CV joints allow smooth transmission of drive to the wheels at all steering and suspension angles. Drive is transmitted by means of a number of steel balls that run in grooves between the two halves of the joint.

On 1.2 and 1.4 litre models, and 1.6 litre automatic transmission models, the inboard CV joint is of tripod type; drive is transmitted across the joint by means of three rollers, mounted on the driveshaft in a tripod arrangement, which is free to slide in the grooved cup. On 1.6 litre models with manual transmission, the inboard CV joint is similar to that of the 1.2 and 1.4 litre models, except that the tripod and rollers are located directly in the differential sun gears, and the rubber gaiters do not rotate with the drive-shaft. The gaiters are secured to the transmission side flanges by clips. On 1.8 litre models, the inboard CV joints are of constant velocity type, like the outer joints, and are bolted to drive flanges on the left-hand side of the transmission and on the right-hand end of the intermediate shaft.

The joint rubber gaiters are packed with grease, to provide permanent lubrication. If wear is detected in the joint, it can be detached from the driveshaft and renewed. Normally, the CV joints do not require additional lubrication, unless they have been overhauled or the rubber gaiters have been damaged, allowing the grease to become contaminated. Refer to Chapter 1, Section 10, for guidance on checking the condition of the driveshaft gaiters.

2.3 Removing the driveshaft securing nut (hub nut)

Both driveshafts are splined at their outer ends, to accept the wheel hubs, and are threaded so that the hubs can be fastened to the driveshafts by means of a large, staked nut.

2 Driveshafts - removal and refitting

Note: *A balljoint separator tool will be required to separate the steering track-rod end from the hub carrier.*

Removal

1 Remove the wheel trim from the appropriate wheel, then loosen the driveshaft securing nut with the vehicle resting on its wheels and the handbrake firmly applied. The nut is very tight and an extension bar may be necessary to loosen it. Also loosen the wheel bolts half a turn.

2 Apply the handbrake, then jack up the front of the vehicle and support it on axle stands (see *Jacking and vehicle support*). Remove the appropriate roadwheel. Note that improved access to the driveshaft may be gained by removing the wheel arch liner from under the relevant front wing.

3 Unscrew and remove the driveshaft securing nut (hub nut) and discard it - a new one must be used on refitting **(see illustration)**.

4 Unscrew the nut securing the steering track-rod end to the hub carrier steering arm. Using a balljoint removal tool, separate the track-rod end from the arm.

5 Support the suspension lower arm with a

2.6 Extracting the driveshaft from the hub carrier

trolley jack, then unscrew and remove the bolts securing the hub carrier to the bottom of the strut (see Chapter 10). Note which way round the bolts are fitted, and note the location of the spacers.

6 Pull out the top of the hub carrier and lower the jack at the same time. Take care not to stretch the hydraulic brake hose. Press the driveshaft from the splined hub **(see illustration)**. If it is tight, use a mallet to drive out the driveshaft.

1.2 and 1.4 litre models and 1.6 litre models (automatic transmission)

7 Position a container beneath the transmission to catch spilt oil/fluid. Lever out the driveshaft, using a suitable lever and piece of thin wood to protect the transmission casing. Withdraw the driveshaft from the car.

1.6 litre models (manual transmission)

8 Position a container beneath the transmission to catch spilt oil. Loosen the clip and release the driveshaft gaiter from the transmission side flange. There is no need to remove the flange bolted to the left-hand side of the transmission. Carefully withdraw the driveshaft inner joint tripod from the transmission differential sun gear, then withdraw the driveshaft from the car **(see illustrations)**.

1.8 litre models

9 Using a long extension and Allen key, unscrew and remove the bolts securing the driveshaft inner joint to the transmission (LHS) or intermediate (RHS) drive flange **(see illustration)**. Withdraw the driveshaft from the car.

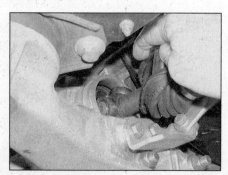

2.8a Removing the driveshaft inner joint tripod from the transmission

2.8b Driveshaft inner joint tripods removed from the transmission

2.9 On 1.8 litre models, unscrew the driveshaft Allen bolts (right-hand driveshaft shown)

Refitting

1.2 and 1.4 litre models and 1.6 litre models (automatic transmission)

10 Before inserting the driveshaft, check the condition of the oil seal in the transmission casing, and if necessary renew it with reference to Chapter 7A or 7B. Briefly, the work involves unbolting the side flange, hooking out the old oil seal, then driving in the new oil seal using a suitable socket or metal tube on the hard outer surface, and finally refitting the flange.

11 Carefully insert the inner end of the driveshaft so that it engages the splines of the differential gears, then press it firmly inwards until the circlip is felt to engage the groove in the gear.

1.6 litre models (manual transmission)

12 Before refitting the driveshaft, check the condition of the gaiter and if necessary renew it with reference to Section 3.

13 Clean the flange on the side of the transmission, then insert the driveshaft inner joint tripod into the differential sun gear. Locate the gaiter on the transmission flange, and tighten the clip.

1.8 litre models

14 Clean the drive flange then locate the driveshaft inner joint on it and insert the bolts. Tighten the bolts securely in a progressive manner.

All models

15 Locate the outer end of the driveshaft in the splined hub and press in the top of the hub carrier.

16 Engage the hub carrier with the bottom of the strut, then insert the bolts together with the spacers. The heads of the bolts face the rear of the car. Tighten the bolts to the specified torque.

17 Reconnect the steering track-rod end with the hub carrier steering arm, then refit and tighten the nut. If the track-rod end stub turns in the steering arm, press down on it while tightening the nut.

18 Screw on the new driveshaft (hub) nut and tighten it moderately at this stage **(see illustration)**.

19 Refit the roadwheel and lower the car to the ground.

2.18 Fitting a new driveshaft nut

20 Tighten the roadwheel bolts to the specified torque, then tighten the hub nut to the specified torque. Stake the rim of the hub nut into the machined recess in the end of the driveshaft using a hammer and punch **(see illustrations)**. Refit the wheel trim.

21 Check and top-up the transmission oil/fluid with reference to Chapter 1.

3 Driveshaft overhaul and rubber gaiter renewal

1.2 and 1.4 litre models and 1.6 litre models (automatic transmission)

Dismantling

1 Remove the driveshaft from the vehicle as described in Section 2, and mount it in a vice.

2 Release the clips and move the gaiter away from the driveshaft inner joint housing. Slide the inner joint housing from the tripod joint.

3 At the inboard end of the driveshaft, use a hammer and centre punch to mark the relationship between the shaft and tripod joint. Remove the circlip with a pair of circlip pliers, then using a three-legged puller if required, draw the tripod joint off the end of the driveshaft. Ensure that the legs of the puller bear upon the cast centre section of the joint, not the roller bearings **(see illustration)**.

4 At the outer end of the driveshaft, release

2.20a Tighten the driveshaft nut to the specified torque (roadwheel removed for clarity)

the clips and move the gaiter away from the driveshaft outer joint housing.

5 Mark the relationship between the outer joint and the driveshaft using a scriber or a dab of paint.

6 Using a pair of circlip pliers, expand the circlip that holds the joint in place and withdraw the joint from the end of the driveshaft. Note that the circlip is captive in the joint, and need not be removed, unless it appears damaged or worn.

7 Slide both rubber gaiters off the driveshaft. It is recommended that the gaiters are renewed whenever removed from the driveshaft.

8 If necessary, the damping weight may be removed from the right-hand driveshaft, however note its fitted position first.

Inspection

9 Thoroughly clean the driveshaft splines, and CV joint components with paraffin or a suitable solvent, taking care not to destroy any alignment marks made during removal. It is not recommended that the joint is completely dismantled, however, if it falls apart accidentally, it is important that it is correctly reassembled. The small webs of the hub must align with the large webs of the housing, and vice versa.

10 Examine the CV joint components for wear and damage. In particular, check the balls and corresponding grooves for pitting and corrosion. If evidence of wear is visible, then the joint must be renewed.

11 Examine the tripod joint components for wear. Check that the three rollers are free to

2.20b Stake the rim of the nut into the recess in the driveshaft

2.20c Recess machined into end of the driveshaft

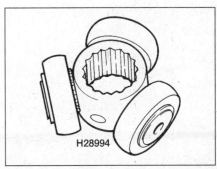

H28994

3.3 Draw the tripod joint off the end of the driveshaft

3.23a Extract the circlip . . .

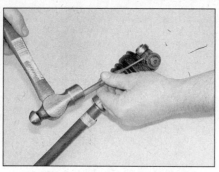

3.23b . . . then use a soft-metal punch to . . .

3.23c . . . remove the tripod joint

rotate without resistance and are not worn, damaged or corroded. If wear is discovered, the tripod joint and housing must be renewed.

Reassembly

12 Refit the damping weight to the right-hand driveshaft, making sure it is located in its previously noted position as given in the Specifications.

13 Fit a new rubber gaiter to the inboard end of the driveshaft and secure it in place on the shaft with a clip.

14 Using the alignment marks made during removal, fit the tripod joint onto the splines of the driveshaft and tap it fully onto the shaft. To ensure that the tripod joint rollers and driveshaft splines are not damaged, use a socket with an internal diameter slightly larger

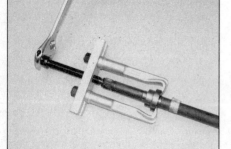

3.24 Using a puller to remove the sealed bearing from the inner end of the driveshaft

than that of the driveshaft as a drift. Refit the circlip.

15 Pack the tripod joint, inner joint housing and gaiter with grease from the service kit, then locate the housing over the tripod joint. Position the gaiter on the housing and secure with the clip.

16 Fit a new rubber gaiter to the outboard end of the driveshaft and secure it in place with a clip.

17 Pack the CV joint and gaiter with grease from the service kit, pushing it into the joint ball grooves and expelling any air that may be trapped underneath.

18 Lubricate the splines of the drive shaft with a smear of grease, then slide the CV joint onto the shaft splines while observing the alignment marks made during removal. Press on the joint until the circlip engages the groove. Pull on the shaft to check that it is held firmly in position.

19 Position the rubber gaiter onto the outer joint housing. Briefly lift the lip of the gaiter to expel all the air from the joint, then secure it in place with a clip.

20 Wipe any excess grease from the drive-shaft, then refit the driveshaft as described in Section 2.

1.6 litre models (manual transmission)

Dismantling

21 Remove the driveshaft from the vehicle as described in Section 2, and mount it in a vice.

22 Release the clip, then move the inner gaiter along the driveshaft away from the inner joint tripod joint and off of the bearing.

23 Use a hammer and centre punch to mark the relationship between the shaft and tripod joint. Remove the circlip with a pair of circlip pliers, then using a three-legged puller if required, draw the tripod joint off the end of the driveshaft. Ensure that the legs of the puller bear upon the cast centre section of the joint, not the roller bearings. Alternatively, use a soft-metal punch to drive the joint from the driveshaft **(see illustrations)**.

24 Note the fitted position of the sealed bearing on the driveshaft - there are two possibilities for each side as given in the Specifications. Using the puller, draw the bearing off the inner end of the driveshaft **(see illustration)**.

25 At the outer end of the driveshaft, release the clips and move the gaiter away from the driveshaft outer joint housing **(see illustration)**.

26 Mark the relationship between the outer joint and the driveshaft using a scriber or a dab of paint. Using a pair of circlip pliers, expand the circlip that holds the joint in place and drive the joint from the end of the driveshaft **(see illustration)**. Note that the circlip is captive in the joint, and need not be removed, unless it appears damaged or worn.

27 Slide both rubber gaiters off the driveshaft **(see illustration)**. It is recommended that the gaiters are renewed whenever removed from the driveshaft.

3.25 Release the clips from the outer joint gaiter

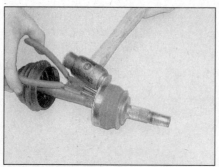

3.26 Removing the outer joint from the driveshaft

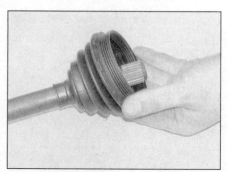

3.27 Removing the gaiters

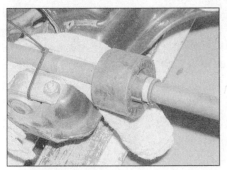

3.28 Damping weight on the right-hand driveshaft

3.35 Locating a new clip and rubber gaiter onto the inboard end of the driveshaft

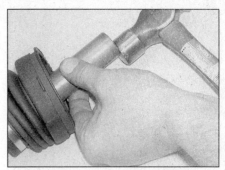

3.36 Driving the sealed bearing onto the inner end of the driveshaft

28 If necessary, the damping weight may be removed from the right-hand driveshaft, however note its fitted position first **(see illustration)**.

Inspection

29 Thoroughly clean the driveshaft splines, and CV joint components with paraffin or a suitable solvent, taking care not to destroy any alignment marks made during removal. It is not recommended that the joint is completely dismantled, however, if it falls apart accidentally, it is important that it is correctly reassembled. The small webs of the hub must align with the large webs of the housing, and vice versa.

31 Examine the CV joint components for wear and damage. In particular, check the balls and corresponding grooves for pitting and corrosion. If evidence of wear is visible, then the joint must be renewed.

32 Examine the tripod joint components for wear. Check that the three rollers are free to rotate without resistance and are not worn, damaged or corroded. If wear is discovered, the tripod joint must be renewed, however, if wear is found on the tripod joint location in the differential gears, more extensive work may be required on the transmission itself (see Chapter 7A or 7B).

33 Examine the gaiter bearing for wear and if necessary renew it.

Reassembly

34 Refit the damping weight to the right-hand driveshaft, making sure it is located in its previously noted position (see Specifications).

35 Locate a new clip and rubber gaiter onto the inboard end of the driveshaft **(see illustration)**.

36 Using a metal tube, drive the sealed bearing onto the inner end of the driveshaft, making sure that its closed end faces towards the outer bearing position and its position from the inner end of the driveshaft is as given in the Specifications **(see illustration)**. The tube must only locate on the inner race of the bearing as it is being fitted.

37 Using the alignment marks made during removal, fit the tripod joint onto the splines of the driveshaft and tap it fully onto the shaft. To ensure that the tripod joint rollers and driveshaft splines are not damaged, use a socket with an internal diameter slightly larger than that of the driveshaft as a drift. Refit the circlip.

38 Locate the gaiter on the bearing and secure with the clip.

39 Fit a new rubber gaiter to the outboard end of the driveshaft and secure it in place with a clip.

40 Pack the CV joint and gaiter with grease from the service kit, pushing it into the joint ball grooves and expelling any air that may be trapped underneath **(see illustration)**.

41 Lubricate the splines of the drive shaft with a smear of grease, then slide the CV joint onto the shaft splines while observing the alignment marks made during removal. Press on the joint until the circlip engages the groove. Pull on the shaft to check that it is held firmly in position.

42 Position the rubber gaiter onto the outer joint housing. Briefly lift the lip of the gaiter to

expel all the air from the joint, then secure it in place with a clip. Note that the clips supplied with the new gaiters require a special tool to tighten the clip **(see illustration)**.

43 Wipe any excess grease from the driveshaft, then refit the driveshaft as described in Section 2.

1.8 litre models

Dismantling

44 Remove the driveshaft from the vehicle as described in Section 2, and mount it in a vice.

45 At the outer end of the driveshaft, release the clips and move the gaiter away from the driveshaft outer joint housing.

46 Mark the relationship between the outer joint and the driveshaft using a scriber or a dab of paint. Using a pair of circlip pliers, expand the circlip that holds the joint in place and withdraw the joint from the end of the driveshaft. Note that the circlip is captive in the joint, and need not be removed, unless it appears damaged or worn. Alternatively, remove the joint by tapping it with a mallet, or by using a slide hammer attached to the hub nut threads on the end of the driveshaft.

47 Remove the protective cup from the inner end of the driveshaft, then release the two clips from the gaiter, and move the gaiter away from the inner joint.

48 Mark the relationship between the inner joint and the driveshaft using a scriber or a dab of paint. Using a pair of circlip pliers, expand the circlip that holds the joint in place and withdraw the joint from the end of the driveshaft. Note that the circlip is captive in the joint, and need not be removed, unless it appears damaged or worn.

49 Remove the inner and outer driveshaft gaiters.

50 Identify the damping weight for position so that it can be refitted in exactly the same place. Undo the screws and remove the weight half shells from the driveshaft, then slide off the rubber buffer.

Inspection

51 Thoroughly clean the driveshaft splines, and CV joint components with paraffin or a suitable solvent, taking care not to destroy any alignment marks made during removal. It is not recommended that the joint is

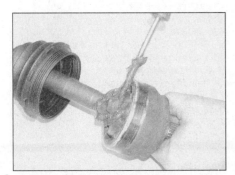

3.40 Packing the CV joint with grease from the service kit

3.42 Using the special tool to tighten the clip onto the outer joint housing

4.7 Unbolt the intermediate shaft from the support bracket

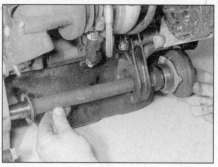

4.8a Withdraw the intermediate shaft from the transmission . . .

4.5b . . . and recover the dust seal

completely dismantled, however, if it falls apart accidentally, it is important that it is correctly reassembled. The small webs of the hub must align with the large webs of the housing, and vice versa.

52 Examine the CV joint components for wear and damage. In particular, check the balls and corresponding grooves for pitting and corrosion. If evidence of wear is visible, then the joint must be renewed.

Reassembly

53 Refit the damping weight to the right-hand driveshaft, making sure it is located in its previously noted position.

54 Fit a new rubber gaiter onto the inner end of the driveshaft and secure it in place with a clip.

55 Pack the CV joint and gaiter with grease from the service kit, pushing it into the joint ball grooves and expelling any air that may be trapped underneath.

56 Lubricate the splines of the drive shaft with a smear of grease, then slide the CV joint onto the shaft splines while observing the alignment marks made during removal. Press on the joint until the circlip engages the groove. Pull on the shaft to check that it is held firmly in position.

57 Position the rubber gaiter onto the inner joint housing. Briefly lift the lip of the gaiter to expel all the air from the joint, then secure it in place with a clip. Refit the protective cup onto the inner joint housing.

58 Fit a new rubber gaiter onto the outer end of the driveshaft and secure it in place with a clip.

59 Pack the CV joint and gaiter with grease from the service kit, pushing it into the joint ball grooves and expelling any air that may be trapped underneath.

60 Lubricate the splines of the drive shaft with a smear of grease, then slide the CV joint onto the shaft splines while observing the alignment marks made during removal. Press on the joint until the circlip engages the groove. Pull on the shaft to check that it is held firmly in position.

61 Position the rubber gaiter onto the inner joint housing. Briefly lift the lip of the gaiter to expel all the air from the joint, then secure it in place with a clip.

62 Wipe any excess grease from the driveshaft, then refit the driveshaft as described in Section 2.

---

4 Intermediate shaft - removal, inspection and refitting

Removal

Note: *This procedure applies only to 1.8 litre models. Note also that the intermediate shaft and bearing are not available as separate spares and can only be renewed as a complete assembly.*

Removal

1 Apply the handbrake, then jack up the front of the vehicle and support it on axle stands (see *Jacking and vehicle support*). Remove the right-hand front roadwheel.

2 Undo the screws and remove the wheel arch liner from beneath the right-hand front wing.

3 Unscrew the nut securing the steering track-rod end to the hub carrier steering arm. Using a balljoint removal tool, separate the track-rod end from the arm.

4 Unbolt and remove the vertical link for access to the rear of the engine.

5 Refer to Section 2 and unbolt the inboard end of the right hand driveshaft from the intermediate shaft flange. Suspend the disconnected end of the driveshaft from a convenient point on the subframe, using wire or a cable-tie, to avoid straining the joint and gaiter.

6 Drain the oil from the transmission, with reference to Chapters 1 and 7A.

7 Unbolt the intermediate shaft from the support bracket on the rear of the engine **(see illustration)**.

8 Withdraw the intermediate shaft flange from

the support bracket, and draw the splined end of the shaft out of the transmission. If it is tight, attach a slide hammer to the shaft. Take care to avoid damaging the oil seal. Recover the dust seal **(see illustrations)**.

9 A modified (solid) intermediate shaft was fitted in 1997, replacing the previous tubular type. Where the modified type is fitted, undo the screws and remove the damping weight shells, then slide off the rubber buffer.

Inspection

10 Examine the oil seal in the transmission for signs of damage or deterioration and, if necessary, renew it with reference to Chapter 7A.

11 Spin the bearing on the intermediate shaft and check for roughness or seizing. If the bearing is worn or damaged, the complete shaft must be renewed.

12 Where applicable, check the rubber buffer for condition and renew it if necessary.

Refitting

13 On the modified intermediate shaft, refit the rubber buffer and damping weight shells, and tighten the screws securely.

14 Thoroughly clean the intermediate shaft splines and the aperture in the transmission. Fit a new dust seal to the shaft, then apply a thin film of grease to the oil seal lips, and to the intermediate shaft splines and shoulders.

15 Insert the shaft squarely into the transmission, taking care to avoid damaging the oil seal. Align the intermediate shaft bearing with the support bracket, then insert the bolts and tighten them securely.

16 Refit the right hand driveshaft to the intermediate shaft with reference to Section 2.

17 Refit the vertical link and steering track-rod end, and tighten the nuts/bolts.

18 Refit the wheel arch liner.

19 Refit the roadwheel and lower the vehicle to the ground. Tighten the roadwheel bolts to the specified torque.

20 On completion refill the transmission with the specified quantity and grade of oil with reference to Chapters 1 and 7A.

Chapter 9
Braking system

Contents

Degrees of difficulty

Easy, suitable for novice with little experience	**Fairly easy,** suitable for beginner with some experience	**Fairly difficult,** suitable for competent DIY mechanic	**Difficult,** suitable for experienced DIY mechanic	**Very difficult,** suitable for expert DIY or professional

Specifications

Front brakes

Type	Disc with single-piston sliding calipers
Disc diameter	257 mm
Disc thickness (new):	
1.2, 1.4 and 1.6 litre (manual) models	11.80 to 12.10 mm
1.6 litre (automatic) and 1.8 litre models	19.80 to 20.10 mm
Minimum disc machining thickness:	
1.2, 1.4 and 1.6 litre (manual) models	11.10 mm
1.6 litre (automatic) and 1.8 litre models	18.55 mm
Minimum disc thickness (wear limit):	
1.2, 1.4 and 1.6 litre (manual) models	10.20 mm
1.6 litre (automatic) and 1.8 litre models	18.20 mm
Maximum disc runout	0.15 mm (2.0 mm from outer edge)
Brake pad friction material minimum thickness	1.5 mm

Rear drum brakes

Drum inner diameter (new):	
1.2 and 1.4 litre models (without ABS)	180.00 to 180.25 mm
1.2 and 1.4 litre models (with ABS)	203.10 to 203.40 mm
1.6 and 1.8 litre models	203.10 to 203.40 mm
Maximum drum machining diameter:	
1.2 and 1.4 litre models (without ABS)	180.95 mm
1.2 and 1.4 litre models (with ABS)	204.10 mm
1.6 and 1.8 litre models	204.10 mm
Maximum drum diameter (wear limit):	
1.2 and 1.4 litre models (without ABS)	181.35 mm
1.2 and 1.4 litre models (with ABS)	204.70 mm
1.6 and 1.8 litre models	204.70 mm
Minimum shoe lining thickness	1.5 mm

Anti-lock braking system

Type .... Teves MK20

Torque wrench settings

	Nm	lb ft
Bleed screw	6	4
Brake disc locating studs	12	9
Brake drum locating studs	12	9
Brake pedal pivot bolt	30	22
Brake pipe union	14	10
Caliper heat shield securing bolts	5	4
Front caliper bracket-to-hub carrier bolts	53	39
Front caliper-to-caliper bracket guide bolts	12	9
Hub carrier to strut	70	52
Pedal bracket mounting	15	11
Rear wheel cylinder mounting bolts	10	7
Roadwheel bolts	86	63

1 General information

1 The braking system is of vacuum servo-assisted, dual-circuit hydraulic type. The arrangement of the hydraulic system is such that each circuit operates one front and one rear brake from a tandem master cylinder. Under normal circumstances, both circuits operate in unison. However, in the event of hydraulic failure in one circuit, full braking force will still be available at two diagonally-opposite wheels.

2 All models are fitted with front disc brakes and rear drum brakes. The front disc brakes are actuated by single-piston sliding type calipers. The rear drum brakes incorporate leading and trailing shoes, which are actuated by twin-piston wheel cylinders. A self-adjust mechanism is incorporated, to automatically compensate for brake shoe wear. As the brake shoe linings wear, the footbrake operation automatically operates the adjuster mechanism, which effectively lengthens the shoe strut and repositions the brake shoes, to remove the lining-to-drum clearance.

3 The mechanical handbrake linkage operates the brake shoes via a lever attached to the trailing brake shoe.

4 Load sensitive proportioning valves operate on the rear brake hydraulic circuits, to prevent the possibility of the rear wheels locking before the front wheels under heavy braking.

Note: *When servicing any part of the system, work carefully and methodically; also observe scrupulous cleanliness when overhauling any part of the hydraulic system. Always renew components (in axle sets, where applicable) if in doubt about their condition, and use only genuine FIAT replacement parts, or at least those of known good quality. Note the warnings given in Safety first! and at relevant points in this Chapter concerning the dangers of asbestos dust and hydraulic fluid.*

Models with anti-lock braking system (ABS)

5 Available as an option on certain models, the anti-lock braking system prevents skidding which not only optimises stopping distances but allows full steering control to be maintained under maximum braking. The ABS system is operative while the vehicle is travelling both forwards and rearwards. During aquaplaning the ABS system temporarily switches itself off, as it detects a faulty condition where the driving wheels rotate at a higher speed than the driven wheels.

6 By electronically monitoring the speed of each roadwheel in relation to the other wheels, the system can detect when a wheel is about to lock-up, before control is actually lost. The brake fluid pressure applied to that wheel's brake caliper is then decreased and restored (or modulated) several times a second until control is regained.

7 The system components comprise an Electronic Control Unit (ECU), four wheel speed sensors, a hydraulic unit, recycling pump, brake lines and dashboard mounted warning lamps. The ECU is located beneath the hydraulic unit, and the recycling pump is located on top of the hydraulic unit, the assembly being mounted in the left-hand side of the engine compartment.

8 The hydraulic unit incorporates a tandem master cylinder, a valve block which modulates the pressure in the brake hydraulic circuits during ABS operation, an accumulator which provides a supply of highly pressurised brake fluid, a hydraulic pump to charge the accumulator and an integral electronic control unit (ECU).

9 The four wheel sensors are mounted on the wheel hubs. The ECU uses the signals produced by the sensors to calculate the rotational speed of each wheel.

10 The ECU has a self-diagnostic capability and will inhibit the operation of the ABS if a fault is detected, lighting the dashboard mounted warning lamp. The braking system will then revert to conventional, non-ABS operation. If the nature of the fault is not immediately obvious upon inspection, the vehicle must be taken to a FIAT dealer, who will have the diagnostic equipment required to interrogate the ABS ECU electronically and pin-point the problem.

11 As from 10/97 (chassis number 4535478-on) an additional electronic control was added to the ABS. The system is referred to as EBD (Electronically-operated Brake force Distribution) and it automatically controls the brake pressure between the front and rear brake hydraulic circuits at all times, as against control only during emergency braking for the ABS. Models with EBD are not fitted with a load sensitive proportioning valve.

12 On models with EBD, the failure warning light function is slightly different to that on models with only ABS. Failure of the ABS system only, causes the ABS warning light to come on. Failure of the EBD system causes both the ABS and handbrake warning lights to come on. If the handbrake warning light only comes on, this indicates that the hydraulic brake fluid is low or that the handbrake lever is not fully released.

2 Hydraulic system - bleeding

 Warning: *Hydraulic fluid is poisonous; wash off immediately and thoroughly in the case of skin contact, and seek immediate medical advice if any fluid is swallowed, or gets into the eyes. Certain types of hydraulic fluid are inflammable, and may ignite when allowed into contact with hot components. When servicing any hydraulic system, it is safest to assume that the fluid IS inflammable, and to take precautions against the risk of fire as though it is petrol that is being handled. Hydraulic fluid is also an effective paint stripper, and will attack plastics; if any is spilt, it should be washed off immediately, using copious quantities of fresh water. Finally, it is hygroscopic (it absorbs moisture from the air) - old fluid may be contaminated and unfit for further use. When topping-up or renewing the fluid, always use the recommended type, and ensure that it comes from a freshly-opened sealed container.*

General

1 The correct operation of any hydraulic system is only possible after removing all air from the components and circuit; and this is achieved by bleeding the system.

2 During the bleeding procedure, add only clean, unused hydraulic fluid of the recommended type; never re-use fluid that has already been bled from the system. Ensure that sufficient fluid is available before starting work.

3 If there is any possibility of incorrect fluid being already in the system, the brake components and circuit must be flushed completely with uncontaminated, correct fluid, and new seals should be fitted throughout the system.

4 If hydraulic fluid has been lost from the system, or air has entered because of a leak, ensure that the fault is cured before proceeding further.

5 Park the vehicle on level ground, and switch off the engine. Alternatively, position the car over a pit or on car ramps.

6 Check that all pipes and hoses are secure, unions tight and bleed screws closed. Remove the dust caps (where applicable), and clean any dirt from around the bleed screws.

7 Unscrew the master cylinder reservoir cap, and top-up the master cylinder reservoir to the MAX level line; refit the cap loosely. Remember to maintain the fluid level at least above the MIN level line throughout the procedure, otherwise there is a risk of further air entering the system.

8 There are a number of one-man, do-it-yourself brake bleeding kits currently available from motor accessory shops. It is recommended that one of these kits is used whenever possible, as they greatly simplify the bleeding operation, and also reduce the risk of expelled air and fluid being drawn back into the system. If such a kit is not available, the basic (two-man) method must be used, which is described in detail below.

9 If a kit is to be used, prepare the vehicle as described previously, and follow the kit manufacturer's instructions, as the procedure may vary slightly according to the type being used; generally, they are as outlined below in the relevant sub-section.

10 Whichever method is used, the same sequence must be followed (paragraphs 11 and 12) to ensure the removal of all air from the system.

Bleeding sequence

11 If the system has been only partially disconnected, and suitable precautions were taken to minimise fluid loss, it should be

2.16 Bleeding a rear brake line

necessary to bleed only that part of the system (ie the primary or secondary circuit).

12 If the complete system is to be bled, then it should be done working in the following sequence:

   a) *Left-hand rear wheel.*
   b) *Right-hand front wheel.*
   c) *Right-hand rear wheel.*
   d) *Left-hand front wheel.*

Note: *When bleeding the rear brakes on a vehicle fitted with load proportioning valves: if the rear of the vehicle has been jacked up to allow access to the brake wheel cylinder, the rear suspension must be compressed so that the load proportioning valves remain open throughout the bleeding process.*

Bleeding - basic (two-man) method

13 Collect a clean glass jar, a suitable length of plastic or rubber tubing which is a tight fit over the bleed screw, and a ring spanner to fit the screw. The help of an assistant will also be required.

14 Remove the dust cap from the first screw in the sequence if not already done. Fit a suitable spanner and tube to the screw, place the other end of the tube in the jar, and pour in sufficient fluid to cover the end of the tube.

15 Ensure that the master cylinder reservoir fluid level is maintained at least above the MIN level line throughout the procedure.

16 Unscrew the bleed screw approximately half a turn, then have the assistant fully depress the brake pedal and hold it down. Tighten the bleed screw and have the brake pedal slowly released. The assistant should maintain pedal pressure, following the pedal down to the floor, and should not release the pedal until instructed to do so. When the flow stops, tighten the bleed screw again, have the assistant release the pedal slowly, and recheck the reservoir fluid level **(see illustration)**.

17 Repeat the procedure given in paragraph 16, until the fluid emerging from the bleed screw is free from air bubbles. If the master cylinder has been drained and refilled, and air is being bled from the first screw in the sequence, allow approximately five seconds between cycles for the master cylinder passages to refill. It may also be necessary to 'pump' the brake pedal vigorously initially, in order to force the fluid into the brake lines.

18 When no more air bubbles appear, tighten the bleed screw securely, remove the tube and spanner, and refit the dust cap. Do not overtighten the bleed screw.

19 Repeat the procedure on the remaining screws in the sequence, until all air is removed from the system, and the brake pedal feels firm again.

Bleeding - using a one-way valve kit

20 As their name implies, these kits consist of a length of tubing with a one-way valve fitted, to prevent expelled air and fluid being drawn back into the system; some kits include a translucent container, which can be positioned so that the air bubbles can be

more easily seen flowing from the end of the tube.

21 The kit is connected to the bleed screw, which is then opened. The user returns to the driver's seat, depresses the brake pedal with a smooth, steady stroke, and slowly releases it. This is repeated until the expelled fluid is clear of air bubbles.

22 Note that these kits simplify work so much that it is easy to forget the master cylinder reservoir fluid level. Ensure that this is maintained at least above the MIN level line at all times.

Bleeding - using a pressure-bleeding kit

23 These kits are usually operated by the reservoir of pressurised air contained in the spare tyre. However, note that it will probably be necessary to reduce the pressure to a lower level than normal. Refer to the instructions supplied with the kit.

24 By connecting a pressurised, fluid-filled container to the master cylinder reservoir, bleeding can be carried out simply by opening each screw in turn (in the specified sequence), and allowing the fluid to flow out until no more air bubbles can be seen in the expelled fluid.

25 This method has the advantage that the large reservoir of fluid provides an additional safeguard against air being drawn into the system during bleeding.

26 Pressure-bleeding is particularly effective when bleeding 'difficult' systems, or when bleeding the complete system at the time of routine fluid renewal.

All methods

27 When bleeding is complete, and firm pedal feel is restored, wash off any spilt fluid, tighten the bleed screws securely, and refit their dust caps.

28 Check the hydraulic fluid level in the master cylinder reservoir, and top-up if necessary (*Weekly checks*).

29 Discard any hydraulic fluid that has been bled from the system, as it will not be fit for re-use.

30 Check the feel of the brake pedal. If it feels at all spongy, air must still be present in the system, and further bleeding is required. Failure to bleed satisfactorily after a reasonable repetition of the bleeding procedure may be due to worn master cylinder seals.

31 On models with ABS, the brake hydraulic system is bled using exactly the same method as for non-ABS models, however it will take longer.

3	Hydraulic pipes and hoses - renewal	

Note: *Before starting work, refer to the note at the beginning of Section 2 concerning the dangers of hydraulic fluid.*

1 If any pipe or hose is to be renewed, minimise fluid loss by first removing the

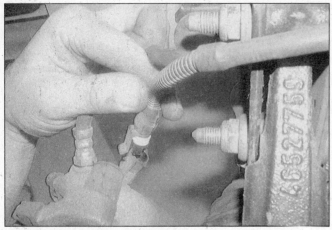

4.2 Disconnecting the brake pad wear sensor wiring

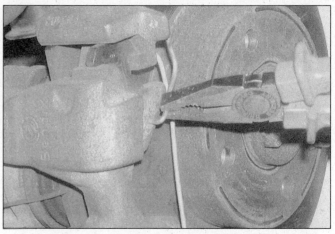

4.3 Removing the anti-rattle spring from the front brake caliper

master cylinder reservoir cap, then tighten the cap down onto a piece of polythene to obtain an airtight seal. Alternatively, flexible hoses can be sealed, if required, using a proprietary brake hose clamp. Metal brake pipe unions can be plugged (if care is taken not to allow dirt into the system) or capped immediately they are disconnected. Place a wad of rag under any union that is to be disconnected, to catch any spilt fluid.

2 If a flexible hose is to be disconnected, unscrew the brake pipe union nut before removing the spring clip which secures the hose to its mounting bracket.

3 To unscrew the union nuts, it is preferable to obtain a special brake pipe split spanner. These are available from most motor accessory shops. Failing this, a close-fitting open-ended spanner will be required, though if the nuts are tight or corroded, their flats may be rounded-off if the spanner slips. In such a case, a self-locking wrench is often the only way to unscrew a stubborn union, but it follows that the pipe and the damaged nuts must be renewed on reassembly. Always clean a union and surrounding area before disconnecting it. If disconnecting a component with more than one union, make a careful note of the connections before disturbing any of them.

4 If a brake pipe is to be renewed, it can be obtained, cut to length and with the union

nuts and end flares in place, from FIAT dealers. All that is then necessary is to bend it to shape, following the line of the original, before fitting it to the vehicle. Alternatively, most motor accessory shops can make up brake pipes from kits, but this requires very careful measurement of the original, to ensure that the replacement is of the correct length. The safest answer is usually to take the original to the shop as a pattern.

5 On refitting, do not overtighten the union nuts. If possible, use a torque wrench to ensure they are tightened correctly.

6 Ensure that the pipes and hoses are correctly routed, with no kinks, and that they are secured in the clips or brackets provided. After fitting, remove the polythene from the reservoir, and bleed the hydraulic system as described in Section 2. Wash off any spilt fluid, and check carefully for fluid leaks.

4 Front brake pads - renewal

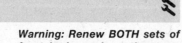

Warning: Renew BOTH sets of front brake pads at the same time - NEVER renew the pads on only one wheel, as uneven braking may result. Note that the dust created by wear of the pads may contain

asbestos, which is a health hazard. Never blow it out with compressed air, and don't inhale any of it. An approved filtering mask should be worn when working on the brakes. DO NOT use petrol or petroleum-based solvents to clean brake parts; use proprietary brake cleaner or methylated spirit only.

1 Apply the handbrake, then jack up the front of the vehicle and support it on axle stands (see *Jacking and vehicle support*). Remove the front roadwheels.

2 If removing the left-hand front brake pads, disconnect the wiring connector from the brake pad wear sensor connector, and release the wire from the clip (see illustration).

3 Using a pair of pliers, unclip the anti-rattle spring and remove it from the brake caliper (see illustration).

4 Release the hydraulic line support grommet from the strut (see illustration).

5 Remove the end caps from the guide bushes to gain access to the caliper guide pin bolts (see illustration).

6 Unscrew and remove the caliper guide bolts, then lift the caliper and inner pad away from the mounting bracket (see illustrations). Tie the caliper to the suspension strut using a piece of wire. Do not allow it to hang unsupported on the flexible brake hose.

7 Unclip the inner pad from the caliper piston

4.4 Releasing the hydraulic line support grommet from the strut

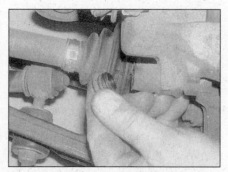

4.5 Removing the guide bush end caps

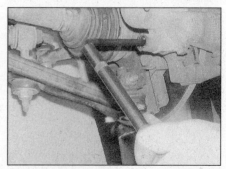

4.6a Unscrew the caliper guide bolts . . .

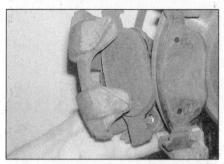

4.6b ... then lift the caliper and inner pad from the mounting bracket

4.7a Unclip the inner pad from the caliper piston ...

4.7b ... and the outer pad from the mounting bracket

and remove the outer pad from the mounting bracket **(see illustrations)**.

8 Measure the thickness of each brake pad's friction material. If either pad is worn at any point to the specified minimum thickness or less, all four pads must be renewed. Also, the pads should be renewed if any are contaminated with oil or grease.

9 If the brake pads are still serviceable, carefully clean them using a clean, fine wire brush or similar, paying particular attention to the sides and back of the metal backing. Clean out the grooves in the friction material, and pick out any large embedded particles of dirt or debris. Clean the pad locations in the caliper mounting bracket.

10 Prior to fitting the pads, check that the guide pin bolts are free to slide easily in the caliper body bushes, and are a reasonably tight fit. Brush the dust and dirt from the caliper and piston, but **do not** inhale it, as it is injurious to health. Inspect the dust seal around the piston for damage, and the piston for evidence of fluid leaks, corrosion or damage. If attention to any of these components is necessary, refer to Section 8.

11 If new brake pads are to be fitted, the caliper piston must be pushed back into the cylinder to make room for them. Either use a G-clamp or similar tool, or use suitable pieces of wood as levers. Provided that the master cylinder reservoir has not been overfilled with hydraulic fluid, there should be no spillage, but keep a careful watch on the fluid level while retracting the piston. If the fluid level rises above the MAX level line at any time, the surplus should be siphoned off or ejected via a plastic tube connected to the bleed screw. **Note:** *Do not*

syphon the fluid by mouth, as it is poisonous; use a syringe or an old poultry baster.

12 Apply a little brake copper grease to the back of the outer brake pad and to the upper and lower edges of both pads which contact the caliper. Do not apply excessive amounts.

13 Clip the inner pad into the caliper piston and fit the outer pad to the mounting bracket, ensuring its friction material is against the brake disc.

14 Manoeuvre the caliper into position over the pads, then apply a little copper grease to the caliper guide bolts, insert them, and tighten them to the specified torque setting.

15 Refit the end caps to the caliper guide bushes and locate the brake pad wear wiring in its clip.

16 Fit the anti-rattle spring, ensuring its ends are correctly located in the caliper body holes.

17 Ensure the wiring is correctly routed then reconnect the brake pad wear wiring to the main loom.

18 Depress the brake pedal repeatedly, until the pads are pressed into firm contact with the brake disc, and normal (non-assisted) pedal pressure is restored.

19 Repeat the above procedure on the remaining front brake caliper.

20 Refit the roadwheels, then lower the vehicle to the ground and tighten the roadwheel bolts to the specified torque setting.

21 Check the hydraulic fluid level as described in *Weekly Checks*.

Note: *New pads will not give full braking efficiency until they have bedded in. Be prepared for this, and avoid hard braking as far as possible for the first hundred miles or so after pad renewal.*

5 Rear brake shoes - renewal

⚠️ *Warning: Renew BOTH sets of rear brake shoes at the same time - NEVER renew the shoes on only one wheel, as uneven braking may result. Note that the dust created by wear of the shoes may contain asbestos, which is a health hazard. Never blow it out with compressed air, and don't inhale any of it. An approved filtering mask should be worn when working on the brakes. DO NOT use petrol or petroleum-based solvents to clean brake parts; use proprietary brake cleaner or methylated spirit only.*

Early models (with round steady springs)

1 Remove the rear brake drums, as described in Section 7.

2 Working on one side of the vehicle, brush the dirt and dust from the brake shoes and backplate, and from the drum. Avoid inhaling the dust, as it may contain asbestos, which is a health hazard.

3 Note the position of each shoe, and the location of the return and steady springs. Also make a note of the adjuster component locations, to aid refitting later. It is advisable, at this stage to wrap a stout rubber band or a cable tie over the wheel cylinder to prevent the pistons from being accidentally ejected.

4 Detach the upper and lower return springs from both brake shoes **(see illustrations)**.

5.4a Detaching the lower return spring

5.4b Detaching the upper return spring from the leading ...

5.4c ... and trailing brake shoes

5.5 Unhook the self-adjuster mechanism return spring from the leading brake shoe

5.6 Carefully pull the leading brake shoe away from the backplate and remove it

5.7a Unhook the self-adjuster mechanism from the trailing shoe . . .

5 Unhook the self-adjuster mechanism return spring from the leading brake shoe **(see illustration)**. Remove the hold-down cup and spring from the leading shoe. The spring cups are a bayonet-style fit - use a large pair of pliers to depress and then turn them through 90°. Remove the pin.

6 Carefully pull the leading brake shoe away from the backplate and remove it **(see illustration)**.

7 Using a suitable pair of pliers, unhook the self-adjuster mechanism from the trailing shoe and remove it **(see illustrations)**.

8 Remove the hold-down cup and spring from the trailing shoe, using a large pair of pliers, as described for the leading shoe.

Remove the pin. Lift the trailing shoe away from the backplate, and disconnect the handbrake cable from the brake shoe lever **(see illustration)**.

9 Thoroughly clean the surface of the backplate using brake component cleaner to remove all traces of dust and old lubricant. Examine all components for signs of corrosion.

10 Apply brake grease sparingly to the shoe contact surfaces of the brake backplate **(see illustration)**.

11 Connect the handbrake cable to the lever on the trailing brake shoe, locate the trailing shoe on the backplate and secure in position with the pin, hold down

spring and cup. Using pliers, turn the cup through 90° and then release it, to lock it in position.

12 Fit the self-adjuster mechanism into the recess in the trailing brake shoe and anchor the retaining spring in the slot provided in the shoe **(see illustration)**.

13 Fit the leading shoe in position on the backplate and secure it with the hold down pin, spring and cup as described for the trailing shoe. Engage the end of the self-adjuster mechanism with the recess in the leading brake shoe. Hook the retaining spring into the slot provided.

14 Fit the upper and lower shoe return springs, engaging them with the slots in the

5.7b . . . and remove it

5.8a Remove the hold-down cup and spring from the trailing shoe

5.8b Lift the trailing shoe away from the backplate . . .

5.8c . . . and disconnect the handbrake cable from the brake shoe lever

5.10 Apply brake grease sparingly to the shoe contact surfaces (arrowed) of the brake backplate

5.12 Fit the self-adjuster mechanism into the recess (arrowed) in the trailing brake shoe

5.14a Lower return spring fitted in place

5.14b Correct location of upper return spring in leading shoe . . .

5.14c . . . and trailing shoe

shoes as shown **(see illustrations)**. Remove the elastic band from the wheel cylinder.

15 Turn the serrated wheel at the end of the self-adjuster mechanism, to retract the brake shoes - this will give additional clearance to allow the drum to pass over the shoes during refitting.

16 Repeat the procedure on the remaining side of the vehicle.

17 Refit the brake drums as described in Section 7. Check and if necessary adjust the operation of the handbrake, as described in Section 14.

18 Apply the brake pedal and handbrake lever several times to settle the self-adjusting mechanism. With both rear roadwheels refitted and the rear of the vehicle still raised,

turn the wheels by hand to check that the brake shoes are not binding.

19 Lower the vehicle to the ground and thoroughly check the operation of the braking system.

Late models
(with square steady springs)

20 Remove the rear brake drums, as described in Section 7.

21 Working on one side of the vehicle, brush the dirt and dust from the brake shoes and backplate, and from the drum. Avoid inhaling the dust, as it may contain asbestos, which is a health hazard.

22 Note the position of each shoe, and the location of the return and steady springs. Also make a note of the adjuster component

locations, to aid refitting later **(see illustration)**. It is advisable, at this stage to wrap a stout rubber band or a cable tie over the wheel cylinder to prevent the pistons from being accidentally ejected.

23 Using a pair of pliers, release the leading brake shoe steady spring from its pin, and remove the pin **(see illustrations)**.

24 Lever the bottom of the leading brake shoe from its anchor, then disconnect the bottom return spring from both brake shoes **(see illustration)**.

25 Move the bottom end of the leading shoe rearwards to expand the top end from the wheel cylinder **(see illustration)**.

26 Unhook and remove the upper return spring from both shoes, then remove the leading brake shoe **(see illustration)**.

5.22 Note the position of the brake shoes and springs before removing them

5.23a Use a pair of pliers to release the leading brake shoe steady spring from its pin . . .

5.23b . . . then remove the spring and pin

5.24 Disconnecting the bottom return spring

5.25 Releasing the top end of the leading shoe from the wheel cylinder

5.26 Unhooking the upper return spring and removing the leading shoe

5.27 Removing the self-adjuster mechanism from the trailing shoe

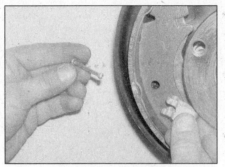

5.28 Removing the trailing brake shoe steady spring and pin

5.29 Disconnecting the handbrake cable from the lever on the back of the trailing shoe

27 Remove the self-adjuster mechanism from the trailing shoe **(see illustration)**.

28 Using the pliers, release the trailing brake shoe steady spring from its pin, and remove the pin **(see illustration)**.

29 Turn over the trailing brake shoe and use a pair of pliers to disconnect the handbrake cable from the lever on the back of the shoe **(see illustration)**.

30 Thoroughly clean the surface of the backplate using brake component cleaner to remove all traces of dust and old lubricant. Examine all components for signs of corrosion.

31 Apply brake grease sparingly to the shoe contact surfaces of the brake backplate **(see illustration 5.10)**.

32 Connect the handbrake cable to the lever on the back of the new trailing brake shoe. Use a pair of long-nosed pliers to hold the spring away from the end of the cable while it is being connected.

33 Offer the trailing shoe up to the backplate and secure in position with the pin and steady spring.

34 Before refitting the self-adjuster mechanism, fully screw in the adjustment screw so that the mechanism is set to its minimum length. Apply a little brake grease to the metal contact faces of both brake shoes, self-adjuster mechanism and handbrake lever **(see illustration)**.

35 Refit the self-adjuster mechanism to the trailing shoe, making sure it is the correct way round.

36 Locate the leading shoe on the backplate

and engage it with the self-adjuster mechanism. Refit the upper return spring.

37 Locate the bottom of the trailing shoe on its anchor, then refit the bottom return spring and lever the leading shoe onto the anchor.

38 Refit the steady spring and pin to the leading shoe. Remove the elastic band from the wheel cylinder.

39 Repeat the procedure on the remaining side of the vehicle.

40 Refit the brake drums as described in Section 7. Check and if necessary adjust the operation of the handbrake, as described in Section 14.

41 Apply the brake pedal and handbrake lever several times to settle the self-adjusting mechanism. With both rear roadwheels refitted and the rear of the vehicle still raised, turn the wheels by hand to check that the brake shoes are not binding.

42 Lower the vehicle to the ground and thoroughly check the operation of the braking system.

---

6 Front brake disc -
inspection, removal
and refitting

⚠️ *Warning: Before starting work, refer to the warning at the beginning of Section 4 concerning the dangers of asbestos dust.*

Inspection

Note: *If either disc requires renewal, BOTH*

should be renewed at the same time, to ensure even and consistent braking. New brake pads should also be fitted.

1 Apply the handbrake, then jack up the front of the car and support it on axle stands. Remove the appropriate front roadwheel.

2 Slowly rotate the brake disc so that the full area of both sides can be checked; remove the brake pads if better access is required to the inboard surface. Light scoring is normal in the area swept by the brake pads, but if heavy scoring or cracks are found, the disc must be renewed.

3 It is normal to find a lip of rust around the disc's perimeter, and this can be scraped off if required. If, however, a lip has formed due to excessive wear of the brake pad swept area, then the disc's thickness must be measured using a micrometer **(see illustration)**. Take measurements at several places around the disc, at the inside and outside of the pad swept area. If the disc has worn at any point to the specified minimum thickness or less, the disc must be renewed.

4 If the disc is thought to be warped, it can be checked for run-out. First make sure that the two disc retaining studs are tight. Either use a dial gauge mounted on any convenient fixed point, while the disc is slowly rotated, or use feeler blades to measure (at several points all around the disc) the clearance between the disc and a fixed point, such as the caliper mounting bracket **(see illustration)**. If the measurements obtained are at the specified maximum or beyond, the disc is excessively

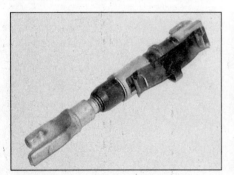

5.34 The rear brake self-adjuster mechanism

6.3 Measuring the brake disc thickness with a micrometer

6.4 Brake disc runout measurement - DTI gauge method

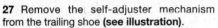

warped, and must be renewed. However, it is worth checking first that the hub bearing is in good condition.

5 Check the disc for cracks, especially around the wheel bolt holes, and any other wear or damage, and renew if necessary.

Removal

6 Remove the brake pads (Section 4) then unbolt and remove the caliper mounting bracket from the hub carrier. Alternatively, leave the caliper attached to the mounting bracket and unbolt the bracket from the hub carrier (see illustrations).

7 Unscrew and remove the two disc retaining studs and withdraw the disc from the hub (see illustrations). If it is tight, lightly tap its rear face with a hide or plastic mallet to free it from the hub.

Refitting

8 Refitting is the reverse of the removal procedure, noting the following points:
 a) Ensure that the mating surfaces of the disc and hub are clean.
 b) If a new disc has been fitted, use a suitable solvent to wipe any preservative coating from the disc, before refitting the caliper. Note that new brake pads should be fitted when the disc is renewed.
 c) Tighten all bolts to the specified torque where given.

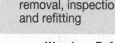

7 Rear brake drum -
removal, inspection and refitting

 Warning: Before starting work, refer to the warning at the beginning of Section 4 concerning the dangers of asbestos dust.

Removal

1 Apply the handbrake, then jack up the front of the vehicle and support it on axle stands (see Jacking and vehicle support). Remove both rear roadwheels. Fully release the handbrake.

2 Unscrew and remove the two studs and pull the drum from the hub. If the drum is binding on the brake shoes, back off the handbrake adjustment nut located on the

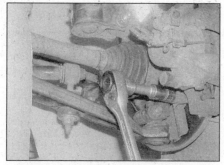
6.6a Unscrew the mounting bolts . . .

6.6b . . . and withdraw the caliper and mounting bracket from the hub carrier

6.7a Unscrew and remove the disc locating studs . . .

6.7b . . . and lift off the disc

handbrake lever and try again. If this is unsuccessful, prise the cover from the inside of the backplate, and use a pair of pliers to disconnect the handbrake cable from the lever on the trailing shoe. Using a screwdriver through one of the roadwheel bolt holes, press the handbrake lever from the outside so that it slides down behind the trailing shoe and retracts the shoes. It should now be possible to remove the drum, however if the drum is rusted to the hub, screw two bolts into the drum at the stud locations (the drum threads are larger than the stud threads), and progressively tighten them to force the drum from the hub (see illustrations).

Inspection

Note: If either drum requires renewal, BOTH should be renewed at the same time, to ensure even and consistent braking. New brake shoes should also be fitted.

3 Brush all traces of brake dust from the drum and shoes, but avoid inhaling the dust, as it is a health hazard.

4 Clean the outside of the drum, and check it for obvious signs of damage. Renew the drum if necessary.

5 Carefully examine the inside of the drum. Light scoring of the friction surface is normal, but if heavy scoring is found, the drum must be renewed.

6 It is usual to find a lip of rust on the drum's inboard edge, which is not in contact with the shoe linings. This rust should be scraped away, otherwise it may cause the brake drum to bind on the shoes when it is being removed at a later date.

7 If the drum is thought to be excessively worn or oval, its internal diameter must be measured at several points using an internal micrometer. Take measurements in pairs, the second at right-angles to the first, and

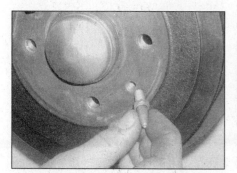
7.2a Removing the drum studs

7.2b Plastic cover on the inside of the backplate

7.2c Using two bolts to force the drum from the hub

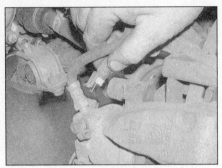

8.4 Disconnecting the wiring connector from the brake pad wear sensor

compare the two, to check for signs of ovality. Provided that it does not enlarge the drum beyond the specified maximum diameter, it may be possible to have the drum refinished by skimming or grinding. If this is not possible, the drums on both sides must be renewed. Note that if the drum is to be skimmed, BOTH drums must be refinished to maintain a consistent internal diameter on both sides.

Refitting

8 If a new brake drum is to be fitted, use a suitable solvent to remove any preservative coating that may have been applied to its internal friction surfaces. Note that it may also be necessary to shorten the adjuster strut length, by rotating the strut wheel, to allow the drum to pass over the brake shoes (see Section 5).

9 Refit the brake drum over the shoes and onto the hub, then insert the two locating studs and tighten securely.

10 Depress the footbrake repeatedly to expand the brake shoes against the drum, and check that normal pedal pressure is restored.

11 Check and if necessary adjust the handbrake cable as described in Section 14.

12 Refit the roadwheels, and lower the vehicle to the ground.

8 **Front brake caliper -**
removal, overhaul and refitting

⚠️ *Warning: Before starting work, refer to the notes at the beginning of Sections 2 and 4 concerning the dangers of handling hydraulic fluid and asbestos dust.*

Removal

1 Apply the handbrake, then jack up the front of the vehicle and support it on axle stands (see *Jacking and vehicle support*). Remove the appropriate front roadwheel.

2 To minimise fluid loss during the following operations, fit a brake hose clamp to the flexible brake hose running to the caliper. Alternatively, remove the master cylinder fluid reservoir cap, and tighten it down onto a

piece of polythene sheeting to obtain an airtight seal.

3 Clean the area around the brake hose union on the caliper, then loosen the union nut half a turn.

4 Disconnect the wiring connector from the brake pad wear sensor connector, and release the wire from the clip **(see illustration).**

5 Using a pair of pliers, unclip the anti-rattle spring and remove it from the brake caliper.

6 Remove the end caps from the guide bushes to gain access to the caliper guide pin bolts.

7 Unscrew and remove the caliper guide bolts, then lift the caliper over the brake pads and away from the mounting bracket.

8 Unscrew the caliper from the hose and place it on the workbench. Plug the hose outlet to prevent loss of brake fluid.

9 Remove the brake pads from the mounting bracket (refer to Section 4 if necessary).

10 Unbolt the caliper mounting bracket from the hub carrier. Note that the bracket mounting bolts are self-locking and should be renewed whenever they are removed.

Overhaul

Note: *Before commencing work, ensure that the appropriate caliper overhaul kit is obtained.*

11 Clean the exterior of the caliper, then mount it in a vice.

12 Place a small block of wood between the caliper body and the piston. Remove the piston by applying a jet of compressed air (such as that produced by a tyre foot pump) to the fluid inlet port.

⚠️ *Warning: Protect your hands and eyes when using compressed air in this manner - brake fluid may be ejected under pressure when the piston pops out of its bore.*

13 Remove the dust seal from the piston, then use a soft, blunt instrument (ie **not** a screwdriver) to extract the piston seal from the caliper bore. Unscrew and remove the bleed screw.

14 Thoroughly clean all components, using only methylated spirit or clean hydraulic fluid. Never use mineral-based solvents such as petrol or paraffin, which will attack the hydraulic system rubber components.

15 The caliper piston seal, the dust seal and the bleed screw dust cap, are only available as part of a seal kit. Since the manufacturers recommend that the piston seal and dust seal are renewed whenever they are disturbed, all of these components should be discarded on disassembly and new ones fitted on reassembly as a matter of course.

16 Carefully examine all parts of the caliper assembly, looking for signs of wear or damage. In particular, the cylinder bore and piston must be free from any signs of scratches, corrosion or wear. If there is any doubt about the condition of any part of the

caliper, the relevant part should be renewed. Note that the piston surface is plated, and **must not** be polished with emery or similar abrasives to remove corrosion or scratches. In addition, the pistons are matched to the caliper bores and can only be renewed as a part of a complete caliper assembly.

17 Check that both guide pins are in good condition and undamaged. They must be a reasonably tight sliding fit in the mounting bracket bores. Remove and clean them, then apply some copper grease and refit them. If necessary, renew the rubber boots.

18 Use compressed air from the tyre pump to blow clear the fluid passages.

⚠️ *Warning: Wear eye protection when using compressed air.*

19 Before commencing reassembly, ensure that all components are spotlessly-clean and dry.

20 Dip the new piston seal in clean hydraulic fluid, and fit it to the groove inside the cylinder bore, using your fingers only to manipulate it into place.

21 Fit the new dust seal to the piston groove, then smear clean hydraulic fluid over the surfaces of the piston and cylinder bore. Insert the piston into the cylinder bore with a twisting action to ensure it enters the internal seal correctly. With the piston fully entered, locate the dust seal in the groove on the caliper.

Refitting

22 Clean the mating surfaces, then refit the caliper mounting bracket to the hub carrier. Insert the new self-locking bolts and tighten to the specified torque. Make sure the guide pins are correctly fitted

23 Carefully screw the caliper onto the hose, and moderately tighten the union nut.

24 Apply a little copper grease to the brake pad backplates as described in Section 4, and locate them on the mounting bracket

25 Locate the caliper over the brake pads, then refit the guide bolts and tighten to the specified torque while holding the pins stationary with a further spanner. **Note:** *Make sure that the flexible brake hose is not twisted. It must not touch any surrounding components throughout its movement from lock to lock.*

26 Fully tighten the hose union nut to the specified torque.

27 Refit the end caps to the guide bushes.

28 Refit the anti-rattle spring making sure that its ends are correctly located in the bracket holes.

29 Reconnect the brake pad wear sensor wiring and secure it in the clip.

30 Remove the brake hose clamp or polythene sheeting, and top up the brake fluid level in the reservoir. Bleed the hydraulic system as described in Section 2. Note that if no other part of the system has been disturbed, it should only be necessary to bleed the relevant front circuit.

9.2 Rear wheel cylinder

9.5 Rear wheel cylinder mounting bolts

31 Refit the roadwheel and lower the vehicle to the ground.
32 Depress the brake pedal repeatedly to bring the pads into contact with the brake disc, and ensure that normal pedal pressure is restored.

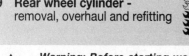
9 Rear wheel cylinder - removal, overhaul and refitting

Warning: Before starting work, refer to the notes at the beginning of Sections 2 and 4 concerning the dangers of handling hydraulic fluid and asbestos dust.

Removal

1 Remove the brake drum as described in Section 7.
2 Remove the brake shoes as described in Section 5. Alternatively, pull the upper ends of the brake shoes apart so that the automatic adjustment mechanism holds them away from the wheel cylinder **(see illustration)**.
3 To minimise fluid loss during the following operations, fit a brake hose clamp to the flexible brake hose running to the rear wheel cylinder. Alternatively, remove the master cylinder fluid reservoir cap, and tighten it down onto a piece of polythene sheeting to obtain an airtight seal.
4 Clean the brake backplate around the wheel cylinder mounting bolts and the hydraulic pipe union, then unscrew the union nut and disconnect the hydraulic pipe. Cover the open ends of the pipe and the master cylinder to prevent dirt ingress.
5 Unscrew the mounting bolts **(see illustration)** then withdraw the wheel cylinder from the backplate.

Overhaul

Note: *Before commencing work, obtain the appropriate wheel cylinder overhaul kit.*
6 Remove both rubber dust covers from the grooves in the wheel cylinder, then use paint or similar to mark one of the pistons so that the pistons are not interchanged on reassembly.

7 Withdraw both pistons and the spring from the wheel cylinder. Unscrew and remove the bleed screw.
8 Remove and discard the rubber piston seals and the dust covers. These should be renewed as a matter of course, and are available as part of an overhaul kit, which also includes the bleed nipple dust cap.
9 Clean the components thoroughly, using only methylated spirit or clean brake fluid.
10 Check the condition of the cylinder bore and piston surfaces which must be free of scratches, scoring and corrosion. Renew the complete wheel cylinder if there is any doubt.
11 Ensure that all components are clean and dry. The pistons, spring and seals should be fitted wet, using hydraulic fluid as a lubricant.
12 Fit the seals to the pistons, ensuring that they are the correct way round. Use only your fingers to manipulate the seals into position.
13 Fit the first piston to the cylinder, taking care not to distort the seal. If the original pistons are being re-used, the marks made on dismantling should be used to ensure that the pistons are refitted to their original bores.
14 Refit the spring and the second piston.
15 Apply a smear of rubber grease to the exposed end of each piston and to the dust cover sealing lips, then fit the dust covers to each end of the wheel cylinder.

Refitting

16 Refitting is a reversal of removal, bearing in mind the following points:
a) *Tighten the mounting bolts to the specified torque.*

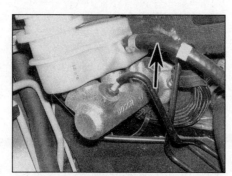

10.7 Clutch fluid supply pipe on the brake fluid reservoir

b) *Refit the brake shoes as described in Section 5, and the brake drum as described in Section 7.*
c) *Before refitting the roadwheel and lowering the vehicle to the ground, bleed the hydraulic system as described in Section 2. Note that if no other part of the system has been disturbed, it should only be necessary to bleed the relevant rear circuit.*

10 Master cylinder - removal, overhaul and refitting

Warning: Before starting work, refer to the note at the beginning of Section 2 concerning the dangers of handling hydraulic fluid.

Removal

Right-hand drive models

1 Loosen the clips and disconnect the throttle body air duct from the air cleaner. Disconnect the crankcase ventilation hose from the duct, then unscrew the nuts and remove the duct from the top of the throttle body.
2 Undo the screw and remove the relay cover.
3 Unscrew the two bolts holding the relay bracket to the bulkhead, then disconnect the small wiring plug beneath it, and move the bracket to one side. Make sure that any electrical terminals are kept insulated from the surrounding components.
4 Release the retaining stud and pull out the lining from the right-hand side of the bulkhead for access to the master cylinder.
5 Disconnect the wiring from the low fluid level unit, then unscrew and remove the cap from the top of the reservoir.
6 Syphon or draw the brake fluid from the reservoir. **Note:** *Do not syphon the fluid by mouth, as it is poisonous; use a syringe or an old poultry baster.* Place some cloth rags beneath the master cylinder to catch any spilt fluid. Alternatively, fit hose clamps to the two supply pipes.
7 On models where the reservoir is located remotely on the bulkhead, using a screwdriver, carefully lever the fluid supply pipes from the top of the master cylinder. On models where the reservoir is located on the master cylinder, loosen the clip and disconnect the clutch fluid supply pipe from the the reservoir **(see illustration)**. Plug the pipe(s) to prevent entry of dust and dirt.

Left-hand drive models

8 Remove the master cylinder fluid reservoir cap, and syphon or draw the hydraulic fluid from the reservoir. **Note:** *Do not syphon the fluid by mouth, as it is poisonous; use a syringe or an old poultry baster.* Alternatively, open any convenient bleed screw in the system, and gently pump the brake pedal to expel the fluid

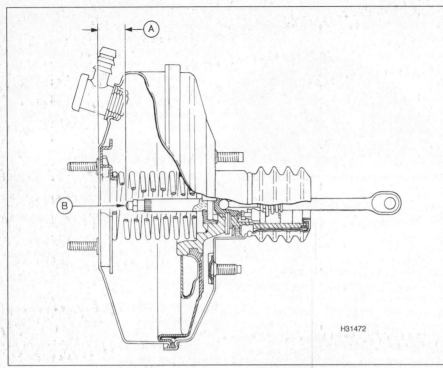

10.13 Cross-sectional view of vacuum servo unit

A 22.45 to 22.65 mm   *B Adjustment nut*

through a tube connected to the screw (see Section 2). Disconnect the wiring connector from the brake fluid level sender unit, and position the reservoir cap to one side.

9 Carefully prise the fluid reservoir from the seals and release it from the top of the master cylinder.

All models

10 Wipe clean the area around the brake pipe unions on the master cylinder. Make a note of the correct fitted positions of the unions, then unscrew the union nuts and carefully withdraw the pipes. Where adapters are bolted to the master cylinder, unscrew the unions from the adapters. Plug or tape over the pipe ends and master cylinder orifices, to minimise the loss of brake fluid, and to prevent the entry of dirt into the system. Wash off any spilt fluid immediately with cold water.

HAYNES HiNT *Cut the finger tips from an old rubber glove and secure them over the open ends of the brake pipes with elastic bands - this will help to minimise fluid loss and prevent the ingress of contaminants.*

11 Unscrew and remove the nuts securing the master cylinder to the vacuum servo unit, then withdraw the unit from the engine compartment.

12 Where applicable, recover the gasket from the rear of the master cylinder, and discard it. Obtain a new one.

13 With the master cylinder removed, check that the distance between the end of the vacuum servo unit pushrod and the master cylinder mating surface is as shown in the diagram. If necessary, the distance may be adjusted by turning the nut at the end of the servo unit pushrod (see illustration).

Overhaul

14 If the master cylinder is faulty, it must be renewed. Repair kits are not available from FIAT dealers.

15 The only items that can be renewed are the mounting seals for the fluid reservoir; obtain new ones if necessary.

Refitting

16 Clean the mating surfaces of the master cylinder and vacuum servo unit, then locate a new gasket on the mounting studs.

17 Refit the master cylinder and secure with the nuts tightened securely.

18 Wipe clean the brake pipe unions, then refit them to the correct master cylinder ports, as noted before removal, and tighten the union nuts securely.

Right-hand drive modelsz

19 Smear a little brake fluid on the supply pipes then press them firmly into the top of the master cylinder.

20 Remove the hose clamps where fitted, then fill the master cylinder reservoir with new fluid, and bleed the complete hydraulic system as described in Section 2.

21 Screw on the cap and reconnect the low fluid level unit wiring.

22 Refit the lining to the bulkhead, and secure with the stud.

23 Refit the relay bracket and tighten the bolts. Reconnect the small wiring plug.

24 Refit the relay cover.

25 Refit the air duct to the throttle body and air cleaner.

Left-hand drive models

26 Locate new mounting seals in the cylinder apertures, then smear some hydraulic fluid on the reservoir port extensions and press the reservoir firmly into position.

27 Reconnect the wiring to the brake fluid level sender unit.

28 Refill the master cylinder reservoir with new fluid, and bleed the complete hydraulic system as described in Section 2.

11 Brake pedal - removal and refitting

Removal

Right-hand drive models

Note: *If it is required to remove the pedal bracket, proceed as described in Section 12 for the removal of the vacuum servo unit.*

1 Unclip and remove the lower fusebox trim panel located beneath the right-hand side of the facia.

2 Disconnect the accelerator cable from the top of the accelerator pedal extension arm, then unscrew the nuts and remove the accelerator pedal (see illustrations).

11.2a Accelerator cable attachment to the top of the pedal extension arm

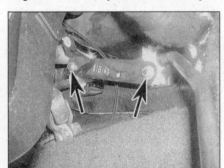

11.2b Accelerator pedal mounting nuts

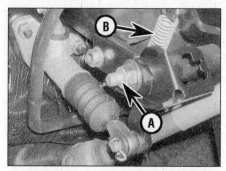

11.5 Pedal pivot bolt (A) and clutch pedal return spring (B)

3 Extract the split pin, and disconnect the clutch master cylinder pushrod from the clutch pedal.
4 Remove the stop-light switch from the pedal bracket with reference to Section 17.
5 Unscrew the pedal pivot bolt and withdraw it slowly to the right until it is possible to remove the clutch pedal from the bracket. Disconnect the clutch pedal return spring **(see illustration)**.
6 Extract the split pin, and disconnect the link from the arm on the brake pedal.
7 Withdraw the pivot bolt and lower the brake pedal from the bracket.
8 If necessary, remove the link and intermediate lever as follows. Extract the split pin, and disconnect the servo unit pushrod from the intermediate lever. Unscrew the pivot bolt and remove the assembly from the pedal bracket.
9 Clean and examine the components for wear and damage **(see illustration)**. Renew as necessary.

Left-hand drive models

10 Extract the split pin, and disconnect the brake servo unit pushrod from the pin on the brake pedal.
11 Position the clutch pedal for access to the brake pedal pivot bolt. Unscrew the bolt and withdraw the pedal from the bracket.
12 Recover the bushes, spacer and washers as necessary.
13 Clean and examine the components for wear and damage. Renew as necessary.

Refitting

14 Refitting is a reversal of removal, but apply a little grease to the pedal bushes before reassembling them.

12 Vacuum servo unit - testing, removal and refitting

Testing

1 To test the operation of the servo unit, depress the footbrake several times to exhaust the vacuum, then start the engine whilst keeping the pedal firmly depressed. As the engine starts, there should be a noticeable

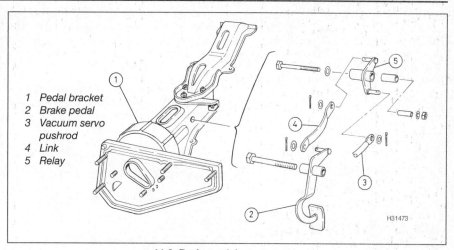

1 Pedal bracket
2 Brake pedal
3 Vacuum servo pushrod
4 Link
5 Relay

11.9 Brake pedal components

give in the brake pedal as the vacuum builds up. Allow the engine to run for at least two minutes, then switch it off. If the brake pedal is now depressed it should feel normal, but further applications should result in the pedal feeling firmer, with the pedal stroke decreasing with each application.
2 If the servo does not operate as described, inspect the servo unit check valve as described in Section 13.
3 If the servo unit still fails to operate satisfactorily, the fault lies within the unit itself. Repairs to the unit are not possible - if faulty, the servo unit must be renewed.

Removal

Right-hand drive models

4 Remove the facia panel from inside the car as described in Chapter 11.
5 Loosen the clips and disconnect the throttle body air duct from the air cleaner. Disconnect the crankcase ventilation hose from the duct, then unscrew the nuts and remove the duct from the top of the throttle body.
6 Undo the screw and remove the relay cover.
7 Unscrew the two bolts holding the relay bracket to the bulkhead, then disconnect the small wiring plug beneath it, and move the bracket to one side. Make sure that any electrical terminals are kept insulated from the surrounding components.
8 Release the retaining stud and pull out the lining from the right-hand side of the bulkhead for access to the master cylinder.
9 Unscrew the two nuts securing the brake master cylinder to the vacuum servo unit. Carefully withdraw the master cylinder from the servo unit taking care not to bend the brake pipes excessively. Move it just enough to provide room to remove the servo unit. There is no need to remove the reservoir cap or disconnect the wiring from the low fluid warning unit.
10 Release the clip and move the fuel injection wiring to one side, then carefully remove the vacuum hose from the servo unit.

The use of a screwdriver may be needed to do this.
11 Working inside the car, undo the screws and remove the footrest located next to the clutch pedal.
12 Unscrew and remove the clamp bolt securing the steering inner column to the steering gear pinion.
13 Remove the steering column as described in Chapter 10.
14 Disconnect the wiring from the stop-light switch located on the brake pedal bracket.
15 Unscrew the accelerator pedal bracket retaining nuts, and unhook the clutch pedal return spring.
16 Disconnect the accelerator cable from the pedal, and withdraw the pedal from the car.
17 Extract the rubber plug from the bonnet opening lever, then disconnect the cable.
18 Extract the split pin and disconnect the pushrod from the clutch pedal.
19 Release the wiring and support from the pedal bracket.
20 Extract the split pin and disconnect the servo unit pushrod from the brake pedal link.
21 Unscrew the mounting nuts and withdraw the pedal bracket and servo unit from inside the car.
22 With the pedal bracket and servo unit on the bench, unscrew the nuts and separate the servo unit from the bracket. Make sure that the washer remains in position on the end of the servo pushrod.

Left-hand drive models

23 Working in the engine compartment, unscrew the nuts securing the master cylinder to the vacuum servo unit. Carefully move the master cylinder away from the servo unit taking care not to bend the brake pipes excessively. Move it just enough to provide room to remove the servo unit. There is no need to remove the reservoir cap or disconnect the wiring from the low fluid warning unit.
24 Carefully lever out the vacuum servo unit check valve from the servo unit with a screwdriver.

25 Working inside the car, reach up over the pedal bracket and disconnect the accelerator cable from the top of the accelerator pedal. Unscrew the nuts and remove the accelerator pedal and plate.

26 Extract the retainers and move the floor covering to one side. **Note:** *The retainers are destroyed during removal, and must be renewed.*

27 Extract the split pin and disconnect the servo pushrod from the pin on the pedal.

28 Unscrew the mounting nuts securing the servo unit to the bulkhead.

29 Working in the engine compartment, withdraw the servo unit from the car.

Refitting

30 Check and if necessary adjust the distance between the end of the vacuum servo unit pushrod and the master cylinder mating surface as described in Section 10.

31 Refitting is a reversal of removal, but apply a little grease to the brake pedal link and clutch pedal pin before reconnecting them. Finally, test the vacuum servo unit as described at the beginning of this Section.

13 Vacuum servo unit check valve - removal, testing and refitting

Removal

1 On some models the valve is an integral part of the servo unit vacuum hose and is not available separately. On other models the valve is fitted separately in the vacuum hose or in the servo unit itself.

2 To remove the valve from the hose, first loosen the clips and disconnect the air inlet duct from between the air cleaner and throttle body. Disconnect the vacuum hoses from each end of the valve and remove the valve. Note which way round it is fitted to ensure correct refitting. The valve should be marked with an arrow pointing towards the inlet manifold.

3 To remove the valve from the servo unit, first disconnect the vacuum hose, then carefully lever the valve from the rubber grommet in the servo unit. Remove the rubber grommet.

4 To remove the complete vacuum hose, first remove the throttle body air duct from the air cleaner, then remove the duct from the top of the throttle body. Remove the relay cover, and move the bracket to one side. Release the retaining stud and pull out the lining from the right-hand side of the bulkhead. Release the wiring from the clip and pull out the vacuum hose from the servo unit. Loosen the clip and disconnect the vacuum hose from the inlet manifold.

Testing

5 The valve may be tested by blowing through it in both directions. Air should flow through the valve in one direction only - when blown through from the servo unit end of the valve. Renew the valve if this is not the case.

6 Examine the servo unit rubber sealing grommet and hose(s) linking the main hose to the inlet manifold for signs of damage or deterioration, and renew as necessary.

Refitting

7 Refitting is a reversal of removal, but make sure that the valve is fitted the correct way round, with the arrow pointing towards the engine inlet manifold.

14 Handbrake - checking and adjustment

Checking

1 Apply the handbrake by pulling it through three clicks of the ratchet mechanism and check that this locks the rear wheels, holding the vehicle stationary on an incline. If not, the handbrake mechanism is need of adjustment.

Adjustment

2 Chock the front wheels, then jack up the rear of the vehicle and support it on axle stands (see *Jacking and vehicle support*).

3 Release the gaiter from the centre console and remove it from the handbrake lever.

4 Unscrew the adjustment nut located under the handbrake lever until the cable is slack.

5 Select neutral, then start the engine and allow it to idle. Fully depress the brake pedal at least 30 times. This will operate the rear brake self-adjusting mechanism and ensure the brake shoes are set at their normal position.

6 Pull the handbrake lever through three clicks of the ratchet mechanism and leave it in this position.

7 Tighten the adjustment nut until the handbrake is fully applied at three or four clicks, and the rear wheels are locked.

8 Release the handbrake lever and check that the rear wheels are free to turn. There should be no binding or dragging.

9 Reapply the handbrake and check the adjustment again.

10 Refit the gaiter and lower the car to the ground.

15 Handbrake lever - removal and refitting

Removal

1 Release the gear lever gaiter from the centre console, then pull the gear lever knob and gaiter together from the top of the gear lever.

2 Chock the rear roadwheels, then fully unscrew the adjustment nut located beneath the handbrake lever.

3 Disconnect the wiring from the handbrake-on warning lamp switch, then undo the screw and remove the switch **(see illustration)**.

4 Jack up the front of the vehicle and support it on axle stands (see *Jacking and vehicle support*).

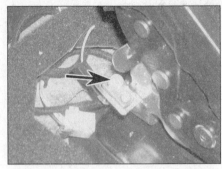

15.3 Handbrake 'on' warning lamp switch

5 Working under the car, unscrew the nuts and remove the exhaust heatshield from its location beneath the handbrake lever.

6 Unscrew the bolts securing the handbrake lever to the underbody. Also unscrew the bolts securing the handbrake cable guide to the underbody.

7 Working inside the car, withdraw the handbrake lever upwards from the floor.

Refitting

8 Refitting is a reversal of removal, but adjust the handbrake as described in Section 14.

16 Handbrake cables - removal and refitting

Removal

1 There is one primary handbrake cable between the lever and equaliser, and two secondary cables between the equaliser and rear brake shoes.

2 Chock the front wheels, then jack up the rear of the vehicle and support it on axle stands (see *Jacking and vehicle support*).

Primary cable

3 Release the gaiter from the centre console and remove it from the handbrake lever.

4 Fully unscrew the adjustment nut located beneath the handbrake lever. Remove the washer and the spring which operates the warning light switch.

5 Working under the car, unscrew the nuts and remove the exhaust heatshield from its location beneath the handbrake lever.

6 Unbolt and remove the handbrake cable guide from the underbody.

7 Unhook the secondary cables from the equaliser bar **(see illustration)**.

8 Remove the rubber grommet from the underbody, then withdraw the primary cable from under the car.

9 Unscrew the nut and remove the equaliser bar from the primary cable.

Secondary cables

10 Release the gaiter from the centre console and remove it from the handbrake lever.

11 Unscrew the adjustment nut located under the handbrake lever until the cable is slack.

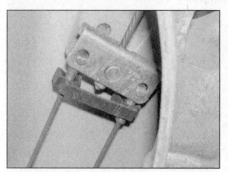

16.7 Handbrake cable equaliser bar

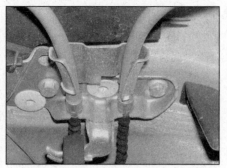

16.14a Rear underbody support for the handbrake cables

16.14b Handbrake cable support on the trailing arms

12 Working under the car, unscrew the nuts and remove the exhaust heatshield from its location beneath the handbrake lever.
13 Unhook the secondary cables from the equaliser bar.
14 Release the cables from the support clips on the underbody **(see illustrations)**. Where necessary, use a screwdriver to prise the clips apart.
15 Prise the covers from the apertures on the inside the rear brake backplates **(see illustration)**.
16 Using a pair of pliers, unhook the inner cables from the levers on the trailing shoes **(see illustration)**. Note the location of the springs on the inner cables. If difficulty is experienced, remove the rear brake shoes as described in Section 5.
17 Pull the outer cables from the rear brake backplates **(see illustration)**. If they are rusted in position, remove the rear brake shoes as described in Section 5, then use a thin punch to drive them out.

Refitting

18 Refitting is a reversal of removal, but adjust the handbrake as described in Section 14.

17 Stop-light switch -
adjustment, removal and refitting

Adjustment

1 The switch plunger operates on a ratchet.

2 If adjustment is required, pull the plunger fully out - the switch then self-adjusts as the brake pedal is applied and released.

Removal

3 Ensure that the ignition is switched to OFF.
4 Unclip and remove the lower fusebox trim panel located beneath the right-hand side of the facia.
5 Disconnect the wiring plug from the switch.
6 Twist the switch anti-clockwise through about 60°, and withdraw the switch from the pedal bracket. If necessary, use a spanner on the hexagon section. Note the position of the spacer and fitting bush.

Refitting

7 Depress the brake pedal and hold it in this position.
8 Fit the bush and spacer over the end of the switch, then insert the switch into its mounting bracket. Rotate the switch body clockwise through 60° until the locating lug is felt to engage in its recess **(see illustration)**.
9 Release the brake pedal and allow it to rest against the switch spacer tab - this adjusts the position of the switch body inside the bush.
10 Now depress the brake pedal again - this has the effect of breaking off the spacer tab and fixes the position of the switch inside the bush. Discard the spacer tab.
11 Reconnect the wiring plug to the switch, and refit the lower fusebox trim panel.
12 Switch on the ignition and test the operation of the brake lights.

16.15 Cover for access to the handbrake cable attachment on the trailing brake shoe

18 Rear brake pressure proportioning valve -
removal and refitting

Note: *Adjustment of a new valve requires a special tool only available at a FIAT dealer.*

Removal

1 Chock the front wheels, then jack up the rear of the vehicle and support it on axle stands (see *Jacking and vehicle support*).

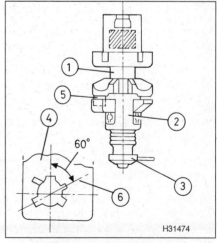

17.8 Brake light switch assembly

1 Hexagonal section	4 Mounting bracket
2 Bush	5 Locating lug
3 Spacer	

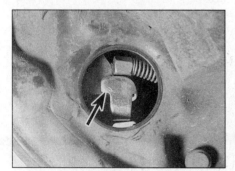

16.16 Unhook the cable end from the brake shoe lever (arrowed)

16.17 Handbrake cable attachment to the rear brake backplates

2 Unbolt the exhaust rear and intermediate mountings from the underbody.

3 Unbolt the heat shield for access to the rear brake pressure proportioning valve.

4 Unscrew the cap from the brake fluid reservoir and tighten it down onto a piece of polythene sheeting. This will help reduce the loss of fluid from the system. Also place a container beneath the valve to catch spilt fluid.

5 Identify the pipe locations on the valve, then unscrew the union nuts and disconnect them. If possible, plug the ends of the pipes to prevent loss of fluid.

6 Disconnect the spring from the lever on top of the valve.

7 Unscrew the mounting bolts and withdraw the valve from under the vehicle **(see illustration)**.

Refitting

8 Refitting is a reversal of removal, but bleed the hydraulic system as described in Section 2, and have the valve adjusted by a FIAT dealer.

19 Anti-lock braking system (ABS) components - removal and refitting

Caution: Disconnect the battery before disconnecting any ABS system hydraulic union and do not reconnect the battery until after the hydraulic system has been reconnected and the fluid reservoir topped up. Failure to take this precaution could lead to air entering the hydraulic unit. New hydraulic units are supplied pre-filled with brake fluid.

Note: *The manufacturers state that the operation of the ABS system should be checked by a FIAT dealer using special test equipment after refitting any of the components in this Section.*

Electro-hydraulic control unit

1 The electro-hydraulic control unit is located on the left-hand side of the engine compartment. The ECU and recycling pump are also part of the control unit.

2 Except on 1.3 and 1.4 litre models, remove the air inlet duct from between the air cleaner and throttle body, by loosening the clips and also disconnecting the crankcase ventilation hose.

3 Remove the battery and battery tray (Chapter 5A), then unbolt and remove the battery mounting bracket. Move the relay holder box to one side after removing the cover and unscrewing the mounting bolts.

4 Unscrew and remove the filler cap from the top of the brake fluid reservoir, then syphon or draw out the hydraulic fluid. Alternatively, fit hose clamps to the hoses attached to the bottom of the reservoir.

5 Unbolt the fluid reservoir from the bulkhead and position it safely to one side.

6 Remove the two fuses located on the side of the fusebox on the left-hand side of the

18.7 Rear brake pressure proportioning valve mounting bolts

bulkhead. Unscrew the mounting nut, and move the fusebox to one side.

7 Identify all the brake pipes attached to the hydraulic unit, then unscrew the union nuts and pull out the pipes so that they are just clear of the unit. Ideally, a split brake pipe spanner should be used to unscrew the nuts.

8 Unscrew the front mounting nut and the side mounting bolt.

9 Pull up the locking device and disconnect the wiring, then withdraw the electro-hydraulic control unit from the engine compartment.

10 Using an Allen key, unscrew the bolts and remove the mounting bracket from the unit.

Refitting

11 Refit the mounting bracket and tighten the bolts.

12 Refit the electro-hydraulic control unit in the engine compartment and tighten the nut and bolt.

13 Reconnect the wiring and secure with the locking device.

14 Reconnect the brake pipes and tighten securely. Do not overtighten them.

15 Refit the fusebox and tighten the nut, then refit the two side fuses.

16 Refit the fluid reservoir to the bulkhead.

17 Refit the battery mounting bracket and tighten the mounting bolts. Refit the relay box.

18 Refit the battery and tray (Chapter 5A).

19 Except on 1.3 and 1.4 litre models, refit the air inlet duct and crankcase ventilation hose.

20 Fill the fluid reservoir with fresh fluid (see *Weekly Checks*).

21 Bleed the complete hydraulic system as described in Section 2. Have the operation of the ABS system checked by a FIAT dealer at the earliest possible opportunity.

Front wheel sensor

Removal

22 Apply the handbrake, then jack up the front of the vehicle and support it on axle stands (see *Jacking and vehicle support*). Remove the appropriate front wheel.

23 At the rear left-hand side of the engine compartment, disconnect the front wheel sensor wiring at the fusebox. Feed the wiring through into the front wheel arch area.

24 Using an Allen key, unscrew the mounting bolt, then withdraw the sensor from the hub carrier.

25 Release the wiring from the support on the bottom of the front suspension strut and remove the front wheel sensor.

Refitting

26 Ensure that the sensor and hub carrier location are clean, then insert the sensor and secure with the bolt.

27 Locate the wiring in the support and feed it through into the engine compartment.

28 Reconnect the wiring at the fusebox.

29 Using a feeler blade, check that the clearance between the wheel sensor and the serrated wheel on the front driveshaft is 0.9 mm ± 0.4 mm. The clearance is not adjustable; if outside the tolerance, check the sensor and serrated wheel for damage.

30 Refit the wheel and lower the vehicle to the ground.

Rear wheel sensor

Removal

31 Chock the front wheels, then jack up the rear of the vehicle and support it on axle stands (see *Jacking and vehicle support*). Remove the appropriate rear wheel.

32 Remove the rear seat cushion as described in Chapter 11, Section 19.

33 Lift the sound proofing material, then disconnect the sensor wiring on the appropriate side.

34 If removing the right-hand side wheel sensor, unbolt the fuel filter cover under the rear of the car.

35 Prise out the rubber grommet and withdraw the sensor wiring from under the car.

36 Remove the brake drum with reference to Section 7. This is not strictly necessary for the removal of the sensor unless it is rusted in position, but it is necessary to check the gap between the sensor and serrated wheel on the hub during refitting.

37 Using an Allen key, unscrew the mounting bolt, then withdraw the sensor from the rear stub axle body and remove from the car.

Refitting

38 Ensure that the sensor and rear stub axle body are clean, then insert the sensor and secure with the bolt.

39 Using a feeler blade, check that the clearance between the wheel sensor and the serrated wheel on the rear hub is 0.9 mm ± 0.4 mm. The clearance is not adjustable; if outside the tolerance, check the sensor and serrated wheel for damage.

40 Refit the brake drum with reference to Section 7.

41 Feed the wiring through the floor into the car, and reposition the rubber grommet.

42 On the right-hand side, refit the fuel filter cover.

43 Reconnect the wiring located beneath the seat cushion, and refit the sound proofing. Refit the rear seat cushion with reference to Chapter 11, Section 19.

44 Refit the rear wheel and lower the car to the ground.

Chapter 10
Suspension and steering systems

Contents

Degrees of difficulty

Easy, suitable for novice with little experience	**Fairly easy,** suitable for beginner with some experience	**Fairly difficult,** suitable for competent DIY mechanic	**Difficult,** suitable for experienced DIY mechanic	**Very difficult,** suitable for expert DIY or professional

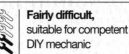

Specifications

Front suspension

Type . . . . Independent, incorporating transverse lower wishbones and coil spring strut units with integral shock absorbers. Anti-roll bar fitted to all models.

Rear suspension

Type . . . . Independent, incorporating trailing arms with telescopic shock absorbers and coil springs. Anti-roll bar fitted to all models.

Steering

Type . . . . Rack-and-pinion, power assisted standard on UK models, but manual on certain other markets

Turns lock-to-lock:
 Pre-1998 models . . . . 2.9 approx.
 1998-on models 3.0

Wheel alignment and steering angles

Front wheel:
 Toe-in . . . . -1.0 to +1.0 mm
 Camber:
  Pre-1998 models . . . . -7' ± 30'
  1998-on models . . . . -33' ± 30'
 Castor:
  Pre-1998 models without PAS . . . . 3° 30' ± 30'
  Pre-1998 models with PAS . . . . 2° 50' ± 30'
  1998-on models . . . . 2° 50' ± 30'
Rear wheel:
 Toe-in:
  Up to chassis number 4.050.319 . . . . -2.5 to +1.5 mm
  From chassis number 4.050.320 . . . . 0 to 4.0 mm
 Camber . . . . 0° 46' ± 30'

Roadwheels

Type . . . . Pressed steel
Size 5½Jx14, 6Jx14, 6Jx15
Tyre pressures . . . . see Weekly Checks

Torque wrench settings

	Nm	lbf ft
Front suspension		
Anti-roll bar clamp nuts	40	30
Anti-roll bar end nuts	70	52
Anti-roll bar link to lower arm	31	23
Hub (driveshaft) nut (M22)	240	177
Lower arm to subframe	69	51
Rear engine mounting and bracket	50	37
Strut:		
Damper rod nut	100	74
Upper mounting bolts	40	30
Strut to hub carrier	70	52
Subframe:		
Front bolt with wide flange	108	80
Rear bolt with normal flange	80	59
Track-rod balljoint to hub carrier	40	30
Rear suspension		
Anti-roll bar:		
End bolt	56	41
Clamp bolt	28	21
Rear axle assembly mounting	108	80
Rear hub nut	280	207
Rear suspension trailing arm pivot bolt	150	111
Shock absorber:		
Upper	60	44
Lower	88	65
Steering		
Lower arm-to-hub carrier clamp bolt	70	52
Power steering gear	70	52
Power steering pump drivebelt tensioner bolt	48	35
Power steering pump mounting bolt:		
M6 and M8 bolt	25	18
M10 bolt	50	37
Power steering pump mounting bracket nut	48	35
Power steering pump pulley	25	18
Return union on steering gear	20	15
Steering column mounting bolts	55	41
Steering wheel nut	50	37
Supply union on steering gear	30	22
Track-rod end balljoint to steering arm on hub carrier	40	30
Universal joint clamp bolts	20	15
Roadwheels		
Wheel bolts	86	63

1 General information

Front suspension

The front suspension is independent, comprising transverse lower wishbones, coil spring strut units with integral shock absorbers, and an anti-roll bar. The hub carriers are bolted to the base of the strut units and are linked to the lower arms by means of balljoints. The entire front suspension assembly is mounted on a subframe, which is in turn bolted to the vehicle body.

Rear suspension

The rear suspension incorporates a torsion beam axle, trailing arms, coil springs and separate telescopic shock absorbers. A rear anti-roll bar is fitted to all models.

Steering

The two-piece steering column assembly is bolted to a bracket mounted on the bulkhead. The upper section of the inner column runs in bearings located in the tubular outer column. The lower section of the column incorporates two universal joints, the lower one being clamped to the splined steering gear pinion.

The steering gear is mounted on the front suspension subframe, and is connected to the steering arms projecting rearwards from the hub carriers. The track-rods are fitted with balljoints at their inner and outer ends, to allow for suspension movement, and are threaded to facilitate adjustment.

Hydraulically-assisted power steering is fitted to all UK models. The hydraulic system is powered by a belt-driven pump, which is driven from the crankshaft pulley.

All models are fitted with an airbag system and seat belt tensioners. Sensors built into the vehicle body are triggered in the event of a front end collision, and prompt an Electronic Control Unit (ECU) to activate the airbag mounted in the centre of the steering wheel and the facia. This reduces the risk of the front seat occupants striking the steering wheel, windscreen or facia during an accident. At the same time the seat belt tensioners are activated.

 Warning: For safety reasons, owners are strongly advised to entrust to an authorised FIAT dealer any work on the airbag system components. The airbag inflation devices contain explosive material and legislation exists to control their handling and storage. In addition, specialised test equipment is needed to check that the airbag system is fully operational following reassembly.

2.5 Splash shield securing bolt on the hub carrier

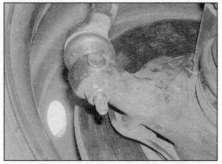

2.6 Nut securing the steering track rod end to the hub carrier steering arm

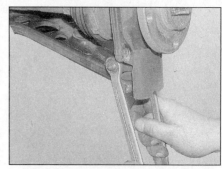

2.8a Unscrew and remove the clamp bolt . . .

2 Front hub bearings - renewal

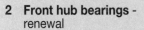

Note: *A balljoint separator tool, and a press or suitable alternative tools (see text) will be required for this operation. The bearing will be destroyed during the removal procedure.*

1 Remove the wheel trim from the appropriate wheel, then loosen the driveshaft/hub nut with the vehicle resting on its wheels and the handbrake firmly applied. The nut is very tight and an extension bar may be necessary to loosen it. Also loosen the wheel bolts half a turn.

2 Apply the handbrake, then jack up the front of the vehicle and support on axle stands (see *Jacking and vehicle support*). Remove the appropriate roadwheel.

3 Unscrew and remove the driveshaft/hub nut and discard it - a new one must be used on refitting.

4 Remove the brake disc and caliper, with reference to Chapter 9. Note that the caliper body can remain bolted to its bracket, and there is no need to disconnect the brake fluid hose from the caliper. Tie the caliper to the coil spring without straining the flexible brake hose.

5 Unbolt and remove the caliper splash shield **(see illustration)**.

6 Unscrew the nut securing the steering track-rod end to the hub carrier steering arm **(see illustration)**. Using a balljoint removal tool, separate the track-rod end from the arm.

7 On models with ABS, undo the screw securing the ABS sensor to the hub carrier. Suspend the sensor away from the working area.

8 Unscrew and remove the clamp bolt from the bottom of the hub carrier, then push the lower arm down and separate the balljoint from the hub carrier **(see illustrations)**.

9 Unscrew and remove the bolts securing the hub carrier to the bottom of the strut, then withdraw the hub carrier from the splined driveshaft **(see illustrations)**. Note which way round the bolts are fitted. If necessary, use a hide mallet to tap the driveshaft from the hub.

Caution: Do not allow the end of the driveshaft to hang down under its own weight, as this places strain on the CV joints; support the end of the shaft using wire or string.

10 At this stage, it is recommended that the hub carrier be taken to an engineering workshop, as the hub and bearing should ideally be removed from the hub carrier using a hydraulic press. Owners wishing to attempt the work themselves should proceed as follows.

11 Support the hub carrier on blocks of wood with the hub drive flange facing downwards. Press or drive the hub from the hub carrier. Alternatively, use a slide hammer to remove the hub **(see illustration)**. Note that the inner race will remain on the hub. To remove the race, initially mount the hub in a vice and use a cold chisel to force it a few millimetres from the shoulder, then use a puller to withdraw it.

12 Extract the bearing circlip from the inside face of the hub carrier, then press or drive out

2.8b . . . then push the lower arm down and separate the balljoint from the base of the hub carrier

2.9a Remove the bolts . . .

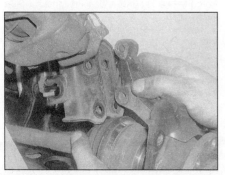

2.9b . . . separate the hub carrier from the bottom of the strut . . .

2.9c . . . and withdraw the hub carrier from the splined driveshaft

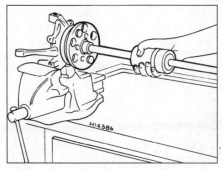

2.11 Using a slide hammer to extract the hub

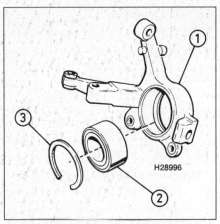

2.12 Wheel bearing components

1 Hub carrier   2 Wheel bearing   3 Circlip

the bearing using a metal tube **(see illustration)**. If necessary, temporarily refit the inner race removed in paragraph before removing the bearing. Note that the flange on the outer side of the carrier means that the bearing can only be driven out in one direction.

13 Before installing the new bearing, thoroughly clean the bearing location in the hub carrier.

14 Fit the new bearing from the inboard side of the hub. Press or drive the bearing into position, applying pressure **only** to the bearing outer race.

15 Fit the bearing retaining circlip to its groove in the hub carrier.

2.16 Typical method of drawing the hub into the wheel bearing using improvised tools

16 Carefully press or draw the hub into the bearing, noting that the bearing inner race **must** be supported during this operation, to prevent it from being separated from the outer race. This can be achieved using a suitable socket, threaded rod, washers and a length of bar **(see illustration)**.

17 Locate the hub on the splined end of the driveshaft, then refit the hub carrier to the bottom of the strut. Insert the bolts as previously noted, and tighten to the specified torque.

18 Locate the lower arm balljoint in the bottom of the hub carrier, then insert the clamp bolt and tighten to the specified torque. Make sure that the bolt enters the groove in the balljoint stub.

19 On models with ABS, refit the ABS sensor and tighten the screw.

20 Refit the steering track-rod end to the hub

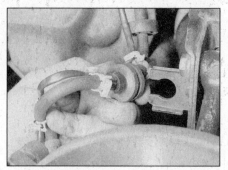

3.2 Release the brake fluid line (and where applicable, the pad wear/ABS sensor wiring) from the strut

carrier steering arm, and tighten the retaining nut to the specified torque.

21 Refit the caliper splash shield and tighten the bolt.

22 Refit the brake caliper and disc with reference to Chapter 9.

23 Screw on the driveshaft/hub nut and moderately tighten it at this stage.

24 Refit the roadwheel and lower the vehicle to the ground.

25 Fully tighten the driveshaft/hub nut to the specified torque.

26 Have the front wheel alignment checked by a FIAT dealer or a tyre specialist at the earliest opportunity.

3 Front suspension strut - removal, overhaul and refitting

⚠️ *Warning: If renewing the strut shock absorber during overhaul, both the left and right hand units should be renewed as a pair, to preserve the handling characteristics of the vehicle.*

Removal

1 Apply the handbrake, then jack up the front of the vehicle and support it on axle stands (see *Jacking and vehicle support*). Remove the relevant roadwheel.

2 Release the brake fluid line (and where applicable, the pad wear/ABS sensor wiring) from the bracket on the base of the strut **(see illustration)**.

3 Remove the two nuts from the bolts securing the lower end of the strut to the hub carrier, noting which way round they are fitted **(see illustrations)**. Withdraw the bolts, and support the hub carrier on a trolley jack.

4 Have an assistant support the strut from under the wheel arch then, working in the engine compartment, unscrew the upper mounting bolts. Note that the location studs ensure the strut can only be fitted in one position. *Do not unscrew the centre damper rod nut yet.* Release the lower end of the strut from the hub carrier, then withdraw the assembly from under the wheel arch **(see illustrations)**.

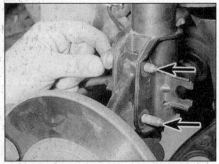

3.3a Remove the two bolts (arrowed) . . .

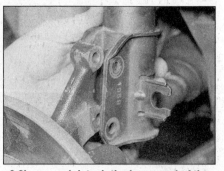

3.3b . . . and detach the lower end of the strut from the hub carrier

3.4a Unscrew the upper mounting bolts . . .

3.4b . . . and withdraw the strut assembly from under the wheel arch

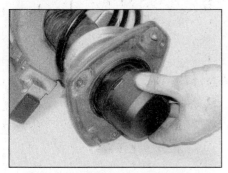

3.5 Remove the plastic protective cap from the top of the strut

3.7a Unscrew the strut upper nut, while counterholding the damper rod with an Allen key . . .

3.7b . . . then remove the nut and cup

3.8a Remove the strut upper mounting plate/bearing . . .

3.8b . . . and seat

3.8c The plate has an arrow formed on its outer edge which is located between the plastic tabs

Overhaul

Note: *Suitable coil spring compressor tools will be required for this operation, and a new strut top nut must be used on reassembly.*

5 Clamp the lower end of the strut in a vice fitted with jaw protectors - take care to avoid deforming the mounting bracket at the lower end of the strut. Remove the protective plastic cap from the top of the strut **(see illustration)**.
6 Fit spring compressor tools to the coil spring, and compress the spring sufficiently to enable the upper spring seat to be turned by hand.

 Warning: Use purpose-made compressor tools, and ensure that the coil spring is compressed sufficiently to remove all the tension from the upper spring seat before attempting to remove the damper rod nut.

7 Unscrew and remove the strut upper nut and cup. Counterhold the damper rod, using a suitable Allen key or hex bit, as the nut is unscrewed **(see illustrations)**. Discard the nut - a new one must be used on reassembly.
8 Withdraw the upper mounting plate/bearing and seat. Note that the plate has an arrow formed on its outer edge which is located between the plastic tabs **(see illustrations)**.
9 Withdraw the spring, complete with the compressors, then withdraw the bump rubber/dust cover **(see illustrations)**.
10 With the strut assembly now dismantled, examine all the components for wear, damage

or deformation. Check the upper bearing for wear and roughness, and check the rubber components for deterioration. Renew any of the components as necessary.
11 Examine the shock absorber for signs of fluid leakage. Check the shock absorber rod for signs of pitting along its entire length, and check the strut body for signs of damage. While holding it in an upright position, test the operation of the shock absorber by moving the rod through a full stroke, and then through short strokes of 50 to 100 mm. In both cases, the resistance felt should be smooth and continuous. If the resistance is jerky, or uneven, or if there is any visible sign of wear or damage to the strut, renewal is necessary. Note that the shock absorber cannot be renewed independently, and if leakage, damage or corrosion is evident, the complete strut/shock

absorber assembly must be renewed. The spring and associated components can be transferred to the new strut.
12 If any doubt exists about the condition of the coil spring, carefully remove the spring compressor tools, and check the spring for distortion and signs of cracking. Renew the spring if there is any doubt about its condition.

 Warning: Coil springs are classified by a coloured paint marking on the central coil (either green or yellow). Both coil springs fitted to the vehicle must be of the same classification to ensure the correct ride height.

13 Clamp the strut body in a vice, as during dismantling, then refit the bump rubber/dust cover.

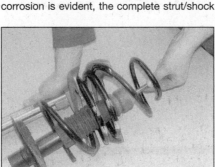

3.9a Remove the coil spring complete with compressor . . .

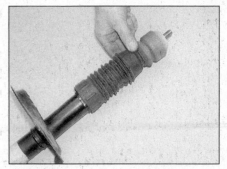

3.9b . . . then remove the bump rubber/dust cover

3.14 Make sure that the lower end of the coil spring is correctly located in the recess on the lower spring seat

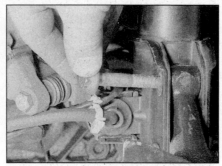

3.19a Fit the securing bolts, noting that the nuts fit on the rear side of the strut . . .

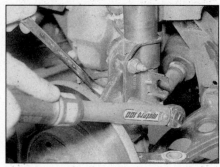

3.19b . . . and tighten them to the specified torque

14 Ensure that the coil spring is compressed sufficiently to enable the upper mounting components to be fitted, then fit the spring onto the strut, ensuring that the lower end of the spring is correctly located in the recess on the lower spring seat **(see illustration)**.

15 Refit the upper mounting plate/bearing followed by the cup and new nut, making sure that the arrow is pointing between the plastic tabs. Ensure that the top end of the spring is correctly located on the upper spring seat.

16 Tighten the nut to the specified torque, counterholding the damper rod in a manner similar to that used during dismantling. Note that a suitable crows-foot adapter will be required to tighten the damper rod top nut to the specified torque.

17 Remove the spring compressor tools, and refit the protective plastic cap to the top of the strut.

Refitting

18 Manoeuvre the strut assembly into position under the wheel arch, and engage the locating studs with the holes in the body turret. Fit the upper mounting bolts, and tighten them to the specified torque.

19 Attach the hub carrier to the bottom of the strut. Insert the bolts the correct way round as previously noted, and tighten to the specified torque **(see illustrations)**.

20 Refit the brake fluid line (and where applicable, the pad wear/ABS sensor wiring) to the bracket on the base of the strut.

21 Refit the roadwheel, and lower the vehicle to the ground.

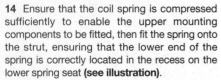

4   Front suspension lower arm - removal and refitting

Removal

Note: *A balljoint separator tool may be required for this operation.*

1 Apply the handbrake, then jack up the front of the vehicle and support it on axle stands (see *Jacking and vehicle support*). Remove the relevant roadwheel.

2 Unscrew and remove the clamp bolt from

the bottom of the hub carrier, then push the lower arm down and separate the balljoint from the hub carrier.

3 Unscrew the nut securing the front anti-roll bar to the lower arm, and remove the washer and rubber. Also unscrew the nut securing the link to the anti-roll bar and remove the washer. Withdraw the link and recover the washer and rubber.

4 Unscrew the mounting bolts and withdraw the lower arm from the subframe.

5 With the lower arm removed, examine the lower arm itself, and the mounting bushes, for wear, cracks or damage.

6 Check the balljoint for wear, excessive play, or stiffness. Also check the balljoint dust boot for cracks or damage.

7 The mounting bushes and balljoint assembly are integral with the lower arm, and cannot be renewed independently. If either the bushes or the balljoint are worn or damaged, the complete lower arm assembly must be renewed.

Refitting

8 Locate the lower arm in the subframe, and refit the mounting bolts. Tighten them to the specified torque.

9 Refit the link, washer and nut to the anti-roll bar, and at the same time refit the rubber and washer and locate the link in the lower arm.

10 Refit the rubber and washer under the lower arm, and fit the nut. Tighten the link nuts to the specified torque.

11 Locate the lower arm balljoint in the

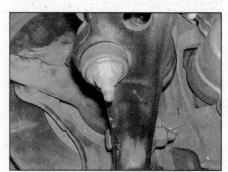

6.2 Nut securing the anti-roll bar to the front suspension lower arm

bottom of the hub carrier, then insert the clamp bolt and tighten to the specified torque. Make sure that the bolt enters the groove in the balljoint stub.

12 Refit the roadwheel and lower the vehicle to the ground.

13 On completion the front wheel alignment should be checked.

5   Front suspension lower arm balljoint - renewal

The balljoint is integral with the suspension lower arm. If the balljoint is worn or damaged, the complete lower arm must be renewed as described in Section 4.

6   Front suspension anti-roll bar - removal and refitting

Removal

1 Apply the handbrake, then jack up the front of the vehicle and support it on axle stands (see *Jacking and vehicle support*). Remove the relevant roadwheels.

2 Unscrew the nuts securing the anti-roll bar links to the front suspension lower arms on each side, and remove the washers and rubbers **(see illustration)**. Note that the convex sides of the washers contact the rubbers.

3 Unscrew the nuts and remove the washers from each end of the anti-roll bar, and remove the links and upper rubbers and washers. Note that the convex sides of the washers contact the rubbers.

4 Mark the top of the anti-roll bar with a dab of paint to ensure correct refitting.

5 Unscrew the anti-roll bar clamp bolts located under the subframe, then withdraw the anti-roll bar from one side of the vehicle. Recover the clamps.

6 Inspect the rubber bushes for cracks or deterioration. If renewal is necessary, slide the old bushes from the bar, and fit the new items, using soapy water as a lubricant. Do

not apply grease or oil as this will attack the rubber.

7 Check the anti-roll bar for signs of damage, wear or serious corrosion.

Refitting

8 Refitting is a reversal of removal, but tighten all nuts and bolts to the specified torque where given.

---

7 Front suspension subframe - removal and refitting

Removal

1 Apply the handbrake, then jack up the front of the vehicle and support it on axle stands (see *Jacking and vehicle support*). Remove both front roadwheels.

2 Remove the exhaust front downpipe with reference to Chapter 4C.

3 Remove both front suspension lower arms as described in Section 4.

4 Remove the anti-roll bar as described in Section 6.

5 Unbolt the rear engine mounting from the subframe, then unbolt the bracket from the transmission and withdraw the mounting and bracket from under the vehicle.

6 Undo the screws and remove the exhaust heatshield from the underbody.

7 Unscrew and remove the two central bolts securing the steering gear to the subframe.

8 Support the weight of the subframe on a trolley jack and length of wood.

9 Unscrew and remove the remaining mounting bolts and lower the subframe to the ground. Withdraw the subframe from under the car.

Refitting

10 Lift the subframe on the trolley jack, and insert the mounting bolts, hand-tight at this stage.

11 Using two 12.0 mm diameter metal rods inserted through the two holes at the rear of the subframe, align the subframe, then tighten the mounting bolts progressively to the specified torque.

12 Insert and tighten the steering gear mounting bolts to the specified torque.

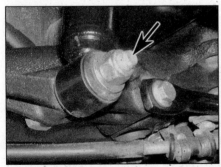

9.3 Rear shock absorber lower mounting bolt

8.4 Prise the dust cap from the hub with a screwdriver

13 Refit the exhaust heatshield.

14 Refit the rear engine mounting and bracket and tighten the bolts to the specified torque.

15 Refit the anti-roll bar with reference to Section 6.

16 Refit both front suspension lower arms with reference to Section 4.

17 Refit the exhaust front downpipe with reference to Chapter 4C.

18 Refit the roadwheels and lower the vehicle to the ground.

---

8 Rear hub bearings - renewal

Note: *A new rear hub nut must be used on refitting.*

1 The rear hub bearings are integral with the hubs themselves, and cannot be renewed separately. If the bearings are worn excessively, the complete hub assembly must be renewed.

2 Chock the front roadwheels, then jack up the rear of the vehicle and support on axle stands (see *Jacking and vehicle support*). Remove the appropriate rear roadwheel.

3 Remove the brake drum as described in Chapter 9. **Do not** depress the brake pedal whilst the brake drum is removed.

4 Prise the dust cap from the hub with a screwdriver **(see illustration)**.

5 Unscrew and remove the hub nut and recover the washer **(see illustration)**.

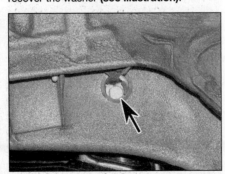

9.4 Rear shock absorber upper mounting bolt

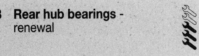

8.5 The rear hub nut

Caution: The nut is tightened to a high torque. Use a socket and long extension bar and ensure that you have access to torque wrench capable of tightening the new nut to the specified torque setting, before removing the existing nut.

6 Withdraw the hub and bearing assembly from the stub axle, and recover the inner washer. Discard the hub nut - a new one must be used on refitting.

7 Thoroughly clean the stub axle, then slide the inner washer and new hub assembly into position.

8 Fit the outer washer, then screw on the new hub nut. Hold the stub axle stationary using a suitable Allen key, then tighten the hub nut to the specified torque.

9 Apply a little grease around the edge of the dust cap, then carefully tap it into the hub. Refit the brake drum with reference to Chapter 9.

10 Refit the roadwheel then lower the vehicle to the ground.

---

9 Rear shock absorber - removal and refitting

Removal

1 Chock the front wheels, then jack up the rear of the vehicle and support on axle stands (see *Jacking and vehicle support*). Remove the relevant rear roadwheel.

2 Using a trolley jack positioned under the trailing arm, raise the trailing arm slightly to compress the coil spring.

3 Unscrew and remove the lower mounting bolt **(see illustration)**.

4 Unscrew and remove the upper mounting bolt using a socket through the access hole **(see illustration)**, then pull the top of the shock absorber from the rear suspension subframe.

Refitting

5 Refitting is a reversal of removal. Tighten the upper and lower mounting bolts to the specified torque with the trolley jack supporting the weight of the car so that the rear suspension is compressed.

13.5 Rear brake hydraulic line and union nut on the underbody in front of the rear axle

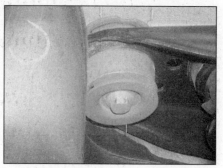

13.9 One of the rear axle mountings

10 Rear suspension coil spring - removal and refitting

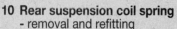

Removal

1 Chock the front wheels, then jack up the rear of the vehicle and support on axle stands (see *Jacking and vehicle support*). Remove the relevant rear roadwheel.

2 Using a trolley jack positioned under the trailing arm, raise the trailing arm slightly to compress the coil spring.

3 Unscrew and remove the shock absorber lower mounting bolt.

4 Lower the trailing arm gradually on the trolley jack, until the coil spring is released from its lower seat on the trailing arm and its upper seat on the subframe. Make a note of the orientation of the coil spring, to ensure correct refitting later.

5 Remove the upper and lower spring seats, and the bump stop rubbers.

Refitting

6 Refitting is a reversal of removal. Tighten the shock absorber lower mounting bolt to the specified torque.

11 Rear suspension trailing arm - removal and refitting

Removal

1 Chock the front wheels, then jack up the rear of the vehicle and support on axle stands (see *Jacking and vehicle support*). Remove the relevant rear roadwheel.

2 Remove the brake drum and rear brake shoes as described in Chapter 9. **Do not** depress the brake pedal whilst the brake drum is removed.

3 Fit a brake hose clamp to the flexible hose leading to the relevant rear brake. Unscrew the union nut from the rear of the rear wheel cylinder, then unbolt the brake line support from the trailing arm.

4 Remove the handbrake cable from the backplate, then unbolt the backplate from the trailing arm.

5 Remove the rear hub (Section 8) and coil spring (paragraphs 6 to 9 of this Section).

6 Unbolt the anti-roll bar from the trailing arm.

7 Unscrew and remove the front pivot bolt and withdraw the trailing arm from the rear suspension subframe.

8 Check the bearings for excessive wear, particularly on the outer bearing. Note that it is not possible to renew the bearings separately; the complete trailing arm must be renewed.

Refitting

9 Refitting is a reversal of removal. Tighten all suspension fixings to the specified torque settings, but delay this operation until the full weight of the vehicle is resting on the roadwheels.

10 On completion, bleed the brake hydraulic system and adjust the operation of the hand-brake, with reference to Chapter 9.

12 Rear suspension anti-roll bar - removal and refitting

Removal

1 Chock the front roadwheels, then jack up the rear of the vehicle and support on axle stands (see *Jacking and vehicle support*). Remove both rear roadwheels.

2 Where fitted, disconnect the rear brake pressure proportioning valve spring from the middle of the rear anti-roll bar.

3 Unscrew the bolts securing the anti-roll bar to the trailing arms, and withdraw it from under the car.

Refitting

4 Refitting is a reversal of removal, but tighten the mounting bolts securely.

13 Rear axle assembly - removal and refitting

Removal

1 Chock the front wheels, then jack up the rear of the vehicle and support on axle stands (see *Jacking and vehicle support*). Remove the relevant rear roadwheel.

2 Remove the fuel tank as described in Chapter 4A or 4B.

3 Remove the rear section of the exhaust system as described in Chapter 4C.

4 Unscrew the filler cap from the brake fluid reservoir, and tighten it down onto a piece of polythene sheeting. This will reduce the loss of fluid when the brake lines are disconnected.

5 Working under the rear of the car, identify for position then unscrew the union nuts and disconnect the rear brake hydraulic lines on the underbody in front of the rear axle **(see illustration)**. Plug the lines to prevent loss of fluid.

6 Back off the handbrake cable adjustment (see Chapter 9), and disconnect the cables from the equaliser bar. Also detach the outer cables from the underbody.

7 Where necessary, unbolt and remove the ABS sensors from each rear brake backplate.

8 Support the rear axle assembly with a trolley jack and length of wood. An assistant would also be helpful to steady the assembly as it is being lowered to the ground.

9 Unscrew the four mounting bolts securing the rear axle assembly to the underbody, then lower it to the floor **(see illustration)**.

10 Remove the component parts of the rear axle assembly with reference to the relevant Sections of this Chapter.

Refitting

11 Refitting is a reversal of removal; tighten all nuts and bolts to the specified torque where given. Bleed the brake hydraulic system and adjust the handbrake cables as described in Chapter 9.

14 Steering wheel - removal and refitting

 Warning: For safety reasons, owners are strongly advised to entrust to an authorised FIAT dealer any work which involves disturbing the airbag system components. The airbag inflation devices contain explosive material and legislation exists to control their handling and storage. In addition, specialised test equipment is needed to check that the airbag system is fully operational following reassembly. The following information is given for the home mechanic who may have access to the necessary equipment and storage.

Removal

1 Disconnect the battery negative (earth) lead (see *Disconnecting the battery*). **Note:** *The ignition must be switched off before*

14.3 Disconnect the horn wiring (white) from the base of the steering wheel

14.6 Unscrew and remove the steering wheel securing nut

14.7 Feed the airbag clockspring and horn wires through the hole when removing the steering wheel

disconnecting the battery leads, then it is important to wait 10 minutes before removing the driver's air bag.

2 Remove the driver's airbag with reference to Chapter 12.

3 Disconnect the horn wiring (white) from the base of the steering wheel **(see illustration)**.

4 Turn the steering wheel to its centre position, so that the roadwheels are pointing straight ahead.

5 Make alignment marks between the steering wheel and the end of the steering column shaft, to aid correct refitting later.

6 Unscrew and remove the steering wheel securing nut **(see illustration)**.

7 Remove the steering wheel from the inner column splines, while feeding the airbag clockspring and horn wires through the hole **(see illustration)**. If the steering wheel is tight, rock it from side to side whilst pulling upwards to release it from the shaft splines. If the wheel is particularly tight, a suitable puller should be used. **Do not** strike the steering wheel.

Refitting

8 Refitting is a reversal of removal, but align the previously made marks, and tighten the securing nut to the specified torque. Make sure that the clockspring wires are pulled completely through the hole in the base of the steering wheel, otherwise they may jam against the plastic location tabs on the clockspring and break them. This would require the renewal of the clockspring.

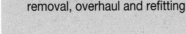

15 Steering column -
removal, overhaul and refitting

Removal

1 Refer to Section 14 and remove the steering wheel.

2 Remove the airbag clockspring unit from the column with reference to Chapter 12. **Note:** *The clockspring incorporates spring tensioned clips which prevent the upper and lower sections of the unit from turning in relation to each other when removed from the column.*

3 Undo the screws and remove the lower steering column shroud, then remove the upper shroud.

4 Remove the combination switch as described in Chapter 12, Section 14.

5 Undo the screws and remove the left foot rest located next to the clutch pedal.

6 At the bottom of the steering column, unscrew and remove the clamp bolt attaching the universal joint to the steering gear pinion shaft **(see illustration)**.

7 Disconnect the wiring plug from the ignition switch.

8 Unclip and remove the lower fusebox trim panel located beneath the right-hand side of the facia.

9 Unbolt the steering column support bar **(see illustration)**.

10 Support the steering column, then unscrew and remove the upper mounting bolts and lower it from the bulkhead **(see illustration)**. Lift the steering column and release the lower universal joint from the steering gear pinion. Note that the pinion has a master spline.

11 Withdraw the steering column from inside the vehicle.

Overhaul

12 The height adjustment mechanism can be removed by removing the nut from the end of the pivot shaft and withdrawing it.

13 The upper and lower bushes are held in position by staking at the ends of the column tube. Relieve the staking using a mallet and punch to extract the bushes.

14 Check for excessive radial and axial play in the universal joints at both ends of the lower steering column. The lower section of the steering column may be renewed separately if required, by slackening the clamp bolt and detaching it from the upper section.

15 If the vehicle has been involved in an accident, check for deformation in all of the steering column components, particularly the mounting bracket and centre tube. Renew as required.

Refitting

16 Refitting is a reversal of removal. Tighten all fixings to the specified torque setting.

15.6 The clamp bolt attaching the steering column universal joint to the steering gear pinion shaft

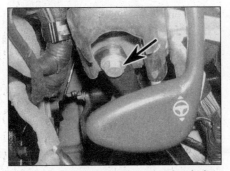

15.9 Steering column support bar bolt

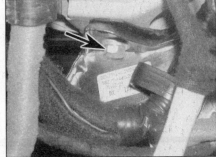

15.10 Steering column upper mounting bolt

16.3 Disconnecting the ignition switch wiring

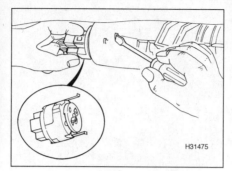

16.4 Depress the two plastic tabs to remove the ignition switch

17.4a With the ignition key in the 'ignition on' position, depress the lug with a screwdriver . . .

16 Ignition switch - removal and refitting

Removal

1 Disconnect the battery negative (earth) lead (see *Disconnecting the battery*), and remove the ignition key from the switch.
2 Undo the screws and remove the lower steering column shroud.
3 Disconnect the ignition switch wiring at the connector beneath the facia **(see illustration)**.
4 Depress the two plastic tabs, using a screwdriver in the lock housing holes, and pull the switch from the steering lock housing **(see illustration)**.

Refitting

5 Refitting is a reversal of removal, but make sure that the ignition key is removed when the switch is inserted in the steering lock housing.

17 Steering column lock and barrel - removal and refitting

Removal

1 Disconnect the battery negative (earth) lead (see *Disconnecting the battery*). Remove the ignition key.
2 Undo the screws and remove the lower

steering column shroud, then undo the screws and remove the upper shroud.
3 Insert the ignition key and turn it to the 'ignition on' position.
4 Using a screwdriver, depress the retaining lug located on the side of the switch housing, then use the key to withdraw the lock and barrel from the housing **(see illustrations)**.
5 With the assembly on the bench, extract the circlip holding the barrel in the lock **(see illustration)**.
6 Depress the parking light button on the lock and turn the ignition key fully anticlockwise (key in the parking light position).
7 Pull out the key approximately 2 or 3 mm so that the retaining tab is released, then withdraw the barrel from the lock **(see illustration)**.
8 To remove the lock housing, use a pin punch to unscrew the shear bolts, then withdraw the housing from the steering column. New shear bolts must be obtained for refitting.

Refitting

9 Locate the lock housing on the steering column, and insert the new shear bolts. Hand-tighten the bolts at this stage.
10 Reassemble the barrel to the lock using a reversal of the dismantling procedure. Before reconnecting the battery negative lead, check that the ignition key can be turned to all positions, then remove the key and check that the steering lock works correctly. Tighten the lock housing shear bolts until their heads are

broken off, then refit the shrouds and reconnect the battery negative lead.

18 Manual steering gear assembly - removal and refitting

Removal

1 Apply the handbrake, then jack up the front of the vehicle and support it on axle stands (see *Jacking and vehicle support*). Remove both front roadwheels.
2 Inside the car, unscrew and remove the clamp bolt at the base of steering column lower universal joint.
3 In the engine compartment, disconnect the link from the gearchange.
4 Unscrew the nuts from the track-rod ends on each side, then use a balljoint removal tool to separate the track-rod ends from the steering arms on the hub carriers.
5 Prise the gear selector rod from the top of the steering gear.
6 Unscrew and remove the steering gear mounting bolts. Withdraw the steering gear through the wheel arch on one side of the car.

Refitting

7 Refitting is a reversal of removal, but tighten all nuts and bolts to the specified torque where given. On completion, have the front wheel alignment checked by a FIAT dealer or tyre specialist.

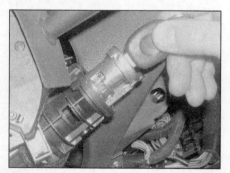

17.4b . . . and withdraw the lock and barrel from the housing

17.5 Extract the circlip holding the barrel in the lock . . .

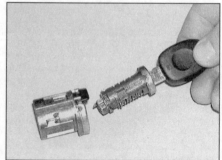

17.7 . . . and withdraw the barrel from the lock

19 Power steering gear assembly - removal and refitting

Removal

1 Apply the handbrake, then jack up the front of the vehicle and support it on axle stands (see *Jacking and vehicle support*). Remove both front roadwheels.
2 Disconnect the battery negative (earth) lead (see *Disconnecting the battery*).
3 Syphon as much fluid as possible from the power steering reservoir, using a pipette or an old poultry baster. Alternatively, fit a hose clamp to the hose leading to the steering gear.
4 Undo the screws and remove the foot rest located next to the clutch pedal.
5 Unscrew and remove the clamp bolt at the base of the steering column, to release the lower universal joint from the steering gear pinion.
6 Unscrew the nuts from the track-rod ends on each side, then use a balljoint removal tool to separate the track-rod ends from the steering arms on the hub carriers.
7 Disconnect the gearchange socket from the ball on the transmission lever, then pull up the clip and disconnect the gearchange outer cable. Position it to one side.
8 Where applicable, disconnect the reverse inhibition wiring from the retaining clip on top of the transmission.
9 On the front of the engine, disconnect the oxygen sensor wiring, then unbolt the exhaust bracket from the cylinder block. Remove the front exhaust downpipe by unscrewing the nuts securing it to the exhaust manifold, and also unscrewing the bolts securing it to the catalytic converter (see Chapter 4C).
10 Support the engine using a trolley jack and piece of wood beneath the sump, then unbolt and remove the rear engine mounting from the transmission and underbody.
11 From under the engine, prise off the gearchange from the transmission mounting.
12 Position a container beneath the steering gear, then unscrew the nut and bolts and detach the hydraulic fluid line support brackets from the subframe and steering gear.
13 Note the location of the hydraulic fluid supply and return lines, then unscrew the union nuts and disconnect the lines from the steering gear **(see illustration)**. Recover the sealing washers. Plug the ends of the lines to prevent loss of fluid.
14 Unscrew and remove the two bolts securing the steering gear to the subframe. Lower the steering gear and disconnect the splined pinion shaft from the bottom of the column universal joint. Note that the pinion shaft has a master spline to ensure it is only fitted in one position.
15 Move the complete steering gear to the

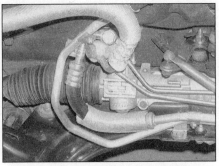

19.13 Hydraulic fluid supply and return lines on the power steering gear

left, then withdraw it downwards from the engine compartment.

Refitting

16 Refitting is a reversal of removal with reference to Chapter 4C where necessary, but tighten the nuts and bolts to the specified torque where given. Refill the hydraulic system with the specified grade and quantity of power steering fluid, then bleed the hydraulic system as described in Section 21. On completion, have the front wheel alignment checked at the earliest opportunity by a FIAT dealer or a tyre specialist.

20 Steering gear rubber gaiters - renewal

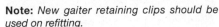

Note: *New gaiter retaining clips should be used on refitting.*

1 Remove the relevant track-rod end as described in Section 23.
2 If not already done, unscrew the track-rod end locknut from the end of the track-rod, but measure the distance from the locknut to the end of the track-rod before removing it.
3 Mark the fitted position of the gaiter on the track-rod, then release the gaiter securing clips. Slide the gaiter from the steering gear, and off the end of the track-rod. Note that on manual steering gear models, it will be necessary to unscrew the nuts and remove the damper and rack bracket for access to the inner gaiter.
4 Thoroughly clean the track-rod and the steering gear housing. Scrape off all the grease from the old gaiter, and apply it to the track-rod inner balljoint. This assumes that grease has not been lost or contaminated as a result of damage to the old gaiter. Use fresh grease if in doubt.
5 Carefully slide the new gaiter onto the track-rod, and locate it on the steering gear housing. Align the outer edge of the gaiter with the mark made on the track-rod prior to removal, then secure it in position with new retaining clips.
6 Screw the track-rod end locknut onto the end of the track-rod.
7 Refit the track-rod end as described in Section 23.

21.3 Power steering hydraulic fluid reservoir at the rear of the engine compartment

21 Power steering hydraulic system - bleeding

General

1 The following symptoms indicate that there is air present in the power steering hydraulic system:
a) *Generation of air bubbles in fluid reservoir.*
b) *Clicking noises from power steering pump.*
c) *Excessive 'buzzing' or 'groaning' from power steering pump.*
2 Note that when the vehicle is stationary, or while moving the steering wheel slowly, a 'hissing' noise may be produced in the steering gear or the fluid pump. This noise is inherent in the system, and does not indicate any cause for concern.

Bleeding

3 Unscrew the filler cap from the power steering fluid reservoir **(see illustration)**, and check that the fluid level is up to the MAX mark on the dipstick. If necessary, top-up the fluid level.
4 Start the engine and allow it to idle.
5 Have an assistant turn the steering from lock to lock, while you observe the fluid level. If the fluid level drops, add more fluid, and repeat the operation until the fluid level no longer drops and there are no visible air bubbles in the fluid.
6 With the fluid level correct, refit and tighten the filler cap.

22 Power steering pump - removal and refitting

Removal

1.2 litre models

1 The power steering pump is located on the front right-hand side of the engine, and is belt-driven from the crankshaft pulley. First, apply the handbrake, then jack up the front of the vehicle and support it on axle stands (see

22.22 Removing the guard from over the power steering pump drivebelt

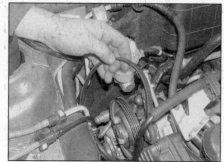

22.24 Removing the drivebelt

22.26a Unscrew the upper pivot bolt . . .

Jacking and vehicle support). Remove the front right-hand roadwheel.

2 Remove the splash guard for access to the power steering pump.

3 Unbolt the shield from over the power steering pump pulley.

4 Loosen the lower lock/pivot bolt securing the pump to the adjustment plate, then back off the adjustment bolt and remove the drivebelt.

5 Drain as much fluid as possible from the power steering fluid reservoir, using a pipette or an old poultry baster. Alternatively, fit a hose clamp to the hydraulic hose leading from the reservoir to the pump.

6 Loosen the clip and disconnect the supply hose from the top of the pump.

7 Unscrew the union nut and disconnect the steering gear pressure supply line from the pump.

8 Unscrew the upper and lower mounting bolts and withdraw the power steering pump from its bracket on the front of the engine.

1.4 litre models

9 Apply the handbrake, then jack up the front of the vehicle and support it on axle stands (see *Jacking and vehicle support*). Remove the right-hand front roadwheel.

10 Drain as much fluid as possible from the power steering fluid reservoir, using a pipette or an old poultry baster. Alternatively, fit a hose clamp to the hydraulic hose leading from the reservoir to the pump.

11 Loosen the clips and remove the air intake

pipe from between the air cleaner and the throttle housing body.

12 From the right-hand side of the engine, unbolt and remove the guard from over the auxiliary drivebelt.

13 Loosen the clip and disconnect the reservoir hose from the pump. Position a suitable container beneath the pump to catch spilled fluid.

14 Unscrew the union nut and disconnect the steering gear pressure supply line from the pump.

15 Remove the fasteners and remove the wheel arch liner from the right-hand side.

16 Loosen the bolts securing the pulley to the power steering pump.

17 Remove the auxiliary drivebelt with reference to Chapter 1.

18 Fully unscrew the bolts and remove the pulley from the pump.

19 Unscrew the mounting bolts and remove the pump.

1.6 litre models

20 Drain as much fluid as possible from the power steering reservoir, using a pipette or an old poultry baster. Alternatively, fit a hose clamp to the hydraulic hose leading from the reservoir to the pump.

21 Release the clips and remove the alternator cooling pipe from the right-hand side of the engine compartment.

22 Unbolt and remove the plastic guard from over the power steering pump drivebelt on the

right-hand side of the engine **(see illustration)**.

23 If necessary, the pulley retaining bolts may be loosened at this stage, and the pulley removed after removing the drivebelt.

24 Loosen the power steering pump pulley bolts, then loosen the locknut and back off the adjustment bolt. Swivel the pump to release the tension, then remove the drivebelt **(see illustration)**.

25 Place a container beneath the pump, then loosen the clip and disconnect the inlet hose from the pump. Unscrew the union nut and disconnect the outlet pressure line from the pump.

26 If the pulley has already been removed, unscrew and remove the mounting bolts and remove the pump from the mounting bracket. Alternatively, unscrew the lower pivot bolt and upper adjustment lock bolt, and remove the pump together with the mounting bracket **(see illustrations)**. Note that the upper bolt also secures the engine lifting eye.

1.8 litre models

27 Apply the handbrake, then jack up the front of the vehicle and support it on axle stands (see *Jacking and vehicle support*). Remove the right-hand front roadwheel.

28 Drain as much fluid as possible from the power steering reservoir, using a pipette or an old poultry baster. Alternatively, fit a hose clamp to the hydraulic hose leading from the reservoir to the pump.

22.26b . . . and lower pivot bolt . . .

22.26c . . . and withdraw the power steering pump from the engine together with the mounting bracket

22.26d Power steering pump

23.2a Balljoint separator tool in use on the track-rod end

23.2b Separate the track-rod end from the steering arm

23.3 Counterhold the track-rod end, then loosen the locknut (arrowed)

29 Loosen the power steering pump pulley bolts.
30 Remove the fasteners and remove the wheel arch liner from the right-hand side.
31 Remove the auxiliary drivebelt with reference to Chapter 1.
32 Fully unscrew the bolts and remove the pulley from the pump.
33 Unbolt the engine support mounting link from the right-hand side of the engine, then unbolt the link bracket from the body.
34 Disconnect the wiring connector and earth wire from over the power steering pump.
35 Loosen the clip and disconnect the reservoir hose from the pump. Position a suitable container beneath the pump to catch spilled fluid.
36 Unscrew the union nut and disconnect the steering gear pressure supply line from the pump.
37 Working beneath the car, unbolt the inlet manifold support bracket from the rear of the engine.
38 Unbolt the alternator mounting bracket from the rear of the engine.
39 Unscrew the mounting bolts and remove the pump.

Refitting

40 Refitting is a reversal of removal, but tighten the nuts and bolts to the specified torque where given. Refill the hydraulic system with the specified grade and quantity of power steering fluid, then bleed the hydraulic system as described in Section 21. Adjust the tension of the power steering pump drivebelt as described in Chapter 1.

23 Track-rod end - removal and refitting

Removal

Note: *A balljoint separator tool will be required for this operation. A new track-rod end nut split pin should be used on refitting.*
1 Apply the handbrake, then jack up the front of the vehicle and support it on axle stands

(see *Jacking and vehicle support*). Remove the relevant front roadwheel.
2 Unscrew the nut securing the track-rod end to the steering arm on the hub carrier. Using a balljoint separator tool, separate the track-rod end from the steering arm **(see illustrations)**.
3 Counterhold the track-rod end using the flats provided, then loosen the track-rod end locknut a quarter turn **(see illustration)**.
4 Unscrew the track-rod end from the track-rod, counting the exact number of turns required to do so. If necessary, mark the relationship between the track-rod end and the track-rod using a dab of paint.

Refitting

5 Check the track-rod end rubber boot for damage, and if necessary obtain a new one. Renew the track-rod end if the movement of the balljoint is either sloppy or too stiff. Also check for other signs of damage such as worn threads.
6 Carefully clean the track-rod end and the track-rod threads.
7 Screw the track-rod end onto the track-rod by the number of turns noted before removal. Tighten the locknut.
8 Ensure that the balljoint taper is clean, then engage the taper in the steering arm on the hub carrier.
9 Refit the balljoint nut, and tighten to the specified torque.
10 Refit the roadwheel, and lower the vehicle to the ground.
11 Have the front wheel alignment checked by a FIAT dealer or tyre specialist at the earliest opportunity.

24 Wheel alignment and steering angles - general information

General information

1 A car's steering and suspension geometry is defined in four basic settings; camber, castor, steering axis inclination, and toe-setting. With the exception of toe setting, all angles are expressed in degrees and are not adjustable. Toe-setting is adjustable.

Front wheel toe setting

Checking

2 Due to the special measuring equipment necessary to check the wheel alignment, and the skill required to use it properly, the checking and adjustment of these settings is best left to a FIAT dealer or similar expert. Most tyre-fitting shops now possess sophisticated checking equipment.
3 For accurate checking, the vehicle must be at the kerb weight specified in *Dimensions and weights*.
4 Before starting work, check first that the tyre sizes and types are as specified, then check tyre pressures and tread wear. Also check roadwheel run-out, the condition of the hub bearings, the steering wheel free play and the condition of the front suspension components (Chapter 1). Correct any faults found.
5 Park the vehicle on level ground, with the front roadwheels in the straight-ahead position. Rock the rear and front ends to settle the suspension. Release the handbrake and roll the vehicle backwards approximately 1 metre, then forwards again, to relieve any stresses in the steering and suspension components.
6 Two methods are available to the home mechanic for checking the front wheel toe setting. One method is to use a gauge to measure the distance between the front and rear inside edges of the roadwheels. The other method is to use a scuff plate, in which each front wheel is rolled across a movable plate which records any deviation, or scuff, of the tyre from the straight-ahead position as it moves across the plate. Such gauges are available in relatively-inexpensive form from accessory outlets. It is up to the owner to decide whether the expense is justified, in view of the small amount of use such equipment would normally receive.
7 Prepare the vehicle as described in paragraphs 3 to 5 above.
8 If the measurement procedure is being used, carefully measure the distance between the front edges of the roadwheel rims and the rear edges of the rims. Subtract the front measurement from the rear measurement,

and check that the result is within the specified range. If not, adjust the toe setting as described in paragraph 10.

9 If scuff plates are to be used, roll the vehicle backwards, check that the road-wheels are in the straight-ahead position, then roll it across the scuff plates so that each front roadwheel passes squarely over the centre of its respective plate. Note the angle recorded by the scuff plates. To ensure accuracy, repeat the check three times, and take the average of the three readings. If the roadwheels are running parallel, there will of course be no angle recorded; if a deviation value is shown on the scuff plates, compare the reading obtained for each wheel with that supplied by the scuff plate manufacturers. If the value recorded is outside the specified tolerance, the toe setting is incorrect, and must be adjusted as follows.

Adjustment

10 Apply the handbrake, then jack up the front of the vehicle and support it securely on axle stands (see *Jacking and vehicle support*). Turn the steering wheel onto full-left lock, and record the number of exposed threads on the right-hand track-rod. Now turn the steering onto full-right lock, and record the number of threads on the left-hand side. If there are the same number of threads visible on both sides, then subsequent adjustment should be made equally on both sides. If there are more threads visible on one side than the other, it will be necessary to compensate for this during adjustment. **Note:** *It is important to ensure that, after adjustment, the same number of threads are visible on the end of each track rod.*

11 First clean the track-rod threads; if they are corroded, apply penetrating fluid before starting adjustment. Release the steering gear rubber gaiter outboard clips, then peel back the gaiters and apply a smear of grease, so that both gaiters are free and will not be twisted or strained as their respective track-rods are rotated.

12 Use a straight-edge and a scriber or similar to mark the relationship of each track-rod to the track-rod end. Working on each track-rod end in turn, unscrew its locking nut.

13 Alter the length of the track-rods, bearing in mind the note in paragraph 10, by screwing them into or out of the track-rod ends. Rotate the track-rod using an open-ended spanner fitted to the flats provided. If necessary, counterhold the track-rod end using a second spanner. Shortening the track-rods (screwing them into their track-rod ends) will reduce toe-in and increase toe-out.

14 When the setting is correct, hold the track-rods and securely tighten the locking nuts. Check that the balljoints are seated correctly in their sockets, and count the exposed threads on the ends of the track-rods. If the number of threads exposed is not the same on both sides, then the adjustment has not been made equally, and problems will be encountered with tyre scrubbing in turns; also, the steering wheel spokes will no longer be horizontal when the wheels are in the straight-ahead position.

15 When the track-rod lengths are the same, lower the vehicle to the ground and re-check the toe setting; readjust if necessary. When the setting is correct, tighten the locking nuts. Ensure that the steering gear rubber gaiters are seated correctly and are not twisted or strained, then secure them in position with the retaining clips.

Chapter 11
Bodywork and fittings

Contents

Degrees of difficulty

| Easy, suitable for novice with little experience | Fairly easy, suitable for beginner with some experience | Fairly difficult, suitable for competent DIY mechanic | Difficult, suitable for experienced DIY mechanic | Very difficult, suitable for expert DIY or professional |

Specifications

Torque wrench settings	Nm	lbf ft
Bumper	20	15
Door hinge centre bolt	15	11
Door hinge-to-door bolt	45	33
Front seat belt pre-tensioner and reel	40	30
Front seat belt pre-tensioner shear bolt	4	3

1 General information

The bodyshell is composed of pressed-steel sections which are welded together, although some use of structural adhesives is made. In addition, the front wings are bolted on.

The bonnet, door and some other panels vulnerable to corrosion are fabricated from zinc-coated metal. A coating of anti-chip primer, applied prior to paint spraying provides further protection.

Extensive use is made of plastic materials, mainly in the interior, but also in exterior components. The outer sections of the front and rear bumpers are injection-moulded from a synthetic material which is very strong, and yet light. Plastic components such as wheel arch liners are fitted to the underside of the

2 Maintenance - bodywork and underframe

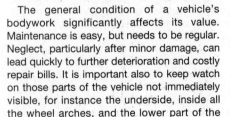

The general condition of a vehicle's bodywork significantly affects its value. Maintenance is easy, but needs to be regular. Neglect, particularly after minor damage, can lead quickly to further deterioration and costly repair bills. It is important also to keep watch on those parts of the vehicle not immediately visible, for instance the underside, inside all the wheel arches, and the lower part of the engine compartment.

The basic maintenance routine for the bodywork is washing - preferably with a lot of water, from a hose. This will remove all the loose solids which may have stuck to the

vehicle, to improve the body's resistance to corrosion.

vehicle. It is important to flush these off in such a way as to prevent grit from scratching the finish. The wheel arches and underframe need washing in the same way, to remove any accumulated mud which will retain moisture and tend to encourage rust. Oddly enough, the best time to clean the underframe and wheel arches is in wet weather, when the mud is thoroughly wet and soft. In very wet weather, the underframe is usually cleaned of large accumulations automatically, and this is a good time for inspection.

Periodically, except on vehicles with a wax-based underbody protective coating, it is a good idea to have the whole of the underframe of the vehicle steam-cleaned, engine compartment included, so that a thorough inspection can be carried out to see what minor repairs and renovations are necessary. Steam-cleaning is available at many garages, and is necessary for the removal of the accumulation of oily grime, which sometimes is allowed to become thick in certain areas. If steam-cleaning facilities are not available, there are some excellent grease solvents available, which can be brush-applied; the dirt can then be simply hosed off. Note that these methods should not be used on vehicles with wax-based underbody protective coating, or the coating will be removed. Such vehicles should be inspected annually, preferably just prior to Winter, when the underbody should be washed down, and any damage to the wax coating repaired using undershield. Ideally, a completely fresh coat should be applied. It would also be worth considering the use of such wax-based protection for injection into door panels, sills, box sections, etc, as an additional safeguard against rust damage, where such protection is not provided by the vehicle manufacturer.

After washing paintwork, wipe off with a chamois leather to give an unspotted clear finish. A coat of clear protective wax polish, will give added protection against chemical pollutants in the air. If the paintwork sheen has dulled or oxidised, use a cleaner/polisher combination to restore the brilliance of the shine. This requires a little effort, but such dulling is usually caused because regular washing has been neglected. Care needs to be taken with metallic paintwork, as special non-abrasive cleaner/polisher is required to avoid damage to the finish. Always check that the door and ventilator opening drain holes and pipes are completely clear, so that water can be drained out. Brightwork should be treated in the same way as paintwork. Windscreens and windows can be kept clear of the smeary film which often appears, by the use of a proprietary glass cleaner. Never use any form of wax or other body or chromium polish on glass.

3 Maintenance - upholstery and carpets

Mats and carpets should be brushed or vacuum-cleaned regularly, to keep them free of grit. If they are badly stained, remove them from the vehicle for scrubbing or sponging, and make quite sure they are dry before refitting. Seats and interior trim panels can be kept clean by wiping with a damp cloth and specialist cleaner. If they do become stained (which can be more apparent on light-coloured upholstery), use a little liquid detergent and a soft nail brush to scour the grime out of the grain of the material. Do not forget to keep the headlining clean in the same way as the upholstery. When using liquid cleaners inside the vehicle, do not over-wet the surfaces being cleaned. Excessive damp could get into the seams and padded interior, causing stains, offensive odours or even rot. If the inside of the vehicle gets wet accidentally, it is worthwhile taking some trouble to dry it out properly, particularly where carpets are involved. *Do not leave oil or electric heaters inside the vehicle for this purpose.*

4 Minor body damage - repair

Repairs of minor scratches in bodywork

If the scratch is very superficial, and does not penetrate to the metal of the bodywork, repair is very simple. Lightly rub the area of the scratch with a paintwork renovator, or a very fine cutting paste, to remove loose paint from the scratch, and to clear the surrounding bodywork of wax polish. Rinse the area with clean water.

Apply touch-up paint to the scratch using a fine paint brush; continue to apply fine layers of paint until the surface of the paint in the scratch is level with the surrounding paintwork. Allow the new paint at least two weeks to harden, then blend it into the surrounding paintwork by rubbing the scratch area with a paintwork renovator or a very fine cutting paste. Finally, apply wax polish.

Where the scratch has penetrated right through to the metal of the bodywork, causing the metal to rust, a different repair technique is required. Remove any loose rust from the bottom of the scratch with a penknife, then apply rust-inhibiting paint to prevent the formation of rust in the future. Using a rubber or nylon applicator, fill the scratch with bodystopper paste. If required, this paste can be mixed with cellulose thinners, to provide a very thin paste which is ideal for filling narrow scratches. Before the stopper-paste in the scratch hardens, wrap a piece of smooth cotton rag around the top of a finger. Dip the finger in cellulose thinners, and quickly sweep it across the surface of the stopper-paste in the scratch; this will ensure that the surface of the stopper-paste is slightly hollowed. The scratch can now be painted over as described earlier in this Section.

Repairs of dents in bodywork

When deep denting of the vehicle's bodywork has taken place, the first task is to pull the dent out, until the affected bodywork almost attains its original shape. There is little point in trying to restore the original shape completely, as the metal in the damaged area will have stretched on impact, and cannot be reshaped fully to its original contour. It is better to bring the level of the dent up to a point which is about 3 mm below the level of the surrounding bodywork. In cases where the dent is very shallow anyway, it is not worth trying to pull it out at all. If the underside of the dent is accessible, it can be hammered out gently from behind, using a mallet with a wooden or plastic head. Whilst doing this, hold a suitable block of wood firmly against the outside of the panel, to absorb the impact from the hammer blows and thus prevent a large area of the bodywork from being 'belled-out'.

Should the dent be in a section of the bodywork which has a double skin, or some other factor making it inaccessible from behind, a different technique is called for. Drill several small holes through the metal inside the area - particularly in the deeper section. Then screw long self-tapping screws into the holes, just sufficiently for them to gain a good purchase in the metal. Now the dent can be pulled out by pulling on the protruding heads of the screws with a pair of pliers.

The next stage of the repair is the removal of the paint from the damaged area, and from an inch or so of the surrounding 'sound' bodywork. This is accomplished most easily by using a wire brush or abrasive pad on a power drill, although it can be done just as effectively by hand, using sheets of abrasive paper. To complete the preparation for filling, score the surface of the bare metal with a screwdriver or the tang of a file, or alternatively, drill small holes in the affected area. This will provide a really good 'key' for the filler paste.

To complete the repair, see the Section on filling and respraying.

Repairs of rust holes or gashes in bodywork

Remove all paint from the affected area, and from an inch or so of the surrounding 'sound' bodywork, using an abrasive pad or a wire brush on a power drill. If these are not available, a few sheets of abrasive paper will do the job most effectively. With the paint removed, you will be able to judge the severity of the corrosion, and therefore decide whether to renew the whole panel (if this is possible) or to repair the affected area. New body panels are not as expensive as most people think, and it is often quicker and more satisfactory to fit a new panel than to attempt to repair large areas of corrosion.

Remove all fittings from the affected area, except those which will act as a guide to the original shape of the damaged bodywork (eg headlight shells, etc). Then, using tin snips or a hacksaw blade, remove all loose metal and any other metal badly affected by corrosion. Hammer the edges of the hole inwards, in order to create a slight depression for the filler paste.

Wire-brush the affected area to remove the powdery rust from the surface of the remaining metal. Paint the affected area with rust-inhibiting paint; if the back of the rusted area is accessible, treat this also.

Before filling can take place, it will be necessary to block the hole in some way. This can be achieved by the use of aluminium or plastic mesh, or aluminium tape.

Aluminium or plastic mesh, or glass-fibre matting, is probably the best material to use for a large hole. Cut a piece to the approximate size and shape of the hole to be filled, then position it in the hole so that its edges are below the level of the surrounding bodywork. It can be retained in position by several blobs of filler paste around its periphery.

Aluminium tape should be used for small or very narrow holes. Pull a piece off the roll, trim it to the approximate size and shape required, then pull off the backing paper (if used) and stick the tape over the hole; it can be overlapped if the thickness of one piece is insufficient. Burnish down the edges of the tape with the handle of a screwdriver or similar, to ensure that the tape is securely attached to the metal underneath.

Bodywork repairs - filling and respraying

Before using this Section, see the Sections on dents, scratches, rust holes and gash repairs.

Many types of bodyfiller are available, but generally speaking, those proprietary kits which contain a tin of filler paste and a tube of resin hardener are best for this type of repair, which can be used directly from the tube. A wide, flexible plastic or nylon applicator will be found invaluable for imparting a smooth and well-contoured finish to the surface of the filler.

Mix up a little filler on a clean piece of card or board - measure the hardener carefully (follow the maker's instructions on the pack), otherwise the filler will set too rapidly or too slowly. Alternatively, a 'no-mix' filler can be used straight from the tube without mixing, but daylight is required to cure it. Using the applicator, apply the filler paste to the prepared area; draw the applicator across the surface of the filler to achieve the correct contour and to level the surface. As soon as a contour that approximates to the correct one is achieved, stop working the paste - if you carry on too long, the paste will become sticky and begin to 'pick-up' on the applicator. Continue to add thin layers of filler paste at 20-minute intervals, until the level of the filler is just proud of the surrounding bodywork.

Once the filler has hardened, the excess can be removed using a metal plane or file. From then on, progressively-finer grades of abrasive paper should be used, starting with a 40-grade production paper, and finishing with a 400-grade wet-and-dry paper. Always wrap the abrasive paper around a flat rubber, cork, or wooden block - otherwise the surface of the filler will not be completely flat. During the smoothing of the filler surface, the wet-and-dry paper should be periodically rinsed in water. This will ensure that a very smooth finish is imparted to the filler at the final stage.

At this stage, the 'dent' should be surrounded by a ring of bare metal, which in turn should be encircled by the finely 'feathered' edge of the good paintwork. Rinse the repair area with clean water, until all of the dust produced by the rubbing-down operation has gone.

Spray the whole area with a light coat of primer - this will show up any imperfections in the surface of the filler. Repair these imperfections with fresh filler paste or bodystopper, and once more smooth the surface with abrasive paper. If bodystopper is used, it can be mixed with cellulose thinners, to form a really thin paste which is ideal for filling small holes. Repeat this spray-and-repair procedure until you are satisfied that the surface of the filler, and the feathered edge of the paintwork, are perfect. Clean the repair area with clean water, and allow to dry fully.

The repair area is now ready for final spraying. Paint spraying must be carried out in a warm, dry, windless and dust-free atmosphere. This condition can be created artificially if you have access to a large indoor working area, but if you are forced to work in the open, you will have to pick your day very carefully. If you are working indoors, dousing the floor in the work area with water will help to settle the dust which would otherwise be in the atmosphere. If the repair area is confined to one body panel, mask off the surrounding panels; this will help to minimise the effects of a slight mis-match in paint colours. Bodywork fittings (eg chrome strips, door handles etc) will also need to be masked off. Use genuine masking tape, and several thicknesses of newspaper, for the masking operations.

Before commencing to spray, agitate the aerosol can thoroughly, then spray a test area (an old tin, or similar) until the technique is mastered. Cover the repair area with a thick coat of primer; the thickness should be built up using several thin layers of paint, rather than one thick one. Using 400-grade wet-and-dry paper, rub down the surface of the primer until it is really smooth. While doing this, the work area should be thoroughly doused with water, and the wet-and-dry paper periodically rinsed in water. Allow to dry before spraying on more paint.

Spray on the top coat, again building up the thickness by using several thin layers of paint. Start spraying at the top of the repair area, and then, using a side-to-side motion, work downwards until the whole repair area and about 2 inches of the surrounding original paintwork is covered. Remove all masking material 10 to 15 minutes after spraying on the final coat of paint.

Allow the new paint at least two weeks to harden, then, using a paintwork renovator or a very fine cutting paste, blend the edges of the paint into the existing paintwork. Finally, apply wax polish.

Plastic components

With the use of more and more plastic body components by the vehicle manufacturers (eg bumpers. spoilers, and in some cases major body panels), rectification of more serious damage to such items has become a matter of either entrusting repair work to a specialist in this field, or renewing complete components. Repair of such damage by the DIY owner is not really feasible, owing to the cost of the equipment and materials required for effecting such repairs. The basic technique involves making a groove along the line of the crack in the plastic, using a rotary burr in a power drill. The damaged part is then welded back together, using a hot air gun to heat up and fuse a plastic filler rod into the groove. Any excess plastic is then removed, and the area rubbed down to a smooth finish. It is important that a filler rod of the correct plastic is used, as body components can be made of a variety of different types (eg polycarbonate, ABS, polypropylene).

Damage of a less serious nature (abrasions, minor cracks etc) can be repaired by the DIY owner using a two-part epoxy filler repair material, Once mixed in equal proportions, this is used in similar fashion to the bodywork filler used on metal panels. The filler is usually cured in twenty to thirty minutes, ready for sanding and painting.

If the owner is renewing a complete component himself, or if he has repaired it with epoxy filler, he will be left with the problem of finding a suitable paint for finishing which is compatible with the type of plastic used. At one time, the use of a universal paint was not possible, owing to the complex range of plastics encountered in body component applications. Standard paints, generally speaking, will not bond to plastic or rubber satisfactorily, but specialist paints, to match any plastic or rubber finish, can be obtained from dealers. However, it is now possible to obtain a plastic body parts finishing kit which consists of a pre-primer treatment, a primer and coloured top coat. Full instructions are normally supplied with a kit, but basically, the method of use is to first apply the pre-primer to the component concerned, and allow it to dry for up to 30 minutes. Then the primer is applied, and left to dry for about an hour before finally applying the special-coloured top coat. The result is a correctly-coloured component, where the paint will flex with the plastic or rubber, a property that standard paint does not normally posses.

5 Major body damage - repair

Where serious damage has occurred, or large areas need renewal due to neglect, it means that complete new panels will need welding-in, and this is best left to professionals. If the damage is due to impact, it will also be necessary to check completely the alignment of the bodyshell, and this can only be carried out accurately by a FIAT dealer using special jigs. If the alignment of the bodyshell is not corrected, the car's handling may be seriously affected. In addition, excessive stress may be imposed on the steering, suspension, tyres or transmission, causing abnormal wear or even complete failure.

6.3 Front bumper upper mounting bolts

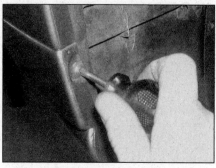

6.4a Undo the screws and remove the fixing studs . . .

6.4b . . . then remove the front sections of the wheel arch liners

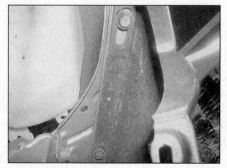

6.5 Front bumper side mounting bolts

6.6 Unscrewing the front bumper lower mounting bolts

6.7 Removing the front bumper

6 Front bumper - removal and refitting

Removal

1 To improve access, apply the handbrake, then jack up the front of the vehicle and support it on axle stands (see *Jacking and vehicle support*). If necessary, remove both front roadwheels.

2 Where applicable, remove the front foglights with reference to Chapter 12, Section 6.

3 Unscrew the bumper upper mounting bolts located on the upper panel in front of the radiator **(see illustration)**.

4 Undo the screws and extract the fixing studs, then remove the front sections of the wheel arch liners for access to the front bumper mounting bolts **(see illustrations)**. Ideally, a forked tool should be used to remove the studs.

5 Unscrew the bumper side mounting bolts **(see illustration)**.

6 Unscrew the lower mounting bolts located along the bottom edge of the bumper **(see illustration)**.

7 With the help of an assistant, withdraw the bumper from the front of the car **(see illustration)**. Where applicable, disconnect the washer tubing and remove the headlight washer jets as described in Chapter 12, Section 17.

Refitting

8 Refitting is a reversal of removal.

7 Rear bumper - removal and refitting

Removal

1 To improve access, chock the front roadwheels, then jack up the rear of the vehicle and support on axle stands (see *Jacking and vehicle support*). If necessary, remove both rear roadwheels.

2 Undo the screws and nuts and remove the wheel arch liners from each side **(see illustrations)**.

3 Working under the rear wheel arches, unscrew the bolts securing the rear bumper to the rear wings **(see illustration)**.

4 Raise the tailgate, then undo the screws

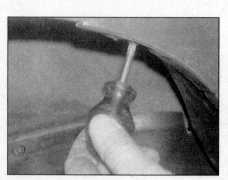

7.2a Undo the screws . . .

7.2b . . . and nuts . . .

7.2c . . . and remove the wheel arch liners from each side

7.3 Removing the bolts securing the rear bumper to the rear wings

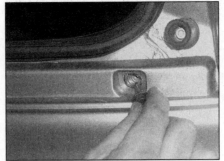

7.4 Removing the screws securing the upper edge of the bumper to the rear valance

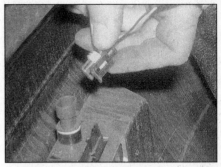

7.5 Disconnecting the wiring from the rear number plate lights

securing the upper edge of the bumper to the rear valance **(see illustration)**.

5 Disconnect the wiring from the rear number plate lights at the connector **(see illustration)**.

6 Unscrew the remaining lower mounting bolts **(see illustration)**.

7 With the help of an assistant, withdraw the bumper from the rear of the car **(see illustration)**.

Refitting

8 Refitting is a reversal of removal.

---

8 Tailgate - removal and refitting

Removal

1 Make sure all lighting and electrical devices are switched off - note, however, that when the tailgate is open, the rear valance electrical interface for the rear wiper and number plate lights will be disconnected. Open the tailgate, then undo the screws securing the trim panel. Note on 5-door models that four of the screws are visible, and four are hidden beneath rubber pads. Prise out the buttons securing the panel to the tailgate lower edge, and withdraw the panel. On 3-door models, use a wide-bladed screwdriver to prise the clips free.

2 Disconnect the pipe from the rear screen washer connection near the rear wiper motor,

then tie a length of string to it. Where fitted, disconnect the wiring from the high-level brake stop light. Draw the pipe and wiring through the tailgate but leave the string in place for refitting. Disconnect the string.

3 Have an assistant support the tailgate in the open position.

4 Detach the upper ends of the support struts from the tailgate as described in Section 9.

5 Unscrew the bolts securing the hinges to the tailgate **(see illustration)**, then lift the tailgate from the vehicle with the help of the assistant.

Refitting

6 Refitting is a reversal of removal, but check the adjustment as given in the following paragraphs.

Adjustment

7 Close the tailgate **carefully**, in case the alignment is incorrect, which may cause scratching on the tailgate or the body as the tailgate is closed, and check for alignment with the adjacent panels. If the gap between the tailgate and surrounding bodywork is not equal, undo the screws and remove the access covers from the rear of the roof headlining for access to the hinge bolts **(see illustrations)**. Loosen the bolts and reposition the tailgate, then tighten them again and refit the covers. **Note:** *If the seal between the hinges and roof is broken during adjustment, it will be necessary to apply new sealant.*

8 Check that the tailgate lock fastens and releases from the striker in a satisfactory manner. If adjustment is necessary, remove

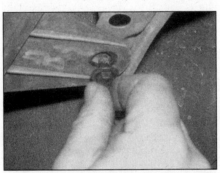

7.6 Removing the rear bumper lower mounting bolts

7.7 Removing the rear bumper

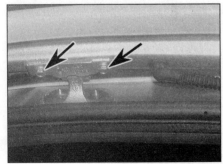

8.5 Tailgate hinge bolts

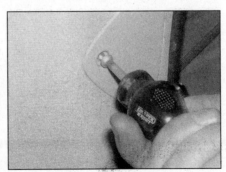

8.7a Undo the screws . . .

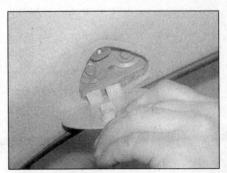

8.7b . . . and remove the access covers to the tailgate hinge bolts

8.8a Remove the covers . . .

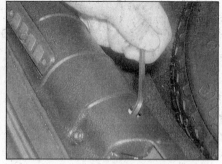

8.8b . . . and loosen the striker bolts with an Allen key

9.2 Lever off the spring clip securing the strut to the balljoint on the tailgate

the covers and loosen the striker mounting bolts then reposition **(see illustrations)**. Tighten the mounting bolts on completion.

9 With the tailgate shut, check that it is held firm by the support rubber buffers located in the lower corners. If necessary, screw them in or out as appropriate.

9 Tailgate strut - removal and refitting

Removal

1 Open the tailgate and support it using suitable wooden props.

2 At the 'lower' end of each strut, lever off the balljoint spring clip using a screwdriver **(see illustration)**. Compress the strut slightly by hand and then prise the strut from the ball stud on the tailgate.

⚠️ **Warning: The strut may still be under tension and could extend suddenly once detached from its mountings.**

3 At the 'upper' end of the strut, lever off the balljoint spring clip using a screwdriver, and release the strut from the ball stud on the body.

4 To remove the ball studs it will be necessary to remove the surrounding trim first, then unscrew the mounting bolts.

Refitting

5 Refitting is a reversal of removal.

10 Tailgate lock components - removal and refitting

Lock

Removal

1 Open the tailgate, then undo the screws securing the trim panel. Note on 5-door models that four of the screws are visible, and four are hidden beneath rubber pads. Prise out the buttons securing the panel to the tailgate lower edge, and withdraw the panel **(see illustrations)**. On 3-door models use a wide-bladed screwdriver to prise free the clips.

2 Unscrew the lock mounting bolts from the lower edge of the tailgate **(see illustration)**.

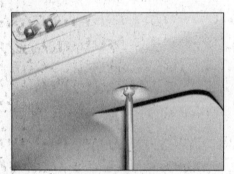

10.1a Undo the screws . . .

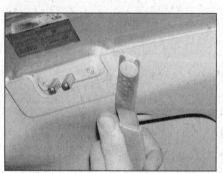

10.1b . . . prise out the buttons . . .

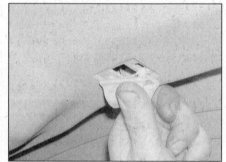

10.1c . . . then remove the rubber pads . . .

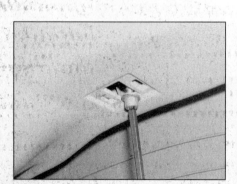

10.1d . . . and undo the remaining screws

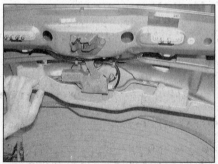

10.1e Removing the tailgate trim panel

10.2 Unscrew the tailgate lock mounting bolts . . .

10.3 . . . then disconnect the lock barrel rod with a pair of pliers

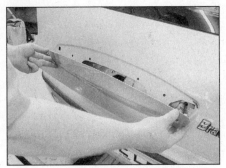

10.6 Removing the handle from the tailgate on 3-door models

10.7a Disconnect the operating rod . . .

3 Carefully withdraw the lock, then disconnect the lock barrel rod by releasing the clip accessible through the lock aperture **(see illustration)**.

Refitting

4 Refitting is a reversal of removal.

Lock cylinder and barrel

Removal

5 Open the tailgate, then undo the screws securing the trim panel. Note that on 5-door models four of the screws are visible, and four are hidden beneath rubber pads. Prise out the buttons securing the panel to the tailgate lower edge, and withdraw the panel. On 3-

door models use a wide-bladed screwdriver to prise free the clips.

6 On 3-door models, remove the lock complete as described in paragraphs 1 to 3, then undo the screws/bolts and remove the tailgate handle by depressing the tabs and pressing the handle out from inside **(see illustration)**.

7 On 5-door models, unscrew the lock cylinder mounting bolts, then withdraw the cylinder and barrel and at the same time disconnect the operating rod by releasing the clip. Alternatively, remove the lock complete, then disconnect the operating rod **(see illustrations)**.

8 On 3-door models, unscrew the bolts and

remove the barrel assembly from the housing. On 5-door models, insert the key in the barrel, then extract the spring clip and withdraw the barrel from the housing **(see illustrations)**.

Refitting

9 Refitting is a reversal of removal.

Striker plate

Removal

10 With the tailgate open, remove the trim from the rear valance in the luggage area **(see illustrations)**.

11 Outline the position of the striker with a pencil or marker pen, then unscrew and remove the mounting bolts, disconnect the

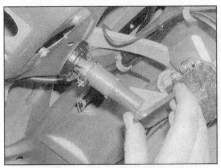

10.7b . . . and remove the lock cylinder and barrel from the tailgate

10.8a On 3-door models, unscrew the bolts to remove the barrel assembly

10.8b With the ignition key inserted, extract the spring clip . . .

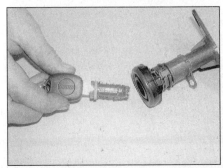

10.8c . . . and withdraw the barrel from the housing

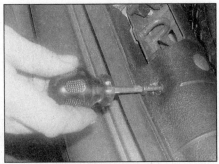

10.10a Undo the screws . . .

10.10b . . . and remove the trim from the rear valance

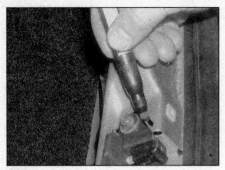

10.11a Outline the position of the tailgate striker with a marker pen

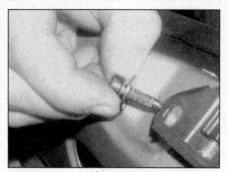

10.11b Unscrew the mounting bolts . . .

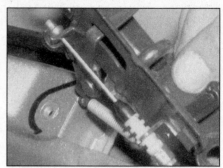

10.11c . . . and disconnect the release cable

release cable, and remove it **(see illustrations)**.

Refitting

12 Refitting is a reversal of removal, but check that the tailgate lock engages the striker correctly when the tailgate is closed. If necessary, reposition the striker by prising out the plastic covers, loosening and mounting bolts, then retightening them **(see illustrations)**.

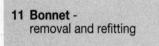

11 Bonnet -
removal and refitting

Removal

Note: *The help of an assistant is required for this work.*
1 Open the bonnet and have the assistant support it.
2 Disconnect the washer jet hoses at the three way joint.
3 Mark the hinges and bolts in relation to each other using a soft pencil or marker pen, to facilitate refitting.
4 Support the bonnet on each side, using the shoulders, then unscrew the mounting bolts and lift it away from the car. Place the bonnet on a dust sheet to protect the paintwork.

Refitting

5 Refitting is a reversal of removal, using the markings made during removal to achieve the correct alignment. Check that the gap between

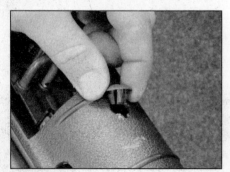

10.12a Remove the plastic covers . . .

the bonnet and surrounding bodywork is identical all the way round. If necessary, loosen the hinge bolts and reposition the bonnet, then tighten the bolts. Check that the bonnet fastens and releases in a satisfactory manner. If necessary, adjust the bonnet lock components, as described in Section 12.

12 Bonnet lock
and safety catch -
removal and refitting

Removal

1 Secure the bonnet in the fully open position using the stay. Disconnect the release cable from the lock behind the engine compartment crossmember.
2 Unscrew the bolts and remove the lock from the crossmember.
3 To remove the safety catch from the bonnet, first mark its position with a soft pencil or marker pen, then unscrew the mounting bolts.

Refitting

4 Refitting is a reversal of removal. Make sure that the height adjustment pin on the safety catch enters the lock centrally. If necessary, loosen the bolts and reposition the safety catch, then retighten the bolts. With the bonnet closed, check that the front edge is level with the surrounding bodywork. If necessary, loosen the locknut and screw the height adjustment pin in or out as required, then retighten the locknut.

10.12b . . . then loosen the striker mounting bolts to adjust the striker

Also check that the rubber buffers hold the front corners of the bonnet firmly - screw them in or out as required.

13 Bonnet release cable -
removal and refitting

Note: *This Section describes the removal of the bonnet release cable on 1.4 litre models. The procedure is similar on other models.*

Removal

1 At the rear of the engine compartment, remove the air inlet duct from between the air cleaner and throttle housing. To do this, loosen the clip at the air cleaner end, then unscrew the nuts and lift the adapter from the throttle housing. Also disconnect the crankcase ventilation hose from the adapter.
2 Unscrew the nut and remove the relay unit protective cover, then unbolt the relay unit from the bulkhead and position it to one side.
3 Prise out the stud, and fold back the noise insulation from the right-hand side of the rear engine panel.
4 Unscrew the nut retaining the bonnet release cable to the bulkhead and remove the guide block.
5 Disconnect the bonnet release cable from the lock behind the engine compartment front crossmember, by unhooking the inner cable from the lever and releasing the outer cable from the lock housing.
6 Working around the engine bay, extract the cable from its securing clips. Also, release the cable from the clip located beneath the injection control unit on the bulkhead.
7 Working beneath the steering wheel, disconnect the inner cable from the release lever by first extracting the cap and moving the cable through the large hole. Also detach the outer cable from the support.
8 Tie a length of string to the cable, and withdraw it into the engine compartment. Untie the string and withdraw the cable from the car.

Refitting

9 Refitting is a reversal of removal. On completion, close the bonnet to check that it locks securely. If necessary, adjust the lock as described in Section 12.

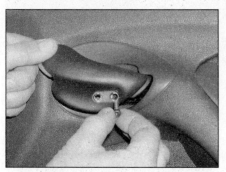

14.1 Removing the interior door handle from the operating lever

14.2a Prise out the electric window switch panel . . .

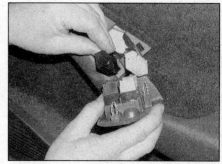

14.2b . . . and disconnect the wiring

14 Door inner trim panel - removal and refitting

Removal

1 Undo the screws and remove the interior door handle from the operating lever **(see illustration)**.

2 On the front doors of models with electric windows, use a screwdriver to carefully prise out the electric window switch panel from the trim panel, then disconnect the wiring. Use a piece of card or cloth to protect the panel while levering on it **(see illustrations)**. On models with manually-operated windows, remove the handle as described for the rear door panel in the following paragraph.

3 On the rear doors, note the position of the window regulator handle when the window is shut, then release the spring clip securing the handle to the regulator shaft by drawing a piece of cloth behind the handle. This will release the spring clip and allow the handle to be removed from the splined shaft. Alternatively, obtain a special removal tool from a car accessory shop and release the spring clip by inserting the tool in line with the end of the handle **(see illustrations)**.

4 Using an Allen key undo the screws securing the trim panel to the door (including the two middle ones on the front door). On the rear door, remove the cover for access to the screw located by the remove door handle **(see illustrations)**.

5 Using a wide-bladed screwdriver or special tool, carefully prise off the trim panel. To prevent damage to the panel, only prise near the retaining clips **(see illustrations)**.

6 Remove the retaining blocks from the front edge of the door by twisting them. If some of the retaining clips have remained in the door, prise them out using a forked tool.

14.3a Using a special removal tool to release the rear door window regulator handle from its splined shaft

14.3b Showing the rear of the window regulator handle

14.4a Removing the inner trim panel front screws . . .

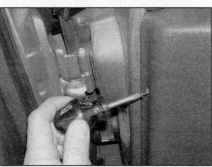

14.4b . . . and middle screws (front door)

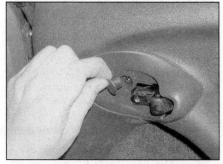

14.4c Removing the cover (rear door)

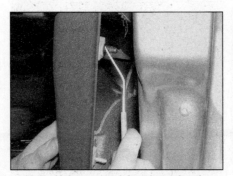

14.5a Using a special tool to prise the inner trim panel from the door

14.5b Lifting the inner trim panel from the door

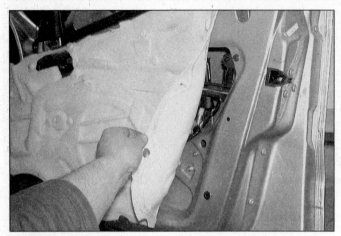

14.7a Removing the plastic sealing sheet from the inside of the front door

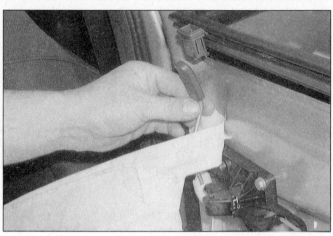

14.7b On the rear door, release the plastic sealing sheet from the locking knob

7 If work is to be carried out on the door internal components, it will be necessary to remove the plastic sealing sheet from the inside of the door. First remove the loudspeaker from the door as described in Chapter 12. Starting at one corner of the sheet, carefully peel it away, using a sharp blade to cut the sealant bead where necessary. On the rear door, release the sheet from the locking knob by lifting the glass inner moulding **(see illustrations)**. Store the detached sealing sheet such that it cannot become contaminated with dust, to allow it to be re-used later.

Refitting

8 Refitting is a reversal of removal, but press the sealing sheet firmly onto the door so that it is sealed all around its edges. If necessary, use new sealant.

15 Door -
removal, refitting and adjustment

Removal

1 Open the door. On the front doors, disconnect the wiring at the front edge of the door by turning the plug anticlockwise **(see illustration)**.

2 Disconnect the check strap from the pillar by driving out the pivot pin **(see illustrations)**. FIAT technicians use a special tool to do this, however a suitable punch may be used to remove it.

3 Unscrew and remove the hinge bolts and lift the door from the brackets on the body **(see illustrations)**.

Refitting

4 Refitting is a reversal of removal. On

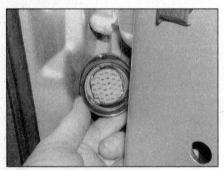

15.1 Disconnecting the wiring from the door

15.2a Tapping out the check strap pivot pin with a hammer

15.2b Removing the check strap pivot pin

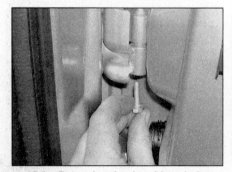

15.3a Removing the door hinge bolts

15.3b Upper hinge on body

15.3c Lower hinge on body

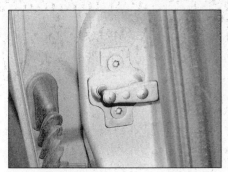

15.6a Front door lock striker

15.6b Rear door lock striker

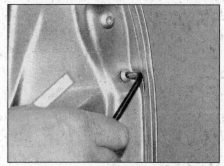

16.2a To remove the front door outer handle, unscrew the screw from the rear edge of the door . . .

completion, tighten the hinge bolts to the specified torque. Check the adjustment of the door as follows.

Adjustment

5 Initially close the door carefully, in case the alignment is incorrect, which may cause scratching on the door or the body, and check the fit of the door with the surrounding panels. If adjustment is required, loosen the socket-headed hinge-to-door bolts then reposition the door as required and retighten the bolts to the specified torque. FIAT technicians use a special bent spanner to do this, due to the position of the bolts, however, it may be possible to make up a suitable tool locally.
6 Check the operation of the door lock. If

necessary, slacken the securing bolts, and adjust the position of the lock striker on the body pillar to achieve satisfactory alignment **(see illustration)**. Tighten the bolts securely on completion.

16 Door handle and lock components - removal and refitting

Outer door handle

Removal

1 Refer to Section 14 and remove the door inner trim panel and sealing sheet.

2 Unscrew the handle securing screw from the rear edge of the door, then unscrew the nut securing the handle to the door, using a socket through the aperture in the inner door panel **(see illustrations)**.
3 Carefully swivel out the front of the handle, then use a screwdriver release the clips and disconnect the operating rods from the handle. Alternatively, on the rear door release the plastic adjustment clip from the operating rod inside the door. Withdraw the handle from the door **(see illustrations)**.

Refitting

4 Refitting is a reversal of removal, but check

16.2b . . . and the nut located through the aperture in the door panel

16.2c To remove the rear door outer handle, unscrew the screw from the rear edge of the door . . .

16.2d . . . and the nut located through the aperture in the door panel . . .

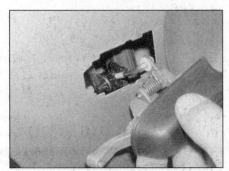

16.2e . . . then swivel out the handle and release the plastic adjustment clip inside the door

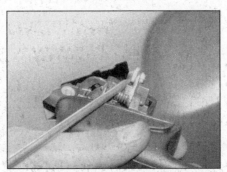

16.3a Using a screwdriver . . .

16.3b . . . to disconnect the operating rods from the front door exterior handle

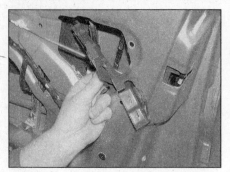

16.10 Removing the security cover from the front door lock operating rods

16.11 Removing the front door lock mounting screws

16.12a Removing the front door lock locking handle

the operation of the door lock before refitting the inner door panel. On the rear door, refit the handle then refit the plastic adjustment clip onto the operating rod.

Outer door lock barrel (driver's door)

Removal

5 Remove the outer door handle as described in paragraphs 1 to 3.
6 Insert the ignition key in the barrel, then carefully extract the retaining spring.
7 With the spring removed, withdraw the barrel from the handle.

Refitting

8 Refitting is a reversal of removal.

Door lock

Removal

9 Remove the outer door handle as described in paragraphs 1 to 3.
10 Undo the screws and remove the security cover from the operating rods **(see illustration)**. If the screws do not unscrew from the inner nuts, the nuts may be turning in the plastic cover, in which case the cover should be pulled from them. After removing the cover, the nuts can be super-glued in position again for refitting.
11 From the rear edge of the door, unscrew and remove the three lock mounting screws **(see illustration)**.
12 Release the clips and disconnect the operating rods (including the locking handle) from the lock. The remote inner door handle

operating rod can be disconnected from the inner handle. Disconnect the wiring plugs (after removing the cover on the front door) and withdraw the lock from inside the door **(see illustrations)**.

Refitting

13 Refitting is a reversal of removal.

Inner door handle

Removal

14 Refer to Section 14 and remove the door inner trim panel and sealing sheet.
15 Unscrew the inner door handle mounting nuts, then withdraw the handle and disconnect the operating rod.

Refitting

16 Refitting is a reversal of removal.

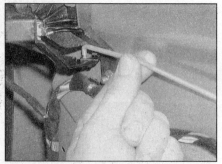

16.12b Disconnecting the remote inner door handle operating rod from the front door exterior handle

16.12c Disconnect the main wiring plug . . .

16.12d . . . then remove the cover . . .

16.12e . . . and disconnect the remaining wiring plug (front door)

16.12f The front door lock removed from the door

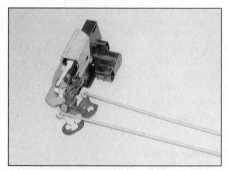

16.12g The rear door lock removed from the door

17.2 Removing the rubber boot and collar from the exterior mirror control knob

17.3 Removing the triangular trim

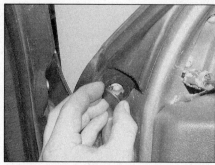

17.4a Remove the cover . . .

17 Exterior mirror components
- removal and refitting

Mirror assembly (manually operated)

Removal

1 Carefully remove the rubber boot from the exterior mirror control knob.

2 Unscrew the locking collar and release the control knob from the door **(see illustration)**. Note that the collar has four cut-outs on its perimeter. If a suitable tool is not available to engage the collar, use a punch to loosen it.

3 Using a screwdriver, carefully prise the triangular trim from the inside of the door **(see illustration)**.

4 Support the exterior mirror, then unscrew the mounting bolts and withdraw the mirror from the outside of the door. Note that one of the mounting bolts is located behind a cover on the front edge of the door **(see illustrations)**.

Refitting

5 Refitting is a reversal of removal.

Mirror assembly (electrically operated)

Removal

6 With the front door open, carefully prise off the triangular trim on the inside of the mirror location.

7 Disconnect the wiring plug leading to the mirror.

8 Support the exterior mirror, then unscrew the mounting bolts and withdraw the mirror from the outside of the door. Note that one of the mounting bolts is located on the front edge of the door.

Refitting

9 Refitting is a reversal of removal.

Mirror glass

Removal

10 Insert a suitable thin plastic or wooden

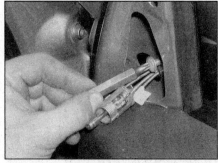

17.4b . . . then unscrew the mounting bolts . . .

tool between the mirror glass and the mirror body, and carefully lever out the glass to release it from the securing clips **(see illustrations)**.

> ⚠ **Warning: Protect your hands and eyes from glass splinters.**

Refitting

11 Carefully push the glass into position to engage the securing clips.

> **HAYNES HINT** *To aid refitting, lightly grease the securing clips on the rear of the mirror glass.*

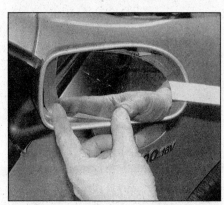

17.10a Use a plastic or wooden tool to prise out the mirror glass

17.4c . . . and withdraw the mirror from the outside of the door

18 Door window glass and regulator -
removal and refitting

Front door window glass

Removal

1 Switch on the ignition, then position the window glass half open.

2 Remove the door inner trim panel and the sealing sheet, as described in Section 14.

3 Working through the aperture in the door inner panel, pull down the plastic fastener clip and release the window glass from the pin on the regulator arm. The clip is on the end of a loop and a pair of pliers may be used to pull

17.10b The mirror has securing clips attached to its rear surface

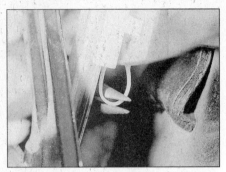

18.3a Using a pair of pliers to unclip the plastic fastener that secures the front window glass to the regulator mechanism

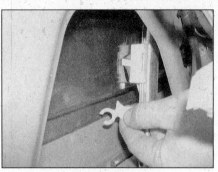

18.3b The plastic clip removed from the end of the plastic pin

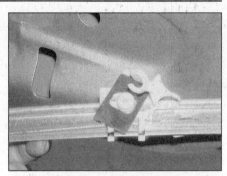

18.3c The front window glass has a hole which engages with the plastic pin on the regulator mechanism

18.5a Remove the front door inner moulding . . .

18.5b . . . and outer moulding . . .

down the loop, however, take care not to break the plastic **(see illustrations)**. If it is tight, spray the clip with a little WD-40 before removing the clip. Support the glass on a block of wood, or use adhesive tape to hold it in its raised position.

4 Unbolt and remove the security plate.

5 Carefully remove the inner and outer mouldings from the upper section of the door, then lower the window and pull up the rear window glass rubber guide moulding from the rear guide channel **(see illustrations)**.

6 Tilt the window glass forwards and withdraw the upper rear corner of the glass from the outside of the door **(see illustration)**.

Refitting

7 Refitting is a reversal of removal. Before refitting the inner trim panel, check the operation of the window by temporarily reconnecting the switch wiring and switching on the ignition.

Front door window regulator

Removal

8 Remove the window glass as described in paragraphs 1 to 5.

9 Disconnect the wiring from the motor on electrically-operated windows, then unscrew the 5 regulator mounting bolts, then withdraw the regulator complete with motor through the aperture in the door inner panel **(see illustrations)**.

18.5c . . . then pull up the rear window glass moulding from the rear guide channel

18.6 Tilt the front window glass forwards and remove it upwards

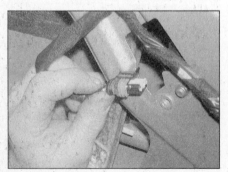

18.9a Disconnect the wiring . . .

18.9b . . . then unscrew the bolts . . .

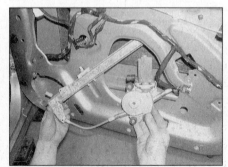

18.9c . . . and withdraw the front door window regulator and motor

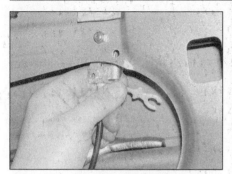

18.13 Disconnecting the plastic clip from the end of the plastic pin

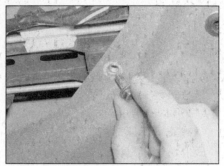

18.14a Unscrew the bolts . . .

18.14b . . . and remove the security plate from the rear door

Refitting

10 Refitting is a reversal of removal.

Rear door window glass

Removal

11 Fully open the window and note the position of the regulator handle.

12 Remove the door inner trim panel and the sealing sheet, as described in Section 14.

13 Working through the aperture in the door inner panel, pull down the plastic fastener clip and release the window glass from the pin on the regulator arm **(see illustration)**. If it is tight, spray the clip with a little WD-40 before removing the clip. Support the glass on a block of wood, or use adhesive tape to hold it in its raised position.

14 Unbolt and remove the security plate **(see illustrations)**.

15 Remove the window glass rear guide channel by unscrewing the retaining bolts located on the rear edge of the door and on the inner panel **(see illustrations)**.

16 Carefully remove the inner and outer mouldings from the upper section of the door. Unbolt the outer triangular plastic cover, then lower the window and pull up the rear window glass rubber guide moulding **(see illustrations)**.

17 Lift the window glass and withdraw it from the outside of the door **(see illustration)**.

Refitting

18 Refitting is a reversal of removal. Before refitting the inner trim panel, check the operation of the window by temporarily refitting the regulator handle.

Rear door window regulator

Removal

19 Fully open the window and note the position of the regulator handle.

20 Remove the door inner trim panel and the sealing sheet, as described in Section 14.

21 Working through the aperture in the door inner panel, pull down the plastic fastener clip and release the window glass from the pin on the regulator arm. If it is tight, spray the clip with a little WD-40 before removing the clip. Support the glass on a block of wood, or use adhesive tape to hold it in its raised position.

22 Unbolt and remove the security plate.

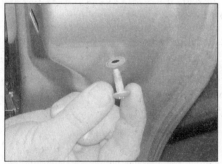

18.15a Unscrew the rear bolt . . .

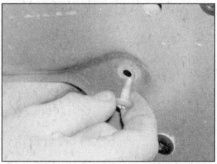

18.15b . . . and inner panel bolt . . .

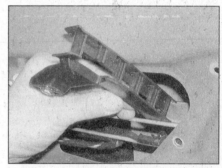

18.15c . . . and remove the rear window glass rear guide channel from the door

18.16a Remove the triangular plastic cover . . .

18.16b . . . then pull up the rear window glass rubber guide moulding

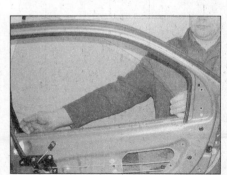

18.17 Removing the rear door window glass

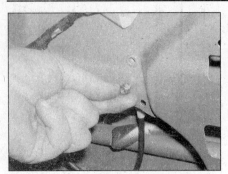

18.23a Unscrew the mounting nuts . . .

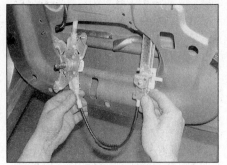

18.23b . . . and withdraw the regulator through the aperture in the door inner panel

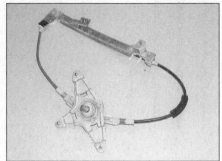

18.23c The rear door window regulator

23 Unscrew the 5 regulator mounting nuts, then withdraw the regulator through the aperture in the door inner panel **(see illustrations)**.

Refitting

24 Refitting is a reversal of removal.

19 Seats - removal and refitting

Front seats

Removal

1 On models fitted with a side airbag and presence sensor in the front passenger seat, disconnect the battery (see *Disconnecting the battery*) then wait approximately 10 minutes before proceeding. This is necessary to ensure the airbag system is completely deactivated and safe.
2 The front seats are secured to the floorpan by four bolts. First, adjust the seat towards the rear of the car to gain access to the two bolts at the front, then unscrew and remove them **(see illustration)**.
3 Adjust the seat fully forwards, then unscrew and remove the two rearmost bolts **(see illustration)**.
4 Tilt the seat backwards for access to its underside. As applicable, disconnect the wiring from the seat heater, lumbar adjuster, and side airbag. Prise off the safety cap and

remove the connector flap, then disconnect the wiring.
5 Lift the seat out of the passenger area. Do not lift on the adjustment bar, otherwise the seat runners may be misaligned.

Refitting

6 Refitting is a reversal of removal. Note that the location pin on the rear of the mounting runner engages with a hole in the floor **(see illustration)**. When reconnecting the battery on models with a side airbag and presence sensor, ensure there is no one inside the vehicle, as a precaution against accidental activation of the airbag. With the driver's door open, reach inside and turn on the ignition, then check the operation of the airbag warning light.

Rear seat backrest

Removal

7 Lower the rear seat backrest onto the cushion, then undo the row of screws securing the luggage compartment floor covering to the bottom of the backrest. Carefully prise out the buttons and fold back the floor covering.
8 At the outer lower corners, undo the two screws on each side securing the backrest to the brackets.
9 Lift the backrest from the passenger area.

Refitting

10 Refitting is a reversal of removal.

Rear seat cushion

Removal

11 Using an Allen key, unscrew and remove the bolts from the mounting brackets on the front edge of the cushion.
12 Lift the rear seat cushion and remove it from the passenger area.

Refitting

13 Refitting is a reversal of removal.

20 Seat belt components - precautions, removal and refitting

Precautions

1 All models covered in this manual are fitted with a front seat belt automatic tensioner system which is integrated in the reel. The tensioner is triggered by a frontal impact above a pre-determined force. Lesser impacts, including impacts from behind, will not trigger the system.
2 When the system is triggered, an internal mass moves to release a gas generator which is forced under spring tension against a percussion pin. This causes combustion of the pyrotechnic charge which forces a piston upwards to the top of the expansion chamber. Attached to the piston is a rod which is wrapped around the reel pulley at its other end, and this retracts and locks the seat belt

19.2 Unscrewing the front mounting bolts from the front seat

19.3 Unscrewing the rear mounting bolts from the front seat

19.6 Location pin on the front seat mounting runner

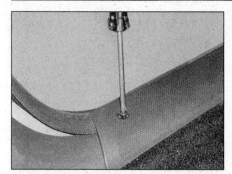

20.11 Removing the door kick-panels

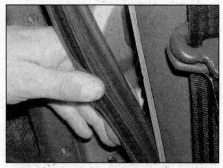

20.12 Pull the door weatherstrips away from the B-pillar

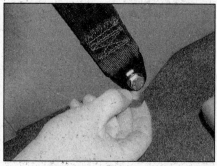

20.13a Prise off the cover . . .

inertia reel in position, holding the front seat occupants firmly in position. Once the tensioner has been triggered, the seat belt will be permanently locked and the assembly must be renewed.

3 To prevent the risk of injury, note the following warnings before contemplating any work on the front seat belts.

 Warning: If the seat belt/ tensioner mechanism is dropped from a height of 1 metre or more, it must be renewed, even if it has suffered no apparent damage. Do not allow any solvents to come into contact with the tensioner cylinder. Do not subject the tensioner cylinder/inertia reel to any form of shock as this could accidentally trigger the mechanism. Do not subject the tensioner cylinder to temperatures in excess of 110°C

Front seat belts

Removal

3-door models

1 Undo the screws and remove the front door kick-panel. The front screw is located beneath the facia and the rear one is located at the bottom of the B-pillar.

2 At the base of the B-pillar undo the screw securing the trim, then prise off the covers, and unscrew the bolts securing the seat belt rail to the side panel.

3 On models with ABS, remove the rear seat cushion as described in Section 19, then disconnect the wiring leading to the rear ABS sensor.

4 Pull out the door weatherstrip from the rear side panel.

5 Undo the screws securing the rear side panel to the sill panel.

6 Prise off the cover and unscrew the bolt securing the seat belt to the floor.

7 Prise out the covers and unscrew the side trim screws. Also unbolt the rear seat lock. Withdraw the side trim.

8 Extract the clip and remove the guide pin from the B-pillar. Release the seat belt at the same time.

9 Break the plastic protective collar around the safety bracket with a screwdriver, and unbolt the bracket from the tensioner. **Note:** *This will invalidate the manufacturer's guarantee.* The bolt is of double-headed shear type and must be renewed together with the bracket. Note that as the bracket is removed, the tensioner will be locked to prevent accidental activation.

10 Unscrew the mounting bolt and withdraw

the tensioner from inside the B-pillar. Handle the unit very carefully and observe the warnings given at the beginning of this Section.

5-door models

11 Undo the screws and remove the front and rear door kick-panels **(see illustration)**. If preferred, the front panel front screw need not be removed.

12 Pull the front and rear door weatherstrips away from the B-pillar **(see illustration)**.

13 Prise off the cover and unscrew the bolt securing the seat belt to the inner sill panel **(see illustrations)**.

14 Pull off the knob from the height adjustment mechanism, then prise off the cover and unscrew the nut securing the seat belt to the mechanism **(see illustrations)**.

15 Remove the cover and undo the screw, then carefully prise the trim away from the B-pillar and release the seat belt from it **(see illustrations)**.

20.13b . . . and unscrew the bolt securing the front seat belt to the inner sill panel

20.14a Remove the knob from the height adjustment mechanism . . .

20.14b . . . then prise off the cover . . .

20.14c . . . and unscrew the nut securing the seat belt to the mechanism

20.15a Remove the cover . . .

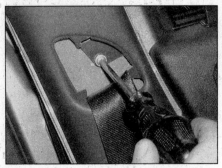

20.15b . . . undo the screw . . .

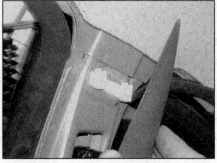

20.15c . . . prise away the trim . . .

20.15d . . . and release the seat belt from it

16 Extract the clip and remove the guide pin from the B-pillar **(see illustration)**. Release the seat belt at the same time.

17 Break the plastic protective collar around

the safety bracket with a screwdriver **(see illustration)**, and unscrew the reel mounting bolt which also secures the safety bracket. **Note:** *This will invalidate the manufacturer's*

guarantee. The bolt is of double-headed shear type and must be renewed together with the bracket. Note that as the bracket is removed, the tensioner will be automatically locked to prevent accidental activation **(see illustration)**.

18 Unscrew the three bolts and withdraw the reel/tensioner and bracket from the B-pillar **(see illustration)**. Handle the unit very carefully and observe the warnings given at the beginning of this Section.

All models

19 To remove the stalk, unbolt it from the inside of the front seat **(see illustration)**. There is no need to remove the plastic cover.

Refitting

20 Carefully locate the tensioner (and bracket on 5-door models) in the B-pillar, and tighten the mounting bolt(s).

21 Refit the safety bracket together with a new double-headed shear bolt. Tighten the shear bolt until its head breaks off. Tighten all remaining bolts securely.

22 The remaining procedure is a reversal of removal.

Rear seat belts

Removal

23 Fold the rear seat cushion forwards, then prise off the cover and unscrew the rear seat belt lower mounting bolt **(see illustration)**.

24 Prise off the cover and unscrew the belt upper anchor mounting bolt **(see illustrations)**.

25 Carefully prise out the speaker grille from

20.16 Seat belt and guide pin on the B-pillar

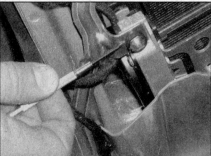

20.17a Breaking this plastic collar will invalidate the manufacturer's guarantee

20.17b When the safety bracket is removed from the reel, the tensioner is automatically disarmed and locked

20.18 One of the bolts securing the reel and bracket to the B-pillar

20.19 Seat belt stalk mounting bolt on the front seat

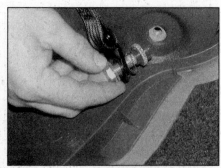

20.23 Unscrewing the rear seat belt lower mounting bolt

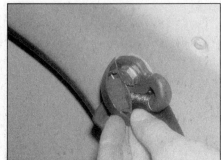

20.24a Prise off the cover . . .

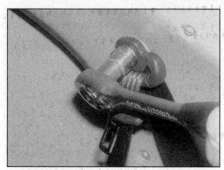

20.24b . . . then unscrew the bolt . . .

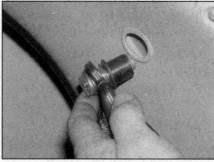

20.24c . . . and remove the rear belt upper anchor mounting bolt

20.25 Removing the rear speaker grille

the side trim panel by depressing the tabs **(see illustration)**.

26 Remove the trim panel for access to the rear seat belt reel mounting bolt **(see illustration)**. Unscrew and remove the bolt.

27 Guide the seat belt through the hole in the rear pillar cover, and remove it complete with the reel **(see illustration)**.

28 To remove the stalk, unbolt it from the rear floor panel beneath the rear seat cushion.

Refitting

29 Refitting is a reversal of removal, but tighten the mounting bolts securely.

21 Sunroof - general information

1 Due to the complexity of the sunroof mechanism, considerable expertise is needed to repair, replace or adjust the sunroof components successfully. Removal of the roof first requires the headlining to be removed, which is a complex and tedious operation, and not a task to be undertaken lightly. Therefore, any problems with the sunroof should be referred to a FIAT dealer.

2 If the sunroof motor fails to operate, first check the relevant fuse. If the fault cannot be traced and rectified, the sunroof can be opened and closed manually as follows.

3 Carefully prise the small covers from the interior light/roof switch housing, and unscrew the two bolts.

4 Remove the special key from the inside of the

courtesy light, then insert it in the drive and turn to move the roof as required **(see illustrations)**.

5 If necessary, the sunroof motor may be removed after removing the interior light/roof switch housing by unscrewing the mounting

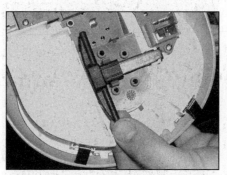

20.26 Rear seat belt reel

21.4a Remove the special key from the inside of the courtesy light . . .

21.5a Remove the mounting bolts/screws . . .

bolts/screws. The sunroof control relay is located next to the motor **(see illustrations)**. Make sure that the motor gear is correctly engaged with the two cables before tightening the mounting bolts/screws.

20.27 Guiding the rear seat belt through the hole in the rear pillar cover

21.4b . . . and insert it in the drive to move the sunroof

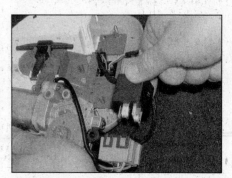

21.5b . . . then lower the sunroof motor and interior light/roof switch from the headlining

21.5c Removing the sunroof control relay

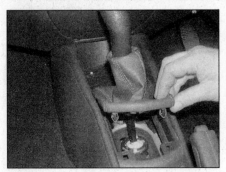

23.3 Releasing the gear lever gaiter from the floor

23.4a Remove the covering from the oddments tray in the centre console . . .

23.4b . . . and undo the hidden screw

22 Windscreen, rear window glass, and fixed window - general information

1 These areas of glass are bonded in position with a special adhesive. Renewal is a difficult, messy and time-consuming task, which is beyond the scope of the home mechanic. Furthermore, the task carries a high risk of breakage; this applies especially to the laminated glass windscreen. In view of this, owners are strongly advised to have this sort of work carried out by one of the many specialist windscreen fitters.

23 Facia and centre console - removal and refitting

Removal

1 Disconnect the battery negative (earth) lead (see *Disconnecting the battery*).
2 Remove the combination switch from the top of the steering column as described in Chapter 12, Section 14. This procedure includes the removal of the steering wheel and shrouds.
3 Release the gear lever gaiter from the floor and pull it up the gear lever **(see illustration)**.
4 Remove the covering from the oddments tray in the centre console, and undo the hidden screw **(see illustrations)**.
5 Prise the ashtray from the rear of the centre console, and undo the hidden screws **(see illustrations)**.
6 Prise the electric rear view mirror switch panel or dummy panel from the centre console and unscrew the hidden screws. Disconnect the wiring where necessary **(see illustrations)**.
7 Release the fasteners (depress the central pins) and undo the screws, then remove the heater side covers. Release the handbrake lever gaiter and remove it from the lever, then withdraw the centre console over the handbrake lever, and remove from inside the car **(see illustrations)**.

23.5a Remove the ashtray . . .

23.5b . . . and undo the hidden screws

23.6a Remove the centre panel . . .

23.6b . . . and unscrew the hidden screws

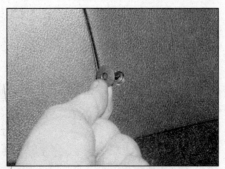

23.7a Release the fasteners and undo the screws . . .

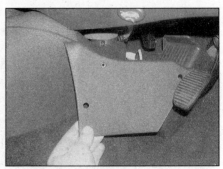

23.7b . . . then remove the heater side covers

23.7c Release the handbrake lever gaiter . . .

23.7d . . . and remove it from the lever . . .

23.7e . . . then withdraw the centre console over the handbrake lever

8 Remove the cover from the fuse holder on the facia, then unscrew the facia mounting bolt accessible through the aperture.

9 Using an Allen key, unscrew the bolts and remove the cowling from the instrument panel. Note that the cowling incorporates the right-hand air vent, which has a securing screw accessed from below.

10 Undo the screws and withdraw the instrument panel from the facia sufficient to disconnect the rear-mounted wiring lugs. With the wiring disconnected, withdraw the instrument panel from the facia.

11 Remove the radio/cassette player as described in Chapter 12.

12 Open the ashtray, then unscrew the heater control panel surround mounting screws. There are two above the ashtray aperture and four in the radio aperture **(see illustrations)**.

13 Carefully pull off the heater ventilation centre control knob (taking care not to drop the retaining spring clip), using a pair of pliers and a piece of card to protect the knob. Unscrew the panel mounting screw located beneath it **(see illustrations)**.

14 Using a small screwdriver, carefully prise out the small covers from each end of the facia switches located above the heater control knobs **(see illustration)**. Also, prise out the cover at the centre of the switches and

23.12a Heater control panel surround mounting screws above the ashtray . . .

23.12b . . . and in the radio aperture

remove the hazard switch (see Chapter 12, Section 14).

15 Undo the screws and withdraw the switch

panel from the front of the facia. Disconnect the wiring and remove the switches from the facia **(see illustrations)**.

23.13a Pull off the heater ventilation centre control knob . . .

23.13b . . . and undo the screw located beneath it

23.14 Prise out the small covers . . .

23.15a Undo the screws . . .

23.15b . . . and withdraw the switch panel from the front of the facia . . .

23.15c ... then disconnect the wiring

23.16 Withdrawing the heater control panel surround from the facia

16 Withdraw the heater control panel surround from the facia **(see illustration)**.

17 With the ashtray closed, undo the lower mounting screws, then open the ashtray lid and unscrew the upper mounting screws. Withdraw the ashtray from the facia and disconnect the wiring from the cigar lighter **(see illustrations)**.

18 Working through the ashtray aperture, unscrew the facia mounting screws securing the facia to the heater housing **(see illustration)**.

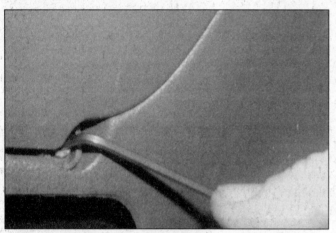

23.17a With the ashtray closed, undo the lower mounting screws ...

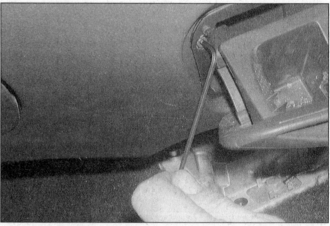

23.17b ... then open the ashtray and unscrew the upper mounting screws

23.17c Disconnecting the wiring from the cigar lighter

23.18 Working through the ashtray aperture, unscrew the facia mounting screws securing the facia to the heater housing

23.19 Removing the screws securing the heater controls to the facia

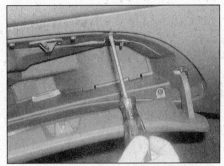

23.20a Undo the screws . . .

23.20b . . . remove the trim . . .

19 Undo the screws securing the heater controls to the facia **(see illustration)**. There are four screws.

20 Open the glovebox lid, then remove the upper trim from inside the glovebox. Unscrew the mounting bolts and withdraw the glovebox from the facia **(see illustrations)**.

21 Remove the left-hand side air vent from the end of the facia, using a screwdriver in the glovebox aperture to unscrew the lower mounting screws **(see illustrations)**.

22 Unscrew the facia mounting bolts accessible through the vent and instrument panel apertures **(see illustration)**.

23 Unscrew the facia lower mounting bolts at each end of the facia **(see illustration)**. If necessary for access to the bolts, undo the screws and remove the trim panels located on the outer sides of the footwells.

24 Carefully prise out the speaker grilles from both sides of the facia, taking care not to damage the facia material.

25 In the grille aperture on each side, unscrew the speaker mounting screws, withdraw the speakers, and disconnect the wiring.

26 With the speakers removed, unscrew the facia mounting bolts now visible **(see illustration)**.

27 Unscrew the centre and top facia mounting bolts **(see illustrations)**.

23.20c . . . and withdraw the glovebox from the facia

23.21a Undo the screws . . .

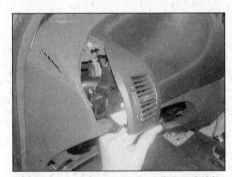

23.21b . . . and remove the left-hand side air vent

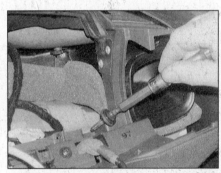

23.22 Removing the facia mounting bolt located in the instrument panel aperture

23.23 Removing the facia lower mounting bolts

23.26 Unscrew the facia mounting bolts in the speaker apertures

23.27a Unscrew the centre bolt . . .

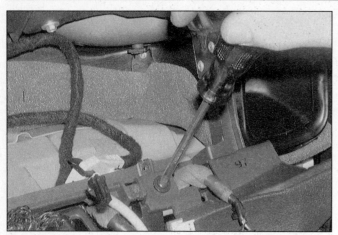

23.27b ... and the bolt in the instrument panel aperture

23.28 Removing the facia-to-steering column bolt

28 Unscrew the bolts securing the facia to the steering column (see illustration).

29 Unscrew the lower mounting nut located near the steering column. Also, unscrew the remaining side bolts and centre bolts (see illustrations).

30 With the help of an assistant, carefully withdraw the facia from the bulkhead slightly. Check that nothing remains connected between the facia and bulkhead, then withdraw it from one side of the car (see illustration).

Refitting

31 Refitting is a reversal of removal. On completion, reconnect the battery negative lead and check the operation of all controls, gauges and instruments disturbed during the removal process, including the ventilation/heating system.

24 Glovebox - removal and refitting

Removal

1 Open the glovebox lid, then on early models undo the two knobs and remove the upper trim from inside the glovebox.

2 Unscrew the mounting bolts and withdraw the glovebox from the facia.

Refitting

3 Refitting is a reversal of removal.

23.29a Bolt located in the radio aperture

23.29b Bolt located above the fusebox

23.29c Bolt located beneath the left-hand side of the facia

23.30 Removing the facia from the bulkhead

Chapter 12
Body electrical systems

Contents

Degrees of difficulty

Easy, suitable for novice with little experience	**Fairly easy,** suitable for beginner with some experience	**Fairly difficult,** suitable for competent DIY mechanic	**Difficult,** suitable for experienced DIY mechanic	**Very difficult,** suitable for expert DIY or professional

Specifications

Note: *The following fuse information is for pre-1998 models. Refer to your handbook for information on later models.*

Main fusebox

Fuse	Amp	Circuit
1	15	Reversing lights, stop lights, direction indicators, instrument panel power supply, check panel power supply, electric mirrors control, radio power supply, remote control power supply
2	10	Radio power supply, internal lighting, glove compartment light, boot light, door lock/unlock remote control power supply, alarm system power supply, clock power supply
3	10	Right side light and left tail light, right number plate light, radio illumination, instrument panel illumination and side/tail lights warning lamp, cigar lighter illumination, switch panel illumination
4	10	Left side light and right tail light, left number plate light, manual climate control/heater controls illumination
5	10	Left dipped beam headlight
6	10	Right dipped beam headlight, headlight alignment control
7	10	Right main beam headlight
8	10	Left main beam headlight, main beam headlight warning light
9	10	Rear foglight
10	10	Hazard lights
11	30	Heated rear window, heated rear window warning light
12	30	Electric climate control motor (manual version)
13	20	Horn
14	20	Windscreen wiper, windscreen washer, rear window wiper, rear window washer, headlamp washers
15	30	Electric heater motor, cigar lighter, manual climate control relay

Fuses above control unit

Fuse	Amp	Circuit
1	20	Electric sunroof, heated seats
2	20	Front foglights
3	20	Door central locking
4	5	Airbag
5	30	Electric windows
6	7.5	Electric mirror defrosting

Fuses behind glovebox

Fuse	Amp	Circuit
1	30	Injection system (1.8 litre engine)
2	15	Fuel pump (1.8 litre engine)

Fuses on left-hand side of engine compartment rear panel

Fuse	Amp	Circuit
1	80	Control unit
2	60	Optional devices
3	40	Ignition switch
4	30	Injection/ignition system
5	60	ABS system

Fuses in front of battery

Fuse	Amp	Circuit
1	20	Headlamp washer
2	5	ABS
3	10	Automatic transmission cooling oil circuit
4	10	Automatic transmission power supply (key)
5	5	Automatic transmission power supply (battery)

Fuses in centre of engine compartment rear panel

Fuse	Amp	Circuit
1	10	1.4 litre engine injection system
2	10	1.4 litre engine fuel pump
3	5	1.6 litre engine injection system
4	25	1.6 litre engine fuel pump

Bulb ratings

	Watts
Headlights (main beam and dipped beam)	55
Front foglight	55
Front sidelight	5
Front direction indicator (orange bulb)	21
Front direction indicator repeater light	5
Rear sidelight	5
Rear direction indicator	21
Rear foglight	21
Stop light	21
High-level stop light	5
Reversing light	21
Rear number plate light	5
Interior light	10
Glovebox light	5
Rear luggage compartment light	5

Torque wrench settings

	Nm	lbf ft
Airbag control unit	8	6
Airbag module to steering wheel	8	6
Passenger airbag module to body	7	5

1 General information and precautions

⚠️ **Warning: Before carrying out any work on the electrical system, read through the precautions given in Safety first! at the beginning of this manual, and in Chapter 5A. Before working on the airbag system, observe the precautions given in Section 21.**

The electrical system is of 12-volt negative earth type. Power for the lights and all electrical accessories is supplied by a lead/acid type battery, which is charged by the alternator.

This Chapter covers repair and service procedures for the various electrical components not associated with the engine. Information on the battery, alternator and starter motor can be found in Chapter 5A.

It should be noted that, prior to working on any component in the electrical system the battery negative terminal should first be disconnected, to prevent the possibility of electrical short-circuits and/or fires. When reconnecting the battery on models with a side airbag and presence sensor, ensure there is no one inside the vehicle, as a precaution against accidental activation of the airbag. With the driver's door open, reach inside and turn on the ignition, then check the operation of the airbag warning light.

2 Electrical fault finding - general information

Note: *Refer to the precautions given in Safety first! and in Section 1 of this Chapter before starting work. The following tests relate to testing of the main electrical circuits, and should not be used to test delicate electronic circuits (such as anti-lock braking systems), particularly where an electronic control module (ECU) is used.*

General

1 A typical electrical circuit consists of an electrical component, any switches, relays, motors, fuses, fusible links or circuit breakers related to that component, and the wiring and connectors which link the component to both the battery and the chassis. To help pinpoint a problem in an electrical circuit, wiring diagrams are included at the end of this manual.

2 Before attempting to diagnose an electrical fault, first study the appropriate wiring diagram, to obtain a more complete understanding of the components included in the particular circuit concerned. The possible sources of a fault can be narrowed down by noting whether other components related to the circuit are operating properly. If several components or circuits fail at one time, the problem is likely to be related to a shared fuse or earth connection.

3 Electrical problems usually stem from simple causes, such as loose or corroded connections, a faulty earth connection, a blown fuse, a melted fusible link, or a faulty relay (refer to Section 3 for details of testing relays). Visually inspect the condition of all fuses, wires and connections in a problem circuit before testing the components. Use the wiring diagrams to determine which terminal connections will need to be checked, in order to pinpoint the trouble-spot.

4 The basic tools required for electrical fault-finding include a circuit tester or voltmeter (a 12-volt bulb with a set of test leads can also be used for certain tests), a self-powered test light (sometimes known as a continuity tester), an ohmmeter (to measure resistance), a battery and set of test leads, and a jumper wire, preferably with a circuit breaker or fuse incorporated, which can be used to bypass suspect wires or electrical components. Before attempting to locate a problem with test instruments, use the wiring diagram to determine where to make the connections.

5 To find the source of an intermittent wiring fault (usually due to a poor or dirty connection, or damaged wiring insulation), a 'wiggle' test can be performed on the wiring. This involves wiggling the wiring by hand, to see if the fault occurs as the wiring is moved. It should be possible to narrow down the source of the fault to a particular section of wiring. This method of testing can be used in conjunction with any of the tests described in the following sub-Sections.

6 Apart from problems due to poor connections, two basic types of fault can occur in an electrical circuit - open-circuit, or short-circuit.

7 Open-circuit faults are caused by a break somewhere in the circuit, which prevents current from flowing. An open-circuit fault will prevent a component from working, but will not cause the relevant circuit fuse to blow.

8 Short-circuit faults are caused by a 'short' somewhere in the circuit, which allows the current flowing in the circuit to 'escape' along an alternative route, usually to earth. Short-circuit faults are normally caused by a breakdown in wiring insulation, which allows a feed wire to touch either another wire, or an earthed component such as the bodyshell. A short-circuit fault will normally cause the relevant circuit fuse to blow.

Finding an open-circuit

9 To check for an open-circuit, connect one lead of a circuit tester or voltmeter to either the negative battery terminal or a known good earth.

10 Connect the other lead to a connector in the circuit being tested, preferably nearest to the battery or fuse.

11 Switch on the circuit, bearing in mind that some circuits are live only when the ignition switch is moved to a particular position.

12 If voltage is present (indicated either by the tester bulb lighting or a voltmeter reading, as applicable), this means that the section of the circuit between the relevant connector and the battery is problem-free.

13 Continue to check the remainder of the circuit in the same fashion.

14 When a point is reached at which no voltage is present, the problem must lie between that point and the previous test point with voltage. Most problems can be traced to a broken, corroded or loose connection.

Finding a short-circuit

15 To check for a short-circuit, first disconnect the load(s) from the circuit (loads are the components which draw current from a circuit, such as bulbs, motors, heating elements, etc).

16 Remove the relevant fuse from the circuit, and connect a circuit tester or voltmeter to the fuse connections.

17 Switch on the circuit, bearing in mind that some circuits are live only when the ignition switch is moved to a particular position.

18 If voltage is present (indicated either by the tester bulb lighting or a voltmeter reading, as applicable), this means that there is a short-circuit.

19 If no voltage is present, but the fuse still blows with the load(s) connected, this indicates an internal fault in the load(s).

Finding an earth fault

20 The battery negative terminal is connected to 'earth' - the metal of the engine/transmission and the car body - and most systems are wired so that they only receive a positive feed, the current returning via the metal of the car body. This means that the component mounting and the body form part of that circuit. Loose or corroded mountings can therefore cause a range of electrical faults, ranging from total failure of a circuit, to a puzzling partial fault. In particular, lights may shine dimly (especially when another circuit sharing the same earth point is in operation), motors (eg wiper motors or the radiator cooling fan motor) may run slowly, and the operation of one circuit may have an apparently-unrelated effect on another. Note that on many vehicles, earth straps are used between certain components, such as the engine/transmission and the body, usually where there is no metal-to-metal contact between components, due to flexible rubber mountings, etc.

21 To check whether a component is properly earthed, disconnect the battery, and connect one lead of an ohmmeter to a known good earth point. Connect the other lead to the wire or earth connection being tested. The resistance reading should be zero; if not, check the connection as follows.

22 If an earth connection is thought to be faulty, dismantle the connection, and clean back to bare metal both the bodyshell and the wire terminal or the component earth

3.2a Main fusebox under the right-hand side of the facia

3.2b Upper fuse block above the main fusebox

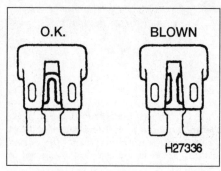

3.6 A blown fuse can be recognised from its melted or broken wire

connection mating surface. Be careful to remove all traces of dirt and corrosion, then use a knife to trim away any paint, so that a clean metal-to-metal joint is made. On reassembly, tighten the joint fasteners securely; if a wire terminal is being refitted, use serrated washers between the terminal and the bodyshell, to ensure a clean and secure connection. When the connection is remade, prevent the onset of corrosion in the future by applying a coat of petroleum jelly, or by spraying on a proprietary ignition sealer, or a water-dispersant lubricant.

3 Fuses and relays - general information

Fuses

1 Fuses are designed to break a circuit when a predetermined current is reached, in order to protect the components and wiring which could be damaged by excessive current flow. Any excessive current flow will be due to a fault in the circuit, usually a short-circuit (see Section 2).

2 The main fuses are located in the fusebox on the driver's side of the facia. To gain access to the fuses, undo the three screws and remove the fusebox cover from its retaining tabs. On later models, the fuses are arranged in two blocks, and access to the fuses in the upper block is gained by releasing the plastic cage **(see illustrations)**.

3 Additional fuses are located behind the glovebox, above the control unit under the facia, and in the engine compartment. Access to the fuses behind the glovebox is gained by removing the trim from inside the glovebox, however on later models the complete glovebox must be removed. Access to the fuses above the control unit is gained by removing the footwell side trim panel. In the engine compartment, additional fuses are located in front of the battery and on the engine compartment rear panel.

4 Refer to the Specifications for the location of fuse circuits, as this varies according to model.

5 Fusible links are located on the left-hand side of the engine compartment rear panel, and are accessed by undoing the upper screw and removing the cover. The links are of 30, 40, 50, 60, and 80 amp rating, according to the circuit protected. It is important to fit a fusible link of the correct rating.

6 A blown fuse can be recognised from its melted or broken wire **(see illustration)**.

7 To remove a fuse, first ensure that the relevant circuit is switched off.

8 Pull the fuse from its location, and fit the new fuse. Spare fuses are provided in the main fusebox.

9 Before renewing a blown fuse, trace and rectify the cause, and always use a fuse of the correct rating. Never substitute a fuse of a higher rating, or make temporary repairs using wire or metal foil, as more serious damage, or even fire, could result.

10 Note that the fuses are colour-coded as follows. Refer to the wiring diagrams for details of the fuse ratings used and the circuits protected.

Colour	Rating
Orange	7.5A
Red	10A
Blue	15A
Yellow	20A
Green	30A

Relays

11 A relay is an electrically-operated switch, which is used for the following reasons:

a) *A relay can switch a heavy current remotely from the circuit in which the current is flowing, therefore allowing the use of lighter-gauge wiring and switch contacts.*

b) *A relay can receive more than one control input, unlike a mechanical switch.*

c) *A relay can have a timer function - for example, the intermittent wiper relay.*

12 The main relays are located together with the fuses behind the facia on the driver's side. The central door locking and sunroof relays are located behind the glovebox. On 1998-on models, additional relays for the air conditioning, headlight washers, and electric cooling fans, are located in front of the battery

in the left-hand front corner of the engine compartment.

13 If a circuit or system controlled by a relay develops a fault, and the relay is suspect, operate the system. If the relay is functioning, it should be possible to hear it click as it is energised. If this is the case, the fault lies with the components or wiring of the system. If the relay is not being energised, then either the relay is not receiving a main supply or a switching voltage, or the relay itself is faulty. Testing is by the substitution of a known good unit, but be careful - while some relays are identical in appearance and in operation, others look similar but perform different functions.

14 To renew a relay, first ensure that the relevant circuit is switched off. The relay can then simply be pulled out from the socket, and the new one pushed firmly into position.

4 Bulbs (exterior lights) - renewal

General

1 Whenever a bulb is renewed, note the following points:

a) *Ensure that the relevant electrical circuit is isolated before removing a bulb.*

b) *Remember that, if the light has just been in use, the bulb may be extremely hot.*

c) *Always check the bulb contacts and holder, ensuring that there is clean metal-to-metal contact. Clean off any corrosion or dirt before fitting a new bulb.*

d) *Where bayonet-type bulbs are fitted, ensure that the live contacts bear firmly against the bulb contacts.*

e) *Always ensure that the new bulb is of the correct rating, and that it is completely clean before fitting it.*

f) *Pay attention to the orientation when fitting multi-filament bulbs (e.g. combined tail/brake light bulbs).*

Headlight

2 Open the bonnet. Press the tab downwards

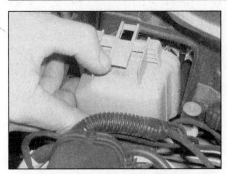

4.2 Removing the plastic cover from the rear of the headlight

4.3 Disconnect the wire . . .

4.4 . . . release the bulb retaining spring clip . . .

to release the clip, then withdraw the plastic cover from the rear of the headlight **(see illustration)**. Note that the inner headlights are for main beam only, whereas the outer headlights are for dipped beam only.

3 Carefully disconnect the wire from the rear of the bulb **(see illustration)**.

4 Release the bulb retaining spring clip and swivel it from the rear of the bulb **(see illustration)**.

5 Withdraw the bulb from the rear of the headlight **(see illustration)**.

6 When handling the new bulb, use a tissue or clean cloth, to avoid touching the glass with the fingers. Moisture and grease from the skin can cause blackening and rapid failure of this type of bulb. If the glass is accidentally touched, wipe it clean using methylated spirit. Avoid knocking or shaking the bulb as this may weaken the filament.

7 Install the new bulb, using a reversal of the removal procedure, ensuring that its locating tabs are correctly located in the light unit cut-outs.

Sidelight

8 Open the bonnet. The sidelight bulbs are located in the outer headlight units. Press the tab downwards to release the clip, then withdraw the plastic cover from the rear of the headlight.

9 Twist the bulbholder to release it from the rear of the light unit **(see illustration)**.

10 The bulb is a push fit in the bulbholder and is removed by pulling it direct from the bulbholder **(see illustration)**.

11 Fit the new bulb using a reversal of the removal procedure.

Front direction indicator

12 Open the bonnet. The front direction indicator bulbs are located in the rear of the headlight/direction indicator light units.

13 Twist the bulbholder anticlockwise through 90° and withdraw it from the rear of the light unit **(see illustration)**.

14 Depress and twist the bulb to remove it from the bulbholder **(see illustration)**.

15 Fit the new bulb using a reversal of the

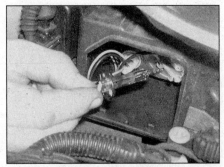

4.5 . . . and withdraw the bulb from the rear of the headlight

removal procedure. Note that an orange coloured bulb must be fitted, not the clear type bulb normally fitted where the lens is coloured orange.

Front direction indicator side repeater

16 The side repeater is held in position by a plastic spring clip on the rear of the light. One method of removing the light without damaging the paintwork is to remove the wheel arch liner first, then reach up behind the wing and depress the clip in order to push out the light from inside. Alternatively, carefully press the side repeater light lens in a rearwards direction, then use a small

4.9 Remove the bulbholder . . .

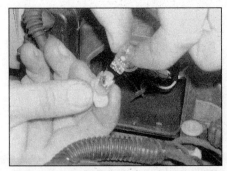

4.10 . . . and pull out the wedge-type bulb

4.13 Twist the front direction indicator anticlockwise and remove it from the rear of the light unit . . .

4.14 . . . then depress and twist the bulb to remove it

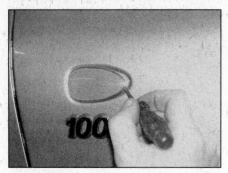

4.16 Carefully release the side repeater front tab with a screwdriver . . .

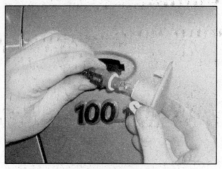

4.17 . . . then twist the bulbholder to release it from the light unit . . .

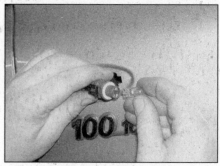

4.18 . . . and pull out the wedge-type bulb

screwdriver to release the front tab from the wing **(see illustration)**.

17 Twist the bulbholder anti-clockwise to release it from the light unit **(see illustration)**.

18 Pull the wedge-type bulb from the bulbholder **(see illustration)**.

19 Fit the new bulb using a reversal of the removal procedure.

Front foglight

20 Unscrew the three screws securing the front foglight to the front bumper. The upper one is located in the light cowl, and the lower two are located on the lower face of the front bumper. With the screws removed, use the screwdriver in the upper screw hole to hook the light unit out from the bumper.

21 Disconnect the wiring from the rear of the

foglight, then turn the cover anticlockwise and remove it.

22 Disconnect the flying lead wire from the rear of the bulb.

23 Release the spring clip, and withdraw the bulb from the rear of the light unit.

24 Fit the new bulb using a reversal of the removal procedure, ensuring that the raised areas engage with the grooves in the light unit.

Rear light cluster bulbs

3-door models

25 Open the tailgate. Working inside the loadspace, undo the screw and remove the cover from the rear of the light cluster.

26 Disconnect the wiring from the rear light cluster bulbholder.

27 Unscrew the two retaining knobs and withdraw the bulbholder.

28 Depress and twist the relevant bulb to remove it **(see illustration)**.

5-door models

29 Open the tailgate. Working inside the loadspace, undo the screw and remove the cover from the rear of the light cluster **(see illustrations)**.

30 Disconnect the wiring from the rear light cluster bulbholder **(see illustration)**.

31 Depress the tabs and withdraw the bulbholder **(see illustration)**.

32 Depress and twist the relevant bulb to remove it **(see illustration)**. The top bulb is for the stop light, the middle bulbs are for the direction indicator and reversing light, and the

4.28 Removing a rear light cluster bulb

4.29a Undo the screw . . .

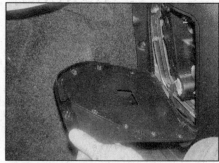

4.29b . . . and remove the cover for access to the rear light cluster bulbs

4.30 Disconnecting the wiring from the rear light cluster

4.31 Withdraw the bulbholder from the rear light cluster

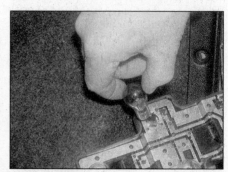

4.32 Removing a bulb from the bulbholder

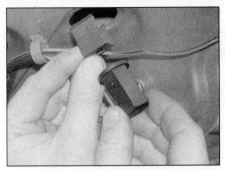

4.35a Brackets are fitted to the middle mounting nuts

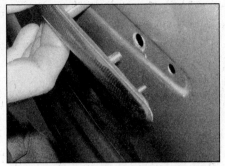

4.35b Withdraw the high-level stop light bulb from the tailgate . . .

4.35c . . . then disconnect the wiring

bottom bulb is of dual filament type for the rear fog light and tail light.

All models

33 Fit the new bulb using a reversal of the removal procedure.

High-level stop light bulb

34 Open the tailgate, then undo the screws securing the trim panel. Note on 5-door models that four of the screws are visible, and four are hidden beneath rubber pads. Prise out the buttons securing the panel to the tailgate lower edge, and withdraw the panel. On 3-door models, use a wide-bladed screwdriver to prise free the clips.
35 Unscrew the plastic nuts inside the tailgate noting that brackets are fitted to the middle nuts. Withdraw the high-level stop

light from the tailgate and disconnect the wiring **(see illustrations)**.
36 Undo the screws and separate the lens from the light unit. Note that it is not possible to remove the bulbs individually **(see illustrations)**.
37 Fit the new bulbs using a reversal of the removal procedure. **Do not** overtighten the light mounting nuts.

Rear number plate light

38 Using a screwdriver, depress the plastic retainer and withdraw the light unit from the rear bumper **(see illustration)**.
39 Twist the bulbholder and remove it from the light body, then pull out the wedge-type bulb **(see illustrations)**.
40 Fit the new bulb using a reversal of the removal procedure.

5 Bulbs (interior lights) - renewal

General

1 Whenever a bulb is renewed, note the following points:

 a) *Ensure that the relevant electrical circuit is isolated before removing a bulb.*
 b) *Remember that, if the light has just been in use, the bulb may be extremely hot.*
 c) *Always check the bulb contacts and holder, ensuring that there is clean metal-to-metal contact. Clean off any corrosion or dirt before fitting a new bulb.*
 d) *Where bayonet-type bulbs are fitted, ensure that the live contacts bear firmly against the bulb contacts.*
 e) *Always ensure that the new bulb is of the correct rating, and that it is completely clean before fitting it.*

Front courtesy light (models without a sunroof)

2 Using a screwdriver, carefully prise out the screw head covers from the courtesy light. Undo the screws and slide the light unit down towards the windscreen. Disconnect the wiring and remove the light unit.
3 Remove the lens by carefully depressing the rear edge.
4 Extract the bulb from the spring contacts.

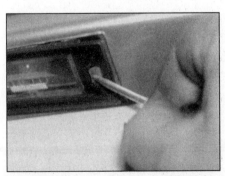

4.36a Undo the screws . . .

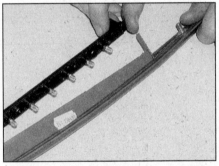

4.36b . . . and separate the lens from the high level light unit

4.38 Use a screwdriver to depress the plastic retainer on the rear number plate light

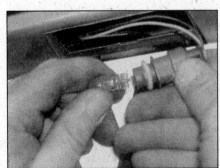

4.39a Twist the bulbholder from the light unit . . .

4.39b . . . then pull out the wedge-type bulb

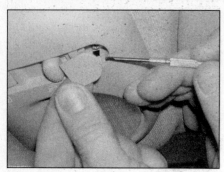

5.6a Prise out the covers . . .

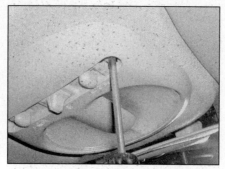

5.6b . . . then undo the screws . . .

5.6c . . . lower the courtesy light . . .

5 Fit the new bulb using a reversal of the removal procedure, but make sure that it is

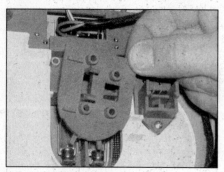

5.6d . . . and disconnect the wiring

held firmly between the spring contacts. If necessary, bend the contacts.

Front courtesy light (models with a sunroof)

6 Using a screwdriver, carefully prise out the screw head covers from the courtesy light. Undo the screws and slide the light unit down towards the windscreen. Disconnect the wiring and remove the light unit (see illustrations).

7 Extract the sunroof key, then push the tab and remove the bulb cover (see illustration).

8 Extract the bulb from the spring contacts (see illustrations).

9 Fit the new bulb using a reversal of the removal procedure, but make sure that it is

held firmly between the spring contacts. If necessary, bend the contacts.

Rear courtesy light

10 Using a screwdriver, carefully prise the light unit from the headlining (see illustration).

11 Extract the bulb from the spring contacts (see illustration).

12 Fit the new bulb using a reversal of the removal procedure, but make sure that it is held firmly between the spring contacts. If necessary, bend the contacts.

Luggage compartment light

13 Using a screwdriver, carefully prise the light unit from the loadspace side trim and let it hang by the wiring (see illustration).

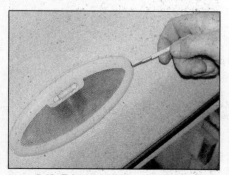

5.7 Remove the bulb cover . . .

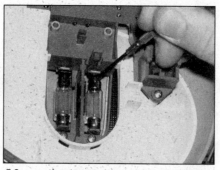

5.8a . . . then use a screwdriver to release the bulb from its contacts . . .

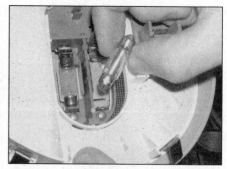

5.8b . . . and withdraw the festoon-type bulb

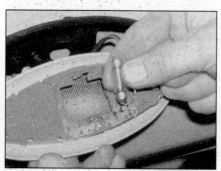

5.10 Prise out the rear courtesy light unit . . .

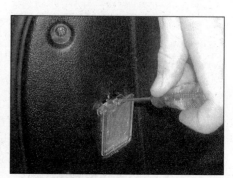

5.11 . . . then extract the festoon-type bulb

5.13 Prise the light unit from the loadspace side trim panel . . .

5.14 ... and extract the festoon-type bulb from the spring contacts

5.21a Turn the bulbholder anticlockwise to remove it ...

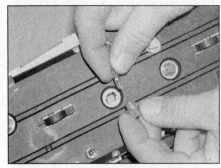

5.21b ... then pull out the wedge-type bulb

5.24a Remove the bulbholder and cover from the surround ...

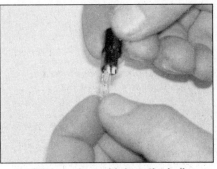

5.24b ... then withdraw the bulb

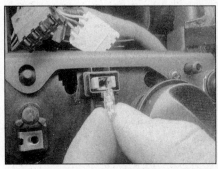

5.27 Removing a heater control panel illumination bulb

14 Extract the festoon-type bulb from the spring contacts **(see illustration)**.

15 Fit the new bulb using a reversal of the removal procedure, but make sure that it is held firmly between the spring contacts. If necessary, bend the contacts.

Glovebox light (where fitted)

16 With the glovebox open, prise out the light using a screwdriver.

17 Disconnect the wiring and remove the light unit. Make sure that the wiring remains in the glovebox.

18 Extract the bulb from the spring contacts.

19 Fit the new bulb using a reversal of the removal procedure, but make sure that it is held firmly between the spring contacts. If necessary, bend the contacts.

Instrument panel illumination

20 Remove the instrument panel as described in Section 7.

21 The bulbs/bulbholders are a bayonet fitting in the rear of the instrument panel. Turn the bulbholder anticlockwise to remove it, then pull out the wedge-type bulb **(see illustrations)**.

22 Fit the new bulb using a reversal of the removal procedure.

Cigarette lighter illumination

23 Remove the cigarette lighter as described in Section 15.

24 Remove the bulbholder and cover from the surround, then withdraw the bulb **(see illustrations)**.

25 Fit the new bulb using a reversal of the removal procedure.

Heater control illumination

26 Remove the heater control surround as described in Chapter 3, Section 9.

27 Pull the wedge-type bulb from its location in the heater control panel **(see illustration)**.

28 Fit the new bulb using a reversal of the removal procedure.

---

6 Exterior light units -
   removal and refitting

Caution: Ensure that the relevant electrical circuit is isolated before removing a light unit. If in doubt, disconnect the battery negative lead before starting work.

Headlight/front direction indicator light

Removal

1 With the bonnet open, disconnect the wiring from the rear of the headlight unit **(see illustration)**. There are wiring plugs for the headlights, sidelights, direction indicator light and beam adjuster.

2 Mark the position of the headlight upper mounting bolts located on the crossmember, then unscrew and remove them **(see illustration)**.

3 Carefully withdraw the headlight unit from

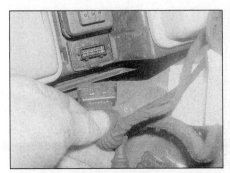

6.1 Disconnecting the wiring from the headlight unit

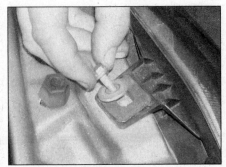

6.2 Removing the headlight upper mounting bolts

6.3a Use a lever . . .

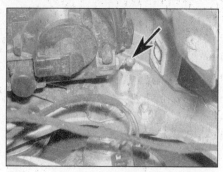

6.3b . . . to lever the headlight location ball from its socket

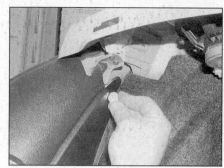

6.12a Using a coin, undo the screw . . .

the front of the car and release the outer location ball from its socket with a suitable lever (see illustrations).

Refitting

4 Refitting is a reversal of removal, but align the upper mounting bolts with the previously-made marks before tightening them. Finally, have the headlight beam alignment checked with reference to Section 8.

Front direction indicator side repeater light

5 The procedure is described as part of the bulb renewal procedure in Section 4.

Front foglight

6 Unscrew the three screws securing the front foglight to the front bumper. The upper one is located in the light cowl, and the lower two are located on the lower face of the front bumper. With the screws removed, use a screwdriver in the upper screw hole to hook the light unit out from the bumper.

7 Disconnect the wiring from the rear of the foglight.

8 To separate the foglight from the mounting bracket/cowl, undo the three crosshead screws.

9 Refitting is a reversal of removal.

10 On completion, check the foglight beam alignment. If necessary, the beam may be altered using the adjustment screw accessible through the hole on the bottom face of the front bumper.

Rear light cluster

3-door models

11 Open the tailgate. Working inside the loadspace, undo the screws and prise out the buttons, then remove the trim panel from the rear valance, using a wide-bladed screwdriver to release the clips.

12 Undo the screw and remove the corner trim panel for access to the rear of the rear light cluster (see illustrations).

13 Disconnect the wiring from the rear light cluster bulbholder. If necessary, remove the bulbholder complete by unscrewing the retaining knobs (see illustration).

14 Support the light cluster from the outside, then unscrew the mounting nuts and withdraw the light unit from the body. If necessary, remove the sealing gasket (see illustrations).

5-door models

15 Open the tailgate. Working inside the loadspace, undo the screws and prise out the buttons, then remove the trim panel from the rear valance.

16 Undo the screw and remove the fastener, then remove the complete corner trim panel for access to the rear of the rear light cluster (see illustration).

17 Disconnect the wiring from the rear light cluster bulbholder. If necessary, remove the bulbholder complete.

18 The light cluster is mounted on a bracket bolted to the inside of the loadspace.

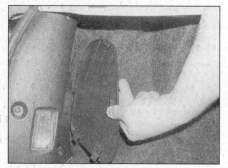

6.12b . . . and remove the corner trim panel

6.13 Disconnecting the wiring from the rear light cluster bulbholder

6.14a Removing the rear light cluster

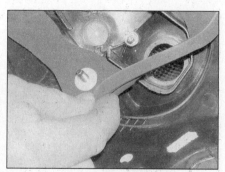

6.14b Removing the sealing gasket

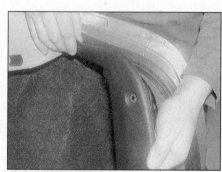

6.16 Removing the corner trim panel

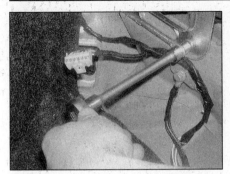

6.18a Unscrew the mounting bolts . . .

6.18b . . . then withdraw the rear light cluster from inside the loadspace

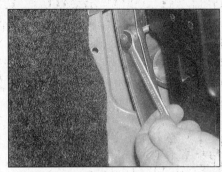

6.19 Adjusting the rear light cluster on its mounting plate

Unscrew the bolts and withdraw the cluster from inside the loadspace **(see illustrations)**.

All models

19 Refitting is a reversal of removal, however, on 5-door models check that the cluster lens is a snug fit on the outer body panel. If necessary, turn the 4 adjustment bolts on the mounting plate to position the lens correctly **(see illustration)**.

High-level stop light bulbs

20 The procedure is described as part of the bulb renewal procedure in Section 4.

Rear number plate light

21 The procedure is described as part of the bulb renewal procedure in Section 4.

7 Instrument panel -
removal and refitting

Right-hand drive models

Removal

1 Disconnect the battery negative (earth) lead (see *Disconnecting the battery*).
2 Undo the screws and remove the lower shroud from the steering column.

3 Undo the screws and remove the upper shroud from the steering column.
4 Undo the screws and remove the cover from the fuses/relays located on the driver's side of the instrument panel **(see illustration)**.
5 Working through the fuse/relay cover hole, undo the screw securing the outer end of the instrument panel surround to the facia **(see illustration)**.
6 Undo the 3 upper and 2 lower screws and withdraw the surround from the facia. Disconnect the wiring from the headlight adjustment and panel lighting rheostats, and place the surround to one side **(see illustrations)**.
7 Undo the four screws and withdraw the instrument panel from the facia, then

7.4 Removing the cover from the fuses/relays

7.5 Removing the instrument panel surround outer screw

7.6a Unscrew the three upper . . .

7.6b . . . and two lower screws . . .

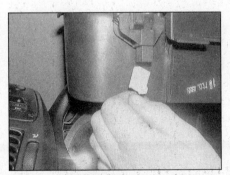

7.6c . . . then disconnect the wiring from the panel lighting rheostat . . .

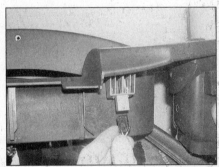

7.6d . . . and headlight adjustment switch

7.7a Undo the upper screws . . .

7.7b . . . and lower screws . . .

7.7c . . . withdraw the instrument panel from the facia . . .

disconnect the wiring plugs from the rear of the panel **(see illustrations)**.
8 The individual gauges and warning lights are illuminated by bulbs. These are a bayonet fit in the rear of the instrument panel and can be removed individually by rotating them through a quarter turn.

Refitting
9 Refitting is a reversal of removal.

Left-hand drive models

Removal
10 Disconnect the battery negative (earth) lead (see *Disconnecting the battery*).
11 Undo the screws and remove the cover from the fuses/relays located on the driver's side of the instrument panel.
12 Working through the fuse/relay cover hole, undo the screw securing the outer end of the instrument panel to the facia.
13 Undo the remaining screws securing the instrument panel surround to the facia. Withdraw the surround and disconnect the wiring from the headlight adjustment and panel lighting rheostats.
14 Undo the four screws and withdraw the instrument panel from the facia, then disconnect the wiring plugs from the rear of the panel.
15 The individual gauges and warning lights are illuminated by bulbs. These are a bayonet fit in the rear of the instrument panel and can be removed individually by rotating them through a quarter turn.

Refitting
16 Refitting is a reversal of removal.

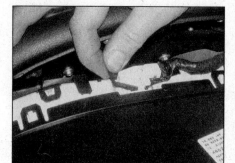

7.7d . . . then lift the clip . . .

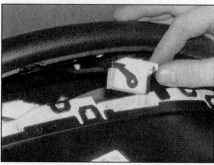

7.7e . . . and disconnect the wiring

8 Headlight beam alignment - general information

Accurate adjustment of the headlight beam is only possible using optical beam-setting equipment, and this work should therefore be carried out by a FIAT dealer or suitably-equipped workshop. Incorrectly adjusted headlamps can dazzle other drivers and cause accidents.

All models are equipped with a headlight aim adjustment switch, located on the facia, which allows the aim of the headlights to be adjusted to compensate for the varying loads carried in the vehicle. The switch should be positioned according to the load being carried in the vehicle. Position 0 is for the driver only or driver and one front passenger. Position 1 is for all seats occupied (5 persons). Position 2 is for all seats occupied plus

some luggage in the rear compartment. Position 3 is for all seats occupied plus the maximum luggage in the rear compartment.

If the headlight beam adjuster is faulty, it may be renewed by twisting it anticlockwise from the rear of the headlight unit **(see illustration)**.

9 Horn - removal and refitting

Removal

1 The horn is mounted beneath the right-hand end of the front bumper. To gain access to the horn, either remove the right-hand headlight unit (see Section 6) or remove the front bumper (see Chapter 11) **(see illustrations)**.

8.3 Removing the headlight beam adjuster from the headlight unit

9.1a The horns viewed with the front bumper removed

9.1b The horns viewed with the right-hand headlight unit removed

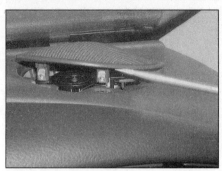

10.2 Prise the speaker grille from the top of the facia . . .

10.3a Undo the speaker mounting screws . . .

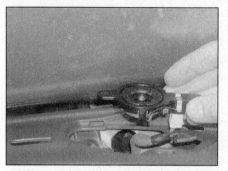

10.3b . . . then withdraw the speaker and disconnect the wiring

10.4 The rear loudspeaker viewed from the luggage compartment

10.6a Undo the screws and remove the loudspeaker from the door . . .

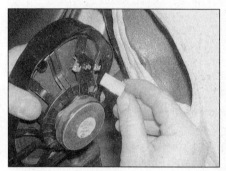

10.6b . . . then disconnect the wiring

2 Disconnect the wiring from the horns.
3 Unscrew the mounting bolts and remove the horns and bracket. Unbolt the horns from the bracket.

Refitting

4 Refitting is a reversal of removal.

10 Loudspeakers - removal and refitting

Removal

1 Ensure that the radio/cassette unit is switched off.

Facia mounted front speaker

2 Carefully prise out the speaker grille from the top of the facia **(see illustration)**.
3 In the grille aperture, undo the speaker mounting screws, withdraw the speaker, and disconnect the wiring **(see illustrations)**.

Rear parcel shelf speakers

4 Working underneath the relevant parcel shelf support bracket, pull back the carpet/trim then undo the securing screws and lower the loudspeaker from the support bracket **(see illustration)**. Unplug the wiring at the connector.

Door-mounted speakers

5 Remove the door inner trim panel as described in Chapter 11.

6 Undo the screws and withdraw the speaker from the door panel, then disconnect the wiring **(see illustrations)**.
7 If necessary, separate the protective grille by releasing the retaining tabs.

Refitting

8 Refitting is a reversal of removal.

11 Radio aerial - removal and refitting

Removal

1 Access to the aerial is gained by removing the interior light/roof switch housing. Carefully prise out the end covers, then undo the two

11.3 Prise off the metal cover and disconnect the aerial lead . . .

screws and lower the housing from the headlining.
2 Undo the sunroof motor screws and disengage the gear from the two cables. Lower the motor from the roof.
3 With the motor removed, prise off the metal cover using a screwdriver, then disconnect the aerial lead **(see illustration)**.
4 Unscrew the mounting nut and withdraw the aerial from the roof **(see illustration)**.
5 Removal of the aerial lead requires removal of the radio/cassette player as described in Section 12, then removal of the interior trim as necessary.

Refitting

6 Refitting is a reversal of removal, but ensure that seal between the aerial housing and the roof panel is in good condition.

11.4 . . . then unscrew the aerial mounting nut

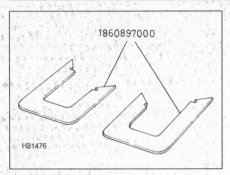

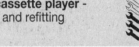

12.2a Fiat radio/cassette removal tools

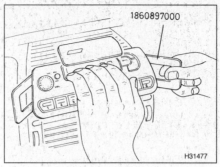

12.2b Using the Fiat tools to remove the radio/cassette

12.2c Using feeler blades to remove the radio/cassette

12 Radio/cassette player - removal and refitting

Caution: If the radio/cassette player fitted has an anti-theft facility, make sure you have the security code before disconnecting the battery.

Removal

1 Disconnect the battery negative (earth) lead (see *Disconnecting the battery*).
2 The radio/cassette player is retained by 4 clips (2 on each side). FIAT technicians use two special tools which are inserted between the sides of the unit and the facia surround, and the tools effectively press the upper clips down, and the lower clips up. These tools may be supplied with the vehicle tool kit. An alternative method to using the special tools is to insert two feeler blades on each sides shown (see illustrations), and to press down the upper blade and press up the lower blade. This will release the unit from the surround, one side at a time.
3 Lift the cassette flap, then pull the unit out from the facia (see illustration).
4 Disconnect the wiring plugs and the aerial lead from the rear of the unit (see illustrations).

Refitting

5 Refitting is a reversal of removal.

13 Speedometer sender unit - removal and refitting

Removal

1 The speedometer sender unit is mounted on the top of the transmission, above the final drive position. First remove the battery and battery tray as described in Chapter 5A for access to the sender. Move the relay holder box to one side after removing the cover and unscrewing the mounting bolts. Also unbolt and remove the battery mounting bracket.
2 Disconnect the wiring from the sender unit.
3 On early models, the sender may be removed from the pinion by unscrewing the large nut. On later models, however, the sender unit is manufactured as a single unit.
4 On manual transmission models, use an Allen key to unscrew the lockbolt from the rear of the transmission casing.
5 On automatic transmission models, unscrew the bolt securing the unit to the top of the transmission casing.
6 Carefully, lift the sender unit and pinion from the casing. Make sure that the pinion remains in the sender unit while it is being removed otherwise it may fall into the transmission.
7 Remove the O-ring seal from the groove in the body of the sender unit. Obtain a new O-ring seal.

Refitting

8 Refitting is a reversal of removal, but fit a new O-ring seal, and make sure that the pinion remains in the body of the sender unit as it is being inserted. The top of the pinion has a square drive which engages a dog inside the unit, and it may be necessary to turn the unit slightly to ensure the dog enters the drive. On manual transmission models it will be necessary to align the hole in the sender body with the lockbolt hole; apply suitable sealant to the threads of the lockbolt before inserting it.

14 Switches - removal and refitting

Steering column combination switch

Removal

1 Disconnect the battery negative (earth) lead (see *Disconnecting the battery*). Wait approximately 10 minutes before proceeding as a precaution against accidental activation of the airbag (see Section 21). Turn the steering wheel so that the roadwheels are pointing in the straight-ahead position.
2 Remove the steering wheel as described in Chapter 10.
3 Remove the airbag clockspring unit from the column with reference to Section 22 of this Chapter. **Note:** *The clockspring*

12.3 Removing the radio/cassette from the facia

12.4a Disconnecting the wiring plugs . . .

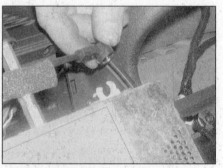

12.4b . . . and aerial plug from the rear of the radio/cassette

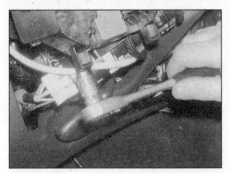

14.4a Using an Allen key, undo the collar retaining screw from the bottom of the switch . . .

14.4b . . . then disconnect the wiper switch wiring . . .

14.4c . . . and the indicator switch wiring . . .

14.4d . . . and slide the combination switch assembly from the top of the steering column

14.4e The collar on the rear of the combination switch assembly

incorporates spring tensioned clips which prevent the upper and lower sections of the unit from turning in relation to each other when removed from the column.

4 Using an Allen key, undo the collar retaining screw from the bottom of the switch, then disconnect the wiring plugs and slide the combination switch assembly from the top of the steering column **(see illustrations)**. It is not possible to separate each stalk unit and switch.

Refitting

5 Refitting is a reversal of removal, but note that the groove at the top of the switch must be aligned with the raised tab on the steering column. As a precaution against accidental activation of the airbag, ensure no one is inside the vehicle when reconnecting the battery. With the driver's door open, reach inside and turn on the ignition, then check the operation of the airbag warning light.

Headlamp beam adjustment switch

Removal

6 The headlamp beam adjustment switch is located on the instrument panel surround. First, undo the screws and remove the lower shroud from the steering column.

7 Undo the screws and remove the upper shroud from the steering column.
8 Undo the screws and remove the cover from the fuses/relays located on the driver's side of the instrument panel.
9 Working through the fuse/relay cover hole, undo the screw securing the outer end of the instrument panel surround to the facia.
10 Undo the 3 upper and 2 lower screws and withdraw the surround from the facia. Disconnect the wiring from the headlight adjustment and panel lighting rheostat.
11 With the surround on the bench, undo the screws and remove the switch.

Refitting

12 Refitting is a reversal of removal.

Brake stop-light switch

Removal and refitting

13 Refer to Chapter 9.

Electric exterior rear view mirror switch (where fitted)

Removal

14 Prise the electric rear view mirror switch panel from the centre console, and disconnect the wiring.

Refitting

15 Refitting is a reversal of removal.

Courtesy light switch

Removal

16 A separate courtesy light switch is only fitted to early models - the function is incorporated in the central locking switch on later models. Where fitted, open the door to expose the switch in the door B-pillar.
17 Remove the securing screw, then remove the rubber gaiter (where applicable) and withdraw the switch from the door pillar. Disconnect the wiring connector as it becomes accessible.

>
> **HAYNES HiNT**
> *Tape the wiring to the door pillar, or tie a length of string to the wiring, to retrieve it if it falls back into the door pillar.*

Refitting

18 Refitting is a reversal of removal, but ensure that the rubber gaiter is securely seated over the switch.

14.27 Removing the instrument panel illumination rheostat from the surround

14.33a Use a screwdriver to prise the hazard warning switch . . .

14.33b . . . from the heater control surround panel . . .

Electric window switches

Removal

19 Use a screwdriver to carefully prise the electric window switch panel from the door trim panel. Use a piece of card or cloth to protect the panel while levering on it.
20 Disconnect the wiring and remove the switch.

Refitting

21 Refitting is a reversal of removal.

Instrument illumination rheostat

Removal

22 The instrument illumination rheostat is located on the instrument panel surround. First, undo the screws and remove the lower shroud from the steering column.
23 Undo the screws and remove the upper shroud from the steering column.
24 Undo the screws and remove the cover

from the fuses/relays located on the driver's side of the instrument panel.
25 Working through the fuse/relay cover hole, undo the screw securing the outer end of the instrument panel surround to the facia.
26 Undo the 3 upper and 2 lower screws and withdraw the surround from the facia. Disconnect the wiring from the headlight adjustment and panel lighting rheostat.
27 With the surround on the bench, undo the screws and remove the switch **(see illustration)**.

Refitting

28 Refitting is a reversal of removal.

Facia switches

Removal

29 The facia switches are located in the centre of the facia, above the heater control knobs. Using a small screwdriver, carefully prise out the small covers from each end of

the switch position, and the cover at the centre of the switches.
30 Undo the screws and withdraw the switch panel from the front of the facia.
31 Disconnect the wiring and remove the switches from the facia.

Refitting

32 Refitting is a reversal of removal.

Hazard warning switch

Removal

33 Using a screwdriver, carefully prise the hazard warning switch from the heater control surround panel **(see illustrations)**.
34 Disconnect the wiring and remove the switch **(see illustration)**.
35 Refitting is a reversal of removal.

---

15 Cigarette lighter -
removal and refitting

Removal

1 With the ashtray closed, undo the lower mounting screws, then open the ashtray lid and unscrew the upper mounting screws. Withdraw the ashtray from the facia and disconnect the wiring from the cigar lighter.
2 With the ashtray on the bench, use a small drift to drive out the pivot pin, then separate the ashtray lid from the base **(see illustrations)**.
3 Remove the element, then using a small screwdriver, carefully prise the inner metal cylinder from the green plastic outer surround **(see illustrations)**. Press the

14.34 . . . then disconnect the wiring

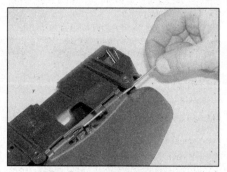

15.2a Remove the pivot pin . . .

15.2b . . . and separate the ashtray lid from the base

15.3a Remove the element . . .

15.3b . . . then use a screwdriver to prise up . . .

15.3c ... and remove the inner metal cylinder

15.4 Removing the cigarette lighter surround and bulbholder

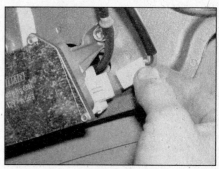

16.4a Disconnecting the wiring from the tailgate wiper motor ...

terminal end of the metal cylinder to assist its removal.

4 Align the raised tooth with the cut-out in the body and remove the surround together with the bulbholder **(see illustration)**.

Refitting

5 Refitting is a reversal of removal.

16 Tailgate wiper motor - removal and refitting

Removal

1 Make sure that the ignition is switched off.
2 Remove the tailgate wiper arm as described in Section 19.
3 With the tailgate open, undo the screws and prise out the retaining studs, then remove the inner trim panel. On 3-door models, use a wide-bladed screwdriver to prise free the clips.
4 Disconnect the wiring from the tailgate wiper motor. Also disconnect the washer tube from the jet adapter located on the spindle housing **(see illustrations)**.
5 Using an Allen key, unscrew the mounting bolts, then withdraw the wiper motor while guiding the jet adapter through the rubber grommet **(see illustrations)**.

Refitting

6 Refitting is a reversal of removal. Refit the wiper arm with reference to Section 19.

17 Windscreen/tailgate/headlight washer system components - removal and refitting

Washer fluid reservoir

Removal

1 The washer fluid reservoir is located on the right-hand side (RHD models) or left-hand side (LHD models) of the engine compartment, next to the coolant reservoir. First syphon out all of the fluid using a pipette.
2 Unscrew the mounting bolts and move the coolant reservoir to one side, away from the coolant reservoir.
3 Disconnect the wiring from the washer pump.
4 Disconnect the washer tubing from the pump, noting where each tube is fitted for correct refitting. Also release the tubing from the support clip.
5 Unscrew the mounting bolts and remove the reservoir from the engine compartment. If necessary, remove the inlet neck from the top of the reservoir.

Refitting

6 Refitting is a reversal of removal.

Washer pump

Removal

7 Unscrew the mounting bolts and move the coolant reservoir to one side, away from the coolant reservoir.

8 Disconnect the wiring from the washer pump.
9 Disconnect the washer tubing from the pump, noting where each tube is fitted for correct refitting.
10 Pull the pump upwards from the rubber grommet, and withdraw from the reservoir. If necessary, extract the rubber grommet.

Refitting

11 Refitting is a reversal of removal.

Windscreen washer nozzle

Removal

12 Open the bonnet, then prise out the fasteners and release the padding in the area beneath the washer nozzles.
13 Release the securing tabs using a suitable screwdriver, then push the nozzle from the bonnet. Disconnect the fluid hose, and withdraw the nozzle.

Refitting

14 Refitting is a reversal of removal, but if necessary adjust the nozzle so that the jets are aimed at a point approximately 250 mm from the upper edge of the windscreen. To do this, insert a thin screwdriver in the adjustment holes on the sides of the nozzles.

Tailgate washer nozzle

Removal

15 The tailgate washer nozzle is located on the tailgate wiper spindle housing. To remove it, first remove the wiper motor as described in Section 16.

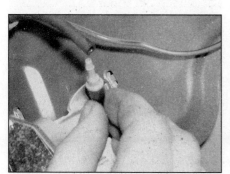

16.4b ... and the washer tube from the tailgate washer jet adapter

16.5a Unscrew the mounting bolts ...

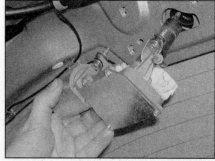

16.5b ... and withdraw the wiper motor from the tailgate

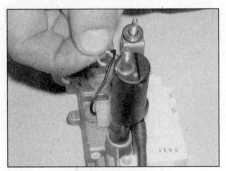

17.16a Extract the circlip . . .

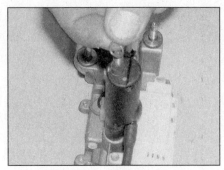

17.16b . . . and washer . . .

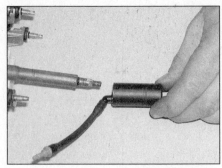

17.16c . . . and pull the nozzle/adapter from the wiper spindle housing

17.16d Removing the washer tube from the nozzle/adapter

18.3a Pull up the weatherstrips . . .

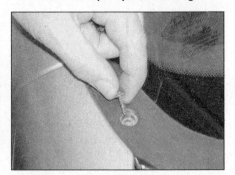

18.3b . . . then undo the screws . . .

16 Extract the circlip and washer, then pull the nozzle/adapter from the wiper spindle housing. If necessary, remove the tube. **(see illustrations)**.

Refitting

17 Refitting is a reversal of removal, but on completion adjust the washer jet using a small screwdriver through the hole in the nozzle/adapter. The jet should be directed towards the upper area of the tailgate wiper wiped area.

Headlight washer nozzle

Removal

18 The headlight washer nozzles are located in the front bumper. First remove the front bumper as described in Chapter 11.
19 Disconnect the tube and adapter from the bottom of the headlight nozzle.

20 Unscrew the nut and withdraw the nozzle from the front bumper.

Refitting

21 Refitting is a reversal of removal.

18 Windscreen wiper motor -
removal and refitting

Removal

1 Make sure that the windscreen wiper motor is in its 'parked' position by briefly switching it on and off. Make sure that the ignition is switched off.
2 Refer to Section 19 and remove both wiper arms.
3 With the bonnet open, pull up the

weatherstrips and undo the screws, then unclip and remove the cowl panel from in front of the windscreen. Note that the two rear screws are accessed by prising out the two covers **(see illustrations)**.
4 Remove the protective cover from the windscreen wiper motor.
5 Disconnect the wiring plug from the motor **(see illustration)**.
6 Unscrew and remove the three mounting bolts, and withdraw the wiper motor assembly from the bulkhead **(see illustrations)**.
7 Unscrew the crank retaining nut, and the three mounting bolts, then separate the wiper motor from the linkage.

Refitting

8 Refitting is a reversal of removal, but ensure that the motor drive is in the 'parked' position before reconnecting the crank arm.

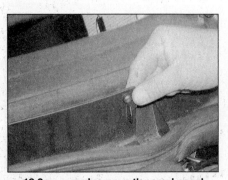

18.3c . . . and remove the cowl panel

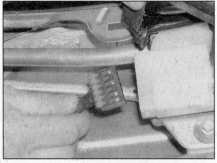

18.5 Disconnect the wiring from the wiper motor

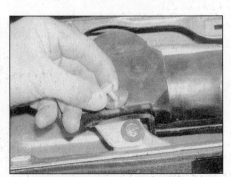

18.6a Wiper mounting bolt located by the motor

18.6b Wiper mounting bolt located on the linkage frame

18.6c Removing the wiper motor assembly from the bulkhead

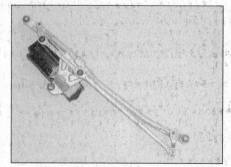

18.6d Wiper motor and linkage removed from the bulkhead

19 Wiper arm -
removal and refitting

Removal

1 Operate the wiper motor, then switch it off so that the wiper arm returns to its 'parked' position.

2 Stick masking tape on the glass, to use as an alignment aid for the rest position of the wiper blade. Note, however, that there is a mark on the tailgate window glass for locating the blade in its 'rest' position **(see illustrations)**.

3 Prise out the wiper arm spindle nut cover, then unscrew and remove the spindle nut. Recover the washer **(see illustrations)**.

4 Lift the blade off the glass, and ease the wiper arm off its spindle, using a rocking action **(see illustrations)**. If both windscreen wiper arms are being removed, note both locations, as different arms are fitted to each side.

Refitting

5 Refitting is a reversal of removal, but ensure that the wiper arm and spindle splines are clean and dry and align the blade with the tape before tightening the spindle nut securely.

20 Anti-theft alarm/engine immobiliser system -
general information

Note: *This information is applicable only to the*

anti-theft alarm system fitted by FIAT as standard equipment.

1 All models are fitted with a FIAT CODE engine immobiliser system as standard equipment. The immobiliser is automatically activated when the ignition key is turned to PARK or STOP, and will also be activated when the key is removed completely from the switch. The ignition key has an integral device which transmits a coded signal to the FIAT CODE unit on the ignition switch, and the unit will only allow the engine to be started if it recognises the signal.

2 Each new car is provided with one master key (burgundy) and two duplicate keys (blue) for normal use. The duplicate keys incorporate a battery on models with remote central locking and an alarm system. The master key should be kept in a safe place, as

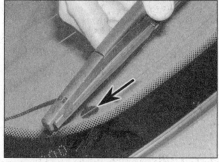

19.2a The 'rest' position mark on the tailgate window glass

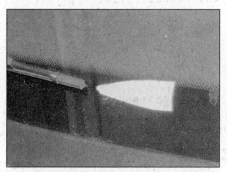

19.2b Stick masking tape on the windscreen to indicate the 'rest' position of the wiper blade

19.3a Prise out the wiper arm spindle nut cover . . .

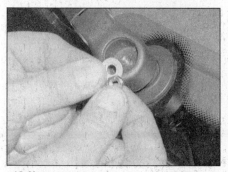

19.3b . . . remove the nut and washer . . .

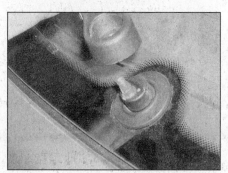

19.4a . . . and remove the tailgate wiper arm from the spindle

19.4b Removing the windscreen wiper arm from its spindle

it is required for making copies in the event of the loss of the duplicate keys.

3 Most models are fitted with an electronic alarm system which enables remote control of the central locking system, together with monitoring of door/tailgate/bonnet opening, movement inside the car, and any hard knocks to the car body. The system is activated when the ignition key is removed from the STOP or PARK positions on the ignition switch. An LED warning light in the middle of the facia flashes for the complete period when the system is activated.

4 The alarm system performs a self-test whenever it is switched on. Should a fault be detected, a second short beep will be heard after the main beep. If this occurs, check that the doors/tailgate/bonnet are closed correctly.

5 When the system is switched on, a single beep will be heard and the direction indicators will light up for approximately three seconds. When the system is switched off, two beeps will be heard and the direction indicators will flash twice.

6 Should the alarm system become faulty, the vehicle should be taken to a FIAT dealer for examination.

7 If a new key is obtained, it will be necessary to transfer the transponder from the old key to the new one. To do this, prise open the old key fob using a small screwdriver. **Note:** *Carry this out over a table, otherwise the transponder may be lost.*

8 Note its location, then use a screwdriver to carefully prise the transponder from the old key **(see illustration)**.

9 Carefully locate the transponder in the new key, then refit the fob halves, pressing the two halves together until they are engaged.

21 Airbag system - precautions and general information

Warning: Note that the airbag must not be subjected to temperatures in excess of 100° C. When the airbag is removed, ensure that it is stored the correct way up to prevent possible inflation. Do not allow any solvents or cleaning agents to contact the airbag assembly. It must be cleaned using only a damp cloth. The airbag and control unit are both sensitive to impact. If either is dropped from a height of 50 cm or more or are damaged they should be renewed. Before working on the airbag components, disconnect the battery and wait approximately 10 minutes. Also remove the airbag fuse from the fusebox.

1 A driver's airbag is fitted as standard on all models, and a passenger airbag is available as an option. Side airbags, fitted in the front seat backrests, are also available on certain models to protect the front seat occupants in

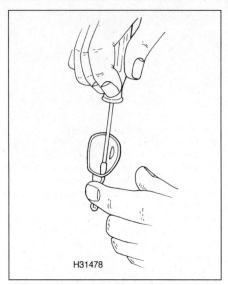

20.8 Removing the transponder from the ignition key fob

the event of a side impact of medium to high level.

2 Where passenger and/or side airbags are fitted, the front passenger seat is fitted with a sensor to detect the presence of a person. If the sensor does not detect a person within approximately 30 seconds, the passenger airbag(s) are deactivated.

3 The airbag system consists of the airbag units complete with gas generators, the control unit with integral deceleration sensor, and a warning light on the instrument panel.

4 The airbag system is triggered in the event of a heavy frontal impact above a predetermined force, depending on the point of impact. The airbag is inflated within milliseconds and forms a safety cushion between the driver and steering wheel and, where fitted, between the passenger and facia. This prevents contact between the upper body and wheel/facia and therefore greatly reduces the risk of injury. The airbag then deflates almost immediately. Note that the front seat belt reels incorporate pretensioners which operate entirely separate to the airbag system and are not connected

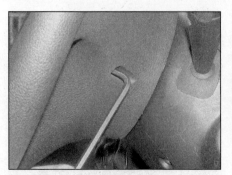

22.2 Unscrew and remove the two airbag retaining screws from the rear of the steering wheel

electrically to the system. The pretensioners are activated by an internal deceleration mechanism.

5 Every time the ignition is switched on, the airbag control unit performs a self-test. The self-test takes approximately 4 seconds and during this time the airbag warning light in the instrument panel is illuminated. After the self-test has been completed the warning light should go out. If the warning light fails to come on, check the bulb first before assuming the system is faulty. If it remains illuminated after 4 seconds or comes on at any time when the vehicle is being driven, there is a fault in the airbag system. The vehicle should be taken to a FIAT dealer for examination at the earliest possible opportunity.

22 Airbag system components - removal and refitting

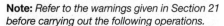

Note: *Refer to the warnings given in Section 21 before carrying out the following operations.*

Driver's airbag

Removal

1 Disconnect the battery negative (earth) lead (see *Disconnecting the battery*). Also remove the airbag fuse from the fusebox. Wait approximately 10 minutes before proceeding, then insert the ignition key and turn it to release the steering lock.

2 Unscrew and remove the two airbag retaining screws from the rear of the steering wheel, rotating the wheel as necessary to gain access to the screws **(see illustration)**.

3 Return the steering wheel to the straight-ahead position then carefully lift the airbag assembly away from the steering wheel. Disconnect the yellow wiring from the rear of the airbag **(see illustrations)**. Note that the airbag must not be knocked or dropped and should be stored the correct way up with its padded surface uppermost.

Refitting

4 Reconnect the wiring to the rear of the airbag and to the horn terminal.

5 Seat the airbag unit centrally in the steering

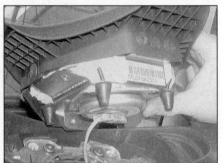

22.3a Carefully lift the airbag assembly away from the steering wheel

22.3b Disconnect the yellow wiring from the rear of the airbag

wheel, making sure the wires do not become trapped. Fit the retaining screws and tighten them to the specified torque setting.

6 Refit the airbag fuse, then reconnect the battery, but as a precaution against accidental activation of the airbag, ensure no one is inside the vehicle. With the driver's door open, reach inside and turn on the ignition, then check the operation of the airbag warning light.

Passenger airbag

Removal

7 Disconnect the battery negative (earth) lead (see *Disconnecting the battery*). Also remove the airbag fuse from the fusebox. Wait approximately 10 minutes before proceeding.

8 Open the glovebox lid, then undo the two knobs and remove the upper trim from inside the glovebox. Unscrew the mounting bolts and withdraw the glovebox from the facia.

9 Working through the glovebox aperture, unscrew and remove the four bolts securing the airbag to the body.

10 Disconnect the wiring and withdraw the airbag from inside the car. Note that the airbag must not be knocked or dropped and should be stored the correct way up with its padded surface uppermost.

11 Note that the complete facia must be removed in order to remove the passenger airbag module cover. Refer to Chapter 11 and remove the facia, then undo the screws and drill out the rivets.

Refitting

12 If removed, refit the module cover and secure with the screws and new rivets.

13 Reconnect the wiring and make sure that the wire is correctly located in the support grommet.

14 Lift the airbag into position and align the holes in the mounting bracket with those in the body. Insert the bolts and tighten to the specified torque.

15 Refit the glovebox and trim.

16 Refit the airbag fuse, then reconnect the battery, but as a precaution against accidental activation of the airbag, ensure no one is inside the vehicle. With the driver's door open, reach inside and turn on the ignition, then check the operation of the airbag warning light.

Front seat side airbag

Removal

17 Remove the front seat as described in Chapter 11.

18 Using a screwdriver, prise the cap from the seat tilt adjustment knob, then pull off the knob.

19 Undo the screws and remove the outer plastic side cover from the seat.

20 On the inside of the seat, undo the screw securing the inner plastic side cover.

21 Using a screwdriver, carefully prise out the rear of the inner plastic cover from the side of the seat taking care not to damage the cover. As it is being removed, the spring washer will be released from the peg on the seat. With the cover removed, press out the spring washer and outer cap.

22 Release and unhook the bottom of the rear cover from the seat rail, disconnect the tensioning rods, and partly pull the upholstery upwards for access to the side airbag mounting nuts.

23 Unscrew the mounting nuts, and carefully withdraw the airbag module from the side of the seat. Carefully disconnect the wiring from the airbag. Note that the airbag must not be knocked or dropped and should be stored with its padded surface uppermost.

Refitting

24 Reconnect the wiring and locate the airbag in the side of the seat. Tighten the mounting nuts to the specified torque.

25 Refit the upholstery and side covers to the seat using a reversal of the removal procedure.

26 Refit the front seat to the car with reference to Chapter 11. When reconnecting the battery, ensure no one is inside the vehicle as a precaution against accidental activation of the airbag. With the driver's door open, reach inside and turn on the ignition, then check the operation of the airbag warning light.

Airbag control unit

Note: *The airbag control unit must always be renewed after a crash which activates an airbag.*

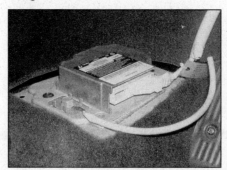

22.28 The airbag control unit is located under the centre of the facia

Removal

27 Disconnect the battery negative (earth) lead (see *Disconnecting the battery*). Also remove the airbag fuse from the fusebox. Wait approximately 10 minutes before proceeding.

28 The airbag control unit is located under the centre of the facia, in front of the centre console **(see illustration)**. Undo the screws and release the fasteners in order to remove the trim panel from the inside of the driver's footwell. Push the centre locking pins of the fasteners in order to release them.

29 Undo the mounting screws then disconnect the wiring and withdraw the control unit.

Refitting

30 Locate the control unit beneath the facia, making sure that the arrow on top of the unit is pointing forwards, then reconnect the wiring and insert the mounting screws. Tighten the screws securely.

31 Make sure that the fasteners are correctly located in the trim panel, with the centre locking pins in their raised position. Refit the trim panel and secure the fasteners by pressing in the centre locking pins until flush. Insert and tighten the screws.

32 Refit the airbag fuse, then reconnect the battery, but as a precaution against accidental activation of the airbag, ensure no one is inside the vehicle. With the driver's door open, reach inside and turn on the ignition, then check the operation of the airbag warning light.

Airbag clock spring

Removal

33 Disconnect the battery negative (earth) lead (see *Disconnecting the battery*). Also remove the airbag fuse from the fusebox. Wait approximately 10 minutes before proceeding.

34 Remove the steering wheel as described in Chapter 10. This procedure includes removal of the driver's airbag described in paragraphs 1 to 3 of this Section. **Note:** *Before removing the steering wheel, make sure it is in its central position with the front wheels pointing straight-ahead.*

35 Undo the screws and remove the lower shroud from the steering column, then undo the screws and remove the upper shroud **(see illustrations)**.

22.35a Undo the screws . . .

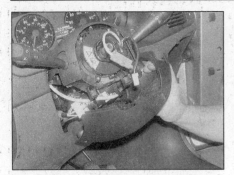

22.35b . . . and remove the lower shroud . . .

22.35c . . . then undo the screws . . .

22.35d . . . and remove the upper shroud from the steering column

36 Next to the ignition switch, disconnect the clock spring wiring, and also disconnect the wiring from the airbag control unit **(see illustration)**.

37 Undo the screws (noting their locations) and remove the clock spring from the combination switch **(see illustration)**. **Note:** *The clockspring incorporates spring tensioned clips which prevent the upper and lower sections of the unit from turning in relation to each other when removed from the column.*

Refitting

38 Make sure the front wheels are pointing in the straight-ahead direction. Refit the clockspring to the combination switch and tighten the screws. Note that there are four holes for the retaining screws, however, only three screws are fitted, to prevent distortion of the clockspring housing. **Note:** *If a new clockspring is being fitted, remove the temporary locking key before locating it on the combination switch.*

22.36 **Disconnecting the clockspring wiring**

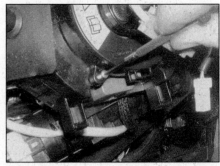

22.37 **Removing the clockspring retaining screws**

39 Reconnect the wiring, and refit the steering column shrouds.

40 Refit the steering wheel and airbag with reference to Chapter 10 and paragraphs 4 to 6 of this Section.

41 Refit the airbag fuse, then reconnect the battery, but as a precaution against accidental activation of the airbag, ensure no one is inside the vehicle. With the driver's door open, reach inside and turn on the ignition, then check the operation of the airbag warning light.

Key to symbols

20	Item number
	Bulb
	Switch
	Multiple contact switch (ganged)
	Fuse/ fusible link
	Solenoid actuator
	Resistor
	Variable resistor
	Internal connection in a component
	Block conection, detachable
	Wire connection, fixed
G/Y	Wire colour (green wire with yellow tracer)
	Interconnecting line (thin line)
	Denotes alternative wiring variation
Diagram 5, Arrow B **RH indicator signal** **B**	Connections to other circuits
G102	Earth point with location code
M	Pump/motor
	Dashed outline denotes part of a larger item, containing in this case an electronic or solid state device
	Gauge/meter

Fiat Brava/Bravo wiring diagrams 1995 to 1999

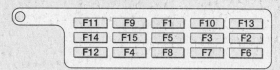

Fuse holder

Fuse allocation

1	15A	Exterior lights - Reversing, stop, direction indicators electric windows, air bag, ABS
2	10A	Front RH side light, rear LH light, RH number plate light, radio lighting, instrument panel lighting, switch panel lighting
3	10A	Front LH side light, heater/air conditioner controls lighting, rear RH light, LH number plate light
4	10A	LH dipped beam
5	10A	RH dipped beam, headlamp adjusters
6	10A	RH main beam
7	10A	LH main beam, main beam warning light
8	10A	Rear fog lamps
9	10A	Hazard warning lights
10	15A	Courtesy light, luggage compartment light, clock, radio, glove compartment light
11	20A	Heated rear window and warning light, heated mirrors
12	-	-
13	20A	Horns
14	20A	Front and rear screen wash/wipe, headlight washer
15	20A	Interior ventilation fan, radiator fan, cigar lighter

Index to diagrams

2	Starting and charging, engine cooling fan, horn, heated rear window, interior ventilation
3	Front and rear screen wash/wipe, headlight wash, Hazard warning lights
4	Direction indicators, brake lights, reversing lights
5	Exterior lights, anti-lock braking system
6	Fog lights - front and rear, electric windows (front)
7	Cigarette lighter, headlight alignment, high level radio
8	Interior lighting, sun roof, heated and adjustable rear view mirrors
9	Weber IAW ignition and injection system (1.6 SX,ELX,HLX)
10	Bosch Mono Motronic ignition and injection system (1.4 S, SX, Team,80)

Earth locations

E1	Battery earth on bodyshell
E2	Left front earth
E3	Left dashboard earth
E4	Right front earth
E5	Left rear earth
E6	Right rear earth
E7	Right dashboard earth
E8	Earth for electronic injection
E9	Earth for electronic ignition

H31692

Wire colours

W	White	O	Orange
R	Red	Lb	Light blue
Y	Yellow		
Br	Brown		
P	Pink		
Bl	Blue		
Gr	Grey		
G	Green		
B	Black		
V	Violet		

H31693

Key to items

1 Battery
2 Power fuse box
  B 40A fuse for ignition system
  D 80A fuse for junction unit
3 Starter motor
4 Alternator
5 Ignition switch
6 Engine cooling fan fuse 40/50A
7 Engine cooling fan
8 Thermostat switch on radiator
9 Steering column switch unit
10 Junction unit
  R1 Ignition relay
  R2 Horn relay
  R3 Heated rear window relay
11 Fan speed switch
12 Fan speed resistors
13 Climate control fan
14 Heater unit light bulbs
15 Horns
16 Heated rear window
17 Switch control panel
  Heated rear window switch with warning light
18 Contact board for rear connections

Diagram 2

Starting and charging

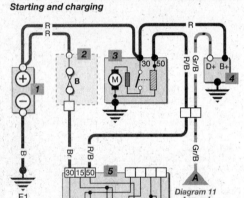

Horn

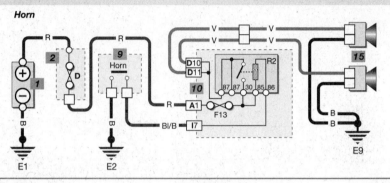

Engine cooling fan

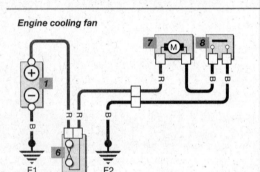

Heated rear window

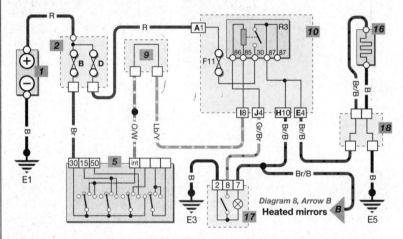

Interior ventilation

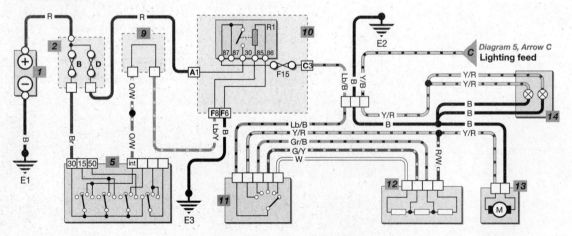

Wire colours

W	White	O	Orange
R	Red	Lb	Light blue
Y	Yellow		
Br	Brown		
P	Pink		
Bl	Blue		
Gr	Grey		
G	Green		
B	Black		
V	Violet		

H31694

Key to items

1 Battery
2 Power fuse box
  B 40A fuse for ignition system
  C 60A fuse for optional extras
  D 80A fuse for junction unit
5 Ignition switch
9 Steering column switch unit
  A windscreen wiper speed control
  B front/rear screen, headlamp
    washer switch

C rear screen wiper switch
D direction indicators/
  hazard lights relay
10 Junction unit
  R1 Ignition relay
18 Contact board for rear connections
20 Front/rear washer pump
21 Windscreen wiper motor
22 Rear screen wiper motor
23 Fuse for headlight washer (20A)

24 Headlight intermittent wash relay
25 Headlight washer pump
26 Hazard warning lights switch

Diagram 3

Front and rear screen wash/wipe

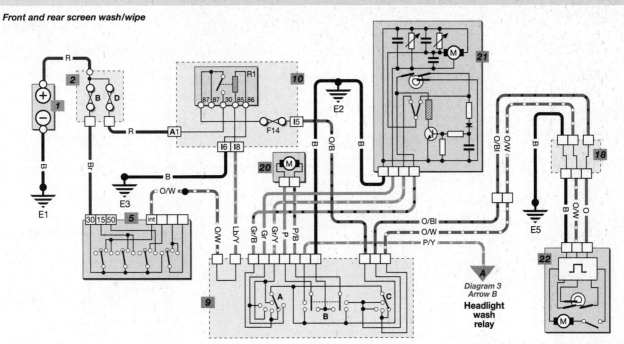

Hazard warning lights

Headlight wash

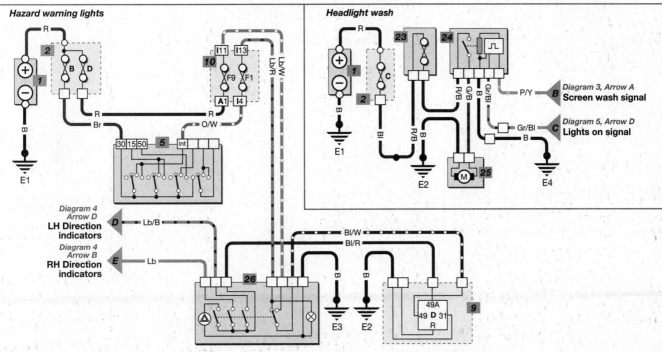

Wire colours

W	White	**O**	Orange
R	Red	**Lb**	Light blue
Y	Yellow		
Br	Brown		
P	Pink		
Bl	Blue		
Gr	Grey		
G	Green		
B	Black		
V	Violet		

H31695

Key to items

1 Battery
2 Power fuse box
   B 40A fuse for ignition system
5 Ignition switch
9 Steering column switch unit
   D direction indicators/
      hazard lights relay
   E Direction indicator switch
10 Junction unit
26 Hazard warning lights switch

27 Front LH light cluster
28 Front RH light cluster
29 Front LH side indicator
30 Front RH side indicator
31 Rear LH light cluster
32 Rear RH light cluster
33 Brake lights switch
34 Additional brake light
35 Reversing light switch

Diagram 4

Direction indicators

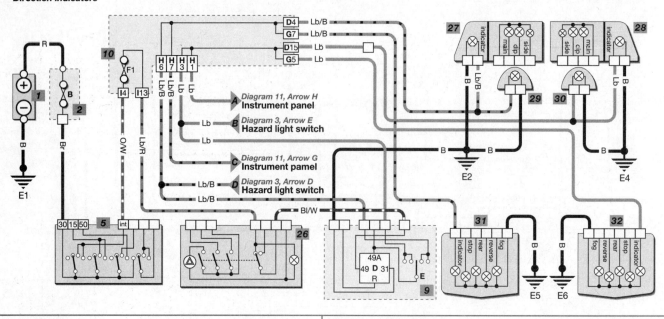

Brake lights

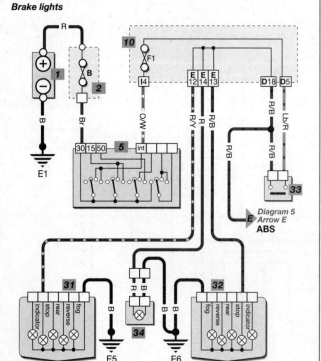

Reversing lights

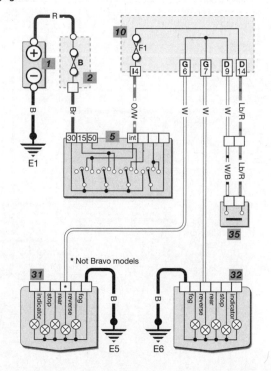

* Not Bravo models

Wire colours

W	White	O	Orange
R	Red	Lb	Light blue
Y	Yellow		
Br	Brown		
P	Pink		
Bl	Blue		
Gr	Grey		
G	Green		
B	Black		
V	Violet		

H31696

Key to items

1 Battery
2 Power fuse box
  B 40A fuse for ignition system
  C 60A fuse for optional extras
5 Ignition switch
9 Steering column switch unit
  F Sidelights switch
  G Headlight dip/main switch
  H Headlight flash
10 Junction unit
27 Front LH light cluster
28 Front RH light cluster

31 Rear LH light cluster
32 Rear RH light cluster
33 Number plate lights
34 Dipped beam relay
35 Fuse (60A)
36 ABS fuse (5A)
37 ABS cintrol unit
38 Diagnostic connection
39 Front LH ABS sensor
40 Front RH ABS sensor
41 Rear LH ABS sensor
42 Rear RH ABS sensor

Diagram 5

Exterior lights

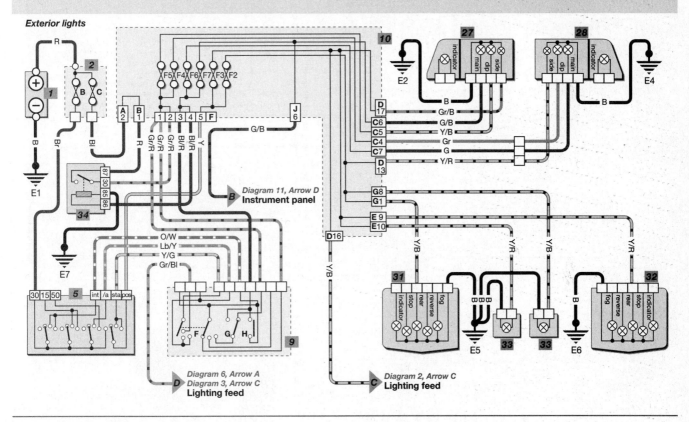

Anti-lock braking system

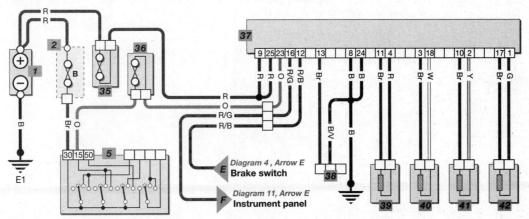

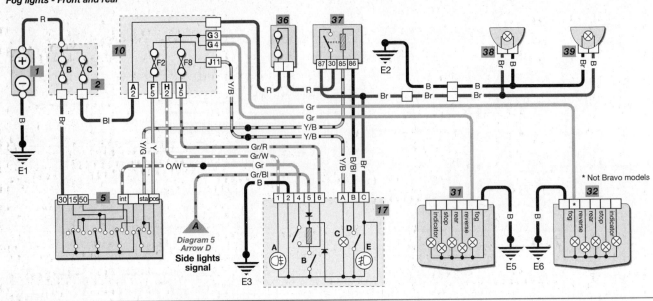

Diagram 6

Wire colours

W	White	O	Orange
R	Red	Lb	Light blue
Y	Yellow		
Br	Brown		
P	Pink		
Bl	Blue		
Gr	Grey		
G	Green		
B	Black		
V	Violet		

H31697

Key to items

1 Battery
2 Power fuse box
  B 40A fuse for ignition system
  C 60A fuse for optional extras
5 Ignition switch
10 Junction unit
17 Switch control panel
  A rear fog lights warning light
  B rear fog lamps switch
  C panel lighting
D fog lights switch
E fog lights warning light
31 Rear LH light cluster
32 Rear RH light cluster
36 Front fog lights fuse 20A
37 Fog lights relay
38 Front LH fog light
39 Front RH fog light
40 Power relay
41 Front windows fuse 30A

42 RH electric window control unit, on LH door
43 LH electric window control unit
44 LH window motor
45 RH window motor
46 RH electric window control unit

Fog lights - Front and rear

Electric windows - front (trim level S - SX)

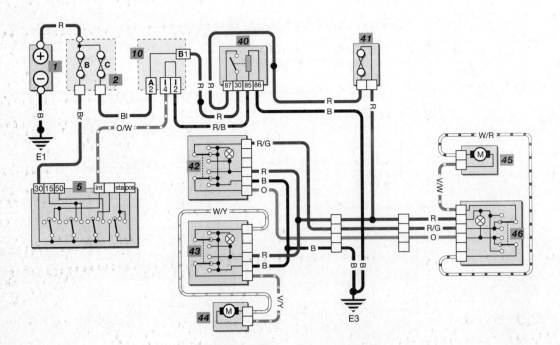

Wire colours

W	White	O	Orange
R	Red	Lb	Light blue
Y	Yellow		
Br	Brown		
P	Pink		
Bl	Blue		
Gr	Grey		
G	Green		
B	Black		
V	Violet		

Key to items

1 Battery
2 Power fuse box
   B 40A fuse for ignition system
   D 80A fuse for junction unit
5 Ignition switch
9 Steering column switch unit
   F Sidelights switch
   G Headlight dip/main switch
   H Headlight flash

10 Junction unit
   R1 Ignition relay
34 Dip beam relay
50 Cigarette lighter
51 High level radio
52 Front LH speaker (Tweeter)
53 Front RH speaker (Tweeter)
54 LH door speaker
55 RH door speaker
56 Rear LH speaker

57 Rear RH speaker
58 LH headlight correction unit
59 RH headlight correction unit
60 Headlight alignment control unit

Diagram 7

Cigarette lighter

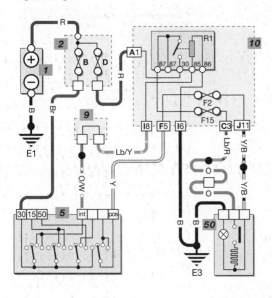

Headlight alignment correction

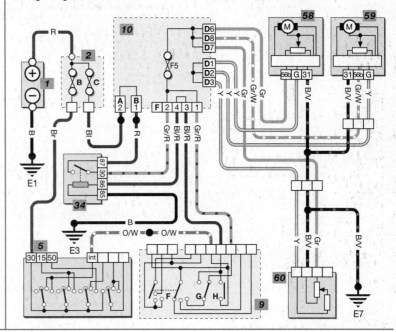

High level Radio

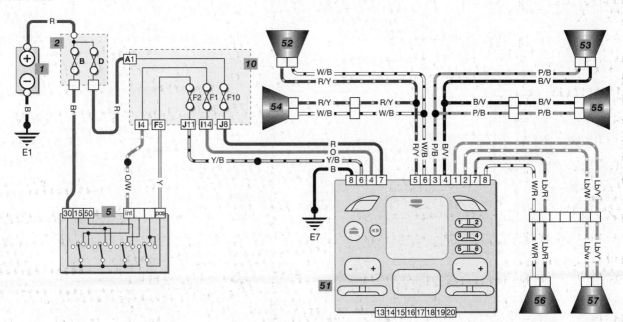

Wire colours

W	White	**O**	Orange
R	Red	**Lb**	Light blue
Y	Yellow		
Br	Brown		
P	Pink		
Bl	Blue		
Gr	Grey		
G	Green		
B	Black		
V	Violet		

S.Tasull
H31699

Key to items

1   Battery
2   Power fuse box
    B 40A fuse for ignition system
    C 60A fuse for optional extras
    D 80A fuse for junction unit
5   Ignition switch
9   Steering column switch unit
    F Sidelights switch
10 Junction unit
    R1 Ignition relay

18 Contact board for rear connections
61 Adjustable mirrors fuse 7.5A
62 Adjustable mirrors control panel
63 LH rear view mirror
64 RH rear view mirror
65 Sun roof control unit
66 Power relay
67 Fuse for sun roof 20A
68 Sun roof motor
69 Sun roof end of travel switch

70 Sun roof control button
71 Instrument panel light dimmer
72 Glove compartment light
73 Courtesy lights
74 Luggage compartment light
75 Front courtesy light switch
76 Rear courtesy light switch

Diagram 8

Interior lights

**   Wiring variation for S-SX trim levels
*** Not on Bravo model

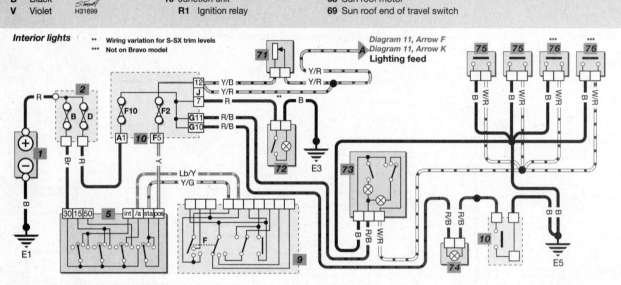

Electrically operated sun roof

Heated/adjustable rear view mirrors

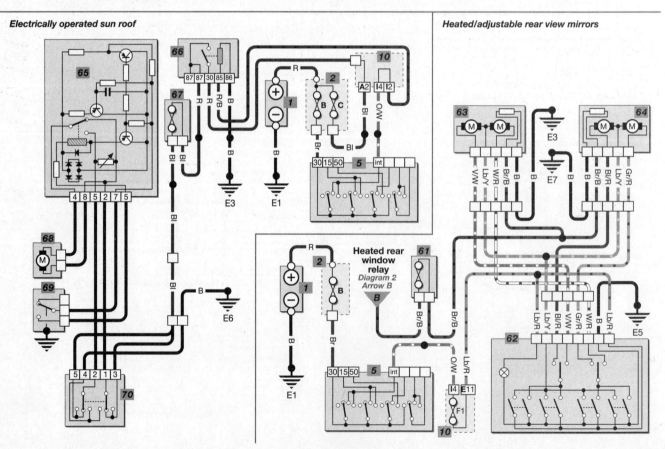

Wire colours

W	White	**O**	Orange
R	Red	**Lb**	Light blue
Y	Yellow		
Br	Brown		
P	Pink		
Bl	Blue		
Gr	Grey		
G	Green		
B	Black		
V	Violet		

H31700

Key to items

1 Battery
2 Power fuse box
  A 30A fuse for injection system
  B 40A fuse for ignition system
5 Ignition switch
10 Junction unit
77 Injection system fuse 25A
78 Injection/ignition control unit
   fuse 5A
79 Water temp. sensor

80 Air temp. sensor
81 RPM and TDC sensor
82 Potentiometer on butterfly valve
83 Timing sensor
84 Heated lambda sensor
85 Injector 1
86 Injector 2
87 Injector 3
88 Injector 4
89 Idle adjustment actuator

90 Absolute pressure sensor
91 Petrol vapour cut out valve
92 Diagnostic sensor
93 Multiple relay
94 Injection/ignition control unit
95 Spark plugs
96 Ignition coils
97 Fuel pump
98 Inertia switch
99 Vehicle speed sensor

Diagram 9

Weber IAW MPI ignition and fuel injection system - 1600 16V models

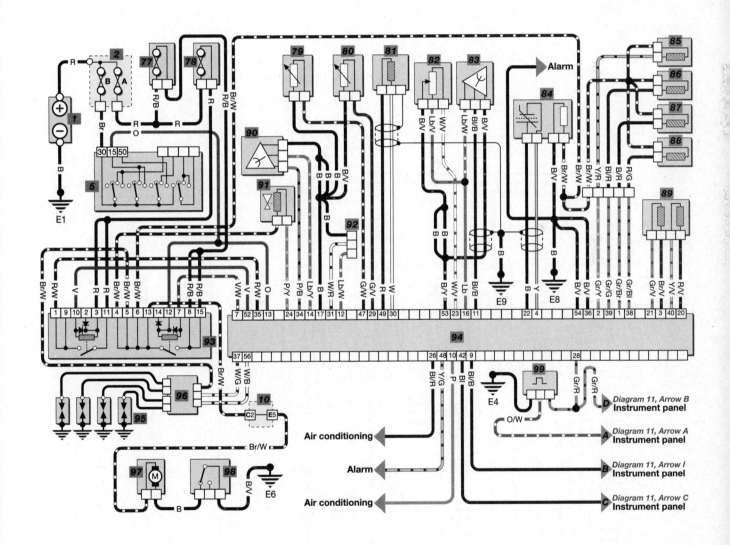

Wire colours

W	White	O	Orange
R	Red	Lb	Light blue
Y	Yellow		
Br	Brown		
P	Pink		
Bl	Blue		
Gr	Grey		
G	Green		
B	Black		
V	Violet		

H31701

Key to items

1 Battery
2 Power fuse box
   A 30A fuse for injection system
   B 40A fuse for ignition system
5 Ignition switch
10 Junction unit
79 Water temp. sensor
81 RPM and TDC sensor
82 Potentiometer on butterfly valve
84 Heated lambda sensor

89 Idle adjustment actuator
91 Petrol vapour cut out valve
92 Diagnostic sensor
94 Injection/ignition control unit
95 Spark plugs
96 Ignition coils
97 Fuel pump
98 Inertia switch
99 Vehicle speed sensor
100 Fuel pump relay

101 Injection relay
102 Injection system fuse 10A
103 Fuel pump/ lambda sensor fuse
     10A
104 Injector and air temp sensor
105 Detonation sensor

Diagram 10

Bosch Mono Motronic ignition and fuel injection system - 1370cc models

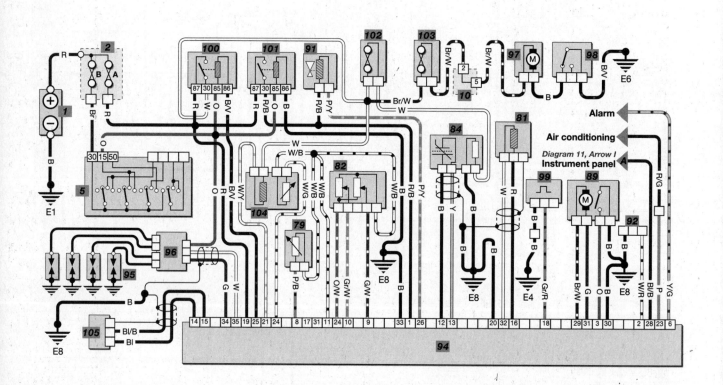

Wire colours

W	White	O	Orange
R	Red	Lb	Light blue
Y	Yellow		
Br	Brown		
P	Pink		
Bl	Blue		
Gr	Grey		
G	Green		
B	Black		
V	Violet		

H31702

Key to items

1 Battery
2 Power fuse box
  B 40A fuse for ignition system
  D 80A fuse for junction unit
5 Ignition switch
10 Junction unit
110 Brake fluid level switch
111 Brake pad wear sensor
112 Oil pressure switch
113 Water temperature sensor
114 Handbrake switch

115 Fuel level sensor
116 Instrument panel
a Battery charging warning lamp
b Injection system failure lamp
c Front brake pad wear lamp
d Low oil pressure warning
e ABS warning lamp
f Water temperature gauge
g Tachometer
h Panel lighting
i Panel lighting

j Handbrake/low brake fluid lamp
k Main beam warning
l Side lights warning
m Fuel gauge
n Fuel reserve control module
o LH indicator
p RH indicator
q Fuel reserve warning
r Speedometer control module
s Speedometer
t Trip meter with reset

Diagram 11

Instrument panel

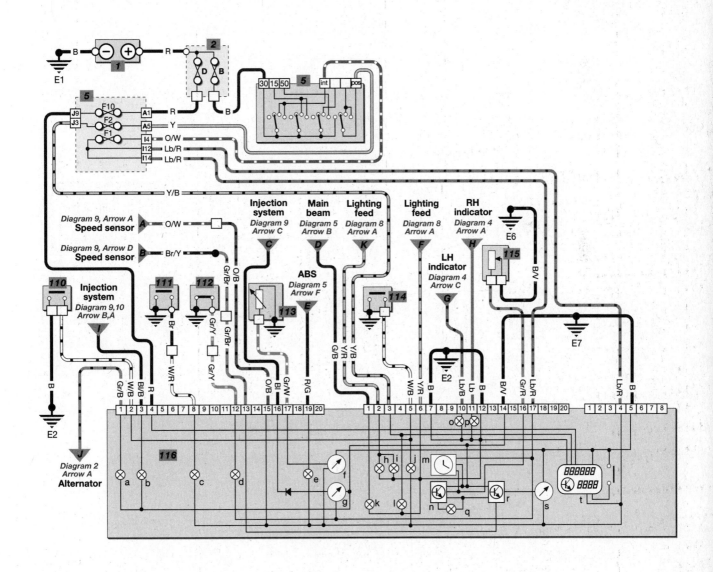

Dimensions and weights

Note: *All figures are approximate, and may vary according to model. Refer to manufacturer's data for exact figures.*

Dimensions

Overall length:
    Bravo . . . . 4025 mm
    Brava . . . . 4187 mm
Overall width:
    Bravo . . . . 1755 mm
    Brava . . . . 1741 mm
Overall height (typical) . . . . 1413 mm
Wheelbase . . . . 2540 mm

Weights

Kerb weight:
    Bravo . . . . 1010 kg (1.2 litre) to 1100 kg (1.8 litre)
    Brava . . . . 1040 kg (1.2 litre) to 1130 kg (1.8 litre)
Maximum roof rack load . . . . 80 kg
Maximum trailer weight:
    Braked . . . . 1000 kg (1.2 litre) to 1200 kg (1.8 litre)
    Unbraked . . . . 400 kg

Length (distance)

Inches (in)	x 25.4	= Millimetres (mm)	x 0.0394	=	Inches (in)
Feet (ft)	x 0.305	= Metres (m)	x 3.281	=	Feet (ft)
Miles	x 1.609	= Kilometres (km)	x 0.621	=	Miles

Volume (capacity)

Cubic inches (cu in; in³)	x 16.387	= Cubic centimetres (cc; cm³)	x 0.061	=	Cubic inches (cu in; in³)
Imperial pints (Imp pt)	x 0.568	= Litres (l)	x 1.76	=	Imperial pints (Imp pt)
Imperial quarts (Imp qt)	x 1.137	= Litres (l)	x 0.88	=	Imperial quarts (Imp qt)
Imperial quarts (Imp qt)	x 1.201	= US quarts (US qt)	x 0.833	=	Imperial quarts (Imp qt)
US quarts (US qt)	x 0.946	= Litres (l)	x 1.057	=	US quarts (US qt)
Imperial gallons (Imp gal)	x 4.546	= Litres (l)	x 0.22	=	Imperial gallons (Imp gal)
Imperial gallons (Imp gal)	x 1.201	= US gallons (US gal)	x 0.833	=	Imperial gallons (Imp gal)
US gallons (US gal)	x 3.785	= Litres (l)	x 0.264	=	US gallons (US gal)

Mass (weight)

Ounces (oz)	x 28.35	= Grams (g)	x 0.035	=	Ounces (oz)
Pounds (lb)	x 0.454	= Kilograms (kg)	x 2.205	=	Pounds (lb)

Force

Ounces-force (ozf; oz)	x 0.278	= Newtons (N)	x 3.6	=	Ounces-force (ozf; oz)
Pounds-force (lbf; lb)	x 4.448	= Newtons (N)	x 0.225	=	Pounds-force (lbf; lb)
Newtons (N)	x 0.1	= Kilograms-force (kgf; kg)	x 9.81	=	Newtons (N)

Pressure

Pounds-force per square inch (psi; lbf/in²; lb/in²)	x 0.070	= Kilograms-force per square centimetre (kgf/cm²; kg/cm²)	x 14.223	=	Pounds-force per square inch (psi; lbf/in²; lb/in²)
Pounds-force per square inch (psi; lbf/in²; lb/in²)	x 0.068	= Atmospheres (atm)	x 14.696	=	Pounds-force per square inch (psi; lbf/in²; lb/in²)
Pounds-force per square inch (psi; lbf/in²; lb/in²)	x 0.069	= Bars	x 14.5	=	Pounds-force per square inch (psi; lbf/in²; lb/in²)
Pounds-force per square inch (psi; lbf/in²; lb/in²)	x 6.895	= Kilopascals (kPa)	x 0.145	=	Pounds-force per square inch (psi; lbf/in²; lb/in²)
Kilopascals (kPa)	x 0.01	= Kilograms-force per square centimetre (kgf/cm²; kg/cm²)	x 98.1	=	Kilopascals (kPa)
Millibar (mbar)	x 100	= Pascals (Pa)	x 0.01	=	Millibar (mbar)
Millibar (mbar)	x 0.0145	= Pounds-force per square inch (psi; lbf/in²; lb/in²)	x 68.947	=	Millibar (mbar)
Millibar (mbar)	x 0.75	= Millimetres of mercury (mmHg)	x 1.333	=	Millibar (mbar)
Millibar (mbar)	x 0.401	= Inches of water (inH₂O)	x 2.491	=	Millibar (mbar)
Millimetres of mercury (mmHg)	x 0.535	= Inches of water (inH₂O)	x 1.868	=	Millimetres of mercury (mmHg)
Inches of water (inH₂O)	x 0.036	= Pounds-force per square inch (psi; lbf/in²; lb/in²)	x 27.68	=	Inches of water (inH₂O)

Torque (moment of force)

Pounds-force inches (lbf in; lb in)	x 1.152	= Kilograms-force centimetre (kgf cm; kg cm)	x 0.868	=	Pounds-force inches (lbf in; lb in)
Pounds-force inches (lbf in; lb in)	x 0.113	= Newton metres (Nm)	x 8.85	=	Pounds-force inches (lbf in; lb in)
Pounds-force inches (lbf in; lb in)	x 0.083	= Pounds-force feet (lbf ft; lb ft)	x 12	=	Pounds-force inches (lbf in; lb in)
Pounds-force feet (lbf ft; lb ft)	x 0.138	= Kilograms-force metres (kgf m; kg m)	x 7.233	=	Pounds-force feet (lbf ft; lb ft)
Pounds-force feet (lbf ft; lb ft)	x 1.356	= Newton metres (Nm)	x 0.738	=	Pounds-force feet (lbf ft; lb ft)
Newton metres (Nm)	x 0.102	= Kilograms-force metres (kgf m; kg m)	x 9.804	=	Newton metres (Nm)

Power

Horsepower (hp)	x 745.7	= Watts (W)	x 0.0013	=	Horsepower (hp)

Velocity (speed)

Miles per hour (miles/hr; mph)	x 1.609	= Kilometres per hour (km/hr; kph)	x 0.621	=	Miles per hour (miles/hr; mph)

Fuel consumption*

Miles per gallon, Imperial (mpg)	x 0.354	= Kilometres per litre (km/l)	x 2.825	=	Miles per gallon, Imperial (mpg)
Miles per gallon, US (mpg)	x 0.425	= Kilometres per litre (km/l)	x 2.352	=	Miles per gallon, US (mpg)

Temperature

Degrees Fahrenheit = (°C x 1.8) + 32   Degrees Celsius (Degrees Centigrade; °C) = (°F - 32) x 0.56

It is common practice to convert from miles per gallon (mpg) to litres/100 kilometres (l/100km), where mpg x l/100 km = 282

Spare parts are available from many sources, including maker's appointed garages, accessory shops, and motor factors. To be sure of obtaining the correct parts, it may sometimes be necessary to quote the vehicle identification number. If possible, it can also be useful to take the old parts along for positive identification. Items such as starter motors and alternators may be available under a service exchange scheme - any parts returned should always be clean.

Our advice regarding spare part sources is as follows:

Officially-appointed garages

This is the best source of parts which are peculiar to your car, and are not otherwise generally available (eg badges, interior trim, certain body panels, etc). It is also the only place at which you should buy parts if the vehicle is still under warranty.

Accessory shops

These are very good places to buy materials and components needed for the maintenance of your car (oil, air and fuel filters, spark plugs, light bulbs, drivebelts, oils and greases, brake pads, touch-up paint, etc). Parts like this sold by a reputable shop are of the same standard as those used by the car manufacturer.

Motor factors

Good factors will stock all the more important components which wear out comparatively quickly and can sometimes supply individual components needed for the overhaul of a larger assembly. They may also handle work such as cylinder block reboring, crankshaft regrinding and balancing, etc.

Tyre and exhaust specialists

These outlets may be independent or members of a local or national chain. They frequently offer competitive prices when compared with a main dealer or local garage, but it will pay to obtain several quotes before making a decision. Also ask what 'extras' may be added to the quote - for instance, fitting a new valve and balancing the wheel are both often charged on top of the price of a new tyre.

Other sources

Beware of parts of materials obtained from market stalls, car boot sales or similar outlets. Such items are not invariably sub-standard, but there is little chance of compensation if they do prove unsatisfactory. In the case of safety-critical components such as brake pads there is the risk not only of financial loss but also of an accident causing injury or death.

Second-hand components or assemblies obtained from a car breaker can be a good buy in some circumstances, but this sort of purchase is best made by the experienced DIY mechanic.

Modifications are a continuing and unpublicised process in vehicle manufacture, quite apart from major model changes. Spare parts manuals and lists are compiled upon a numerical basis, the individual vehicle identification numbers being essential to correct identification of the component concerned.

When ordering spare parts, always give as much information as possible. Quote the model number, chassis number, engine number and, where applicable, the spare parts number, as appropriate.

The vehicle model number and chassis serial number appear on the model plate attached to the front crossmember. The model plate also gives vehicle loading details, engine type, and the FIAT spare parts number. The model and chassis numbers are also stamped in the right-hand front suspension strut top mounting (right as seen from the driver's seat). Some models may also have these numbers etched into the windscreen **(see illustrations)**.

Vehicle paint codes appear on a plate attached to the inside of the tailgate.

Engine type designation and serial numbers are stamped on the upper side of the cylinder block, at the left front corner on all except 1.2 litre models, whose details appear front centre **(see illustration)**. These numbers may also appear on a sticker on the upper timing belt cover.

The transmission identification numbers are located on a plate attached to the transmission casing.

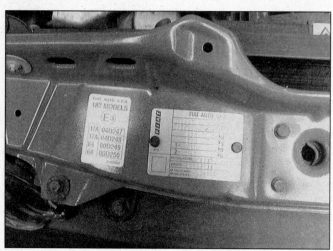

Model plate on front crossmember

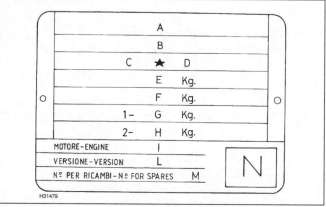

Model plate details

A Manufacturer name
B Homologation number
C Vehicle model number
D Chassis number
E Maximum laden weight
F Maximum laden weight and towing weight

G Maximum 1st axle weight
H Maximum 2nd axle weight
I Engine type
L Bodywork version code
M FIAT spare parts number
N Smoke coefficient (Diesel engines)

Vehicle model number and chassis number on suspension strut mounting

Some models have the vehicle/chassis numbers etched into the windscreen

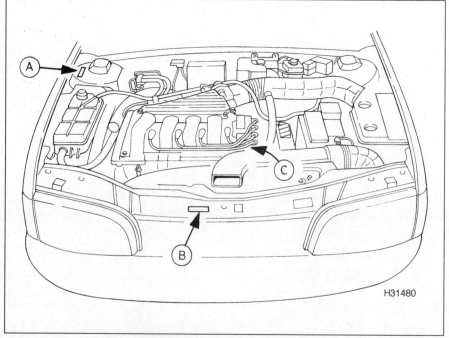

Vehicle identification number locations

A Model and chassis numbers   B Model plate   C Engine number

The jack supplied with the vehicle tool kit should **only** be used for changing the roadwheels in an emergency - see *Wheel changing* at the front of this book. When carrying out any other kind of work, raise the vehicle using a heavy-duty hydraulic (or trolley) jack, and always supplement the jack with axle stands positioned under the vehicle jacking points. If the roadwheels do not have to be removed, consider using wheel ramps - if wished, these can be placed under the wheels once the vehicle has been raised using a hydraulic jack, and the vehicle lowered onto the ramps so that it is resting on its wheels.

Only ever jack the vehicle up on a solid, level surface. If there is even a slight slope, take great care that the vehicle cannot move as the wheels are lifted off the ground. Jacking up on an uneven or gravelled surface is not recommended, as the weight of the vehicle will not be evenly distributed, and the jack may slip as the vehicle is raised.

As far as possible, do not leave the vehicle unattended once it has been raised, particularly if children are playing nearby.

Before jacking up the front of the car, ensure that the handbrake is firmly applied. When jacking up the rear of the car, place wooden chocks in front of the front wheels, and engage first gear (or P).

The jack supplied with the vehicle locates in the sill flanges, at the points marked by two indentations in the sill on each side of the car **(see illustration)**. Ensure that the jack head is correctly engaged before attempting to raise the vehicle.

When using a hydraulic jack or axle stands, the jack head or axle stand head may be placed under one of the jacking points. Always use a block of wood (with a slot cut in its top surface, to locate in the sill flange) between the jack head or axle stand, and the sill. **Do not** jack the vehicle under any other part of the sill, engine sump, floor pan, or directly under any of the steering or suspension components.

To raise the front of the vehicle, the jack can be positioned under the transmission, using a block of wood on top of the jack head to spread the load. The front of the car can also be supported under the subframe to the rear of the engine (**not** under the front suspension arms, attached to the subframe).

Raising the rear of the vehicle can be achieved using the rear jacking points on the sills, or the special bracket on the sill in line with the rear edge of the front doors. If using a hydraulic (trolley) jack, place a block of wood (with a slot cut in its top surface to locate in the sill flange) on top of the jack head, to spread the load. Axle stands (with a block of wood) can be placed under the reinforced

Vehicle jack locates the sill flange at the point marked by two indentations

chassis sections immediately inboard of the rear jacking points. It is not advisable to jack or support under the rear axle tube.

Providing care is taken (and a block of wood is used to spread the load), reinforced areas of the floor pan, particularly those in the region of suspension mountings, may be used as support points. Consult a FIAT dealer for advice before using anything other than the approved jacking points, however.

Never work under, around, or near a raised vehicle, unless it is adequately supported on stands. Do not rely on a jack alone, as even a hydraulic jack could fail under load. Makeshift methods should not be used to lift and support the car during servicing work.

Several of the systems fitted to the Bravo/Brava require battery power to be available at all times (permanent live). This is either to ensure their continued operation (such as the clock), or to maintain electronic memory settings which would otherwise be erased. Whenever the battery is to be disconnected therefore, first note the following points, to ensure there are no unforeseen consequences:

a) Firstly, on any vehicle with central door locking, it is a wise precaution to remove the key from the ignition, and to keep it with you. This avoids the possibility of the key being locked inside the car, should the central locking engage when the battery is reconnected.

b) The radio/cassette unit fitted as standard equipment by FIAT is equipped with a built-in security code, to deter thieves. If the power source to the unit is cut, the anti-theft system will activate. Even if the power source is immediately reconnected, the radio/cassette unit will not function until the correct security code has been entered. Therefore, if you do not know the correct security code for the radio/cassette unit, **do not** disconnect either of the battery terminals, or remove the radio/cassette unit from the vehicle. The code appears on a code card supplied with the car when new. Details for entering the code appear in the vehicle handbook. Should the code have been misplaced or forgotten, on production of proof of ownership, a FIAT dealer or in-car entertainment specialist may be able to help.

c) The engine management system ECU is of the 'self-learning' type, meaning that, as it operates, it adapts to changes in operating conditions, and stores the optimum settings found (this is especially true for idle settings). When the battery is disconnected, these 'learned' settings are lost, and the ECU reverts to the base factory settings. When the engine is restarted, it may idle and run roughly until the ECU has re-learned the best settings. To further this learning process, take the car for a road test of at least 15 minutes' duration, covering as many engine speeds and loads as possible, and concentrating on the 2000 to 4000 rpm range. On completion, let the engine idle for at least 10 minutes, turning the steering wheel occasionally and switching on high-current-draw equipment such as the heater fan or heated rear window.

d) The Bravo/Brava is equipped with an electronic immobiliser system, called FIAT CODE. When new, the car is provided with three keys - a master (burgundy) key, and two normal (blue) keys. To deactivate the CODE system and start the engine, the control unit must recognise a code from the transponder inside the keys. Each blue key must be programmed into the control unit, and if the battery is disconnected, this information may be lost. The master (burgundy) key is essential for programming the blue keys into the control unit memory - if this is not available, use the CODE card supplied with the car (**not** the radio code card) to perform the 'Emergency start-up' procedure detailed in the vehicle handbook. For security reasons, details on reprogramming the blue keys are not given here - refer to a FIAT dealer for advice.

Devices known as 'memory-savers' or 'code-savers' can be used to avoid some of the above problems. Precise details of use vary according to the device used. Typically, it is plugged into the cigar lighter socket, and is connected by its own wiring to a spare battery; the vehicle battery is then disconnected from the electrical system, leaving the memory-saver to pass sufficient current to maintain audio unit security codes and other memory values, and also to run permanently-live circuits such as the clock.

Warning: Some of these devices allow a considerable amount of current to pass, which can mean that many of the vehicle's systems are still operational when the main battery is disconnected. If a memory-saver is used, ensure that the circuit concerned is actually 'dead' before carrying out any work on it!

Whenever servicing, repair or overhaul work is carried out on the car or its components, observe the following procedures and instructions. This will assist in carrying out the operation efficiently and to a professional standard of workmanship.

Joint mating faces and gaskets

When separating components at their mating faces, never insert screwdrivers or similar implements into the joint between the faces in order to prise them apart. This can cause severe damage which results in oil leaks, coolant leaks, etc upon reassembly. Separation is usually achieved by tapping along the joint with a soft-faced hammer in order to break the seal. However, note that this method may not be suitable where dowels are used for component location.

Where a gasket is used between the mating faces of two components, a new one must be fitted on reassembly; fit it dry unless otherwise stated in the repair procedure. Make sure that the mating faces are clean and dry, with all traces of old gasket removed. When cleaning a joint face, use a tool which is unlikely to score or damage the face, and remove any burrs or nicks with an oilstone or fine file.

Make sure that tapped holes are cleaned with a pipe cleaner, and keep them free of jointing compound, if this is being used, unless specifically instructed otherwise.

Ensure that all orifices, channels or pipes are clear, and blow through them, preferably using compressed air.

Oil seals

Oil seals can be removed by levering them out with a wide flat-bladed screwdriver or similar implement. Alternatively, a number of self-tapping screws may be screwed into the seal, and these used as a purchase for pliers or some similar device in order to pull the seal free.

Whenever an oil seal is removed from its working location, either individually or as part of an assembly, it should be renewed.

The very fine sealing lip of the seal is easily damaged, and will not seal if the surface it contacts is not completely clean and free from scratches, nicks or grooves. If the original sealing surface of the component cannot be restored, and the manufacturer has not made provision for slight relocation of the seal relative to the sealing surface, the component should be renewed.

Protect the lips of the seal from any surface which may damage them in the course of fitting. Use tape or a conical sleeve where possible. Lubricate the seal lips with oil before fitting and, on dual-lipped seals, fill the space between the lips with grease.

Unless otherwise stated, oil seals must be fitted with their sealing lips toward the lubricant to be sealed.

Use a tubular drift or block of wood of the appropriate size to install the seal and, if the seal housing is shouldered, drive the seal down to the shoulder. If the seal housing is unshouldered, the seal should be fitted with its face flush with the housing top face (unless otherwise instructed).

Screw threads and fastenings

Seized nuts, bolts and screws are quite a common occurrence where corrosion has set in, and the use of penetrating oil or releasing fluid will often overcome this problem if the offending item is soaked for a while before attempting to release it. The use of an impact driver may also provide a means of releasing such stubborn fastening devices, when used in conjunction with the appropriate screwdriver bit or socket. If none of these methods works, it may be necessary to resort to the careful application of heat, or the use of a hacksaw or nut splitter device.

Studs are usually removed by locking two nuts together on the threaded part, and then using a spanner on the lower nut to unscrew the stud. Studs or bolts which have broken off below the surface of the component in which they are mounted can sometimes be removed using a stud extractor. Always ensure that a blind tapped hole is completely free from oil, grease, water or other fluid before installing the bolt or stud. Failure to do this could cause the housing to crack due to the hydraulic action of the bolt or stud as it is screwed in.

When tightening a castellated nut to accept a split pin, tighten the nut to the specified torque, where applicable, and then tighten further to the next split pin hole. Never slacken the nut to align the split pin hole, unless stated in the repair procedure.

When checking or retightening a nut or bolt to a specified torque setting, slacken the nut or bolt by a quarter of a turn, and then retighten to the specified setting. However, this should not be attempted where angular tightening has been used.

For some screw fastenings, notably cylinder head bolts or nuts, torque wrench settings are no longer specified for the latter stages of tightening, "angle-tightening" being called up instead. Typically, a fairly low torque wrench setting will be applied to the bolts/nuts in the correct sequence, followed by one or more stages of tightening through specified angles.

Locknuts, locktabs and washers

Any fastening which will rotate against a component or housing during tightening should always have a washer between it and the relevant component or housing.

Spring or split washers should always be renewed when they are used to lock a critical component such as a big-end bearing retaining bolt or nut. Locktabs which are folded over to retain a nut or bolt should always be renewed.

Self-locking nuts can be re-used in non-critical areas, providing resistance can be felt when the locking portion passes over the bolt or stud thread. However, it should be noted that self-locking stiffnuts tend to lose their effectiveness after long periods of use, and should then be renewed as a matter of course.

Split pins must always be replaced with new ones of the correct size for the hole.

When thread-locking compound is found on the threads of a fastener which is to be re-used, it should be cleaned off with a wire brush and solvent, and fresh compound applied on reassembly.

Special tools

Some repair procedures in this manual entail the use of special tools such as a press, two or three-legged pullers, spring compressors, etc. Wherever possible, suitable readily-available alternatives to the manufacturer's special tools are described, and are shown in use. In some instances, where no alternative is possible, it has been necessary to resort to the use of a manufacturer's tool, and this has been done for reasons of safety as well as the efficient completion of the repair operation. Unless you are highly-skilled and have a thorough understanding of the procedures described, never attempt to bypass the use of any special tool when the procedure described specifies its use. Not only is there a very great risk of personal injury, but expensive damage could be caused to the components involved.

Environmental considerations

When disposing of used engine oil, brake fluid, antifreeze, etc, give due consideration to any detrimental environmental effects. Do not, for instance, pour any of the above liquids down drains into the general sewage system, or onto the ground to soak away. Many local council refuse tips provide a facility for waste oil disposal, as do some garages. If none of these facilities are available, consult your local Environmental Health Department, or the National Rivers Authority, for further advice.

With the universal tightening-up of legislation regarding the emission of environmentally-harmful substances from motor vehicles, most vehicles have tamperproof devices fitted to the main adjustment points of the fuel system. These devices are primarily designed to prevent unqualified persons from adjusting the fuel/air mixture, with the chance of a consequent increase in toxic emissions. If such devices are found during servicing or overhaul, they should, wherever possible, be renewed or refitted in accordance with the manufacturer's requirements or current legislation.

OIL CARE

FOLLOW THE CODE

OIL BANK LINE
0800 66 33 66
www.oilbankline.org.uk

Note: It is antisocial and illegal to dump oil down the drain. To find the location of your local oil recycling bank, call this number free.

Introduction

A selection of good tools is a fundamental requirement for anyone contemplating the maintenance and repair of a motor vehicle. For the owner who does not possess any, their purchase will prove a considerable expense, offsetting some of the savings made by doing-it-yourself. However, provided that the tools purchased meet the relevant national safety standards and are of good quality, they will last for many years and prove an extremely worthwhile investment.

To help the average owner to decide which tools are needed to carry out the various tasks detailed in this manual, we have compiled three lists of tools under the following headings: *Maintenance and minor repair*, *Repair and overhaul*, and *Special*. Newcomers to practical mechanics should start off with the *Maintenance and minor repair* tool kit, and confine themselves to the simpler jobs around the vehicle. Then, as confidence and experience grow, more difficult tasks can be undertaken, with extra tools being purchased as, and when, they are needed. In this way, a *Maintenance and minor repair* tool kit can be built up into a *Repair and overhaul* tool kit over a considerable period of time, without any major cash outlays. The experienced do-it-yourselfer will have a tool kit good enough for most repair and overhaul procedures, and will add tools from the *Special* category when it is felt that the expense is justified by the amount of use to which these tools will be put.

Maintenance and minor repair tool kit

The tools given in this list should be considered as a minimum requirement if routine maintenance, servicing and minor repair operations are to be undertaken. We recommend the purchase of combination spanners (ring one end, open-ended the other); although more expensive than open-ended ones, they do give the advantages of both types of spanner.

☐ *Combination spanners:*
  Metric - 8 to 19 mm inclusive
☐ *Adjustable spanner - 35 mm jaw (approx.)*
☐ *Spark plug spanner (with rubber insert) - petrol models*
☐ *Spark plug gap adjustment tool - petrol models*
☐ *Set of feeler gauges*
☐ *Brake bleed nipple spanner*
☐ *Screwdrivers:*
  Flat blade - 100 mm long x 6 mm dia
  Cross blade - 100 mm long x 6 mm dia
  Torx - various sizes (not all vehicles)
☐ *Combination pliers*
☐ *Hacksaw (junior)*
☐ *Tyre pump*
☐ *Tyre pressure gauge*
☐ *Oil can*
☐ *Oil filter removal tool*
☐ *Fine emery cloth*
☐ *Wire brush (small)*
☐ *Funnel (medium size)*
☐ *Sump drain plug key (not all vehicles)*

Repair and overhaul tool kit

These tools are virtually essential for anyone undertaking any major repairs to a motor vehicle, and are additional to those given in the *Maintenance and minor repair* list. Included in this list is a comprehensive set of sockets. Although these are expensive, they will be found invaluable as they are so versatile - particularly if various drives are included in the set. We recommend the half-inch square-drive type, as this can be used with most proprietary torque wrenches.

The tools in this list will sometimes need to be supplemented by tools from the *Special* list:

☐ *Sockets to cover range in previous list (including Torx/Ribe sockets)*
☐ *Reversible ratchet drive (for use with sockets)*
☐ *Extension piece, 250 mm (for use with sockets)*
☐ *Universal joint (for use with sockets)*
☐ *Flexible handle or sliding T "breaker bar" (for use with sockets)*
☐ *Torque wrench (for use with sockets)*
☐ *Self-locking grips*
☐ *Ball pein hammer*
☐ *Soft-faced mallet (plastic or rubber)*
☐ *Screwdrivers:*
  Flat blade - long & sturdy, short (chubby), and narrow (electrician's) types
  Cross blade – long & sturdy, and short (chubby) types
☐ *Pliers:*
  Long-nosed
  Side cutters (electrician's)
  Circlip (internal and external)
☐ *Cold chisel - 25 mm*
☐ *Scriber*
☐ *Scraper*
☐ *Centre-punch*
☐ *Pin punch*
☐ *Hacksaw*
☐ *Brake hose clamp*
☐ *Brake/clutch bleeding kit*
☐ *Selection of twist drills*
☐ *Steel rule/straight-edge*
☐ *Allen keys (inc. splined/Torx/Ribe type)*
☐ *Selection of files*
☐ *Wire brush*
☐ *Axle stands*
☐ *Jack (strong trolley or hydraulic type)*
☐ *Light with extension lead*
☐ *Universal electrical multi-meter*

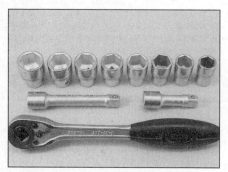

Sockets and reversible ratchet drive

Brake bleeding kit

Torx key, socket and bit

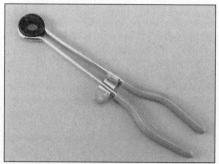

Hose clamp

Angular-tightening gauge

Special tools

The tools in this list are those which are not used regularly, are expensive to buy, or which need to be used in accordance with their manufacturers' instructions. Unless relatively difficult mechanical jobs are undertaken frequently, it will not be economic to buy many of these tools. Where this is the case, you could consider clubbing together with friends (or joining a motorists' club) to make a joint purchase, or borrowing the tools against a deposit from a local garage or tool hire specialist. It is worth noting that many of the larger DIY superstores now carry a large range of special tools for hire at modest rates.

The following list contains only those tools and instruments freely available to the public, and not those special tools produced by the vehicle manufacturer specifically for its dealer network. You will find occasional references to these manufacturers' special tools in the text of this manual. Generally, an alternative method of doing the job without the vehicle manufacturers' special tool is given. However, sometimes there is no alternative to using them. Where this is the case and the relevant tool cannot be bought or borrowed, you will have to entrust the work to a dealer.

- [ ] Angular-tightening gauge
- [ ] Valve spring compressor
- [ ] Valve grinding tool
- [ ] Piston ring compressor
- [ ] Piston ring removal/installation tool
- [ ] Cylinder bore hone
- [ ] Balljoint separator
- [ ] Coil spring compressors (where applicable)
- [ ] Two/three-legged hub and bearing puller
- [ ] Impact screwdriver
- [ ] Micrometer and/or vernier calipers
- [ ] Dial gauge
- [ ] Stroboscopic timing light
- [ ] Dwell angle meter/tachometer
- [ ] Fault code reader
- [ ] Cylinder compression gauge
- [ ] Hand-operated vacuum pump and gauge
- [ ] Clutch plate alignment set
- [ ] Brake shoe steady spring cup removal tool
- [ ] Bush and bearing removal/installation set
- [ ] Stud extractors
- [ ] Tap and die set
- [ ] Lifting tackle
- [ ] Trolley jack

Buying tools

Reputable motor accessory shops and superstores often offer excellent quality tools at discount prices, so it pays to shop around.

Remember, you don't have to buy the most expensive items on the shelf, but it is always advisable to steer clear of the very cheap tools. Beware of 'bargains' offered on market stalls or at car boot sales. There are plenty of good tools around at reasonable prices, but always aim to purchase items which meet the relevant national safety standards. If in doubt, ask the proprietor or manager of the shop for advice before making a purchase.

Care and maintenance of tools

Having purchased a reasonable tool kit, it is necessary to keep the tools in a clean and serviceable condition. After use, always wipe off any dirt, grease and metal particles using a clean, dry cloth, before putting the tools away. Never leave them lying around after they have been used. A simple tool rack on the garage or workshop wall for items such as screwdrivers and pliers is a good idea. Store all normal spanners and sockets in a metal box. Any measuring instruments, gauges, meters, etc, must be carefully stored where they cannot be damaged or become rusty.

Take a little care when tools are used. Hammer heads inevitably become marked, and screwdrivers lose the keen edge on their blades from time to time. A little timely attention with emery cloth or a file will soon restore items like this to a good finish.

Working facilities

Not to be forgotten when discussing tools is the workshop itself. If anything more than routine maintenance is to be carried out, a suitable working area becomes essential.

It is appreciated that many an owner-mechanic is forced by circumstances to remove an engine or similar item without the benefit of a garage or workshop. Having done this, any repairs should always be done under the cover of a roof.

Wherever possible, any dismantling should be done on a clean, flat workbench or table at a suitable working height.

Any workbench needs a vice; one with a jaw opening of 100 mm is suitable for most jobs. As mentioned previously, some clean dry storage space is also required for tools, as well as for any lubricants, cleaning fluids, touch-up paints etc, which become necessary.

Another item which may be required, and which has a much more general usage, is an electric drill with a chuck capacity of at least 8 mm. This, together with a good range of twist drills, is virtually essential for fitting accessories.

Last, but not least, always keep a supply of old newspapers and clean, lint-free rags available, and try to keep any working area as clean as possible.

Micrometers

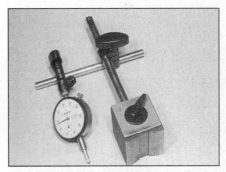

Dial test indicator ("dial gauge")

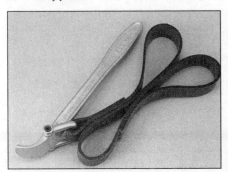

Strap wrench

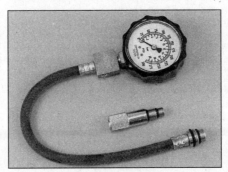

Compression tester

Fault code reader

This is a guide to getting your vehicle through the MOT test. Obviously it will not be possible to examine the vehicle to the same standard as the professional MOT tester. However, working through the following checks will enable you to identify any problem areas before submitting the vehicle for the test.

Where a testable component is in borderline condition, the tester has discretion in deciding whether to pass or fail it. The basis of such discretion is whether the tester would be happy for a close relative or friend to use the vehicle with the component in that condition. If the vehicle presented is clean and evidently well cared for, the tester may be more inclined to pass a borderline component than if the vehicle is scruffy and apparently neglected.

It has only been possible to summarise the test requirements here, based on the regulations in force at the time of printing. Test standards are becoming increasingly stringent, although there are some exemptions for older vehicles.

An assistant will be needed to help carry out some of these checks.

The checks have been sub-divided into four categories, as follows:

1 Checks carried out **FROM THE DRIVER'S SEAT**

2 Checks carried out **WITH THE VEHICLE ON THE GROUND**

3 Checks carried out **WITH THE VEHICLE RAISED AND THE WHEELS FREE TO TURN**

4 Checks carried out on **YOUR VEHICLE'S EXHAUST EMISSION SYSTEM**

---

1 Checks carried out **FROM THE DRIVER'S SEAT**

Handbrake

☐ Test the operation of the handbrake. Excessive travel (too many clicks) indicates incorrect brake or cable adjustment.

☐ Check that the handbrake cannot be released by tapping the lever sideways. Check the security of the lever mountings.

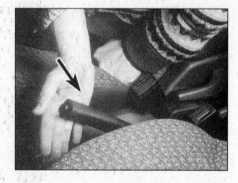

Footbrake

☐ Depress the brake pedal and check that it does not creep down to the floor, indicating a master cylinder fault. Release the pedal, wait a few seconds, then depress it again. If the pedal travels nearly to the floor before firm resistance is felt, brake adjustment or repair is necessary. If the pedal feels spongy, there is air in the hydraulic system which must be removed by bleeding.

☐ Check that the brake pedal is secure and in good condition. Check also for signs of fluid leaks on the pedal, floor or carpets, which would indicate failed seals in the brake master cylinder.

☐ Check the servo unit (when applicable) by operating the brake pedal several times, then keeping the pedal depressed and starting the engine. As the engine starts, the pedal will move down slightly. If not, the vacuum hose or the servo itself may be faulty.

Steering wheel and column

☐ Examine the steering wheel for fractures or looseness of the hub, spokes or rim.

☐ Move the steering wheel from side to side and then up and down. Check that the steering wheel is not loose on the column, indicating wear or a loose retaining nut. Continue moving the steering wheel as before, but also turn it slightly from left to right.

☐ Check that the steering wheel is not loose on the column, and that there is no abnormal

movement of the steering wheel, indicating wear in the column support bearings or couplings.

Windscreen, mirrors and sunvisor

☐ The windscreen must be free of cracks or other significant damage within the driver's field of view. (Small stone chips are acceptable.) Rear view mirrors must be secure, intact, and capable of being adjusted.

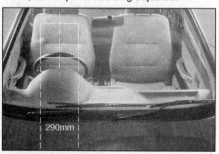

290mm

☐ The driver's sunvisor must be capable of being stored in the "up" position.

Seat belts and seats

Note: *The following checks are applicable to all seat belts, front and rear.*

☐ Examine the webbing of all the belts (including rear belts if fitted) for cuts, serious fraying or deterioration. Fasten and unfasten each belt to check the buckles. If applicable, check the retracting mechanism. Check the security of all seat belt mountings accessible from inside the vehicle.

☐ Seat belts with pre-tensioners, once activated, have a "flag" or similar showing on the seat belt stalk. This, in itself, is not a reason for test failure.

☐ The front seats themselves must be securely attached and the backrests must lock in the upright position.

Doors

☐ Both front doors must be able to be opened and closed from outside and inside, and must latch securely when closed.

2 Checks carried out WITH THE VEHICLE ON THE GROUND

Vehicle identification

☐ Number plates must be in good condition, secure and legible, with letters and numbers correctly spaced – spacing at (A) should be at least twice that at (B).

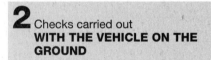

☐ The VIN plate and/or homologation plate must be legible.

Electrical equipment

☐ Switch on the ignition and check the operation of the horn.

☐ Check the windscreen washers and wipers, examining the wiper blades; renew damaged or perished blades. Also check the operation of the stop-lights.

☐ Check the operation of the sidelights and number plate lights. The lenses and reflectors must be secure, clean and undamaged.

☐ Check the operation and alignment of the headlights. The headlight reflectors must not be tarnished and the lenses must be undamaged.

☐ Switch on the ignition and check the operation of the direction indicators (including the instrument panel tell-tale) and the hazard warning lights. Operation of the sidelights and stop-lights must not affect the indicators - if it does, the cause is usually a bad earth at the rear light cluster.

☐ Check the operation of the rear foglight(s), including the warning light on the instrument panel or in the switch.

☐ The ABS warning light must illuminate in accordance with the manufacturers' design. For most vehicles, the ABS warning light should illuminate when the ignition is switched on, and (if the system is operating properly) extinguish after a few seconds. Refer to the owner's handbook.

Footbrake

☐ Examine the master cylinder, brake pipes and servo unit for leaks, loose mountings, corrosion or other damage.

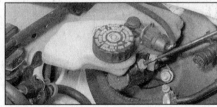

☐ The fluid reservoir must be secure and the fluid level must be between the upper (**A**) and lower (**B**) markings.

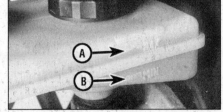

☐ Inspect both front brake flexible hoses for cracks or deterioration of the rubber. Turn the steering from lock to lock, and ensure that the hoses do not contact the wheel, tyre, or any part of the steering or suspension mechanism. With the brake pedal firmly depressed, check the hoses for bulges or leaks under pressure.

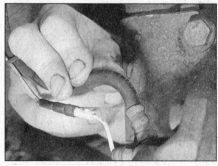

Steering and suspension

☐ Have your assistant turn the steering wheel from side to side slightly, up to the point where the steering gear just begins to transmit this movement to the roadwheels. Check for excessive free play between the steering wheel and the steering gear, indicating wear or insecurity of the steering column joints, the column-to-steering gear coupling, or the steering gear itself.

☐ Have your assistant turn the steering wheel more vigorously in each direction, so that the roadwheels just begin to turn. As this is done, examine all the steering joints, linkages, fittings and attachments. Renew any component that shows signs of wear or damage. On vehicles with power steering, check the security and condition of the steering pump, drivebelt and hoses.

☐ Check that the vehicle is standing level, and at approximately the correct ride height.

Shock absorbers

☐ Depress each corner of the vehicle in turn, then release it. The vehicle should rise and then settle in its normal position. If the vehicle continues to rise and fall, the shock absorber is defective. A shock absorber which has seized will also cause the vehicle to fail.

Exhaust system

☐ Start the engine. With your assistant holding a rag over the tailpipe, check the entire system for leaks. Repair or renew leaking sections.

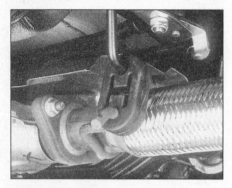

3 Checks carried out
WITH THE VEHICLE RAISED AND THE WHEELS FREE TO TURN

Jack up the front and rear of the vehicle, and securely support it on axle stands. Position the stands clear of the suspension assemblies. Ensure that the wheels are clear of the ground and that the steering can be turned from lock to lock.

Steering mechanism

☐ Have your assistant turn the steering from lock to lock. Check that the steering turns smoothly, and that no part of the steering mechanism, including a wheel or tyre, fouls any brake hose or pipe or any part of the body structure.
☐ Examine the steering rack rubber gaiters for damage or insecurity of the retaining clips. If power steering is fitted, check for signs of damage or leakage of the fluid hoses, pipes or connections. Also check for excessive stiffness or binding of the steering, a missing split pin or locking device, or severe corrosion of the body structure within 30 cm of any steering component attachment point.

Front and rear suspension and wheel bearings

☐ Starting at the front right-hand side, grasp the roadwheel at the 3 o'clock and 9 o'clock positions and rock gently but firmly. Check for free play or insecurity at the wheel bearings, suspension balljoints, or suspension mountings, pivots and attachments.
☐ Now grasp the wheel at the 12 o'clock and 6 o'clock positions and repeat the previous inspection. Spin the wheel, and check for roughness or tightness of the front wheel bearing.

☐ If excess free play is suspected at a component pivot point, this can be confirmed by using a large screwdriver or similar tool and levering between the mounting and the component attachment. This will confirm whether the wear is in the pivot bush, its retaining bolt, or in the mounting itself (the bolt holes can often become elongated).

☐ Carry out all the above checks at the other front wheel, and then at both rear wheels.

Springs and shock absorbers

☐ Examine the suspension struts (when applicable) for serious fluid leakage, corrosion, or damage to the casing. Also check the security of the mounting points.
☐ If coil springs are fitted, check that the spring ends locate in their seats, and that the spring is not corroded, cracked or broken.
☐ If leaf springs are fitted, check that all leaves are intact, that the axle is securely attached to each spring, and that there is no deterioration of the spring eye mountings, bushes, and shackles.

☐ The same general checks apply to vehicles fitted with other suspension types, such as torsion bars, hydraulic displacer units, etc. Ensure that all mountings and attachments are secure, that there are no signs of excessive wear, corrosion or damage, and (on hydraulic types) that there are no fluid leaks or damaged pipes.
☐ Inspect the shock absorbers for signs of serious fluid leakage. Check for wear of the mounting bushes or attachments, or damage to the body of the unit.

Driveshafts (fwd vehicles only)

☐ Rotate each front wheel in turn and inspect the constant velocity joint gaiters for splits or damage. Also check that each driveshaft is straight and undamaged.

Braking system

☐ If possible without dismantling, check brake pad wear and disc condition. Ensure that the friction lining material has not worn excessively, (A) and that the discs are not fractured, pitted, scored or badly worn (B).

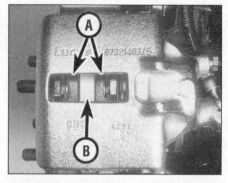

☐ Examine all the rigid brake pipes underneath the vehicle, and the flexible hose(s) at the rear. Look for corrosion, chafing or insecurity of the pipes, and for signs of bulging under pressure, chafing, splits or deterioration of the flexible hoses.
☐ Look for signs of fluid leaks at the brake calipers or on the brake backplates. Repair or renew leaking components.
☐ Slowly spin each wheel, while your assistant depresses and releases the footbrake. Ensure that each brake is operating and does not bind when the pedal is released.

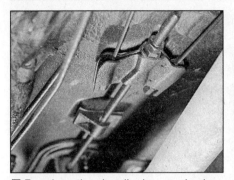

☐ Examine the handbrake mechanism, checking for frayed or broken cables, excessive corrosion, or wear or insecurity of the linkage. Check that the mechanism works on each relevant wheel, and releases fully, without binding.

☐ It is not possible to test brake efficiency without special equipment, but a road test can be carried out later to check that the vehicle pulls up in a straight line.

Fuel and exhaust systems

☐ Inspect the fuel tank (including the filler cap), fuel pipes, hoses and unions. All components must be secure and free from leaks.

☐ Examine the exhaust system over its entire length, checking for any damaged, broken or missing mountings, security of the retaining clamps and rust or corrosion.

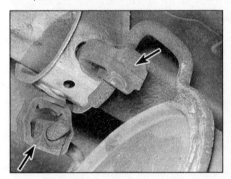

Wheels and tyres

☐ Examine the sidewalls and tread area of each tyre in turn. Check for cuts, tears, lumps, bulges, separation of the tread, and exposure of the ply or cord due to wear or damage. Check that the tyre bead is correctly seated on the wheel rim, that the valve is sound and properly seated, and that the wheel is not distorted or damaged.

☐ Check that the tyres are of the correct size for the vehicle, that they are of the same size and type on each axle, and that the pressures are correct.

☐ Check the tyre tread depth. The legal minimum at the time of writing is 1.6 mm over at least three-quarters of the tread width. Abnormal tread wear may indicate incorrect front wheel alignment.

Body corrosion

☐ Check the condition of the entire vehicle structure for signs of corrosion in load-bearing areas. (These include chassis box sections, side sills, cross-members, pillars, and all suspension, steering, braking system and seat belt mountings and anchorages.) Any corrosion which has seriously reduced the thickness of a load-bearing area is likely to cause the vehicle to fail. In this case professional repairs are likely to be needed.

☐ Damage or corrosion which causes sharp or otherwise dangerous edges to be exposed will also cause the vehicle to fail.

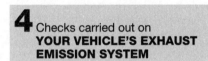

4 Checks carried out on **YOUR VEHICLE'S EXHAUST EMISSION SYSTEM**

Petrol models

☐ Have the engine at normal operating temperature, and make sure that it is in good tune (ignition system in good order, air filter element clean, etc).

☐ Before any measurements are carried out, raise the engine speed to around 2500 rpm, and hold it at this speed for 20 seconds. Allow the engine speed to return to idle, and watch for smoke emissions from the exhaust tailpipe. If the idle speed is obviously much too high, or if dense blue or clearly-visible black smoke comes from the tailpipe for more than 5 seconds, the vehicle will fail. As a rule of thumb, blue smoke signifies oil being burnt (engine wear) while black smoke signifies unburnt fuel (dirty air cleaner element, or other carburettor or fuel system fault).

☐ An exhaust gas analyser capable of measuring carbon monoxide (CO) and hydrocarbons (HC) is now needed. If such an instrument cannot be hired or borrowed, a local garage may agree to perform the check for a small fee.

CO emissions (mixture)

☐ At the time of writing, for vehicles first used between 1st August 1975 and 31st July 1986 (P to C registration), the CO level must not exceed 4.5% by volume. For vehicles first used between 1st August 1986 and 31st July 1992 (D to J registration), the CO level must not exceed 3.5% by volume. Vehicles first

used after 1st August 1992 (K registration) must conform to the manufacturer's specification. The MOT tester has access to a DOT database or emissions handbook, which lists the CO and HC limits for each make and model of vehicle. The CO level is measured with the engine at idle speed, and at "fast idle". The following limits are given as a general guide:

> *At idle speed -*
> CO level no more than 0.5%
> *At "fast idle" (2500 to 3000 rpm) -*
> CO level no more than 0.3%
> (Minimum oil temperature 60ºC)

☐ If the CO level cannot be reduced far enough to pass the test (and the fuel and ignition systems are otherwise in good condition) then the carburettor is badly worn, or there is some problem in the fuel injection system or catalytic converter (as applicable).

HC emissions

☐ With the CO within limits, HC emissions for vehicles first used between 1st August 1975 and 31st July 1992 (P to J registration) must not exceed 1200 ppm. Vehicles first used after 1st August 1992 (K registration) must conform to the manufacturer's specification. The MOT tester has access to a DOT database or emissions handbook, which lists the CO and HC limits for each make and model of vehicle. The HC level is measured with the engine at "fast idle". The following is given as a general guide:

> *At "fast idle" (2500 to 3000 rpm) -*
> HC level no more than 200 ppm
> (Minimum oil temperature 60ºC)

☐ Excessive HC emissions are caused by incomplete combustion, the causes of which can include oil being burnt, mechanical wear and ignition/fuel system malfunction.

Diesel models

☐ The only emission test applicable to Diesel engines is the measuring of exhaust smoke density. The test involves accelerating the engine several times to its maximum unloaded speed.

Note: *It is of the utmost importance that the engine timing belt is in good condition before the test is carried out.*

☐ The limits for Diesel engine exhaust smoke, introduced in September 1995 are:

Vehicles first used before 1st August 1979:
> Exempt from metered smoke testing, but must not emit "dense blue or clearly visible black smoke for a period of more than 5 seconds at idle" or "dense blue or clearly visible black smoke during acceleration which would obscure the view of other road users".

Non-turbocharged vehicles first used after
> *1st August 1979:* 2.5m^{-1}

Turbocharged vehicles first used after
> *1st August 1979:* 3.0m^{-1}

☐ Excessive smoke can be caused by a dirty air cleaner element. Otherwise, professional advice may be needed to find the cause.

Engine

- ☐ Engine fails to rotate when attempting to start
- ☐ Engine rotates but will not start
- ☐ Engine difficult to start when cold
- ☐ Engine difficult to start when hot
- ☐ Starter motor noisy or excessively-rough in engagement
- ☐ Engine starts but stops immediately
- ☐ Engine idles erratically
- ☐ Engine misfires at idle speed
- ☐ Engine misfires throughout the driving speed range
- ☐ Engine hesitates on acceleration
- ☐ Engine stalls
- ☐ Engine lacks power
- ☐ Engine backfires
- ☐ Oil pressure warning light illuminated with engine running
- ☐ Engine runs-on after switching off
- ☐ Engine noises
- ☐ Engine oil consumption excessive

Cooling system

- ☐ Overheating
- ☐ Overcooling
- ☐ External coolant leakage
- ☐ Internal coolant leakage
- ☐ Corrosion

Fuel and exhaust systems

- ☐ Excessive fuel consumption
- ☐ Fuel leakage and/or fuel odour
- ☐ Excessive noise or fumes from exhaust system

Clutch

- ☐ Pedal travels to floor - no pressure or very little resistance
- ☐ Clutch fails to disengage (unable to select gears)
- ☐ Clutch slips (engine speed increases with no increase in vehicle speed)
- ☐ Judder as clutch is engaged
- ☐ Noise when depressing or releasing clutch pedal

Manual transmission

- ☐ Noisy in neutral with engine running
- ☐ Noisy in one particular gear
- ☐ Difficulty engaging gears
- ☐ Jumps out of gear
- ☐ Vibration
- ☐ Lubricant leaks

Automatic transmission

- ☐ Fluid leakage
- ☐ Transmission fluid brown, or has burned smell
- ☐ Transmission will not downshift (kickdown) with accelerator pedal fully depressed
- ☐ General gear selection problems
- ☐ Engine will not start in any gear, or starts in gears other than Park or Neutral
- ☐ Transmission slips, is noisy, or has no drive in forward or reverse gears

Driveshafts

- ☐ Clicking or knocking noise on turns (at slow speed on full lock)
- ☐ Vibration when decelerating or accelerating

Braking system

- ☐ Vehicle pulls to one side under braking
- ☐ Noise (grinding or high-pitched squeal) when brakes applied
- ☐ Excessive brake pedal travel
- ☐ Brake pedal feels spongy when depressed
- ☐ Excessive brake pedal effort required to stop vehicle
- ☐ Judder felt through brake pedal or steering wheel when braking
- ☐ Brakes binding

Suspension and steering systems

- ☐ Vehicle pulls to one side
- ☐ Wheel wobble and vibration
- ☐ Excessive pitching and/or rolling around corners, or during braking
- ☐ Wandering or general instability
- ☐ Excessively-stiff steering
- ☐ Excessive play in steering
- ☐ Lack of power assistance
- ☐ Tyre wear excessive

Electrical system

- ☐ Battery will not hold a charge for more than a few days
- ☐ Ignition/no-charge warning light remains illuminated with engine running
- ☐ Ignition/no-charge warning light fails to come on
- ☐ Lights inoperative
- ☐ Instrument readings inaccurate or erratic
- ☐ Horn inoperative, or unsatisfactory in operation
- ☐ Windscreen/tailgate wipers inoperative or unsatisfactory in operation
- ☐ Windscreen/tailgate washers inoperative, or unsatisfactory in operation
- ☐ Electric windows inoperative, or unsatisfactory in operation
- ☐ Central locking system inoperative, or unsatisfactory in operation

Introduction

The vehicle owner who does his or her own maintenance according to the recommended service schedules should not have to use this section of the manual very often. Modern component reliability is such that, provided those items subject to wear or deterioration are inspected or renewed at the specified intervals, sudden failure is comparatively rare. Faults do not usually just happen as a result of sudden failure, but develop over a period of time. Major mechanical failures in particular are usually preceded by characteristic symptoms over hundreds or even thousands of miles. Those components which do occasionally fail without warning are often small and easily carried in the vehicle.

With any fault-finding, the first step is to decide where to begin investigations. Sometimes this is obvious, but on other occasions, a little detective work will be necessary. The owner who makes half a dozen haphazard adjustments or replacements may be successful in curing a fault (or its symptoms), but will be none the wiser if the fault recurs, and ultimately may have spent more time and money than was necessary. A calm and logical approach will be found to be more satisfactory in the long run. Always take into account any warning signs or abnormalities that may have been noticed in the period preceding the fault - power loss, high or low gauge readings, unusual smells, etc - and remember that failure of components such as fuses or spark plugs may only be pointers to some underlying fault.

The pages which follow provide an easy-reference guide to the more common problems which may occur during the operation of the vehicle. These problems and their possible causes are grouped under headings denoting various components or systems, such as Engine, Cooling system, etc. The general Chapter which deals with the problem is also shown in brackets; refer to the relevant Part of that Chapter for system-specific information. Whatever the fault, certain basic principles apply. These are as follows:

Verify the fault. This is simply a matter of being sure that you know what the symptoms are before starting work. This is particularly important if you are investigating a fault for someone else, who may not have described it very accurately.

Don't overlook the obvious. For example, if the vehicle won't start, is there petrol in the tank? (Don't take anyone else's word on this particular point, and don't trust the fuel gauge either!) If an electrical fault is indicated, look for loose or broken wires before digging out the test gear.

Cure the disease, not the symptom. Substituting a flat battery with a fully-charged one will get you off the hard shoulder, but if the underlying cause is not attended to, the new battery will go the same way. Similarly, changing oil-fouled spark plugs for a new set will get you moving again, but remember that the reason for the fouling (if it wasn't simply an incorrect grade of plug) will have to be established and corrected.

Don't take anything for granted. Particularly, don't forget that a 'new' component may itself be defective (especially if it's been rattling around in the boot for months), and don't leave components out of a fault diagnosis sequence just because they are new or recently fitted. When you do finally diagnose a difficult fault, you'll probably realise that all the evidence was there from the start.

Consider what work, if any, has recently been carried out. Many faults arise through careless or hurried work. For instance, if any work has been performed under the bonnet, could some of the wiring have been dislodged or incorrectly routed, or a hose trapped? Have all the fasteners been properly tightened? Were new, genuine parts and new gaskets used? There is often a certain amount of detective work to be done in this case, as an apparently-unrelated task can have far-reaching consequences.

Engine

Engine fails to rotate when attempting to start

☐ Battery terminal connections loose or corroded (*Weekly checks*).
☐ Battery discharged or faulty, or electrolyte level low (Chapter 1 or 5A).
☐ Broken, loose or disconnected wiring in the starting circuit (Chapter 5A).
☐ Defective starter solenoid or switch (Chapter 5A).
☐ Defective starter motor (Chapter 5A).
☐ Starter pinion or flywheel ring gear teeth loose or broken (relevant part of Chapter 2 or 5A).
☐ Engine/transmission earth leads broken or disconnected (Chapter 2E or 5A).
☐ Automatic transmission not in Park/Neutral position, or selector cable adjustment incorrect (Chapter 7B).

Engine rotates but will not start

☐ Fuel tank empty.
☐ Fuel pump not working, or fuel lines blocked/damaged (Chapter 4A or 4B).
☐ Fuel filter blocked, where applicable (Chapter 1).
☐ Fuel injector wiring disconnected or damaged (Chapter 4A or 4B).
☐ Battery discharged, or electrolyte level low (engine rotates slowly) (Chapter 1 or 5A).
☐ Battery terminal connections loose or corroded (*Weekly checks*).
☐ Ignition components damp or damaged (Chapter 1 or 5B).
☐ Broken, loose or disconnected wiring in the ignition circuit (Chapter 1 or 5B).
☐ Immobiliser fault (Chapter 12, or *Disconnecting the battery*).
☐ Worn, faulty or incorrectly-gapped spark plugs (Chapter 1).
☐ Low cylinder compressions (relevant part of Chapter 2).
☐ Major mechanical failure (eg timing belt broken) (relevant part of Chapter 2).

Engine difficult to start when cold

☐ Battery discharged or faulty, or electrolyte level low (Chapter 1 or 5A).
☐ Battery terminal connections loose or corroded (*Weekly checks*).
☐ Worn, faulty or incorrectly-gapped spark plugs (Chapter 1).
☐ Other ignition system fault (Chapter 1 or 5B).
☐ Engine management system fault (Chapter 1, 4A, 4B or 5B).
☐ Low cylinder compressions (relevant part of Chapter 2).

Engine difficult to start when hot

☐ Air cleaner element dirty or clogged (Chapter 1).
☐ Engine management system fault (Chapter 1, 4A, 4B or 5B).
☐ Low cylinder compressions (relevant part of Chapter 2).

Starter motor noisy or excessively-rough in engagement

☐ Starter pinion or flywheel ring gear teeth loose or broken (Chapter 2 or 5A).
☐ Starter motor mounting bolts loose or missing (Chapter 5A).
☐ Starter motor internal components worn or damaged (Chapter 5A).

Engine starts but stops immediately

☐ Loose or faulty electrical connections in the ignition circuit (Chapter 1 or 5B).
☐ Engine management system fault (Chapter 1, 4A, 4B or 5B).
☐ Vacuum leak at the inlet manifold or associated hoses (Chapter 1, 4A or 4B).

Engine idles erratically

☐ Engine management system fault (Chapter 1, 4A, 4B or 5B).
☐ Fuel injectors partially blocked (Chapter 4A or 4B).
☐ Air cleaner element dirty or clogged (Chapter 1).
☐ Crankcase breather hoses blocked or damaged (Chapter 1 or 5B).
☐ Vacuum leak at the inlet manifold or associated hoses (Chapter 1, 4A or 4B).
☐ Worn, faulty or incorrectly-gapped spark plugs (Chapter 1).
☐ Uneven or low cylinder compressions (relevant part of Chapter 2).
☐ Camshaft lobes worn (relevant part of Chapter 2).

Engine misfires at idle speed

☐ Worn, faulty or incorrectly-gapped spark plugs (Chapter 1).
☐ Faulty spark plug HT leads, where applicable (Chapter 5B).
☐ Engine management system fault (Chapter 1, 4A, 4B or 5B).
☐ Fuel injector(s) partially blocked (Chapter 4A or 4B).
☐ Vacuum leak at the inlet manifold or associated hoses (Chapter 1, 4A or 4B).
☐ Uneven or low cylinder compressions (relevant part of Chapter 2).
☐ Disconnected, leaking or perished crankcase breather hoses (Chapter 1 or 5B).
☐ Crankshaft sensor dirty or damaged (Chapter 5B).

Engine (continued)

Engine misfires throughout the driving speed range

- ☐ Fuel filter choked (Chapter 1).
- ☐ Fuel pump faulty (relevant part of Chapter 4).
- ☐ Fuel tank vent blocked or fuel pipes restricted (relevant part of Chapter 4).
- ☐ Vacuum leak at the inlet manifold or associated hoses (Chapter 1, 4A or 4B).
- ☐ Worn, faulty or incorrectly-gapped spark plugs (Chapter 1).
- ☐ Faulty spark plug HT leads, where applicable (Chapter 5B).
- ☐ Engine management system fault (Chapter 1, 4A, 4B or 5B).
- ☐ Fuel injector(s) partially blocked (Chapter 4A or 4B).
- ☐ Uneven or low cylinder compressions (relevant part of Chapter 2).
- ☐ Crankshaft sensor dirty or damaged (Chapter 5B).

Engine hesitates on acceleration

- ☐ Worn, faulty or incorrectly-gapped spark plugs (Chapter 1).
- ☐ Engine management system fault (Chapter 1, 4A, 4B or 5B).
- ☐ Fuel injector(s) partially blocked (Chapter 4A or 4B).
- ☐ Vacuum leak at the inlet manifold or associated hoses (Chapter 1, 4A or 4B).

Engine stalls

- ☐ Engine management system fault (Chapter 1, 4A, 4B or 5B).
- ☐ Fuel injector(s) partially blocked (Chapter 4A or 4B).
- ☐ Vacuum leak at the inlet manifold or associated hoses (Chapter 1, 4A or 4B).
- ☐ Fuel filter choked (Chapter 1).
- ☐ Fuel pump faulty (relevant part of Chapter 4).
- ☐ Fuel tank vent blocked or fuel pipes restricted (Chapter 4A or 4B).
- ☐ Crankshaft sensor dirty or damaged (Chapter 5B).

Engine lacks power

- ☐ Engine management system fault - possibly in 'limp-home' mode (Chapter 1, 4A, 4B or 5B).
- ☐ Fuel injector(s) partially blocked (Chapter 4A or 4B).
- ☐ Timing belt incorrectly fitted (relevant part of Chapter 2)
- ☐ Fuel filter choked (Chapter 1).
- ☐ Fuel pump faulty (relevant part of Chapter 4).
- ☐ Knock sensor faulty - ignition retarded (Chapter 5B).
- ☐ Uneven or low cylinder compressions (relevant part of Chapter 2).
- ☐ Worn, faulty or incorrectly-gapped spark plugs (Chapter 1).
- ☐ Vacuum leak at the inlet manifold or associated hoses (Chapter 1, 4A or 4B).
- ☐ Brakes binding (Chapter 1 or 9).
- ☐ Clutch slipping (Chapter 6).
- ☐ Automatic transmission fluid level incorrect (Chapter 1).

Engine backfires

- ☐ Engine management system fault (Chapter 1, 4A, 4B or 5B).
- ☐ Spark plug HT leads incorrectly fitted (Chapter 5B).
- ☐ Timing belt incorrectly fitted (relevant part of Chapter 2).
- ☐ Vacuum leak at the inlet manifold or associated hoses (Chapter 1, 4A or 4B).
- ☐ Emission control system fault (Chapter 4C).

Oil pressure warning light illuminated with engine running

- ☐ Low oil level or incorrect oil grade (Chapter 1).
- ☐ Faulty oil pressure switch (relevant part of Chapter 2).
- ☐ Worn engine bearings and/or oil pump (relevant part of Chapter 2).
- ☐ High engine operating temperature (Chapter 3).
- ☐ Oil pump pressure relief valve defective (relevant part of Chapter 2).
- ☐ Oil pick-up pipe strainer clogged (relevant part of Chapter 2).

Engine runs-on after switching off

- ☐ Engine management system fault (Chapter 1, 4A, 4B or 5B).
- ☐ Excessive carbon build-up on cylinder head/piston crowns (relevant part of Chapter 2).
- ☐ High engine operating temperature (Chapter 3).

Engine noises

Pre-ignition (pinking) or knocking during acceleration or under load

- ☐ Incorrect grade of fuel (Chapter 4A or 4B).
- ☐ Knock sensor faulty (Chapter 5B).
- ☐ Vacuum leak at the inlet manifold or associated hoses (Chapter 1, 4A or 4B).
- ☐ Excessive carbon build-up on cylinder head/piston crowns (relevant part of Chapter 2).

Whistling or wheezing noises

- ☐ Leaking inlet manifold gasket (Chapter 4A or 4B).
- ☐ Leaking exhaust manifold gasket or front pipe-to-manifold joint (Chapter 4C).
- ☐ Leaking vacuum hose (Chapter 1, 4, 5B or 9).
- ☐ Blowing cylinder head gasket (relevant part of Chapter 2).

Tapping or rattling noises

- ☐ Worn valve gear or camshafts (relevant part of Chapter 2).
- ☐ Worn or faulty hydraulic tappets (relevant part of Chapter 2).
- ☐ Worn timing belt, tensioner, or idler pulleys (relevant part of Chapter 2).
- ☐ Ancillary component fault (coolant pump, alternator, etc) (Chapter 3 or 5A).

Knocking or thumping noises

- ☐ Worn big-end bearings (regular heavy knocking, perhaps less under load) (Chapter 2E).
- ☐ Worn main bearings (rumbling and knocking, perhaps worsening under load) (Chapter 2E).
- ☐ Piston slap (most noticeable when cold - engine worn) (Chapter 2E).
- ☐ Ancillary component fault (coolant pump, alternator, etc) (Chapter 3 or 5A).

Engine oil consumption excessive

- ☐ Wrong grade of oil, or oil level too high (*Weekly checks*).
- ☐ Oil filter or sump drain plug loose (Chapter 1).
- ☐ Oil seal leaking (relevant part of Chapter 2).
- ☐ Camshaft cover seal leaking (Chapter 2B or 2D).
- ☐ Sump seal leaking (relevant part of Chapter 2).
- ☐ Cylinder head gasket leaking (relevant part of Chapter 2).
- ☐ Engine burning oil - piston ring or cylinder bore wear (Chapter 2E).

Cooling system

Overheating

☐ Insufficient coolant in system (*Weekly checks*).
☐ Thermostat faulty - not opening (Chapter 3).
☐ Radiator core blocked or grille restricted (Chapter 3).
☐ Radiator electric cooling fan(s) or coolant temperature sensor faulty (Chapter 3).
☐ Engine management system fault (Chapter 1, 4A, 4B or 5B).
☐ Pressure cap faulty (Chapter 3).
☐ Auxiliary drivebelt worn or slipping (Chapter 1).
☐ Airlock in cooling system (Chapter 1, Section 31).

Overcooling

☐ Thermostat faulty - not closing, or thermostat missing (Chapter 3).
☐ Inaccurate coolant temperature sensor (Chapter 3).

External coolant leakage

☐ Deteriorated or damaged hoses or hose clips (Chapter 1).
☐ Radiator core or heater matrix leaking (Chapter 3).
☐ Pressure cap faulty (Chapter 3).
☐ Coolant pump seal leaking (Chapter 3).
☐ Boiling due to overheating (Chapter 3).

Internal coolant leakage

☐ Leaking cylinder head gasket (relevant part of Chapter 2).
☐ Cracked cylinder head or cylinder bore (Chapter 2E).

Corrosion

☐ Infrequent draining and flushing (Chapter 1).
☐ Incorrect antifreeze mixture, or inappropriate antifreeze type (Chapter 1 or 3).

Fuel and exhaust systems

Excessive fuel consumption

☐ Unsympathetic driving style, or adverse conditions.
☐ Air cleaner filter element dirty or clogged (Chapter 1).
☐ Engine management system fault (Chapter 1, 4A, 4B or 5B).
☐ Fuel injector(s) partially blocked (Chapter 4A or 4B).
☐ Tyres under-inflated (*Weekly checks*).

Fuel leakage and/or fuel odour

☐ Damaged or corroded fuel tank, pipes or connections (Chapter 1).

Excessive noise or fumes from exhaust system

☐ Leaking exhaust system or manifold joints (Chapter 1 or 4C).
☐ Leaking, corroded or damaged silencers or pipe (Chapter 1 or 4C).
☐ Broken mountings, causing body or suspension contact (Chapter 1 or 4C).

Clutch

Note: *The clutch is actuated either by a cable, or by hydraulics (using a master and slave cylinder). Refer to Chapter 6 and establish which type is fitted.*

Pedal travels to floor - no pressure or very little resistance

- ☐ Air in clutch hydraulic system (Chapter 6).
- ☐ Faulty clutch slave cylinder (Chapter 6).
- ☐ Faulty clutch master cylinder (Chapter 6).
- ☐ Clutch cable broken (Chapter 6).
- ☐ Pedal return spring detached or broken (Chapter 6).
- ☐ Broken diaphragm spring in clutch pressure plate (Chapter 6).

Clutch fails to disengage (unable to select gears)

- ☐ Air in clutch hydraulic system (Chapter 6).
- ☐ Faulty clutch slave cylinder (Chapter 6).
- ☐ Faulty clutch master cylinder (Chapter 6).
- ☐ Clutch cable incorrectly adjusted (Chapter 6).
- ☐ Clutch disc sticking on transmission mainshaft splines (Chapter 6).
- ☐ Clutch disc sticking to flywheel or pressure plate (Chapter 6).
- ☐ Faulty pressure plate assembly (Chapter 6).
- ☐ Clutch release mechanism worn or incorrectly assembled (Chapter 6).

Clutch slips (engine speed increases with no increase in vehicle speed)

- ☐ Clutch cable incorrectly adjusted (Chapter 6).
- ☐ Clutch disc linings excessively worn (Chapter 6).
- ☐ Clutch disc linings contaminated with oil or grease (Chapter 6).
- ☐ Faulty pressure plate or weak diaphragm spring (Chapter 6).

Judder as clutch is engaged

- ☐ Clutch disc linings contaminated with oil or grease (Chapter 6).
- ☐ Clutch disc linings excessively worn (Chapter 6).
- ☐ Faulty or distorted pressure plate or diaphragm spring (Chapter 6).
- ☐ Worn or loose engine/transmission mountings (relevant part of Chapter 2).
- ☐ Clutch disc hub or transmission input shaft splines worn (Chapter 6).

Noise when depressing or releasing clutch pedal

- ☐ Worn clutch release bearing (Chapter 6).
- ☐ Worn or dry clutch pedal bushes (Chapter 6).
- ☐ Faulty pressure plate assembly (Chapter 6).
- ☐ Pressure plate diaphragm spring broken (Chapter 6).
- ☐ Broken clutch disc cushioning springs (Chapter 6).
- ☐ Clutch cable sticking or damaged (Chapter 6).

Manual transmission

Noisy in neutral with engine running

- ☐ Mainshaft bearings worn (noise apparent with clutch pedal released, but not when depressed) (Chapter 7A).*
- ☐ Clutch release bearing worn (noise apparent with clutch pedal depressed, possibly less when released) (Chapter 6).

Noisy in one particular gear

- ☐ Worn, damaged or chipped gear teeth (Chapter 7A).*
- ☐ Worn bearings (Chapter 7A).*

Difficulty engaging gears

- ☐ Clutch fault (Chapter 6).
- ☐ Selector cables out of adjustment (Chapter 7A).
- ☐ Worn synchroniser assemblies (Chapter 7A).*

Jumps out of gear

- ☐ Selector cables out of adjustment (Chapter 7A).
- ☐ Worn synchroniser assemblies (Chapter 7A).*
- ☐ Worn selector forks (Chapter 7A).*

Vibration

- ☐ Lack of oil (Chapter 1).
- ☐ Worn bearings (Chapter 7A).*

Lubricant leaks

- ☐ Leaking driveshaft/transmission oil seal (Chapter 7A).
- ☐ Leaking housing joint (Chapter 7A).*
- ☐ Leaking input shaft oil seal (Chapter 7A).

* Although the corrective action necessary to remedy the symptoms described is beyond the scope of the home mechanic, the above information should be helpful in isolating the cause of the condition, so that the owner can communicate clearly with a professional mechanic.

Automatic transmission

Note: *Due to the complexity of the automatic transmission, it is difficult for the home mechanic to properly diagnose and service this unit. For problems other than the following, the vehicle should be taken to a dealer service department or automatic transmission specialist.*

Fluid leakage

☐ Automatic transmission fluid is usually dark in colour. Fluid leaks should not be confused with engine oil, which can easily be blown onto the transmission by airflow.

☐ To determine the source of a leak, first remove all built-up dirt and grime from the transmission housing and surrounding areas, using a degreasing agent, or by steam-cleaning. Drive the vehicle at low speed, so airflow will not blow the leak far from its source. Raise and support the vehicle, and determine where the leak is coming from. The following are common areas of leakage:
a) *Transmission fluid sump (Chapter 1 or 7B).*
b) *Dipstick tube (Chapter 1 or 7B).*
c) *Transmission-to-fluid cooler pipes/unions (Chapter 1 or 7B).*
d) *Transmission fluid seals (Chapter 7B).*

Transmission fluid brown, or has burned smell

☐ Transmission fluid level low, or fluid in need of renewal (Chapter 1).

Transmission will not downshift (kickdown) with accelerator pedal fully depressed

☐ Low transmission fluid level (Chapter 1).
☐ Incorrect selector cable adjustment (Chapter 1 or 7B).
☐ Automatic transmission ECU or sensor fault (Chapter 7B).

General gear selection problems

☐ Checking and adjusting the selector cable is covered in Chapter 1 and 7B. The following are common problems which may be caused by a poorly-adjusted cable:
a) *Engine starting in gears other than Park or Neutral.*
b) *Indicator on gear selector lever pointing to a gear other than the one actually being used.*
c) *Vehicle moves when in Park or Neutral.*
d) *Poor gear shift quality or erratic gear changes.*
Refer to Chapter 7B for the selector cable adjustment procedure.

Engine will not start in any gear, or starts in gears other than Park or Neutral

☐ Incorrect selector cable adjustment (Chapter 7B).
☐ Automatic transmission ECU or sensor fault (Chapter 7B).

Transmission slips, is noisy, or has no drive in forward or reverse gears

☐ There are many probable causes for the above problems, but the home mechanic should be concerned with only one possibility - fluid level. Before taking the vehicle to a dealer or transmission specialist, check the fluid level and condition of the fluid as described in Chapter 1. Correct the fluid level as necessary, or change the fluid if needed. If the problem persists, professional help will be necessary.

Driveshafts

Clicking or knocking noise on turns (at slow speed on full lock)

☐ Lack of constant velocity joint lubricant, possibly due to damaged gaiter (Chapter 8).
☐ Worn outer constant velocity joint (Chapter 8).

Vibration when decelerating or accelerating

☐ Worn inner constant velocity joint (Chapter 8).
☐ Bent or distorted driveshaft (Chapter 8).

Braking system

Note: *Before assuming that a brake problem exists, make sure that the tyres are in good condition and correctly inflated, that the front wheel alignment is correct, and that the vehicle is not loaded with weight in an unequal manner. Apart from checking the condition of all brake pipes/hoses and electrical connections, any faults occurring on the Anti-lock Braking System (ABS) should be referred to a FIAT dealer for repair.*

Vehicle pulls to one side under braking

- ☐ Worn, defective, damaged or contaminated front brake pads (or rear brake shoes) on one side (Chapter 9).
- ☐ Seized or partially-seized front brake caliper piston or rear wheel cylinder (Chapter 9).
- ☐ A mixture of brake pad/shoe lining materials fitted between sides (Chapter 9).
- ☐ Brake caliper mounting bolts loose (Chapter 9).
- ☐ Worn or damaged steering or suspension components (Chapter 10).

Noise (grinding or high-pitched squeal) when brakes applied

- ☐ Brake friction material worn down to metal backing (Chapter 9).
- ☐ Excessive corrosion of brake disc (may be apparent after the vehicle has been standing for some time) (Chapter 9).

Excessive brake pedal travel

- ☐ Faulty master cylinder (Chapter 9).
- ☐ Air in hydraulic system (Chapter 9).
- ☐ Rear brake shoe adjuster mechanism seized or faulty (Chapter 9).

Brake pedal feels spongy when depressed

- ☐ Air in hydraulic system (Chapter 9).
- ☐ Deteriorated flexible rubber brake hoses (Chapter 9).
- ☐ Master cylinder mounting nuts loose (Chapter 9).
- ☐ Faulty master cylinder (Chapter 9).

Excessive brake pedal effort required to stop vehicle

- ☐ Faulty vacuum servo unit (Chapter 9).
- ☐ Disconnected, damaged or insecure brake servo vacuum hose (Chapter 9).
- ☐ Primary or secondary hydraulic circuit failure (Chapter 9).
- ☐ Seized brake caliper piston(s) or rear wheel cylinder(s) (Chapter 9).
- ☐ Brake pads/shoes incorrectly fitted (Chapter 9).
- ☐ Incorrect grade of brake pads/shoes fitted (Chapter 9).
- ☐ Brake pad/shoe linings contaminated (Chapter 9).

Judder felt through brake pedal or steering wheel when braking

- ☐ Excessive run-out or distortion of front discs or rear drums (Chapter 9).
- ☐ Brake pad/shoe linings worn (Chapter 9).
- ☐ Brake caliper mounting bolts loose (Chapter 9).
- ☐ Wear in suspension or steering components or mountings (Chapter 10).

Brakes binding

- ☐ Seized brake caliper piston(s) or rear wheel cylinder(s) (Chapter 9).
- ☐ Faulty handbrake mechanism (Chapter 9).
- ☐ Faulty master cylinder (Chapter 9).

Suspension and steering systems

Note: *Before diagnosing suspension or steering faults, be sure that the trouble is not due to incorrect tyre pressures, mixtures of tyre types, or binding brakes.*

Vehicle pulls to one side

- ☐ Defective tyre (*Weekly checks*).
- ☐ Excessive wear in suspension or steering components (Chapter 10).
- ☐ Incorrect front or rear wheel alignment (Chapter 10).
- ☐ Accident damage to steering or suspension components (Chapter 10).

Wheel wobble and vibration

- ☐ Front roadwheels out of balance (vibration felt mainly through the steering wheel) (*Weekly checks*).
- ☐ Rear roadwheels out of balance (vibration felt throughout the vehicle) (*Weekly checks*).
- ☐ Roadwheels damaged or distorted (*Weekly checks*).
- ☐ Faulty or damaged tyre (*Weekly checks*).
- ☐ Worn steering or suspension joints, bushes or components (Chapter 10).
- ☐ Roadwheel bolts loose (Chapter 1).

Excessive pitching and/or rolling around corners, or during braking

- ☐ Defective shock absorbers (Chapter 10).
- ☐ Broken or weak coil spring and/or suspension component (Chapter 10).
- ☐ Worn or damaged anti-roll bar or mountings (Chapter 10).

Wandering or general instability

- ☐ Incorrect wheel alignment (Chapter 10).
- ☐ Worn steering or suspension joints, bushes or components (Chapter 10).
- ☐ Roadwheels out of balance (*Weekly checks*).
- ☐ Faulty or damaged tyre (*Weekly checks*).
- ☐ Roadwheel bolts loose (Chapter 1).
- ☐ Defective shock absorbers (Chapter 10).

Excessively-stiff steering

- ☐ Broken or slipping steering pump (auxiliary) drivebelt (Chapter 1).
- ☐ Steering pump faulty (Chapter 10).
- ☐ Seized track rod end balljoint or suspension balljoint (Chapter 10).
- ☐ Incorrect front wheel alignment (Chapter 10).
- ☐ Steering rack or column bent or damaged (Chapter 10).

Excessive play in steering

- ☐ Worn steering column universal joint(s) (Chapter 10).
- ☐ Worn steering track rod end balljoints (Chapter 10).
- ☐ Worn steering gear (Chapter 10).
- ☐ Worn steering or suspension joints, bushes or components (Chapter 10).

Lack of power assistance

- ☐ Broken or slipping steering pump (auxiliary) drivebelt (Chapter 1).
- ☐ Incorrect fluid level (*Weekly checks*).
- ☐ Restriction in fluid hoses (Chapter 10).
- ☐ Faulty steering pump (Chapter 10).
- ☐ Faulty steering gear (Chapter 10).

Tyre wear excessive

Tyres worn on inside or outside edges

- ☐ Tyres under-inflated (*Weekly checks*).
- ☐ Incorrect camber or castor angles (wear on one edge only) (Chapter 10).
- ☐ Worn steering or suspension joints, bushes or components (Chapter 10).
- ☐ Excessively-hard cornering.
- ☐ Accident damage.

Tyre treads exhibit feathered edges

- ☐ Incorrect toe setting (Chapter 10).

Tyres worn in centre of tread

- ☐ Tyres over-inflated (*Weekly checks*).

Tyres worn on inside and outside edges

- ☐ Tyres under-inflated (*Weekly checks*).

Tyres worn unevenly

- ☐ Tyres out of balance (*Weekly checks*).
- ☐ Excessive wheel or tyre run-out (*Weekly checks*).
- ☐ Worn shock absorbers (Chapter 10).
- ☐ Faulty tyre (*Weekly checks*).

Electrical system

Note: *For problems associated with the starting system, refer to the faults listed under* **Engine** *earlier in this Section.*

Battery will not hold a charge for more than a few days

- [ ] Battery defective internally (Chapter 5A).
- [ ] Battery electrolyte level low (Chapter 1).
- [ ] Battery terminal connections loose or corroded (*Weekly checks*).
- [ ] Auxiliary drivebelt worn or slipping (Chapter 1).
- [ ] Alternator not charging at correct output (Chapter 5A).
- [ ] Alternator or voltage regulator faulty (Chapter 5A).
- [ ] Short-circuit causing continual battery drain (Chapter 5A or 12).

Ignition/no-charge warning light remains illuminated with engine running

- [ ] Auxiliary drivebelt worn or slipping (Chapter 1).
- [ ] Alternator brushes worn, sticking, or dirty (Chapter 5A).
- [ ] Alternator brush springs weak or broken (Chapter 5A).
- [ ] Internal fault in alternator or voltage regulator (Chapter 5A).
- [ ] Broken, disconnected, or loose wiring in charging circuit (Chapter 5A).

Ignition/no-charge warning light fails to come on

- [ ] Warning light bulb blown (Chapter 12).
- [ ] Broken, disconnected, or loose wiring in warning light circuit (Chapter 12).
- [ ] Alternator faulty (Chapter 5A).

Lights inoperative

- [ ] Bulb blown (Chapter 12).
- [ ] Corrosion of bulb or bulbholder contacts (Chapter 12).
- [ ] Blown fuse (Chapter 12).
- [ ] Faulty relay (Chapter 12).
- [ ] Broken, loose, or disconnected wiring (Chapter 12).
- [ ] Faulty switch (Chapter 12).

Instrument readings inaccurate or erratic

Instrument readings increase with engine speed

- [ ] Faulty instrument panel control components or circuitry (Chapter 12).

Tachometer gives no reading, or gives inaccurate reading

- [ ] Faulty instrument panel control components or circuitry (Chapter 12).
- [ ] Faulty crankshaft sensor (Chapter 5B).
- [ ] Engine management system fault (Chapter 4A, 4B or 5B).
- [ ] Wiring open-circuit (Chapter 12).
- [ ] Faulty gauge (Chapter 12).

Fuel or temperature gauges give no reading

- [ ] Faulty instrument panel control components or circuitry (Chapter 12).
- [ ] Engine management system fault (Chapter 4A, 4B or 5B).
- [ ] Faulty gauge sender unit (Chapter 3, 4A or 4B).
- [ ] Wiring open-circuit (Chapter 12).
- [ ] Faulty gauge (Chapter 12).

Fuel or temperature gauges give continuous maximum reading

- [ ] Faulty instrument panel control components or circuitry (Chapter 12).
- [ ] Faulty gauge sender unit (Chapter 3, 4A or 4B).
- [ ] Wiring short-circuit (Chapter 12).
- [ ] Faulty gauge (Chapter 12).

Horn inoperative, or unsatisfactory in operation

Horn fails to operate

- [ ] Blown fuse (Chapter 12).
- [ ] Steering wheel wiring connections loose, broken or disconnected (Chapter 10).
- [ ] Faulty horn (Chapter 12).

Horn emits intermittent or unsatisfactory sound

- [ ] Steering wheel cable connections loose, broken or disconnected (Chapter 10).
- [ ] Horn mountings loose (Chapter 12).
- [ ] Faulty horn (Chapter 12).

Horn operates all the time

- [ ] Horn push either earthed or stuck down (Chapter 10).
- [ ] Steering wheel cable connections earthed (Chapter 10).

Windscreen/tailgate wipers inoperative or unsatisfactory in operation

Wipers fail to operate, or operate very slowly

- [ ] Wiper blades stuck to screen, or linkage seized or binding (Chapter 12).
- [ ] Blown fuse (Chapter 12).
- [ ] Wiring or connections loose, broken or disconnected (Chapter 12).
- [ ] Faulty relay (Chapter 12).
- [ ] Faulty wiper motor (Chapter 12).

Wiper blades sweep over too large or too small an area of the glass

- [ ] Wiper arms incorrectly positioned on spindles (Chapter 12).
- [ ] Excessive wear of wiper linkage (Chapter 12).
- [ ] Wiper motor or linkage mountings loose or insecure (Chapter 12).

Wiper blades fail to clean the glass effectively

- [ ] Wiper blade rubbers worn or perished (*Weekly checks*).
- [ ] Wiper arm tension springs broken, or arm pivots seized (Chapter 12).
- [ ] Insufficient windscreen washer additive to adequately remove road film (*Weekly checks*).

Windscreen/tailgate washers inoperative, or unsatisfactory in operation

One or more washer jets inoperative

- [ ] Blocked washer jet (Chapter 12).
- [ ] Disconnected, kinked or restricted fluid hose (Chapter 12).
- [ ] Insufficient fluid in washer reservoir (*Weekly checks*).

Washer pump fails to operate

- [ ] Broken or disconnected wiring or connections (Chapter 12).
- [ ] Blown fuse (Chapter 12).
- [ ] Faulty washer switch (Chapter 12).
- [ ] Faulty washer pump (Chapter 12).

Washer pump runs for some time before fluid is emitted from jets

- [ ] Faulty one-way valve in fluid supply hose (Chapter 12).

Electrical system (continued)

Electric windows inoperative, or unsatisfactory in operation

Window glass will only move in one direction

☐ Faulty switch (Chapter 12).

Window glass slow to move

☐ Incorrectly-adjusted door glass guide channels (Chapter 11).
☐ Regulator seized or damaged, or in need of lubrication (Chapter 11).
☐ Door internal components or trim fouling regulator (Chapter 11).
☐ Faulty motor (Chapter 12).

Window glass fails to move

☐ Incorrectly-adjusted door glass guide channels (Chapter 11).
☐ Blown fuse (Chapter 12).
☐ Faulty relay (Chapter 12).
☐ Broken or disconnected wiring or connections (Chapter 12).
☐ Faulty motor (Chapter 12).

Central locking system inoperative, or unsatisfactory in operation

Complete system failure

☐ Blown fuse (Chapter 12).
☐ Faulty relay (Chapter 12).
☐ Broken or disconnected wiring or connections (Chapter 12).

Latch locks but will not unlock, or unlocks but will not lock

☐ Faulty door lock microswitch (Chapter 11).
☐ Broken or disconnected latch operating rods or levers (Chapter 11).
☐ Faulty relay (Chapter 12).

One lock motor fails to operate

☐ Broken or disconnected wiring or connections (Chapter 12).
☐ Faulty lock motor (Chapter 11).
☐ Broken, binding or disconnected latch operating rods or levers (Chapter 11).
☐ Fault in door latch (Chapter 11).

A

ABS (Anti-lock brake system) A system, usually electronically controlled, that senses incipient wheel lockup during braking and relieves hydraulic pressure at wheels that are about to skid.

Air bag An inflatable bag hidden in the steering wheel (driver's side) or the dash or glovebox (passenger side). In a head-on collision, the bags inflate, preventing the driver and front passenger from being thrown forward into the steering wheel or windscreen.

Air cleaner A metal or plastic housing, containing a filter element, which removes dust and dirt from the air being drawn into the engine.

Air filter element The actual filter in an air cleaner system, usually manufactured from pleated paper and requiring renewal at regular intervals.

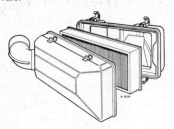

Air filter

Allen key A hexagonal wrench which fits into a recessed hexagonal hole.

Alligator clip A long-nosed spring-loaded metal clip with meshing teeth. Used to make temporary electrical connections.

Alternator A component in the electrical system which converts mechanical energy from a drivebelt into electrical energy to charge the battery and to operate the starting system, ignition system and electrical accessories.

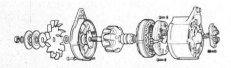

Alternator (exploded view)

Ampere (amp) A unit of measurement for the flow of electric current. One amp is the amount of current produced by one volt acting through a resistance of one ohm.

Anaerobic sealer A substance used to prevent bolts and screws from loosening. Anaerobic means that it does not require oxygen for activation. The Loctite brand is widely used.

Antifreeze A substance (usually ethylene glycol) mixed with water, and added to a vehicle's cooling system, to prevent freezing of the coolant in winter. Antifreeze also contains chemicals to inhibit corrosion and the formation of rust and other deposits that would tend to clog the radiator and coolant passages and reduce cooling efficiency.

Anti-seize compound A coating that reduces the risk of seizing on fasteners that are subjected to high temperatures, such as exhaust manifold bolts and nuts.

Anti-seize compound

Asbestos A natural fibrous mineral with great heat resistance, commonly used in the composition of brake friction materials. Asbestos is a health hazard and the dust created by brake systems should never be inhaled or ingested.

Axle A shaft on which a wheel revolves, or which revolves with a wheel. Also, a solid beam that connects the two wheels at one end of the vehicle. An axle which also transmits power to the wheels is known as a live axle.

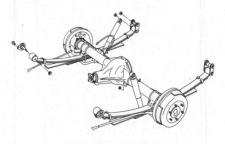

Axle assembly

Axleshaft A single rotating shaft, on either side of the differential, which delivers power from the final drive assembly to the drive wheels. Also called a driveshaft or a halfshaft.

B

Ball bearing An anti-friction bearing consisting of a hardened inner and outer race with hardened steel balls between two races.

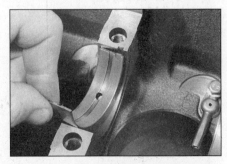

Bearing

Bearing The curved surface on a shaft or in a bore, or the part assembled into either, that permits relative motion between them with minimum wear and friction.

Big-end bearing The bearing in the end of the connecting rod that's attached to the crankshaft.

Bleed nipple A valve on a brake wheel cylinder, caliper or other hydraulic component that is opened to purge the hydraulic system of air. Also called a bleed screw.

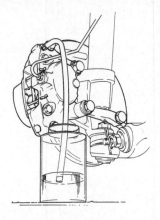

Brake bleeding

Brake bleeding Procedure for removing air from lines of a hydraulic brake system.

Brake disc The component of a disc brake that rotates with the wheels.

Brake drum The component of a drum brake that rotates with the wheels.

Brake linings The friction material which contacts the brake disc or drum to retard the vehicle's speed. The linings are bonded or riveted to the brake pads or shoes.

Brake pads The replaceable friction pads that pinch the brake disc when the brakes are applied. Brake pads consist of a friction material bonded or riveted to a rigid backing plate.

Brake shoe The crescent-shaped carrier to which the brake linings are mounted and which forces the lining against the rotating drum during braking.

Braking systems For more information on braking systems, consult the *Haynes Automotive Brake Manual*.

Breaker bar A long socket wrench handle providing greater leverage.

Bulkhead The insulated partition between the engine and the passenger compartment.

C

Caliper The non-rotating part of a disc-brake assembly that straddles the disc and carries the brake pads. The caliper also contains the hydraulic components that cause the pads to pinch the disc when the brakes are applied. A caliper is also a measuring tool that can be set to measure inside or outside dimensions of an object.

Camshaft A rotating shaft on which a series of cam lobes operate the valve mechanisms. The camshaft may be driven by gears, by sprockets and chain or by sprockets and a belt.

Canister A container in an evaporative emission control system; contains activated charcoal granules to trap vapours from the fuel system.

Canister

Carburettor A device which mixes fuel with air in the proper proportions to provide a desired power output from a spark ignition internal combustion engine.

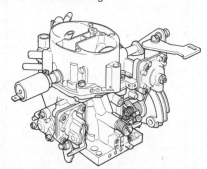

Carburettor

Castellated Resembling the parapets along the top of a castle wall. For example, a castellated balljoint stud nut.

Castellated nut

Castor In wheel alignment, the backward or forward tilt of the steering axis. Castor is positive when the steering axis is inclined rearward at the top.

Catalytic converter A silencer-like device in the exhaust system which converts certain pollutants in the exhaust gases into less harmful substances.

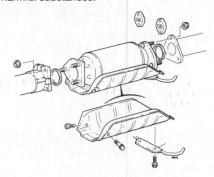

Catalytic converter

Circlip A ring-shaped clip used to prevent endwise movement of cylindrical parts and shafts. An internal circlip is installed in a groove in a housing; an external circlip fits into a groove on the outside of a cylindrical piece such as a shaft.

Clearance The amount of space between two parts. For example, between a piston and a cylinder, between a bearing and a journal, etc.

Coil spring A spiral of elastic steel found in various sizes throughout a vehicle, for example as a springing medium in the suspension and in the valve train.

Compression Reduction in volume, and increase in pressure and temperature, of a gas, caused by squeezing it into a smaller space.

Compression ratio The relationship between cylinder volume when the piston is at top dead centre and cylinder volume when the piston is at bottom dead centre.

Constant velocity (CV) joint A type of universal joint that cancels out vibrations caused by driving power being transmitted through an angle.

Core plug A disc or cup-shaped metal device inserted in a hole in a casting through which core was removed when the casting was formed. Also known as a freeze plug or expansion plug.

Crankcase The lower part of the engine block in which the crankshaft rotates.

Crankshaft The main rotating member, or shaft, running the length of the crankcase, with offset "throws" to which the connecting rods are attached.

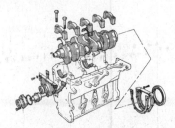

Crankshaft assembly

Crocodile clip See Alligator clip

D

Diagnostic code Code numbers obtained by accessing the diagnostic mode of an engine management computer. This code can be used to determine the area in the system where a malfunction may be located.

Disc brake A brake design incorporating a rotating disc onto which brake pads are squeezed. The resulting friction converts the energy of a moving vehicle into heat.

Double-overhead cam (DOHC) An engine that uses two overhead camshafts, usually one for the intake valves and one for the exhaust valves.

Drivebelt(s) The belt(s) used to drive accessories such as the alternator, water pump, power steering pump, air conditioning compressor, etc. off the crankshaft pulley.

Accessory drivebelts

Driveshaft Any shaft used to transmit motion. Commonly used when referring to the axleshafts on a front wheel drive vehicle.

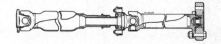

Driveshaft

Drum brake A type of brake using a drum-shaped metal cylinder attached to the inner surface of the wheel. When the brake pedal is pressed, curved brake shoes with friction linings press against the inside of the drum to slow or stop the vehicle.

Drum brake assembly

E

EGR valve A valve used to introduce exhaust gases into the intake air stream.

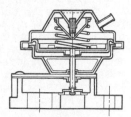

EGR valve

Electronic control unit (ECU) A computer which controls (for instance) ignition and fuel injection systems, or an anti-lock braking system. For more information refer to the *Haynes Automotive Electrical and Electronic Systems Manual*.

Electronic Fuel Injection (EFI) A computer controlled fuel system that distributes fuel through an injector located in each intake port of the engine.

Emergency brake A braking system, independent of the main hydraulic system, that can be used to slow or stop the vehicle if the primary brakes fail, or to hold the vehicle stationary even though the brake pedal isn't depressed. It usually consists of a hand lever that actuates either front or rear brakes mechanically through a series of cables and linkages. Also known as a handbrake or parking brake.

Endfloat The amount of lengthwise movement between two parts. As applied to a crankshaft, the distance that the crankshaft can move forward and back in the cylinder block.

Engine management system (EMS) A computer controlled system which manages the fuel injection and the ignition systems in an integrated fashion.

Exhaust manifold A part with several passages through which exhaust gases leave the engine combustion chambers and enter the exhaust pipe.

Exhaust manifold

F

Fan clutch A viscous (fluid) drive coupling device which permits variable engine fan speeds in relation to engine speeds.

Feeler blade A thin strip or blade of hardened steel, ground to an exact thickness, used to check or measure clearances between parts.

Feeler blade

Firing order The order in which the engine cylinders fire, or deliver their power strokes, beginning with the number one cylinder.

Flywheel A heavy spinning wheel in which energy is absorbed and stored by means of momentum. On cars, the flywheel is attached to the crankshaft to smooth out firing impulses.

Free play The amount of travel before any action takes place. The "looseness" in a linkage, or an assembly of parts, between the initial application of force and actual movement. For example, the distance the brake pedal moves before the pistons in the master cylinder are actuated.

Fuse An electrical device which protects a circuit against accidental overload. The typical fuse contains a soft piece of metal which is calibrated to melt at a predetermined current flow (expressed as amps) and break the circuit.

Fusible link A circuit protection device consisting of a conductor surrounded by heat-resistant insulation. The conductor is smaller than the wire it protects, so it acts as the weakest link in the circuit. Unlike a blown fuse, a failed fusible link must frequently be cut from the wire for replacement.

G

Gap The distance the spark must travel in jumping from the centre electrode to the side

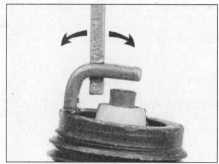

Adjusting spark plug gap

electrode in a spark plug. Also refers to the spacing between the points in a contact breaker assembly in a conventional points-type ignition, or to the distance between the reluctor or rotor and the pickup coil in an electronic ignition.

Gasket Any thin, soft material - usually cork, cardboard, asbestos or soft metal - installed between two metal surfaces to ensure a good seal. For instance, the cylinder head gasket seals the joint between the block and the cylinder head.

Gasket

Gauge An instrument panel display used to monitor engine conditions. A gauge with a movable pointer on a dial or a fixed scale is an analogue gauge. A gauge with a numerical readout is called a digital gauge.

H

Halfshaft A rotating shaft that transmits power from the final drive unit to a drive wheel, usually when referring to a live rear axle.

Harmonic balancer A device designed to reduce torsion or twisting vibration in the crankshaft. May be incorporated in the crankshaft pulley. Also known as a vibration damper.

Hone An abrasive tool for correcting small irregularities or differences in diameter in an engine cylinder, brake cylinder, etc.

Hydraulic tappet A tappet that utilises hydraulic pressure from the engine's lubrication system to maintain zero clearance (constant contact with both camshaft and valve stem). Automatically adjusts to variation in valve stem length. Hydraulic tappets also reduce valve noise.

I

Ignition timing The moment at which the spark plug fires, usually expressed in the number of crankshaft degrees before the piston reaches the top of its stroke.

Inlet manifold A tube or housing with passages through which flows the air-fuel mixture (carburettor vehicles and vehicles with throttle body injection) or air only (port fuel-injected vehicles) to the port openings in the cylinder head.

J

Jump start Starting the engine of a vehicle with a discharged or weak battery by attaching jump leads from the weak battery to a charged or helper battery.

L

Load Sensing Proportioning Valve (LSPV) A brake hydraulic system control valve that works like a proportioning valve, but also takes into consideration the amount of weight carried by the rear axle.

Locknut A nut used to lock an adjustment nut, or other threaded component, in place. For example, a locknut is employed to keep the adjusting nut on the rocker arm in position.

Lockwasher A form of washer designed to prevent an attaching nut from working loose.

M

MacPherson strut A type of front suspension system devised by Earle MacPherson at Ford of England. In its original form, a simple lateral link with the anti-roll bar creates the lower control arm. A long strut - an integral coil spring and shock absorber - is mounted between the body and the steering knuckle. Many modern so-called MacPherson strut systems use a conventional lower A-arm and don't rely on the anti-roll bar for location.

Multimeter An electrical test instrument with the capability to measure voltage, current and resistance.

N

NOx Oxides of Nitrogen. A common toxic pollutant emitted by petrol and diesel engines at higher temperatures.

O

Ohm The unit of electrical resistance. One volt applied to a resistance of one ohm will produce a current of one amp.

Ohmmeter An instrument for measuring electrical resistance.

O-ring A type of sealing ring made of a special rubber-like material; in use, the O-ring is compressed into a groove to provide the sealing action.

O-ring

Overhead cam (ohc) engine An engine with the camshaft(s) located on top of the cylinder head(s).

Overhead valve (ohv) engine An engine with the valves located in the cylinder head, but with the camshaft located in the engine block.

Oxygen sensor A device installed in the engine exhaust manifold, which senses the oxygen content in the exhaust and converts this information into an electric current. Also called a Lambda sensor.

P

Phillips screw A type of screw head having a cross instead of a slot for a corresponding type of screwdriver.

Plastigage A thin strip of plastic thread, available in different sizes, used for measuring clearances. For example, a strip of Plastigage is laid across a bearing journal. The parts are assembled and dismantled; the width of the crushed strip indicates the clearance between journal and bearing.

Plastigage

Propeller shaft The long hollow tube with universal joints at both ends that carries power from the transmission to the differential on front-engined rear wheel drive vehicles.

Proportioning valve A hydraulic control valve which limits the amount of pressure to the rear brakes during panic stops to prevent wheel lock-up.

R

Rack-and-pinion steering A steering system with a pinion gear on the end of the steering shaft that mates with a rack (think of a geared wheel opened up and laid flat). When the steering wheel is turned, the pinion turns, moving the rack to the left or right. This movement is transmitted through the track rods to the steering arms at the wheels.

Radiator A liquid-to-air heat transfer device designed to reduce the temperature of the coolant in an internal combustion engine cooling system.

Refrigerant Any substance used as a heat transfer agent in an air-conditioning system. R-12 has been the principle refrigerant for many years; recently, however, manufacturers have begun using R-134a, a non-CFC substance that is considered less harmful to the ozone in the upper atmosphere.

Rocker arm A lever arm that rocks on a shaft or pivots on a stud. In an overhead valve engine, the rocker arm converts the upward movement of the pushrod into a downward movement to open a valve.

Rotor In a distributor, the rotating device inside the cap that connects the centre electrode and the outer terminals as it turns, distributing the high voltage from the coil secondary winding to the proper spark plug. Also, that part of an alternator which rotates inside the stator. Also, the rotating assembly of a turbocharger, including the compressor wheel, shaft and turbine wheel.

Runout The amount of wobble (in-and-out movement) of a gear or wheel as it's rotated. The amount a shaft rotates "out-of-true." The out-of-round condition of a rotating part.

S

Sealant A liquid or paste used to prevent leakage at a joint. Sometimes used in conjunction with a gasket.

Sealed beam lamp An older headlight design which integrates the reflector, lens and filaments into a hermetically-sealed one-piece unit. When a filament burns out or the lens cracks, the entire unit is simply replaced.

Serpentine drivebelt A single, long, wide accessory drivebelt that's used on some newer vehicles to drive all the accessories, instead of a series of smaller, shorter belts. Serpentine drivebelts are usually tensioned by an automatic tensioner.

Serpentine drivebelt

Shim Thin spacer, commonly used to adjust the clearance or relative positions between two parts. For example, shims inserted into or under bucket tappets control valve clearances. Clearance is adjusted by changing the thickness of the shim.

Slide hammer A special puller that screws into or hooks onto a component such as a shaft or bearing; a heavy sliding handle on the shaft bottoms against the end of the shaft to knock the component free.

Sprocket A tooth or projection on the periphery of a wheel, shaped to engage with a chain or drivebelt. Commonly used to refer to the sprocket wheel itself.

Starter inhibitor switch On vehicles with an automatic transmission, a switch that prevents starting if the vehicle is not in Neutral or Park.

Strut See MacPherson strut.

T

Tappet A cylindrical component which transmits motion from the cam to the valve stem, either directly or via a pushrod and rocker arm. Also called a cam follower.

Thermostat A heat-controlled valve that regulates the flow of coolant between the cylinder block and the radiator, so maintaining optimum engine operating temperature. A thermostat is also used in some air cleaners in which the temperature is regulated.

Thrust bearing The bearing in the clutch assembly that is moved in to the release levers by clutch pedal action to disengage the clutch. Also referred to as a release bearing.

Timing belt A toothed belt which drives the camshaft. Serious engine damage may result if it breaks in service.

Timing chain A chain which drives the camshaft.

Toe-in The amount the front wheels are closer together at the front than at the rear. On rear wheel drive vehicles, a slight amount of toe-in is usually specified to keep the front wheels running parallel on the road by offsetting other forces that tend to spread the wheels apart.

Toe-out The amount the front wheels are closer together at the rear than at the front. On front wheel drive vehicles, a slight amount of toe-out is usually specified.

Tools For full information on choosing and using tools, refer to the *Haynes Automotive Tools Manual*.

Tracer A stripe of a second colour applied to a wire insulator to distinguish that wire from another one with the same colour insulator.

Tune-up A process of accurate and careful adjustments and parts replacement to obtain the best possible engine performance.

Turbocharger A centrifugal device, driven by exhaust gases, that pressurises the intake air. Normally used to increase the power output from a given engine displacement, but can also be used primarily to reduce exhaust emissions (as on VW's "Umwelt" Diesel engine).

U

Universal joint or U-joint A double-pivoted connection for transmitting power from a driving to a driven shaft through an angle. A U-joint consists of two Y-shaped yokes and a cross-shaped member called the spider.

V

Valve A device through which the flow of liquid, gas, vacuum, or loose material in bulk may be started, stopped, or regulated by a movable part that opens, shuts, or partially obstructs one or more ports or passageways. A valve is also the movable part of such a device.

Valve clearance The clearance between the valve tip (the end of the valve stem) and the rocker arm or tappet. The valve clearance is measured when the valve is closed.

Vernier caliper A precision measuring instrument that measures inside and outside dimensions. Not quite as accurate as a micrometer, but more convenient.

Viscosity The thickness of a liquid or its resistance to flow.

Volt A unit for expressing electrical "pressure" in a circuit. One volt that will produce a current of one ampere through a resistance of one ohm.

W

Welding Various processes used to join metal items by heating the areas to be joined to a molten state and fusing them together. For more information refer to the *Haynes Automotive Welding Manual*.

Wiring diagram A drawing portraying the components and wires in a vehicle's electrical system, using standardised symbols. For more information refer to the *Haynes Automotive Electrical and Electronic Systems Manual*.

Note: *References through-out this index are in the form "**Chapter number**" • "**Page number**"*

Notes

Notes

Haynes Manuals – The Complete List

Title	Book No.
ALFA ROMEO Alfasud/Sprint (74 - 88) up to F *	0292
Alfa Romeo Alfetta (73 - 87) up to E *	0531
AUDI 80, 90 & Coupe Petrol (79 - Nov 88) up to F	0605
Audi 80, 90 & Coupe Petrol (Oct 86 - 90) D to H	1491
Audi 100 & 200 Petrol (Oct 82 - 90) up to H	0907
Audi 100 & A6 Petrol & Diesel (May 91 - May 97) H to P	3504
Audi A3 Petrol & Diesel (96 - May 03) P to 03	4253
Audi A4 Petrol & Diesel (95 - Feb 00) M to V	3575
AUSTIN A35 & A40 (56 - 67) up to F *	0118
Austin/MG/Rover Maestro 1.3 & 1.6 Petrol (83 - 95) up to M	0922
Austin/MG Metro (80 - May 90) up to G	0718
Austin/Rover Montego 1.3 & 1.6 Petrol (84 - 94) A to L	1066
Austin/MG/Rover Montego 2.0 Petrol (84 - 95) A to M	1067
Mini (59 - 69) up to H *	0527
Mini (69 - 01) up to X	0646
Austin/Rover 2.0 litre Diesel Engine (86 - 93) C to L	1857
Austin Healey 100/6 & 3000 (56 - 68) up to G *	0049
BEDFORD CF Petrol (69 - 87) up to E	0163
Bedford/Vauxhall Rascal & Suzuki Supercarry (86 - Oct 94) C to M	3015
BMW 316, 320 & 320i (4-cyl) (75 - Feb 83) up to Y*	0276
BMW 320, 320i, 323i & 325i (6-cyl) (Oct 77 - Sept 87) up to E	0815
BMW 3- & 5-Series Petrol (81 - 91) up to J	1948
BMW 3-Series Petrol (Apr 91 - 96) H to N	3210
BMW 3-Series Petrol (Sept 98 - 03) S to 53	4067
BMW 520i & 525e (Oct 81 - June 88) up to E	1560
BMW 525, 528 & 528i (73 - Sept 81) up to X *	0632
BMW 5-Series 6-cyl Petrol (April 96 - Aug 03) N to 03	4151
BMW 1500, 1502, 1600, 1602, 2000 & 2002 (59 - 77) up to S *	0240
CHRYSLER PT Cruiser Petrol (00 - 03) W to 53	4058
CITROËN 2CV, Ami & Dyane (67 - 90) up to H	0196
Citroën AX Petrol & Diesel (87 - 97) D to P	3014
Citroën Berlingo & Peugeot Partner Petrol & Diesel (96 - 05) P to 55	4281
Citroën BX Petrol (83 - 94) A to L	0908
Citroën C15 Van Petrol & Diesel (89 - Oct 98) F to S	3509
Citroën C3 Petrol & Diesel (02 - 05) 51 to 05	4197
Citroën CX Petrol (75 - 88) up to F	0528
Citroën Saxo Petrol & Diesel (96 - 04) N to 54	3506
Citroën Visa Petrol (79 - 88) up to F	0620
Citroën Xantia Petrol & Diesel (93 - 01) K to Y	3082
Citroën XM Petrol & Diesel (89 - 00) G to X	3451
Citroën Xsara Petrol & Diesel (97 - Sept 00) R to W	3751
Citroën Xsara Picasso Petrol & Diesel (00 - 02) W to 52	3944
Citroën ZX Diesel (91 - 98) J to S	1922
Citroën ZX Petrol (91 - 98) H to S	1881
Citroën 1.7 & 1.9 litre Diesel Engine (84 - 96) A to N	1379
FIAT 126 (73 - 87) up to E *	0305
Fiat 500 (57 - 73) up to M *	0090
Fiat Bravo & Brava Petrol (95 - 00) N to W	3572
Fiat Cinquecento (93 - 98) K to R	3501
Fiat Panda (81 - 95) up to M	0793
Fiat Punto Petrol & Diesel (94 - Oct 99) L to V	3251
Fiat Punto Petrol (Oct 99 - July 03) V to 03	4066
Fiat Regata Petrol (84 - 88) A to F	1167
Fiat Tipo Petrol (88 - 91) E to J	1625
Fiat Uno Petrol (83 - 95) up to M	0923
Fiat X1/9 (74 - 89) up to G *	0273
FORD Anglia (59 - 68) up to G *	0001

Title	Book No.
Ford Capri II (& III) 1.6 & 2.0 (74 - 87) up to E *	0283
Ford Capri II (& III) 2.8 & 3.0 V6 (74 - 87) up to E	1309
Ford Cortina Mk III 1300 & 1600 (70 - 76) up to P *	0070
Ford Escort Mk I 1100 & 1300 (68 - 74) up to N *	0171
Ford Escort Mk I Mexico, RS 1600 & RS 2000 (70 - 74) up to N *	0139
Ford Escort Mk II Mexico, RS 1800 & RS 2000 (75 - 80) up to W *	0735
Ford Escort (75 - Aug 80) up to V *	0280
Ford Escort Petrol (Sept 80 - Sept 90) up to H	0686
Ford Escort & Orion Petrol (Sept 90 - 00) H to X	1737
Ford Escort & Orion Diesel (Sept 90 - 00) H to X	4081
Ford Fiesta (76 - Aug 83) up to Y	0334
Ford Fiesta Petrol (Aug 83 - Feb 89) A to F	1030
Ford Fiesta Petrol (Feb 89 - Oct 95) F to N	1595
Ford Fiesta Petrol & Diesel (Oct 95 - Mar 02) N to 02	3397
Ford Fiesta Petrol & Diesel (Apr 02 - 05) 02 to 54	4170
Ford Focus Petrol & Diesel (98 - 01) S to Y	3759
Ford Focus Petrol & Diesel (Oct 01 - 04) 51 to 54	4167
Ford Galaxy Petrol & Diesel (95 - Aug 00) M to W	3984
Ford Granada Petrol (Sept 77 - Feb 85) up to B *	0481
Ford Granada & Scorpio Petrol (Mar 85 - 94) B to M	1245
Ford Ka (96 - 02) P to 52	3570
Ford Mondeo Petrol (93 - Sept 00) K to X	1923
Ford Mondeo Petrol & Diesel (Oct 00 - Jul 03) X to 03	3990
Ford Mondeo Diesel (93 - 96) L to N	3465
Ford Orion Petrol (83 - Sept 90) up to H	1009
Ford Sierra 4-cyl Petrol (82 - 93) up to K	0903
Ford Sierra V6 Petrol (82 - 91) up to J	0904
Ford Transit Petrol (Mk 2) (78 - Jan 86) up to C	0719
Ford Transit Petrol (Mk 3) (Feb 86 - 89) C to G	1468
Ford Transit Diesel (Feb 86 - 99) C to T	3019
Ford 1.6 & 1.8 litre Diesel Engine (84 - 96) A to N	1172
Ford 2.1, 2.3 & 2.5 litre Diesel Engine (77 - 90) up to H	1606
FREIGHT ROVER Sherpa Petrol (74 - 87) up to E	0463
HILLMAN Avenger (70 - 82) up to Y	0037
Hillman Imp (63 - 76) up to R *	0022
HONDA Civic (Feb 84 - Oct 87) A to E	1226
Honda Civic (Nov 91 - 96) J to N	3199
Honda Civic Petrol (Mar 95 - 00) M to X	4050
HYUNDAI Pony (85 - 94) C to M	3398
JAGUAR E Type (61 - 72) up to L *	0140
Jaguar MkI & II, 240 & 340 (55 - 69) up to H *	0098
Jaguar XJ6, XJ & Sovereign; Daimler Sovereign (68 - Oct 86) up to D	0242
Jaguar XJ6 & Sovereign (Oct 86 - Sept 94) D to M	3261
Jaguar XJ12, XJS & Sovereign; Daimler Double Six (72 - 88) up to F	0478
JEEP Cherokee Petrol (93 - 96) K to N	1943
LADA 1200, 1300, 1500 & 1600 (74 - 91) up to J	0413
Lada Samara (87 - 91) D to J	1610
LAND ROVER 90, 110 & Defender Diesel (83 - 95) up to N	3017
Land Rover Discovery Petrol & Diesel (89 - 98) G to S	3016
Land Rover Freelander Petrol & Diesel (97 - 02) R to 52	3929
Land Rover Series IIA & III Diesel (58 - 85) up to C	0529
Land Rover Series II, IIA & III 4-cyl Petrol (58 - 85) up to C	0314
MAZDA 323 (Mar 81 - Oct 89) up to G	1608
Mazda 323 (Oct 89 - 98) G to R	3455
Mazda 626 (May 83 - Sept 87) up to E	0929
Mazda B1600, B1800 & B2000 Pick-up Petrol (72 - 88) up to F	0267

Title	Book No.
Mazda RX-7 (79 - 85) up to C *	0460
MERCEDES-BENZ 190, 190E & 190D Petrol & Diesel (83 - 93) A to L	3450
Mercedes-Benz 200D, 240D, 240TD, 300D & 300TD 123 Series Diesel (Oct 76 - 85) up	1114
Mercedes-Benz 250 & 280 (68 - 72) up to L *	0346
Mercedes-Benz 250 & 280 123 Series Petrol (Oct 76 - 84) up to B *	0677
Mercedes-Benz 124 Series Petrol & Diesel (85 - Aug 93) C to K	3253
Mercedes-Benz C-Class Petrol & Diesel (93 - Aug 00) L to W	3511
MG A (55 - 62) *	0475
MGB (62 - 80) up to W	0111
MG Midget & Austin-Healey Sprite (58 - 80) up to W *	0265
MINI Petrol (July 01 - 05) Y to 05	4273
MITSUBISHI Shogun & L200 Pick-Ups Petrol (83 - 94) up to M	1944
MORRIS Ital 1.3 (80 - 84) up to B	0705
Morris Minor 1000 (56 - 71) up to K	0024
NISSAN Almera Petrol (95 - Feb 00) N to V	4053
Nissan Bluebird (May 84 - Mar 86) A to C	1223
Nissan Bluebird Petrol (Mar 86 - 90) C to H	1473
Nissan Cherry (Sept 82 - 86) up to D	1031
Nissan Micra (83 - Jan 93) up to K	0931
Nissan Micra (93 - 02) K to 52	3254
Nissan Primera Petrol (90 - Aug 99) H to T	1851
Nissan Stanza (82 - 86) up to D	0824
Nissan Sunny Petrol (May 82 - Oct 86) up to D	0895
Nissan Sunny Petrol (Oct 86 - Mar 91) D to H	1378
Nissan Sunny Petrol (Apr 91 - 95) H to N	3219
OPEL Ascona & Manta (B Series) (Sept 75 - 88) up to F *	0316
Opel Ascona Petrol (81 - 88)	3215
Opel Astra Petrol (Oct 91 - Feb 98)	3156
Opel Corsa Petrol (83 - Mar 93)	3160
Opel Corsa Petrol (Mar 93 - 97)	3159
Opel Kadett Petrol (Nov 79 - Oct 84) up to B	0634
Opel Kadett Petrol (Oct 84 - Oct 91)	3196
Opel Omega & Senator Petrol (Nov 86 - 94)	3157
Opel Rekord Petrol (Feb 78 - Oct 86) up to D	0543
Opel Vectra Petrol (Oct 88 - Oct 95)	3158
PEUGEOT 106 Petrol & Diesel (91 - 04) J to 53	1882
Peugeot 205 Petrol (83 - 97) A to P	0932
Peugeot 206 Petrol & Diesel (98 - 01) S to X	3757
Peugeot 306 Petrol & Diesel (93 - 02) K to 02	3073
Peugeot 307 Petrol & Diesel (01 - 04) Y to 54	4147
Peugeot 309 Petrol (86 - 93) C to K	1266
Peugeot 405 Petrol (88 - 97) E to P	1559
Peugeot 405 Diesel (88 - 97) E to P	3198
Peugeot 406 Petrol & Diesel (96 - Mar 99) N to T	3394
Peugeot 406 Petrol & Diesel (Mar 99 - 02) T to 52	3982
Peugeot 505 Petrol (79 - 89) up to G	0762
Peugeot 1.7/1.8 & 1.9 litre Diesel Engine (82 - 96) up to N	0950
Peugeot 2.0, 2.1, 2.3 & 2.5 litre Diesel Engines (74 - 90) up to H	1607
PORSCHE 911 (65 - 85) up to C	0264
Porsche 924 & 924 Turbo (76 - 85) up to C	0397
PROTON (89 - 97) F to P	3255
RANGE ROVER V8 Petrol (70 - Oct 92) up to K	0606
RELIANT Robin & Kitten (73 - 83) up to A *	0436
RENAULT 4 (61 - 86) up to D *	0072

* Classic reprint

Title	Book No.
Renault 5 Petrol (Feb 85 - 96) B to N	1219
Renault 9 & 11 Petrol (82 - 89) up to F	0822
Renault 18 Petrol (79 - 86) up to D	0598
Renault 19 Petrol (89 - 96) F to N	1646
Renault 19 Diesel (89 - 96) F to N	1946
Renault 21 Petrol (86 - 94) C to M	1397
Renault 25 Petrol & Diesel (84 - 92) B to K	1228
Renault Clio Petrol (91 - May 98) H to R	1853
Renault Clio Diesel (91 - June 96) H to N	3031
Renault Clio Petrol & Diesel (May 98 - May 01) R to Y	3906
Renault Clio Petrol & Diesel (June 01 - 04) Y to 54	4168
Renault Espace Petrol & Diesel (85 - 96) C to N	3197
Renault Laguna Petrol & Diesel (94 - 00) L to W	3252
Renault Laguna Petrol & Diesel (01 - 05) X to 05	4283
Renault Mégane & Scénic Petrol & Diesel (96 - 98) N to R	3395
Renault Mégane & Scénic Petrol & Diesel (Apr 99 - 02) T to 52	3916
Renault Megane Petrol & Diesel (Oct 02 - 05) 52 to 55	4284
Renault Scenic Petrol & Diesel (Sept 03 - 06) 53 to 06	4297
ROVER 213 & 216 (84 - 89) A to G	1116
Rover 214 & 414 Petrol (89 - 96) G to N	1689
Rover 216 & 416 Petrol (89 - 96) G to N	1830
Rover 211, 214, 216, 218 & 220 Petrol & Diesel (Dec 95 - 99) N to V	3399
Rover 25 & MG ZR Petrol & Diesel (Oct 99 - 04) V to 54	4145
Rover 414, 416 & 420 Petrol & Diesel (May 95 - 98) M to R	3453
Rover 45 / MG ZS	4384
Rover 618, 620 & 623 Petrol (93 - 97) K to P	3257
Rover 75 / MG ZT Petrol & Diesel (Feb 99 - 05) T to 05	4292
Rover 820, 825 & 827 Petrol (86 - 95) D to N	1380
Rover 3500 (76 - 87) up to E *	0365
Rover Metro, 111 & 114 Petrol (May 90 - 98) G to S	1711
SAAB 95 & 96 (66 - 76) up to R *	0198
Saab 90, 99 & 900 (79 - Oct 93) up to L	0765
Saab 900 (Oct 93 - 98) L to R	3512
Saab 9000 (4-cyl) (85 - 98) C to S	1686
Saab 9-5 4-cyl Petrol (97 - 04) R to 54	4156
SEAT Ibiza & Cordoba Petrol & Diesel (Oct 93 - Oct 99) L to V	3571
Seat Ibiza & Malaga Petrol (85 - 92) B to K	1609
SKODA Estelle (77 - 89) up to G	0604
Skoda Fabia (00 - 06) W to 06	4376
Skoda Favorit (89 - 96) F to N	1801
Skoda Felicia Petrol & Diesel (95 - 01) M to X	3505
Skoda Octavia Petrol & Diesel (98 - Apr 04) R to 04	4285
SUBARU 1600 & 1800 (Nov 79 - 90) up to H *	0995
SUNBEAM Alpine, Rapier & H120 (67 - 74) up to N *	0051
SUZUKI SJ Series, Samurai & Vitara (4-cyl) Petrol (82 - 97) up to P	1942
Suzuki Supercarry & Bedford/Vauxhall Rascal (86 - Oct 94) C to M	3015
TALBOT Alpine, Solara, Minx & Rapier (75 - 86) up to D	0337
Talbot Horizon Petrol (78 - 86) up to D	0473
Talbot Samba (82 - 86) up to D	0823
TOYOTA Avensis Petrol (Nov 97 - Jan 03) R to 52	4264
Toyota Carina E Petrol (May 92 - 97) J to P	3256
Toyota Corolla (80 - 85) up to C	0683

Title	Book No.
Toyota Corolla (Sept 83 - Sept 87) A to E	1024
Toyota Corolla (Sept 87 - Aug 92) E to K	1683
Toyota Corolla Petrol (Aug 92 - 97) K to P	3259
Toyota Corolla Petrol (June 97 - 01) P to 51	4286
Toyota Hi-Ace & Hi-Lux Petrol (69 - Oct 83) up to A	0304
Toyota Yaris Petrol (99 - 05) T to 05	4265
TRIUMPH GT6 & Vitesse (62 - 74) up to N *	0112
Triumph Herald (59 - 71) up to K *	0010
Triumph Spitfire (62 - 81) up to X	0113
Triumph Stag (70 - 78) up to T *	0441
Triumph TR2, TR3, TR3A, TR4 & TR4A (52 - 67) up to F *	0028
Triumph TR5 & 6 (67 - 75) up to P *	0031
Triumph TR7 (75 - 82) up to Y *	0322
VAUXHALL Astra Petrol (80 - Oct 84) up to B	0635
Vauxhall Astra & Belmont Petrol (Oct 84 - Oct 91) B to J	1136
Vauxhall Astra Petrol (Oct 91 - Feb 98) J to R	1832
Vauxhall/Opel Astra & Zafira Petrol (Feb 98 - Apr 04) R to 04	3758
Vauxhall/Opel Astra & Zafira Diesel (Feb 98 - Apr 04) R to 04	3797
Vauxhall/Opel Calibra (90 - 98) G to S	3502
Vauxhall Carlton Petrol (Oct 78 - Oct 86) up to D	0480
Vauxhall Carlton & Senator Petrol (Nov 86 - 94) D to L	1469
Vauxhall Cavalier Petrol (81 - Oct 88) up to F	0812
Vauxhall Cavalier Petrol (Oct 88 - 95) F to N	1570
Vauxhall Chevette (75 - 84) up to B	0285
Vauxhall/Opel Corsa Diesel (Mar 93 - Oct 00) K to X	4087
Vauxhall Corsa Petrol (Mar 93 - 97) K to R	1985
Vauxhall/Opel Corsa Petrol (Apr 97 - Oct 00) P to X	3921
Vauxhall/Opel Corsa Petrol & Diesel (Oct 00 - Sept 03) X to 53	4079
Vauxhall/Opel Frontera Petrol & Diesel (91 - Sept 98) J to S	3454
Vauxhall Nova Petrol (83 - 93) up to K	0909
Vauxhall/Opel Omega Petrol (94 - 99) L to T	3510
Vauxhall/Opel Vectra Petrol & Diesel (95 - Feb 99) N to S	3396
Vauxhall/Opel Vectra Petrol & Diesel (Mar 99 - May 02) T to 02	3930
Vauxhall/Opel 1.5, 1.6 & 1.7 litre Diesel Engine (82 - 96) up to N	1222
VOLKSWAGEN 411 & 412 (68 - 75) up to P *	0091
Volkswagen Beetle 1200 (54 - 77) up to S	0036
Volkswagen Beetle 1300 & 1500 (65 - 75) up to P	0039
Volkswagen Beetle 1302 & 1302S (70 - 72) up to L *	0110
Volkswagen Beetle 1303, 1303S & GT (72 - 75) up to P	0159
Volkswagen Beetle Petrol & Diesel (Apr 99 - 01) T to 51	3798
Volkswagen Golf & Jetta Mk 1 Petrol 1.1 & 1.3 (74 - 84) up to A	0716
Volkswagen Golf, Jetta & Scirocco Mk 1 Petrol 1.5, 1.6 & 1.8 (74 - 84) up to A	0726
Volkswagen Golf & Jetta Mk 1 Diesel (78 - 84) up to A	0451
Volkswagen Golf & Jetta Mk 2 Petrol (Mar 84 - Feb 92) A to J	1081
Volkswagen Golf & Vento Petrol & Diesel (Feb 92 - Mar 98) J to R	3097
Volkswagen Golf & Bora Petrol & Diesel (April 98 - 00) R to X	3727
Volkswagen Golf & Bora 4-cyl Petrol & Diesel (01 - 03) X to 53	4169

Title	Book No.
Volkswagen LT Petrol Vans & Light Trucks (76 - 87) up to E	0637
Volkswagen Passat & Santana Petrol (Sept 81 - May 88) up to E	0814
Volkswagen Passat 4-cyl Petrol & Diesel (May 88 - 96) E to P	3498
Volkswagen Passat 4-cyl Petrol & Diesel (Dec 96 - Nov 00) P to X	3917
Volkswagen Passat Petrol & Diesel (Dec 00 - May 05) X to 05	4279
Volkswagen Polo & Derby (76 - Jan 82) up to X	0335
Volkswagen Polo (82 - Oct 90) up to H	0813
Volkswagen Polo Petrol (Nov 90 - Aug 94) H to L	3245
Volkswagen Polo Hatchback Petrol & Diesel (94 - 99) M to S	3500
Volkswagen Polo Hatchback Petrol (00 - Jan 02) V to 51	4150
Volkswagen Scirocco (82 - 90) up to H *	1224
Volkswagen Transporter 1600 (68 - 79) up to V	0082
Volkswagen Transporter 1700, 1800 & 2000 (72 - 79) up to V *	0226
Volkswagen Transporter (air-cooled) Petrol (79 - 82) up to Y *	0638
Volkswagen Transporter (water-cooled) Petrol (82 - 90) up to H	3452
Volkswagen Type 3 (63 - 73) up to M *	0084
VOLVO 120 & 130 Series (& P1800) (61 - 73) up to M *	0203
Volvo 142, 144 & 145 (66 - 74) up to N *	0129
Volvo 240 Series Petrol (74 - 93) up to K	0270
Volvo 262, 264 & 260/265 (75 - 85) up to C *	0400
Volvo 340, 343, 345 & 360 (76 - 91) up to J	0715
Volvo 440, 460 & 480 Petrol (87 - 97) D to P	1691
Volvo 740 & 760 Petrol (82 - 91) up to J	1258
Volvo 850 Petrol (92 - 96) J to P	3260
Volvo 940 Petrol (90 - 96) H to N	3249
Volvo S40 & V40 Petrol (96 - Mar 04) N to 04	3569
Volvo S70, V70 & C70 Petrol (96 - 99) P to V	3573
Volvo V70 / S80 Petrol & Diesel (98 - 05) S to 55	4263

AUTOMOTIVE TECHBOOKS

Title	Book No.
Automotive Air Conditioning Systems	3740
Automotive Electrical and Electronic Systems Manual	3049
Automotive Gearbox Overhaul Manual	3473
Automotive Service Summaries Manual	3475
Automotive Timing Belts Manual – Austin/Rover	3549
Automotive Timing Belts Manual – Ford	3474
Automotive Timing Belts Manual – Peugeot/Citroën	3568
Automotive Timing Belts Manual – Vauxhall/Opel	3577

DIY MANUAL SERIES

Title	Book No.
The Haynes Air Conditioning Manual	4192
The Haynes Manual on Bodywork	4198
The Haynes Manual on Brakes	4178
The Haynes Manual on Carburettors	4177
The Haynes Car Electrical Systems Manual	4251
The Haynes Manual on Diesel Engines	4174
The Haynes Manual on Engine Management	4199
The Haynes Manual on Fault Codes	4175
The Haynes Manual on Practical Electrical Systems	4267
The Haynes Manual on Small Engines	4250
The Haynes Manual on Welding	4176

* Classic reprint

CL20.3/06

Preserving Our Motoring Heritage

< *The Model J Duesenberg Derham Tourster. Only eight of these magnificent cars were ever built – this is the only example to be found outside the United States of America*

Almost every car you've ever loved, loathed or desired is gathered under one roof at the Haynes Motor Museum. Over 300 immaculately presented cars and motorbikes represent every aspect of our motoring heritage, from elegant reminders of bygone days, such as the superb Model J Duesenberg to curiosities like the bug-eyed BMW Isetta. There are also many old friends and flames. Perhaps you remember the 1959 Ford Popular that you did your courting in? The magnificent 'Red Collection' is a spectacle of classic sports cars including AC, Alfa Romeo, Austin Healey, Ferrari, Lamborghini, Maserati, MG, Riley, Porsche and Triumph.

A Perfect Day Out

Each and every vehicle at the Haynes Motor Museum has played its part in the history and culture of Motoring. Today, they make a wonderful spectacle and a great day out for all the family. Bring the kids, bring Mum and Dad, but above all bring your camera to capture those golden memories for ever. You will also find an impressive array of motoring memorabilia, a comfortable 70 seat video cinema and one of the most extensive transport book shops in Britain. The Pit Stop Cafe serves everything from a cup of tea to wholesome, home-made meals or, if you prefer, you can enjoy the large picnic area nestled in the beautiful rural surroundings of Somerset.

> *John Haynes O.B.E., Founder and Chairman of the museum at the wheel of a Haynes Light 12.*

< *Graham Hill's Lola Cosworth Formula 1 car next to a 1934 Riley Sports.*

The Museum is situated on the A359 Yeovil to Frome road at Sparkford, just off the A303 in Somerset. It is about 40 miles south of Bristol, and 25 minutes drive from the M5 intersection at Taunton.

Open 9.30am - 5.30pm (10.00am - 4.00pm Winter) 7 days a week, *except Christmas Day, Boxing Day and New Years Day*

Special rates available for schools, coach parties and outings Charitable Trust No. 292048